Theories of Team Cognition
Cross-Disciplinary Perspectives

SERIES IN APPLIED PSYCHOLOGY

Jeanette N. Cleveland, Colorado State University
Kevin R. Murphy, Landy Litigation and Colorado State University
Series Editors
Edwin A. Fleishman, Founding series editor (1987–2010)

Gregory Bedny and David Meister
The Russian Theory of Activity: Current Applications to Design and Learning

Winston Bennett, David Woehr, and Charles Lance
Performance Measurement: Current Perspectives and Future Challenges

Michael T. Brannick, Eduardo Salas, and Carolyn Prince
Team Performance Assessment and Measurement: Theory, Research, and Applications

Jeanette N. Cleveland, Margaret Stockdale, and Kevin R. Murphy
Women and Men in Organizations: Sex and Gender Issues at Work

Aaron Cohen
Multiple Commitments in the Workplace: An Integrative Approach

Russell Cropanzano
Justice in the Workplace: Approaching Fairness in Human Resource Management, Volume 1

Russell Cropanzano
Justice in the Workplace: From Theory to Practice, Volume 2

David V. Day, Stephen Zaccaro, and Stanley M. Halpin
Leader Development for Transforming Organizations: Growing Leaders for Tomorrow's Teams and Organizations

Stewart I. Donaldson, Mihaly Csikszentmihalyi, and Jeanne Nakamura
Applied Positive Psychology: Improving Everyday Life, Health, Schools, Work, and Safety

James E. Driskell and Eduardo Salas
Stress and Human Performance

Sidney A. Fine and Steven F. Cronshaw
Functional Job Analysis: A Foundation for Human Resources Management

Sidney A. Fine and Maury Getkate
Benchmark Tasks for Job Analysis: A Guide for Functional Job Analysis (FJA) Scales

J. Kevin Ford, Steve W. J. Kozlowski, Kurt Kraiger, Eduardo Salas, and Mark S. Teachout
Improving Training Effectiveness in Work Organizations
Jerald Greenberg
Organizational Behavior: The State of the Science, Second Edition
Jerald Greenberg
Insidious Workplace Behavior

Edwin Hollander
Inclusive Leadership: The Essential Leader-Follower Relationship
Jack Kitaeff
Handbook of Police Psychology
Uwe E. Kleinbeck, Hans-Henning Quast, Henk Thierry, and Hartmut Häcker
Work Motivation
Laura L. Koppes
Historical Perspectives in Industrial and Organizational Psychology
Ellen Kossek and Susan Lambert
Work and Life Integration: Organizational, Cultural, and Individual Perspectives
Martin I. Kurke and Ellen M. Scrivner
Police Psychology into the 21st Century
Joel Lefkowitz
Ethics and Values in Industrial and Organizational Psychology
Manuel London
Job Feedback: Giving, Seeking, and Using Feedback for Performance Improvement, Second Edition
Manuel London
How People Evaluate Others in Organizations

Manuel London
Leadership Development: Paths to Self-Insight and Professional Growth
Robert F. Morrison and Jerome Adams
Contemporary Career Development Issues
Michael D. Mumford, Garnett Stokes, and William A. Owens
Patterns of Life History: The Ecology of Human Individuality
Michael D. Mumford
Pathways to Outstanding Leadership: A Comparative Analysis of Charismatic, Ideological, and Pragmatic Leaders

Kevin R. Murphy
Validity Generalization: A Critical Review
Kevin R. Murphy
A Critique of Emotional Intelligence: What Are the Problems and How Can They Be Fixed?
Kevin R. Murphy and Frank E. Saal
Psychology in Organizations: Integrating Science and Practice
Susan E. Murphy and Ronald E. Riggio
The Future of Leadership Development
Susan E. Murphy and Rebecca J. Reichard
Early Development and Leadership: Building the Next Generation of Leaders
Margaret A. Neal and Leslie Brett Hammer
Working Couples Caring for Children and Aging Parents: Effects on Work and Well-Being
Robert E. Ployhart, Benjamin Schneider, and Neal Schmitt
Staffing Organizations: Contemporary Practice and Theory, Third Edition
Steven A.Y. Poelmans
Work and Family: An International Research Perspective
Erich P. Prien, Jeffery S. Schippmann, and Kristin O. Prien
Individual Assessment: As Practiced in Industry and Consulting
Robert D. Pritchard, Sallie J. Weaver, and Elissa L. Ashwood
Evidence-Based Productivity Improvement: A Practical Guide to the Productivity Measurement and Enhancement System
Ned Rosen
Teamwork and the Bottom Line: Groups Make a Difference
Eduardo Salas, Stephen M. Fiore, and Michael P. Letsky
Theories of Team Cognition: Cross-Disciplinary Perspectives
Heinz Schuler, James L. Farr, and Mike Smith
Personnel Selection and Assessment: Individual and Organizational Perspectives
John W. Senders and Neville P. Moray
Human Error: Cause, Prediction, and Reduction
Lynn Shore, Jacqueline Coyle-Shapiro, and Lois E. Tetrick
The Employee-Organization Relationship: Applications for the 21st Century
Kenneth S. Shultz and Gary A. Adams

Aging and Work in the 21st Century
Frank J. Smith
Organizational Surveys: The Diagnosis and Betterment of Organizations
Through Their Members
Dianna Stone and Eugene F. Stone-Romero
The Influence of Culture on Human Resource Processes and Practices
Kecia M. Thomas
Diversity Resistance in Organizations
George C. Thornton III and Rose Mueller-Hanson
Developing Organizational Simulations: A Guide for Practitioners and
Students
George C. Thornton III and Deborah Rupp
Assessment Centers in Human Resource Management: Strategies for Prediction, Diagnosis, and Development
Yoav Vardi and Ely Weitz
Misbehavior in Organizations: Theory, Research, and Management
Patricia Voydanoff
Work, Family, and Community
Mark A. Wilson, Winston Bennett, Shanan G. Gibson, and George M.
Alliger
The Handbook of Work Analysis: Methods, Systems, Applications and
Science of Work Measurement in Organizations

Theories of Team Cognition
Cross-Disciplinary Perspectives

Edited by
Eduardo Salas
University of Central Florida
Orlando, Florida

Stephen M. Fiore
University of Central Florida
Orlando, Florida

Michael P. Letsky
Office of Naval Research
Arlington, Virginia

Routledge
Taylor & Francis Group
New York London

Routledge
Taylor & Francis Group
52 Vanderbilt Avenue,
New York, NY 10017

Routledge
Taylor & Francis Group
27 Church Road
Hove, East Sussex BN3 2FA

© 2012 by Taylor & Francis Group, LLC
Routledge is an imprint of Taylor & Francis Group, an Informa business

Version Date: 20110817

International Standard Book Number: 978-0-415-87413-7 (Hardback)

For permission to photocopy or use material electronically from this work, please access www.copyright.com (http://www.copyright.com/) or contact the Copyright Clearance Center, Inc. (CCC), 222 Rosewood Drive, Danvers, MA 01923, 978-750-8400. CCC is a not-for-profit organization that provides licenses and registration for a variety of users. For organizations that have been granted a photocopy license by the CCC, a separate system of payment has been arranged.

Trademark Notice: Product or corporate names may be trademarks or registered trademarks, and are used only for identification and explanation without intent to infringe.

Library of Congress Cataloging-in-Publication Data

Theories of team cognition : cross-disciplinary perspectives / editors, Eduardo Salas ... [et al.].
    p. cm. -- (Series in applied psychology ; 49)
  Includes bibliographical references and index.
  ISBN 978-0-415-87413-7 (hbk. : alk. paper)
  1. Teams in the workplace--Psychological aspects. 2. Cognition. 3. Small groups--Psychological aspects. 4. Organizational behavior. I. Salas, Eduardo.

HD66.T463 2012
658.4'022019--dc23   2011033808

Visit the Taylor & Francis Web site at
http://www.taylorandfrancis.com

and the Psychology Press Web site at
http://www.psypress.com

Contents

Series Foreword.. xiii
    Jeannette N. Cleveland and Kevin R. Murphy
Preface xv
Acknowledgments xvii
About the Editors xix
Contributors.. xxi

SECTION I   Team Cognition as a Field

Chapter 1   Why Cross-Disciplinary Theories of Team
Cognition? 3

    Eduardo Salas, Stephen M. Fiore, and Michael P. Letsky

Chapter 2   Macrocognition, Team Learning, and Team
Knowledge: Origins, Emergence, and Measurement..... 19

    Steve W. J. Kozlowski and Georgia T. Chao

SECTION II   Organizational Behavior Perspectives

Chapter 3   Reasoning About Intentions in Complex
Organizational Behaviors: Intentions in Surgical
Handoffs 51

    Eugene Santos, Jr., Joseph Rosen, Keum Joo Kim, Fei Yu, Deqing
    Li, Yufan Guo, Elizabeth Jacob, Samuel Shih, Jean Liu, and
    Lindsay B. Katona

Chapter 4   Time and Team Cognition: Toward Greater
Integration of Temporal Dynamics 87

    Susan Mohammed, Rachel Tesler, and Katherine Hamilton

ix

x • *Contents*

Chapter 5 Leadership and Emergent Collective Cognition 117

Toshio Murase, Christian J. Resick, Miliani Jiménez, Elizabeth Sanz, and Leslie A. DeChurch

Chapter 6 Elaborating Cognition in Teams: Cognitive Similarity Configurations 145

Joan R. Rentsch and Ioana R. Mot

SECTION III Human Factors and Cognitive Engineering Pespectives

Chapter 7 A Cognitive Systems Engineering Perspective on Shared Cognition: Coping With Complexity 173

Emily S. Patterson and Robert J. Stephens

Chapter 8 Theoretical Underpinning of Interactive Team Cognition 187

Nancy J. Cooke, Jamie C. Gorman, Christopher Myers, and Jasmine Duran

Chapter 9 Articulating Collaborative Contributions to Activity Awareness 209

John M. Carroll, Marcela Borge, Craig H. Ganoe, and Mary Beth Rosson

SECTION IV Cognitive and Computer Science Perspectives

Chapter 10 Combinations of Contributions for Sharing Cognitions in Teams 245

Verlin B. Hinsz and Jared L. Ladbury

Contents • xi

Chapter 11 Considering the Influence of Task Complexity on Macrocognitive Team Processes 271

Rebecca Lyons, Heather Lum, Stephen M. Fiore, Eduardo Salas, Norman Warner, and Michael P. Letsky

Chapter 12 Team Knowledge: Dimensional Structure and Network Representation 289

J. Alberto Espinosa and Mark A. Clark

Chapter 13 Intelligent Agents as Teammates.................................. 313

Gita Sukthankar, Randall Shumaker, and Michael Lewis

Chapter 14 Looking at Macrocognition Through a Multimethodological Lens 345

Michael D. McNeese and Mark S. Pfaff

Chapter 15 Gaining Insight Into Team Processes on Cognitive Tasks With Member Expectations and the Social Relations Model.. 373

Jared L. Ladbury and Verlin B. Hinsz

SECTION V   Social Psychology, Communication, and Developmental Perspectives

Chapter 16 Team Cognition and the Accountabilities of the Tool Pass 405

Timothy Koschmann, Gary Dunnington, and Michael Kim

Chapter 17 Transactive Memory Theory and Teams: Past, Present, and Future.. 421

Andrea B. Hollingshead, Naina Gupta, Kay Yoon, and David P. Brandon xii • *Contents*

Chapter 18 Team Cognition, Communication, and Sharing.......... 457

Marshall Scott Poole

Chapter 19 Team Cognition, Communication, and Message
Interdependence.. 471

Stephenson J. Beck and Joann Keyton

Chapter 20 Team Reason: Between Team Cognition and
Societal Knowledge.. 495

Peter Musaeus

Chapter 21 Group Cognition in Online Teams.............................. 517

Gerry Stahl and Carolyn Penstein Rosé

Chapter 22 Facilitating Effective Mental Model Convergence:
The Interplay Among the Team's Task, Mental
Model Content, Communication Flow, and Media..... 549

Sara A. McComb and Deanna M. Kennedy

SECTION VI The Road Ahead

Chapter 23 Commentary on the Coordinates of Coordination
and Collaboration 571

John Elias and Stephen M. Fiore

Chapter 24 Some More Reflections on Team Cognition 597

Olivia C. Riches and Eduardo Salas

Author Index.. 607

Subject Index... 623

Series Foreword

Jeanette N. Cleveland
Colorado State University

Kevin R. Murphy
Landy Litigation and Colorado State University

WHY CROSS-DISCIPLINARY THEORIES OF TEAM COGNITION?

There is a compelling need for innovative approaches to the solution of many pressing problems involving human relationships in today's society. Such approaches are more likely to be successful when they are based on sound research and applications. This Series in Applied Psychology offers publications that emphasize state-of-the-art research and its applications to important issues of human behavior in a variety of social settings. The objective is to bridge both academic and applied interests.

We welcome the Salas, Fiore, and Letsky book to the Applied Psychology Series. This volume brings together an impressive set of scholars studying team cognition, an area that bridges the emerging fields of macrocognition, group cognition, and distributed cognition. These authors build and apply theories of shared cognitition to help us understand how teams respond to complex challenges that require the skills and inputs of multiple members. Its approach exemplifies the unique strengths and challenges of applied psychology. The application of solid science to solving real-world problems has led to fundamental advances in theory as well as delivering methods and technologies for improving team performance in the field.

This book tackles a daunting set of problems, including measuring and defining team knowledge, assessing team members' intentions and decision making processes, developing an understanding of the role of time pressure in team decision making and performance, explicating the links between leadership and team cognition, modeling shared knowledge and

xiii

cognitive similarity, developing technologies to facilitate collaboration, using team tasks to test and expand models of shared cognition, and developing a better understanding of the demands that different types of tasks place on teams. The authors of this volume show how theories of shared cognition contribute to the development of computerized agents that can be used as virtual collaborators in performing complex tasks. They illustrate the development and application of team-related simulations, which have emerged as fundamental tools in both research and application.

This volume poses fundamental questions about the meaning of cognition and the science of teams. It presents a compelling case that the current models of cognition as an activity that happens within individuals need to be broadened, and that the development of a better understanding of how cognition functions as a shared activity will lead to a different understanding of what a team is and how a team functions. Drawing on theory and models from communications, computer-mediated cognition, and collaboration, the authors of this volume show how cross-disciplinary research holds the potential to redefine our understanding of how individuals, groups, and even man–machine systems process, share, and come to understand information.

This book will appeal to undergraduate and graduate students in psychology, sociology, communication, computer science, and cognitive science. It will challenge and inform researchers in all of these fields and is likely to become a standard reference tool for cross-disciplinary work in a number of areas that touch upon the challenges and opportunities associated with studying shared information processing. Professionals and practitioners who work with teams will find this volume extremely useful, laying out a roadmap of where team research and interventions designed to help teams function effectively are likely to go in the coming decade. This is an exciting and challenging addition to the Applied Psychology Series.

Preface

We know that many scholars from an array of disciplines are interested in team cognition. We all recognize the importance of cognitive processes in teams, and so there has been some progress in understanding what matters in team cognition. The science of team cognition is in its early stages of maturity, and one way to motivate more research is by creating a forum where different thinking and theories can be discussed, debated, and learned from. This book aims to do just that. This book provides such a forum for leading scholars to share their ideas, theories, models, and conceptions about what matters in team cognition.

The book has been divided into sections that were formed on the basis of similarity and relatedness of theory and contribution. Section I, Team Cognition as a Field, lays the foundation for the topics and discussions that are included in the book. Chapter 1 discusses the various contributions presented in the book. Chapter 2 examines underlying constructs that drive the field as a whole. Section II is composed of information that is derived from the perspectives found in organizational behavior. In Chapter 3, team cognition is conceptualized in a medical context, and the authors present a tool by which surgeons can better understand the intentions of others and enhance patient care. Time and the important consideration of temporal dynamics are broken down and considered in Chapter 4. Leadership and its important influence on team cognition is the topic of Chapter 5. Finally, Chapter 6 elaborates on the concept of similar meanings and presents methodologies that are appropriate for their investigation.

Section III focuses on perspectives found in human factors and cognitive systems engineering (CSE). Beginning with Chapter 7, the concept of coordination is discussed from the stance of CSE. In Chapter 8, interactive team cognition (ITC) is introduced and explained. Finally, Chapter 9 explores activity awareness and presents collaborative competencies that enable it, as well as tools that can develop and enhance the competencies.

Section IV transitions the discussion to cognitive and computer science perspectives. The section opens with Chapter 10, which views sharing cognition from the lens of the combinations-of-contributions theory. Chapter 11 explains macrocognition in teams and addresses the influence

xv

xvi • *Preface*

of task complexity. In Chapter 12, the benefits of using network analysis approaches to represent team knowledge are described. Chapter 13 reviews current research and evaluates future potential concerning the use of agents in teams. An interdisciplinary understanding of different aspects of macrocognition is presented in Chapter 14. The final chapter in this section, Chapter 15, explores the dynamics of expectations of team members in relation to team interaction processes and outcomes.

Section V explores team cognition from social psychology, communication, and developmental perspectives. Beginning with Chapter 16, a "hybrid" approach to studying teams is offered and elaborated upon. Chapter 17 addresses the concept of transactive memory, expanding on its theoretical foundation as well as possible implications for team research. Next, in Chapter 18, sharing is understood as co-orientation of perspectives, and through the incorporation of research from communication and psychology, different meanings that sharing can have are explored from multiple dimensions. Chapter 19 furthers the notion that because team cognition has its basis in communication, it can be exposed by examining interdependent messages that take place during team interactions. In Chapter 20, the gap in the literature that exists with regards to long-term and short-term knowledge is exposed and addressed. From a computer-supported collaborative learning (CSCL) perspective, Chapter 21 identifies factors that foster discussions within which learning occurs. Chapter 22 presents a taxonomy that illustrates the relationships that exist between a team's task and their communication.

Section VI serves as a concluding section that pulls together the ideas and concepts presented in the book, outlining the road ahead as far as progress for the field of team cognition is concerned. Chapter 23 elaborates upon the concept of coordination and addresses the critical role that it plays in team cognition. Chapter 24 concludes the book by identifying several themes that have surfaced throughout the chapters. It further reflects upon those themes and interprets them in a way that aims to direct future efforts in the field of team cognition.

Acknowledgments

It is our hope that the ideas and contributions that make up this book promote a more robust science of team cognition. We would like to thank the Office of Naval Research for their support in this book. This book originated from a workshop held at the University of Central Florida funded under the ONR MURI Grant #N000140610446. We would like to thank Mike Letsky and Norm Warner for their support and the many scholars that make up the team-cognition community.

xvii

About the Editors

Eduardo Salas is University Trustee Chair and Pegasus Professor of Psychology at the University of Central Florida (UCF) and Program Director for the Human Systems Integration Research Department at UCF's Institute for Simulation and Training. Salas is a Fellow of the American Psychological Association (Society for Industrial and Organization Psychology and Divisions 19, 21, and 49), the Human Factors and Ergonomics Society, and the Association for Psychological Science. He was editor of *Human Factors* from 2000 to 2004. For 15 years, he was a Senior Research Psychologist and head of the Training Technology Development Branch of NAVAIR-Orlando. Salas served as a principal investigator for numerous research and development programs focusing on teamwork, team training, simulation-based training, decision-making under stress, learning methodologies, and performance assessment. He helps organizations foster teamwork, design and implement team-training strategies, facilitate training effectiveness, manage decision-making under stress, develop performance-measurement tools, and design learning- and simulation-based environments. Salas has coauthored more than 330 journal articles and book chapters and has coedited 20 books. He has served as an editorial board member for numerous journals and is an associate editor of the *Journal of Applied Psychology*. He received a PhD in industrial and organizational psychology from Old Dominion University in 1984.

Stephen M. Fiore is a faculty member at the University of Central Florida's (UCF) Cognitive Sciences Program in the Department of Philosophy and Director of the Cognitive Sciences Laboratory at UCF's Institute for Simulation and Training. He earned his PhD in Cognitive Psychology from the University of Pittsburgh, Learning Research and Development Center. He maintains a multidisciplinary research interest that incorporates aspects of the cognitive, social, and computational sciences in the investigation of learning and performance in individuals and teams. He is coeditor of the recent titles *Team Cognition* (American Psychological Association, 2004), *Toward a Science of Distributed Learning* (American Psychological Association, 2007), and *Macrocognition in Teams* (Ashgate, 2008), and he has coauthored more than 100 scholarly publications in the

xix

xx • *About the Editors*

areas of learning, memory, and problem solving at the individual and group levels. As Principal Investigator and Co-Principal Investigator at the University of Central Florida he has helped to secure and manage approximately $15 million in research funding from organizations such as the National Science Foundation, the Office of Naval Research, the Air Force Office of Scientific Research, and the Department of Homeland Security.

Michael P. Letsky is currently Program Officer for the Collaboration and Knowledge Interoperability Program at the Office of Naval Research (ONR) in Arlington, Virginia. He manages a research program of academic grants and innovative small business projects seeking to understand team cognition and team performance. He previously worked for the Army Research Institute of the Behavioral and Social Sciences where he developed their long range strategic research plan and also served on the Army Science Board on Highly Maneuverable Forces. Dr. Letsky's education includes a BS in Electrical Engineering (Northeastern University) and an MBA and DBA in Operations Research (George Washington University).

Contributors

Stephenson J. Beck
Department of Communication
North Dakota State University
Fargo, North Dakota

Marcela Borge
College of Information Sciences
and Technology
The Pennsylvania State University
University Park, Pennsylvania

David P. Brandon
Beckman Institute for Advanced
Science and Technology
University of Illinois Urbana-
Champaign
Urbana, Illinois

John M. Carroll
College of Information Sciences
and Technology
The Pennsylvania State University
University Park, Pennsylvania

Georgia T. Chao
Department of Management
Michigan State University
East Lansing, Michigan

Mark A. Clark
Kogod School of Business
American University
Washington, DC

Nancy J. Cooke
Cognitive Science and
Engineering, Technological
Entrepreneurship and
Innovation Management
Arizona State University
Polytechnic
Mesa, Arizona

Leslie A. DeChurch
Department of Psychology
University of Central Florida
Orlando, Florida

Gary Dunnington
Department of Surgery
Southern Illinois University
School of Medicine
Springfield, Illinois

Jasmine Duran
Lumir Research Institute
Grayslake, Illinois

John Elias
Institute for Simulation and
Training
University of Central Florida
Orlando, Florida

J. Alberto Espinosa
Kogod School of Business
American University
Washington, DC

xxi

xxii • *Contributors*

Craig H. Ganoe
College of Information Sciences
and Technology
The Pennsylvania State University
University Park, Pennsylvania

Jamie C. Gorman
Psychology Department
Texas Tech University
Lubbock, Texas

Yufan Guo
Thayer School of Engineering
Dartmouth College
Hanover, New Hampshire

Naina Gupta
Nanyang Business School
Nanyang Technological University
Nanyang, Singapore

Katherine Hamilton
College of Information Sciences
and Technology
The Pennsylvania State University
University Park, Pennsylvania

Andrea B. Hollingshead
Annenberg School for
Communication and
Journalism
University of Southern California
Los Angeles, California

Verlin B. Hinsz
Department of Psychology
North Dakota State University
Fargo, North Dakota

Elizabeth Jacob
Thayer School of Engineering
Dartmouth College
Hanover, New Hampshire

Miliani Jiménez
Department of Psychology
University of Central Florida
Orlando, Florida

Lindsay B. Katona
Thayer School of Engineering
Dartmouth College
Hanover, New Hampshire

Deanna M. Kennedy
University of Washington Bothell
Bothell, Washington

Joann Keyton
Department of Communication
North Carolina State University
Raleigh, North Carolina

Keum Joo Kim
Thayer School of Engineering
Dartmouth College
Hanover, New Hampshire

Michael Kim
School of Medicine
University of Rochester
Rochester, New York

Timothy Koschmann
Department of Medical Education
Southern Illinois University School
of Medicine
Springfield, Illinois

Contributors • xxiii

Steve W. J. Kozlowski
Department of Psychology
Michigan State University
East Lansing, Michigan

Jared L. Ladbury
Department of Psychology
North Dakota State University
Fargo, North Dakota

Michael Lewis
School of Information Sciences
University of Pittsburgh
Pittsburgh, Pennsylvania

Deqing Li
Thayer School of Engineering
Dartmouth College
Hanover, New Hampshire

Jean Liu
Veterans Affairs Medical Center
White River Junction, Vermont

Heather Lum
Department of Psychology
University of Central Florida
Orlando, Florida

Rebecca Lyons
Institute for Simulation and Training
University of Central Florida
Orlando, Florida

Sara A. McComb
School of Nursing and School of
  Industrial Engineering
Purdue University
West Lafayette, Indiana

Michael D. McNeese
College of Information Sciences
  and Technology
The Pennsylvania State University
University Park, Pennsylvania

Susan Mohammed
Department of Psychology
The Pennsylvania State University
University Park, Pennsylvania

Ioana R. Mot
University of Phoenix Online
Houston, Texas

Toshio Murase
Department of Psychology
University of Central Florida
Orlando, Florida

Peter Musaeus
Center for Medical Education
Aarhus University
Aarhus, Denmark

Christopher Myers
Performance and Learning
  Models Team
Cognitive Models and Agents
  Branch (RHAC)
Wright-Patterson Air Force Base,
  Ohio

Emily S. Patterson
College of Medicine
School of Allied Medical
  Professions
Ohio State University
Columbus, Ohio

xxiv • *Contributors*

Mark S. Pfaff
School of Informatics
Indiana University
Indianapolis, Indiana

Marshall Scott Poole
Department of Communication
University of Illinois
Urbana, Illinois

Joan R. Rentsch
Department of Management
The University of Tennessee
Knoxville, Tennessee

Christian J. Resick
LeBow College of Business
Drexel University
Philadelphia, Pennsylvania

Olivia C. Riches
Institute for Simulation and
    Training
University of Central Florida
Orlando, Florida

Carolyn Penstein Rosé
Languages Technologies Institute
Carnegie Mellon University
Pittsburgh, Pennsylvania

Joseph Rosen
Thayer School of Engineering
Dartmouth College
Hanover, New Hampshire

Mary Beth Rosson
College of Information Sciences
    and Technology
The Pennsylvania State University
University Park, Pennsylvania

Eugene Santos, Jr.
Thayer School of Engineering
Dartmouth College
Hanover, New Hampshire

Elizabeth Sanz
Department of Psychology
University of Central Florida
Orlando, Florida

Samuel Shih
Thayer School of Engineering
Dartmouth College
Hanover, New Hampshire

Randall Shumaker
University of Central Florida
Orlando, Florida

Gerry Stahl
Drexel University
Philadelphia, Pennsylvania

Robert J. Stephens
National Center for Human
    Factors in Healthcare
MedStar Health
Washington, District of Columbia

Gita Sukthankar
Department of Electrical
 Engineering and Computer
 Science
University of Central Florida
Orlando, Florida

Rachel Tesler
Department of Psychology
The Pennsylvania State University
University Park, Pennsylvania

Norman Warner
Naval Air Systems Command
White Haven, Pennsylvania

Kay Yoon
College of Communication
DePaul University
Chicago, Illinois

Fei Yu
Thayer School of Engineering
Dartmouth College
Hanover, New Hampshire

Section I

Team Cognition as a Field

1

Why Cross-Disciplinary Theories of Team Cognition?

Eduardo Salas, Stephen M. Fiore, and Michael P. Letsky

Teamwork, by its very definition, is achieved when members interact interdependently and work together toward shared and valued goals. Further, expert teamwork involves the adaptation of collaboration strategies through coordination, cooperation, and communication, as well as a collective understanding of the task so that the team can reach its goals (Salas & Cannon-Bowers, 2000). Cognitive psychology has substantially influenced the study of teams, and it has been over a decade since the original applications of constructs from cognitive psychology were used to foster the development of the team cognition movement (e.g., Cannon-Bowers, Salas, & Converse, 1993; Hutchins, 1991; Orasanu, 1990). Since then, much cross-disciplinary attention has focused on determining how cognitive processes contribute to effective team performance. What is invariant across these disciplines is the notion that shared information processing among group members has both inter- and intraindividual outcomes (e.g., Levine, Resnick, & Higgins, 1993), whereby constructs such as encoding, storage, and retrieval of information are thought to be equally applicable to both individuals and groups (e.g., Hinsz, Tindale, & Vollrath, 1997; Larson & Christensen, 1993; Tindale & Kameda, 2000).

Although there have been recent multidisciplinary integrations in investigations of team process and performance (Salas & Fiore, 2004), there is much to be learned with regard to cross-disciplinary interaction between researchers in team cognition and emerging areas such as macrocognition, group cognition, distributed cognition, and team cognition. The overarching purpose of this book is to provide an outlet for leading scientists in the field of shared cognition to discuss their own and related work. Across these disciplines, shared cognition can involve a variety of factors. For example, it can encompass differing levels of complexity

4 • *Theories of Team Cognition*

of cognitive processes. It can describe the manifestation of cognition in the real world versus the laboratory. It can also involve varying levels of analysis—from the individual to the team. Additionally, teams in shared cognition research can range from well-established teams to ad hoc and rapidly formed teams who have to deal with difficult situations as they present themselves in the short term. Additionally, given the complexity of the problems these teams face, they are often quite heterogeneous, possessing unique skills and knowledge. These teams may also work within environments that are ill defined and that often carry grave consequences for mistakes. Regardless of the situation, the focus is the cognitive processes that arise during the complex and dynamic interaction of teams.

In consideration of this general context, our objective with this volume is to codify some of the foundational theoretical issues associated with shared cognition and help the scientific community move forward in its attempts to understand this complex issue. Contributors to this book will discuss how it is that team process and performance are impacted by interindividual and intraindividual factors, in the context of a variety of complex environments. We next summarize the contributions to this volume to illustrate the breadth of disciplinary perspectives.

CROSS-DISCIPLINARY PERSPECTIVES ON TEAM COGNITION

In Chapter 2, Kozlowski and Chao (a) present a theoretical approach for conceptualizing the process of team learning; (b) develop theoretical representations of resulting team knowledge as a means to drive measurement of its formation, emergence, and manifestation at the collective level of analysis; and (c) sketch theoretical processes that are likely to shape team knowledge acquisition and emergence. They first highlight the theoretical foundation and key conceptual drivers of the approach, founded on a distinction between learning processes and knowledge outcomes, the iterative process of knowledge acquisition and formation, and the origins of learning and knowledge both at the individual level and at the collective level of the team. The authors then develop a taxonomy to represent team knowledge conceptually linked to corresponding techniques for measuring it. The goal of this theoretical and operational effort is to develop a robust conceptualization of team knowledge emergence as collective phenomena and a set of measurement tools to capture it that can be applied across a wide range of team task situations. Finally, they focus on what they believe are core theoretical processes—team member networks and team regulation—that are likely to influence team knowledge acquisition and its emergence in the team. In combination, the knowledge conceptual foundation, team knowledge measurement tools, and the processes that influence knowledge acquisition and emergence constitute an integrated framework to guide research on how teams can be shaped to generate new knowledge efficiently and effectively.

In situations such as combat casualty care, understanding the medical environments, where surgeons must make crucial decisions under the pressures of limited time and information as well as a multitude of competing demands and distractions, is essential to improving the chances of the injured patient's survival. The surgeons who understand their coworkers and such environments can make better decisions for patients, families, and care providers. In Chapter 3, Santos et al. provide a computational tool to assist a surgeon's decision making by inferring others' intentions from his observations and perceptions. Through modeling an individual surgeon's decision-making processes and integrating these under the overall team intent regarding patient care, they contribute to a better attainment of the target organizational intent and patient care. In particular, this can be implemented by detecting and minimizing errors that arise from a number of situations including communications failure among individuals within a team, as well as from handoffs between teams. The authors describe their approach to modeling intent, which includes reasoning with Bayesian Knowledge Bases, and to validating the models built through a real-world test case.

In Chapter 4, Mohammed, Tesler, and Hamilton address the crucial and often overlooked role of time in the process of shared cognition. From its inception, shared cognition was designed to account for the implicit coordination frequently observed in effective teams. Although the importance of coordination and timing are inherent in the broad conceptualization of many types of shared cognition (e.g., team mental models, transactive memory, shared situational awareness), the role of time has been largely downplayed in past research. Although an understanding of the "what" and the "who" are indeed critical to team functioning, a failure to understand the "when" can seriously jeopardize final team outcomes. Therefore,

6 • Theories of Team Cognition

our understanding of shared cognition should be broadened to include shared perceptions of temporal milestones and the pacing of actions. Not only has time been downplayed in the conceptualization of shared cognition, but measurement techniques have been temporally deficient as well. Although there are clearly examples of empirical studies that have tracked the longitudinal development of shared cognition over time, temporal reference points can as yet be more directly and explicitly included in the measures of shared cognition. For example, the authors suggest that future research could be sharpened conceptually and operationally by explicitly defining team mental models as shared, organized mental representations of who is going to do *what* (taskwork), with *whom* (teamwork), and *when*.

Leadership plays a pivotal role in shaping and reshaping the cognitive states that emerge and underpin collective performance. Although both the leadership (Weick, 1995) and team (Burke, Stagle, Salas, Pierce, & Kendall, 2006; Randall, Resick, & DeChurch, 2009) literatures have begun to explicitly examine the role of leadership in shaping collective cognition, these two research areas have progressed largely in silos. In Chapter 5, Murase, Resick, Jiménez, Sanz, and DeChurch develop an integrated framework linking leadership functions to the emergence of collective cognition. They begin by examining the forms of collective cognition that have implications for collective-level success. Next, they propose that six forms of leadership are particularly important facilitators of collective cognition; for each type of leadership, they discuss specific mechanisms that facilitate the emergence of collective cognition and develop propositions intended to stimulate future research. The authors conclude with a discussion of practical and theoretical implications.

In Chapter 6, Rentsch and Mot detail a model of configurations of cognitive similarity in intense problem-solving teams (i.e., teams of experts solving complex problems in difficult contexts). Rentsch, Delise, and Hutchinson (2008) defined cognitive similarity as "forms of related meanings or understandings attributed to and utilized to make sense of and interpret internal and external events including affect, behavior, and thoughts of self and others that exist amongst individuals" (p. 130). Multiple types of cognitive similarity exist, definable by the intersection of three features: (1) form of the cognition, (2) form of similarity, and (3) cognitive content domain. Types of cognitive similarity in combination produce configurations of cognitive similarity (Rentsch, Small, & Hanges, 2008). Rentsch and Mot describe the relevance of cognitive similarity configuration for intense problem-solving teams as they adapt and engage in internalized and externalized cognitive processes to achieve viable solutions. Literature drawn from the research in organizational behavior, industrial organizational psychology, social psychology, cognitive psychology, and human factors psychology supports the model. Questions such as the following serve as the impetus for developing the model: What is team cognition? How are cognitive configurations developed? What cognitive configurations are most relevant to intense problem-solving teams?

Patterson and Stephens, in Chapter 7, address macrocognitive processes in the context of technological extension and interaction. From their perspective, cognition at the macro level is conducted by humans supported by technological aids to effectively cope with complexity in the world. Common elements are (a) joint activity distributed over time and space, (b) coordinated to meet complex, dynamic demands, (c) in an uncertain, event-driven environment with (d) complementary and conflicting goals and high consequences for failure, (e) made possible by effective expertise in roles, and (f) shaped by organizational (blunt end) constraints, which produce emergent phenomena such as automation surprises, groupthink, mental simulations, escalation, and knowledge shielding. Cognitive functions include (a) detecting anomalies, (b) assessing explanations, (c) committing to decisions, (d) making sense of the big picture, (e) replanning in response to obstacles and opportunities, and (f) flexibly executing a plan. All cognitive functions are supported by collaboration functions. Functions can be triggered by events in the world, communication episodes, or internal cognitive processing. Certain factors can increase the complexity of functions, such as *red herrings*, hidden couplings between activities, and distributed knowledge and expertise across roles that do not usually directly interact.

Teams are a special kind of group, one that has members who play heterogeneous but interdependent roles to work toward common objectives (Salas, Dickinson, Converse, & Tannenbaum, 1992). Thus, a typing pool of individuals doing the same task, each independently, is a small group that can be contrasted with a surgical team (nurse, surgeon, anesthesiologist), the members of which each have distinct but interdependent roles. Furthermore, teams increasingly perform cognitive tasks such as planning, decision making, designing, assessing situations, and solving problems. In Chapter 8, Cooke, Gorman, Myers, and Duran describe one perspective on team cognition, interactive team cognition (ITC), which is a different perspective on team cognition that has arisen in response to limitations

8 • *Theories of Team Cognition*

of shared cognition, data inconsistent with shared cognition, and a set of psychological theories that are seen by some as alternatives to information processing psychology and others as a focus on inextricable interconnectedness between animals and their environment to produce cognitive processing (Cooke, Gorman, & Rowe, 2009; Cooke, Gorman, & Winner, 2007). ITC views team cognition not as a knowledge collective, but as an activity. It is the joint activity that teams engage in when they coordinate, communicate, and make decisions (Galantucci & Sebanz, 2009).

In complex and creative task contexts, collaborators must attain and maintain reciprocal awareness of partners through significant spans of time and across many levels of team functioning to coordinate and perform effectively. This requirement is difficult to achieve in relatively routine, face-to-face teamwork interactions and remains highly problematic when teams are faced with one-of-a-kind situations and supported by contemporary collaborative systems and software. In Chapter 9, Carroll, Borge, Ganoe, and Rosson present an analysis of the collaborative competencies required for teams to attain and maintain awareness of their own shared activity and discuss tools and activities they are building to support development of these competencies.

Sharing cognitions is important for understanding cognitive task performance in teams. In Chapter 10, Hinsz and Ladbury take the perspective of information processing in teams and combinations-of-contributions theory as organizing frameworks for sharing cognition in teams. They propose that team performance can be predicted based on the cognitive contributions members bring to their team and the ways these cognitions are combined and shared. In addition, combinations-of-contributions theory proposes that the context in which the team performs the task and the correspondence of the members' cognitive contributions to task demands help predict team performance. Research on shared mental models and information sharing in teams is used to show how combinations-of-contributions theory helps us understand the unique nature of sharing cognition. In addition, the authors describe a social cognition–based approach for team interaction and task performance, which proposes that the expectations team members hold about how teams operate mediate the relationships between team interaction and team functioning and outcomes. The importance of these expectations for understanding team cognitive performance is highlighted. By using combinations of contributions, information processing in teams, and expectations for team interactions perspectives, Chapter 10 describes a number of conceptual approaches for comprehending how cognitions are shared in teams.

In Chapter 11, Lyons, Lum, Fiore, Salas, Warner, and Letsky argue that theory and methods from the cognitive and organizational sciences can be integrated with ideas on task complexity to produce a fuller understanding of the macrocognitive processes involved in problem solving within complex collaborative environments. The authors first describe the characteristics embedded within complex collaborative environments. They then discuss the development of the macrocognition construct within naturalistic research environments and briefly discuss research on task complexity. They conclude by providing a set of research propositions to guide empirical examination of how task complexity may impact macrocognitive processes.

Team knowledge research has traditionally focused on small, real-time teams. However, many extant team knowledge constructs and measures are not applicable for asynchronous tasks performed by larger teams, particularly when team members are geographically dispersed. In Chapter 12, Espinosa and Clark propose a multidimensional network approach to representing and measuring team knowledge effectively in large teams with relatively complex tasks. This approach is based on several concepts: (1) a given type of team knowledge can be represented and measured at the dyad level using current methods; (2) various types of team knowledge (e.g., task, durable, fleeting) can be reduced to fundamental underlying dimensions that can help reconcile the abundance of constructs in the literature (e.g., team mental models, transactive memory, team awareness); (3) these dimensions can be individual (about team members) or relational (about the knowledge relationship in a dyad); (4) team boundaries (e.g., distance, time zones) can be represented as relational attributes; and (5) team knowledge for larger teams can be represented and measured using social network methods with individual attributes (of team members) and relationship attributes (of dyads), such that configuration measures such as knowledge isolates, cliques, and centrality can help explain variance beyond simple aggregate measures.

Macrocognition has been defined as the high-level cognitive processes, both internalized and externalized, that teams engage in to create new knowledge. Expressions of externalized processes are related to other team members' reference/interpretation systems, such as language, icons, gestures, and boundary objects, among others. By this definition, computerized agents that do such things as identify targets, filter information, or communicate through messages are exhibiting externalized macrocognition at the same ontological level as the humans they serve. Software agents have been designed to fill a variety of roles within teams, including supporting individual team members, being a teammate, and supporting the team as a whole (Stasser, Stewart, & Wittenbaum, 1995). Many of the facets of human agent teamwork models, such as communication protocols for forming mutual intelligibility, performing team monitoring to assess progress, forming joint goals, and addressing task interdependencies in hybrid teamwork, are still unexplored. In Chapter 13, Sukthankar, Shumaker, and Lewis review research on multiagent systems, mixed initiative control, and agent interaction within human teams to evaluate the potential of developing agents to serve as bona fide team members.

The last several decades of research have resulted in a symbiotic understanding of complex team performance and how intelligent tools may aid teams. This has generated an interdisciplinary, emergent view of macrocognition that emphasizes the interactive and mutually constraining roles of cognition and context as they shape situated action in highly complex environments. In Chapter 14, McNeese and Pfaff elaborate on a shared cognitive systems approach through the Living Laboratory Framework, tracing historical perspectives. The framework is used to review how shared cognitive systems have been studied and developed through multiple theoretical lenses, ethnographic fieldwork activities, scaled world simulations, and distributed artifacts and tools. Inherent in this view are the influences of cognitive science and cognitive engineering perspectives that jointly determine how shared cognitive systems produce adaptive behavior in emergent, dynamic teamwork. In particular, the chapter portrays and analyzes several team-related simulations (e.g., TRAP, CITIES, JASPER, NeoCITIES, R-CAST) used to look at the mutual integration of theory, information, technology, and people for a variety of domains. Important themes for macrocognition, such as affective/belief states, perceptual differentiation, transactive memory, temporal mental models, collective induction, situated learning, and hidden knowledge profiles, are described in light of intelligent support mechanisms (agents, aids, and geo-visual analytics).

When exploring collaboration in teams, the inherent difficulties that impede efforts aimed at understanding team processes should not be discounted. Moreover, these complications should be identified so that effective ways to address them or work around them can be established. In

Why Cross-Disciplinary Theories of Team Cognition? • 11

Chapter 15, Ladbury and Hinsz attend to this need and propose a conceptualization of team functioning that incorporates how team member expectations lead to team interaction outcomes. In defining expectations, the authors focus on the cognitive beliefs that team members have about their team, its behaviors and interactions, and its outcomes. Using a social relations approach, Ladbury and Hinsz propose how team processes that lead to team outcomes can be quantified, providing valuable insight into how teams complete tasks. They discuss the social relations model (SRM) and how it allows team researchers to not only understand how expectations influence team functioning, but also how a variety of other factors underlying team processes can impact team functioning. The authors conclude with an overview of different areas of research on teams and small groups that would benefit from investigations using the SRM.

Teamwork lies at the nexus of a variety of disciplines' interests. Cognitive and social psychology, organization science, human factors research, and communication studies, to name a few, all have scholarly interests related to the functioning of groups and teams. Given this convergence of interest, it would seem mutually advantageous to find ways of sharing insights across fields. The current volume seeks to engender just such a conversation, one intended to eventually lead to a *science of teams*, a science that would eventually enable us to make positive recommendations regarding how teams should function. This would require establishing an agreed upon theoretical vocabulary and set of measurement methods. Taken for granted within this larger enterprise is a shared allegiance to a way of conducting research that entails: (a) formulating an abstract model of what counts as the phenomenon of interest, (b) constructing operational means of measurement, and (c) using these measures to test hypotheses about how the matter, so construed, might be done better. The disciplines currently participating in the conversation on teamwork (i.e., cognitive and social psychology, management science, communication studies) all have a strong psychological orientation. As we expand the circle of participation and reach out to other disciplines, however, some problems begin to emerge. It becomes apparent that this strategy of beginning from a base of theoretical constructions is not one that is universally embraced across the human sciences. Indeed, some social scientists reject this kind of approach categorically and on principle. In Chapter 16, Koschmann, Dunnington, and Kim examine one critique of formal theorizing in the social sciences and point out its relevance to the task of constructing a science of teams.

12 • *Theories of Team Cognition*

They offer a sample of an alternative form of analysis and suggest a framework for what might be termed a *hybrid* approach to studying teams.

Using the theory of transactive memory as a way of explaining how people share information in groups has become increasingly popular among researchers across a wide array of disciplines. A transactive memory system is a group-level memory system that often develops in close relationships and work teams. It involves the division of responsibility among group members with respect to the encoding, storage, retrieval, and communication of information from different knowledge areas and a shared awareness among group members about each member's knowledge responsibilities (or *who knows what*). Evidence of transactive memory systems has been documented in a variety of relationships and groups, including married couples, dating couples, families, friends, coworkers, and project teams in both organizational and laboratory settings. In Chapter 17, Hollingshead, Gupta, Yoon, and Brandon describe the original theory and its extensions over time, how the theory has been tested, the various ways of measuring transactive memory, and where the theory may be heading in the future.

In Chapter 18, Poole focuses on the various meanings that sharing can have, drawing on the literature in communication and psychology. An important factor that shapes shared cognition is interaction among group members. Through interaction, members exchange information about the situation and how they frame it, learn from each other, diagnose points of disagreement or divergence, attempt to repair misaligned cognitive frames, and exchange information on the status of *sharedness* in the group. Indeed, at an operational level, what is shared is what is openly discussed in group interaction. The degree to which cognition is shared in groups will be conceptualized in terms of the degree of co-orientation among group members about critical topics. Co-orientation—an essential property of interpersonal communication systems—refers to the degree to which members agree, understand they agree, and understand that others understand agreement. Co-orientation is a multilevel concept that can be used as a metric for shared cognition, and its variation over time can be used to describe the state of shared cognition in a group at any point in time. Several communication processes that enact shared cognition systems and that build and repair them through increasing co-orientation are discussed.

Teamwork is achieved when members interact interdependently and work together toward shared goals. That interdependence can be observed in what teams do (behavior) and what messages they send to one another (talk). For teams whose tasks are primarily cognitive ones (i.e., problem solving, decision making, creating strategy) and for which no known solution exists, the interdependence of team members' talk reveals not only how group outcomes are developed, but also the functional strategies used by members to get their ideas considered by others. What team members say and how and when they say it relative to other team members' contributions are crucial variables to consider in teamwork processes. In Chapter 19, Beck and Keyton argue that macrocognition, or team cognition, is communicatively based and can be tracked in team members' message interdependence. Transcripts of jury deliberations of a death penalty murder trial are used to explore how individual positions are managed through conversation to create a group decision. A jury is a problem-solving team formed with zero history to deliberate on complex information. Moreover, a jury can only return a guilty verdict when sufficient shared meaning about their task and facts of the case is achieved. Theoretical propositions are advanced, extending from current research and theory.

In Chapter 20, Musaeus explores an important tension in team and macrocognitive research between long-term knowledge and short-term knowledge. Short-term knowledge can be understood as fleeting knowledge associated with team situational awareness (Cooke, Salas, Kiekel, & Bell, 2004). This might be conceived as a type of team cognition in the here and now, for instance, in regard to team coordination, workspace awareness, or up-to-the-moment understanding (Fiore, Rosen, Salas, Burke, & Jentsch, 2008). However, team cognition also draws from the notion of long-term knowledge conceived as team cognitive structures such as mental models and "knowledge of the nature and causes of the problem" (Fiore et al., 2008, p. 153) referring to problems relating to the situation. Orasanu and Fischer (1992, p. 189) argued that although professional teams clearly have shared background knowledge, as also argued earlier in terms of scientific knowledge, the fact that accidents and errors occur illustrates the need for something besides shared background knowledge, namely a shared team understanding of the current situation. But errors do not occur because teams have a shared knowledge background, and they do not disappear regardless of how many shared team models a team might have; after all, the models could be wrong. An ethnographic video study by Xiao and Moss (2001) on trauma resuscitation teams found that the teams were characterized by a high degree of shared responsibility to prevent failures. The teams practiced a checks and balances system where team members were expected to register and speak out loud the vital signs of the patient. However, in order for such a system of mutual group checking to function, the team must share an idea about what knowledge is, what signs are worth communicating, and why they are doing this. Thus, team reason is a precondition for a check and balance system. Individual cognition, macrocognition, and team cognition are social phenomena, not foremost because knowledge is shared and can be made public, but because team cognition is unthinkable without social practices such as natural science or art that provide means for team members to think and reason with. Thus, what members of society take to be rational, that is to say, mediated by societal institutions and with goals, norms, and underlying assumptions amenable to critical scrutiny, might shape what a high-reliability team takes to be worth pursuing. Therefore, the notion of team reason aims to describe how societal institutions validate and shape knowledge, goals, tools, and ideas relevant for high-reliability team problem solving.

In Chapter 21, Stahl and Rosé present a disciplinary perspective from computer-supported collaborative learning (CSCL), an interdisciplinary field concerned with leveraging technology for education and analyzing cognitive processes such as learning and meaning making in small groups of students (Stahl, Koschmann, & Suthers, 2006). *Group cognition* is a theory developed to support CSCL research by describing how collaborative groups of students could achieve cognitive accomplishments together and how that could benefit the individual learning of the participants (Stahl, 2006). Group cognition can then be seen as what transforms groups into factories for the creation of new knowledge. The types of problems that have been the focus of exploration within the group cognition paradigm have thus not been routine, well-structured problems where every participant can know exactly what their piece of the puzzle is up front in such a way that the team can function as a well-oiled machine. The processes that are the concern of group cognition research have not primarily been those that are related to efficiency of problem solving (as in some other chapters of this volume). Rather, the focus has been on the pivotal moments where a creative spark or a process of collaborative knowledge building occurs through interaction. Here, the authors consider insights from group cognition in light of synergistic ideas from subcommunities within CSCL, with a focus on identifying the conditions under which these moments of inspiration are triggered and with the goal of facilitating this process of group innovation and collaborative knowledge creation.

Why Cross-Disciplinary Theories of Team Cognition? • 15

In Chapter 22, McComb and Kennedy conceive team cognition in problem-solving teams as deeply linked to team communication, such that the unfolding of the convergence process can be examined through the information conveyed by team members as they collaborate (Kennedy & McComb, 2010). The medium over which communication is carried out is a salient issue for researchers interested in mental model convergence, particularly because the medium is uniquely capable of limiting the amount and flow of information transmission among team members. Face-to-face communication provides a rich social medium through which many channels are open for information sharing (Short, Williams, & Christie, 1976). As such, the high social presence of team members may create a cooperative communication environment that, in turn, brings about concerted efforts in discussions (De Dreu, 2007). Such concerted efforts may, in turn, lead to more effective mental model convergence. Computer-mediated communication, in contrast, is a lean media that prompts users to be concise and efficient with their communication (Short et al., 1976). The lack of communication channels, however, creates an environment with low social presence prone to interruptions and less information sharing (e.g., Graetz, Boyle, Kimble, Thompson, & Garlock, 1998). This environment may lead to delayed, or an outright lack of, mental model convergence. Initiating team activities face to face before shifting to computer-mediated collaboration might provide the necessary sociotechnical environment to engender effective and efficient communication that facilitates the shared cognitive processing required for mental model convergence. Thus, team researchers interested in mental model convergence may benefit from incorporating the communication media used by teams. Moreover, by synthesizing research comparing the cognitive processes of face-to-face, computer-mediated, and mixed-media problem-solving teams, researchers may develop a more meaningful portrayal of the interrelationships among social presence, information sharing, and the mental model convergence process.

There are moments in any scientific exploration when the concepts employed themselves become the objects of inquiry, in the conceptual clarification that goes hand in hand with proper empirical investigation. For, after all, the questions we ask come conceptualized, and so direct, or misdirect, us towards the answers we seek. Thus it is obviously important to get the questions right in order for the right answers to follow. In Chapter 23, Elias and Fiore analyze and clarify the central concepts of *coordination* and *collaboration*, using a mix of etymological inquiry and

16 • *Theories of Team Cognition*

critical exposition of current usage to position the terms in relation to one another to better understand their similarities and distinctions. Specifically, the authors propose a reconceptualization of *explicit* and *implicit* coordination in terms of *collaboration* and *coordination*, which they argue captures the dynamics of autonomy and authority at play in coordinative processes in a way that other descriptions do not. They conclude by tracing connections with the rest of the contributions in this volume.

The chapters that comprise this volume have much to offer the growing field of team cognition. They clearly evidence how team cognition is a topic that both influences and is informed by a number of disciplines. This characteristic offers ample opportunity for growth of the field, yet at the same time, can have many negative implications for collaboration among scholars and integration of ideas. In Chapter 24, Riches and Salas expand and reflect upon several common threads that are suggested, both explicitly and implicitly, by each chapter. In doing so, the authors attend to aspects of team cognition where progress has been made and where more attention is needed. Moreover, they challenge team cognition scholars to continue to identify and address such themes that surface in the team cognition literature. Such efforts are critical because they will motivate research, while at the same time, continue to close the gaps that exist among the different disciplines in the field of team cognition.

SUMMARY

As our understanding of the shared cognition concept matures, we can pursue the development of theoretically driven and empirically based guidelines for designing, managing, and developing teams, as well as examine how these theories and findings apply to differing domains. This book represents one step toward integrating theories across disciplines so as to lead to a better understanding of shared cognition in complex collaborative contexts. In order for shared cognition research to achieve the broad power and scope necessary for it to benefit performance in real-world environments, theory and methods in one domain must be examined in relation to a variety of domains. Toward this end, our aim with this book is to promote interdisciplinary thinking in shared cognition so as to advance a dialogue between researchers from differing disciplines.

Only in this way can we hope to address the variety of needs surrounding dynamic team functioning.

ACKNOWLEDGMENTS

This research was supported by the Office of Naval Research (ONR) Collaboration and Knowledge Interoperability (CKI) Program and ONR Multidisciplinary University Research Initiative Grant No. N000140610446 (Dr. Michael P. Letsky, Program Manager). We thank John Elias for help in preparing this manuscript.

REFERENCES

Burke, C. S., Stagl, K. C., Salas, E., Pierce, L., & Kendall, D. L. (2006). Understanding team adaptation: A conceptual analysis and model. *Journal of Applied Psychology, 91,* 1189–1207.

Cannon-Bowers, J., Salas, E., & Converse, S. (1993). Shared mental models in expert team decision making. In N. J. Castellan Jr. (Ed.), *Individual and group decision making: Current issues* (pp. 221–246). Hillsdale, NJ: Lawrence Erlbaum Associates.

Cooke, N. J., Gorman, J. C., & Rowe, L. J. (2009). An ecological perspective on team cognition. In E. Salas, G. F. Goodwin, & C. S. Burke (Eds.), *Team effectiveness in complex organizations* (pp. 157–182). New York: Routledge, Taylor & Francis Group.

Cooke, N. J., Gorman, J., & Winner, J. L. (2007). Team cognition. In F. T. Durso, R. S. Nickerson, S. T. Dumais, S. Lewandowsky, & T. J. Perfect (Eds.), *Handbook of applied cognition* (2nd ed., pp. 239–268). Hoboken, NJ: John Wiley.

Cooke, N. J., Salas, E., Kiekel, P. A., & Bell, B. (2004). Advances in measuring team cognition. In E. Salas & S. M. Fiore (Eds.), *Team cognition* (pp. 83–106). Washington, DC: American Psychological Association.

De Dreu, C. K. W. (2007). Cooperative outcome interdependence, task reflexivity, and team effectiveness: A motivated information processing perspective. *Journal of Applied Psychology, 92,* 628–638.

Fiore, S. M., Rosen, M. A., Salas, E., Burke, C. S., & Jentsch, F. (2008). Processes in complex team problem solving: Parsing and defining the theoretical problem space. In M. Letsky, N. Warner, S. M. Fiore, & C. Smith (Eds.), *Macrocognition in teams: Theories and methodologies* (pp. 143–163). London: Ashgate Publishers.

Galantucci, B., & Sebanz, N. (2009). Joint action: Current perspectives. *Topics in Cognitive Science, 1,* 255–259.

Graetz, K., Boyle, E., Kimble, C., Thompson, P., & Garlock, J. (1998). Information sharing in face-to-face, teleconferencing, and electronic chat groups. *Small Group Research, 29,* 714–743.

Hinsz, V. B., Tindale, R. S., & Vollrath, D. A. (1997). The emerging conceptualization of groups as information processors. *Psychological Bulletin, 121,* 43–64.

18 • *Theories of Team Cognition*

Hutchins, E. (1991). The social organization of distributed cognition. In L. B. Resnick & J. M. Levine (Eds.), *Perspectives on socially shared cognition* (pp. 283–307). Washington, DC: American Psychological Association.

Kennedy, D., & McComb, S. (2010). Merging internal and external processes: Examining the mental model convergence process through team communication. *Theoretical Issues in Ergonomic Science, 11*, 339–356.

Larson, J. R., & Christensen, C. (1993). Groups as problem-solving units: Toward a new meaning of social cognition. *British Journal of Social Psychology, 32*, 5–30.

Levine, J. L., Resnick, L. B., & Higgins, E. T. (1993). Social foundations of cognition. *Annual Review of Psychology, 44*, 585–612.

Orasanu, J. (1990). *Shared mental models and crew performance* (Cognitive Science Laboratory Report No. 46). Princeton, NJ: Princeton University.

Orasanu, J., & Fischer, U. (1992). Distributed cognition in the cockpit: Linguistic control of shared problem solving. In *Proceedings of the Fourteenth Annual Conference of the Cognitive Science Society* (pp. 189–194). Hillsdale, NJ: Erlbaum.

Randall, K. R., Resick, C. J., & DeChurch, L. A. (2009). *Building adaptive capacity in teams: External leader sense-giving and team composition.* Unpublished working paper.

Rentsch, J. R., Delise, L. A., & Hutchinson, S. (2008). Transferring meaning and developing cognitive similarity in decision-making teams: Collaboration and meaning analysis process. In M. P. Letsky, N. W. Warner, S. M. Fiore, & C. Smith (Eds.), *Macrocognition in teams: Theories and methodologies* (pp. 127–142). London, UK: Ashgate.

Rentsch, J. R., Small, E. E., & Hanges, P. J. (2008). Cognitions in organizations and teams: What is the meaning of cognitive similarity? In B. Smith (Ed.), *The people make the place* (pp. 129–157). Mahwah, NJ: Lawrence Erlbaum.

Salas, E., & Cannon-Bowers, J. A. (2000). The anatomy of team training. In S. Tobias & J. D. Fletcher (Eds.), *Training and retraining: A handbook for business, industry, government, and the military* (pp. 312–335). New York: Macmillan Reference.

Salas, E., Dickinson, T. L., Converse, S. A., & Tannenbaum, S. I. (1992). Toward an understanding of team performance and training. In R. J. Swezey & E. Salas (Eds.), *Teams: Their training and performance* (pp. 3–29). Norwood, NJ: Ablex.

Salas, E., & Fiore, S. M. (Eds.). (2004). *Team cognition: Understanding the factors that drive process and performance.* Washington, DC: American Psychological Association.

Short, J., Williams, E., & Christie, B. (1976). *The social psychology of telecommunications.* New York, NY: John Wiley.

Stahl, G. (2006). *Group cognition: Computer support for building collaborative knowledge.* Cambridge, MA: MIT Press.

Stahl, G., Koschmann, T., & Suthers, D. (2006). Computer-supported collaborative learning: An historical perspective. In R. K. Sawyer (Ed.), *Cambridge handbook of the learning sciences*. Cambridge, UK: Cambridge University Press.

Stasser, G., Stewart, D., & Wittenbaum, G. (1995). Expert roles and information exchange during discussion: The importance of knowing who knows what. *Journal of Experimental Social Psychology, 31*, 244–265.

Tindale, R. S., & Kameda, T. (2000). "Social sharedness" as a unifying theme for information processing in groups. *Group Processes & Intergroup Relations, 3*, 123–140.

Weick, K. (1995). *Sensemaking in organizations.* Thousand Oaks, CA: Sage Publications.

Xiao, Y., & Moss, J. (2001). Practices of high reliability teams: Observations in trauma resuscitation. In *Proceedings of the Human Factors and Ergonomics Society 45th Annual Meeting* (pp. 395–399). Santa Monica, CA: Human Factors and Ergonomics Society.

2

Macrocognition, Team Learning, and Team Knowledge: Origins, Emergence, and Measurement[*]

Steve W. J. Kozlowski and Georgia T. Chao

Macrocognition is an emerging multidisciplinary area of theory development and research activity that is focused on understanding how groups, teams, and other collective entities learn, develop meaningful knowledge, and apply it to resolve significant and challenging problems. The literature on team effectiveness has also exhibited considerable interest in team learning and cognitive representations of team knowledge such as team mental models, transactive memory, and knowledge stocks (Edmondson, Dillon, & Roloff, 2007). However, the origins and process of team learning remain conceptually murky, and there is considerable diversity in the ways that researchers have attempted to represent and measure team (and higher level) knowledge (DeChurch & Mesmer-Magnus, 2010; Klimoski & Mohammed, 1995; Rentsch, Small, & Hanges, 2008; Salas & Wildman, 2009) and the processes by which it is acquired, emerges, and manifests as a team-level property. Indeed, a recent monograph concluded that although there is high interest in these phenomena and promising research progress, much more conceptual clarity is needed to enhance understanding of the nature of team learning and to advance useful and robust theoretical representations to drive the measurement of collective knowledge constructs (Kozlowski & Ilgen, 2006).

This chapter (a) presents a theoretical approach for conceptualizing the process of team learning; (b) develops theoretical representations of resulting team knowledge as a means to drive measurement of its formation, emergence, and manifestation at the collective level of analysis; and

---

[*] Any opinions, findings, and conclusions or recommendations expressed are those of the authors and do not necessarily reflect the views of the Office of Naval Research.

19

20 • *Theories of Team Cognition*

(c) sketches theoretical processes that are likely to shape team knowledge acquisition and emergence. We first highlight the theoretical foundation and key conceptual drivers of the approach. They are founded on a distinction between learning processes and knowledge outcomes, the iterative process of knowledge acquisition and formation, the origins of learning and knowledge at the psychological level (i.e., individual), and the pattern of emergence and manifestation at the collective level of the team. In other words, team learning and team knowledge are multilevel in nature (Kozlowski & Klein, 2000). We then develop a typology to represent team knowledge conceptually linked to corresponding techniques for measuring it. The goal of this theoretical and operational effort is to develop a robust conceptualization of team knowledge emergence as collective phenomena and a set of measurement tools to capture it that can be applied across a wide range of team task situations. Finally, we focus on what we believe are core theoretical processes—team member networks and team regulation—that are likely to influence team knowledge acquisition and its emergence in the team. In combination, the knowledge conceptual foundation, team knowledge measurement tools, and the processes that influence knowledge acquisition and emergence constitute an integrated framework to guide research on how teams can be shaped to generate new knowledge efficiently and effectively.

THEORETICAL FOUNDATION AND CONCEPTUAL DRIVERS

Learning is a process; knowledge is an outcome. Much of the research on team (or collective) learning has not carefully distinguished learning as a *process* from knowledge, and changes in knowledge over time, as learning outcomes. For the most part, outcomes of learning processes, such as a collective pool of knowledge, shared (team) mental models, and transactive memory, have been treated or described as if they were synonymous with team learning, rather than outcomes of learning as a process (Edmondson, 1999; Kozlowski & Bell, 2008; Kozlowski & Ilgen, 2006). This lack of conceptual clarity has contributed to a weak conceptualization of team learning processes and has also tended to promote cross-sectional research that yields a static perspective on team learning and resulting team knowledge. Thus, an important aspect of our approach is to carefully distinguish learning as a process from different forms of knowledge that are the result of that process and to consider how knowledge emerges over time.

The process of learning is iterative and cyclical. Self-regulation is currently the dominant model of learning, motivation, and performance in psychology and has amassed considerable support in the literature (Kanfer, Chen, & Pritchard, 2008; Karoly, 1993). Models of self-regulation reference goals as mechanisms for directing attention and effort, and strategies as ways to shape the process of goal striving. As illustrated in Figure 2.1, progress toward goal accomplishment is monitored, discrepancies revealed via feedback are diagnosed, and goals and strategies are revised in an iterative process directed toward learning, knowledge compilation, and skill acquisition, which yields performance improvements and goal accomplishment. Over time, this iterative and cyclical process of goal striving accounts for individual learning, motivation, and performance.

Knowledge formation compiles over iterations of the regulation process. Research on complex skill acquisition demonstrates that knowledge compiles with experience from the initial formation of declarative knowledge (i.e., facts, raw data), to procedural knowledge (i.e., categorized/contextualized knowledge, application of conditional if–then rule relations), to

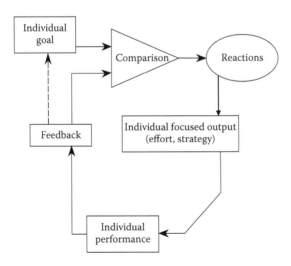

FIGURE 2.1
Individual self-regulation heuristic. (DeShon, R. P., Kozlowski, S. W. J., Schmidt, A. M., Milner, K. R., & Wiechmann, D. [2004]. A multiple goal, multilevel model of feedback effects on the regulation of individual and team performance. *Journal of Applied Psychology, 89*, 1035–1056. Published by the American Psychological Association. Adapted with permission.)

22 • *Theories of Team Cognition*

strategic knowledge (i.e., synthesis; inference to guide resource allocation for decision making, problem solving, and behavioral action), and finally, to adaptive knowledge (i.e., generalization, innovation, invention) (Anderson, 1982; Kozlowski & Bell, 2007). Note that this model, depicted in Figure 2.2, exhibits Guttman scale properties such that more basic forms of knowledge are necessary conditions for the acquisition of more complex forms.

This psychological conceptualization of skill acquisition and the formation of expertise integrates readily with the data, information, and knowledge typology (DIK-T) proposed by Fiore et al. (2010). *Data* is knowledge of discrete facts, which is equivalent to the concept of *declarative knowledge* (e.g., a NATO international crisis response coalition has been established with American, British, and Polish members). Simulation-based tasks are composed of a fixed (closed) domain of facts that capture the important characteristics of a problem domain or synthetic world emulated by the simulation. In that sense, the total *fact space* can be specified and used as a referent to gauge the extent to which team members have acquired the fact space. Real-world tasks, of course, are not closed worlds, although the necessary pool of facts that need to be known (whether they are known or not) can usually be specified in advance.

Information is data that has been organized, structured, or categorized with respect to a problem context. This conceptualization is equivalent to *procedural knowledge*, which represents the intersection of facts with other facts, decisions, or behaviors given the problem state. Facts may connect to each other (if this fact, then that fact), with decisions (if this fact, then that decision), or with behaviors (if this fact, then that act, where the act can be a behavior, communication, etc.). Although this is somewhat abstract, specification of a task provides the basis to define the domain of procedural knowledge and to anchor it to specific if–then connections for facts, decisions, and acts. Related to the previous data example on the international team, examples of information include the following: "If people are located in their home countries, the Americans and Poles have the greatest time difference," and "If the military team operates in Iraq, access to Arabic translators is needed." This defines an *information space* that can be assessed with situational test questions or with actual decisions and/or behavioral acts.

Knowledge represents an integration or synthesis of "two or more categories of information into something that did not explicitly exist before and which has been made actionable by being related to the problem solving context" (Table 2, Fiore et al., 2010, p. 212). For example, information on

	Basic			Advanced
		Knowledge and skill complexity →		
Knowledge type	Declarative knowledge [Data]	Procedural knowledge and skill [Information]	Strategic knowledge and skill [Knowledge]	Adaptive knowledge and skill [Adaptation]
Knowledge capability	Facts, concepts, rules; Definition, meaning (*What?*)	Contexualized rule application; Conditional if-then rules (*How?*)	Synthesis; Task contingencies; Selective resource allocation (*When, where, why?*)	Generalization of task rules, principles, and contingencies to new situations (*What now, what next?*)

FIGURE 2.2

Knowledge compilation. (Kozlowski, S. W. J., & Bell. B. S. [2007]. A theory-based approach for designing distributed learning systems. In S. M. Fiore & E. Salas [Eds.], *Where is the learning in distance learning? Toward a science of distributed learning and training* [pp. 15–39]. Washington, DC: APA Books. © Copyright 2002, 2010 S. W. J. Kozlowski and B. S. Bell. Adapted with permission.)

24 • *Theories of Team Cognition*

different government programs to reduce its military presence, combined knowledge of force capabilities, and intelligence on enemy strongholds can be combined to form new knowledge on military strategies and their likely impact. In essence, it is an *inference* and is very similar to the concept of *strategic knowledge* (Kozlowski & Bell, 2007), which represents a synthesis of information to draw an inference—an inference goes beyond the information—that can guide the allocation of resources (appropriate prioritization) given current task contingencies. Knowledge or strategic knowledge can be captured via test questions and/or by discrete behavioral acts that signal the application of specific strategies given the current task state (e.g., Bell & Kozlowski, 2002, 2008).

Learning and knowledge formation in teams are emergent multilevel phenomena. The formation and compilation of knowledge (i.e., *change* in knowledge capability) *originate* at the individual level (within person) but are shaped and amplified by interactions with team members such that they *emerge* over time and manifest as team-level knowledge. *"A phenomenon is emergent when it originates in the cognition, affect, behaviors, or other characteristics of individuals, is amplified by their interactions, and manifests as a higher-level, collective phenomenon"* (Kozlowski & Klein, 2000, p. 55, italics in original). Research by DeShon, Kozlowski, Schmidt, Milner, and Wiechmann (2004) has shown that individual regulatory (i.e., learning) processes and outcomes in a team context yield emergent and parallel team-level regulatory processes and outcomes. As illustrated in Figure 2.3, in a team setting, individuals regulate attention and effort around individual goals *and* team goals, dynamically switching resources to manage discrepancies on both goals. As this regulatory process iterates over time, team regulation emerges as a parallel regulatory process at the collective level that accounts for team learning and performance. Regulation, learning, and performance in teams are multilevel phenomena, and learning takes time (Salas & Wildman, 2009).

Moreover, once the team-level process has emerged, it serves as a context for individual behavior. In other words, as individuals engage in self-regulation within the team, a parallel team-regulation process emerges, which then shapes and influences subsequent individual regulation and performance. Chen, Kanfer, DeShon, Mathieu, and Kozlowski (2009) demonstrated these multilevel effects in research that in part reanalyzed data from DeShon et al. (2004). Thus, there is a reciprocal pattern of relations between individual learning and motivation, and the emergence of team

Macrocognition, Team Learning, and Team Knowledge • 25

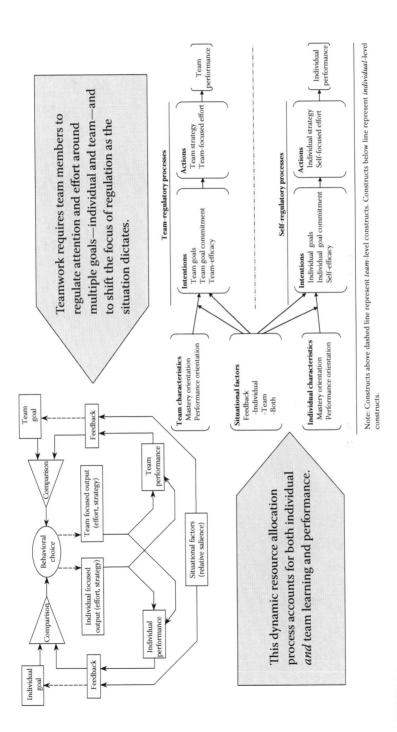

FIGURE 2.3
A multiple goal, multilevel model of individual and team regulation. (DeShon, R. P., Kozlowski, S. W. J., Schmidt, A. M., Milner, K. R., & Wiechmann, D. [2004]. A multiple goal, multilevel model of feedback effects on the regulation of individual and team performance. *Journal of Applied Psychology, 89,* 1035–1056. Published by the American Psychological Association. Adapted with permission.)

learning and motivation, with subsequent effects on individual learning and motivation.

Team knowledge can emerge in different ways (i.e., forms of emergence), which influence how it should be represented conceptually and, thus, how it should be measured. As illustrated in Figure 2.4, Kozlowski and Klein (2000) describe different "ideal" forms of emergence—composition and compilation—that characterize distinctly different types of emergence processes at opposite ends of a continuum. *Composition*, based on assumptions of isomorphism, describes phenomena that are essentially the same as they emerge upward across levels. Composition emergence represents

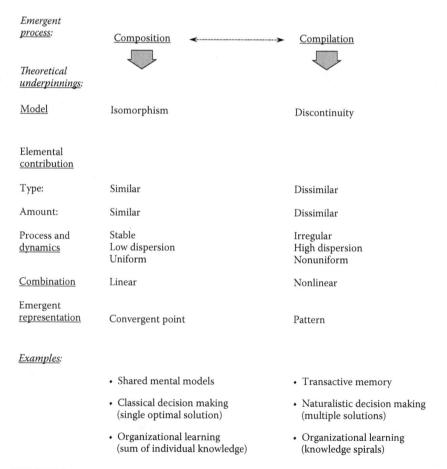

FIGURE 2.4
"Ideal" forms of emergence. (Copyright © 1999, 2010 S. W. J. Kozlowski. All rights reserved. With permission.)

Macrocognition, Team Learning, and Team Knowledge • 27

the coalescence of *identical* lower level properties—that is, the convergence of similar lower level characteristics to yield a higher level property that is essentially the same as its constituent elements (e.g., a *shared* team mental model). *Compilation*, based on assumptions of discontinuity, describes phenomena that comprise a common domain but are distinctively different as they emerge across levels. The concepts are functionally equivalent; that is, they occupy essentially the same role in models at different levels, but they are not identical as in composition. Compilation processes describe the combination of related but *different* lower-level properties—that is, the configuration of different lower-level characteristics to yield a higher-level property that is functionally equivalent with its constituent elements (e.g., a *distributed* transactive team memory or a configuration of knowledge distributed across team members). There is meta-analytic support for the usefulness of these conceptual distinctions in forms of emergence for collective cognitive constructs (DeChurch & Mesmer-Magnus, 2010). For the most part, team research has tended to examine these distinctly different conceptualizations of team knowledge as either/or—*either* composition forms of team knowledge (i.e., shared mental models) *or* compilation forms (i.e., transactive memory). However, a range of emergent forms spanning between composition and compilation are likely (Kozlowski & Klein, 2000). Our interest is in capturing that range.

REPRESENTING THE ACQUISITION AND EMERGENCE OF INDIVIDUAL AND TEAM KNOWLEDGE

Foundation and Assumptions

Based on the foregoing theoretical foundation, collective knowledge representation should be grounded in the underlying theoretical processes of knowledge acquisition and the expected form of collective knowledge emergence, which then should drive a corresponding approach to measurement (Kozlowski & Klein, 2000). Core theoretical features of our approach to conceptualizing team knowledge include the following:

- Learning processes and data, information, and knowledge as outcomes are theoretically and empirically distinct.

28 • *Theories of Team Cognition*

- Learning as a psychological process is rooted in self-regulation and team regulation, which unfold iteratively over time.
- The acquisition of data, information, and knowledge compile in a phased sequence.
- Data, information, and knowledge emerge from the individual to the team level such that the process is multilevel.
- The form of data, information, and knowledge emergence can vary across teams and is important to capture.

Thus, our approach views team learning as an iterative individual and team-level regulatory process with data, information, and knowledge as phased emergent outcomes of the process and the form of emergence as a characteristic of interest for distinguishing teams. To ground the knowledge representations, it is necessary to specify basic assumptions. First, we assume a collaborative team task wherein members have individual responsibilities (goals) that require data, information, and knowledge acquisition and also team responsibilities (goals), with discretion (Steiner, 1972) as to how much and how they will contribute to building team knowledge. Second, we assume that team members will begin their collaboration with access to *common* data, information, and knowledge (i.e., access available to all members) that define key aspects of the problem space, but also access to *unique* data, information, and knowledge that are matched to their role and expertise (i.e., access linked to a specific member) and that are also important to the problem space (Mesmer-Magnus & DeChurch, 2009; Stasser & Titus, 1985, 1987). An important aspect of team collaboration will be the acquisition of relevant data, information, and knowledge. Third, we assume that to effectively resolve the problem, team members will have to appropriately align data, information, and knowledge from both the common and unique domains with an optimal solution. For purposes of representation, the *total pool* of data, information, or knowledge is defined by the sum of the elements comprising the common and unique domains that are relevant to resolving the problem space.

Knowledge Representation Typology

The conceptual approach begins with the knowledge types shown in Figure 2.2, which are consistent with the DIK-T model (Fiore et al., 2010). Data, information, and knowledge are distinctive and arrayed such that the acquisition of more basic types provides a necessary foundation for the acquisition of more advanced types. We next draw on Kozlowski and Klein's (2000) typology of emergence forms, which are expansions of the ideal types ranging between composition and compilation illustrated in Figure 2.4, to specify emergence forms and potential measurement approaches. In particular, we focus on forms of emergence that represent (a) the *pooling* of individual and team DIK types, (b) patterns or *configurations* of the knowledge pool, and (c) within- and between-team *variances in the rates* of knowledge acquisition and rates of knowledge emergence from the individual to the team level. Note that the specific operationalization of the measures is dependent on the specific task involved, but the *conceptual representation* is designed to generalize across a wide range of collaborative tasks. Given a common underlying knowledge representation, rates of knowledge acquisition and rates of emergence can be compared across different collaborative tasks.

Finally, we draw upon the framework for macrocognition in teams (Figure 1 in Fiore et al., 2010). In this heuristic, individual knowledge building, or what we conceptualize as the learning process, links to internalized knowledge, or knowledge acquired by individual team members and the team collectively. Individualized knowledge links to subsequent individual learning and also to team knowledge building, or what we conceptualize as team learning processes. Team learning links to externalized team knowledge. We conceptualize this as knowledge that has been explicitly shared (i.e., communicated, discussed) that is subsequently learned by other team members who did not previously hold it and is then captured as internalized team knowledge. In the heuristic, team learning and externalized knowledge are the key antecedents of team problem-solving effectiveness. Team learning and problem solving are entwined; learning is the process by which knowledge and solutions emerge.

For ease of presentation, our typology references "knowledge"; however, each of the representations is applicable to data, information, and knowledge; that is, the conceptual representations generalize across the DIK types. The elements used to operationalize a measure will vary depending on whether they index data, information, or knowledge, but the conceptual representations will not vary. In addition, our descriptions assume a team of three members for presentation ease. However, the representations are scalable to larger teams. The different forms of

30 • *Theories of Team Cognition*

emergence described earlier yield several useful metrics and are illustrated in Figure 2.5. Specific metrics for a particular type of task would necessarily be bound by that task's constraints. For illustrative purposes, examples of these metrics are presented within the context of a three-member new product development team. The three members have different roles related to market research, product design, and production. Their unique expertise has to be combined to develop a new product that consumers want, that is technically innovative, and that can be produced at high quality for a reasonable cost.

Knowledge metrics	Brief description	Example	
Individual knowledge	The proportion of the total pool of possible knowledge possessed by each team member separately	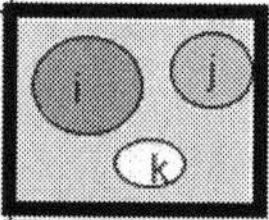	The amount of knowledge individuals i, j, and k each possess within the problem space
Knowledge pool	The proportion of the total pool of possible knowledge possessed by the team collectively	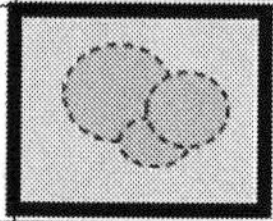	The proportion of the total knowledge among individual team members accounting for overlap
Knowledge configuration	The proportion of the total pool shared in common by team members and the pattern of unique knowledge held across individuals	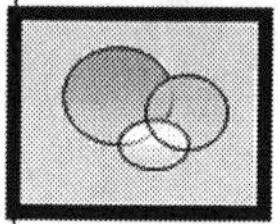	Understanding what is common and what is unique knowledge among team members
Knowledge acquisition	The rate of knowledge compiled by each team member over time	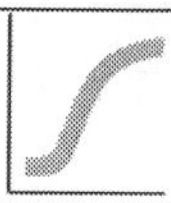	How fast an individual learns (expands a circle in above Venn diagrams)
Knowledge variability	Within team variance in the rates of knowledge acquisition	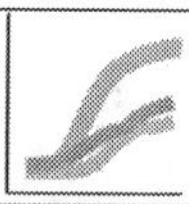	Different rates of knowledge acquisition can affect a team's learning
Knowledge emergence (within team)	The rates of growth for knowledge pool and knowledge configuration	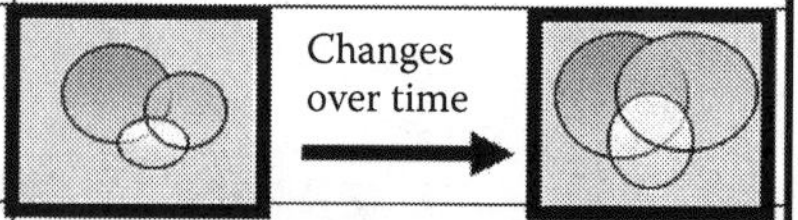	Changes over time
Knowledge emergence (between teams)	Comparing growth rates for knowledge variability, knowledge pool, and knowledge configuration across teams	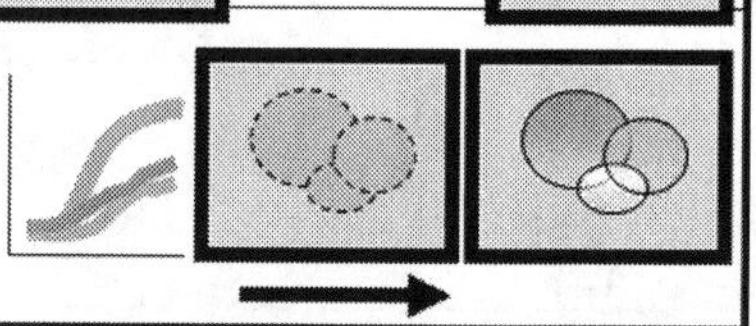	

FIGURE 2.5

Knowledge representation typology. (Copyright © 2010 S. W. J. Kozlowski & G. T. Chao. All rights reserved worldwide. With permission.)

Individual Knowledge

Based on our assumptions about the design of the collaborative decision-making task, each team member has access to common and unique knowledge defining the problem space, and the sum of the common and unique knowledge defines the total pool of knowledge relevant for solving the problem at hand. Thus, one can represent the amount of knowledge possessed by any one individual team member at any given point in time as the proportion of the total knowledge pool possessed by that member. Members may overlap (or not) in the knowledge they possess, but that is not relevant to representing individual knowledge acquisition. This is an individual-level measure of internalized knowledge. Figure 2.5 illustrates an example of three team members, each possessing different amounts of individual knowledge that do not overlap with the knowledge of any other member.

In the example of the new product development team, individual knowledge can be measured by what each team member knows that is relevant to the task. The market researcher has knowledge about consumer preferences; the design engineer has knowledge about innovative product features; and the production manager has knowledge about available production equipment and capabilities. These examples represent unique knowledge if held by only one team member. General knowledge about the organization's current product lines and financial support for new products can represent common knowledge accessible to all team members.

Knowledge Pool

Individual knowledge provides a solid assessment of what any one team member knows, but it is not informative about the collective because it does not carry information about the degree of knowledge overlap among members. In other words, merely summing individual knowledge would provide an inaccurate representation of team knowledge. To represent team knowledge accurately, it is necessary to account for the degree of aggregate overlap among members. That is, in some teams, members may have acquired predominantly the same knowledge across members, whereas in other teams, members may have acquired different areas of the knowledge pool. Thus, this representation captures the proportion of the total knowledge pool possessed by the team collectively. This is a team-level *composition* measure that can be used to represent internalized and

32 • *Theories of Team Cognition*

externalized knowledge. Figure 2.5 illustrates how three team members' knowledge is considered together as a set, comprising the knowledge pool. The sum of all unique knowledge from individual team members, plus the knowledge shared across team members, represent the knowledge pool at the team level.

Knowledge Configuration

Understanding the proportion of the total knowledge pool held by the team is informative, but as an aggregate measure, it does not convey precise information as to *how* knowledge is distributed across team members. That is, because team members ultimately have to possess collective knowledge that is relevant to resolving the problem space, it is useful to have a representation that can capture knowledge that is held by one, two, or more members of the team. Thus, the configuration of team knowledge is represented by the set of proportions of the total pool that is possessed by one, two, or more members (Figure 2.5). This is a team-level *compilation* measure that can be used to represent internalized and externalized knowledge.

Metrics for knowledge configuration are dynamic, changing as teams share information and generate new knowledge. Over time, the expertise relevant to one team member becomes increasingly collective across team members as they communicate to solve their mutual problem. That shifting pattern of knowledge being compiled across team members can be tracked over time.

Knowledge Acquisition

The representations described previously capture individual knowledge, team knowledge composition, and team knowledge compilation. An important aspect of our conceptualization is that learning is distinct from knowledge outcomes and, as an iterative regulatory process, learning advances in the knowledge acquired by team members over time. Obviously, how learning takes place is constrained by the collaborative task, but in essence, team members acquire knowledge as they study briefing materials and collect information about the problem space *and* as they interact, converse, and share information they have acquired. Thus, one can represent individual knowledge acquisition as the growth rate of individual knowledge (i.e., the proportion of the total pool held by an individual team member) across a time line. This growth rate would be indicative of the quality of learning and team collaboration. This is a within-individual measure of internalized knowledge. Figure 2.5 shows a typical S-shaped learning curve, with learning and time on the vertical and horizontal axes, respectively. The steeper the slope of the learning curve, the faster is the rate of knowledge acquisition.

Metrics for knowledge acquisition include the rate at which a team member learns about the problem context, features, and constraints and the extent to which team members communicate their knowledge and expertise to others. In the new product development team example, a team member who actively listens to others can be more effective in using his or her own expertise to solve the problem. Thus, the design engineer might quickly learn from the market researcher what design features are attractive to prospective consumers. This knowledge acquisition can focus the design engineer's innovations and stimulate a need for knowledge from the production manager regarding production feasibility for a particular innovation.

Knowledge Variability

Depending on a number of individual difference factors (e.g., cognitive ability, motivation) and team factors (e.g., team composition, team cohesion), different team members may learn and acquire knowledge at very similar rates in some teams and at very different rates in others. A basic principle of team learning (Kozlowski & Bell, 2008) is that the most rapid rates of knowledge acquisition with low *within-team variance* yield optimum team learning. Thus, within-team variance in the rates of knowledge acquisition is likely to impede team knowledge-building processes, the development of externalized team knowledge, and team problem-solving outcomes. Metrics would include the variance across team members in rates of knowledge acquisition. This is a team-level, internalized knowledge measure.

Figure 2.5 shows three team members with different rates of knowledge acquisition. Given the (likely) deleterious effects of within-team variance in rates of knowledge acquisition and the likelihood that it is commonplace, it is important to examine the boundary conditions of the effects. Consider that it is possible that the team member with the highest rate of knowledge acquisition may be able to advance the rate of other team members or to

34 • *Theories of Team Cognition*

compensate for other members. For example, the design engineer may be able to identify a good new product by him- or herself, once the other members have shared enough information. However, it is possible that the team member with the lowest rate of knowledge acquisition may drain resources and limit the rate of knowledge acquisition of other team members. For example, the market researcher may have a low rate of knowledge acquisition and be unable to share critical information that the team needs in order to come up with an optimal solution for a new product.

Knowledge Emergence (Within Team)

Within-team variance on knowledge acquisition provides an overall indication of how well team members will be able to collaborate effectively and will certainly influence emergence. A more direct representation of knowledge emergence is provided by examining the growth rates for the knowledge pool and knowledge configuration, which are both team-level measures that can capture internalized knowledge and externalized knowledge. In particular, we would expect the knowledge configuration growth rate, because of its greater precision, to be most diagnostic of team decision-making effectiveness. Figure 2.5 depicts knowledge emergence as enlarged areas of individual knowledge in Venn diagrams from one time period to another.

Metrics for knowledge emergence track how quickly the team's knowledge pool approximates the total knowledge pool over a period of time. When comparing internalized and externalized team knowledge, metrics for knowledge emergence track how the team's knowledge configuration shifts from primarily unique knowledge held by one team member to knowledge held by most or all team members.

Knowledge Emergence (Between Teams)

Finally, the team-level representations can be compared across teams. That is, one would anticipate that different team compositions, team factors, or interventions would influence how well teams learned, acquired knowledge, and rendered decisions. A between-team examination of the rates of growth for knowledge variability, knowledge pool, and knowledge configuration would provide an evaluative yardstick for comparing the quality of collaborative learning and knowledge outcomes (Figure 2.5).

These measures are at the system level (i.e., between teams) and capture internalized and externalized knowledge.

Metrics for knowledge emergence between teams might involve 10 new product development teams, each charged with different missions to improve and expand the organization's product portfolio. Teams' growth rates in knowledge variability, knowledge pool, and knowledge configuration would be expected to be related to team processes, such as team cohesion, or team outcomes, such as decision-making effectiveness.

SHAPING KNOWLEDGE ACQUISITION AND EMERGENCE IN TEAMS

Among the more interesting aspects to examine with respect to team learning are the ways in which formal task or informal social configurations influence how knowledge propagates across team members as individuals acquire data, information, and knowledge and share what they have learned with teammates. Although team knowledge emergence is often regarded as an additive aggregation process that is consistent with composition emergence, Kozlowski and Klein (2000) suggest that team knowledge emergence is more likely to be a pattern or configuration consistent with compilation emergence.

In this last section of the chapter, we consider two core factors—the network of connections that link team members and the regulatory processes that undergird learning—that are primary leverage points for shaping the ways in which data, information, and knowledge are shared, learned, and acquired within teams and, hence, the nature of knowledge emergence in teams. Thus, in combination with the foregoing conceptual foundation and team knowledge measurement typology, we will specify an integrated theoretical framework for understanding, capturing, and shaping knowledge acquisition and emergence in teams.

Leveraging Team Member Network Linkages

Team Composition and Team Networks

Teams are composed of an assembly of individuals who bring with them a collection of individual differences on demographics, ability, and personality that are described in the literature as *team composition*. (Note that this is not the same form of composition discussed with respect to emergence.) Chao and Moon (2005) suggest that network patterns (formal—dictated by task design, and informal—based on social relations) are likely to play a major role in the ways that knowledge is acquired and emerges in teams. This perspective is useful in understanding the process of knowledge emergence and for validating the measures of team knowledge. Social identity theory describes how an individual's memberships in various groups can shape that person's self-concept (Tajfel, 1982). Group memberships can vary along demographic, geographic, or associative lines (Chao & Moon, 2005). Social identities based on demographic characteristics such as age, race, and gender typically serve as immediate cues to guide interpersonal behaviors. Geographically based groups (e.g., rural/urban, coastal/inland, temperate/tropical) can form the basis for regional values. Finally, social identities based on associations with particular groups (e.g., profession, organization, religion) are linked to distinct cultures. Each group embodies specific values and characteristics that help define in-groups from out-groups. Multiple group identities allow individuals to connect to others in different ways. An example of a cultural mosaic among five individuals within an international military context is illustrated in Figure 2.6. A female Army officer

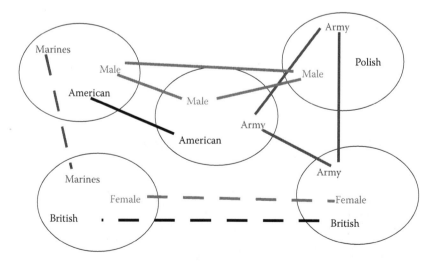

FIGURE 2.6
An example of a cultural mosaic. (Copyright © 2004, 2010 G. T. Chao. All rights reserved worldwide. With permission.)

may link with a female Marine through a gender group identity, and she can link with a male Army officer through a professional group identity. Conversely, a male Polish Army officer may distance himself from a female British Marine because few social identities are shared. Among the five individuals depicted in Figure 2.6, several links can be based on gender, nationality, and military force. Additional links can be based on mosaic tiles that are not shown in Figure 2.6, such as military rank, training, and education. The number of cultural tiles and their relationships with one another are many and complex. Research on social identities has found that group identities can be formed with nominal information. Furthermore, even loose associations with a group can have a powerful impact on behavior. Individuals are more likely to favor their in-group members over out-group members. Social identity theory argues that members in one group compare their relative standings with other groups in order to reconfirm their group memberships and to guide interactions with members of other groups (Chao, 2000).

Cultural mosaics among team members can be viewed as a network of multiple social identities that link team members along different cultural tiles. The number and type of ties each member has with other members can be powerful antecedents to information sharing and team learning. For example, centrality in networks is likely to affect the acquisition and emergence of individual and team knowledge (Freeman, 1977; Kilduff & Tsai, 2003). *Degree centrality* measures the number of ties a team member has to other team members, and *betweenness centrality* measures the frequency with which a team member connects two unconnected members. Individuals who are high on degree and/or betweenness centrality are in position to control the flow of data, information, and knowledge to others and, thus, have disproportionate potential to facilitate *or* inhibit the rate of knowledge acquisition and emergence in a team. At the team level, *network density* is the proportion of ties in a team network relative to the total number of possible links (sparse versus dense networks). Teams with dense networks are more likely to propagate knowledge more quickly and, thus, are expected to exhibit rapid knowledge acquisition and emergence. Conversely, teams with sparse networks and/or antagonistic social identities may encounter slower rates of information sharing, information acquisition, and team knowledge emergence. Thus, network configurations are potentially useful antecedents to patterns in team knowledge acquisition and emergence.

38 • *Theories of Team Cognition*

One network configuration that has been linked to team learning is the formation of a subgroup within a team. Gibson and Vermeulen (2003) have shown how these subgroups can affect the team's learning behaviors. Subgroups are often found in diverse teams when members are drawn to other members because of one or more shared identities. Members in a subgroup often support each other and provide a climate that encourages participation. Thus, the subgroup can offer some psychological safety for team members to express opinions, experiment, and learn (Edmondson, 1999). Conversely, subgroups can also highlight differences between in-group and out-group members, and tensions between individuals or subgroups can inhibit members from learning as a team. The research on organizational silence (Morrison & Milliken, 2000) illustrates how some individuals may withhold information from others due to perceived negative repercussions. Individuals may be less likely to mention problems or offer constructive criticism to others with higher status or rank.

The current literature on team composition and team performance is mixed (Williams & O'Reilly, 1998). Heterogeneous groups are valued for their diversity in knowledge and experience (Lovelace, Shapiro, & Weingart, 2001), yet they are often encumbered by poor communication and social integration (Zenger & Lawrence, 1989). The cultural mosaic provides a tool for understanding how networks and subgroups develop within a team learning context. Dense networks are more likely when there are multiple ties linking members by demographic, geographic, and associative cultural identities. Subgroups are more likely when the diversity among all members makes salient specific cultural identities that are shared by only a few members. Gibson and Vermeulen (2003) found that optimal learning occurred in groups with moderately strong demographic subgroups. The subgroups enabled information and insights to emerge; however, they did not overpower differing opinions and insights from other team members. Moreover, teams with no subgroups or strong subgroups could overcome these structural limitations with good leadership that emphasized empowerment and knowledge management systems.

Leveraging Team Regulation and Knowledge Compilation

Theoretical Foundation

Kozlowski, Gully, Nason, and Smith (1999) have applied a process perspective to develop a normative model of *team compilation* with self-regulatory underpinnings that integrates learning and team performance with the principles of multilevel theory. Their theoretical framework is characterized by three key conceptual features that center on: (1) episodic task cycles, (2) temporal development with attention to distinct learning content and knowledge and skill outcomes, and (3) transitions in the focus of learning as it emerges from the individual to the team level. The theory is illustrated in Figure 2.7.

First, episodic task cycles capture the effects of multiple task episodes and the regulatory processes that energize individual and team learning. Task variations prompt individual regulatory processes, providing experiences for learning and skill acquisition. With repeated experiences, skill acquisition in the team context begins to shift from individual regulation to multilevel regulation (DeShon et al., 2004). This enables the compilation process.

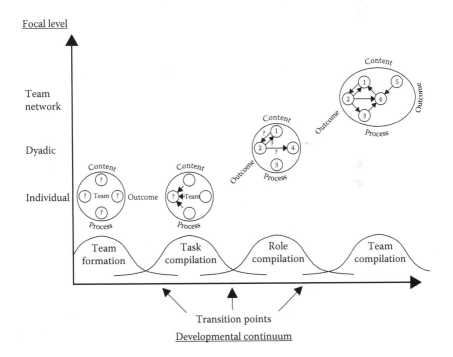

FIGURE 2.7
Team compilation model. (Kozlowski, S. W. J., Gully, S. M., Nason, E. R., & Smith, E. M. [1999]. Developing adaptive teams: A theory of compilation and performance across levels and time. In D. R. Ilgen & E. D. Pulakos [Eds.], *The changing nature of work performance: Implications for staffing, personnel actions, and development* [pp. 240–292]. San Francisco: Jossey-Bass. Copyright © 1997, 2006, 2010 S. W. J. Kozlowski. All rights reserved worldwide. Used with permission)

40 • *Theories of Team Cognition*

Second, developmental processes capture the compilation of knowledge and skills. This is partly modeled on the way individual expertise is acquired. As novices make the transition to experts, they progress through a series of learning phases during which their knowledge and skills compile into qualitatively different forms—from declarative, to procedural, to strategic (Anderson, 1982; Ford & Kraiger, 1995), to adaptive (Kozlowski & Bell, 2007). Similarly, team capabilities improve developmentally, thereby prompting transition to more advanced phases of skill acquisition that entail distinct learning content and knowledge outcomes.

Third, team compilation is viewed as an emergent multilevel phenomenon. In a team context, knowledge and skill compilation have emergent manifestations at multiple levels of analysis. Knowledge, skills, and performance capabilities compile across focal levels from an individual self-focus to a focus on developing the team as a collective entity. Team members transition from a focus on the self (e.g., what do I need to do to perform my task) to a focus on the team as an entity (e.g., how do we coordinate and adapt).

This model readily integrates with the knowledge typology presented previously. Guided by this model, we sketch a set of interventions that map the team learning sequence, beginning with interventions that provide basic team skills and bond members to the team and then shifting to more advanced knowledge and skills that help team members learn more effectively. The first two interventions, teamwork skills and team cohesion training, focus on enhancing social linkages to improve knowledge sharing. The second two interventions, team learning orientation and team metacognition, focus on enhancing the learning process directly. These four interventions are not the only ones to influence the team learning sequence, but are presented here to illustrate potential ways to shape team learning and problem-solving effectiveness:

- *Teamwork skills* training to enhance basic teamwork skills underlying team communication, collaboration, and development that should, in turn, enhance team knowledge acquisition
- *Team cohesion*—by stimulating a tightly coupled team network (Chao & Moon, 2005)—to enhance team member bonding to the team and its task, trust formation, and information sharing that should, in turn, enhance team knowledge acquisition

- *Team learning orientation* that focuses team member attention on learning goals and processes (versus performance goals and processes) that should enhance learning of the deeper and more complex strategic forms of team knowledge (Bunderson & Sutcliffe, 2003)
- *Team metacognition*, which is an intervention designed to sensitize the team to the regulatory processes underlying learning—setting goals, monitoring performance, diagnosing discrepancies, managing affect, and appropriately revising strategies and reallocating effort—that should, in turn, enhance team knowledge acquisition and performance (DeShon et al., 2004)

Teamwork Skills

Teamwork skills represent competencies that members possess that are relevant to interacting and working effectively with others (Stevens & Campion, 1994). Unlike the typical selection focus on knowledge, skills, and abilities (KSAs) that underlie *taskwork*, the KSAs identified by Stevens and Campion (1994) focus on *teamwork* skills, the presumption being that teams composed of members higher on teamwork KSAs will be more effective. Stevens and Campion (1994) conducted a broad review of the literature, inferring individual KSAs generic to teamwork. Their typology consists of two primary dimensions, each with subdimensions (i.e., interpersonal KSAs of conflict resolution, collaborative problem solving, and communication; self-management KSAs of goal setting and performance management, planning, and task coordination). Research has shown that teamwork skills based on the Stevens and Campion (1994) typology can be trained efficiently (Ellis, Bell, Ployhart, Hollenbeck, & Ilgen, 2005). Ellis et al. (2005) conducted a laboratory experiment to evaluate the effectiveness of teamwork skill training on cognitive and skill-based outcomes using a simulated command and control task operated by four-person teams. Naïve team members trained on the teamwork skills were compared to control condition teams who did not receive teamwork skills training. The findings indicated that teamwork training improved collaboration, communication, and coordination. Although these findings do not focus on team knowledge per se, we believe that the approach is a promising one for providing team members with the skills needed to quickly build bonds (i.e., the interpersonal subdimension) and the regulatory skills (i.e., the self-management subdimension) needed to support learning.

Team Cohesion

Team cohesion captures the extent to which team members are attracted to the team (social cohesion) and its mission (task cohesion). Task cohesion is defined as a team's shared commitment to a group goal; it increases commitment to the task and effort exerted by team members. Social cohesion is defined as the group members' attraction to or liking of the group; it allows groups to have less inhibited communication and to effectively coordinate their efforts. Meta-analyses have established that both task and social cohesion are related to team performance, particularly for more complex and interdependent tasks (Beal, Cohen, Burke, & McLendon, 2003; Gully, Devine, & Whitney, 1995). Although there has been much research on the relation between cohesion and team performance, there is little research on the antecedents of team cohesion (Kozlowski & Ilgen, 2006). However, one promising theoretical approach is offered by Chao and Moon (2005), who postulated that team identity, cohesion, and trust can be enhanced by making salient the underlying commonalities that link different individuals together. This network of links or *mosaic* of connections is thought to promote the mutual attraction among team members and their commitment to the team mission. Chao and Moon (2005) describe how specific tiles of the mosaic can be primed to activate or make salient a network of connections by identifying similarities (in background, individual differences, or preferences) linking team members and making them explicit as a means to quickly build team cohesion, with expected influences on trust, collaboration, and information sharing, and subsequent effects on team knowledge acquisition and emergence.

Theory indicates that knowledge and skill acquisition can be enhanced by actively stimulating processes of learning, metacognition, and self-regulation that are central to learning (Bell & Kozlowski, 2008; Kozlowski et al., 2001). Features relevant to promoting these learning processes include: (a) stimulating a learning orientation via goal frames and specific learning goals, and (b) prompting metacognition and augmenting feedback. These interventions are implemented by instructions given to team members, simulation design, or task feedback.

Learning Orientation

Learning orientation represents the way individuals and teams view their goals in a novel achievement situation. Their views are shaped by the way the goal is framed and by the content of the goal (Kozlowski & Bell, 2006). *Goal frames* represent the emphasis on learning versus performance or on approach (goals) versus avoidance (errors). Learning frames are more effective during skill acquisition when attention needs to be directed to learning and comprehension, whereas performance frames are more effective after skills have been acquired and attention needs to be applied to task accomplishment. Learning frames are designed to motivate learning and are implemented by instructing teams to focus on understanding task features and operation. Performance frames motivate performance and are implemented by instructing trainees to focus on task performance.

Goal content is designed to focus attention on key features, principles, and strategies of the task domain. Learning goals are relevant during skill acquisition when learners need to master deep task principles and relations. Nonspecific learning goals or performance goals tend to direct attention to surface characteristics and inhibit deep learning. Specific learning goals are implemented by instructing learners to learn and explore particular types of task information (learn cue values), task features (learn how to change the range of your sensors), and task strategies (learn how to establish priorities). Nonspecific learning goals are implemented by instructing learners to do their best to learn the task. Performance goals are implemented by instructing learners to process a particular number of contacts or to score a particular number of points. Although there is a rich literature on the effects of learning versus performance goals on individual learning and skill acquisition, there is only limited, although promising, evidence for similar effects at the team level (Bunderson & Sutcliffe, 2003).

Team Metacognition

Metacognition is a cognitive control process at the heart of learning, knowledge acquisition, and task performance (Flavell, 1979). Metacognition is awareness of and conscious control over one's cognitive processes involved in regulating attention and effort to learn a task and accomplish goals. Key elements of metacognition include setting goals, monitoring performance via feedback, diagnosing discrepancies between the goal and current performance, managing affective reactions, and revising one's strategy and reallocating effort. Metacognitive probes (questions) directed at these activities can be used to enhance metacognitive awareness and processes (Kozlowski et al., 2007).

44 • *Theories of Team Cognition*

In addition, feedback is essential to learning and can be augmented to support metacognition. Feedback augmentation refers to techniques designed to improve the diagnostic value of feedback or focus learners on specific information relevant to learning objectives. Feedback can be augmented by several features embedded in a task simulation. Learners may be given a continuous readout of their score, which indicates their performance progress. They may be given feedback at the point of each decision, which indicates how well they have learned and applied information. They may be given feedback specific to their progress on specific learning objectives, which may reference goals they are striving to achieve, their prior performance, or normative performance. Ultimately, the combination of inductions to prompt a learning orientation, prime metacognitive processes, and augment feedback is expected to help team members and teams acquire knowledge more rapidly and to enable more consistent rates of knowledge emergence.

CONCLUSION

Among the many challenges facing researchers of team macrocognition are the needs to (a) better understand the process of team learning, (b) clearly distinguish it from resulting team knowledge outcomes, (c) incorporate the reality that learning and knowledge formation are temporal phenomena that emerge across levels (individual to team), and (d) capture the ways in which emergent knowledge in teams can manifest in different forms (composition and compilation) (Kozlowski & Bell, 2008; Kozlowski & Klein, 2000; Salas & Wildman, 2009). The purpose of this chapter was to present an integrated theoretical framework for addressing these challenges.

We first outlined our theoretical foundation, which incorporated the needs discussed previously. We distinguished learning as a process from knowledge outcomes (Kozlowski & Bell, 2003, 2008); highlighted the iterative, self-regulatory nature of learning (Karoly, 1993); noted the sequence of knowledge compilation (Anderson, 1982) and its connection to the DIK typology (Fiore et al., 2010); and described the multilevel and temporal nature of knowledge emergence (Kozlowski & Klein, 2000). Based on this conceptual foundation, we next developed a typology of knowledge representations that are designed to capture how domain-relevant knowledge (i.e., data, information, and knowledge) is distributed across team members and held collectively, how it is acquired over time, and how it emerges across multiple levels (individuals, dyads, and the team) and in different ways (composition and compilation). More specifically, our typology developed forms of knowledge emergence that capture (a) the *pooling* of individual and team data, information, and knowledge; (b) patterns or *configurations* of the knowledge pool; and (c) within- and between-team *variance in the rates* of knowledge acquisition and knowledge emergence from the individual to the team level. Finally, we sketched core theoretical processes including team member network linkages and team regulation processes that have the potential to shape how knowledge in teams is acquired and disseminated. We view these three theoretically driven aspects of our approach as comprising an integrated conceptual–operational framework for understanding, capturing, and shaping knowledge acquisition and emergence in teams.

We believe our framework approach offers several important contributions to team macrocognitive theory and research. First, it meets key challenges specified in the literature to distinguish process and outcome, incorporate time, and examine emergence as a multilevel phenomenon. Second, it integrates the literature on learning processes, skill acquisition, and multilevel emergence with a theoretical framework for macrocognition in teams (Fiore et al., 2010). That is, the knowledge representation typology is consistent with the data, information, and knowledge typology and captures the macrocognition heuristic features of individual and team knowledge-building processes, internalized individual and team knowledge, and externalized team knowledge. It provides a means to validate the core processes and outcomes inherent in the team macrocognitive theoretical framework and, potentially, ways to extend the theory. Third, our theoretical models addressing team member networks and team regulation identify promising leverage points for improving knowledge acquisition, emergence, and macrocognitive problem solving in teams. Finally, although specific operationalization of the knowledge representation measures is constrained by the specific team task under examination, the *conceptual representation* incorporated in the typology is designed to generalize across a wide range of collaborative tasks, thus imbuing it with high application potential. That is, the knowledge representation typology has the potential to be used to guide a common measurement approach across different laboratory tasks, tasks employed for application development, and tasks used in an operational environment. This comparability

46 • *Theories of Team Cognition*

in the underlying measurement conceptualization would allow for direct comparisons of, for example, a particular intervention (e.g., a tool to improve communication) examined across different laboratory tasks or in different operational tasks using a common measurement framework. Given the inherent complexity in studying macrocognition, we believe this general applicability has important integrative potential.

ACKNOWLEDGMENTS

We gratefully acknowledge the Office of Naval Research, Collaborative Knowledge and Interoperability (CKI) Program (N00014-09-1-0519, S. W. J. Kozlowski and G. T. Chao, Principal Investigators) for support that, in part, assisted the composition of this chapter.

REFERENCES

Anderson, J. R. (1982). The acquisition of cognitive skill. *Psychological Review, 89,* 369–406.

Beal, D. J., Cohen, R. R., Burke, M. J., & McLendon, C. L. (2003). Cohesion and performance in groups: A meta-analytic clarification of construct relations. *Journal of Applied Psychology, 88,* 989–1004.

Bell, B. S., & Kozlowski, S. W. J. (2002). Adaptive guidance: Enhancing self-regulation, knowledge, and performance in technology-based training. *Personnel Psychology, 55,* 267–307.

Bell, B. S., & Kozlowski, S. W. J. (2008). Active learning: Effects of core training design elements on self-regulatory processes, learning, and adaptability. *Journal of Applied Psychology, 93,* 296–316.

Bunderson, J. S., & Sutcliffe, K. A. (2003). Management team learning orientation and business unit performance. *Journal of Applied Psychology, 88,* 552–560.

Chao, G. T. (2000). Multilevel issues and culture: An integrative view. In K. J. Klein & S. W. J. Kozlowski (Eds.), *Multilevel theory, research, and methods in organizations: Foundations, extensions, and new directions* (pp. 308–346) (SIOP Frontiers Series). San Francisco, CA: Jossey-Bass.

Chao, G. T., & Moon, H. (2005). The cultural mosaic: A metatheory for understanding the complexity of culture. *Journal of Applied Psychology, 90,* 1128–1140.

Chen, G., Kanfer, R., DeShon, R. P., Mathieu, J. E., & Kozlowski, S. W. J. (2009). The motivating potential of teams: Test and extension of Chen and Kanfer's (2006) cross-level model of motivation in teams. *Organizational Behavior and Human Decision Processes, 110,* 45–55.

DeChurch, L. A., & Mesmer-Magnus, J. R. (2010). The cognitive underpinnings of effective teamwork. *Journal of Applied Psychology, 95,* 32–53.

DeShon, R. P., Kozlowski, S. W. J., Schmidt, A. M., Milner, K. R., & Wiechmann, D. (2004). A multiple goal, multilevel model of feedback effects on the regulation of individual and team performance. *Journal of Applied Psychology, 89,* 1035–1056.

Macrocognition, Team Learning, and Team Knowledge • 47

Edmondson, A. (1999). Psychological safety and learning behavior in work teams. *Administrative Science Quarterly, 44*, 350–383.

Edmondson, A., Dillon, J. R., & Roloff, K. S. (2007). Three perspectives on team learning. *The Academy of Management Annuals, 1*, 269–314.

Ellis, A. P. J., Bell, B. S., Ployhart, R. E., Hollenbeck, J. R., & Ilgen, D. R. (2005). An evaluation of generic teamwork skills training with action teams: Effects on cognitive and skill-based outcomes. *Personnel Psychology, 58*, 641–672.

Fiore, S. M., Rosen, M. A., Smith-Jentsch, K. A., Salas, E., Letsky, M., & Warner, N. (2010). Toward an understanding of macrocognition in teams: Predicting processes in complex collaborative contexts. *Human Factors, 52*, 203–224.

Flavell, J. H. (1979). Metacognition and cognitive monitoring: A new area of cognitive-developmental inquiry. *American Psychologist, 34*, 906–911.

Ford, J. K., & Kraiger, K. (1995). The application of cognitive constructs to the instructional systems model of training: Implications for needs assessment, design, and transfer. *International Review of Industrial and Organizational Psychology, 10*, 1–48.

Freeman, L. C. (1977). A set of measures of centrality based on betweenness. *Sociometry, 40*, 35–41.

Gibson, C., & Vermeulen, F. (2003). A healthy divide: Subgroups as a stimulus for team learning behavior. *Administrative Science Quarterly, 48*, 202–239.

Gully, S. M., Devine, D. J., & Whitney, D. J. (1995). A meta-analysis of cohesion and performance: Effects of levels of analysis and task interdependence. *Small Group Research, 26*, 497–520.

Kanfer, R., Chen, G., & Pritchard, R. (2008). Work motivation: Forging new perspectives and directions in the post-millennium. In R. Kanfer, G. Chen, & R. D. Pritchard (Eds.), *Work motivation: Past, present, and future* (pp. 601–632). New York, NY: Routledge.

Karoly, P. (1993). Mechanisms of self-regulation: A systems view. *Annual Review of Psychology, 44*, 23–52.

Kilduff, M., & Tsai, W. (2003). *Social networks and organizations.* Thousand Oaks, CA: Sage.

Klimoski, R., & Mohammed, S. (1995). Team mental model: Construct or metaphor? *Journal of Management, 20*, 403–437.

Kozlowski, S. W. J., & Bell, B. S. (2003). Work groups and teams in organizations. In W. C. Borman, D. R. Ilgen, & R. J. Klimoski (Eds.), *Handbook of psychology: Industrial and organizational psychology* (Vol. 12, pp. 333–375). London, UK: Wiley.

Kozlowski, S. W. J., & Bell, B. S. (2006). Disentangling achievement orientation and goal setting: Effects on self-regulatory processes. *Journal of Applied Psychology, 91*, 900–916.

Kozlowski, S. W. J., & Bell. B. S. (2007). A theory-based approach for designing distributed learning systems. In S. M. Fiore & E. Salas (Eds.), *Where is the learning in distance learning? Toward a science of distributed learning and training* (pp. 15–39). Washington, DC: APA Books.

Kozlowski, S. W. J., & Bell, B. S. (2008). Team learning, development, and adaptation. In V. I. Sessa & M. London (Eds.), *Group learning* (pp. 15–44). Mahwah, NJ: LEA.

Kozlowski, S. W. J., DeShon, R. P., Park, G., Curran, P., Kuljanin, G., & Firth, B. (2007). *Dynamic resource allocation in teamwork* (final performance report). Arlington, VA: Air Force Office of Scientific Research.

Kozlowski, S. W. J., Gully, S. M., Nason, E. R., & Smith, E. M. (1999). Developing adaptive teams: A theory of compilation and performance across levels and time. In D. R. Ilgen & E. D. Pulakos (Eds.), *The changing nature of work performance: Implications for staffing, personnel actions, and development* (pp. 240–292). San Francisco, CA: Jossey-Bass.

48 • *Theories of Team Cognition*

Kozlowski, S. W. J., & Ilgen, D. R. (2006). Enhancing the effectiveness of work groups and teams [Monograph]. *Psychological Science in the Public Interest, 7,* 77–124.

Kozlowski, S. W. J., & Klein, K. J. (2000). A multilevel approach to theory and research in organizations: Contextual, temporal, and emergent processes. In K. J. Klein & S. W. J. Kozlowski (Eds.), *Multilevel theory, research and methods in organizations: Foundations, extensions, and new directions* (pp. 3–90). San Francisco, CA: Jossey-Bass.

Kozlowski, S. W. J., Toney, R. J., Mullins, M. E., Weissbein, D. A., Brown, K. G., & Bell, B. S. (2001). Developing adaptability: A theory for the design of integrated-embedded training systems. In E. Salas (Ed.), *Advances in human performance and cognitive engineering research* (Vol. 1, pp. 59–123). Amsterdam: JAI/Elsevier Science.

Lovelace, D., Shapiro, D. L., & Weingart, L. R. (2001). Maximizing cross-functional new product teams' innovativeness and constraint adherence: A conflict communications perspective. *Academy of Management Journal, 44,* 779–793.

Mesmer-Magnus, J. R., & DeChurch, L. A. (2009). Information sharing and team performance: A meta-analysis. *Journal of Applied Psychology, 94,* 535–546.

Morrison, E. W., & Milliken, F. J. (2000). Organizational silence: A barrier to change and development in a pluralistic world. *Academy of Management Review, 25,* 706–725.

Rentsch, J. R., Small, E. E., & Hanges, P. J. (2008). Cognitions in organizations and teams: What is the meaning of cognitive similarity? In B. Smith (Ed.), *The people make the place: Exploring dynamic linkages between individuals and organizations.* New York, NY: Psychology Press.

Salas, E., & Wildman, J. L. (2009). Ten critical research questions: The need for new and deeper explorations. In E. Salas, G. F. Goodwin, & C. S. Burke (Eds.), *Team effectiveness in complex organizations: Cross-disciplinary perspectives and approaches* (pp. 525–546). New York, NY: Routledge Academic.

Stasser, G., & Titus, W. (1985). Pooling of unshared information in group decision making: Biased information sampling during discussion. *Journal of Personality and Social Psychology, 48,* 1467–1478.

Stasser, G., & Titus, W. (1987). Effects of information load and percentage of shared information on the dissemination of unshared information during group discussion. *Journal of Personality and Social Psychology, 53,* 81–93.

Steiner, I. D. (1972). *Group process and productivity* (pp. 14–66). New York, NY: Academic Press.

Stevens, M. J., & Campion, M. A. (1994). The knowledge, skill, and ability requirements for teamwork: Implications for human resource management. *Journal of Management, 20,* 503–530.

Tajfel, H. (1982). Social psychology of intergroup relations. *Annual Review of Psychology, 33,* 1–39.

Williams, K., & O'Reilly, C. A. (1998). Demography and diversity in organization. In B. M. Staw & R. I. Sutton (Eds.), *Research in organizational behavior* (pp. 77–140). New York, NY: Elsevier/JAI Press.

Zenger, T. R., & Lawrence, B. S. (1989). Organizational demography: The differential effects of age and tenure distributions on technical communication. *Academy of Management Journal, 32,* 353–377.

Section II

Organizational Behavior Perspectives

3

Reasoning About Intentions in Complex Organizational Behaviors: Intentions in Surgical Handoffs

Eugene Santos, Jr., Joseph Rosen, Keum Joo Kim, Fei Yu, Deqing Li, Yufan Guo, Elizabeth Jacob, Samuel Shih, Jean Liu, and Lindsay B. Katona

INTRODUCTION

Naturally, military hospitals must accommodate large numbers of injured soldiers in and from the battlefield in a short time period. To enhance the soldiers' chances of survival, a significant effort has been devoted to providing a better health care environment that is able to manage uncontrolled patient volume and the variable acuity of medical encounters effectively (McNeil & Pratt, 2008). One major effort has been to provide more operating room (OR) and intensive care unit (ICU) capability to satisfy the required medical and surgical needs (for examples in Iraq, see Eastridge, Jenkins, Flaherty, Schiller, & Holcomb, 2006; Montgomery, Swiecki, & Shriver, 2005). However, this solution only addresses one aspect of the problem and does not improve the injured soldiers' chances of survival in the battlefield, where environments are too complicated to be controlled as desired. Furthermore, in the ORs of both military and civilian hospitals, physicians must frequently make complicated clinical decisions with limited time and information while faced with a great number of competing demands and distractions (Kovacs & Croskerry, 1999; McIntyre, Stiegmann, & Eiseman, 2004). In addition, patients have often been transferred thousands of miles, passing through multiple teams of doctors at various places; for example,

52 • *Theories of Team Cognition*

a severely injured U.S. soldier in the Middle East would likely travel through several hospitals in the region before ultimately returning to a hospital in the United States. During these transitions, the patient's information with respect to medical treatments can be easily lost or corrupted. This happens often, especially in unpredictable battlefield situations (Horwitz, Krumholz, Green, & Huot, 2006).

The OR is a critical and complex work environment that includes a wide spectrum of people, devices, and tools, in addition to various activities and events. Its complexity can be clearly demonstrated in the patient and treatment protocol, as well as in the high technologies applied and the management skills required to effectively cope with dynamically changing conditions. As noted by Christian et al. (2006) and Dalton, Samaropoulos, and Dalton (2008), there have been various studies analyzing complex health care environments such as the ICU, OR, and emergency room. In particular, they have focused on the influence of interactions among components with respect to performance on quality of care and patient safety. Among the many key components that impact patient safety, communication failure among medical care providers is common in transitional care, where the patient is moved from one place to another (e.g., the OR to the recovery room) and is handed off from one care provider to another (Landro, 2006).

Using the definitions from the Institute of Medicine, a medical error is "the failure of a planned action to be completed as intended or the use of a wrong plan to achieve an aim," whereas an adverse event is "an injury caused by medical management rather than the underlying condition of the patient" (Kohn, Corrigan, & Donaldson, 2000, p. 54). Errors in the OR can have catastrophic consequences for patients, families, and care providers (Hurwitz & Sheikh, 2009). Retained sponges, wrong-site operations, and mismatched organ transplants or blood transfusions are examples of adverse events, and only by having effective methods for detecting medical errors can they be prevented from happening. Medical errors have been known to cause from 44,000 to 98,000 deaths and more than one million injuries each year in the United States (Kohn et al., 2000). A significant portion of these deaths and injuries are preventable (Dalton et al., 2008). In addition, communication failure was recently identified as the leading cause of many adverse events by The Joint Commission (Parush et al., 2010), and much literature reports that communication failure within health

Reasoning About Intentions in Complex Organizational Behaviors • 53

care teams increases error rates and the number of adverse events (Alvarez & Coiera, 2006; Lingard et al., 2004). In the report by Wilson, Runciman, and Gibberd (1995), communication failure was associated with medical errors twice more frequently than inadequate medical skills. Bhasale, Miller, and Reid (1998) noted that medical errors due to communication breakdown accounted for 50% of all detected adverse events. An interesting study has recently investigated breakdowns in situation-related communication as a cause of medical errors in open-heart surgeries (Parush et al., 2010).

All aforementioned studies show that teamwork is an essential component to promoting patient safety in the OR and is "an important surrogate of patient safety" (Makary et al., 2006, p. 746). Due to the widespread recognition and significance of teamwork regarding patient safety, training and working in teams have been studied intensively (Guise, 2008). However, most studies published up to now are limited to developing theories rather than providing a useful framework to facilitate the medical care members who are involved in cooperative tasks.

The goal of our work is to promote patient safety by enhancing medical care members' team performance. To realize this, we provide a computational cognitive framework that represents the individuals' clinical decision-making processes and assists the medical care members' understanding of their coworkers throughout the cooperative operations.

By inferring the intentions of team members from the actions observed and environments perceived, we can capture their intent behind actions and predict future actions. In addition, we can detect potential errors caused by discrepancies among OR team members by comparing their intentions and others' beliefs about them. In particular, we focus here on individual differences and interactions among them in modeling the members' reasoning because both of these elements are critical to inferring their intentions accurately.

In this chapter, we present the cognitive architecture that forms the basis of our surgical intent modeling. Our experiments are designed to validate whether our models are a true representation of real surgeons' decision-making processes and, as such, whether they are capable of detecting medical errors. Therefore, we will show how the potential errors caused by discrepancies among OR team members can be identified through our surgical intent modeling approach, focusing on the errors resulting from communication failure between surgeons.

54 • *Theories of Team Cognition*

We begin our discussion by providing background on intent modeling and Bayesian Knowledge Bases as the mechanisms for modeling the decision-making process. Then, we model beliefs, goals, and intentions of surgeons (and any other team member). Next, we describe our real-world case study, followed by our experimental results. Finally, we provide our conclusions and directions for future research.

INTENT INFERENCING AND BAYESIAN KNOWLEDGE BASES

Originally a psychological concept, individual intent is considered as a conscious subject. Intentional states are composed of multiple "psychological modes" and specify "the conditions of satisfaction" (Searle, 1983, pp. 12, 18). Although the individual intent can be realized in various ways, it is clear that the intent leads to a course of actions. Team (organizational) intent is shaped by the individuals to pursue cooperative tasks. It is "bound to be collective to a degree, because a team consists of multiple members" (Manterea & Sillinceb, 2007, p. 411). Such collective intent can be promoted by an interconnection of individual intentions where "individuals need to be aware of, and adjust to, intentions of other members of the team" (Manterea & Sillinceb, 2007, p. 411). Although strong and consistent shared intent among team members enhances the performance of the team to achieve the cooperative goals, inconsistent team intent can cause catastrophic damage in some circumstances, especially where the common goal is urgent and highly complicated, such as in the surgical practice (Williams, Rose, & Simon, 1999).

Surgeons' intentions can be inferred from individuals' course of actions and perceptions of the environments. The team intent can be driven by collecting and comparing these individuals' intentions. For modeling individuals' intentions, each individual's knowledge and perceptions need to be represented appropriately. Among many knowledge representation systems, we choose Bayesian Knowledge Bases (BKBs) due to their simplicity in construction, sound semantics in modeling the human decision-making process, and low computational complexity in reasoning. In BKBs, individual differences can be implemented through various instantiations of random variables and probabilistic distributions among them.

Bayesian Knowledge Bases

BKBs are directed graphs that represent the causal relationship between knowledge (Santos & Santos, 1999). Similar to Bayesian Networks (BNs) (Pearl, 1988), BKBs integrate together graph and probability theories but provide a better formalism to handle uncertainty and incompleteness in decision making. The directed graph representation presents a formal yet visual expression of causality, whereas probability theory guarantees the semantic soundness in decision making under uncertainty. BKBs are composed of two types of nodes (I-nodes and S-nodes) and one type of directional arc. Figure 3.1 depicts a small BKB example. Knowledge is stored through random variables. A pair consisting of a random variable and an instantiation (also called state) is uniquely represented by an I-node, which is depicted as a white oval in Figure 3.1. The dependencies between I-nodes are encoded by conditional probabilities through S-nodes, indicating the likelihood of the child I-node given that a parent I-node is observed. Black dots in Figure 3.1 represent S-nodes, and the weights on S-nodes represent the conditional probabilities. As mentioned previously, individual differences in the surgical intent modeling can be represented through instantiating random variables using I-nodes and probabilistic distributions of S-nodes. I-nodes are directed by arcs to demonstrate causality (e.g., if $B = b_1$, then $A = a_1$ with 80% chance). Some S-nodes, such as the nodes feeding into $B = b_1$ and $B = b_2$, have no parents. In this case, the weights refer to the prior probability of the I-nodes, that is, the probability of $B = b_1$ (or $B = b_2$) without any observation.

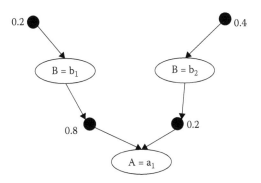

FIGURE 3.1
Bayesian Knowledge Base fragment.

56 • *Theories of Team Cognition*

BKBs are framed in this way to preserve both simplicity and expressiveness (Santos & Santos, 1999; Santos, Santos, & Shimony, 2003). BNs, on the other hand, do not explicitly model conditional probability rules in the graph and thus have to supply a conditional probability table that stores the conditional probabilities among all states of connected random variables. This is in contrast to BKBs, which do not require complete knowledge and the high complexity in interpreting the graph through the compact structure. In addition, BKBs are capable of handling cyclic knowledge and multiple information sources (Santos, Wilkinson, & Santos, 2009).

Reasoning in BKBs is based on the structure of the knowledge, which includes the if–then rules, the evidence that includes pieces of information observed prior to the reasoning, and the chain rule as shown in Equation 3.1.

$$P(X_1, X_2, \ldots, X_n) = \prod_1^n P(X_i \mid parents\,(X_i)) \qquad (1)$$

There are two forms of reasoning in BKBs: belief updating and belief revision. Belief updating computes the posterior probability of each single I-node using Bayes' theorem with given evidence. It answers questions such as, "What is the probability of a random variable given the evidence?" On the other hand, belief revision solves questions such as, "What is the most probable state of the world?" In belief revision, combinations of each state of the random variables together with the evidence form a possible world, and the likelihood of the world is the joint probability of the I-nodes as calculated by the chain rule. The algorithm then searches for a world that maximizes the likelihood. Algorithms for performing belief revision and belief updating in BKBs have been discussed in detail (Santos, 1991; Santos & Santos, 1987, 1999). The major difference between belief updating and belief revision is that belief updating does not account for the joint behavior of different random variables, whereas belief revision assumes that only one state of each random variable can be true in any possible world. Moreover, belief updating computes the posterior probabilities of random variables with given evidence, whereas belief revision generates the ranks of all possible worlds. Because these worlds are inferred from the same set of evidence, the joint probabilities are used to rank all the possible worlds. Consequently, the posterior joint probabilities are expected to be small. Furthermore, the probabilities of the worlds may even be smaller than expected due to the incomplete knowledge. Therefore, modelers should keep in mind that the inferred solution is one possible solution among all others that supports the evidence most and is only valid with respect to the information available. In inferring surgeons' intentions, belief revision is more appropriate because we are interested in all possible worlds of a surgeon's reasoning, which is composed of all aspects of his behavior. This also includes the comparison of all possible behaviors of a surgeon, some of which are relevant to potential medical errors caused by the surgeon's mistakes.

Intent Inference

With BKBs as the basis for capturing reasoning and decision making, we now describe our underlying approach for modeling intent. In particular, our approach is based on explicitly representing an entity's beliefs, goals, actions, and intentions and has been successfully applied in a number of domains such as user modeling (Santos & Nguyen, 2009), adversarial modeling (Santos, 2003; Santos & Zhao, 2006), and commander's intent modeling (Pioch et al., 2009). We first describe intent inferencing followed by its application to surgical intent modeling.

Because intent is an explanation of people's activities, it can be defined as the combination of the goal(s) that is being pursued, the support for the goal, and the plan to achieve the goal. A system containing these components and capable of reasoning through them is regarded as a computational representation of human intent. To capture the major elements in human intent, we incorporate the components of intent into the structure of BKBs. In particular, we categorize the I-nodes into axioms, beliefs, goals, and actions (Santos & Zhao, 2006). Axioms represent what a person believes about him- or herself; beliefs represent what a person believes about others (including other people and the world); goals represent what results a person wants to achieve; and actions represent what actions a person will take to realize his or her goal. Axioms and beliefs may influence themselves or each other. Both axioms and beliefs can contribute to goals. An action needs the support of goals and beliefs (or axioms). Actions can lead to other actions (mostly subactions). The hierarchy of interactions between the types of nodes is shown in Figure 3.2. Compliance with the hierarchy is not critical to the reasoning process but is enforced to

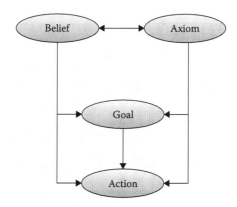

FIGURE 3.2
Hierarchy of interaction between four types of nodes in intent models.

encourage modelers to check for logical flaws, think more thoroughly about the structure of the model, and then systematically organize and correctly categorize their knowledge. After the dependencies between I-nodes are determined, the probabilities of S-nodes need to be estimated by experts first and then are further validated through experiments in general. Rules of thumb for constructing intent models can be found in Pioch et al. (2009) and Santos and Negri (2004).

Reasoning in intent models, called intent inferencing, follows the reasoning schemes of BKBs, which are (a) belief updating that calculates the posterior probability of individual I-nodes, and (b) belief revision that obtains the most probable state of the world. In particular, two tasks are frequently used: causal reasoning and diagnostic reasoning. Causal reasoning focuses on the direction of causality and infers the effects based on causes by extending the evidence forward to the currently unknown states of the world. In contrast, diagnostic reasoning infers the causes back from the known effects. Consequently, causal reasoning helps predict the behavior of a person based on what the person thinks, and diagnostic reasoning explains one's intent by inferring what was on the person's mind according to what the person had done (the observations).

An intent model is a representation of a person's knowledge about him- or herself and about others based on his or her perceptions, which may or may not be consistent with others' views or even with the real world. The behavior inferred from observables may serve as the input to the intent model of others or to the world.

SURGICAL INTENT MODELING

In general, a surgery involves multiple steps, which are implemented by surgeons, nurses, and other supporting care members. To better achieve the common goal of improving patients' health, all medical care members need to coordinate with each other when undertaking their medical activities. To improve team performance by enhancing communication and team members' situation awareness, we propose a computational cognitive framework representing surgeons' knowledge. This is different from other methods that have been studied for detecting adverse events and medical errors, as mentioned in Murff, Patel, Hripcsak, and Bates (2003), such as chart review, detecting adverse events using coded data, and free-text clinical narratives. Although there are individual differences among medical care members, we can detect potential errors and enhance the capability of achieving the common goal by considering individual intentions together with respect to the common goal of patient safety. By simulating each individual's reasoning process starting from diagnosing the patient and continuing to each single activity in the medical procedure, we expect to understand the underlying decision-making process.

Behaviors of the medical team members can also be influenced by incidents that occur prior to, during, or after the operation. Therefore, predicting the care members' actions by considering all possibilities, even though all of them may impact the team members' decision directly or indirectly, is a complicated task, and handling uncertainty and incompleteness is essentially required. By using the BKB's capability to represent uncertainty, we capture the uncertainty in team members' reasoning by the probabilistic dependency among elements of intent.

The key modules implemented to represent surgical intent are as follows: beliefs about the condition of the patient, axioms about one's own capability in performing (or assisting with, as in the case of a nurse) the surgery, goals regarding choice of procedures, and actions that are taken to perform the procedures. Sometimes the dependency between elements or the prior knowledge of an element is unattainable (e.g., it is known that surgeon A's malpractice in procedure B is low, but there is no record about his malpractice in procedure C). Because this kind of incompleteness is common, we leave the incomplete knowledge as it is through the compact and modular representation of BKBs. Because surgeons have the greatest

60 • *Theories of Team Cognition*

authority in performing medical procedures, we have initially detailed the process of building an intent model for a surgeon in this chapter.

- The condition of the patient has the highest priority in determining the surgeon's choice of procedure (Healey & Jacobson, 1994). The condition refers to the patient's disease and the risk of performing the medical procedure. The patient's condition is not restricted to the diagnosed illness, but also includes any related symptoms that may help the surgeons make decisions. The risk of performing the surgery includes all factors that may reduce the patient's chance of surviving the surgery such as age, allergy, pregnancy, and medical history. Patients may also take tests to assess their candidacies in the procedure such as a blood test. Both of these elements are encoded as the surgeons' beliefs as depicted in Figure 3.3, which is a snippet of a surgical intent model built for our case study (described in the next section) in which *(B)* stands for belief and *(G)* stands for goal. The surgeon's belief in the patient's candidacy in procedure *19180* is determined by the patient's bleeding status (*Coagulation_Profile_PT*, *Coagulation_Profile_INR*, and *Coagulation_Profile_PTT*), and the decision on the procedure directly depends on the patient's disease (*ICD_V07.5* and *ICD_610.1*).
- A surgeon confirms the procedure determined in the previous module depending on his or her personal competence. Usually the surgeon first considers the complexity of the procedure. The least complex procedure is most preferred due to the low risk and high success rate. When a complex procedure is inevitable, a surgeon prefers what he or she is more familiar with as well as more skilled in performing. Thus, the complexity of the procedure and the surgeon's experience (as well as malpractice history) in conducting the procedure serve as effective measures of the surgeon's preference. Complexity of procedures are represented as beliefs, whereas experience and malpractice are represented as axioms. This module can be extended by integrating the surgeon's confidence and fatigue as additional entities to represent the surgeon's personality and status of controlling capability. A BKB example of this dependency is shown in Figure 3.4. All three factors are concerned with the surgeon's competence and thus are modularized by an axiom (*competence_in_19180*). The competence influences the chances of staying with the original plan

Reasoning About Intentions in Complex Organizational Behaviors • 61

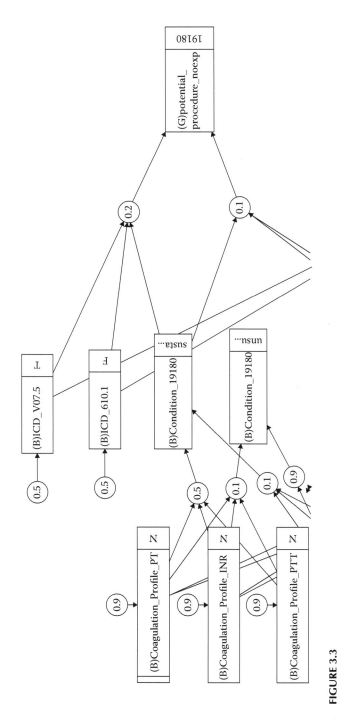

FIGURE 3.3
Example of Surgical Intent Model I.

62 • *Theories of Team Cognition*

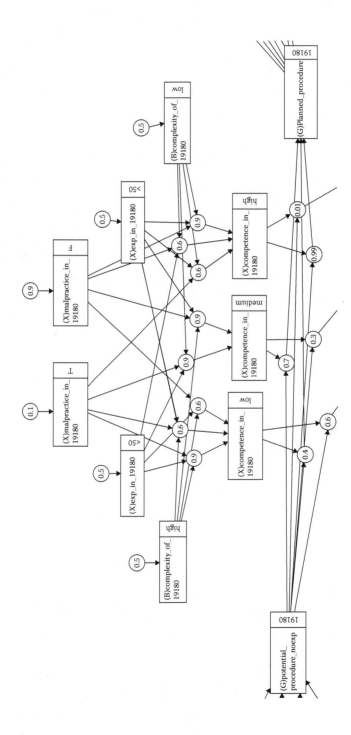

FIGURE 3.4
Example of Surgical Intent Model II.

(*Planned_Procedure=19180*) or switching to the alternative (*Planned_Procedure=19182*).

- In the surgical intent model, goals refer to the surgeon's intended procedures, and actions refer to the sequence of activities involved in the procedure. As the only observable in the OR, action is directly determined by the surgeon's goal. The status of an operation is determined by the previous actions and their completeness and is implemented by adding belief nodes indicating the actions as completed. As Figure 3.5 shows, together with the goal (*Planned_Procedure*), the belief nodes (*Completed_IAD*) contribute to the selection of the next action (*Action*).

The construction of the intent model is subject to change depending on the specific case and the role and characteristics of the surgeon (or other team member). Elements in each module are not restricted to the ones we propose here. As a simple extension, the fatigue of the surgeon can be integrated into the competence module. Also note that it is possible to take actions out of order due to the surgeon's incompetence.

CASE STUDY

To demonstrate the practical aspects of our intent modeling approach, we consider a handoff case where the patient, a 45-year-old woman having breast pain, is transferred from one surgeon to another. Such a handoff is particularly vulnerable to information loss. This case can be described in three stages: pre-op, intra-op, and post-op. The woman was diagnosed with idiopathic breast pain from fibrocystic disease. Her pain is related to fibrocystic disease but with no evidence of breast cancer. Some patients have chronic pain that is not relieved through nonsurgical methods and therefore require surgical removal of the involved breast tissue, but this usually does not involve the nipple–areola complex. In the case of breast cancer, the nipple–areola complex is removed, but when the breast pain is a result of noncancerous causes, the nipple–areola complex can be left intact.

Two surgeons were involved in the care of this patient. The general surgeon expected to do a subcutaneous mastectomy (or skin-sparing

64 • *Theories of Team Cognition*

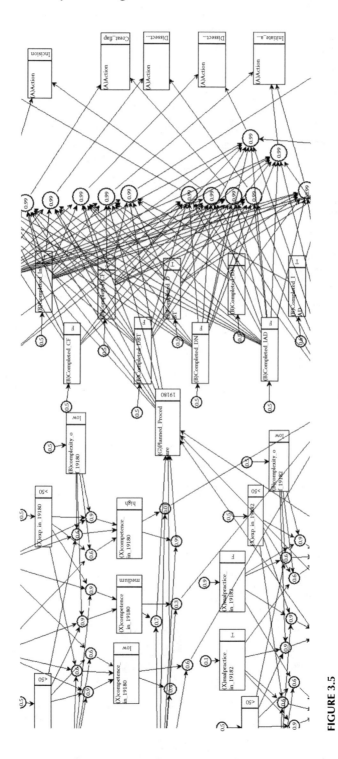

FIGURE 3.5
Example of Surgical Intent Model III.

Reasoning About Intentions in Complex Organizational Behaviors • 65

mastectomy); this can be done in either one of two ways—leaving the nipple–areola attached via a small pedicle for blood supply, or removing it entirely (separating it from the patient and re-attaching it as a full-thickness graft). Unfortunately, the plastic surgeon thought the general surgeon's mastectomy included the removal of the nipple–areola complex and believed that this was a case of breast disease that involved breast cancer or a severe case of fibrocystic disease. The plastic surgeon felt that the general surgeon was going to perform a simple mastectomy, which involves the removal of the breast tissue and the nipple–areola complex. There was confusion over the accepted definitions of simple mastectomy and subcutaneous mastectomy. The patient was seen by the general surgeon, and a decision was made by the general surgeon to do a subcutaneous mastectomy. This was defined to the patient as removing the breast tissue but *not* the nipple–areola complex. The patient was referred to the plastic surgeon to assist in the reconstruction, but no clear discussion occurred of what would happen to the nipple—whether the nipple–areola complex would be saved or whether it would be removed and replaced with a reconstructed nipple. The patient was seen preoperatively by the general surgeon but not by the plastic surgeon. The patient gave signed permission to operate but only gave combined consent, rather than an agreement to each surgeon's procedure.

The patient was brought into the OR, where the nurse explained what operation was going to be done; the surgeon agreed with this and proceeded. This was *not* repeated when the second surgeon (plastic surgeon) came into the room. The general surgeon performed bilateral subcutaneous mastectomies, removing the breast tissue along with the nipple–areola complexes. These were passed to the back table where the tissue remained until the plastic surgeon came into the room after the general surgeon had left. The plastic surgeon assumed that the specimen was to go to pathology, and the specimen included breast tissue and nipple–areola complex. However, in this case, he should have known that in a subcutaneous mastectomy, the nipple–areola can be saved and put back onto the patient. The operation that the plastic surgeon had planned and had previously had the patient sign for was the immediate replacement of the removed breast tissue for breast implants. He assumed that the nipple–areola complex would go to pathology and, at a later time, he would reconstruct new nipple–areola complexes, as is done in breast reconstruction surgery. The plastic surgeon was asked repeatedly by

66 • *Theories of Team Cognition*

the nurses if he wanted to save the nipples from the specimens, but he told them *no*, that this was not necessary, and he would be making a nipple later. There was a communication loss between the general surgeon, nurses, and plastic surgeon. The nurses should have known that, in this case, the nipples should have been kept. However, the confusing part for the plastic surgeon was that the nipple–areola came off with the specimen rather than being left attached to the breast. The patient left the OR without her nipple–areola complexes; they instead went unnecessarily to pathology for a patient with breast pain and not cancer. Although a subcutaneous mastectomy is an uncommon procedure, most surgeons are aware of it. However, sometimes it is confused with a simple mastectomy because a simple mastectomy is performed more frequently.

The patient was not aware that she had lost her nipples until several days later when the dressings were taken off by the general surgeon. This quickly set the tone of the follow-up care. When the plastic surgeon saw the patient, he tried to explain that he could make nipples better than her original, but this was not a satisfactory solution to the patient. Subsequently, she had multiple complications with tissue loss, partly related to the closure under tension due to the large size of the implants placed, the loss of the additional tissue (the nipple–areola), and the patient's persistent smoking, overall resulting in the patient being a breast cripple.

EXPERIMENTAL STUDY

Our empirical study is aimed at validating the capability of the intent model to represent a real case in medical practice with the purpose of enhancing patient safety. To model the surgeons' reasoning and intentions in the case study, we built BKBs from the behavioral patterns and the perceptions of the general and plastic surgeons. Table 3.1 shows the size of BKBs built for the general and plastic surgeons. With the BKBs, each surgeon's intent was inferred by computing the most probable instantiation of the world composed of random variables under consideration. Because we assumed that the surgeons' goals are the same as their procedures to carry out the patient's treatment, we set

TABLE 3.1

Size of Bayesian Knowledge Bases

	Random Variables	I-Nodes	Connectivity	S-Nodes (Rules)	Average Condition for Each Rule
General surgeon	25	57	5.5	91	2.4
Plastic surgeon	27	57	4.5	84	2.0

our target variable with *planned_procedure* representing the surgeon's decision. Because the two surgeons are involved in the overall breast care at different time intervals, their observations and perceptions are different. Naturally, the observations used to infer each surgeon's intent are different.

Experimental Setup

The sets of evidence used for validating the two surgeons' models are different because the two surgeons are involved in the operation at different times with different tasks to accomplish. To validate the general surgeon's model, we set the evidence with the patient's conditions, the surgeon's competence, and the status of completed actions, whereas we used the patient's condition, the status of the patient's nipple, and the surgeon's experience for the plastic surgeon's model. The target variable (*planned_procedure*) represents the procedure planned by the surgeon in both models. By comparing the value inferred with our expected values, we confirmed the model's correctness when obtaining identical values.

The evidence is chosen based on its causal relationship with the target variable. The patient condition includes whether the patient has breast pain or cancer. The surgeon's competence for a procedure is determined by a combination of his experience, malpractice history, and the complexity of the procedure. The course of actions for the mastectomy is shown in Figure 3.6, where P19357.1 and 19357.2 represent the breast reconstruction with reattaching the nipple complexes and the breast reconstruction without reattaching the nipple complexes, respectively (American Medical Association, 2004). For the subcutaneous mastectomy, dissecting and removing the nipple–areola complexes is optional, as shown in Figure 3.6.

68 • *Theories of Team Cognition*

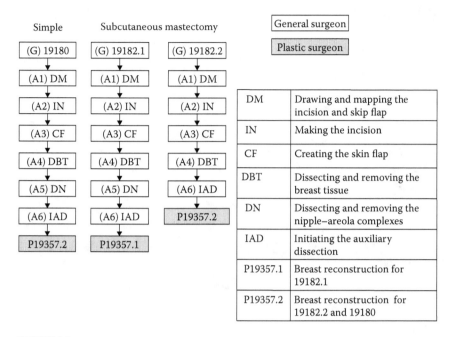

FIGURE 3.6
Course of actions in a mastectomy.

To validate the surgical intent models, deviations between the model and the real intent of the surgeon are indicative of conflicts between the results obtained from simulation and the hypotheses we had expected during modeling. It may come from the conditional probabilities, the causal rules, or the violation of the hierarchy of the four types of nodes. Model reconstruction and validation should be iteratively performed until the model is verified to be consistent with the hypotheses. The validation of BKBs is extensively studied in Santos and Dinh (2008) and Santos (2001). The consistency of the models built for the case study is confirmed by the tool used in Santos and Dinh (2008).

The following experiments are designed to investigate the model's applicability in detecting or removing potential errors in real medical situations. We checked whether we could recognize the error occurring in the case study when simulating the case through our models. As shown in the following section, all our experimental results support that our models represent the two surgeons' decision making correctly. In addition, we observed the communication failure when we compared each individual's intent with others' belief on the individual.

Experimental Results

Our experimental results are presented here from two perspectives. First, the results are arranged to show that our model is a true representation of the surgeon's diagnosis of the patient as having certain medical conditions. Second, the experimental results are provided with respect to the case study, and the potential error is detected by comparing individual intents and beliefs inferred from the surgeon's observations and perceptions.

The patient's conditions are the first determinant of the choice of procedure (*potential_procedure*), whereas the decision (*planned_procedure*) is confirmed by the surgeon's competence level later. To validate whether the general surgeon's (GS) model truly represents the surgeon's decision making, we hypothesized that when the patient has breast pain and is appropriate for a subcutaneous mastectomy, that procedure is chosen because it is a better treatment for curing breast pain than the simple mastectomy. The "most probable potential procedure" refers to the chosen procedure that is not deterministic but most likely among all the possible procedures. The patient's condition includes her disease and her candidacy for each procedure. The evidence representing the patient's disease is set with *ICD_V07.5* (breast cancer) and *ICD_610.1* (breast pain), whereas the evidence on the patient's candidacy is set with *condition_19182* (patient's condition in subcutaneous mastectomy) and *condition_19180* (patient's condition in simple mastectomy). We vary the patient's disease and her candidacy in the subcutaneous mastectomy or the simple mastectomy. The detailed experimental settings are listed in Table 3.2. In each of the settings, belief revision is conducted searching for the most probable world with the given evidence. In this particular experiment, we focus on the state of the potential procedure in each possible world. The result shows that the expectations are satisfied, which justifies the general surgeon's choice of potential procedure based on the patient's condition.

The confirmation of the procedure to be performed is influenced by both the potential procedure and the surgeon's competence. In other words, the final decision is weighed by the surgeon's preference in addition to the patient's condition. The elements that determine a surgeon's competence are his experience in conducting the procedure (*experience_in_##*, where ## represents the code of a procedure), his malpractice history (*malpractice_in_##*), and the complexity of the procedure

70 • *Theories of Team Cognition*

TABLE 3.2

Validation With the Patient Condition

		Evidence		Expectation of Potential
(B) ICD_610.1	**(B)** ICD_V07.5	**(B)** condition_ 19182	**(B)** condition_ 19180	*Procedure* (G) potential_procedure
T	F	Appropriate	N/A	19182
		Inappropriate	N/A	Unknown
F	T	N/A	Appropriate	19180
		N/A	Inappropriate	Unknown

Note: N/A = not applicable.

(*complexity_of_##*). These elements form the set of evidence in this test. We validate the surgeon's competence in two parts: the inference of competence and the influence of competence. In the inference of competence, we test how different factors, including personal factors and procedural factors, influence the competence of a surgeon in a particular procedure; whereas in the influence of competence, we target the joint effect of the potential procedure and competence on the planned procedure. The settings of the inference of competence are provided in Table 3.3. Overall, we expect that high competence results from ample experience, low malpractice, and low complexity and that low competence results from the opposite states of these factors. With both personal factors contributing to low

TABLE 3.3

Validation With the Inference of the General Surgeon's Competence

	Evidence		Expectation of
(X) exp_in_##	**(X)** malpractice_in_##	**(B)** complexity_of_##	*Competence in ##* (X) competence_in_##
>50	F	Low	High
<50	F	Low	High
>50	T	Low	High
<50	T	Low	Medium
>50	F	High	Medium
<50	T	High	Low
>50	T	High	Low
<50	F	High	Low

competence and the complexity of the procedure being low, the surgeon is regarded as medium in competence.

To test the influence of the general surgeon's competence, we fix the potential procedure, vary the general surgeon's competences in subcutaneous mastectomy and simple mastectomy, and observe the planned procedure. Although it is inappropriate to set competence as evidence because competence is not an external observable (although it can be inferred from the evidence of experience, etc.), we use it as evidence here for the purpose of focusing on the direct impact of competence on the surgeon's decision making. Given that the potential procedure is subcutaneous mastectomy, the general surgeon is expected to plan a subcutaneous mastectomy if his competence in it is high, regardless of the competence in a simple mastectomy. However, if the general surgeon's competence in the subcutaneous mastectomy procedure is low, he will select the simple mastectomy procedure unless his competence in the latter is low as well. If the general surgeon's competence in subcutaneous mastectomy is medium, he is expected to stick to the original choice of procedure. If the surgeon's competence in simple mastectomy is higher than that in subcutaneous mastectomy, which heavily depends on the characteristics of the particular surgeon (although all other expectations are also subject to individual difference), the general surgeon is expected to perform a simple mastectomy with the highest probability. Table 3.4 details the evidence setting for this experiment. Both the inference of competence and the influence of competence are confirmed by the results obtained.

In this experiment, we are particularly interested in the cases where the general surgeon's competences in the two procedures are equally high or equally low. When he is equally competent in the two procedures, he is expected to have enough knowledge about both procedures and sound judgment in choosing the most effective procedure that is least biased by his personal factors. In contrast, when he is not competent in a procedure, his final choice of procedure is heavily biased and even may override the condition of the patient. Our result shows that when the general surgeon's competence in subcutaneous mastectomy is low, he always tends to choose the simple mastectomy regardless of his competence in performing a simple mastectomy. In the case of both being low, the general surgeon is diffident in choosing the appropriate procedure and fluctuates between the two procedures. We show the joint probability of the both-low case in Table 3.5.

72 • *Theories of Team Cognition*

TABLE 3.4

Validation With the Influence of the General Surgeon's Competence

	Evidence		
(G) potential_ procedure	**(X) competence_ in_19182**	**(X) competence_ in_19180**	***Expectation of Planned Procedure* (G) planned_procedure**
19182	High	High	19182
		Medium	19182
		Low	19182
	Medium	High	19182
		Medium	19182
		Low	19182
	Low	High	19180
		Medium	19180
		Low	19182 or 19180 with similar probability

The last validation on the general surgeon's model tests the order of actions because following the correct order of actions is critical when performing a medical procedure. By testing the order of actions, we make sure that (a) the surgeon's actions are in correct order, and (b) the surgeon is doing what he is supposed to do. The second point concerns whether the surgeon is carrying out his planned procedure and whether his actions are consistent with other surgeons' actions. In this case study, although the general surgeon plans a simple mastectomy, it is necessary to dissect the patient's nipple, but if he plans a subcutaneous mastectomy, whether to dissect the nipple is partially determined by his belief about the plastic

TABLE 3.5

Validation With the Influence of the General Surgeon's Competence

	Evidence			Result
(G) potential_ procedure	**(X) competence_ in_19182**	**(X) competence_ in_19180**	**(G) planned_ procedure**	**Joint probability**
19182	Low	Low	19180	7.49114e–06
			19182	4.99409e–06

Reasoning About Intentions in Complex Organizational Behaviors • 73

surgeon's (PS) procedure. Therefore, when the planned procedure is determined, the most probable actions are investigated depending on the status of the overall operations. The target variable is *action*, and the evidence is *planned_procedure*, *PS_procedure* (general surgeon's belief on plastic surgeon's procedure), and *completed_XX* (the completeness of action *XX*, where *XX* represents the abbreviation of an action). Because the evidence setting of the experiment regarding simple mastectomy is subsumed by that of subcutaneous mastectomy, we assume that the subcutaneous mastectomy is planned. We vary the belief about the plastic surgeon's procedure and the completed actions. At each instant, we observe that the action that is being carried out by the general surgeon follows the correct order of actions in each procedure as shown in Figure 3.6. Table 3.6 lists the details of this experimental setting.

To validate the inference of target variables (*GS_procedure* and *potential_procedure*) on the plastic surgeon's model, we examined them with a varying set of evidence as shown in Table 3.7. *GS_procedure* denotes the plastic surgeon's belief on the general surgeon's procedure, and *potential_procedure* represents the procedure the plastic surgeon plans to carry out. First, we collected the status of the target variables when *GS_nipple_removal* is the only evidence given to the plastic surgeon, and the results obtained are shown in Table 3.7. When the nipple is removed, the plastic surgeon considers both the simple (19180) and the subcutaneous (19182) mastectomies as the general surgeon's procedure with the same highest probability. Thinking that the general surgeon plans the simple mastectomy (19180), the plastic surgeon plans the breast reconstruction without nipple reattachment (19357.2) with the highest probability. If he believes that the general surgeon plans the subcutaneous mastectomy (19182), he needs to consider two ways to reconstruct the breast—with (19357.1) or without (19357.2) reattaching the nipple complexes. When the nipple is not removed by the general surgeon, the plastic surgeon can easily plan the breast reconstruction without reattaching the nipple (19357.2) with the highest probability regardless of his belief on the general surgeon's procedure. Because the evidence of *GS_nipple_removal* is independent from *GS_procedure*, which is inferred from the patient condition, both the simple and the subcutaneous mastectomies can be chosen with the same probability when the nipple complexes are left behind.

Table 3.7 shows the results obtained from our experiments, and all of them fit to our expectations, where *No. of answers* and *First rank*

TABLE 3.6

Action Prediction

		Evidence						
(G) planned_ procedure	**(B) PS_ procedure**	**(B) completed_ DM**	**(B) completed_ IN**	**(B) completed_ CF**	**(B) completed_ DBT**	**(B) completed_ DN**	**(B) completed_ IAD**	***Most Probable Next Action* (A) action**
19182	19357.1	F	F	F	F	F	F	Draw_Map
		T	F	F	F	F	F	Incision
		T	T	F	F	F	F	Create_Flap
		T	T	T	F	F	F	Dissect_Breast_Tissue
		T	T	T	T	F	F	Dissect_Nipple
		T	T	T	T	T	F	Initiate_Auxiliary_ Dissection
		T	T	T	T	T	T	Close_Wound
	19357.2	F	F	F	F	F	F	Draw_Map
		T	F	F	F	F	F	Incision
		T	T	F	F	F	F	Create_Flap
		T	T	T	F	F	F	Dissect_Breast_Tissue
		T	T	T	T	F	F	Initiate_Auxiliary_ Dissection
		T	T	T	T	F	T	Close_Wound

probability denote the possible number of states of the world and the highest probability obtained, respectively. For example, we can get 2,688 possible states of the world represented by the BKB by setting the evidence *GS_nipple_removal* with *T*. Among them, 44 states are highly probable, and both alternatives have the same number of possible states of the world, which means that the plastic surgeon considers both the simple (19180) and the subcutaneous (19182) mastectomies as the general surgeon's procedure with the same highest probability (1.03003e–08). Thinking that the general surgeon plans the simple mastectomy (19180), the plastic surgeon plans the breast reconstruction without nipple reattachment (19357.2) in 20 possible states of the world. If he believes that the general surgeon plans the subcutaneous mastectomy (19182), he needs to consider two ways to reconstruct the breast, with reattaching the nipple complexes (19357.1) in 12 possible states or without reattaching the nipple complexes (19357.2) in 10 possible states.

The plastic surgeon believes the subcutaneous mastectomy (19182) is planned by the general surgeon because it is the common procedure for the patient with breast pain (*ICD_610.1*) not cancer (*ICD_v07.5*), as shown in Table 3.8. Because the nipple can be removed or kept with the same probability, the plastic surgeon plans the breast reconstruction with reattaching the nipple complexes (19357.1) and the breast reconstruction without reattaching the nipple (19357.2) with the same probability. When

TABLE 3.7

Inference With Status of the Patient's Nipple

Evidence	*Target Variables*				
GS_ nipple_ removal	(B) GS_ procedure	(G) potential_ procedure	Total no. of answers	No. of answers in first rank	First rank probability
T	19180	19357.1	2,688	0/42	1.03003e–08
	19180	19357.2		20/42	
	19182	19357.1		12/42	
	19182	19357.2		10/42	
F	19180	19357.1	2,560	0/40	1.03003e–08
	19180	19357.2		20/40	
	19182	19357.1		0/40	
	19182	19357.2		20/40	

76 • *Theories of Team Cognition*

TABLE 3.8

Inference With Patient Conditions

Evidence		Target Variables			No. of	
ICD_610.1	ICD_ V07.5	(B) GS_ procedure	(G) potential_ procedure	Total No. of Answers	Answers in First Rank	First Rank Probability
T	F	19180	19357.1	2,624	0/42	1.03003e–08
		19180	19357.2		0/42	
		19182	19357.1		12/42	
		19182	19357.2		30/42	
F	T	19180	19357.1	2,624	0/40	1.03003e–08
		19180	19357.2		40/40	
		19182	19357.1		0/40	
		19182	19357.2		0/40	

ICD_V07.5 is *T,* which means that the patient has a cancer rather than just breast pain, the plastic surgeon believes the simple mastectomy (191820) is planned by the general surgeon. To follow the general surgeon's procedure, the plastic surgeon plans the breast reconstruction (19357.2) with the highest probability.

When the subcutaneous mastectomy (19182) is inferred as the general surgeon's procedure, the nipple complexes can be removed or not with the same probability due to the two types of subcutaneous mastectomy, which are described in Table 3.9. If the nipple complexes are removed by the general surgeon, the plastic surgeon needs to reattach them (19357.1). Otherwise, the plastic surgeon plans the breast reconstruction without the reattachment (19357.2). When the simple mastectomy (19180) is inferred as the general surgeon's procedure, the plastic surgeon plans the breast reconstruction without reattaching the nipple complexes (19357.2) with the highest probability regardless of the nipple removal. However, the plastic surgeon may doubt the evidence given to him because the nipple complexes are always expected to be removed during the simple mastectomy (19180) even if his designated plan (19357.2) remains the same.

To further investigate the impact of the plastic surgeon's experience on his decision making, we use four random variables as the evidence in inferring the plastic surgeon's belief and goal. As previously mentioned, the *GS_procedure* is inferred from the patient profile and does not count on the status

TABLE 3.9

Inference With Patient Information Combined

Evidence			Target Variables		Total No. of Answers	No. of Answers in First Rank	First Rank Probability
ICD_610.1	ICD_V07.5	Nipple_removal	(B) GS_procedure	(G) potential_procedure			
T	F	T	19182	19357.1	1,344	12/22	1.03003e-08
			19182	19357.2		10/22	
		F	19182	19357.2	1,280	20/20	1.03003e-08
F	T	T	19180	19357.2	1,344	20/20	1.03003e-08
		F	19180	19357.2	1,280	20/20	1.03003e-08

78 • *Theories of Team Cognition*

of the patient's nipple and the plastic surgeon's experience. However, the plastic surgeon's belief on the general surgeon's procedure can change by additional evidence such as the nipple complexes being removed and his own experience in the procedure. To represent the belief changed by additional evidence, we add another target variable (*GS_procedure_post*) and investigate how this variable changes when some of the evidence conflicts with other evidence, as shown in Table 3.10.

When the plastic surgeon believes that the general surgeon plans the subcutaneous mastectomy (19182) from the patient profile and finds that the patient's nipple complexes are removed, there are two possible cases. First, he can change his belief from *GS_procedure* to *GS_procedure_post* that the general surgeon plans the simple mastectomy (19180) and not the subcutaneous mastectomy (19182). However, if he has more experience/ knowledge in the subcutaneous mastectomy (19182), he can bring up a type of subcutaneous mastectomy (19182.1) that includes dissecting and reattaching the nipple complexes, and plans the breast reconstruction including the nipple reattachment (19357.1) with the highest probability. However, if the nipple complexes are not removed, the plastic surgeon confirms that the general surgeon plans the subcutaneous mastectomy (19182) and plans his own procedure, the breast reconstruction without the reattachment (19357.2). In this situation, the communication between the two surgeons can be cleared easily, and the level of the plastic surgeon's experience does not change his previous belief and final goal.

When the plastic surgeon believes that the general surgeon plans the simple mastectomy (19180), the removed nipple complexes support his previous belief. Therefore, the plastic surgeon confirms his belief on the general surgeon's procedure and plans his own procedure, the breast reconstruction without reattaching the nipple complexes (19357.2), with the highest probability. However, when the nipple complexes are left behind, the plastic surgeon has difficulty in understanding the general surgeon's plan. Although the plastic surgeon believes that the simple mastectomy (19180) should be chosen to cure the patient's cancer with the highest probability, the nipple complexes remaining make him wonder as to whether the general surgeon plans another alternative procedure, which is represented as 19180.1 in Table 3.10. We represent this with *GS_procedure_post*, which represents the plastic surgeon's belief on the general surgeon's procedure after considering additional evidence, the status of the patient's nipple. However, because he believes that the breast

TABLE 3.10

Inference out of Considering Experience

Evidence				Target Variables				No. of	
ICD_610.1	ICD_ V07.5	Nipple_ removal	Experience	(B) GS_procedure	(B) GS_ procedure (post)	(G) potential_ procedure	Total No. of Answers	Answers in First Rank	First Rank Probability
T	F	T	Low	19182	19180	19357.2	640	10	1.03003e−08
			High	19182	19182.1	19357.1	704	12	1.03003e−08
T	F	F	Low	19182	19182	19357.2	640	10	1.03003e−08
			High	19182	19182	19357.2	640	10	1.03003e−08
F	T	T	Low	19180	19180	19357.2	640	10	1.03003e−08
			High	19180	19180	19357.2	704	10	1.03003e−08
F	T	F	Low	19180	19180.1	19357.2	640	10	1.03003e−08
			High	19180	19180.1	19357.2	640	10	1.03003e−08

80 • *Theories of Team Cognition*

reconstruction without reattaching the nipple complexes (19357.2) is the most appropriate procedure, he keeps his plan with the highest probability despite the discrepancy.

Errors in the Case Study

The errors in the case study came from two conflicts: One is the conflict between the general surgeon's planned procedure and the plastic surgeon's belief of the general surgeon's procedure, and the other is the conflict between the plastic surgeon's planned procedure and the general surgeon's belief of the plastic surgeon's procedure. By combining individual models, which represent the two surgeons separately in our case study, and comparing one's belief with the other's intent inferred, we can recognize the communication gap between the two surgeons.

Tables 3.11 and 3.12 show the evidence and the target variables used for this experiment. Although the breast pain T means that $ICD\_610.1 = T$ and $ICD\_V07.5 = F$, the drawing and mapping T means that the general surgeon completed the action "drawing and mapping the incision and skin flap," which is one of the actions included in the mastectomy. Therefore, the breast pain represents the patient's condition, and the drawing and mapping denote the completeness of the actions by the general surgeon at a certain time. In the same stream, the plastic surgeon plans his procedure

TABLE 3.11

Evidence for the Overall Inference

Evidence				Specialty
Breast pain	T	F	T	G, P
Breast cancer	F	T	F	G, P
Drawing and mapping	T	T	T	G
Create flap	T	T	T	G
Dissecting breast tissue	T	T	T	G
Dissecting nipple	F	F	F	G
Initiate auxiliary dissection	F	F	F	G
PS procedure	19357.1	19357.2	19357.2	G
GS_nipple_removal	T	T	F	P
Exp_in_19182	Low High	Low High	Low High	P
SET ID	1.1 1.2	2	3	

Reasoning About Intentions in Complex Organizational Behaviors • 81

TABLE 3.12

Results Inferred With Evidence Given in Table 3.11

Target Variables					Specialty
(A) Action		Dissecting nipple		Initiate auxiliary dissection	G
(G) Planned_procedure		19182	19180	19182	G
(B) GS_procedure	19180	19182	19180	19182	P
(G) Planned_procedure	19357.2	19357.1	19357.2	19357.2	P
SET ID	1.1	1.2	2	3	

based on the patient profile and the status of the patient's nipple complexes. The far right columns of each table represent to which surgeon the evidence is given or from which surgeon the value of the target variable is inferred during the experiments. G represents the general surgeon, and P represents the plastic surgeon. With the given evidence including his belief on the plastic surgeon's procedure, the general surgeon's intent was inferred to the subcutaneous mastectomy or the simple mastectomy depending on the patient condition and the status of completed actions. When the general surgeon plans to dissect the patient's nipple, he can plan the subcutaneous mastectomy when he believes that the plastic surgeon will reattach it, which is the case with SET ID 1.1 and 1.2. The plastic surgeon's belief on the general surgeon's procedure is varied depending on his experience in the subcutaneous mastectomy. He changes his belief to the simple mastectomy when he considers the patient's nipple being removed as an obvious outcome of the simple mastectomy due to his lack of experience (i.e., $exp\_in\_19182 = low$), although the simple mastectomy is not the appropriate treatment for the patient having a breast pain in general, which is addressed with SET ID 1.1 in Tables 3.11 and 3.12. However, an experienced plastic surgeon (i.e., $exp\_in\_19182 = high$) keeps his belief and plans nipple reattachment, which is addressed with SET ID 1.2. When the patient has breast cancer and the nipple complexes are removed, the plastic surgeon believes that the general surgeon plans the simple mastectomy and plans his procedure without any difficulty, which is represented with SET ID 2. This is same as when the patient has breast pain and the nipple complexes remain; the plastic surgeon believes that the general surgeon plans the subcutaneous mastectomy and plans his procedure easily, which corresponds to SET ID 3.

82 • *Theories of Team Cognition*

When we compare both surgeons' inference results, the error happens when the general surgeon believes that the plastic surgeon plans the breast reconstruction with reattaching the nipple (19357.1), while the plastic surgeon does not consider the reattachment at all (19257.2) due to his lack of knowledge/experience, which corresponds to SET ID 1.1. However, it can also be explained by the plastic surgeon being unaware of the fact that the general surgeon plans the subcutaneous mastectomy (19182) due to his lack of knowledge. Both of these interpretations can fit the communication failure that occurred between the two surgeons in the patient's care.

CONCLUSION AND FUTURE WORK

Our main contribution here is to provide the cognitive architecture that forms the basis of surgical intent modeling and a principled approach for realizing and creating the model. In addition, we apply our models to improving team coordination by considering individuals' intents and beliefs associated with others. To validate our model, we chose a real-world patient handoff case and modeled each surgeon's reasoning by considering his behavioral patterns and his perceptions associated with the case. In particular, we implemented the surgeons' intents, which were interpreted as their goal in treating the patient, inferred from their observations and perceptions.

Given our current results obtained from models built for this case study, we identified the following issues for future research.

- Level of detail: In our current implementation, we have considered sets of actions for the simple mastectomy, the subcutaneous mastectomy, and the breast reconstruction. It was reasonable to consider specific actions when the overall patient care included only a few procedures carried out by a small number of surgeons. However, some cases require several procedures, and critical communication failures occur during the transition time between any pair of consecutive procedures. Therefore, considering the surgeons' reasoning in the procedure level seems more appropriate for modeling in general.
- Order of actions/procedures: Some actions/procedures are preemptive and reversible, whereas others are not. The actions/procedures

in the case study were considered irreversibly and nonpreemptively, and partial orders were not considered. This is because the actions in the mastectomy result in adverse medical events if they are performed out of order. In order to perform procedures without causing any harmful effect in practice when they are out of order, partial orders should be considered if the target case permits this.

- Roles in the overall patient care: The plastic surgeon's decision making begins at a different time point from that of the general surgeon because the plastic surgeon enters the OR after the general surgeon has left the OR in the case study. Although all observations of the plastic surgeon are associated with the general surgeon's actions, the models built for the two surgeons have little commonality because their specialties are very unique. However, some surgeons can have very similar knowledge, and models for these surgeons are expected to be very similar. In general, the level of specification of modeling individuals is difficult to be clarified.

REFERENCES

Alvarez, G., & Coiera, E. (2006). Interdisciplinary communication: An uncharted source of medical error? *Journal of Critical Care, 21*, 236–242.

American Medical Association. (2004). *Current procedural terminology (CPT)* (Standard ed.). Chicago, IL: Author.

Bhasale, A., Miller, G., & Reid, S. (1998). Analysing potential harm in Australian general practice: An incident-monitoring study. *Medical Journal of Australia, 169*, 73–76.

Christian, C. K., Gustafson, M. L., Roth, E. M., Sheridan, T. B., Gandhi, T. K., Dwyer, K., et al. (2006). A prospective study of patient safety in the operating room. *Surgery, 139*, 159–173.

Dalton, G. D., Samaropoulos, X. F., & Dalton, A. C. (2008). Improvements in the safety of patient care can help end the medical malpractice crisis in the United States. *Health Policy, 86*, 153–162.

Eastridge, B. J., Jenkins, D., Flaherty, S., Schiller, H., & Holcomb, J. B. (2006). Trauma system development in a theater of war: Experiences from Operation Iraqi Freedom and Operation Enduring Freedom. *Journal of Trauma, 61*, 1366–1372.

Guise, J. M. (2008). Teamwork in obstetric critical care. *Best Practice & Research Clinical Obstetrics and Gynaecology, 22*, 937–951.

Healey, P. M., & Jacobson, E. J. (1994). *Common medical diagnoses: An algorithmic approach* (2nd ed.). Philadelphia, PA: W.B. Saunders Co.

Horwitz, L. I., Krumholz, H. M., Green, M. L., & Huot, S. J. (2006). Transfers of patient care between house staff on internal medicine wards: A national survey. *Archives of Internal Medicine, 166*, 1173–1177.

84 • Theories of Team Cognition

Hurwitz, B., & Sheikh, A. (2009). *Health care errors and patient safety* (1st ed.). Boston, MA: BMJ Books.

Kohn, L., Corrigan, J., & Donaldson, M. (2000). *To err is human.* Washington, DC: National Academy Press.

Kovacs, G., & Croskerry, P. (1999). Clinical decision making: An emergency medicine perspective. *Academic Emergency Medicine, 6,* 947–952.

Landro, L. (2006, June 28). Hospitals combat errors at the "hand-off." *The Wall Street Journal.*

Lingard, L., Espin, S., Whyte, S., Regehr, G., Bajer, G., Reznick, R., et al. (2004). Communication failure in the operating room: Observational classification of recurrent types and effects. *Quality and Safety in Healthcare, 13,* 330–334.

Makary, M. A., Sexton, J. B., Freischlag, J. A., Holzmueller, C. G., Millman, E. A., Rowen, L., et al. (2006). Operating room teamwork among physicians and nurses: Teamwork in the eye of the beholder. *Journal of the American College of Surgeons, 202,* 746–752.

Manterea, S., & Sillinceb, J. A. (2007). Strategic intent as a rhetorical device. *Scandinavian Journal of Management, 23,* 406–423.

McIntyre, R., Stiegmann, G. V., & Eiseman, B. (2004). *Surgical decision making* (5th ed.). Philadelphia, PA: Saunders.

McNeil, J. D., & Pratt, J. (2008). Combat casualty care in an Air Force theater hospital: Perspectives of recently developed cardiothoracic surgeons. *Seminars in Thoracic and Cardiovascular Surgery, 20,* 78–84.

Montgomery, S. P., Swiecki, C. W., & Shriver, C. D. (2005). The evaluation of casualties from Operation Iraqi Freedom on return to the continental United States from March to June 2003. *Journal of the American College of Surgeons, 201,* 7–12.

Murff, H. J., Patel, V. L., Hripcsak, G., & Bates, D. W. (2003). Detecting adverse events for patient safety research: A review of current methodologies. *Journal of Biomedical Informatics, 36,* 131–143.

Parush, A., Kramer, C., Foster-Hunt, T., Momtahan, K., Hunter, A., & Sohmer, B. (2010, April 8). Communication and team situation awareness in the OR: Implications for augmentative information display. *Journal of Biomedical Informatics* [Epub ahead of print].

Pearl, J. (1988). *Probabilistic reasoning in intelligent systems.* San Francisco, CA: Morgan Kaufmann.

Pioch, N. J., Melhuish, J., Seidel, A., Santos, E., Jr., Li, D., & Gorniak, N. (2009). Adversarial intent modeling using embedded simulation and temporal Bayesian knowledge bases. *SPIE Defense, Security and Sensing, 7348,* 1–14.

Rosen, T., Shimony, S., & Santos, E., Jr. (2004). Reasoning with BKBs: Algorithms and complexity. *Annals of Mathematics and Artificial Intelligence, 40,* 403–425.

Santos, E., Jr. (1991). On the generation of alternative explanations with implications for belief revision. *Proceedings of the Seventh Conference on Uncertainty in Artificial Intelligence,* 337–347.

Santos, E., Jr. (2001). Verification and validation of knowledge-bases under uncertainty. *Data and Knowledge Engineering, 37,* 307–329.

Santos, E., Jr. (2003). A cognitive architecture for adversary intent inferencing: Knowledge structure and computation. *Proceedings of the SPIE 17th Annual International Symposium on Aerospace/Defense Sensing and Controls: AeroSense 2003,* 182–193.

Santos, E., Jr., & Dinh, H. T. (2008). Automatic knowledge validation for Bayesian knowledge bases. *Data and Knowledge Engineering, 64,* 218–241.

Santos, E., Jr., & Negri, A. (2004). Constructing adversarial models for threat intent prediction and inferencing. *Proceedings of the SPIE Defense & Security Symposium, 5423,* 77–88.

Santos, E., Jr., & Nguyen, H. (2009). Modeling users for adaptive information retrieval by capturing user intent. In M. Chevalier, C. Julien, & C. Soule-Depuy (Eds.), *Collaborative and social information retrieval and access: Techniques for improved user modeling* (pp. 88–118). New York: Information Science Reference.

Santos, E., Jr., & Santos, E. E. (1999). A framework for building knowledge-based under uncertainty. *Journal of Experimental and Theoretical Artificial Intelligence, 11,* 265–286.

Santos, E., Jr., Santos, E. E., & Shimony, S. E. (2003). Implicitly preserving semantics during incremental knowledge base acquisition under uncertainty. *International Journal of Approximate Reasoning, 33,* 71–94.

Santos, E., Jr., Wilkinson, J. T., & Santos, E. E. (2009). Bayesian knowledge fusion. In *22nd International FLAIRS Conference.* Menlo Park, CA: AAAI Press.

Santos, E., Jr., & Zhao, Q. (2006). Adversarial models for opponent intent inferencing. In A. Kott & W. McEneaney (Eds.), *Adversarial reasoning: Computational approaches to reading the opponents mind* (pp. 1–22). London, UK: Chapman & Hall/CRC.

Santos, E. S., & Santos, E., Jr. (1987). Reasoning with uncertainty in a knowledge-based system. *Proceedings of the Seventeenth International Symposium on Multiple-Valued Logic,* 75–81.

Searle, J. R. (1983). *Intentionality: An essay in the philosophy of mind.* Cambridge, UK: Cambridge University Press.

Williams, K. A., Rose, W. D., & Simon, R. (1999). Teamwork in emergency medical services. *Air Medical Journal, 18,* 149–153.

Wilson, R., Runciman, W., & Gibberd, R. (1995). The quality in Australian health care study. *Medical Journal of Australia, 163,* 458–471.

4

Time and Team Cognition: Toward Greater Integration of Temporal Dynamics[*]

Susan Mohammed, Rachel Tesler, and Katherine Hamilton

Since the early 1990s, there has been an exciting proliferation of team cognition research across disciplinary boundaries. Team cognition is a broad term referring to the collective cognitions of a group (Tindale, Meisenhelder, Dykema-Engblade, & Hogg, 2001). In delineating the potential benefits of team cognition, Cannon-Bowers and Salas (2001) noted its role as an explanatory mechanism in distinguishing between effective and ineffective teams, its ability to predict team preparedness, and its diagnostic value in surfacing team problems and identifying points for intervention. Empirical research has gleaned support for the positive relationship between enhanced team process and/or performance and various forms of team cognition, including group learning (e.g., Edmondson, 1999), transactive memory (e.g., Liang, Moreland, & Argote, 1995), team mental models (e.g., Mathieu, Heffner, Goodwin, Salas, & Cannon-Bowers, 2000), team situation awareness (e.g., Artman, 1999), and cognitive consensus (e.g., Mohammed & Ringseis, 2001). Indeed, a recent meta-analysis of 65 independent studies concluded that team cognition positively predicts team processes, motivational states, and performance (DeChurch & Mesmer-Magnus, 2010a).

Since the early 1990s, there has also been increased awareness of the role of time in various team phenomena and the importance of explicitly incorporating temporal dynamics in conceptual and empirical work (e.g., Arrow, Poole, Henry, Wheelan, & Moreland, 2004; Ballard, Tschan, & Waller, 2008; McGrath, 1991; Mohammed & Zhang, 2009). For example,

---

[*] The opinions expressed in this chapter are those of the authors only and do not necessarily represent the official position of the Office of Naval Research, the U.S. Navy, the U.S. Department of Defense, or the Pennsylvania State University.

87

88 • *Theories of Team Cognition*

groups have been characterized as complex systems that change systematically over time and exhibit processes with temporal patterns and nonlinear dynamics (Arrow et al., 2004). In addition, empirical findings from teams investigated only in the short term may not hold over time (type I error), and findings from longer-term teams may not occur in short-term teams (type II error; McGrath, Arrow, Gruenfeld, Hollingshead, & O'Connor, 1993). Therefore, a temporal focus should inform conceptual as well as methodological team research choices (Ballard et al., 2008).

In this chapter, we address the conceptual and empirical research intersecting time and team cognition. From the standpoint of practical significance, there are plenty of applied indicators in support of the critical interplay between time and team cognition. For example, the consequences of teams of cooks and servers achieving (or failing to achieve) high levels of temporal coordination are played out daily in restaurant kitchens all over the world. Specifically, "timing food reflects a concern with synchronization—a division of labor among cooks and servers. The cook must internalize the ordering and timing of dishes to permit the production of fifteen different dishes, each at the peak of quality, and *must believe that other cooks are acting similarly*" (Fine, 1996, p. 62, italics added). Moreover, investigations of several military, government, and natural disasters have been blamed on team cognition failures (Foushee, 1984; Wilson, Salas, Priest, & Andrews, 2007), and many include a significant temporal component. Using Hurricane Katrina as an illustration, delays by U.S. federal officers in gaining situational awareness about levee breaches and delays in providing buses to evacuate shelters contributed to the largest natural disaster in recent U.S. history (Moynihan, 2007). "With limited time, the Katrina network largely failed to coordinate itself, or to improve response until after terrible suffering occurred" (Moynihan, 2007, p. 18). Indeed, coordination includes a temporal component that is not present in other types of team processes, such as communication and cooperation.

From these practical examples, it is clear that establishing and maintaining congruence in team members' temporal perceptions is a nontrivial task that deserves research attention. Nevertheless, despite its ubiquitous and fundamental nature, time has been referred to as "perhaps the most neglected critical issue" in team research (Kozlowski & Bell, 2003, p. 364). Although considerable progress has been made in answering questions of *what* factors contribute to team effectiveness and *why* some groups are more successful than others, team research has been deficient regarding *when* groups are more and less effective (Ilgen, Hollenbeck, Johnson, & Jundt, 2005; Mohammed, Hamilton, & Lim, 2009). Lamentably, the temporal criticisms levied against team research in general can also be more specifically directed toward team cognition research. Although temporal dynamics are implicit in the conceptualization of many types of team cognition (e.g., team situation awareness, team mental models), the role of time has been largely downplayed in the extant research. Therefore, the purpose of the current chapter is to review past and current work to consider how future team cognition research can more comprehensively incorporate temporal dynamics conceptually and empirically.

Because it is beyond the scope of this chapter to cover all team cognition constructs, we focus on perceptual team cognition, team mental models, and team situation awareness. Each construct captures unique aspects of team cognition and is couched in emerging literatures that have been contrasted in recent reviews (e.g., Mohammed, Ferzandi, & Hamilton, 2010) as well as combined in current models of macrocognition (Letsky & Warner, 2008; Warner & Letsky, 2008). Furthermore, although by no means abundant, existing work on perceptual team cognition, team mental models, and team situation awareness has begun to integrate temporal dynamics.

The sections on perceptual team cognition, team mental models, and team situation awareness are organized according to a four-part framework proposed in a recent review of the literature on time and teams (Mohammed et al., 2009). According to Mohammed et al. (2009), the first and most popular category representing the treatment of time is the use of longitudinal design (variables measured at multiple time points). In addition to longitudinal research, a comprehensive incorporation of temporal issues involves explicitly including time as part of the content of the construct. For example, variables such as time urgency (Mohammed & Nadkarni, 2010) and temporal reminders (Gevers, van Eerde, & Rutte, 2009) are naturally time related in their conceptualization and measurement. The third category integrates the first two by examining constructs with temporal properties longitudinally. The fourth and final category regards time as part of the temporal context by considering the potential influence of deadlines, time pressure, and the time-related aspects of the larger organizational and cultural environment in which teams are embedded.

90 • *Theories of Team Cognition*

PERCEPTUAL TEAM COGNITION

Overview

Perceptual team cognition comprises a subset of constructs that have two general characteristics. First, perceptual team cognition constructs assess beliefs (desired states of nature that are preferred or evaluative) as opposed to knowledge (descriptive states of nature that one knows to be true; Mohammed, Klimoski, & Rentsch, 2000). To illustrate, requesting one's subjective opinion on whether a team member should be assigned to the operations crew (beliefs) is different from requesting the rules underlying operating procedures (knowledge). Second, perceptual team cognition constructs assess perceived as opposed to actual sharing among team members. For example, asking individuals to rate the extent to which their team holds similar views on teamwork would constitute perceptual team cognition, whereas measuring each member's knowledge structures and then directly comparing them to the rest of the team would not.

A variety of specific constructs fall under the purview of perceptual team cognition, including shared task representations, cognitive consensus, and strategic consensus. Shared task representations capture "any task/situation-relevant concept, norm, perspective, or cognitive process that is shared by most or all of the group members" (Tindale, Smith, Thomas, Filkins, & Sheffey, 1996, p. 84). Using an experimental design, van Ginkel and van Knippenberg (2008) found that groups with shared task representations who also realized that they shared representations engaged in more information elaboration (exchange, consideration, and integration) and had higher decision quality than other conditions.

Also, framed in a decision-making context, cognitive consensus describes similarity in the way that group members conceptualize key issues and can be measured as assumptions, broad categories (e.g., threat, opportunity), content domains (e.g., political, strategic), or causal maps (Mohammed, 2001). Operationalized as shared assumptions underlying decisions, Mohammed and Ringseis (2001) found that cognitive consensus positively affected expectations regarding decision implementation and satisfaction. Moreover, unanimity-decision-rule groups achieved more cognitive consensus than majority-rule groups in a sample of student groups participating in a multi-issue decision-making exercise (Mohammed & Ringseis, 2001).

Strategic consensus refers to a shared understanding of strategic goals and priorities and has been traditionally assessed using top management teams (Kellermanns, Walter, Lechner, & Floyd, 2005). Organizational performance has been a key outcome variable, but some studies have shown a positive linkage with top management team consensus (e.g., Bourgeois, 1980), whereas others have not (e.g., Ensley & Pearce, 2001). In terms of predictors, cognitive conflict (Ensley & Pearce, 2001) and agreement seeking (Knight et al., 1999) have been found to increase strategic consensus in top management teams, but functional and educational diversity decreases strategic consensus (Knight et al., 1999).

Perceptual Team Cognition Over Time: Longitudinal Research

To our knowledge, no studies have assessed shared task representations, cognitive consensus, or strategic consensus longitudinally. Because of the nascent stage of empirical work on shared task representations and cognitive consensus, the emphasis has been on establishing the constructs in a nomological network of antecedents and consequences. Therefore, the lack of longitudinal work at this juncture is not surprising. However, even in the more developed strategic consensus literature, a recent review noted the neglect of temporal issues and the focus on agreement at single points in time (Kellermanns et al., 2005). According to Priem (1990, p. 475), the "cross-sectional, correlation-based nature of consensus-performance studies performed to date does not allow causal inferences to be drawn or lag effects to be examined." The difficulty of obtaining multiple measures from management samples, especially those at the top of the organization, may put longitudinal designs out of reach for most studies. As such, much remains to be known about how strategic consensus changes over time (Kellermanns et al., 2005).

Time as Part of the Construct Content: Shared Temporal Cognition

Shared cognitions on time (Bartel & Milliken, 2004; Gevers, Rutte, & van Eerde, 2004), temporal consensus (Gevers et al., 2009), and shared temporal cognition (Gevers, Rutte, & van Eerde, 2006) are all terms that have

92 • *Theories of Team Cognition*

been used to describe when team members have common views about the time-related aspects of executing collective tasks. Consistent with the extant research, these terms will be used interchangeably (Gevers et al., 2006; Gevers et al., 2009). Although there is consensus on the general definition, differences exist regarding the specific components of shared temporal cognition. For example, Bartel and Milliken (2004) hypothesized three time-related cognitions: individuals' time orientations toward the present and future, perceived time pressure by outside parties, and organizational norms about time management. Although also including time orientation, Standifer and Bluedorn (2006) suggested that a shared temporal perspective encompasses entrainment, pace, cycle, and dominant rhythms. Representing another perspective, Gevers et al. (2004) posited that sharing temporal cognition consists of team members agreeing on temporal milestones and schedules as well as attaching equal importance to temporal reference points on interdependent tasks. In a later article, these authors further specify that shared cognitions on time include a common understanding of "the importance of meeting the deadline, (sub) task completion times, and appropriate timing and pacing of task activities" (Gevers et al., 2006, p. 54). That is, team members should agree on specific deadlines, how the work should be scheduled over time, and how fast the team should work to meet the deadlines (Gevers et al., 2009).

When team members hold conflicting temporal expectations about interdependent tasks (e.g., different interpretations of deadline flexibility/rigidity, the pace at which subtasks should be completed), coordination problems can result, which may affect the timeliness and quality of the team output (Bartel & Milliken, 2004; Gevers et al., 2009). Contrastingly, establishing a common temporal perspective is thought to facilitate the process by which team members adapt to each other's actions as well as to external temporal demands (Gevers et al., 2004). Thus, Gevers et al. (2004) theorized that shared temporal cognition is a primary mechanism through which teams achieve coordinated action. Similarly, shared cognition on time has been proposed to lead to temporal synchronization, "a condition in which work group members agree on the rate at which group activities should occur and align the pace at which they work to complete individual and shared tasks" (Bartel & Milliken, 2004, p. 88). As such, it is especially important that group members achieve congruence in temporal perceptions when tasks are highly interdependent and require intense collaboration and information sharing (Bartel & Milliken, 2004;

Standifer & Bluedorn, 2006). Extending beyond the team level of analysis, the significance of shared temporal cognition among leaders of component teams has also been discussed in the context of multiteam systems (Standifer, 2012).

Studies measuring the extent to which team members experience congruence in temporal perceptions are limited in number but have shown promising results. In an exploratory study of 104 face-to-face groups from 92 different organizational contexts, Bartel and Milliken (2004) found that group members were more likely to develop similar temporal perceptions derived from the situation (time pressure and scheduling norms) than the person (present versus future time orientation). Credited with the largest concentration of empirical work, Gevers and colleagues conducted a series of studies identifying the precursors and consequences of member consensus regarding the temporal aspects of task execution (Gevers & Peeters, 2009; Gevers, Rutte, van Eerde, & Roe; 2005; Gevers et al., 2006, 2009). In each of these studies, shared temporal cognition was operationalized as the group mean on a four-item scale assessing the extent to which members had similar thoughts about meeting deadlines, the best way to use time, how to allocate the time available, and the time it takes to perform certain tasks.

In terms of antecedents, both implicit (e.g., pacing style, conscientiousness) and explicit (e.g., temporal reminders, temporal planning) mechanisms were found to predict shared temporal cognition (Gevers & Peeters, 2009; Gevers et al., 2006, 2009). For example, dissimilarity in conscientiousness and pacing styles (individual differences for time allocation under deadline conditions) among team members related to lower levels of shared temporal cognition (Gevers & Peeters, 2009; Gevers et al., 2006). In contrast, exchanging temporal reminders (prompting each other to finish tasks on time) fostered higher shared cognition in a sample of 31 Dutch student teams performing two case analyses. A recent study of 48 engineering student teams working on a business project replicated the earlier results regarding temporal reminders and also found that temporal planning (determining the order of actions and discussing time constraints) had a positive influence on temporal consensus (Gevers et al., 2009). Contrary to hypotheses, temporal reflexivity (evaluating and communicating adjustments in plans to meet temporal milestones) was not found to contribute to higher levels of shared temporal cognition (Gevers et al., 2009).

94 • *Theories of Team Cognition*

In terms of consequences, Gevers et al. (2005) demonstrated that shared temporal cognition contributed unique variance to meeting deadlines over and above shared teamwork and taskwork cognition. Across two studies, student and organizational teams with higher temporal consensus were more likely to complete their projects on time (Gevers et al., 2005, 2009). However, in both cases, the relationship was mediated. In an organizational sample, group potency (the generalized belief that a group can be effective) mediated the relationship between shared temporal cognition and meeting deadlines (Gevers et al., 2005). However, coordinated action mediated the relationship between temporal consensus and meeting deadlines among student project teams (Gevers et al., 2009). Also among student project teams, Gevers and Peeters (2009) found that greater temporal consensus predicted greater levels of coordinated action, which then contributed to team member satisfaction. In another study, some support was also found for the notion that temporal consensus is positively associated with meeting deadlines when members start their work early, but is negatively associated with meeting deadlines when members wait until the last minute (Gevers et al., 2006).

Although shared temporal cognition enhances a team's ability to complete its projects on time, Gevers et al. (2005) did not find the parallel relationship with output quality. In contrast, results from Mohammed and Nadkarni (2010) showed that shared temporal cognition (measured with the same scale as Gevers) exerted a positive, direct influence on the quality and quantity of team performance in a sample of 71 organizational teams in India. In addition, diversity of time urgency (feeling chronically hurried) and polychronicity (preference to engage in more than one task concurrently) were more positively related to team performance when shared temporal cognition was higher than lower (Mohammed & Nadkarni, 2010).

Teams Over Time: Shared Temporal Cognition

Through longitudinal measurement over multiple studies, Gevers et al. (2005, 2006, 2009) were able to compare temporal consensus developed early and late in a team's tenure. Using difference scores, Gevers et al. (2005) found that shared temporal cognition did not change significantly when the measure was collected three times over an average of 32 weeks. However, in this longitudinal field study, teams that had high levels of shared temporal cognition within the first few weeks of a project were more likely to complete the project on time. Moreover, meeting deadlines was further enhanced when temporal consensus increased from Time 1 to Time 2 as well as from Time 2 to Time 3 (Gevers et al., 2005). These results were later replicated in a sample of engineering student teams. Specifically, teams were better able to achieve timely completion when they had higher temporal consensus early on and when they experienced increases in the level of temporal consensus over time (Gevers et al., 2009).

Longitudinal effects were also evidenced with respect to the antecedents of shared cognition about temporal demands. For example, similarity in pacing styles was found to be positively related to shared temporal cognition only in the project's early stages, whereas the use of temporal reminders was positively related to shared temporal cognition only later in the project (Gevers et al., 2006). In a subsequent study conducted over 13 weeks, a similar pattern of results occurred when increases in temporal reminders predicted temporal consensus over the course of the project, but temporal planning predicted temporal consensus in the initial stages (Gevers et al., 2009).

Time as Part of the General Context: Team Temporal Environment

The temporal demands imposed by the group, organizational, and societal context as well as how these demands are perceived by team members through time pressure have not received adequate attention in the perceptual team cognition literature. In addition, although timeliness is recognized as an important part of team effectiveness conceptually (e.g., Hackman, 1990) and practically (e.g., Freeman & Beele, 1992), meeting deadlines is often ignored empirically as a component of the temporal context. These criticisms have been levied against team research in general (Mohammed et al., 2009), and team cognition studies have also fallen short in this regard. As a notable exception, however, timely work completion was the primary dependent variable in the shared temporal cognition studies conducted by Gevers et al. (2005, 2006, 2009).

Summary of Time and Perceptual Team Cognition

In light of the paucity of longitudinal studies measuring perceptual team cognition and the general lack of emphasis given to the team temporal

96 • *Theories of Team Cognition*

context, the integration of time as part of the construct content is the rising star of this research stream. Specifically, the extant work on shared temporal cognition has shown promising results with respect to establishing a nomological network of antecedents (pacing style, temporal reminders, temporal planning), consequences (meeting deadlines, performance quality), and moderated effects (Gevers et al., 2005, 2006, 2009; Mohammed & Nadkarni, 2010). Indeed, it is noteworthy that Gevers et al. (2005, 2006, 2009) infused a temporal focus into all of the categories we have described: time as part of the construct content, longitudinal measurement, and the team temporal environment. Nevertheless, given that shared temporal cognition is in a nascent stage, additional conceptual and empirical research is clearly needed. The variety of terms used to describe the general notion of team members having common views of temporal demands creates conceptual confusion. In addition, refinement and consensus are required to elaborate the specific components of shared temporal cognition. A key agenda item is to significantly expand the body of empirical work in this area. We now turn our attention to another type of team cognition, namely team mental models.

TEAM MENTAL MODELS

Overview

Team mental models (TMMs) are team members' shared, organized understanding and mental representation of knowledge about key elements of the team's relevant environment (Klimoski & Mohammed, 1994). The central assumption underlying this research is that teams will be more effective when members share and have an adequate understanding of taskwork (e.g., work goals, performance requirements) and teamwork (e.g., interpersonal interaction requirements; Cannon-Bowers, Salas, & Converse, 1993) domains. TMMs have two primary properties: sharedness (the degree to which members' mental models are consistent with one another) and accuracy (the degree to which members' mental models converge with experts' mental models or a *true score*), although sharedness has received the most research emphasis (e.g., Mathieu, Heffner, Goodwin, Cannon-Bowers, & Salas, 2005).

In contrast to perceptual forms of team cognition, TMMs assess knowledge (as opposed to beliefs) and measure actual (as opposed to perceived) sharing among team members. Furthermore, through incorporating what needs to be accomplished (taskwork) as well as how work needs to be accomplished (teamwork), TMMs cover a broader array of cognitive content than other forms of team cognition (Mohammed et al., 2010). In addition to the breadth of cognitive content as a point of conceptual distinction, the measurement of structure operationally differentiates TMMs from other forms of team cognition (Mohammed et al., 2010). Because organized knowledge is central to the definition of TMMs, TMM measurement involves the additional step of examining the relationship between concepts in addition to capturing cognitive content. Paired comparison ratings (e.g., Lim & Klein, 2006), concept mapping (e.g., Ellis, 2006), and card sorting (e.g., Smith-Jentsch, Cannon-Bowers, Tannenbaum, & Salas, 2008) are commonly used TMM measurement techniques that capture both content and structure.

Since 1995, a growing number of empirical studies have consistently shown that TMMs are of substantial benefit to both team processes and performance (e.g., Edwards, Day, Arthur, & Bell, 2006; Ellis, 2006; Lim & Klein, 2006; Mathieu et al., 2000; Rentsch & Klimoski, 2001). Two meta-analyses (DeChurch & Mesmer-Magnus, 2010a, 2010b) and a qualitative review (Mohammed et al., 2010) have similarly concluded that one of the keys to team effectiveness lies with TMMs. Given the remarkable growth of the construct in the past decade, TMMs have been identified as "one of the more developed collective cognition literature streams" (Mathieu, Maynard, Rapp, & Gilson, 2008, p. 429).

TMMs Over Time: Longitudinal Research

Although individual-level modifications are expected to occur more quickly, TMM similarity and accuracy are expected to change over time (Cooke, Salas, Cannon-Bowers, & Stout, 2000). However, existing conceptual models have said little regarding the speed with which TMMs develop or their rate of change once they are formed. An exception is McComb (2008), who suggested that convergence on TMM content may occur faster than convergence on TMM structure. In addition, Cannon-Bowers et al. (1993) proposed that the rate of change would depend on TMM content. Specifically, equipment models (knowledge about tools

98 • *Theories of Team Cognition*

and technology) were projected to be the most stable, followed by task (understanding of work procedures) and team interaction models (awareness of role interdependencies and member responsibilities), which were expected to be moderately stable. TMMs capturing teammates' habits and preferences were anticipated to be the most malleable (Cannon-Bowers et al., 1993). Because many studies measure only one type of TMM content and/or are cross-sectional, these propositions have largely remained untested. However, two studies have suggested some support in that taskwork mental models showed no changes over sessions, but teamwork knowledge improved over time (Cooke, Kiekel, & Helm, 2001; Cooke et al., 2003).

Empirical TMM longitudinal research has been limited in volume as well as scope. Given the resource-intensive nature of assessing TMMs, administering multiple measures over time may become prohibitive, especially for field studies. When longitudinal research is conducted, TMM convergence is generally measured two or three times over a multihour period in the context of undergraduates performing computer simulations (e.g., Cooke et al., 2001, 2003; Edwards et al., 2006; Marks, Zaccaro, & Mathieu, 2000; Mathieu et al., 2000, 2005). To our knowledge, only two longitudinal TMM studies have reported longer time frames. In a field sample of government employees, Smith-Jentsch, Campbell, Milanovich, and Reynolds (2001) administered a teamwork card sort twice over the course of 2 successive days. Levesque, Wilson, and Wholey (2001) collected teamwork and taskwork surveys (no structural data) from student software development teams at 1, 2, and 3.5 months. Therefore, little is known about TMM stability in teams that have a long history of working together.

A common assumption is that team members' mental models will converge over time because of greater levels of interaction (e.g., Rentsch & Hall, 1994). However, a mixed pattern of empirical results has emerged. Whereas some studies have found no significant differences over time (Edwards et al., 2006; Mathieu et al., 2000, 2005; Smith-Jentsch et al., 2001), others have found increases in sharedness over time (e.g., Marks et al., 2000). One study even found a decrease in sharedness over time, which was attributed to progressively more specialized roles and reduced team interaction over several months (Levesque et al., 2001). Comparisons across studies are complicated by the variety of TMM measurement techniques (e.g., card sort, concept mapping), time spans (e.g., hours, days, months), and contexts (e.g., field, classroom, laboratory) investigated.

Nevertheless, these results underscore that time alone does not guarantee the development of TMMs (Kang, Yang, & Rowley, 2006).

Time as Part of the Construct Content: Temporal TMMs

At the individual level, there has been active dialogue at the intersection of mental models and time, including long-term memory for temporal mental models (Baguley & Payne, 2000), the role of time in situation models (Radvansky, Zwaan, Federico, & Franklin, 1998), temporal order in mental models (Mandler, 1986), and temporal reasoning in mental model development (Schaeken, Johnson-Laird, & d'Ydewalle, 1996). Regrettably, the parallel discussion at the team level has been much sparser. From its inception, the TMM construct was designed to account for the implicit coordination frequently observed in effective teams (Cannon-Bowers et al., 1993). However, although the importance of coordination and timing is inherent in the broad conceptualization of a TMM, the role of time has not been given adequate attention in past research. Thus far, TMM studies have emphasized teamwork and taskwork as two broad categories of mental model content (e.g., Mathieu et al., 2000). Although an understanding of the "what" and the "how" are indeed critical to team functioning, failure to understand "when" can seriously jeopardize final team outcomes.

Notably, a few researchers have discussed the need for TMMs to explicitly include temporality (e.g., Millward, 2006; Mohammed et al., 2009; Standifer & Bluedorn, 2006). For example, Millward (2006) identified shared conceptions of being on schedule as a facet of TMMs. In addition, Standifer and Bluedorn (2006) advocated that team interaction models be enhanced to include shared meanings about temporal concepts. Specifically, shared temporal mental models represent an "awareness, acceptance, and intentional blending of each member's temporal perspective" (Standifer & Bluedorn, 2006, p. 918). Shared temporal mental models were proposed to enable alliance management teams to achieve greater consensus regarding entrainment (rhythmic patterns adjust to align with the rhythm of another activity), pace, rhythm, and time orientation (Standifer & Bluedorn, 2006).

Despite the conceptual recognition that TMMs should be enhanced to include temporality, studies measuring temporal TMMs are practically nonexistent. This research paucity is, in no small part, due to the fact that

100 • *Theories of Team Cognition*

popular TMM measurement techniques have been temporally deficient. Therefore, Mohammed et al. (2009) recommended that time-based referents be added to TMM techniques such as paired comparison ratings and concept mapping to increase measurement precision. Answering this call, a recent study empirically examined temporal TMMs, which were defined as agreement among group members concerning deadlines for task completion, the pacing or speed at which activities take place, and the sequencing of tasks (Hamilton, Mohammed, et al., 2010). In the context of a crisis management simulation involving police, fire, and hazardous material units, team members coordinated the timing of their arrival on the scene of events (e.g., all units need to be on site by 3:30) as well as temporal ordering (e.g., fire first, police second, hazmat third). Temporal TMMs were measured in two ways. First, with paired comparison ratings, participants judged the similarity between pairs of temporal concepts (e.g., deadline, speed). Second, concept mapping involved team members identifying the sequence by which units needed to arrive on the scene of events.

Teams Over Time: Temporal TMMs

Given that research on temporal TMMs is in its formative stages, it is not surprising that studies that both add time-based referents to TMM measurement techniques *and* administer them over time are limited. To the author's knowledge, there is no relevant empirical work to describe in this section. Thus, longitudinal research on temporal TMMs is a key agenda item for future research.

Time as Part of the General Context: TMM Temporal Environment

According to Cannon-Bowers et al. (1993), TMMs exist within dynamic environments and are especially critical to team performance in time-constrained situations when high levels of adaptability are required by team members. Indeed, TMMs were prominently featured in a recent model of team adaptation, which involves changes in performance (Burke, Stagle, Salas, Pierce, & Kendall, 2006). On a similar note, Rico, Sanchez-Manzanares, Gil, and Gibson (2008) proposed team situation models as dynamic knowledge structures that capture moment-by-moment changes in understanding regarding the environment, team, and task. Regrettably, however, little empirical work has measured TMMs under varying temporal conditions such as time pressure, deadlines, and the organizational temporal context. Although team performance has been the dominant criterion variable of TMM research (Mohammed et al., 2010), most outcome measures have focused on quality and quantity dimensions, ignoring the timeliness of task completion (e.g., Kellermans, Floyd, Pearson, & Spencer, 2008; Marks et al., 2000; Mathieu et al., 2000). As an exception, a qualitative study found that high-performing nuclear power plant crews engaged in less attention to time during TMM development than low-performing crews (Waller, Gupta, & Giambatista, 2004).

Summary of Time and TMMs

Although there is consensus that TMMs are worthy of study and growing in research popularity, a recent review of the TMM literature identified greater integration of temporal dynamics as a key agenda item for future research (Mohammed et al., 2010). Relative to temporal content and context as categories, most empirical work at the intersection of time and TMM has been conducted longitudinally. Nevertheless, the limited and mixed research findings speak to the need for additional studies to clarify our understanding of TMM stability and how TMMs are revised over time. In addition, future research should expand the definition and measurement of TMMs to shared, organized mental representations of who is going to do what, with whom, and *when*. As such, TMM assessment techniques should be enhanced with time-based referents, and longitudinal work on temporal TMMs also needs to be conducted. Furthermore, increased conceptual and empirical attention should be devoted to the temporal context in which TMMs develop.

TEAM SITUATION AWARENESS

Overview

Unfortunately, there is no universally accepted definition of situation awareness (SA) (Salas, Prince, Baker, & Shrestha, 1995; Salmon et al., 2008; Shrestha, Prince, Baker, & Salas, 1995). For example, Smith and Hancock

102 • *Theories of Team Cognition*

(1995) view it as a perceptual cycle of cognitive processes, whereas Bedny and Meister (1999) define it as conscious dynamic reflections on the situation. Furthermore, some researchers do not view SA as a construct that is limited to the human mind, but rather as an interaction of human cognition and artifacts such as devices/displays (Salmon, Stanton, Walker, Jenkins, & Rafferty, 2010; Stanton, Salmon, Walker, & Jenkins, 2010).

Among all of the definitions of SA, Endsley's (1995a) three-level model is the most cited and used (Salmon et al., 2008). Three hierarchical levels represent the progressive development of SA. In Level 1, elements in the environment are physically perceived (e.g., noticing an image displayed on a radar screen). In Level 2, elemental information is put together to elicit comprehension of the current situation in relation to the observer's task/goals (e.g., understanding that the Level 1 data represent a rapidly approaching aircraft). Finally, in the highest level, Level 3, the knowledge from the lower levels is used to project future events and environmental states (e.g., the two planes will crash in 1 minute if courses are not corrected; Endsley, 1995a).

Team SA involves the interaction of individual SA with processes such as coordination and information sharing (Endsley, 1995a; Salas et al., 1995). More specifically, team members may enhance their SA by communicating about aspects of the task such as requirements and goals, or they may share and modify their SA knowledge with each other in a cyclical fashion (Salas et al., 1995; Salmon et al., 2008). For example, Bolman (1979) coined the concept of the theory of the situation, whereby team members collect and share task information and come together to endorse a particular theory about a given situation. As time elapses and inconsistencies between theory and reality arise, the collective theory must be reviewed and revised.

SA researchers generally agree that in teams, individuals' SA areas should overlap, and the overlap corresponds to team coordination (Endsley, 1995a; Salas et al., 1995; Wellens, 1993). Thus, there should be an optimal balance of individual and overlapping SA in teams. For some researchers, individual and overlapping SA represent the concepts of team and shared SA, respectively. For example, team SA has been defined as "the degree to which each team member possesses the SA required for his or her responsibilities" (Endsley, 1995a, p. 39), whereas shared SA can represent "the degree to which team members possess the same SA on shared SA requirements" (Endsley & Jones, 2001, p. 48). However, there is still ambiguity regarding the distinction between these two terms, and they appear to be often used interchangeably (Salmon et al., 2008). For example, Wellens (1993, p. 6) defined "the sharing of a common perspective [on the three levels of SA]" as team SA, despite the definition's focus on overlapping, or shared, SA. Furthermore, researchers have discussed the concept of distributed SA, in which they argue that no two agents, whether human or artifact, share the exact same perception of a situation, and thus only need to have *compatible* SA rather than *shared* SA (Salmon et al., 2010; Stanton et al., 2006, 2010). Given the inconsistencies in the literature, we use the term *team SA* to encompass all of the aforementioned constructs.

Overall, the situation awareness global assessment technique (SAGAT) appears to be the most commonly used measure of SA and has the most validation evidence (Salmon, Stanton, Walker, & Green, 2006). SAGAT involves freezing the task and administering multiple-choice and/or open-ended questions assessing SA at each of the three levels of Endsley's (1995b) model. In addition to SAGAT, whose queries elicit responses that can be objectively assessed as correct or incorrect, a number of self-report and observational measures have also been developed (Salmon et al., 2006). There has also recently been growing interest in using propositional network models for measuring team SA, as this qualitative approach does not simply measure the aggregate of individual team members' SA, but rather uses a systems perspective (Salmon et al., 2010; Stanton et al., 2006).

Team SA Over Time: Longitudinal Research

SA can build up and change over time as one gains more exposure to the situation and/or as the situation changes, consequently affecting future projections. Therefore, various researchers have recommended that SA be measured multiple times in real time during the course of a task to observe changes and to better pinpoint what incites those changes (e.g., Endsley, 1995a; Salas et al., 1995; Sarter & Woods, 1991). Solely measuring team SA after the task will not elucidate the unique progression of the construct up until that point (Endsley, 1995b; Sarter & Woods, 1991). Furthermore, although a single posttask administration is less intrusive on the task itself, accurate recall may be more difficult, especially if participants are asked to recollect several different moments in the task (Endsley, 1995b; Salmon et al., 2006; Sarter & Woods, 1991).

104 • *Theories of Team Cognition*

However, what is encompassed within the realm of longitudinal SA studies is unclear. Within a given task, multiple measurements could potentially be used to assess changes in SA. In the case of self-report measures, the same scale items can be administered multiple times, but because SAGAT is context specific, different questions would typically need to be assessed over the course of a task. Thus, it is uncertain whether a study should be considered longitudinal when different questions referring to different situations are used at each administration. Furthermore, Patrick and Morgan (2010) contend that the acquisition of SA is largely context driven, and thus "any statement about a person having poor or good SA does not imply similar psychological skill that may generalize from one situation to another, or even within performance of the same task" (p. 47). In other words, it may be difficult to determine whether changes in SA are a function of individual differences or contextual differences.

There have been a few recent efforts to measure SA over time and address these conceptual difficulties (Patrick, James, Ahmed, & Halliday, 2006; Saner, Bolstad, Gonzalez, & Cuevas, 2009). For example, Saner et al. (2009) used the SAGAT tool to measure individual and team SA during five military rescue operation simulations across the course of 3 days. Interestingly, there was no discernable pattern, demonstrating that SA did not simply increase over time as the context of each scenario changed. This finding led the authors to conclude that learning effects could not account for the changes in SA over time. Likewise, although Patrick et al. (2006) relied on observational SA measures, they also found that there was no consistent pattern for team SA over the course of three training simulations at a nuclear reactor site. Therefore, they concluded that their results support the situation-specific perspective of SA.

Despite these recent studies, overall, published studies empirically assessing team SA at even a single occurrence are limited, despite many researchers voicing this need (e.g., Endsley, 1995a; Salas et al., 1995; Sarter & Woods, 1991). Thus, the notion of multiple measurements of team SA over time is one that warrants elaboration and future research.

Time as Part of Team SA Content: Future Projections

SA has a temporal proclivity toward both the past and the future (Endsley, 1995a; Salas et al., 1995). In other words, although SA reflects one's environmental awareness at a given point in time, this information can also accumulate over time. In turn, reviewing this accumulated knowledge from the past may facilitate the prediction of future states of the environment (Endsley, 1995a). In their review of the numerous conceptualizations of SA, Shrestha et al. (1995) concluded that temporal awareness and anticipating future events are themes common to almost all definitions, further illustrating the importance of time in SA. Endsley's (1995a, 1995b) three-level SA model and the corresponding SAGAT tool have an inherent temporal focus in that Level 3 deals with future projections. Specifically, Level 3 refers to "the ability to project the future actions of the elements in the environment" (Endsley, 1995a, p. 37). These projections of the near future can be assessed by multiple-choice or open-ended questions. For example, Endsley and Kiris (1995) used SAGAT questions such as "Which aircraft must be handed off to another sector/facility within the next 2 minutes?" and "Enter the aircraft that will violate special airspace separation standards if they stay on their current (assigned) path" to assess participants' ability to integrate SA Levels 1 and 2 and consequently make predictions about the near future.

Overall, Level 3 SA appears to have been investigated at the team level sparingly, despite being most pertinent to temporal considerations. However, Wellens (1993) devised an experiment to measure projection in team SA using a simulation called C^3 Interactive Task for Identifying Emerging Situations (CITIES) (Wellens & Ergener, 1988). In this simulation of an emergency response center, two 2-person teams were assigned to either a police-tow or fire-rescue decision-making unit, where they could allocate appropriate resources in response to emergency events. In a "Visiting Senator" scenario within the simulation, police-tow and fire-rescue events of increasing intensity were introduced over the course of 30 minutes. In addition, the police-tow team received written information at the start of the scenario about the times and places a senator would be during the shift. The object of the simulation was for police tow to realize that events were tied to the senator's travel path and to then share that information with fire rescue and preemptively allocate resources to the next location on the itinerary. Team SA and, in particular, the temporal component/Level 3 were assessed via a postsession questionnaire by virtue of whether both teams could "accurately report the connection between the senator's movements and major emergency events" (Wellens & Ergener, 1988, p. 279). Other similar scenarios also addressed the same concept of preallocating resources based on a projection of future events.

106 • *Theories of Team Cognition*

Another study that addressed the temporal/projection aspect of team SA involved visual information acquisition during the training of air traffic controller students (Hauland, 2008). Hauland (2008) focused on the distribution of attention between current- and future-oriented air traffic information, assessed via eye-tracking equipment. More specifically, some information on the students' screens pertained to current information, and some information was more relevant to conducting planning for future events. It was assumed that if members were focusing on planning-related information on the screen, then they were using that information to create projections in response to probes that were administered during the experiment. Team SA was deemed to be present when there was congruence of visual attention across members (i.e., members proportionally looking at the same things on the screen for the same amount of time). Hauland (2008) noted that in abnormal/nonroutine scenarios, teams spent less time attending to future-oriented information on the screen, thus representing lower levels of Level 3 team SA.

Finally, using an updated version of CITIES (Wellens, 1993), a recent study investigated team SA in a crisis management simulation called NeoCITIES involving police, fire, and hazardous material units (Hamilton, Mancuso, et al., 2010). The scenarios within the simulation were designed to emphasize temporal sequencing (fire first, police second, hazmat third) and pacing (all units need to arrive on scene within 60 seconds). Following Endsley's (1995b) guidelines for SAGAT, the simulation was frozen mid-task, and participants were asked multiple-choice and open-ended questions assessing all three levels of SA. For Level 3, questions assessing the participants' ability to make future projections based on past events were constructed. Sample Level 3 items included: "Based on the event description, what would MOST likely happen if units didn't arrive on scene within 60 seconds in the case of the tanker collision?" and "Given the pattern in the order of sequenced events, who will most likely need to arrive FIRST at the next event?"

Teams Over Time: Future Projections

Although there have been recommendations to study team SA as an overall construct over time (e.g., Endsley, 1995a; Salas et al., 1995), this has been rarely accomplished, perhaps partially due to the previously noted difficulties of conceptualizing longitudinal team SA. Likewise, to our knowledge, there has not been any empirical research specifically targeting the changes in Level 3 team SA (i.e., future projections) over time. Thus, longitudinal studies on team SA in general, and temporally related team SA in particular, represent key focal points for future research.

Time as Part of the General Context: Team Temporal Environment

SA is a construct that is constantly being changed and updated, reflecting the dynamic nature of the environment and the cues to which the observer is attending (Endsley, 1995a; Salas et al., 1995). For example, team SA may decrease or become more narrowly focused due to contextual effects such as time pressure, stress, or cognitive overload (e.g., Endsley, 1995a; Sarter & Woods, 2001). Although there has been some research conducted on SA that focuses on task complexity/overload as a contextual feature (e.g., Blandford & Wong, 2004), time pressure appears to have been largely ignored. Clearly, the team's temporal environment is deeply intertwined with the measurement of team SA and, as such, should be taken into consideration in future empirical studies.

Summary of Time and Team SA

Conceptualizations of SA commonly incorporate temporal awareness and anticipating future events (Shrestha et al., 1995), thus demonstrating that time is a construct that warrants careful attention in SA research. In fact, Level 3 of Endsley's (1995a) popularly cited three-level model of SA specifically pertains to "projected future states of the environment that are valuable for decision making" (p. 37). Despite this pervasive theme in SA, there has been little empirical research specifically targeting its temporal components (cf. Hauland, 2008; Wellens, 1993). Furthermore, although there have been numerous recommendations to study team SA over multiple points in time to more accurately reflect the dynamic nature of both the environment and resulting SA (e.g., Endsley, 1995a; Salas et al., 1995; Sarter & Woods, 1991), there have been few longitudinal studies of this nature.

In light of the apparent scarcity of team SA research with respect to temporal dynamics, future research should pursue this matter further.

108 • *Theories of Team Cognition*

For example, additional methods of measuring Level 3 team SA should be developed. Visual attention to future-oriented information (Hauland, 2008) and preemptive allocation of resources (Wellens, 1993) have been used, but there is plenty of room for additional creative solutions. Specifically, Hauland (2008) measured whether team members attended to current or future-related information on an air traffic controller simulation, concluding that more attention to future-related information signaled higher levels of Level 3 SA. Wellens (1993) assessed the presence of future-oriented team SA by noting whether teammates all recognized a pattern of events in an emergency management simulation and preemptively allocated resources to prevent the next anticipated event in the pattern. However, neither of these studies directly assessed Level 3 team SA, but rather inferred it from the participants' actions, and neither study used longitudinal measures. Thus, creating new methods of directly measuring Level 3 team SA over time should be prioritized on the research agenda.

A temporally related area of interest is how teams handle repeatedly performed routine tasks that result in automaticity, or a decrease in active processing of information (Endsley, 1995a). For example, in some situations, automaticity can reduce awareness of novel stimuli in the environment, thus reducing SA (Endsley, 1995a). Thus, one may not notice a newly erected stop sign on the route home from work because driving that route has become so familiar that the driver is not on the lookout for changes in the environment. However, because automated tasks can reduce cognitive load, there is a possibility that more cognitive resources could become available for accumulating SA (Endsley, 1995a). Thus, research could be conducted to investigate how the process of developing automaticity affects team SA over time and whether there are any factors that moderate/mediate this relationship. Researchers may also be interested in investigating how teams correct SA errors and related mental models, particularly with respect to Level 3 SA. Conceptually, awareness of SA error can affect whether one chooses a new mental model or modifies an existing one (Endsley, 1995a). Thus, one could measure SA Level 3 error awareness and its relation to subsequent changes in both team Level 3 SA and team temporal mental models, thereby incorporating multiple measures over time. By taking these temporal research recommendations into consideration, team SA will transition more from abstraction to substantiation.

CONCLUSION

As was increasingly evident throughout the chapter, more temporal research is needed on perceptual team cognition, TMMs, and team SA across each of the four temporal categories discussed. Compared with perceptual cognition and team SA, the TMM literature has the greatest volume of longitudinal work, but the conclusions that can be gleaned from the extant body of work are less than satisfying. Apart from the need to measure team cognition over time, an issue that deserves greater attention is when measures should be collected to align with when critical processes are occurring. A time-sensitive task analysis may aid in determining the optimal intervals to collect team cognition data (e.g., Tschan et al., 2009).

Because team research is already logistically difficult and operationalizing team cognition can add significant challenges, the addition of a longitudinal design component may prove infeasible in many contexts. Nevertheless, we strongly urge that researchers continually seek out opportunities to measure cognitive constructs over time. However, longitudinal design is not the only avenue toward integrating temporal effects. Incorporating time-based referents and examining the temporal context offer additional opportunities to be pursued in team cognition research. Regarding time as part of the content of the construct, the most popular definition and operationalization of SA explicitly incorporates the notion of future projection (Endsley, 1995a; Salmon et al., 2008). However, future projections are perhaps the most difficult to assess of the three levels. Due in no small part to the pioneering work of Gevers et al. (2005, 2006, 2009), the work on perceptual team cognition has most fully incorporated temporal dynamics as compared to TMMs and team SA. Not only has the notion of shared temporal cognition received some theoretical attention (Bartel & Milliken, 2004; Gevers et al., 2004), but several studies have examined the construct longitudinally in a temporally relevant context (Gevers et al., 2005, 2006, 2009). The development of a generic, perceptually based Likert scale that can be used in multiple settings (Gevers et al., 2005, 2006, 2009) has promulgated empirical research in this area. In contrast, TMMs and the most popular team SA measure (SAGAT) require contextually tailored assessment, making measurement more challenging

110 • *Theories of Team Cognition*

in practice (Mohammed & Hamilton, in press). Across all three of the team cognition constructs reviewed in this chapter, there is a need for empirical research to explore the role of deadlines, time pressure, and the larger temporal context.

Given the growth in the team cognition literature in recent years as well as the concurrent interest in team temporal dynamics, some of the most fruitful research streams of the future may occur at the intersection of these two streams. This chapter contributes to this effort by revealing several opportunities for time-related research on perceptual team cognition, TMMs, and team SA.

ACKNOWLEDGMENT

Work on this chapter was supported by Grant No. N000140810887 from the Office of Naval Research.

REFERENCES

Arrow, H., Poole, M. S., Henry, K. B., Wheelan, S., & Moreland, R. (2004). Time, change, and development: The temporal perspective on groups. *Small Group Research, 35,* 73–104.

Artman, H. (1999). Situation awareness and co-operation within and between hierarchical units in dynamic decision making. *Ergonomics, 42,* 1404–1417.

Baguley, T., & Payne, S. J. (2000). Long-term memory for spatial and temporal mental models includes construction processes and model structure. *The Quarterly Journal of Experimental Psychology, 53,* 479–512.

Ballard, D. I., Tschan, F., & Waller, M. J. (2008). All in the timing: Considering time at multiple stages of group research. *Small Group Research, 39,* 328–351.

Bartel, C. A., & Milliken, F. J. (2004). Perceptions of time in work groups: Do members develop shared cognitions about their temporal demands? In S. Blount (Ed.), *Research on managing groups and teams: Time in groups* (Vol. 6, pp. 87–109). New York: Elsevier.

Bedny, G., & Meister, D. (1999). Theory of activity and situation awareness. *International Journal of Cognitive Ergonomics, 3,* 63–72.

Blandford, A., & Wong, B. L. W. (2004). Situation awareness in emergency medical dispatch. *International Journal of Human-Computer Studies, 61,* 421–452.

Bluedorn, A. C., & Standifer, R. L. (2004). Groups, boundary spanning, and the temporal imagination. In S. Blount (Ed.), *Research on managing groups and teams: Time in groups* (Vol. 6, pp. 159–182). New York: Elsevier.

Bolman, L. (1979). Aviation accidents and the theory of the situation. In G. E. Cooper, M. D. White, & J. K. Laubers (Eds.), *Resource management in the cockpit*. Moffett Field, CA: NASA Ames Research Center (NASA Conference Publication 2120).

Bourgeois, L. J. (1980). Performance and consensus. *Strategic Management Journal, 1*, 227–248.

Burke, C. S., Stagle, K. C., Salas, E., Pierce, L., & Kendall, D. (2006). Understanding team adaptation: A conceptual analysis and model. *Journal of Applied Psychology, 91*, 1189–1207.

Cannon-Bowers, J. A., & Salas, E. (2001). Reflections on shared cognition. *Journal of Organizational Behavior, 22*, 195–202.

Cannon-Bowers, J. A., Salas, E., & Converse, S. (1993). Shared mental models in expert team decision making. In N. J. Castellan, Jr. (Ed.), *Individual and group decision making: Current issues* (pp. 221–246). Hillsdale, NJ: Lawrence Erlbaum.

Cooke, N. J., Kiekel, P. A., & Helm, E. E. (2001). Measuring team knowledge during skill acquisition of a complex task. *International Journal of Cognitive Ergonomics, 5*, 297–315.

Cooke, N. J., Kiekel, P. A., Salas, E., Stout, R., Bowers, C., & Cannon-Bowers, J. (2003). Measuring team knowledge: A window to the cognitive underpinnings of team performance. *Group Dynamics: Theory, Research, and Practice, 7*, 179–199.

Cooke, N. J., Salas, E., Cannon-Bowers, J. A., & Stout, R. J. (2000). Measuring team knowledge. *Human Factors, 421*, 151–173.

DeChurch, L. A., & Mesmer-Magnus, J. R. (2010a). The cognitive underpinnings of effective teamwork: A meta-analysis. *Journal of Applied Psychology, 95*, 32–53.

DeChurch, L. A., & Mesmer-Magnus, J. R. (2010b). Measuring shared team mental models: A meta-analysis. *Group Dynamics: Theory, Research, & Practice, 14*, 1–14.

Edmondson, A. (1999). Psychological safety and learning behavior in work teams. *Administrative Science Quarterly, 44*, 350–383.

Edwards, B. D., Day, E. A., Arthur, W., & Bell, S. T. (2006). Relationships among team ability composition, team mental models, and team performance. *Journal of Applied Psychology, 91*, 727–736.

Ellis, A. P. J. (2006). System breakdown: The role of mental models and transactive memory in the relationship between acute stress and team performance. *Academy of Management Journal, 49*, 576–589.

Endsley, M. R. (1995a). Toward a theory of situation awareness in dynamic systems. *Human Factors, 37*, 32–64.

Endsley, M. R. (1995b). Measurement of situation awareness in dynamic systems. *Human Factors, 37*, 65–84.

Endsley, M. R., & Jones, W. M. (2001). A model of inter- and intrateam situation awareness: Implications for design, training, and measurement. In M. McNeese, E. Salas, & M. Endsley (Eds.), *New trends in cooperative activities: Understanding system dynamics in complex environments* (pp. 46–67). Santa Monica, CA: Human Factors and Ergonomics Society.

Endsley, M. R., & Kiris, E. O. (1995). *Situation awareness global assessment technique (SAGAT) TRACON air traffic control user guide*. Lubbock, TX: Texas Tech University.

Ensley, M. D., & Pearce, C. L. (2001). Shared cognition in top management teams: Implications for new venture performance. *Journal of Organizational Behavior, 22*, 145–160.

Fine, G. A. (1996). *Kitchens: The culture of restaurant work*. Berkeley, CA: University of California Press.

112 • Theories of Team Cognition

Foushee, H. C. (1984). Dyads and triads and 35000 feet: Factors affecting group process and aircrew performance. *American Psychologist, 39*, 885–893.

Freeman, M., & Beele, P. (1992). Measuring project success. *Project Management Journal, 23*, 8–17.

Gevers, J. M. P., & Peeters, M. A. G. (2009). A pleasure working together? The effects of dissimilarity in team member conscientiousness on team temporal processes and individual satisfaction. *Journal of Organizational Behavior, 30*, 379–400.

Gevers, J. M. P., Rutte, C. G., & van Eerde, W. (2004). How project teams achieve coordinated action: A model of shared cognitions on time. In S. Blount (Ed.), *Research on managing groups and teams: Time in groups* (Vol. 6, pp. 67–85). New York, NY: Elsevier.

Gevers, J. M. P., Rutte, C. G., & van Eerde, W. (2006). Meeting deadlines in work groups: Implicit and explicit mechanisms. *Applied Psychology: An International Review, 55*, 52–72.

Gevers, J. M. P., Rutte, C. G., van Eerde, W., & Roe, R. A. (2005, August). *Meeting deadlines in project teams: A longitudinal study on the effects of shared cognitions.* Paper presented at the annual meeting of the Academy of Management, Honolulu, HI.

Gevers, J. M. P., van Eerde, W., & Rutte, C. G. (2009). Team self-regulation and meeting deadlines in project teams: Antecedents and effects of temporal consensus. *European Journal of Work and Organizational Psychology, 18*, 295–321.

Gorman, J. C., Cooke, N. J., & Winner, J. L. (2006). Measuring team situation awareness in decentralized command and control environments. *Ergonomics Special Issue: Command and Control, 49*, 1312–1325.

Hackman, J. R. (Ed.). (1990). *Groups that work (and those that don't).* San Francisco, CA: Jossey-Bass.

Hauland, G. (2008). Measuring individual and team situation awareness during planning tasks in training of en route air traffic control. *The International Journal of Aviation Psychology, 19*, 290–304.

Hamilton, K., Mancuso, V., Minotra, D., Hoult, R., Mohammed, S., McNeese, M., et al. (2010, September). *Using the NeoCITIES 3.0 simulation to study and measure team cognition.* Paper presented at the 54th Annual Meeting of the Human Factors and Ergonomics Society, San Francisco, CA.

Hamilton, K., Mohammed, S., Mancuso, V., Hoult, R., Minotra, D., & McNeese, M. (2010, July). *It's about time: The conceptualization and operationalization of temporal team mental models.* Paper presented at the Fifth Annual Meeting of the Interdisciplinary Network of Group Researchers (INGRoup), Washington, DC.

Ilgen, D. R., Hollenbeck, J. R., Johnson, M., & Jundt, D. (2005). Teams in organizations: From input-process-output models to IMOI models. *Annual Review of Psychology, 56*, 517–543.

Kang, H. R., Yang, H. D., & Rowley, C. (2006). Factors in team effectiveness: Cognitive and demographic similarities of software development team members. *Human Relations, 59*, 1681–1710.

Kellermanns, F. W., Floyd, S. W., Pearson, A. W., & Spencer, B. (2008). The contingent effect of constructive confrontation on the relationship between shared mental models and decision quality. *Journal of Organizational Behavior, 29*, 119–137.

Kellermanns, F. W., Walter, J., Lechner, C., & Floyd, S. W. (2005). The lack of consensus about strategic consensus: Advancing theory and research. *Journal of Management, 31*, 719–737.

Klimoski, R., & Mohammed, S. (1994). Team mental model: Construct or metaphor? *Journal of Management, 20*, 403–437.

Knight, D., Pearce, C. L., Smith, K. G., Olian, J. D., Sims, H. P., Smith, K. A., et al. (1999). Top management team diversity, group process, and strategic consensus. *Strategic Management Journal, 20*, 445–465.

Kozlowski, S. W. J., & Bell, B. S. (2003). Work groups and teams in organizations. In W. C. Borman, D. R. Ilgen, & R. J. Klimoski (Eds.), *Handbook of psychology: Industrial and organizational psychology* (Vol. 12, pp. 333–375). New York, NY: Wiley.

Letsky, M., & Warner, N. W. (2008). Macrocognition in teams. In M. Letsky, N. Warner, S. M. Fiore, & C. Smith (Eds.), *Macrocognition in teams: Theories and methodologies* (pp. 1–14). London, UK: Ashgate Publishers.

Levesque, L. L., Wilson, J. M., & Wholey, D. R. (2001). Cognitive divergence and shared mental models in software development project teams. *Journal of Organizational Behavior, 22*, 135–144.

Liang, D. W., Moreland, R. L., & Argote, L. (1995). Group versus individual training and group performance: The mediating role of transactive memory. *Personality and Social Psychology Bulletin, 21*, 384–393.

Lim, B. C., & Klein, K. J. (2006). Team mental models and team performance: A field study of the effects of team mental model similarity and accuracy. *Journal of Organizational Behavior, 27*, 403–418.

Mandler, J. M. (1986). On the comprehension of temporal order. *Language and Cognitive Processes, 1*, 309–320.

Marks, M. A., Zaccaro, S. J., & Mathieu, J. E. (2000). Performance implications of leader briefings and team-interaction training for team adaptation to novel environments. *Journal of Applied Psychology, 85*, 971–986.

Mathieu, J. E., Heffner, T. S., Goodwin, G. F., Cannon-Bowers, J. A., & Salas, E. (2005). Scaling the quality of teammates' mental models: Equifinality and normative comparisons. *Journal of Organizational Behavior, 26*, 37–56.

Mathieu, J. E., Heffner, T. S., Goodwin, G. F., Salas, E., & Cannon-Bowers, J. A. (2000). The influence of shared mental models on team process and performance. *Journal of Applied Psychology, 85*, 273–283.

Mathieu, J. E., Maynard, M. T., Rapp, T., & Gilson, L. (2008). Team effectiveness 1997–2007: A review of recent advancements and a glimpse into the future. *Journal of Management, 34*, 410–476.

McComb, S. A. (2008). Shared mental models and their convergence. In M. Letsky, N. Warner, S. M. Fiore, & C. Smith (Eds.), *Macrocognition in teams: Theories and methodologies* (pp. 35–50). London, UK: Ashgate Publishers.

McGrath, J. E. (1991). Time, interaction, and performance (TIP): A theory of groups. *Small Group Research, 22*, 147–174.

McGrath, J. E., Arrow, H., Gruenfeld, D. H., Hollingshead, A. B., & O'Conner, K. M. (1993). Groups, tasks, and technology: The effects of experience and change. *Small Group Research, 24*, 406–420.

Millward, S. M. (2006). Do you know your stuff? Training collaborative modelers. *Team Performance Management, 12*, 225–236.

Mohammed, S. (2001). Toward an understanding of cognitive consensus in a group decision making context. *Journal of Applied Behavioral Science, 37*(4), 408–425.

Mohammed, S., Ferzandi, L., & Hamilton, K. (2010). Metaphor no more: A 15 year review of the team mental model construct. *Journal of Management, 36*, 876–910.

114 • *Theories of Team Cognition*

Mohammed, S., & Hamilton, K. (in press). Studying team cognition: The good, the bad, and the practical. Chapter prepared for A. B. Hollingshead & M. S. Poole (Eds.), *Research methods for studying groups: A behind-the-Scenes guide*. New York, NY: Taylor & Francis/Routledge.

Mohammed, S., Hamilton, K., & Lim, A. (2009). The incorporation of time in team research: Past, current, and future. In E. Salas, G. F. Goodwin, & C. S. Burke (Eds.), *Team effectiveness in complex organizations: Cross-disciplinary perspective and approaches* (pp. 321–348). New York, NY: Taylor & Francis/Routledge.

Mohammed, S., Klimoski, R., & Rentsch, J. (2000). The measurement of team mental models: We have no shared schema. *Organizational Research Methods, 3*, 123–165.

Mohammed, S., & Nadkarni, S. (2010, August). *Shared temporal cognition as a moderator of the temporal diversity-team performance relationship*. Paper presented at the annual meeting of the Academy of Management Conference, Montreal, Quebec, Canada.

Mohammed, S., & Ringseis, E. (2001). Cognitive diversity and consensus in group decision making: The role of inputs, processes, and outcomes. *Organizational Behavior and Human Decision Processes, 85*, 310–335.

Mohammed, S., & Zhang, Y. (2009). Providing timely assistance: Temporal measurement guidelines for the study of virtual teams. In D. Schmorrow, J. Cohn, & D. Nicholson (Eds.), *Handbook of virtual environments for training and education: Developments for the military and beyond* (Vol. 1, pp. 376–389). Westport, CT: Praeger Security International.

Moynihan, D. P. (2007). *From forest fires to hurricane Katrina: Case studies of incident command systems*. Washington, DC: IBM Center for the Business of Government.

Patrick, J., James, N., Ahmed, A., & Halliday, P. (2006). Observational assessment of situation awareness, team differences and training implications. *Ergonomics, 49*, 393–417.

Patrick, J., & Morgan, P. L. (2010). Approaches to understanding, analyzing and developing situation awareness. *Theoretical Issues in Ergonomics Science, 11*, 41–57.

Priem, R. L. (1990). Top management team group factors, consensus, and firm performance. *Strategic Management Journal, 11*, 469–478.

Radvansky, G. A., Zwaan, R. A., Federico, T., & Franklin, N. (1998). Retrieval from temporally organized situation models. *Journal of Experimental Psychology: Learning, Memory, and Cognition, 24*, 1224–1237.

Rentsch, J. R., & Hall, R. J. (1994). Members of great teams think alike: A model of team effectiveness and schema similarity among team members. In M. M. Beyerlein & D. A. Johnson (Eds.), *Advances in interdisciplinary studies of work teams: Theories of self-managing work teams* (Vol. 1, pp. 223–261). Greenwich, CT: Elsevier Science/ JAI Press.

Rentsch, J. R., & Klimoski, R. J. (2001). Why do "great minds" think alike? Antecedents of team member schema agreement. *Journal of Organizational Behavior, 22*, 107–120.

Rico, R., Sanchez-Manzanares, M., Gil, F., & Gibson, C. (2008). Team implicit coordination processes: A team knowledge-based approach. *Academy of Management Review, 33*, 163–184.

Salas, E., Prince, C., Baker, D. P., & Shrestha, L. (1995). Situation awareness in team performance: Implications for measurement and training. *Human Factors Special Issue: Situation Awareness, 37*, 123–136.

Salmon, P. M., Stanton, N. A., Walker, G. H., Baber, C., Jenkins, D. P., McMaster, R., et al. (2008). What really is going on? Review of situation awareness models for individuals and teams. *Theoretical Issues in Ergonomics Science, 9*, 297–323.

Salmon, P. M., Stanton, N. A., Walker, G. H., & Green, D. (2006). Situation awareness measurement: A review of applicability for C4i environments. *Applied Ergonomics, 37*, 225–238.

Salmon, P. M., Stanton, N. A., Walker, G. H., Jenkins, D. P., & Rafferty, L. (2010). Is it really better to share? Distributed situation awareness and its implications for collaborative system design. *Theoretical Issues in Ergonomics Science, 11*, 58–83.

Saner, L. D., Bolstad, C. A., Gonzalez, C., & Cuevas, H. M. (2009). Measuring and predicting shared situation awareness in teams. *Journal of Cognitive Engineering and Decision Making, 3*, 280–308.

Sarter, N. B., & Woods, D. D. (1991). Situation awareness: A critical but ill-defined phenomenon. *The International Journal of Aviation Psychology, 1*, 45–57.

Schaeken, W., Johnson-Laird, P. N., & d'Ydewalle, G. (1996). Mental models and temporal reasoning. *Cognition, 60*, 205–234.

Schwartz, D. (1990). *Training for situational awareness.* Houston, TX: Flight Safety International.

Shrestha, L. B., Prince, C., Baker, D. P., & Salas, E. (1995). Understanding situation awareness: Concepts, methods, and training. *Human Factors, 37*, 45–83.

Smith, K., & Hancock, P. A. (1995). Situation awareness is adaptive, externally directed consciousness. *Human Factors Special Issue: Situation Awareness, 37*, 137–148.

Smith-Jentsch, K. A., Campbell, G. E., Milanovich, D. M., & Reynolds, A. M. (2001). Measuring teamwork mental models to support training needs assessment, development, and evaluation: Two empirical studies. *Journal of Organizational Behavior, 22*, 179–194.

Smith-Jentsch, K. A., Cannon-Bowers, J. A., Tannenbaum, S. I., & Salas, E. (2008). Guided team self-correction: Impacts on team mental models, processes, and effectiveness. *Small Group Research, 39*, 303–327.

Standifer, R. L. (2012). The emergence of temporal coordination within multi-team systems. In S. J. Zaccaro, L. A. DeChurch, & M. A. Marks (Eds.), *Multi-team systems: An organization form for dynamic and complex environments* (pp. 395–427). New York, NY: Taylor & Francis/Routledge.

Standifer, R., & Bluedorn, A. (2006). Alliance management teams and entrainment: Sharing temporal mental models. *Human Relations, 59*, 903–927.

Stanton, N. A., Salmon, P. M., Walker, G. H., & Jenkins, D. P. (2010). Is situation awareness all in the mind? *Theoretical Issues in Ergonomics Science, 11*, 29–40.

Stanton, N. A., Stewart, R., Harris, D., Houghton, R. J., Baber, C., McMaster, R., et al. (2006). Distributed situation awareness in dynamic systems: Theoretical development and application of an ergonomics methodology. *Ergonomics, 49*, 1288–1311.

Stout, R. J., Carson, R., & Salas, E. (1991, August). *Can team process behaviors enhance performance?* Paper presented at the annual meeting of the American Psychological Association, Washington, DC.

Tindale, R. S., Meisenhelder, H. M., Dykema-Engblade, A. A., & Hogg, M. A. (2001). Shared cognition in small groups. In M. A. Hogg & R. Tindale (Eds.), *Blackwell handbook of social psychology: Group processes* (pp. 1–30). Malden, MA: Blackwell Publishers.

Tindale, R. S., Smith, C. M., Thomas, L. S., Filkins, J., & Sheffey, S. (1996). Shared representations and symmetric social influence processes in small groups. In E. Witte & J. H. Davis (Eds.), *Understanding group behavior: Consensual action by small groups* (Vol. 1). Hillsdale, NJ: Erlbaum.

116 • *Theories of Team Cognition*

Tschan, F., McGrath, J. E., Semmer, N. K., Aramett, M., Bogenstatter, Y., & Marsch, S. U. (2009). Temporal aspects of processes in ad-hoc groups: A conceptual schema and some research examples. In R. A. Roe, M. J. Waller, & S. R. Clegg (Eds.), *Time in organizational research* (pp. 42–61). New York, NY: Taylor & Francis/Routledge.

van Ginkel, W. P., & van Knippenberg, D. (2008). Group information elaboration and group decision making: The role of shared task representations. *Organizational Behavior and Human Decision Processes, 105*, 82–97.

Waller, M. J., Gupta, N., & Giambatista, R. C. (2004). Effects of adaptive behaviors and shared mental models on control crew performance. *Management Science, 50*, 1534–1544.

Warner, N. W., & Letsky, M. (2008). Empirical model of team collaboration focus on macrocognition. In M. Letsky, N. Warner, S. M. Fiore, & C. Smith (Eds.), *Macrocognition in teams: Theories and methodologies* (pp. 15–34). London, UK: Ashgate Publishers.

Wellens, A. R. (1993). Group situation awareness and distributed decision making: From military to civilian applications. In N. J. Castellan, Jr. (Ed.), *Individual and group decision making: Current issues* (pp. 267–291). Hillsdale, NJ: Lawrence Erlbaum Associates.

Wellens, A. R., & Ergener, D. (1988). The C.I.T.I.E.S. game: A computer-based situation assessment task for studying distributed decision making. *Simulation and Games, 19*, 304–327.

Wilson, K. A., Salas, E., Priest, H., & Andrews, D. (2007). Errors in the heat of the battle: Taking a closer look at shared cognition breakdowns through teamwork. *Human Factors, 49*, 243–256.

5

Leadership and Emergent Collective Cognition[*]

Toshio Murase, Christian J. Resick, Miliani Jiménez, Elizabeth Sanz, and Leslie A. DeChurch

Leadership is ... about the ability to make others feel part of a larger thing. It's part of being able to articulate the social architecture in a way that others can understand, believe in and follow.

—Kevin Sharer
CEO Amgen (quoted in Bryant, 2009, p. BU2)

Leadership plays a pivotal role in shaping and reshaping the cognitive states that emerge and underpin collective performance. Although both the leadership (e.g., Weick, 1995) and teams (Burke, Stagle, Salas, Pierce, & Kendall, 2006; Randall, Resick, & DeChurch, 2009) literatures have begun to explicitly examine the role of leadership in shaping collective cognition, these two research areas have progressed largely in silos. This chapter develops an integrated framework linking leadership functions to the emergence of collective cognition. We begin by examining the forms of collective cognition that have implications for collective-level success. Next, we propose that six forms of leadership are particularly important facilitators of collective cognition; for each type of leadership, we discuss specific mechanisms that facilitate the emergence of collective cognition and develop propositions intended to stimulate future research. We conclude with a discussion of the practical and theoretical implications.

---

[*] The views expressed in this work are those of the authors and do not necessarily reflect official Army or university policy.

118 • *Theories of Team Cognition*

EMERGENT COLLECTIVE COGNITION

In recent years, team cognition has become an increasingly central focus of team effectiveness research as both theory and empirical evidence underscore the important roles of team mental models and transactive memory systems for effective team performance. However, since Schneider's (1975) seminal paper on organizational climate, researchers have been examining the emergence and implications of team or organizational members' shared perceptions of work environmental factors. A central tenet of this line of theory and inquiry is that the perceptions and knowledge held by individuals emerge to become a property of a team (or even organization) as members interact with one another. These shared perceptions and shared knowledge serve to regulate members' behaviors and enable individual members to function as a unified entity.

Twenty years of team effectiveness research definitively links team cognitive architectures to their performance capacity (DeChurch & Mesmer-Magnus, 2010a). Although the relationship is moderated by specific underpinnings of cognition, DeChurch and Mesmer-Magnus (2010b) found that team cognition contributes uniquely to team performance after controlling for behavioral processes such as coordination and backup behavior (Marks, Mathieu, & Zaccaro, 2001) and motivational states such as cohesion (Gully, Devine, & Whitney, 1995). The field we now describe under the lexicon of team cognition actually grew out of three relatively independent research streams: the first one on shared team mental models (Cannon-Bowers, Salas, & Converse, 1993), the second one on team transactive memory (Liang, Moreland, & Argote, 1995), and the last one on organizational climate (Schneider, 1975).

In reflecting back on the discovery of mental models in teams, Eduardo Salas remarked that, "20 years ago we began a long journey to understand teams and team performance in naturalistic environments ... we were perplexed why some teams under heavy workload could still maintain performance without communicating. Our explanation was—they have a shared understanding of what is going on and what needs to happen; they have a shared mental model" (E. Salas, personal communication, September 8, 2009).

Leadership and Emergent Collective Cognition • 119

Indeed, since Salas and colleagues' original observations, a deluge of both conceptual and empirical research has investigated the role of *thinking alike* in integrated team performance.

At around the same time, Moreland and colleagues were developing the team transactive memory concept—an extension of Wegner's 1986 notion of shared memory in romantic couples (Liang et al., 1995; Moreland, Argote, & Krishnan, 1996). Transactive memory consists of a differentiated set of knowledge relevant to the team's task that is distributed across team members, coupled with an understanding of who possesses particular sets of knowledge. Through this collective system for encoding and retrieving information, teams have access to a large body of information because members specialize in particular subsets of information needed for teamwork; essentially, this increases the information-processing capacity of the team (Hinsz, Tindale, & Vollrath, 1997). Team transactive memory has been empirically linked to better team processes by allowing team members to have better coordination, reducing the amount of information that individual members are responsible for by knowing which members have specific expertise, and aiding in the sharing of task-relevant information (Lewis, 2003).

Team climate is the perception about the group environment that is shared among team members and develops through socialization and interaction with the environment and one another (Lindell & Brandt, 2000). The team climate literature has demonstrated relationships between team-level perceptions and specific behaviors that those perceptions emphasize such as service-oriented and safety behavior (e.g., Schneider, Ehrhart, Mayer, Saltz, & Niles-Jolly, 2005; Zohar & Luria, 2004).

Although these research streams developed somewhat independently, they offer diagnostic and predictive capability in teams. As an integrated construct, team cognition encompasses various arrangements of knowledge that teams use "to make sense of, attribute meaning to, and interpret internal and external events, including affect, behavior, and thoughts of self and others" (Rentsch, Small, & Hanges, 2008, p. 144). A recent meta-analytic integration synthesized these previously disjointed research streams on various emergent cognitive constructs (DeChurch & Mesmer-Magnus, 2010b) in terms of three meaningful underpinnings of team cognition: nature of emergence, form of cognition, and content of cognition. Of the three, the nature of emergence was the most critical moderator of relationships between shared cognition and team performance.

120 • *Theories of Team Cognition*

Nature of Emergence

Team cognition originates in team members' (i.e., individual-level) patterned knowledge. In this way, it can be characterized as a bottom-up emergent construct, where new meaning is present at the team level beyond what was apparent in the individual-level cognitive content (Kozlowski & Klein, 2000). Kozlowski and Klein (2000) distinguish different forms of emergence according to the extent to which the higher level emergent construct is different, nonisomorphic in form and function, and patterned in comparison to the individual or lower level content from which it originates. The nature of emergence is a critical distinction between team mental model research and transactive memory research. In essence, these two approaches to the study of team cognition represent different types of emergence. The team mental model concept represents compositional emergence; here, the structure of cognition at the individual level is similar in form to the structured arrangement of cognition examined at the team level. In contrast, team transactive memory represents compilational emergence; the knowledge held by individuals is not patterned in the same way as it is at the team level. The team transactive memory system is composed of individuals' knowledge sets, but the meaningful team-level construct reflects the patterned, differentiated knowledge.

Composition variables are often aggregated using the sum or average of the components from each individual, with researchers justifying the aggregation of such scores due to high interrater agreement indices (Klein & Kozlowski, 2000). This type of emergence has been criticized as having "limited the development of bottom-up multilevel theory and research" (Kozlowski & Klein, 2000, p. 5). In contrast, compilation variables are different at higher levels of analysis than at lower levels of analysis (i.e., individual level). Compilation variables arise from the pattern of cognition among members rather than a simple aggregate. The components of cognition serve the same purpose at each level; however, they are not the same in pattern. Compilation variables are often aggregated using the distribution of component scores, such as the variance of individual scores for a particular component. Importantly, the meta-analytic study by DeChurch and Mesmer-Magnus (2010a) found stronger relationships between cognition and team behavioral processes and performance when cognition was measured as compilational emergence as compared to compositional emergence.

Form of Cognition

Rentsch et al. (2008) posited that there are three categories in which cognition can be classified: perceptual, structured, and interpretive. Although most of the literature to date has examined perceptual and structured cognition (DeChurch & Mesmer-Magnus, 2010b), each form of cognition adds to our understanding of how teams function in dynamic environments.

Focus on team members' beliefs, values, attitudes, perceptions, and expectations is referred to as perceptual cognition. This form of cognition draws from team members' past experiences/observations as the basis for such knowledge construction and is shaped through interactions with one's team members and environment (DeChurch & Mesmer-Magnus, 2010b, p. 12; Rentsch et al., 2008). However, a shortcoming of perceptual cognition is that it does not allow researchers to examine relationships among different constructs (i.e., structure) because perceptual cognition is more of a reaction to stimuli (e.g., event, person, entity). Climate is an example of perceptual cognition. Although most extant research has measured climate as a compositional variable, researchers are beginning to realize the value of compilational variables, and more research examining the patterning of shared perceptions is focusing largely on the direction of perceptions and strength of perceptions (e.g., Dickson, Resick, & Hanges, 2006; Lindell & Brandt, 2000; Schneider, Salvaggio, & Subirats, 2002). Other examples of perceptual cognition include psychological safety (e.g., Walumbwa & Schaubroeck, 2009) and perceived similarity (e.g., Huang & Iun, 2006).

Structured cognition has an underlying organizational scheme and is represented by the patterning of knowledge organization, which provides information on cognitive linkages. Schemas are a type of structured knowledge or cognition that direct an individual's attention toward critical pieces of information and enhance an individual's ability to make sense of situations and stimuli based on previously developed mental architectures (Rentsch et al., 2008). Examples of structured cognition would be team mental models (e.g., Mathieu, Heffner, Goodwin, Salas, & Cannon-Bowers, 2000) and transactive memory systems (e.g., Austin, 2003; Lewis, 2003). A recent meta-analysis of team mental model studies revealed that structured cognition is more predictive of teamwork processes than perceptual cognition; however, both perceptual cognition and structured cognition were equally predictive of team performance

(DeChurch & Mesmer-Magnus, 2010b). DeChurch and Mesmer-Magnus (2010b) also found that cognitive congruence exhibited a stronger relationship with processes when the form of cognition was structured rather than perceptual; however, this relationship was reversed when cognitive accuracy was assessed rather than cognitive congruence, and therefore, perceptual cognition was the condition in which the cognition–process relationship was the strongest.

Interpretive cognition serves to make meaning or sense of the environment or situation. Interpretive cognition uses individuals' past experiences to construct meaning to current experiences through the interaction of the current environment and individuals (along with one's past experiences). As previously mentioned, most research has been conducted on the aforementioned forms of cognition. Rentsch et al. (2008) use sensemaking and collective learning as two examples of interpretive cognition. Sensemaking is the process in which group members create an agreed upon explanation or logical rationale for current or past events (e.g., Fiss & Zajac, 2006). Previous studies have found that all three forms of cognition have been linked to various types of outcomes, such as affective/motivational (Meglino, Ravlin, & Adkins, 1989), behavioral (Zohar & Luria, 2004), and objective (Schneider et al., 2005).

Content of Cognition

When Cannon-Bowers et al. (1993) first proposed the content areas for mental models, they posited that there are four content domains for cognition: knowledge of the task, team interactions (teamwork), equipment, and knowledge regarding teammates. Mathieu et al. (2000) suggested that these four categories could be condensed into two: team focused and task focused.

Team-focused content refers to knowledge of one's team members' roles, skills, expertise, preferences, and social interaction norms within one's team. Team knowledge allows members to interpret behavior from their teammates in a similar manner and behave in ways that are consistent with group expectations, thereby shaping both one's own behavior and the interpretation/reaction to others' behavior (Mathieu et al., 2000). The second content of cognition, task-focused content, refers to knowledge regarding the task that is being performed (often can be ascertained through a job or task analysis). Task content includes knowledge about task procedures, if–then scenarios, task strategies, task-relevant situations, and task component relationships. As noted by Mathieu et al. (2000), task content knowledge is critical when tasks are dynamic and are susceptible to change.

A third content of cognition, strategic, has been receiving more attention in recent years. Strategic cognition, or strategic consensus, is "the shared understanding of strategic priorities among managers at the top, middle, and/or operating levels of the organization" (Kellermanns, Walter, Lechner, & Floyd, 2005, p. 721). Said another way, strategic consensus refers to the strategies that are to be enacted to reach the team's goal. Research on strategic content has typically been performed using top management teams. Research has found that not only is a shared understanding of the plans and goals important, but also a shared understanding of the reasoning behind such plans is needed in order for managers to act according to the overall plan while not directly in contact with upper management (Kellermanns et al., 2005). Furthermore, among knowledge-based teams, Randall et al. (2009) found that both the similarity and accuracy of team strategic mental models were predictive of adaptive performance. This brings us to the effects of collective cognition on outcomes beyond team processes, which have been previously noted.

COGNITION, LEADERSHIP, AND EFFECTIVENESS

The effectiveness of collectives is a complex, multidimensional construct involving performance outcomes, behavioral processes such as adaptability, and beliefs such as team satisfaction or viability (Kozlowski & Ilgen, 2006; Sundstrom, DeMuse, & Futrell, 1990). One important indicator of team effectiveness is the extent to which the team is successful at accomplishing its goals. In addition, the team's ability to successfully coordinate efforts, back each other up, and remain a viable entity in the future are also important indicators of collective effectiveness (Kozlowsky & Ilgen, 2006; Sundstrom et al., 1990). A number of studies have examined the relationships between compositional collective cognition (e.g., Edwards, Day, Arthur, & Bell, 2006; Marks, Sabella, Burke, & Zaccaro, 2002; Resick, Dickson, Mitchelson, Allison, & Clark, 2010) and compilational collective cognition (e.g., Austin, 2003; Lewis, 2003; Zhang, Hempel, Han, &

124 • *Theories of Team Cognition*

Tjosvold, 2007). DeChurch and Mesmer-Magnus (2010a) meta-analyzed effects of compilational and compositional forms on team performance and found evidence that collective cognition is strongly related to both subjective and objective types of performance indicators. Overall coefficients of compositional and compilational emergence are .26 and .42 for objective performance and .42 and .50 for subjective performance, respectively. These relationships are moderated by different factors such as study setting, team types, and interdependence levels.

To understand teamwork, scholars have been searching for factors that influence teamwork through collective cognition. Among many, leadership has been theorized and identified to influence both collective cognition and team functioning (Zaccaro, Rittman, & Marks, 2001). However, the recent trend in the leadership literature was found to be more focused on leadership effects on dyadic relationships than collective process (Kaiser, Hogan, & Craig, 2008). For years, leadership scholars have defined leadership as the process of influencing collective action in order to achieve a collective goal (Stogdill, 1950). There has not been alignment between theoretical interests of the field and accumulated knowledge. Research on understanding how leadership influences team effectiveness through collective cognition is still an underresearched but promising area.

COGNITIVE ASPECTS OF LEADERSHIP THEORIES

Although numerous leadership theories and approaches submit that leaders influence collective perception and similar cognitive constructions, research on leadership has not yet fully incorporated the advances of team cognition in their empirical inquiry. The next section delves into the five approaches to leadership that have strong theoretical connections to emergent collective cognition. Table 5.1 summarizes the leadership literature and distinct cognitive aspects of the five major theories discussed in the following section.

Behavioral Perspectives

Seminal studies of leadership were conducted by researchers at Ohio State University and University of Michigan, separately, that identified

TABLE 5.1

Cognitive Aspects of Five Major Approaches to Organizational Leadership

Forms of Leadership	Forms of Cognition Contained in Theory	Summary of Prior Findings
Behavioral		
Behavior is more broadly defined than the Ohio State University two-factor model. Yukl (2002) identifies 12 behavioral dimensions and Fleishman et al. (1991) identify 13 dimensions.	Specific behavioral dimensions influence different types of cognition development such as mental models, team norm, and role ambiguity.	Schneider, Ehrhart, Mayer, Saltz, and Niles-Jolly (2005) found a link between leader behavior emphasizing service climate and staff service-oriented climate. DeChurch, Marks, and Murase (2009) found that leader strategy and coordinating behavior impacted mental model similarity in multiteam systems.
Strategic		
Encompasses the top executives of organizations and the top management team whose aim is to influence organizational outcomes.	Strategic leadership facilitates followers' identification with a collective level and development of understanding of critical issues among subsystems.	Fiss and Zajac (2006) found that leader sensemaking influenced cognitive frameworks. Walumbwa and Schaubroeck (2009) found that strategic leader ethical leadership influenced the development of psychological safety. Randall, Resick, and DeChurch (2009) found that external leader sensegiving influenced team strategy-focused mental model similarity and accuracy.
Transformational		
Leaders inspire followers to transcend their self-interest and increase their awareness in valued outcomes by engaging in charismatic leadership, individual consideration, and intellectual stimulation (Bass, 1985).	Transformational leaders encourage followers to self-identify with the task and collective goals and share vision.	Schippers, Den Hartog, Koopman, and van Knippenberg (2008) found that transformational leadership was related to the formation of a shared vision.

continued

126 • *Theories of Team Cognition*

TABLE 5.1 (CONTINUED)

Cognitive Aspects of Five Major Approaches to Organizational Leadership

Forms of Leadership	Forms of Cognition Contained in Theory	Summary of Prior Findings
		Kearney and Gebert (2009) found that transformational leadership influenced collective team identification. Resick, Whitman, Weingarden, and Hiller (2009) found that chief executive officer transformational leadership was related to the performance of core teams within the firm.
Functional		
It is the function of the leader "to do, or get done, whatever is not being adequately handled for group needs" (McGrath, 1962, p. 5).	Functional leadership entails the cognitive leadership process of surveying group conditions and information to design plans and consistently negotiate group conditions (Kane, Zaccaro, Tremble, & Masuda, 2002).	Marks, Zaccaro, and Mathieu (2000) found that leader briefings influenced the accuracy and similarity of team members' mental models.
Shared Team Leadership		
Involves the process by which all members of a team engage as the leader of the team (Gronn, 2002; Pearce & Conger, 2003; Pearce, Manz & Sims, 2008)	Team members need to have some form of shared understanding/consensus of their fellow team members' specialized expertise. It is through this shared understanding of each other's expertise that team members will be willing to trust a team member who takes on the leader role during a task.	Hiller, Day, and Vance (2006) found that shared leadership influenced collectivism attitudes.

two dimensions of leader behavior. At Ohio State, these dimensions were termed Initiating Structure (IS) and Consideration (C), whereas at the University of Michigan, they were termed relationship oriented, which shows support and acceptance of subordinates, versus task oriented, which indicates behavior aimed at attainment of the group's goal. These dimensions of leader behavior are positively linked to many valued organizational outcomes including subordinate performance, group and organizational performance, subordinate job attitudes, and turnover (House & Aditya, 1997; Judge, Piccolo, & Ilies, 2004).

Also influential in the domain of leader behavior are taxonomic efforts specifying more narrowly defined behaviors (Yukl, Gordon, & Taber, 2002). Yukl et al. (2002) have proposed a taxonomy of 12 behavioral dimensions, and Fleishman et al. (1991) developed 13 behavioral categories. Both the Yukl et al. (2002) and Fleishman et al. (1991) taxonomies include behaviors that guide followers to understand the environment and develop a similar cognitive schema. In particular, Yukl et al. (2002) describe three behaviors that should promote collective cognition: planning and organization, clarifying roles and objectives, and informing. Similarly, Fleishman et al. (1991) include two emergent cognition-relevant behaviors: planning and coordinating and communicating information. These behavioral categories are directly aimed at influencing and changing followers' cognition. In turn, the teams literature provides various cognitive variables that make theoretically sound linkages to those leadership behaviors.

Role clarification is defined as specifying responsibilities and setting up goals (Yukl, 2002). Planning is defined as making decisions about objectives, priorities, assignments of responsibilities, and coordination of activities (Yukl, 2002). Once leaders have identified separate, distinct actions, they must develop a plan that considers timely coordination (Morse & Wagner, 1978). Leaders and members must clearly understand their unique function and contribution to the team. With clear directions, they can exert energy on information critical to their roles. However, leaders must coordinate such individuals with different specialties. In planning, members recognize which members are specialized in what functions and how they should coordinate with one another at different points. Recognition of interdependence improves transactive memory because in a planning process, members must understand each unique role and how they are connected to accomplish a mission (Zhang

128 • *Theories of Team Cognition*

et al., 2007). In addition, leaders must manage information internal and external to the team. Identifying and relaying appropriate information to members enhances coordination timing and members' unique roles. As the environment changes, leaders need to update their agenda and develop a new coordination plan. As they adjust their plans, leaders must engage in communication with members to alter their collective cognitions and make them fit the changing environment (Morgeson, 2005). Leaders must allocate information to the right members based on their responsibilities to avoid having members cognitively overloaded (Littlepage, Hollingshead, Drake, & Littlepage, 2008). As members obtain unique information that may not be shared with others, their cognitive schema will be altered. These three leader behaviors interact with each other to create conversion and differentiation in members' knowledge at the team level.

> *Proposition 1: Team leader planning behavior positively influences team members' development of task-, team-, and strategy-focused compositional forms of emergent cognition.*
> *Proposition 2: Team leader role clarification behavior positively influences team members' development of compilational forms of emergent cognition.*
> *Proposition 3: Team leader informational communication behavior positively influences team members' development of task-, team-, and strategy-focused compositional forms of emergent cognition.*

Strategic Leadership

Understanding the impact of strategic leadership is a core goal of organizational science research because senior executives can and do have a company-wide impact and mistakes can lead to catastrophic consequences. Strategic leadership theory and research focus on individuals at the apex of an organization, and topics can range widely from traits to behaviors to even the succession process (e.g., Jensen & Zajac, 2004; Nutt, 1987; Tushman & Rosenkopf, 1996). Upper echelon theory and an argument for legitimizing the use of observed data of executives' traits by Hambrick and Mason (1984) have spawned many studies that explore how top managers' traits influence their actions. Researchers have found empirical evidence that the characteristics and actions of strategic leaders are related to more distal outcomes such as firm strategy and performance, as well as the relationships with and the performance of teams within the organization (e.g., Chatterjee & Hambrick, 2007; Peterson, Smith, Martorana, & Owens, 2003; Resick, Whitman, Weingarden, & Hiller, 2009).

Strategic leaders must coordinate actions and effort from multiple constituents at multiple layers to attain organizational outcomes (Lord, 2001). Formulating effective strategies is important but not sufficient. Constructing a collective mental schema is equally as necessary for any collective action. Cognitive diversity influences effectiveness of strategy at least in two stages. First, members at the top have diverse functions, which lend them different lenses to view the business world and make them focus on different parts of information. Studies show that cognitive diversity among top managers inhibits development of comprehensive and extensive strategic planning (Miller, Burke, & Glick, 1998). In addition, companies with well-developed strategies sometimes face negative consequences if they cannot implement them. Middle and first-line managers must understand the meaning of strategies in order to implement them at the operational levels (Balogun & Johnson, 2004). Thus, the main function of strategic leadership is to develop similar, collective cognition among constituents at different levels and cultivate support for strategies. Executives must provide a vision and framework (Balogun & Johnson, 2004; Fiss & Zajac, 2006; Rapert, Velliquette, & Garretson, 2002) and cultivate collective identity (Lord & Brown, 2001; Shamir, House, & Arthur, 1993) to maintain and orchestrate subsystems while institutionalizing new policies and regulations and developing adapting structures to dynamic environments (Bernard, 1938).

Sensegiving and development of culture have been found to be important mechanisms that enhance convergence of individual cognitive schema on critical issues. Executives' vertical communication with top middle managers allows them to be involved in strategic planning, enhances convergence of their cognitive schema with top managers, and improves the understanding of priorities (Rapert et al., 2002; Wooldridge & Floyd, 1990). Executive leaders also use culture as a vehicle to develop and maintain certain collective cognitive patterns in their organizations (Giberson et al., 2009; Schein, 2004).

A culture is a set of socially constructed rules and values shared by members that determines thought process, perceptions, and behaviors

130 • *Theories of Team Cognition*

(Schein, 2004). Several recent studies have shown that leaders play a critical role in developing and changing culture (Giberson et al., 2009; Schneider et al., 2005). Executive leaders use culture as a tool to send signals as to their emphasis on certain values and to integrate individual different schemas into a unified one (Grojean, Resick, Dickson, & Smith, 2004; Zohar & Luria, 2004). For example, members in an organization use the culture as a standard to judge whether behaviors or their values are appropriate. It is a powerful tool that influences collective cognition and behavior (Mayer, Kuenzi, Greenbaum, Bardes, & Salvador, 2009; Salvaggio et al., 2007). Through these mechanisms, executive leaders enhance the convergence of collective cognitive schema at the organization level.

> *Proposition 4: Strategic leader sensegiving behavior positively influences team members' strategy-focused compositional and perceptual forms of emergent cognition.*

Transformational Leadership Theory

In proposing transformational leadership (TL) theory, Bass (1985) suggested that transformational leaders incite followers to transcend their self-interest and increase their awareness of valued outcomes by engaging in four types of behaviors: idealized influence, inspirational motivation, intellectual simulation, and individual consideration (Bass & Avolio, 1993). Within the literature, both idealized influences and inspirational motivation are combined to create what is known as charismatic leadership or a leader's ability to provide followers with a strong vision of the future. Individual consideration focuses on a leader's ability to attend to the unique developmental needs of followers. Lastly, intellectual stimulation involves leaders encouraging followers to think *outside the box* and challenge organizational norms (Bass, 1985; Bono & Judge, 2004).

Research on leaders who exhibit TL behaviors has found that followers are more aware of organizational goals (Berson & Avolio, 2004) and share similar views on the importance of goals (Colbert, Kristof-Brown, Bradley, & Murray, 2008). The effects of TL go beyond individual influence as recent studies have begun to focus on the effects of TL behaviors on collective cognition. For instance, leaders who engage in TL behaviors have the ability to influence collective team identification (Kearney & Gebert, 2009) and unit climate by networking among followers (Zohar & Tenne-Gazit, 2008). Schippers, Den Hartog, Koopman, and van Knippenberg (2008) and Jansen, George, Van den Bosch, and Volberda (2008) found that leaders who engaged in TL behaviors had followers with similar team shared vision. Furthermore, because transformational chief executive officers have been found to impact the performance of core teams within their organizations (Resick et al., 2009), TL behaviors exhibited by strategic leadership may have a cascading effect on leadership at lower levels and teams throughout the firm.

Although many studies have looked at the mechanisms leaders influence that promote team outcomes, the linkage between TL and followers' collective cognition has yet to be investigated. Although shared vision encompasses followers adopting a leader's vision and working toward that vision, it does not fully encompass collective cognitive processes. One of the more commonly studied TL behaviors is the ability for TL to influence and create a shared vision among followers. We argue that shared vision simply implies that a leader persuades or encourages the follower to agree with his or her vision, but it does not incorporate important aspects such as the degree of agreement between followers or whether the vision followers adopt is accurate. Future research should focus on the impact TL behaviors have on collective cognition and, more specifically, on how leaders who inspire a shared vision among followers can help teams develop collective cognition.

Proposition 5: TL behaviors positively influence team members' strategy-focused compositional forms of emergent cognition.

Functional Leadership Theory

Functional leadership has been developed uniquely in the teams literature and often neglected in the traditional leadership literature (e.g., Avolio, Walumbwa, & Weber, 2009; House & Aditya, 1997). The main distinction from other leadership approaches is its focus on leadership behaviors that fulfill team needs in order to attain goals instead of traditional leadership definitions focusing on what leaders should do (Morgeson, 2005; Zaccaro et al., 2001). Unlike traditional models of leadership, this role can be fulfilled by any member who is capable of executing requirements for

132 • *Theories of Team Cognition*

the team function (Lord, 1977; Morgeson, Lindoerfer, & Loring, 2009). Relative to the other leadership approaches, the literature is still scant. More research is necessary to fully understand what behaviors functional leaders engage in and how members occupy this role or share it.

Researchers have proposed different models that indicate linkages to collective cognitive processes. Lord (1977) has proposed 13 behavioral dimensions for task-related and socioemotionally related behavior, and Morgeson et al. (2009) have identified 13 behavioral dimensions based on the team taxonomy of Marks et al. (2001), whereas Zaccaro et al. (2001) have used Fleishman et al.'s (1991) 13 behavioral dimensions to explain linkages to collective cognition. Among these models, we find substantial overlap of distinct functional behaviors that can be linked to collective cognition. They recognize the importance of planning and sensegiving and identification of problems and needs. Zaccaro et al. (2001) have explicitly delineated theoretical linkages between these behaviors and team cognitive processes such as shared mental models, collective information sharing, and team metacognition. Other research suggests that functional leadership leads to enhanced convergence on collective cognition (Marks, Zaccaro, & Mathieu, 2000; Morgeson et al., 2009).

Studies have supported the effect of functional leadership on collective cognition. Mission analysis provides a main framework within which members form expectations, priorities, and tasks. Identification with leaders makes members accept the same understanding of strategy and priorities. Like other leadership approaches, sensemaking behavior and the leader exchanging information with followers process help develop similar understanding of priorities (Donnellon, Gray, & Bougon, 1986; Morgeson, 2005). The teams literature has provided empirical support for direct effect of leader's behaviors on collective cognition. Because members have unique cognitive schema due to their functional training and experiences, it is important for them to construct a similar mental model that guides the coordination of their actions effectively (Mathieu et al., 2000). Leader briefing behavior has been found to influence the development of shared mental models in teams and multiple teams (DeChurch, Marks, & Murase, 2009; Marks et al., 2000). In addition, teams must work as a unified entity in a dynamic environment. As the environment changes, they must change their patterns of coordination and adapt (Harrison, Mohammed, McGrath, Florey, & Vanderstoep,

Leadership and Emergent Collective Cognition • 133

2003). Thus, leaders must continuously schedule meetings where they can clarify any confusion about member roles that arises due to environmental change and develop a new strategic plan to facilitate coordination (Lant & Hewlin, 2002). Without a central member giving a framework that they can all share to interpret the environment in a similar manner, the team cannot function (Marks et al., 2000; Morgeson, 2005). Leader sensegiving has been found to positively influence the similarity and accuracy of strategic mental models, which in turn influence the extent to which teams adapt to a dynamic environment (Randall et al., 2009). Because functional leadership is defined in terms of behaviors that satisfy team needs (Morgeson et al., 2009), sources of empirical supports for the theoretical linkages overlap with those for the behavioral leadership approach. Functional leadership must differentiate specialty across members and show important issues on which members have consensus by engaging in role clarification and planning.

> *Proposition 6: Team leaders who engage in functional leadership behaviors involving (a) mission briefings, and (b) team preparation positively influence team members' development of task-, team-, and strategy-focused compositional forms of emergent cognition and compilational forms of emergent cognition.*

Shared and Distributed Leadership

With the prevalence of work teams in organizations, nontraditional forms of leadership have become commonplace. These forms of leadership go beyond the conventional view that a single member of a team is appointed as a leader by a more established member of the organization. For instance, shared leadership is viewed in team settings where multiple members of a collective take on or transfer the "leader" role among team members in order to take advantage of each member's strengths in an effort to attain the overall team goal (Burke, Fiore, & Salas, 2003; Hiller, Day, & Vance, 2006; Pearce & Conger, 2002). In shared leadership, the empowerment of multiple team members is based on expertise relevance and context. In other words, the leadership is disseminated between members based on the needs of the team at a specific time in its life cycle. Thus, when a team member's expertise contributes to the overall team goal, that individual "steps up" and takes on the leadership role. Similar to shared leadership is

134 • *Theories of Team Cognition*

distributed leadership, which acknowledges that leadership is composed of a collection of behaviors that can be rotated among the members of the group (Barry, 1991; Erez, LePine, & Elms, 2002). Distributed leadership does not require a member to emerge based on the expertise he or she possesses and how it contributes to the team goal. Instead, distributed leadership occurs when the team members dispose of it. It can come about when the existing leader is overwhelmed with his or her responsibilities, or it can be predetermined by the team, such as with a set schedule. Thus, distributed leadership enables team members to rotate leadership responsibilities, such as coordination and acting as liaisons to other teams (Erez et al., 2002).

Although new to the field of leadership, shared leadership and distributed leadership have been found to be associated with collectivism attitudes (e.g., focus on group welfare, success, and loyalty; Hiller et al., 2006). In addition, shared leadership and distributed leadership have been linked to a number of important team outcomes, such as increased organizational citizenship, member satisfaction, team effectiveness, and team performance (Carson, Tesluk, & Marrone, 2007; Erez et al., 2002; Hiller et al., 2006).

Limited research has focused on the relationship between shared and distributed leadership and collective cognition. Burke et al. (2003) proposed the influence of collective cognition on shared leadership, suggesting that the more team members have overlapping mental models, the stronger the team's understanding of when a team member should rise as the team leader. Teams function in a complex network where diverse members contribute unique information to the decision-making task and thus require collaboration and coordination among these members for successful performance. The impact leaders can have in shaping the knowledge sharing, task understanding, and coordination within a team is a critical key that researchers need to investigate. Thus, how shared and distributed leadership can detract or contribute to team performance is another avenue that must be considered. Does the impact of having multiple leaders over time actually strengthen a team's collective cognition, or do distinct perspectives actually break it down? We believe that as teams exchange leadership roles, they are more inclined to have a better understanding of other team members' task responsibilities. This, in turn, will translate to the development of better collective cognitive processes.

Proposition 7: Shared and distributed leadership within a team positively influence team members' development of task- and team-focused compositional forms of emergent cognition.

Proposition 8: Shared leadership and distributed leadership within a team positively influence team members' development of compilational forms of emergent cognition.

APPLIED IMPLICATION

Stogdill (1950) defined leadership as "the process of influencing the activities of an organized group in its efforts toward goal setting and goal achievement" (p. 4). Although this classic definition explicitly recognizes the importance of leadership on collective actions, the leadership literature and training programs tend to focus on developing skills that enhance one's quality or skills to influence followers' affective components (Day, 2000; DeChurch, Hiller, Murase, Doty, & Rohre, 2009). Although these training programs improve leaders' behaviors, the essence of leadership should be recognized in the extent to which leaders orchestrate followers' actions and efforts to achieve a collective goal and orchestrate individual actions to achieve it.

Based on recent meta-analytic findings, we should expand our understanding of leaders' influence beyond simply motivational and behavioral team processes (DeChurch & Mesmer-Magnus, 2010a). To achieve higher goals, leaders must realize or be trained on how to influence collective cognitive mechanisms that enhance orchestration and coordination of individual actions. Years of team literature suggest that collective cognition is the key to smooth coordination among members (DeChurch & Mesmer-Magnus, 2010a; Mohammed, Ferzandi, & Hamilton, 2010). Drawing on the model of Marks et al. (2001), Morgeson, DeRue, and Karam (2010) summarize that in the transition phase, leaders must help members establish similar cognitive schemas by defining the mission, establishing expectations and goals, and planning for action. Training focused on leadership behaviors that influence collective cognition seems to be promising but underestablished. Many leadership behaviors have been proposed and linked to collective cognition (see Table 5.2 and Figure 5.1). Thus, for practitioners to fully take

TABLE 5.2

Linking Forms of Leadership and Emergent Cognition

Forms	Leadership — Specific variables	Emergent Cognition	Proposition
Behavior	Planning	Compositional	1. Team leader planning behavior positively influences team members' development of task-, team-, and strategy-focused compositional forms of emergent cognition.
	Role clarification	Compilational	2. Team leader role clarification behavior positively influences team members' development of compilational forms of emergent cognition.
	Communicating information	Compositional	3. Team leader informational communication behavior positively influences team members' development of task-, team-, and strategy-focused compositional forms of emergent cognition.
Strategic	Sensemaking	Compositional and perceptual	4. Strategic leader sensegiving behavior positively influences team members' strategy-focused compositional and perceptual forms of emergent cognition.
Transformational	All core transformational	Compositional	5. TL behaviors positively influence team members' strategy-focused compositional forms of emergent cognition.
Functional	Briefing behavior and preparation	Compositional and compilational	6. Team leaders who engage in functional leadership behaviors involving (a) mission briefings, and (b) team preparation positively influence team members' development of task-, team-, and strategy-focused compositional forms of emergent cognition and compilational forms of emergent cognition.
Shared	Role clarification	Compositional and compilational	7. Shared and distributed leadership within a team positively influence team members' development of task- and team-focused compositional forms of emergent cognition.
			8. Shared and distributed leadership within a team positively influence team members' development of compilational forms of emergent cognition.

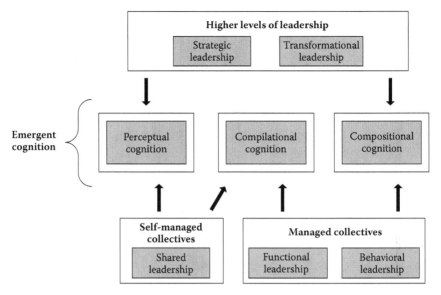

FIGURE 5.1
Relationships between types of leadership and collective cognition.

advantage of this research, we must identify specific linkages from different behaviors to appropriate types of team cognition. Future research focusing on the effects of leadership on collective cognition can help us add another piece to the puzzle that will allow us to strengthen the impact of teams and, furthermore, of organizations.

CONCLUSIONS

We have much to celebrate when it comes to the body of scientific evidence that has accumulated over the past few decades regarding the nature and importance of both leadership and collective cognition. Although we have come a long way, greater attention needs to be devoted to understanding the linkages between leadership and collective cognition. Despite the fact that the leadership literature has proposed theoretical and empirical linkages between the two (e.g., Fiss & Zajac, 2006; Morgeson et al., 2010; Weick, 1995; Zaccaro et al., 2001), recent reviews summarizing 20 years of leadership (DeChurch, Hiller, et al., 2009) and 15 years of shared mental models research (Mohammed et al., 2010) indicate that relatively few studies

138 • *Theories of Team Cognition*

have examined the relationships between various forms of leadership and various forms of collective cognition. In this chapter, we present a set of propositions to guide empirical research in this area. Implicit in this set of propositions is the need for multilevel methodologies to examine the leadership cognition relationships within and across organizational levels. Also implicit in this set of propositions is the need for time-lagged designs to examine temporal issues associated with the emergence of collective cognition, emergence of shared leadership, and the importance of various leadership functions, processes, and behaviors.

Kozlowski and Klein (2000) have argued that emergence cognition should be characterized as compositional and compilational in form. This distinction is particularly important for understanding how various types of cognition form and emerge at higher levels. In this chapter, we examine the linkages between leadership and the development and emergence of both compositional and compilational forms of cognition. We further argue that the empirical study of this alignment is critical to the continued evolution of the leadership and collective cognition literatures.

To perform effectively and become or remain viable, members must share strategic objectives and expectations but also maintain their own unique perceptual lens arising from their roles and functions. The challenge for leaders is to satisfy complex demands for developing and maintaining conversion as well as diversion on collective cognition. These demands come from various sources: (a) strategic objectives and plans; (b) internal resources, capabilities, and weaknesses; (c) individual and collective task responsibilities; (d) social norms and expectations; and (e) beliefs about the unit itself. These areas represent various forms of collective cognition, each of which plays some role in enhancing the interactions or ultimate effectiveness of the collective unit. Developing conversion on these sources may not always be beneficial for the team because it may lead to negative consequences such as groupthink (Janis, 1971). Research on relationships between specific leadership behaviors and types of collective cognition will significantly advance the understanding of collective process influencing its performance.

Leadership has long been considered a unique property of teams (Stogdill, 1950), and both leaders' influence and power have been recognized for a long time. However, leadership in the teams literature is often overlooked, as is the relationship between leadership and collective cognition. However, recent studies provide some indication that organizational science researchers are paying greater attention to the linkages between leadership and collective cognition (e.g., Giberson et al., 2009; Randall et al., 2009). This is an encouraging trend, and we encourage both leadership and team cognition researchers to examine the specific leadership functions and behaviors that play a role in the formation and emergence of specific forms of collective cognition. In the 1990s, Cannon-Bowers and Salas posited that team cognition was a critical piece of the teamwork puzzle we needed to further consider. Many studies have examined team cognition and demonstrated its utility. Therefore, our next step is to integrate the knowledge and capabilities from both the leadership and collective cognition fields in order to develop a better understanding of how different forms of team cognition can be developed and influence teamwork.

ACKNOWLEDGMENT

This work was supported in part by funding from the Army Research Institute for the Behavioral and Social Sciences (Contract No. W91WAW-08-C-0028).

REFERENCES

Austin, J. R. (2003). Transactive memory in organizational groups: The effects of content, consensus, specialization, and accuracy on group performance. *Journal of Applied Psychology, 88*, 866–878.

Avolio, B. J., Walumbwa, F. O., & Weber, T. J. (2009). Leadership: Current theories, research, and future directions. *Annual Review of Psychology, 60*, 421–449.

Balogun, J., & Johnson, G. (2004). Organizational restructuring and middle manager sensemaking. *Academy of Management Journal, 47*, 523–549.

Barry, D. (1991) Managing the bossless team: Lessons in distributed leadership. *Organizational Dynamics, 20*, 31–47.

Bass, B. M. (1985). *Leadership and performance beyond expectations*. New York, NY: Free Press.

Bass, B. M., & Avolio, B. J. (1993). Transformational leadership: A response to critique. In M. M. Chemers & R. Ayman (Eds.), *Leadership theory and research: Perspective and directions* (pp. 49–88). San Diego, CA: Academic Press.

Bernard, C. (1938). *The function of the executive*. Cambridge, MA: Harvard University Press.

Berson, Y., & Avolio, B. J. (2004). Transformational leadership and the dissemination of organizational goals: A case study of a telecommunication firm. *Leadership Quarterly, 15*, 625–646.

140 • *Theories of Team Cognition*

Bono, J. E., & Judge, T. A. (2004). Personality and transformational and transactional leadership: A meta-analysis. *Journal of Applied Psychology, 89,* 901–910.

Bryant, A. (2009, March 28). Feedback in heaping helpings. *The New York Times,* p. BU2. Retreieved June 3, 2011, from http://www.nytimes.com/2009/03/29/business/29corner.html

Burke, C. S., Fiore, S. M., & Salas, E. (2003). The role of shared cognition in enabling shared leadership and team adaptability. In C. L. Pearce & J. A. Conger (Eds.), *Shared leadership: Reframing the hows and whys of leadership* (pp. 103–122). Thousand Oaks, CA: Sage.

Burke, C. S., Stagle, K. C., Salas, E., Pierce, L., & Kendall, D. (2006). Understanding team adaptation: A conceptual analysis and model. *Journal of Applied Psychology, 91,* 1189–1207.

Cannon-Bowers, J. A., Salas, E., & Converse, S. (1993). Shared mental models in expert team decision making. In N. J. Castellan (Ed.), *Individual and group decision making: Current issues* (pp. 221–246). Hillsdale, NJ: Lawrence Erlbaum Associates.

Carson, J. B., Tesluk, P. E., & Marrone, J. A. (2007). Shared leadership in teams: An investigation of antecedent conditions and performance. *Academy of Management Journal, 50,* 1217–1234.

Chatterjee, A., & Hambrick, D. C. (2007). It's all about me: Narcissistic CEOs and their effects on company strategy and performance. *Administrative Science Quarterly, 52,* 351–386.

Colbert, A. E., Kristof-Brown, A. L., Bradley, B. H., & Murray, R. (2008). CEO transformational leadership: The role of goal importance congruence in top management teams. *Academy of Management Journal, 51,* 81–96.

Day, D. V. (2000). Leadership development: A review in context. *Leadership Quarterly, 11,* 581–613.

DeChurch, L. A., Hiller, N., Murase, T., Doty, D., & Rohre, D. (2009, August). *The inferential capacity of leadership research: A 20-year review.* Poster session presented at the Annual Conference of Academy of Management, Chicago, IL.

DeChurch, L. A., Marks, M. A., & Murase, T. M. (2009). *Leading the team, and above: Leader mental models and multiteam system effectiveness.* Unpublished working paper.

DeChurch, L. A., & Mesmer-Magnus, J. R. (2010a). The cognitive underpinnings of team effectiveness: A meta-analysis. *Journal of Applied Psychology, 95,* 32–53.

DeChurch, L. A., & Mesmer-Magnus, J. R. (2010b). Measuring shared team mental models: A meta-analysis. *Group Dynamics: Theory, Research, and Practice, 14,* 1–14.

Dickson, M. W., Resick, C. J., & Hanges, P. J. (2006). When organizational climate is unambiguous, it is also strong. *Journal of Applied Psychology, 91,* 351–364.

Donnellon, A., Gray, B., & Bougon, M. G. (1986). Communication, meaning, and organized action. *Administrative Science Quarterly, 31,* 43–55.

Edwards, B. D., Day, E. A., Arthur, W., & Bell, S. T. (2006). Relationships among team ability composition, team mental models, and team performance. *Journal of Applied Psychology, 91,* 727–736.

Erez, A., LePine, J. A., & Elms, H. (2002). Effects of rotated leadership and peer evaluation on the functioning and effectiveness of self-managed teams: A quasi-experiment. *Personnel Psychology, 55,* 929–948.

Fiss, P. C., & Zajac, E. J. (2006). The symbolic management of strategic change: Sensegiving via framing and decoupling. *Academy of Management Journal, 49,* 1173–1193.

Fleishman, E. A., Mumford, M. D., Zaccaro, S. J., Levin, K. Y., Korotkin, A. L., & Hein, M. B. (1991). Taxonomic efforts in the description of leader behavior: A synthesis and functional interpretation. *Leadership Quarterly, 2,* 245–287.

Leadership and Emergent Collective Cognition • 141

Giberson, T. R., Resick, C. J., Dickson, M. W., Mitchelson, J. K., Randall, K. R., & Clark, M. A. (2009). Leadership and organizational culture: Linking CEO characteristics to cultural values. *Journal of Business Psychology, 24*, 123–137.

Grojean, M. W., Resick, C. J., Dickson, M. W., & Smith, D. B. (2004). Leaders, values, and organizational climate: Examining leadership strategies for establishing an organizational climate regarding ethics. *Journal of Business Ethics, 55*, 223–241.

Gronn, P. (2002). Distributed leadership as a unit of analysis. *Leadership Quarterly, 13*, 423–451.

Gully, S. M., Devine, D. J., & Whitney, D. J. (1995). A meta-analysis of cohesion and performance: Effects of levels of analysis and task interdependence. *Small Group Research, 26*, 497–520.

Hambrick, D. C., & Mason, P. A. (1984). Upper echelons: The organization as a reflection of its top managers. *Academy of Management Review, 9*, 193–206.

Harrison, D. A., Mohammed, S., McGrath, J. E., Florey, A. T., & Vanderstoep, S. W. (2003). Time matters in team performance: Effects of member familiarity, entrainment, and task discontinuity on speed and quality. *Personnel Psychology, 56*, 633–669.

Hiller, N. J., Day, D. V., & Vance, R. J. (2006). Collective enactment of leadership roles and team effectiveness: A field study. *The Leadership Quarterly, 17*, 387–397.

Hinsz, V. B., Tindale, R. S., & Vollrath, D. A. (1997). The emerging conceptualization of groups as information processors. *Psychological Bulletin, 121*, 43–64.

House, R. J., & Aditya, R. N. (1997). The social scientific study of leadership: Quo vadis? *Journal of Management, 23*, 409–473.

Huang, X., & Iun, J. (2006). The impact of subordinate-supervisor similarity in growth-need strength on work outcomes: The mediating role of perceived similarity. *Journal of Organizational Behavior, 27*, 1121–1148.

Iaquinto, A. L., & Fredrickson, J. W. (1997). Top management team agreement about the strategic decision process: A test of some of its determinants and consequences. *Strategic Management Journal, 18*, 63–75.

Janis, I. L. (1971, November). Groupthink. *Psychology Today*, 43–46, 74–76.

Jansen, J. J. P., George, G., Van den Bosch, F. A. J., & Volberda, H. W. (2008). Senior team attributes and organizational ambidexterity: The moderating role of transformational leadership. *Journal of Management, 45*, 982–1007.

Jensen, M., & Zajac, E. J. (2004). Corporate elites and corporate strategy: How demographic preferences and structural position shape the scope of the firm. *Strategic Management Journal, 25*, 507–524.

Judge, T. A., Piccolo, R. F., & Ilies, R. (2004). The forgotten ones? A re-examination of consideration, initiating structure, and leadership effectiveness. *Journal of Applied Psychology, 89*, 36–51.

Kaiser, R., Hogan, R., & Craig, S. (2008). Leadership and the fate of organizations. *American Psychologist, 63*, 96–110.

Kane T. D., Zaccaro S. J., Tremble T. R., & Masuda, A. D. (2002). An examination of the leader's regulation of groups. *Small Group Research, 33*, 65–120.

Kearney, E., & Gebert, D. (2009). Managing diversity and enhancing team outcomes: The promise of transformational leadership. *Journal of Applied Psychology, 94*, 77–89.

Kellermanns, F. W., Walter, J., Lechner, C., & Floyd, S. W. (2005). The lack of consensus about strategic consensus: Advancing theory and research. *Journal of Management, 31*, 719–737.

142 • *Theories of Team Cognition*

Klein, K. J., & Kozlowski, S. W. J. (2000). From micro to meso: Critical steps in conceptualizing and conducting multilevel research. *Organizational Research Methods, 3*, 211–236.

Kozlowski, S. W. J., & Ilgen, D. R. (2006). Enhancing the effectiveness of work groups and teams. *Psychological Science in the Public Interest, 7*, 77–124.

Kozlowski, S. W. J., & Klein, K. J. (2000). A multilevel approach to theory and research in organizations: Contextual, temporal, and emergent properties. In K. L. Klein & S. W. J. Kozlowski (Eds.), *Multilevel theory, research, and methods in organizations: Foundations, extensions, and new directions* (pp. 3–90). San Francisco, CA: Jossey-Bass.

Lant, T. K., & Hewlin, P. F. (2002). Information cues and decision making: The effects of learning, momentum, and social comparison in competing teams. *Group & Organization Management, 27*, 374–407.

Lewis, K. (2003). Measuring transactive memory systems in the field: Scale development and validation. *Journal of Applied Psychology, 88*, 587–604.

Liang, D. W., Moreland, R., & Argote, L. (1995). Group versus individual training and group performance: The mediating factor of transactive memory. *Personality and Social Psychology Bulletin, 21*, 384–393.

Lindell, M. K., & Brandt, C. J. (2000). Climate quality and climate consensus as mediators of the relationship between organizational antecedents and outcomes. *Journal of Applied Psychology, 85*, 331–348.

Littlepage, G. E., Hollingshead, A. B., Drake, L. R., & Littlepage, A. M. (2008). Transactive memory and performance in work groups: Specificity, communication, ability differences, and work allocation. *Group Dynamics: Theory, Research, and Practice, 12*, 223–241.

Lord, R. G. (1977). Functional leadership behavior: Measurement and relation to social power and leadership perceptions. *Administrative Science Quarterly, 22*, 114–133.

Lord, R. G. (2001). Collective construction of a theory of executive leadership. In S. J. Zaccaro & R. J. Klimoski (Eds.), *The nature of organizational leadership: Understanding the performance imperatives confronting today's leaders* (pp. 413–436). San Francisco, CA: Jossey-Bass.

Lord, R. G., & Brown, D. J. (2001). Leadership, values, and subordinate self-concepts. *Leadership Quarterly, 12*, 133–152.

Marks, M. A., Mathieu, J. E., & Zaccaro, S. J. (2001). A temporally based framework and taxonomy of team processes. *Academy of Management Review, 26*, 356–376.

Marks, M. A., Sabella, M. J., Burke, C. S., & Zaccaro, S. J. (2002). The impact of cross-training on team effectiveness. *Journal of Applied Psychology, 87*, 3–13.

Marks, M. A., Zaccaro, S. J., & Mathieu, J. E. (2000). Performance implications of leader briefings and team-interaction training for team adaptation to novel environments. *Journal of Applied Psychology, 85*, 971–986.

Mathieu, J. E., Heffner, T. S., Goodwin, G. F., Salas, E., & Cannon-Bowers, J. A. (2000). The influence of shared mental models on team process and performance. *Journal of Applied Psychology, 85*, 273–283.

Mayer, D. M., Kuenzi, M., Greenbaum, R., Bardes, M., & Salvador, R. (2009). How low does ethical leadership flow? Test of a trickle-down model. *Organizational Behavior and Human Decision Processes, 108*, 1–13.

McGrath, J. E. (1962). *Leadership behavior: Some requirements for leadership training*. Washington, DC: U.S. Civil Service Commission, Office of Career Development.

Meglino, B. M., Ravlin, E. C., & Adkins, C. L. (1989). A work values approach to corporate culture: A field test of the value congruence process and its relationship to individual outcomes. *Journal of Applied Psychology, 3*, 424–432.

Miller, C. C., Burke, L. M., & Glick, W. H. (1998). Cognitive diversity among upper-echelon executives: Implications for strategic decision processes. *Strategic Management Journal, 19,* 39–58.

Mohammed, S., Ferzandi, L., & Hamilton, K. (2010). Metaphor no more: A 15-year review of the team mental model construct. *Journal of Management, 36,* 876–910.

Moreland, R. L., Argote, L., & Krishnan, R. (1996). Socially shared cognition at work: Transactive memory and group performance. In J. L. Nye & A. M. Brower (Eds.), *What's social about social cognition? Research on socially shared cognition in small groups* (pp. 57–84). Thousand Oaks, CA: Sage.

Morgeson, F. P. (2005). The external leadership of self-managing teams: Intervening in the context of novel and disruptive events. *Journal of Applied Psychology, 90,* 497–508.

Morgeson, F. P., DeRue, D. S., & Karam, E. P. (2010). Leadership in teams: A functional approach to understanding leadership structures and processes. *Journal of Management, 36,* 5–40.

Morgeson, F. P., Lindoerfer, D., & Loring, D. (2009). Developing team leadership capability. In E. Van Velsor, C. McCauley, & M. Ruderman (Eds.), *The Center for Creative Leadership handbook of leadership development* (3rd ed.). San Francisco, CA: Jossey-Bass.

Morse, J. J., & Wagner, F. R. (1978). Measuring the process of managerial effectiveness. *Academy of Management Journal, 21,* 23–35.

Nutt, P. C. (1987). Identifying and appraising how managers install strategy. *Strategic Management Journal, 8,* 1–14.

Pearce, C. L., & Conger, J. A. (Eds.). (2002). *Shared leadership: Reframing the how's and why's of leadership.* Thousand Oaks, CA: Sage.

Pearce, C. L., Manz, C. C., & Sims, H. P. (2008). The roles of vertical and shared leadership in the enactment of executive corruption: Implications for research and practice. *Leadership Quarterly, 19,* 353–359.

Peterson, R., Smith, D. B., Martorana, P., & Owens, P. (2003). The impact of chief executive officer personality on top management team dynamics: One mechanism by which leadership affects organizational performance. *Journal of Applied Psychology, 88,* 795–808.

Randall, K. R., Resick, C. J., & DeChurch, L. A. (2009). *Building adaptive capacity in teams: External leader sense-giving and team composition.* Unpublished working paper.

Rapert, M. I., Velliquette, A., & Garretson, J. A. (2002). The strategic implementation process: Evoking strategic consensus through communication. *Journal of Business Research, 55,* 301–310.

Rentsch, J. R., Small, E. E., & Hanges, P. J. (2008). Cognition in organizations and teams: What is the meaning of cognitive similarity? In D. B. Smith (Ed.), *The people make the place: Dynamic linkages between people and organizations* (pp. 127–155). New York, CA: Lawrence Erlbaum.

Resick, C. J., Dickson, M. W., Mitchelson, J. K., Allison, L. K., & Clark, M. A. (2010). Team composition, cognition, and effectiveness: Examining mental model similarity and accuracy. *Group Dynamics: Theory, Research, and Practice, 14,* 174–191.

Resick, C. J., Whitman, D. S., Weingarden, S. M., & Hiller, N. J. (2009). The bright-side and the dark-side of CEO personality: Examining core self-evaluations, narcissism, transformational leadership, and strategic influence. *Journal of Applied Psychology, 94,* 1365–1381.

Salvaggio, A. N., Schneider, B., Nishii, L. H., Mayer, D. M., Ramesh, A., & Lyon, J. S. (2007). Manager personality, manager service quality orientation, and service climate: Test of a model. *Journal of Applied Psychology, 92,* 1741–1750.

144 • *Theories of Team Cognition*

Schein, E. H. (1990). Organizational culture. *American Psychologist, 45,* 109–119.

Schein, E. H. (2004). *Organizational culture and leadership* (3rd ed.). San Francisco, CA: Jossey-Bass.

Schippers, M. C., Den Hartog, D. N., Koopman, P. L., & van Knippenberg, D. (2008). The role of transformational leadership in enhancing team reflexivity. *Human Relations, 61,* 1593–1616.

Schneider, B. (1975). Organizational climate: An essay. *Personnel Psychology, 28,* 447–479.

Schneider, B., Ehrhart, M. G., Mayer, D. M., Saltz, J. L., & Niles-Jolly, K. (2005). Understanding organization-customer links in service settings. *Academy of Management Journal, 48,* 1017–1032.

Schneider, B., Salvaggio, A. N., & Subirats, M. (2002). Climate strength: A new quality for climate research. *Journal of Applied Psychology, 87,* 220–229.

Shamir, B., House, R. J., & Arthur, M. B. (1993). The motivational effects of charismatic leadership: A self-concept based theory. *Organization Science, 4,* 577–594.

Smith-Jentsch, K. A., Mathieu, J. E., & Kraiger, K. (2005). Investigating linear and interactive effects of shared mental models on safety and efficiency in a field setting. *Journal of Applied Psychology, 3,* 523–535.

Stogdill, R. M. (1950). Leadership, membership and organization. *Psychological Bulletin, 47,* 1–14.

Sundstrom, E., DeMeuse, K., & Futrell, D. (1990). Work teams: Applications and effectiveness. *American Psychologist, 45*(2), 120–133.

Tushman, M. L., & Rosenkopf, L. (1996). Executive succession, strategic reorientation and performance growth: A longitudinal study in the US cement industry. *Management Science, 42,* 939–953.

Walumbwa, F. O., & Schaubroeck, J. (2009). Leader personality traits and employee voice behavior: Mediating roles of ethical leadership and work group psychological safety. *Journal of Applied Psychology, 5,* 1275–1286.

Wegner, D. M. (1986). Transactive memory: A contemporary analysis of the group mind. In B. Mullen & G. R. Goethals (Eds.), *Theories of group behavior* (pp. 185–208). New York, NY: Springer-Verlag.

Weick, K. E. (1995). *Sensemaking in organizations.* Thousand Oaks, CA: Sage.

Wooldridge, B., & Floyd, S. W. (1990). The strategy process, middle management involvement, and organizational performance. *Strategic Management Journal, 11,* 231–241.

Yukl, G. (2002). *Leadership in organizations* (4th ed.). Upper Saddle River, NJ: Prentice Hall.

Yukl, G., Gordon, A., & Taber, T. (2002). A hierarchical taxonomy of leadership behavior: Integrating a half century of behavior research. *Journal of Leadership & Organizational Studies, 9,* 15–32.

Zaccaro, S. J., Rittman, A. L., & Marks, M. A. (2001). Team leadership. *The Leadership Quarterly, 12,* 451–483.

Zhang, Z., Hempel, P. S., Han, Y., & Tjosvold, D. (2007). Transactive memory system links work team characteristics and performance. *Journal of Applied Psychology, 92,* 1722–1730.

Zohar, D., & Luria, G. (2004). Climate as a social-cognitive construct of supervisory safety practices: Scripts as proxy of behavior patterns. *Journal of Applied Psychology, 89,* 322–333.

Zohar, D., & Tenne-Gazit, O. (2008). Transformational leadership and group interaction as climate antecedents: A social network analysis. *Journal of Applied Psychology, 93,* 744–757.

6

Elaborating Cognition in Teams: Cognitive Similarity Configurations

Joan R. Rentsch and Ioana R. Mot

Through selection, socialization, social construction, and negotiation processes, individuals working together will form similar understandings or interpretations of events occurring within and around the work unit including those related to their tasks, other individuals, leaders, the work environment, and so on. Similar interpretations or meanings of events are functional for people in groups and for groups of people. For example, they can smooth interactions, facilitate task completion, and enhance knowledge transfer (e.g., Dyer, 1984; Nieva, Fleishman, & Reick, 1985; Rentsch, Delise, & Hutchison, 2008). Indeed, similar interpretations may become reified to the extent that people (and groups and organizations) forget that they, themselves, control their similar interpretations and, instead, become controlled by them (e.g., Berger & Luckmann, 1966). Because of their power, similar meanings have garnered the interest of organizational behavior researchers, who have studied them at the organizational, unit, and team levels of analysis, and who have identified them by such terms as schema similarity, climate, culture, shared mental models, and shared meanings.

A fair amount of research has increased the understanding of antecedents and outcomes associated with similar meanings. Recently, researchers have advocated elaborating the conceptualizations of similar cognitions (e.g., Rentsch, Small, & Hanges, 2008) and expanding the methodological approaches to studying similar cognitions (e.g., Schulte, Ostroff, Shmulyian, & Kinicki, 2009). The purpose of this chapter is to continue this discussion, particularly with respect to the study of cognition in teams. In this chapter, we summarize common conceptualizations of variables associated with the phenomenon of similar meanings and present the notion of cognitive similarity configurations. We present common methods for operationalizing cognitive similarity and several examples

145

146 • *Theories of Team Cognition*

from the empirical research literature, including examples of cognitive similarity configurations. Then, we discuss several potential cognitive similarity configuration points for future research.

CONCEPTUALIZATIONS OF SIMILAR COGNITIONS IN THE STUDY OF TEAMS

Similar meanings have been conceptualized to several degrees of abstraction and complexity. Two common conceptualizations can be categorized as perceptual cognition and structured cognition.

The perceptual approach conceptualizes similar meanings as beliefs, expectations, and perceptions that become "shared" among individuals. Beliefs are cognitions (thoughts or philosophy) possessed by individuals that may become held in common. For example, shared beliefs regarding the team task and understanding how to respond to failure are thought to be important team cognition variables (e.g., Cannon & Edmondson, 2001; Kirkman, Tesluk, & Rosen, 2001). Collective efficacy, a team's "collective belief in its capability to perform a task" (Gibson, 2003, p. 2153), is another form of shared belief considered relevant to teams. Shared beliefs have been examined separately from shared expectations (Earley & Mosakowski, 2000), another type of perception. Expectations, the anticipation of a future event or predicted standards, represent another form of cognition that is hypothesized to become similar among individuals and affect behavior. For example, the effects of expectations for attendance on absence behavior have been examined in groups (Xie & Johns, 2000).

The perceptual approach is perhaps best characterized by the research on organizational and team climate. Climate researchers have studied perceptual meanings held in common among organizational and team/ group members (e.g., Bain, Mann, & Pirola-Merlo, 2001; Colquitt, Noe, & Jackson, 2002; Naumann & Bennett, 2000, 2002; Zohar, 2000; Zohar & Luria, 2005). Climate has been defined as shared perceptions of policies, practices, and procedures that are rewarded, supported, and expected (Schneider, 1975; Schneider & Reichers, 1983). Most climate researchers refer to "shared" perceptions (e.g., Anderson & West, 1998; Hofmann, Morgeson, & Gerras, 2003; Naumann & Bennett, 2000, 2002) and follow Schneider's recommendation to specify the domain content of the shared perceptions. Therefore, the domain content of the cognition is identified in climate studies as the "climate for..." (Schneider, 1975). Climates for innovation, safety, leadership, and service have been examined in organizations (e.g., Chen & Bliese, 2002; Gonzalez-Roma, Peiro, & Tordera, 2002; Schneider, White, & Paul, 1998; Zohar & Luria, 2005). Climates for innovation, creativity, safety, and procedural justice have been examined in teams (e.g., Anderson & West, 1998; Bain et al., 2001; Colquitt et al., 2002; Naumann & Bennett, 2000, 2002; Pirola-Merlo & Mann, 2004; Zohar, 2000; Zohar & Luria, 2005). Some researchers argue that the most relevant cognitive content is likely to be the individual's interpretation of the environment's influence on his or her well-being (e.g., Glisson & James, 2002).

The perceptual conceptualization of similar cognitions focuses on the overlap or agreement among individuals' beliefs, expectations, and perceptions that they develop to interpret events. Usually the researchers who examine these types of cognitions assume that individuals generate meanings that then become held in common through interactions and problem solving. The interest is in "shared" perceptions, which are typically assessed by aggregating individual responses on measures of beliefs, expectations, or perceptions. The perceptual approach focuses primarily on the issue of cognitive content but does not address the issue of cognitive structure.

Another set of conceptualizations of similar meanings is related to cognitive structure and emerged from the research on cognition in teams. A common approach to structured cognition has been to examine mental models. Mental models are defined as "mechanisms whereby humans are able to generate descriptions of system purpose and form, explanations of system functioning and observed system states, and predictions of future systems states" (Rouse & Morris, 1986, p. 351). In human factors psychology, mental models of organizing knowledge systems, responses to systems, and system environments are of research interest. Team researchers have investigated mental models that team members develop in common representing understandings of the team's purpose, process (Marks, Sabella, Burke, & Zaccaro, 2002), and task. Training is expected to be a key antecedent of team mental models.

Structured meaning has also been examined as schema similarity. Schemas are knowledge structures that serve to organize information about a specific domain (e.g., teamwork, team members, task). They generate interpretations and provide meaning (Rumelhart, 1980; Rumelhart,

148 • *Theories of Team Cognition*

Smolensky, McClelland, & Hinton, 1988), making schemata powerful interpretive devices. Through socialization processes, interaction, training, and biographical experiences, team members are expected to develop similar schemas regarding content domains relevant to teams, such as teamwork, team members, and team tasks (e.g., Rentsch & Klimoski, 2001).

The structured cognition approach focuses on the overlap or agreement among individuals' structured cognition. In this approach, the individual is assumed to be the source of the cognition. This approach also places a strong emphasis on recognizing various cognitive content domains.

The theoretical and empirical research based on the perceptual and structured cognition conceptualizations tends not to overlap. However, several consistencies exist among these approaches. First, in both approaches, the individual is assumed to be the source of cognition. Second, the congruent form of similarity represented by commonality, agreement, or overlap is emphasized. Third, both approaches recognize that cognition covers multiple content domains; therefore, the necessity of specifying the cognitive content domain of interest is recognized as essential in both approaches.

Although these consistencies exist, the approaches also have important differences. Differences in the approaches include the following: (a) either structure (structured cognition approach) or content (perceptual approach) is typically emphasized; and (b) primary emphasis is placed on different antecedents (e.g., social interaction, leadership, and social construction as antecedents of perceptions and training and biographical experience as antecedents of structured cognition).

Both of these approaches have contributed to the understanding of cognition in teams. Perhaps a major reason for the differentiation of the research using these approaches is due to the available methodologies. In the next section, examples of how these conceptualizations are operationalized are presented.

OPERATIONALIZING PERCEPTUAL AND STRUCTURED COGNITION

Research designed to test hypotheses about perceptual meaning operationalized congruent perceptions using individuals' responses to survey items. The individual responses were typically aggregated to the team or unit level of analysis (e.g., Bain et al., 2001; Beersma & De Dreu, 2002; Choi, Price, & Vinokur, 2003; Ensley & Pearce, 2001) using some index such as analysis of variance, r_{wg}, or intraclass correlations to justify aggregation (e.g., Anderson & West, 1998; Cannon & Edmondson, 2001; Ensley & Pearce, 2001; Glisson & James, 2002; Hofmann et al., 2003; Kirkman et al., 2001; Levesque, Wilson, & Wholey, 2001; Mason & Griffin, 2003; Naumann & Bennett, 2000, 2002; Xie & Johns, 2000). Typically, the primary operationalization, the rating level (or elevation), is the indicator of the similar cognitions. This approach focuses the operationalization on the content of the cognition but does not address the degree of similarity (and that is the type of cognitive congruence typically of interest). Thus, the questions addressed using this type of operationalization focus more on the point on the scale team members use to describe (interpret) the domain than on how much similarity, overlap, or congruence exists among members. Therefore, researchers were testing theoretical relationships between the level of the shared perceptions (e.g., how much justice or safety was valued in the team) and other variables (e.g., Naumann & Bennett, 2002; Zohar, 2000; Zohar & Luria, 2005). More recently, researchers have begun to place more emphasis on the degree of similarity, which they sometimes refer to as consensus (Schulte et al., 2009), assessing it using variance or an interrater agreement index (e.g., r_{wg}, coefficient of variation, standard deviation) (e.g., Austin, 2003; Colquitt et al., 2002; Isabella & Waddock, 1994; Levesque et al., 2001; Mohammed & Ringseis, 2001). Alternatively, researchers have asked individuals to explicitly rate the level of agreement among team members (e.g., Mason & Griffin, 2003; Xie & Johns, 2000), thereby producing a subjective assessment of perceptual agreement.

Climate research was initiated long before (Schneider & Bartlett, 1968) the structured cognition research was applied to teams (Cannon-Bowers, Salas, & Converse, 1993). Although methods should not drive conceptualization, empirical research is in fact restricted by available methodology. Since the initiation of organizational climate research in the late 1960s, the advance of computer technology has made programs running complex statistics (e.g., network analysis and multidimensional scaling [MDS]) readily available to organizational researchers. The climate research tradition has not routinely incorporated the more recently available methods (see Rentsch, 1990, for an exception). However, research on team cognition

150 • *Theories of Team Cognition*

began in force in the 1990s, and teamwork researchers took advantage of these methods. Moreover, these methods may have contributed to the ways in which cognitive similarity has been conceptualized.

Although aggregated responses to Likert-type scales have also been used to operationalize structured cognition (e.g., Ensley & Pearce, 2001; Levesque et al., 2001), structured cognition is typically operationalized using structural assessments. One approach involves analyzing responses to paired comparison judgments using UCINET, Pathfinder, or MDS (e.g., Marks et al., 2002; Mathieu, Heffner, Goodwin, Salas, & Cannon-Bowers, 2000; Rentsch, Heffner, & Duffy, 1994; Rentsch & Klimoski, 2001). The advantage of these approaches is that the congruence of the structure of the cognition is evaluated. However, the degree or elevation of ratings along specific content dimensions is typically not addressed (see Rentsch, 1990, for an exception). Other techniques, such as concept maps (e.g., Carley, 1997; Marks, Zaccaro, & Mathieu, 2000; Marks et al., 2002; Rentsch et al., 1994) enable assessment of the degree of content and structural congruence among individuals.

In summary, in operationalizing perceptual and structured cognition, the complexity of the current measurement issues continues to present challenges for future researchers (e.g., Langan-Fox, Code, & Langfield, 2000; Mathieu, Heffner, Goodwin, Cannon-Bowers, & Salas, 2005; Mohammed, Klimoski, & Rentsch, 2000). The operationalization within the perceptual approach reveals more information about content, whereas the structured assessment approach reveals greater insight into structure. The ability to differentiate between these two features enables researchers to articulate the variable of interest clearly and to achieve close alignment between conceptualizations and operationalizations. However, each approach has traded off information about content or structure in favor of the other. Thus, both are lacking to some degree. It is important to note that, because cognition is aimed at understanding, interpreting, and attributing meaning to stimuli, cognitive content and structure are entangled in the assessment process (Rentsch & Small, 2007). Because the ability to differentiate between these two features enables researchers to articulate the variable of interest clearly and to achieve close alignment between conceptualizations and operationalizations, future studies should attempt to bridge the existing research gap by explicitly examining specific cognitive content and structure. Next, research related to this emerging area is highlighted and related to several areas for further research.

MOVING TOWARD COGNITIVE SIMILARITY CONFIGURATIONS

Currently, perceptual and structured research approaches remain separate. However, in combination, they may present potent understanding. These forms of cognition are important, and for the purposes of this chapter, the generic term *cognitive similarity* will be used to refer to meanings and interpretations (including perceptual and structured cognition) that are alike among individuals and that individuals apply to make sense of, attribute meaning to, and interpret internal and external events including affect, behavior, and thoughts of self and others (Rentsch, Small, et al., 2008). Following convention, cognitive similarity at the team level is referred to as team cognition.

Rentsch, Delise, et al. (2008) urged researchers to clearly articulate the type of cognitive similarity under investigation regardless of the level of analysis. Cognitive similarity types are defined by the content domain of the cognition, the form of cognition, and the form of similarity. First, as described earlier, the content domain of the cognition must be identified to specify a type of cognitive similarity, and for the most part, researchers do a good job of specifying the cognition content domain. Second, conceptualization or form of cognition is critical in defining a specific type of cognitive similarity. As described earlier, the form of cognition may be perceptual (e.g., beliefs) or structured (e.g., schemas), and it may take other forms, such as interpretive. Third, the form of the "similarity" should be specified. For example, cognitions between individuals may be congruent, accurate, complementary, and so on. Congruent cognitions are those that match when there is no target. Within the perceptual conceptualization, "shared" or "agreement" is used to refer to the congruence of cognition among individuals. Within the structured cognition perspective, researchers who studied schema preferred the term "similar" to identify cognitions among team members that were somehow alike, whereas those who studied team mental models preferred the term "shared" to refer to congruent cognitions. Accurate cognitions exist to the extent cognitions match a target. Accurate schemas (Jenkins & Rentsch, 1995) and accurate mental models (Smith-Jentsch, Mathieu, & Kraiger, 2005) have been studied to examine accurate cognitions. Complementary cognitions exist when team members contribute unique cognitions to the whole. These

152 • *Theories of Team Cognition*

cognitive contributions fit together like puzzle pieces (e.g., team members contribute unique expertise to solve problems). In addition, cognitions among individuals may be similar in other ways.

Researchers have done well to articulate cognitive similarity types, which are defined by the intersection of form of similarity (e.g., congruent or accurate), form of cognition (e.g., perceptual or structured), and content domain (e.g., creativity or teamwork; Rentsch, Small, et al., 2008). However, additional research is needed to theorize about and empirically examine cognition similarity configurations, which are combinations of cognitive similarity types (Rentsch, Small, et al., 2008). For example, a cognitive similarity configuration that includes complementary schemas of the task, accurate perceptions of team members' areas of expertise, and congruent interpretations of team members' interaction may increase a cross-functional team's effectiveness (Rentsch & Staniewicz, 2012).

Additional theoretical work is needed to guide future research. We urge theorists to develop models that include specific cognitive similarity types and configurations. The relevance of cognitive similarity types will likely depend on team type, membership (e.g., rotating, diverse, expert), work cycles, and team development. Challenges to be addressed by this work will likely include issues related to multiple and dynamic cognitive similarity configurations associated with various outcomes. Although additional specific theory is needed, research is moving toward cognitive similarity configurations. In the next section, we highlight research conducted on various types of cognitive similarity. Although much is being learned about cognitive similarity using these approaches, little systematic work has been done to examine cognitive similarity configurations. However, there has been a trend toward this type of approach, and samples of those efforts are highlighted.

ASSESSING COGNITIVE SIMILARITY

Perceptual Approach

The perceptual approach has been used at the dyad, team, unit, or organizational level. Within the team literature, Colquitt et al. (2002) examined several antecedents (team size, demographic diversity, and team collectivism) and outcomes (team performance and absenteeism) of procedural justice climate at the team level of analysis. The researchers measured two forms of cognitive similarity, level (climate level) and consensus (climate strength). The procedural justice climate level was assessed as the group mean, whereas climate level was measured as the within-group variance. Team size and collectivism predicted climate level. In addition, climate level was shown to be related to both outcomes of interest: team performance and absenteeism. Team size and demographic diversity were revealed as significant antecedents of climate strength. Moreover, climate strength moderated the effect of climate level on both team performance and absenteeism.

Clearly, the example just provided demonstrates the importance of measuring more than one form of cognitive similarity. Different forms of similarity revealed further information about the relationships between team and/or organizational antecedents and outcomes. In the following sections, the discussion focuses primarily on studies performed at the organizational level of analysis with relevance to the team level of analysis.

The study by Colquitt et al. (2002) is just one example of the trend toward the study of cognitive configurations. However, there is even greater potential for this type of investigation. The perceptual approach has been used to examine cognitive similarity in a wide variety of organizations spanning the gamut of occupations from the military (Zohar & Tenne-Gazit, 2008) to the business, financial, manufacturing, and telecommunications industries (Dickson, Resick, & Hanges, 2006; Schneider, Salvaggio, & Subirats, 2002; Sorensen, 2002; van Dyck, Frese, Baer, & Sonnentag, 2005; Zohar & Luria, 2005). Within the variety of organizations and occupations, the cognitive content domains to be studied are potentially infinite. The cognitive content domains relevant to organizations can encompass knowledge regarding the individual, team members, the task, organizational members' actions and roles, leadership, national culture, appropriate responses to the environment, justice, innovation, and so on. Cognitive variables are expected to be predictive of outcome variables, and examples of those investigated in connection to organizational climate span a wide variety of domains depending on the researchers' scope. For example, the perceptual approach is taken to gain understanding of variables such as helping behaviors (Naumann & Bennett, 2000); behavior-dependent, on-the-job minor injury rates in groups (Zohar, 2000); and firm performance (Collins & Smith, 2006).

154 • *Theories of Team Cognition*

As mentioned earlier, the most common form of measurement connected to the perceptual approach is the use of aggregated scale scores. The typical climate survey measure is composed of anywhere from approximately 3 to 22 items measured on 5- to 7-point scales (e.g., Dickson et al., 2006; Gonzalez-Roma et al., 2002; Zohar & Luria, 2005). Forms of cognition are developed based on these data. Climate level is operationalized as the aggregated ratings of climate perception for a particular aspect of performance. To justify aggregation, the researchers must demonstrate a sound theoretical basis or rationale for their use. Subsequently, agreement among raters must be established, which is usually accomplished by computing interrater agreement indices (e.g., intraclass correlations and/or r_{wg}). Researchers must observe within-group agreement to justify aggregation to the unit or organizational level. After meeting these stated conditions, the ratings are then aggregated to form the organizational climate level indices (e.g., Dickson et al., 2006; Zohar & Tenne-Gazit, 2008). These indices provide an assessment of level but do not reflect degree of similarity.

More recently, climate strength has become of interest. Climate strength is a measure of within-group variability in climate perceptions. Climate strength refers to the employees' perceptual agreement (variability), and it is generally operationalized as the standard deviation in employees' perceptions. Climate strength adds another component to our understanding of teams and organizations. Rather than climate level, climate strength recognizes individual differences (e.g., in beliefs, attitudes, values). These individual differences play an important part in determining members' climate perceptions. Additionally, climate strength does not necessarily have the same correlates as climate level. Moreover, climate strength has also been shown to moderate climate level, such that level effects are stronger when climates are strong rather than when they are weak (Lindell & Brandt, 2000).

The focus of measurement in the studies of interest is another aspect that deserves closer attention. Regardless of content domain, the obtained aggregated scores are a reflection of the perceptual content covered in the items. According to James, James, and Ashe (1990), climate is a product of personal values and remains a property of the individuals, whereas culture is engendered by system values and is a property of the collective. Glisson and James (2002) point out the importance of items clearly noting the point of reference. According to the researchers, depending on the referent being rated, either shared perceptions (climate) or normative beliefs and shared expectations (culture) are measured. Because perceptions (climate) originate within individuals, items should clearly reference the individual (e.g., "I feel that..."). Conversely, because the normative beliefs (culture) are a function of the organization, the items should reference the group or organization (e.g., "Members of organizational unit encourage safety behaviors"). Although some researchers followed this principle (Zohar, 2000), others did not (Anderson & West, 1998). Future research studies should heed the call of Glisson and James (2002) and clearly delineate the focus of their investigation (individual or group). The results should be interpreted at the same level as the unit of measurement. When using aggregate measures to observe group differences, the interpretation of the results should be at the group level.

Cognitive similarity in teams is more apt to be studied under controlled conditions using lab experiments, whereas organizational or unit-level studies are necessarily performed in their naturally occurring environments. It is important that the instruments be tailored for the specific organizations under study. Furthermore, there are numerous factors that need to be accounted for, measured, and controlled in order to eliminate contamination. The majority of studies mentioned control for some types of such variables. However, researchers should be cautious in their degree of generalization of the results.

Structured Approach

The majority of studies investigating cognitive structure are currently being performed at the team level of analysis. For example, Marks et al. (2002) studied shared team-interaction mental models. Mental model similarity was defined as the extent to which mental models are shared among team members. Team members were asked to provide pair comparison relatedness ratings for 10 "critical task concepts" (e.g., "identify enemy," "adjust speed"). Using Pathfinder, the researchers computed the "C" statistic, which was used as an index of team mental model similarity. The results of the study confirmed that higher levels of shared knowledge regarding team interaction resulted in better coordination.

Studies of cognitive structure can focus on any number of variables. For example, studies of structured cognition have the potential to investigate the causal, relational, and explanatory linkages among cognitive content

156 • *Theories of Team Cognition*

nodes. Typically, individuals provide data regarding the connections between these content nodes (e.g., card sorts, paired comparison ratings). These data are analyzed in comparison with analogous data from others on the team (or in the organizational unit), and the similarity of their cognitive structures is computed. It is possible to analyze characteristics of the structure using measures of directionality, centrality, and density, which have not received much research attention. Forms of content typically investigated in the structural approach include team- or task-relevant content. For example, with respect to teamwork, it is proposed that individuals develop mental models of team characteristics such as its purpose, connections between members' actions and roles, and the necessary actions needed to complete the team's collective task (Marks et al., 2002).

Schema structure similarity has been studied in connection with multiple outcomes such as team satisfaction (Mason & Griffin, 2003), team effectiveness (Kirkman et al., 2001), absenteeism (Colquitt et al., 2002), and helping behavior (Naumann & Bennett, 2000). Schema centrality and schema density have not been the subject of much investigation in team research; however, they represent opportunities for future work on cognitive similarity. Assessing cognitive structure is difficult, and the most common measurement issues associated with the structural approach are related to the topics of researcher bias, item numbers, and data collection methods (e.g., Langan-Fox et al., 2000; Mohammed et al., 2000).

Researcher bias is of concern in relation to the items chosen to be included in comparison ratings. Because the items are not always generated by research subjects, and thus sometimes they are researcher provided, a certain level of care should be ensured during their selection. The items should demonstrate a clear content relevance and should be comparable to previously validated measures. However, unlike other measurement techniques, one of the advantages of using MDS and Pathfinder is the minimization of researcher influence on data manipulation. Pathfinder, for example, has a built-in measure, the coherence coefficient, that detects a participant's cognitive inability or unwillingness to respond appropriately to the scale items. Very low coherence coefficients (less than 0.20) indicate that participants did not (or could not) take the rating task seriously (Schvaneveldt, 1990) or that they had no well-formed schema (i.e., novice). Such an index is useful in identifying haphazardly provided ratings that can be eliminated from the analyses.

The number of items to be included in the scales should also be carefully considered. The number of items varies. However, 15 items are generally sufficient. This allows for enough items in order to map the cognitive structure of interest while at the same time minimizing participants' fatigue while making ratings. To obtain the comparison ratings, the items of interest are presented either side by side or in a grid/matrix format. One of the concerns posed is that the matrix format may be too cognitively complex and participants may prefer a more intuitive type of question presentation (side-by-side paired comparisons). Although the matrix format may require more detailed instructions and guidance, the side-by-side comparisons may "feel" like more work is required on the part of the subjects. The choice of format should also take into consideration the population of interest. The matrix format may not be appropriate in certain cultures and/or for younger participants. There are advantages and disadvantages to both formats, and the choice ultimately rests with the researcher who must make an informed decision (Mot, 2008).

Summary

In summary, to assess cognitive similarity configurations, each cognitive similarity type may be assessed using a different methodology. Thus, assessing configurations will involve a variety of assessment techniques potentially including variance or interrater agreement indices (e.g., r_{wg}, coefficient of variation, standard deviation) of perceptual agreement, and structural assessments involving complex analyses (e.g., network, MDS, or Pathfinder analyses). In addition, theoretical specificity should be developed based on research drawn from a wide variety of domains.

POTENTIAL LINKAGES BETWEEN COGNITIVE SIMILARITY CONFIGURATIONS AND TEAM VARIABLES

Organizational and team researchers within each approach are beginning to consider cognitive similarity configurations. Several examples are provided in this section. It should be noted that a common terminology

158 • *Theories of Team Cognition*

is being developed. For example, climate quality and climate level refer to the level of cognitive similarity and are usually operationalized as the group mean climate rating. Climate strength and climate consensus refer to cognitive consensus and are measured by group variability on the climate measures of interest.

Gonzalez-Roma et al. (2002) investigated the relationship between three facets of climate strength (innovation, goal orientation, and support) and work unit social interactions. Climate strength was conceptualized as "the degree of within-unit agreement among unit members' climate perceptions" (Gonzalez-Roma et al., 2002, p. 465), or cognitive consensus. Social interaction between work unit members was significantly correlated with climate strength in goals orientation and innovation, but not in support. Moreover, climate strength/cognitive consensus moderated the relationship between a unit's score on climate scales and the aggregate work satisfaction and organizational commitment.

Climate, more specifically safety climate, has also been investigated in relation to on-the-job injury rates (Zohar, 2000). After controlling for hazard/risk level, team-level safety climate predicted behavior-dependent injury rates in groups. Subsequently, Zohar and Tenne-Gazit (2008) concluded that the density of the group communication network mediates the relationship between transformational leadership and climate strength (or cognitive consensus). The researchers also found support for the incremental effects on climate strength over transformational leadership exerted by group centralization of the communication (negative relationship) and friendship networks (positive relationship).

Dickson et al. (2006) investigated two antecedents of climate strength: mechanistic and organic organizational forms. After controlling for societal and industry differences, they found that mechanistic (rather than organic) organizational forms resulted in greater climate strength. Moreover, clearly defined organizational forms, regardless of type, resulted in greater climate strength than ambiguous ones. Shared values were found to moderate the relationship between climate level and climate strength.

Each of the studies just described portray different correlates for one type of cognitive similarity, namely consensus. However, numerous studies are also concerned with the interplay between cognitive consensus (agreement), the level of cognitive similarity (or shared perceptions), and other variables of interest.

For example, Zohar and Luria (2005) performed a multilevel (group and organizational) study of safety climate. Group climate level (or the level of group shared perceptions) was found to mediate the relationship between organizational climate (cognitive similarity level) and safety behavior. Higher constraints placed on supervisors to implement formal organizational procedures moderated the relationship between organizational climate strength (cognitive consensus) resulting from procedural coherence and group climate strength (cognitive consensus). Between groups, climate variability in organizations was negatively related to organization climate strength and procedural formalization.

Lindell and Brandt (2000) also assessed the interaction between the two different types of cognitive similarity. The researchers assessed both cognitive similarity types based on the answers to one climate scale. Climate quality was assessed by computing the average climate ratings, and climate consensus was assessed by computing the variance of the climate ratings. It was expected that both quality (cognitive similarity level) and consensus (cognitive consensus) would be related to external contextual variables (e.g., community resources and elected official support for local emergency planning committees [LEPCs]) and internal structural variables (e.g., role formalization and meeting frequency of LEPCs). The researchers found that climate quality (e.g., leader consideration, team coordination, team pride) was related to several contextual variables (e.g., support from elected officials) and internal structural variables (e.g., meeting formalization). Moreover, climate quality was shown not to be affected by organizational size, thereby suggesting that in organizations such as the one in this study, adding more members would not have an undesirable effect on organizational climate. Although climate quality was shown to mediate the relationship between some antecedents (e.g., subcommittees) and outcomes (job satisfaction) completely, climate consensus did not. The lack of unique contribution by climate consensus in predicting both individual- and organizational-level outcomes is puzzling. The researchers noted that the results were atypical and could be due to the nature of the groups under study (volunteer groups). Therefore, besides providing the different interconnected relationships for climate quality, Lindell and Brandt's (2000) study points out the possibility that cognitive consensus (climate consensus) may not uniquely contribute to the prediction

160 • *Theories of Team Cognition*

of individual- and organizational-level outcomes in organizations and groups where interdependence of tasks is not required or essential.

Smith-Jentsch et al. (2005) also investigated the effectiveness of two types of shared mental models (SMMs) in an air traffic control environment. The mental models were defined as the "organized understanding or mental representation of knowledge shared by team members" (Smith-Jentsch et al., 2005, p. 523) and were assessed through both consistency and agreement. The researchers investigated the consistency and agreement of two types of SMMs (positional-goal interdependencies and cue-strategy associations) and hypothesized that they would each be positively related to air traffic control tower safety and efficiency. Furthermore, they predicted that the two types of SMMs would interact with respect to both tower safety and tower efficiency. No effects were found for agreement. However, they observed the highest outcomes (efficiency and safety rates) when participants exhibited consistent SMMs of both types (positional-goal interdependencies and cue-strategy associations). Additionally, and quite unexpectedly, they also observed that it was better to have inconsistent rather than consistent mental models of both types.

In light of the previously mentioned studies, it is evident that similar cognitions at the organizational, unit level, or team levels have multiple correlates in terms of outcomes. For example, a climate for safety, goal orientation, innovation, or support provides valuable pieces of information with regard to multiple organizational outcomes.

Within the organizational arena, Schulte et al. (2009) examined the relationships between different configurations of unit-level climate dimensions and different internal (e.g., employee affect and intentions to stay) and external (e.g., customer satisfaction and financial performance) organizational outcomes. The results of their studies emphasized the need to take into consideration the effects of multiple climate dimensions, taken together as a higher order system. The researchers examined elevation, variability, and the shape of climate configurations. Four different climate shapes emerged through cluster analysis. The researchers received support for the hypothesized relationships. Overall, climate elevation (overall score across climate dimensions) was strongly related to internal effectiveness outcomes (e.g., employee affect) but not to external effectiveness outcomes. Conversely, climate shape was related to external outcomes (e.g., customer satisfaction and financial performance) but not to internal employee-centered effectiveness outcomes. The results of this study underline the importance of considering the different climate profile characteristics and their different effects on internal and external outcomes. Considering the overall organizational climate system provides information above and beyond that provided by individual climate dimensions.

MDS has been applied by Rentsch et al. (1994) in schema research in teams. In their study, the researchers endeavored to ascertain the connections between teamwork schemas and team experience by using MDS and freehand-generated schemas. The researchers demonstrated that individuals with higher experience working in teams (experts) tended to organize knowledge systematically and to chunk more information in memory than individuals with limited team experience (novices). Relative to novices, experts were able to acquire information more quickly and easily, and their schemas were characterized as deep and multileveled with many connections between and within levels. Novices, however, possessed shallow schemas consisting of many details connected to a few general ideas and tended to categorize problems based on concrete surface features. In summary, the researchers showed that experts tended to converge on concepts and novices did not.

Mathieu et al. (2000) investigated the effect of team members' shared team and task mental models on team performance and team processes. Mental model convergence (level of sharedness) was assessed using online, individually completed, paired comparison matrices analyzed using UCINET. Both types of mental models were positively related to team processes and performance. Moreover, the researchers substantiated the fact that the relationship between mental model convergence and team effectiveness was fully mediated by team processes.

Marks et al. (2000) examined the impact of leader briefings and team interaction training on team member knowledge structures related to routine and novel environment effective performance. The researchers investigated both the similarity and the accuracy of mental models. Similarity was defined as the extent to which "mental models are shared among team members," and accuracy was defined as "the correctness of the knowledge structures maintained by team members" (Marks et al., 2000, p. 973). Concept mapping was used to assess the participants' knowledge structures. Knowledge structure similarity was calculated by assessing the overlap in the concepts selected by each team member. Knowledge structure accuracy was assessed by judges. The researchers found that

162 • *Theories of Team Cognition*

both manipulations (briefings and training) affected the development of mental models. Consequently, the mental models were positively related to team communication processes and team performance. Performance was better predicted by mental models in novel rather than in routine environments, thus emphasizing the fact that the strength of the relationship between mental models and various outcomes of interest may differ based on environmental factors.

Most structural studies focus solely on the interconnectedness of mental model content nodes. Just as perceptual studies have provided an abundance of antecedents and outcomes of organizational members' cognitive consensus and agreement, structural researchers have scrutinized the different mental model contents, number of links, antecedents, susceptibility or resistance to training, outcomes, and so on. Although, the number of studies investigating cognitive similarity is growing, the void between the perceptual and the structured approaches has not been bridged.

DEVELOPING COGNITIVE SIMILARITY CONFIGURATIONS: BRIDGING PAST AND FUTURE RESEARCH

Evidence of potential cognitive configurations is emerging in the literature. For example, procedural justice climate strength moderated the effect of climate level on team performance and absenteeism (Colquitt et al., 2002). Schema structure similarity has connected with team satisfaction (Mason & Griffin, 2003), team effectiveness (Kirkman et al., 2001), absenteeism (Colquitt et al., 2002), and helping behavior (Naumann & Bennett, 2000). Perhaps these cognitive types form a useful configuration that explains team performance, absence, process, and attitudes.

In addition, the examples provided in the previous sections illustrate the potential for increased understanding offered by the study of cognitive configurations for teams and organizations. Recently, the notion has been applied to the study of multiteam systems. A component team within a multiteam system may rely on configurations of cognitive similarity as coordinating mechanisms, and these configurations may be related to the nature of the interdependence among team members. For example, team members who have reciprocal process interdependence may benefit by possessing complementary task schemas (i.e., team members understand the task in complementary ways) such that team members are able to make unique contributions to the task. However, these complementary cognitions may be useful only to the extent they are coordinated by team members also possessing congruent schemas regarding the teamwork process (e.g., agreeing on how to work effectively with others on the team; Rentsch & Staniewicz, 2012).

Another example is hypothesized with respect to problem-solving teams in which conflict is likely to occur due to team members misinterpreting their teammates' behaviors (Baron, 1997; Ensley & Pearce, 2001). For example, when team members disagree with one another or express opposing opinions, some members may believe they are being personally attacked, when in fact, these types of behaviors are aimed at creating integrative problem solutions. A cognitive configuration that contains congruent teamwork schemas that interpret debate, openness, and so on as behaviors that support collaborative decision making and accurate team member schemas that contain knowledge regarding teammates' expertise and preferences may alleviate misinterpretations and facilitate team effectiveness in decision-making teams (Rentsch & Zelno, 2003). In terms of facilitating team problem solving, one of these types of cognitive similarity alone will most likely not be as effective as the configuration including both types.

Cognitive similarity configurations consist of cognitive domains, forms of cognition, and similarity forms. As described earlier, a trend toward studying cognitive configurations is beginning to emerge. Also obvious from previous discussion is the realization that the perceptual and structured approaches tend to operate within reach of each other with little cross-fertilization.

Cognitive Content Domains

Clearly, cognitive content domain is limitless. However, aspects of cognitive domains should be articulated to better define the content of cognitions. One notion of cognitive content reflects a network of organized knowledge structures. Thus, cognitive content domain perhaps is best described as the dense, well-organized, or as Rentsch and Small (2007) put it, the "more solidly constructed" (p. 165) portion of the cognitive structure—that is,

164 • *Theories of Team Cognition*

that portion of the knowledge structure that contains concentrated knowledge or interpretive information related to a given content domain. The challenge for researchers is to define the qualitative aspect of the content (e.g., cognition about leadership, teams, or justice) and to define the relevant underlying dimensions of the content domain (e.g., degree of abstraction, level of articulation [depth], breadth, functionality, stability, and malleability).

For example, the stability of domains may vary. Perhaps newcomers' cognitive content regarding leadership is malleable upon entry to a new organization. As they begin to obtain information about leadership in the organization, their understanding about leadership may change. Perhaps they enter the organization defining leadership as facilitating and rewarding success, but learn that in that particular organization, "leadership" is defined by deceitful, unethical, demeaning, and defensive behaviors. Stability or malleability of cognitive content may be indicative of commitment or adaptability.

Quality or functionality of cognitive content is another feature that should be addressed (e.g., Mathieu et al., 2005; Rentsch & Hall, 1994). Similarity of dysfunctional cognitive content will be predictive of different outcomes than functional content. Furthermore, the content considered functional or dysfunctional may depend on the context. For example, competitiveness may be functional in some contexts but dysfunctional within a university management department.

Forms of Cognition

Perceptual and structured cognition are only two forms of cognition. Rentsch, Delise, et al. (2008) also described interpretative cognition. Processes related to cognition may also be of interest. Clearly, the form of cognition should be articulated, but in addition, the underlying feature of the cognition may also be of theoretical interest. For example, structured cognition may be defined in terms of the degree of differentiation that characterizes the structure. Differentiated cognitive structures are characteristic of cognitive complexity. Centrality is a feature of cognitive structures that has been examined. For example, the centrality of specific concepts in schemas of leadership is related to culture differences (Hanges, Dorfman, Shteynberg, & Bates, 2006; Hanges et al., 2001; Mot, 2008; Nishii, Gelfand, Ang, Lange, & Taveesin, 2004).

Elaborating Cognition in Teams • 165

Schema structure density and the directionality or causality of linkages will also provide additional information regarding understanding and meaning that is currently not being addressed in the team cognition research. For example, a very dense structure would consist of many connections among all or most content nodes, reflecting a high degree of integration among concepts in the content domain. This may also be indicative of cognitive flexibility. Several of the features that may be related to cognitive flexibility require advanced measurement techniques and research designs in order to address the dynamic aspect of the cognition. A single measurement approach may miss important features of the cognition.

Forms of Similarity

As discussed earlier, similarity may take many forms including congruent, accurate, and complementary forms. Most research focuses on congruence and accuracy (for an exception, see Mohammed & Ringseis, 2001). Other forms include those that may be derived from other theories such as the social relations model (Rentsch & Woehr, 2004), a theory of person perception. Within the social relations model, person perceptions are differentiated based on influences due to the perceiver, the target, and the interaction of the perceiver and the target (Kenny, 1994). Using the social relations model, interesting questions relevant to team cognition can be generated (Rentsch & Woehr, 2004), such as questions related to meta-accuracy (e.g., do team members know how they are perceived by their teammates?) and reciprocity (e.g., do team members perceive each other in the same manner?).

In addition to qualitatively different forms of similarity, dimensions associated with the form of similarity should be articulated. The perceptual approach has made some strides in this area by examining profiles of perceptions that capture the elevation, variability, and salience/strength (e.g., Colquitt et al., 2002; Xie & Johns, 2000). However, we urge researchers to push even more in this area. For example, similarity with respect to cognitive structures may be described in terms of stability, reliability, variability, salience, consensus, and strength. Specific cognitive similarity profile shapes may be highly predictive of specific outcomes. In addition, all forms of similarity may be related to various cognitive forms (e.g., perceptual, structured, interpretive)

166 • *Theories of Team Cognition*

and various cognitive content domains (e.g., work environment, task, equipment, rewards).

AIMING FOR THE FUTURE

Cognitive similarity has been established as a useful predictor in the literature, as is evidenced by the research cited in this chapter. The challenge is to fully articulate and examine its potential. Meeting theoretical and methodological challenges will require researchers to triangulate on team cognition using multiple conceptualizations and methods. Future research should explore the usefulness of cognitive similarity configurations for predicting specific outcomes. For example, various sets of cognitive similarity configurations may have differential significant effects on specific input, process, and outcome variables. Boundary and contextual variables, such as team type and team development, will play major roles in theories that include cognitive similarity configurations. Questions to be addressed include: What are the best "shapes" or sets of cognitive similarity configurations in predicting specific variables and their relations in specific types of teams at specific levels of development? What are the optimal levels of each form of similarity? Many such questions require investigation, and addressing them will result in a fine-grained understanding of teams.

ACKNOWLEDGMENT

The contribution of Joan R. Rentsch was funded in part by Office of Naval Research Award No. N00014-05-1-0624.

REFERENCES

Anderson, N. R., & West, M. A. (1998). Measuring climate for work group innovation: Development and validation of the team climate inventory. *Journal of Organizational Behavior, 19*, 235–258.

Austin, J. R. (2003). Transactive memory in organizational groups: The effects of content, consensus, specialization, and accuracy on group performance. *Journal of Applied Psychology, 88*, 866–878.

Bain, P. G., Mann, L., & Pirola-Merlo, A. (2001). The innovation imperative: The relationships between team climate, innovation, and performance in R&D teams. *Small Group Research, 32*, 55–73.

Baron, R. A. (1997). Positive effects of conflict: Insights from social cognition. In C. K. W. De Dreu, & E. Van de Vliert (Eds.), *Using conflict in organizations* (pp. 177–191). London, UK: Sage Publications.

Beersma, B., & De Dreu, C. K. W. (2002). Integrative and distributive negotiation in small groups: Effects of task structure, decision rule, and social motive. *Organizational Behavior and Human Decision Processes, 87*, 227–252.

Berger, P. L., & Luckmann, T. (1966). *The social construction of reality*. New York, NY: Doubleday.

Cannon, M. D., & Edmondson, A. C. (2001). Confronting failure: Antecedents and consequences of shared beliefs about failure in organizational work groups. *Journal of Organizational Behavior, 22*, 161–177.

Cannon-Bowers, J. A., Salas, E., & Converse, S. A. (1993). Shared mental models in expert team decision making. In N. J. Castellan, Jr. (Ed.), *Individual and group decision making: Current issues* (pp. 221–246). Hillsdale, NJ: Erlbaum.

Carley, K. M. (1997). Extracting team mental models through textual analysis. *Journal of Organizational Behavior, 18*, 533–558.

Chen, G., & Bliese, P. D. (2002). The role of different levels of leadership in predicting self- and collective efficacy: Evidence for discontinuity. *Journal of Applied Psychology, 87*, 549–556.

Choi, J. N., Price, R. H., & Vinokur, A. D. (2003). Self-efficacy changes in groups: Effects of diversity, leadership, and group climate. *Journal of Organizational Behavior, 24*, 357–372.

Collins, C. J., & Smith, K. G. (2006). Knowledge exchange and combination: The role of human resource practices in the performance of high-technology firms. *Academy of Management Journal, 49*, 544–560.

Colquitt, J. A., Noe, R. A., & Jackson, C. L. (2002). Justice in teams: Antecedents and consequences of procedural justice climate. *Personnel Psychology, 55*, 83–109.

Dickson, M. W., Resick, C. J., & Hanges, P. J. (2006). When organizational climate is unambiguous, it is also strong. *Journal of Applied Psychology, 91*, 351–364.

Dyer, J. L. (1984). Team research and team training: A state-of-the-art review. In F. A. Muckler (Ed.), *Human factors review* (pp. 285–323). Santa Monica, CA: The Human Factors Society, Inc.

Earley, P. C., & Mosakowski, E. (2000). Creating hybrid team cultures: An empirical test of transnational team functioning. *Academy of Management Journal, 43*, 26–49.

Ensley, M. D., & Pearce, C. L. (2001). Shared cognition in top management teams: Implications for new venture performance. *Journal of Organizational Behavior, 22*, 145–160.

Gibson, C. B. (2003). The efficacy advantage: Factors related to the formation of group efficacy. *Journal of Applied Social Psychology, 33*, 2153–2186.

Glisson, C., & James, L. R. (2002). The cross-level effects of culture and climate in human service teams. *Journal of Organizational Behavior, 23*, 767–794.

Gonzalez-Roma, V., Peiro, J. M., & Tordera, N. (2002). An examination of the antecedents and moderator influences of climate strength. *Journal of Applied Psychology, 87*, 465–473.

Hanges, P. J., Dorfman, P. W., Shteynberg, G., & Bates, A. L. (2006). Culture and leadership: A connectionist information processing model. *Advances in Global Leadership, 4*, 7–37.

168 • *Theories of Team Cognition*

Hanges, P. J., Higgins, M., Dyer, N. G., Smith-Major, V., Dorfman, P. W., Brodbeck, F. C., et al. (2001, April). *Influence of cultural values on leadership schema structure.* Paper presented at the 16th Annual Society of Industrial and Organizational Psychology Conference, San Diego, CA.

Hofmann, D. H., Morgeson, F. P., & Gerras, S. J. (2003). Climate as a moderator of the relationship between LMX and content specific citizenship: Safety climate as an exemplar. *Journal of Applied Psychology, 88,* 170–178.

Isabella, L. A., & Waddock, S. A. (1994). Top management team certainty: Environmental assessments, teamwork, and performance implications. *Journal of Management, 20,* 835–858.

James, L. R., James, L. A., & Ashe, D. K. (1990). The meaning of organizations: The role of cognition and values. In B. Schneider (Ed.), *Organizational climate and culture* (pp. 40–84). San Francisco, CA: Jossey-Bass.

Jenkins, N. M., & Rentsch, J. R. (1995, May). *The effects of teamwork schema similarity on team performance and fairness perceptions.* Paper presented at the annual meeting of the Society for Industrial and Organizational Psychology, Orlando, FL.

Kenny, D. A. (1994). Using the social relations model to understand relationships. In R. Erber & R. Gilmour (Eds.), *Theoretical frameworks for personal relationships* (pp. 111–127). Hillsdale, NJ: Lawrence Erlbaum.

Kirkman, B. L., Tesluk, P. E., & Rosen, B. (2001). Assessing the incremental validity of team consensus ratings over aggregation of individual-level data in predicting team effectiveness. *Personnel Psychology, 54,* 645–667.

Langan-Fox, J., Code, S., & Langfield, K. (2000). Team mental models: Techniques, methods, and analytic approaches. *Human Factors, 42,* 242–271.

Levesque, L. L., Wilson, J. M., & Wholey, D. R. (2001). Cognitive divergence and shared mental models in software development project teams. *Journal of Organizational Behavior, 22,* 135–144.

Lindell, M. K., & Brandt, C. J. (2000). Climate quality and climate consensus as mediators of the relationship between organizational antecedents and outcomes. *Journal of Applied Psychology, 85,* 331–348.

Marks, M. A., Sabella, M. J., Burke, C. S., & Zaccaro, S. J. (2002). The impact of cross-training on team effectiveness. *Journal of Applied Psychology, 87,* 3–13.

Marks, M. A., Zaccaro, S. J., & Mathieu, J. E. (2000). Performance implications of leader briefings and team-interaction training for team adaptation to novel environments. *Journal of Applied Psychology, 85,* 971–986.

Mason, C. M., & Griffin, M. A. (2003). Identifying group task satisfaction at work. *Small Group Research, 34,* 413–442.

Mathieu, J. E., Heffner, T. S., Goodwin, G. F., Cannon-Bowers, J. A., & Salas, E. (2005). Scaling the quality of teammates' mental models: Equifinality and normative comparisons. *Journal of Organizational Behavior, 26,* 37–56.

Mathieu, J. E., Heffner, T. S., Goodwin, G. F., Salas, E., & Cannon-Bowers, J. A. (2000). The influence of shared mental models on team process and performance. *Journal of Applied Psychology, 85,* 273–283.

Mohammed, S., Klimoski, R., & Rentsch, J. R. (2000). The measurement of team mental models: We have no shared schema. *Organizational Research Methods, 3,* 123–165.

Mohammed, S., & Ringseis, E. (2001). Cognitive diversity and consensus in group decision making: The role of inputs, processes, and outcomes. *Organizational Behavior and Human Decision Processes, 85,* 310–335.

Elaborating Cognition in Teams • 169

Mot, I. R. (2008). *Conceptualizations of teamwork and leadership: A cross-cultural analysis.* Unpublished doctoral dissertation, The University of Tennessee, Knoxville.

Naumann, S. E., & Bennett, N. (2000). A case for procedural justice climate: Development and test of a multilevel model. *Academy of Management Journal, 43,* 881–889.

Naumann, S. E., & Bennett, N. (2002). The effects of procedural justice climate on work group performance. *Small Group Research, 33,* 361–377.

Nieva, V. F., Fleishman, E. A., & Reick, A. (1985). *Team dimensions: Their identity, their measurement, and their relationships.* Washington, DC: Advanced Research Resources Organization.

Nishii, L. H., Gelfand, M. J., Ang, S., Lange, S., & Taveesin, J. (2004). *Culture, systems of thought, and leadership: Holistic and analytical thinking and the structure of leadership schemas in the U.S., Germany, Singapore, and Thailand.* Unpublished manuscript.

Pirola-Merlo, A., & Mann, L. (2004). The relationship between individual creativity and team creativity: Aggregating across people and across time. *Journal of Organizational Behavior, 25,* 235–257.

Rentsch, J. R. (1990). Climate and culture: Interaction and qualitative differences in organizational meanings. *Journal of Applied Psychology, 75,* 668–681.

Rentsch, J. R., Delise, L. A., & Hutchison, S. (2008). Cognitive similarity configurations in teams: In search of the team mindmeld. In E. Salas, G. F. Goodwin, & C. S. Burke (Eds.), *Team effectiveness in complex organizations: Cross-disciplinary perspectives and approaches* (pp. 241–266). New York, NY: Routledge.

Rentsch, J. R., & Hall, R. J. (1994). Members of great teams think alike: A model of team effectiveness and schema similarity among team members. In M. M. Beyerlein, D. A. Johnson, & S. T. Beyerlein (Eds.), *Advances in interdisciplinary studies of work teams: Theories of self-managing work teams* (Vol. 1, pp. 223–261). Greenwich, CT: JAI Press.

Rentsch, J. R., Heffner, T. S., & Duffy, L. T. (1994). What you know is what you get from experience: Team experience related to teamwork schemas. *Group and Organization Management, 19,* 450–474.

Rentsch, J. R., & Klimoski, R. J. (2001). Why do "great minds" think alike? Antecedents of team member schema agreement. *Journal of Organizational Behavior, 22,* 107–120.

Rentsch, J. R., & Small, E. E. (2007). Understanding team cognition: The shift to cognitive similarity configurations. In F. J. Yammarino & F. Dansereau (Eds.), *Research in multi-level issues* (Vol. 6, pp. 159–174). San Diego, CA: Elsevier.

Rentsch, J. R., Small, E. E., & Hanges, P. J. (2008). Cognitions in organizations and teams: What is the meaning of cognitive similarity? In B. Smith (Ed.), *The people make the place: Exploring dynamic linkages between individuals and organizations* (pp. 127–156). New York, NY: Lawrence Erlbaum Associates.

Rentsch, J. R., & Staniewicz, M. J. (2012). Cognitive similarity configurations in multi-team systems. In S. J. Zaccaro, L. DeChurch, & M. Marks (Eds.), *Multiteam systems: An organization form for dynamic and complex environments* (pp. 225–252). New York, NY: Taylor & Francis/Routledge.

Rentsch, J. R., & Woehr, D. J. (2004). Quantifying congruence in cognition: Social relations modeling and team member schema similarity. In E. Salas & S. M. Fiore (Eds.), *Team cognition: Understanding the factors that drive process and performance* (pp. 11–31). Washington, DC: American Psychological Association.

Rentsch, J. R., & Zelno, J. A. (2003). The role of cognition in managing conflict to maximize team effectiveness. In M. A. West, D. Tjosvold, & K. G. Smith (Eds.), *International handbook of organizational teamwork and cooperative working* (pp. 131–150). New York, NY: John Wiley & Sons.

170 • *Theories of Team Cognition*

Rouse, W. B., & Morris, N. M. (1986). On looking into the black box: Prospects and limits in the search for mental models. *Psychological Bulletin, 100,* 349–363.

Rumelhart, D. E. (1980). On evaluating story grammars. *Cognitive Science, 4,* 313–316.

Rumelhart, D. E., Smolensky, P., McClelland, J. L., & Hinton, G. E. (1988). Schemata and sequential thought processes in PDP models. In A. M. Collins & E. E. Smith (Eds.), *Readings in cognitive science: A perspective from psychology and artificial intelligence* (pp. 224–249). San Mateo, CA: Morgan Kaufmann, Inc.

Schneider, B. (1975). Organizational climates: An essay. *Personnel Psychology, 28,* 447–479.

Schneider, B. (1990). The climate for service: An application of the climate construct. In B. Schneider (Ed.), *Organizational climate and culture* (pp. 383–412), San Francisco, CA: Jossey-Bass.

Schneider, B., & Bartlett, C. J. (1968). Individual differences and organizational climates: 1. The research plan and questionnaire development. *Personnel Psychology, 11,* 323–333.

Schneider, B., & Reichers, A. E. (1983). On the etiology of climates. *Personnel Psychology, 36,* 19–39.

Schneider, B., Salvaggio, A. N., & Subirats, M. (2002). Climate strength: A new direction for climate research. *Journal of Applied Psychology, 87,* 220–229.

Schneider, B., White, B., & Paul, M. C. (1998). Linking service climate and customer perceptions of service quality: Tests of a causal model. *Journal of Applied Psychology, 83,* 150–163.

Schulte, M., Ostroff, C., Shmulyian, S., & Kinicki, A. (2009). Organizational climate configurations: Relationships to collective attitudes, customer satisfaction, and financial performance. *Journal of Applied Psychology, 94,* 618–634.

Schvaneveldt, R. W. (1990). *Pathfinder associative networks: Studies in knowledge organization.* Norwood, NJ: Ablex Publishing Corporation.

Smith-Jentsch, K. A., Mathieu, J. E., & Kraiger, K. (2005). Investigating linear and interactive effects of shared mental models on safety and efficiency in a field setting. *Journal of Applied Psychology, 90,* 523–535.

Sorensen, J. B. (2002). The strength of corporate culture and the reliability of firm performance. *Administrative Science Quarterly, 47,* 70–91.

van Dyck, C., Frese, M., Baer, M., & Sonnentag, S. (2005). Organizational error management culture and its impact on performance: A two-study replication. *Journal of Applied Psychology, 90,* 1228–1240.

Xie, J. L., & Johns, G. (2000). Interactive effects of absence culture salience and group cohesiveness: A multi-level and cross-level analysis of work absenteeism in the Chinese context. *Journal of Occupational and Organizational Psychology, 73,* 31–52.

Zohar, D. (2000). A group-level model of safety climate: Testing the effect of group climate on microaccidents in manufacturing jobs. *Journal of Applied Psychology, 85,* 587–596.

Zohar, D., & Luria, G. (2005). A multi-level model of safety climate: Cross-level relationships between organization and group-level climates. *Journal of Applied Psychology, 90,* 616–628.

Zohar, D., & Tenne-Gazit, O. (2008). Transformational leadership and group interaction as climate antecedents: A social network analysis. *Journal of Applied Psychology, 93,* 744–757.

Section III

Human Factors and Cognitive Engineering Pespectives

7

A Cognitive Systems Engineering Perspective on Shared Cognition: Coping With Complexity*

Emily S. Patterson and Robert J. Stephens

INTRODUCTION

In this chapter, we provide an overview of a cognitive systems engineering (CSE) perspective on shared cognition, including a set of team coordination patterns and factors that trigger them. From a CSE perspective, macrocognition is conducted by teams of humans supported by technological aids to effectively cope with complexity in the world. The term "macrocognition" is defined as "how cognition adapts to complexity" (Klein, 2010, p. 71; Klein et al., 2003). The "macro" in macrocognition emphasizes that the perspective is based on studying real-world settings across multiple individuals using tools and shared resources, as contrasted with microcognition, which is done "between the ears" of an isolated individual at a discrete point in time (Letsky, Warner, Fiore, & Smith, 2009; Roth, Woods, & Gallagher, 1986; Woods, 1987; Woods and Roth, 1986). We use the term "team" to cover a broad range of human–human–machine configurations, including physically and temporally distributed members, ad hoc groups that form and then disband once an objective has been met, and anonymous interactions with others who have common or interacting goals without any sense of shared identity.

The CSE perspective is bounded by the following assumptions (Patterson, Ebright, & Saleem, 2011):

---

* The views expressed are those of the authors and do not necessarily represent the views of the Office of Naval Research.

174 • *Theories of Team Cognition*

- The adaptation of cognition to complexity
- Coordinated to meet complex, dynamic demands
- In an uncertain, event-driven environment with conflicting goals and high consequences for failure
- Made possible by effective expertise in roles
- Shaped by organizational (blunt end) constraints
- That emergently generates phenomena that can be scientifically investigated at both the individual and team levels of analysis

Five macrocognition functions have been previously identified across a wide variety of settings (Klein et al., 2003; Patterson et al., 2011):

1. *Detecting:* This is noticing that events may be taking an unexpected (positive or negative) direction. This change requires explanation and might signal a need or opportunity to reframe how a situation is conceptualized (sensemaking) and/or revise ongoing plans (planning) in progress.
2. *Sensemaking:* This is collecting, corroborating, and assembling information and assessing how the information maps onto potential explanations. This includes generating new potential hypotheses to consider and revisiting previously discarded hypotheses in the face of new evidence.
3. *Planning:* This is adaptively responding to changes in objectives from supervisors and peers, obstacles, opportunities, events, or changes in predicted future trajectories. When ready-to-hand default plans are applicable, there is still a need to adapt a prespecified plan into actions within a window of opportunity. When ready-to-hand default plans are not applicable to the situation, this can include creating a new strategy for achieving one or more goals or desired end states. This function includes adapting procedures, based on possibly incomplete guidance, to an evolving situation where multiple procedures need to be coordinated, when not all procedures that have been started have been completed, or when steps in a procedure may occur out of sequence or interact with other actions. Executing a plan is never distinguished from replanning, even when the individual or team that generates a plan is different from the individuals or teams who perform the actions to execute it (Klein, 2007a, 2007b).

A Cognitive Systems Engineering Perspective on Shared Cognition • 175

4. *Deciding:* This is committing to one or more course of action options. The commitment may constrain the ability to reverse courses of action. This function is inherently a continuous process conducted under time pressure. It involves reexamining embedded default decisions in ongoing plan trajectories for the predicted impact on meeting objectives, including whether to sacrifice decisions to which agents were previously committed based on considering trade-offs. This function may involve a single individual or might require consensus across distributed actors with different stances toward decisions. This function is far more complex than classical discussions of decision making, including increased uncertainty about when a decision can be modified, the level of commitment to a future planned action, distributed perspectives with associated goal trade-off tendencies negotiating an agreement, and temporal dynamics, including rallying points, changes in the ability to modify an action, and impacts of changes to plans of other stakeholders (Hoffman & Yates, 2005).

5. *Coordinating:* This is managing interdependencies of activity and communication across individuals acting in roles that have common, overlapping, or interacting (and possibly conflicting) goals.

These macrocognitive functions can be triggered by events in the world, communication episodes, or internal cognitive processing. These functions are only partially decomposable. Therefore, although focusing on a particular function can be important for gaining traction in conducting research, there will still be a need to consider interactions with other activities, such as monitoring the environment for changes, adapting a procedure to fit the dynamic situation, interpreting the guidance of distant supervisors as to the intent of an original procedure that cannot be executed in order to adapt it, assessing whether a plan in progress can be done within the anticipated window of opportunity, coordinating the implementation of multiple procedures, and timing activities so that they do not negatively interact with other activities (Hollnagel & Woods, 2005; Woods & Hollnagel, 2006).

In this chapter, we focus on the coordinating function; propose a set of patterns that have been observed "in the wild" in multiple complex, sociotechnical settings; and suggest factors that trigger the patterns.

COORDINATING: THE CASE FOR DISTRIBUTING COGNITION

Coordinating is defined as managing interdependencies across multiple individuals acting in roles that have common, overlapping, or interacting goals. This definition is strongly influenced by coordination theory (Crowston, Rubleske, & Howison, 2006), which defines several aspects of coordination that must be managed in order for multiagent systems to be successful: shared resources, producer/consumer relationships (e.g., prerequisites), interdependency and synchronization, and task/subtask relationships.

Implicit in the definition is that coordinating is a "cost." If one individual does an entire task, then the need to manage interdependencies across individuals is eliminated. Therefore, one might ask: Why is coordinating a necessary, let alone desirable, function?

The CSE perspective reflects research performed in complex, sociotechnical domains where no one individual could physically conduct at one time all of the operations needed, such as nuclear power generation, aviation, and industrial process control. Many of the settings divide work into "shifts," which necessarily requires transferring responsibility across shift boundaries to allow personnel to sleep. Another common element is that these complex work environments have specialized practitioners performing distinct roles at different levels of expertise and capability. Distributing cognition across tasks can also balance workloads so that the capabilities of the systems as a whole are maximized and so that agents perceive that tasks are justly (relatively evenly) distributed across personnel resources. One of the benefits of distributing cognition is to better manage an efficient workflow; by having multiple individuals perform tasks simultaneously, workflow bottlenecks can be mitigated. Finally, an often overlooked benefit of distributing cognition is the ability for a "fresh perspective" to identify erroneous assumptions, plans, and actions (Patterson, Woods, Cook, & Render, 2007).

COORDINATION PATTERNS AND TRIGGERS

In this chapter, the main contribution is a set of coordinating patterns and factors that trigger them (Table 7.1). These patterns are similar in that they are all strategies to obtain benefits of coordinating while reducing costs.

A Cognitive Systems Engineering Perspective on Shared Cognition • 177

TABLE 7.1

Coordination Patterns, Triggers, and Examples

Pattern	Trigger	Example
Escalation of activity	Detection and communication to a group regarding an unusual or unexpected event.	Calling in additional personnel to manage an anomaly with the mechanical systems on the space shuttle.
Proactive investment in coming up to speed	Increased likelihood that a person will be impacted by the work of others.	Nurses participate in physician rounds.
Emergent workload balancing	People respond to signals that a person has a high workload by offering aid.	A nurse puts up a red flag on a medication cart to request voluntary support from other nurses.
Role-based communication	Increased potential for consequences for delay due to confusion about which individual is performing a particular role.	Health care personnel are called using a dedicated "code pager" to respond to heart attacks in a hospital.
Dropping or delaying lower priority tasks during bottlenecks	Judgment that a person is a bottleneck in workflow, prediction that a bottleneck period will occur in the future.	Documentation that a patient was discharged from the emergency department is delayed until after a new patient is admitted.
Reducing the priority of tasks that do not directly benefit the agent or reduce status or power	Perception that a task does not have an immediate personal benefit and/or signals a reduction in status or power.	A nurse does not document a justification for a late medication administration.
Increased communication during nonroutine events	Recognition that a future or current event is nonroutine, which increases uncertainty.	A new chemotherapy order written on the weekend triggers numerous communications to verify the plan.

Source: Adapted from Patterson, E. S., Woods, D. D., Sarter, N. B., & Watts-Perotti, J., COOP, '98, *Third International Conference on the Design of Cooperative Systems*. May 1998.

Pattern 1: Escalation of Activity

The pattern of escalation of activity is triggered by detection and communication to a group of agents regarding an unusual or unexpected event. This pattern can give rise to several problems because of a fundamental relationship: The greater the trouble in the underlying system or the higher

178 • *Theories of Team Cognition*

the tempo of operations, the greater the information processing activities required to cope with the trouble or pace of activities (Woods & Patterson, 2001). For example, demands for monitoring, attentional control, information, and communication among team members (including human–machine communication) all go up with the unusualness (situations at or beyond margins of normality or beyond textbook situations), tempo, and criticality of situations. This means that the burden of interacting with other people or an interface tends to be concentrated at the very times when the person can least afford new tasks, new memory demands, or diversions of his or her attention away from the job at hand.

As an illustrative example, during a space shuttle launch, there was a hydraulic leak that triggered escalations in activity (Watts-Perotti & Woods, 2009). One of the ground-based mission controllers responsible for the mechanical systems noticed an unexpected drop in hydraulic fluid. His team immediately calculated the leak rate in order to recommend an action to the astronauts. Because the leak was small enough not to require immediate action, the team then focused on how to best configure the mechanical systems in order to obtain additional diagnostic information. In parallel, they analyzed if any actions could be taken to protect other interconnected systems. Throughout the period of escalation, controllers were constantly updating members of their immediate team, the flight director, and other support controllers who were calling in. In addition, they were giving instructions to be relayed to the astronauts through another mission controller. Even before the astronauts entered the orbit phase and shut down the auxiliary power units, additional support personnel were called in to help assess the impacts of the anomaly on mission plans.

Pattern 2: Proactive Investment in Coming Up to Speed

The pattern of proactively investing in developing an understanding of a situation occurs when there is an increased likelihood that an agent will be impacted by the work of other agents. At some organizations, proactive investments are institutionalized. For example, space shuttle mission controllers designated as "on-call" are required to check in once a day to obtain an update on the mission status. Similarly, some health care institutions require attendance of nurses during physician rounds in intensive care units so that they can learn about predicted activities earlier, such as when patients will be transferred to other units. Finally, some nursing shift changes include listening to audio-taped handoffs from the prior shift as a group so that all of the nurses can be familiar with information about other nurses' patients to allow them to more effectively provide aid in an emergency situation. For example, nurses would know the do not resuscitate (DNR) status in the event of a heart attack.

Pattern 3: Emergent Workload Balancing

With this pattern, people respond to signals that a person has a high workload by offering aid without first going through a supervisor hierarchy to obtain permission. Signals include body language indicators of stress and anxiety, which occur naturally and so do not require additional work on the part of the signaler.

At the Pittsburgh Regional Health Institute (2007), this pattern was systematically encouraged to increase nursing staff retention on an abdominal transplantation unit. Individual nurses were allowed to hoist red flags when they were feeling overwhelmed, which was an explicit signal for nurses or nurse managers to help. Balls and sticks with green, yellow, and red flags were provided on each medication cart, with an understanding that posting in yellow or red would signal the need for help, with immediate help requested at the red level. With this system, nursing turnover was reduced from 12% to no turnover at 6 months after the intervention, and the system spread to other units.

Pattern 4: Role-Based Communication

Most social interactions are based on a personal history of interactions, where referents (names), contact information, and expectations for behavior depend on an individual's preferences and predispositions. In complex settings where multiple individuals can fulfill an organizational role, keeping track of what individuals are scheduled to perform a particular role and how to contact them can carry a high cost. Particularly when there are high consequences for delay due to confusion about which individual agent is performing a particular role, some organizations use role-based interaction techniques rather than individual-based interactions.

Examples include having one phone number to reach the primary clerk at the emergency department of a hospital. That phone number is

180 • *Theories of Team Cognition*

independent of what individual is performing the clerk's duties, unlike using a personal pager or cell phone to contact the clerk. "Code pagers" and "charge nurse cell phones" similarly use role-based means of contact. This strategy is particularly helpful when someone is filling in for another person or when there is uncertainty about the exact time a role transfer will take place. In space shuttle mission control, it is viewed as impolite to "plug in" a headset to the primary position on the voice loop console until after the previous team has been dismissed. This protocol makes it easy for others to see at a glance which person is actively filling the role around a transition time.

In space shuttle mission control, names are not used to get the attention of someone filling a particular role. Rather, the convention is to name the role of the person to whom they wish to speak followed by the role that the person is filling. For example, a mechanical systems controller (Mech) would contact her supervisor (MMACS—Maintenance, Mechanical, Arm, and Crew Systems) on the voice loop system by saying "MMACS, Mech" and then wait for the response "Go ahead" before saying the content of the communication. Similarly, trauma teams will sometimes refer to "Nurse Left" and "Nurse Right" to highlight the role that the nurse is filling rather than using the nurse's name.

Pattern 5: Dropping or Delaying Lower Priority Tasks During Bottlenecks

Based on a synthesis of research on "stacking" activities in nursing (Patterson et al., 2011), we have created a prioritization hierarchy of task importance in complex, sociotechnical settings (Figure 7.1). During work-load bottlenecks or during a pattern of escalating activities, the assumption is that the normative behavior is that lower priority tasks will be dropped, delayed, or performed less well to protect the quality and completion of higher priority tasks. Therefore, this pattern of dropping or delaying lower priority tasks such as personal breaks, cleaning the workspace, or documentation activities is triggered by a judgment that an agent is a bottleneck in workflow, or a prediction that a bottleneck period will occur in the future.

An example of this pattern is an emergency department clerk delaying documentation that one patient has been discharged until a new patient has been admitted. At one hospital where this pattern was observed,

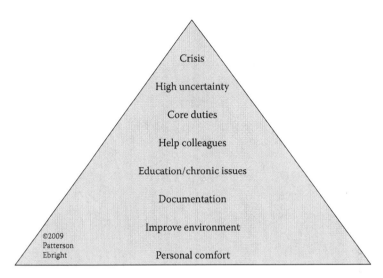

FIGURE 7.1
Hierarchy of task priorities.

patients were required to be admitted to the hospital by the clerk before physicians could access the patient's electronic health record, which is needed by physicians to do core duty activities, such as writing orders.

Pattern 6: Reducing the Priority of Tasks That Do Not Directly Benefit the Agent or That Are Associated With a Reduction in Status

Another pattern is reducing the priority of tasks that do not directly benefit the agent or that are associated with a reduction in status or power. These decisions can be surprising to administrative members of an organization. Analysis has tended to reveal that, from the perspective of a "sharp end" worker, this behavior is locally rational.

For example, individuals predictably respond by failing to prioritize a new task that does not have an immediate personal benefit or indicates a reduction in power. The pattern of failing to adopt technology not perceived to have a personal benefit was coined by Donald Norman (1993) as Grudin's Law: "When those who benefit are not those who do the work, then the technology is likely to fail or, at least, be subverted" (Grudin, 1994, p. 113). For example, physicians may choose not to type in reasons for orders that are helpful to pharmacists, nurses,

182 • *Theories of Team Cognition*

and patients in order to have a more efficient use of a computerized order entry system.

Similarly, individuals predictably fail to prioritize a new task that is associated with a reduction in power or status. For example, jotting handwritten annotations on manual whiteboards has been observed to be preferred to typing information displayed on an electronic version of a whiteboard. Historically, typing was done by "clerks," who were perceived as having a lower status than licensed professionals. Similarly, a requirement to type a justification for a "late" medication administration was often dropped as a task partially because of the frequent perception that the software was "blaming" the nurse for being "late."

Pattern 7: Increased Communication During Nonroutine Events

The final pattern is that there is increased communication during nonroutine events. Unlike strategies that emphasize increased communication for building trust, the CSE literature highlights how little communication there usually is in highly functioning teams. During nonroutine events, the amount of communication spikes.

Patterson, Cook, Woods, and Render (2004) provide a detailed example of a nonroutine event, the initiation of a new chemotherapy regimen over the weekend. In summary, a routine event would have avoided any direct communication between team members. A physician types an order into the patient's electronic health record, which would be automatically routed to the pharmacist for verification using an electronic signature, followed by dispensing by a pharmacy staff member, and administration by a nurse. In this case:

- The physician called the pharmacist to let him know the order was coming.
- The pharmacist requested that a handwritten order be hand delivered by the ordering physician, during which interaction they again communicated.
- The pharmacist called the physician while preparing the medication.
- The pharmacist walked the medication to the nurse and commented that there were numerous bags and the dose appeared high; the nurse then requested that the pharmacist again call the physician to verify the order.

A Cognitive Systems Engineering Perspective on Shared Cognition · 183

- After administering the medication, the nurse called the physician to inform him of how the patient reacted to the medication; the physician then canceled a related medication administration.

CONCLUSION

There are powerful regularities to be described at a level of analysis that transcends the details of the specific domain, but the regularities are not about the domain specific details, they are about the nature of human cognition in human activity.

—Hutchins
as cited in Patterson, Miller, Roth, & Woods, 2010, p. xii

Coordinating supports the accomplishment of cognitive work that is necessarily distributed across people and time. Coordinating manages interdependencies of activity and communication for individuals in specialized roles with related (including sometimes conflicting) goals. To support coordinating, it is helpful to have knowledge of repeating patterns that reduce the costs of coordinating and that transcend the details of a particular setting.

The patterns in this chapter provide insight into coordination strategies for the following:

- Negotiating conflicts
  - Dropping or delaying tasks that do not provide a direct personal benefit
  - Dropping or delaying tasks that are perceived to reduce power or status
  - Prioritizing competing tasks by importance and interactions with other tasks
- Synchronizing activities
  - During escalations following anomalous events
  - When preparing for workload bottlenecks
  - When balancing workload
- Communicating
  - Using role-based communication technology

184 • *Theories of Team Cognition*

- Using common ground to reduce communication
- Increasing communication during nonroutine events

Although the patterns identified in this chapter were derived from research conducted in a wide variety of real-world settings, the theoretical foundations permit the identification of recurring patterns. By comparing these patterns to the phenomena studied under more highly controlled conditions and stemming from different conceptual roots, such as is described in the other chapters of this book, the hope is to triangulate with methods and findings upon a solid theoretical foundation. This foundation is needed to enable principled improvement in the design of systems and training to improve cognitive performance in domains with all of their inherent "messy complexity."

ACKNOWLEDGMENT

This research was supported by the Office of Naval Research (GRT000 12190) at The Ohio State University.

REFERENCES

Crowston, K., Rubleske, J., & Howison, J. (2006). Coordination theory. In P. Zhang & D. Galletta (Eds.), *Human-computer interaction and management information systems: Foundations* (p. 120). Armonk, NY: M.E. Sharpe, Inc.

Grudin, J. (1994). Computer-supported cooperative work: History and focus. *IEEE Computer, 27*, 19–27.

Hoffman, R. R., & Yates, J. F. (2005). Decision(?)-making(?). *IEEE: Intelligent Systems, 20*, 76–83.

Hollnagel, E., & Woods, D. D. (2005). *Joint cognitive systems: Foundations of cognitive systems engineering.* New York, NY: Taylor & Francis.

Klein, G. (2007a). Flexecution as a paradigm for replanning, part 1. *IEEE Intelligent Systems, 22*, 79–83.

Klein, G. (2007b). Flexecution, part 2: Understanding and supporting flexible execution. *IEEE Intelligent Systems, 22*, 108–112.

Klein, G. (2010). Macrocognitive measures for evaluating cognitive work. In E. S. Patterson & J. Miller (Eds.), *Macrocognition metrics and scenarios: Design and evaluation for real-world teams* (pp. 47–64). Burlington, VT: Ashgate Publishing.

Klein, G. A., Ross, K. G., Moon, B. M., Klein D. E., Hoffman, R. R., & Hollnagel E. (2003). Macrocognition. *IEEE Intelligent Systems, 18*, 81–85.

Letsky, M. P., Warner, N. W., Fiore, S. M., & Smith, C. A. P. (Eds.). (2009). *Macrocognition in teams: Theories and methodologies*. Burlington, VT: Ashgate Publishing Company.

Norman, D. A. (1993). *Things that make us smart: Defending human attributes in the age of the machine*. Reading, MA: Addison-Wesley.

Patterson, E. S., Cook, R. I., Woods, D. D., & Render, M. L. (2004). Examining the complexity behind a medication error: Generic patterns in communication. *IEEE Transactions on Systems, Man and Cybernetics—Part A: Systems and Humans, 34*, 749–756.

Patterson, E. S., Ebright, P. R., & Saleem, J. J. (2011, February 17). Investigating stacking: How do registered nurses prioritize their activities in real-time? *International Journal of Industrial Ergonomics, Special Issue on Human Factors and Ergonomics in Healthcare Delivery* [Epub ahead of print].

Patterson, E. S., Miller, J., Roth, E. M., & Woods, D. D. (2010). Macrocognition: Where do we stand? In E. S. Patterson & J. Miller (Eds.), *Macrocognition metrics and scenarios: Design and evaluation for real-world teams* (pp. i–xv). Burlington, VT: Ashgate Publishing.

Patterson, E. S., Watts-Perotti, J., & Woods, D. D. (1999). Voice loops as coordination aids in space shuttle mission control. *Computer Supported Cooperative Work: The Journal of Collaborative Computing, 8*, 353–371.

Patterson, E. S., Woods, D. D., Cook, R. I., & Render, M. L. (2007). Collaborative cross-checking to enhance resilience. *Cognition, Technology and Work, 9*, 155–162.

Patterson, E. S., Woods, D. D., Sarter, N. B., & Watts-Perotti, J. (1998, May). Patterns in cooperative cognition. *COOP, '98, Third International Conference on the Design of Cooperative Systems*, 13–23.

Pittsburgh Regional Health Institute. (2007). *PRHI executive summary, January/February 2007* (Newsletter). Retrieved June 3, 2011, from http://www.prhi.org/docs/Executive_Summary_Jan_Feb_2007.pdf

Roth, E. M., Woods, D. D., & Gallagher, J. M., Jr. (1986). Analysis of expertise in a dynamic control task. *Proceedings of the Human Factors Society 30th Annual Meeting*, 179–181.

Watts-Perotti, J., & Woods, D. D. (2009). Cooperative advocacy: An approach for integrating diverse perspectives in anomaly response. *Computer Supported Cooperative Work, 18*, 175–198.

Woods, D. D. (1987). Commentary: Cognitive engineering in complex and dynamics worlds. *International Journal of Man-Machine Studies, 27*, 571–585.

Woods, D. D., & Hollnagel, E. (2006). *Joint cognitive systems: Patterns in cognitive systems engineering*. New York, NY: Taylor & Francis.

Woods, D. D., & Patterson, E. S. (2001). How unexpected events produce an escalation of cognitive and coordinative demands. In P. A. Hancock & P. A. Desmond (Eds.), *Stress, workload, and fatigue* (pp. 290–304). Hillsdale, NJ: Lawrence Erlbaum Associates.

Woods, D. D., & Roth, E. M. (1986). *The role of cognitive modeling in nuclear power plant personnel activities* (NUREG-CR-4532). Washington, DC. U.S. Nuclear Regulatory Commission.

8

Theoretical Underpinning of Interactive Team Cognition

Nancy J. Cooke, Jamie C. Gorman, Christopher Myers, and Jasmine Duran

Teams are a special kind of group, one that has members who play heterogeneous but interdependent roles to work toward common objectives (Salas, Dickinson, Converse, & Tannenbaum, 1992). Thus a typing pool of individuals doing the same task, each independently, is a small group that can be contrasted with a surgical team (nurse, surgeon, and anesthesiologist) who each have distinct although interdependent roles. Furthermore, teams increasingly perform cognitive tasks such as planning, decision making, designing, assessing situations, and solving problems. We label this cognitive activity of teams "team cognition." The purpose of this chapter is to describe one perspective on team cognition, interactive team cognition (ITC), and its theoretical underpinnings.

We begin this chapter by motivating the study of team cognition and describing the more traditional shared cognition perspective. We then present some arguments for another perspective, that of ITC, which we describe along with three key assumptions. In the remainder of the chapter, we provide theoretical background aligned with each of the three assumptions of ITC and suggest that this perspective accounts for a body of data and has implications for measurement and team effectiveness interventions.

Why is team cognition important? We assume that the cognitive activity carried out by teams has important implications for team performance outcomes and team effectiveness. Hence we can attribute some extraordinary consequences to failures of team cognition that have led to incorrect decisions, actions, or even inaction. For instance, the Vincennes tragedy in which an Iranian Airbus was accidentally shot down by a U.S. Naval warship has been attributed to failures in team situation awareness,

188 • *Theories of Team Cognition*

coordination, communication, and decision making (Collyer & Malecki, 1998). Ultimately, the decision to shoot down the civilian aircraft was a wrong decision and was attributable to failures of a team rather than the failure of any individual. Similarly, the poor response to Hurricane Katrina has been at least partially blamed on deficiencies in team coordination, communication, and planning (Leonard & Howitt, 2006). In contrast, the "Miracle on the Hudson," in which bird strikes and subsequent engine failures led to passengers deplaning unharmed on the Hudson River, is an example of exceptional team communication, coordination, and decision making (McFadden, 2009). Therefore, it is important to understand team cognition so that it can be assessed, predicted, trained, and improved.

One way to think about team cognition is to view the team as an aggregate of cognitive entities (human or synthetic). For example, a surgical team's cognition can be captured in the aggregate of the nurse, surgeon, and anesthesiologist specialty knowledge. Concepts such as shared situation awareness and shared mental models are aligned with this view, which is largely inspired by information processing theories of cognition (Cooke, Gorman, & Rowe, 2009; Cooke, Gorman, & Winner, 2007). Shared mental models are thought to develop as individuals become more similar in their knowledge of the task and the team (Converse, Cannon-Bowers, & Salas, 1991; Langan-Fox, Code, & Langfield-Smith, 2000). Cognition of team members with a shared mental model is thought to be identical or overlapping, and this commonality, or *sharedness*, leads to superior team performance. The intuitive appeal of this shared cognition perspective is that team members must be *on the same page* for effective team performance. On the surface, this is a reasonable goal.

However, the shared cognition perspective tends to be poorly aligned with concepts of team heterogeneity and with relatively large teams (e.g., a team of 50 versus a team of 3). Furthermore, this perspective also tends to focus on knowledge more than processes associated with teammate interaction, such as coordination and communication. For a surgical team to be *on the same page*, each of the team members must not only know his or her own job, but also what the other team members are doing and intend to do. But, does it really make sense for the surgeon, nurse, and anesthesiologist to have the same or nearly the same knowledge of past, current, and possible future events in an operating room? A better goal beyond matching knowledge bases is, perhaps, effective communication of specialty knowledge.

In any case, there are empirical results that are at odds with a shared cognition perspective. For example, Mathieu, Goodwin, Heffner, Salas, and Cannon-Bowers (2000) failed to find mental model convergence among team members over time, and Levesque, Wilson, and Wholey (2001) actually found decreasing similarity of knowledge over time. In our research, we have seen evidence of improvements in team performance unaccompanied by changes in knowledge. Instead, we find that changes in team processes accompany team learning (Cooke, Kiekel, & Helm, 2001; Cooke, Shope, & Kiekel, 2001). We have also found that teams with experience working in teamwork settings who were naïve regarding an experimental task were nonetheless superior to other teams that formed at the time of the experiment (Cooke, Gorman, Duran, & Taylor, 2007). In addition, retention of team skill was better predicted by change in team process (e.g., coordination) than change in team knowledge (Cooke, Gorman, Duran, Myers, & Andrews, in press). These results are problematic for any theory of team cognition that relies heavily on knowledge-based explanations for superior team performance. Importantly, the aforementioned results suggest that team processes and interactions are at least partially responsible for team performance.

ITC is a different perspective on team cognition that has arisen in response to limitations of shared cognition and data inconsistent with shared cognition. As a result, a set of psychological theories that are alternatives to information-processing psychology and others that focus on inextricable interconnectedness between animals and their environment to produce cognitive processing have been embraced as theoretical forerunners of phenomenological team cognition (Cooke et al., 2009; Cooke, Gorman, & Winner, 2007). ITC views team cognition not as a knowledge collective (or aggregate), but as an activity or, better, an *interactivity*. Team cognition is essentially the joint activity that teams engage in when they coordinate, communicate, and make decisions (Galantucci & Sebanz, 2009). Interactions, often in the form of verbal communications, make up a large portion of this activity. Thus, the interactive perspective on team cognition views team interactions as team cognition. ITC also assumes that team cognition is inextricably tied to context. Consequently, team cognition is determined mostly by team member interaction in the context of the task environment. Furthermore, this perspective assumes that teams are the correct unit of analysis for studying team cognition and that it is not necessary, and perhaps even undesirable, to measure and

190 • *Theories of Team Cognition*

TABLE 8.1

Two Caricatures of Perspectives on Team Cognition

	Shared Cognition	Interactive Team Cognition
Focus	Static knowledge	Dynamic activity
Drives team cognition	Shared mental models	Team interactions
Primary locus of team cognition	Intracranial	Extracranial
Unit of analysis	Aggregation of individual data	Team level

aggregate individual data. Caricatures of the shared cognition and ITC perspectives are presented in Table 8.1.

ITC accounts for significant data in the literature and from our research. ITC and its three main assumptions are inspired by many similar perspectives in psychology and cognitive science listed in Table 8.2. A deep analysis of each is beyond the scope of this chapter. In this chapter, we describe the three key assumptions of ITC and three representative theories that are at the basis of these assumptions.

ITC ASSUMPTIONS AND THEORETICAL UNDERPINNINGS

Assumption 1: Team Cognition Is Dynamic

Generally, ITC theory assumes that team cognition is inherently dynamic. Team cognition, like individual cognition, changes over time, but not in discrete intervals and not in random or completely fixed ways: Team cognition at one moment is not completely independent from the prior moments, nor is it completely specified by prior moments. Team cognition is continuous, however, just as a person's life cycle is continuous. The metaphor of a stream used by William James (1890/1950) is an appropriate characterization of the dynamic nature of team cognition: The stream is unbroken; it can meander around the structures of its environment—a rock, the riverbed; it can become briefly fixed in an eddy—from moment to moment; but the "structure" of the stream is inherently dynamic and continuous. Try to pick up the flowing stream with your hand and it ceases to flow. Team cognition is just a special case of this.

TABLE 8.2

Theories and Schools of Thought That Have Inspired Interactive Team Cognition Theory and That Underlie Each of Three Main Assumptions

Theory and Schools of Thought	Citations	Team Cognition Is Dynamic	Team Cognition Is Tied to Context	Teams as Unit of Cognitive Analysis
Activity theory	Bannon & Bødker (1991); Cheyne & Tarulli (1999); Vygotsky (1978); Wertsch (1991, 1994)			
Functionalism	James (1890/1950)			
Dynamical/ complex systems	Abraham & Shaw (1992); Alligood, Sauer, & Yorke (1996); Nicolis & Prigogine (1989)			
Direct perception	Gibson (1966, 1986)			
Ecological psychology	Gibson (1966, 1986); Brunswik & Kamiya (1953)			
Distributed cognition	Hutchins (1995a, 1995b, 2000)			
Situated cognition/action	Greeno (1998)			
Embodied cognition	Wilson (2002)			
Multilevel modeling	Kozlowski & Klein (2000)			
Time scales of human activity	Newell (1990)			
Macrocognition	Klein et al. (2003)			

Just as the ripples of a stream form patterns as they pass over the riverbed, in team cognition, dynamic pattern formation occurs as people interact with each other and their surroundings. Construed in this way, team cognition is activity—activity in the form of team interactions that are often observable. Pattern formation tends to constrain the interaction of lower level components of cognitive systems—in the present chapter, the team members—and can also provide a landscape (substrate) for future cognitive activity. We provide an introduction to aspects of dynamical systems thinking that have been particularly influential to our theory of team cognition.

192 • *Theories of Team Cognition*

We provide several ways of thinking about the relation between dynamics and team cognition: The broad field of complex systems is described briefly; this is followed by a discussion of synergetics and coordination dynamics; and finally, the concept of fractal dynamics and its relation to cognitive activity are described. These dynamical concepts are then considered with respect to recent research on team coordination and collaboration dynamics. One concept that is essential to each of these descriptions is the notion of a system whose components do not completely determine system behavior. One can find explanations in component behavior, but it is often not as satisfying as an explanation based on system behavior. Just as a team is made up of the heterogeneously skilled members, interrelated components make up such systems. Just as in teams, however, component properties do not fully account for system behavior.

Complexity

Perhaps the most essential concept related to complex systems is the concept of emergence. Put simply, emergence is the idea that system-level behavior is nonreducible to the properties of system components. Rather, system-level behavior emerges from the interactions of system components as the system interacts with the environment. One of the most often cited examples of complexity is the formation of convection rolls in a dish of oil as the oil is heated from below (Nicolis & Prigogine, 1989). At low heat, heat is dissipated through conduction, the transfer of heat from molecule to molecule. As the heat is increased, conduction ceases to be a stable mode of dissipation, and convection rolls—counter-rotating pockets of molecules—emerge. Convection rolls are not a property intrinsic to the oil or its molecular components. Convection patterns emerge due to the increasing upward transfer of heat and gravity acting on the topmost molecules. Thus, pattern formation, namely, the appearance of rolls, is not deterministically related to the molecular properties of oil. In fact, whether the rolls will turn to the right or left is not knowable a priori—they *self-organize* (Nicolis & Prigogine, 1989). Once the rolls form however, they constrain the molecules to interact in a particular way. Pattern formation drives, and is driven by, stable molecular interactions of the oil as the heat gradient—the environment—changes.

That emergence of pattern can be observed in a dish of oil does not appear to be related to cognition. What does complexity mean for team cognition? The concepts of complexity, constraint, and emergence have been applied to cognitive activity at both the individual level and relatively large scales. For instance, Juarrero (1999) argued that emergent constraints play a causal role in intentional action. Juarrero's view of "constraints as causes" (p. 131) runs counter to many long-standing mechanical notions of causality in purposive action: Rather than a billiard ball–like predetermined sequence of actions, constraints create new possibilities for action by making components interdependent in novel ways. Therefore, complexity provides an explanation for creativity in performatory behavior. The establishment of modern human civilization has also been described as a complex system with humans as the atomic components. Iberall (1987) characterized the growth of human culture as a series of phase transitions from hunter–gatherer to agricultural settlements through diffusion (roaming) and condensation (settling) processes to cities with infrastructures and central governments through convection (trade) processes.

In between the individual and societal levels of analysis, we have observed that team cognition can also be characterized as an emergent phenomenon. In particular, we have found that team member interactions are regulated by both local interactions and constraints that emerge over relatively long time scales. Analyses of team coordination dynamics in three-person teams in an uninhabited aerial vehicle (UAV) simulation, quantified using an order parameter (described in the section "Synergetics and Coordination Dynamics"), revealed long-range dependencies that span greater than one 40-minute UAV mission (Cooke & Gorman, 2009; Gorman, 2006; Gorman, Amazeen, & Cooke, 2010; see also Gorman, 2005). It is likely that team members were unaware of the emergence of these long-range patterns, although these patterns constrained their interactions. Similar to how the molecular interactions were constrained by the emergence of convection rolls, local team member interactions that take place on the order of minutes are constrained by larger, global patterns of behavior that can span hours.

Synergetics and Coordination Dynamics

In this section, we first describe the central concepts of synergetics and coordination dynamics. We then briefly describe some findings on intra- and interpersonal coordination. Finally, we describe some recent research on team coordination dynamics.

194 • *Theories of Team Cognition*

Synergetics (Haken, 1977) is the study of general principles governing the emergence of patterns in complex systems. Inspired by synergetics, coordination dynamics (Jirsa & Kelso, 2004) is the study of how coordinated patterns form and adapt to changes in the environment. A central concept of this approach is information compression across components of the system. Rather than needing to describe the behavior of all system components (lots of information), at points of instability their behavior can be described by very low dimensional quantities (little information), the *order parameters*. Environmental conditions are quantified using *control parameters*. As environmental conditions change by scaling a control parameter, the state of the order parameter becomes increasingly unstable until a phase transition occurs and a new, more stable pattern of coordination emerges. Thus, pattern formation and phase transition are quantified in terms of qualitative changes in the order parameters. The *slaving principle* states that once pattern formation at the macro level occurs, then interactions at the micro level are constrained to interact in certain ways in order to maintain the pattern at the macro level. Therefore, the role of the slaving principle is to describe the up–down circular causality of complex systems. Once the order parameter is fixed and the components are enslaved, then information expansion occurs: It suffices to identify the relatively low-dimensional behavior of the order parameter (little information) in order to describe the high-dimensional component behavior (lots of information).

In motor coordination, relative phasing φ between two limbs is an order parameter that has led to more than 20 years of research on coordination dynamics (e.g., Haken, Kelso, & Bunz, 1985; Jirsa & Kelso, 2004; Kelso, 1995). If an individual flexes and extends their right and left index fingers in the sagittal plane, for example, the temporal relationship between the endpoints of these fingers is a measure of φ. One of the most robust findings is that the relative phase between two limbs in monofrequency (1:1) coordination has two stable states (inphase—moving together—phase difference of 0°, and antiphase—moving apart—phase difference of 180°). The most stable state depends on the value of a control parameter, movement frequency. At relatively slow movement frequency, both inphase and antiphase are stable; the system is bistable. As movement frequency increases, antiphase becomes critically unstable, and a phase transition occurs after which only inphase is stable. Thus, people who are performing antiphase movements spontaneously shift to inphase as movement frequency is increased. However, a corresponding shift from inphase to antiphase as movement frequency decreases does not occur. This phenomenon, known as hysteresis, means the future behavior of the system depends critically on the prior behavior and conditions of the system, or in other words, the system has memory. These findings have been replicated in interlimb coordination dynamics *across* people (Schmidt, Bienvenu, Fitzpatrick, & Amazeen, 1998). The stable states, phase transitions, and hysteresis effects are, therefore, not simply properties of physical coupling between limbs. Informational coupling between different people's limbs produces the same coordination dynamics.

In a series of experiments on teams operating in a UAV simulated task environment, we have quantified team coordination using an order parameter that captures the temporal relationships between a set of team member interactions. The component measures that feed into the calculation of the order parameter include behaviors that team members perform individually but that the team assembles dynamically (Gorman et al., 2010). We have observed that the scaling of team control parameters (e.g., team member familiarity) changes the stable state of team coordination, and teams may become more or less prone to adapt to novel situations with the scaling of a control parameter. Thus, we can use a relatively low-dimensional order parameter (information compression) to describe relatively complicated team behavior (information expansion). Furthermore, by finding transitions between stable states, the tuning of control parameters is one mechanism for creating teams that are flexible yet stable as they encounter an uncertain, changing task environment.

Fractal Dynamics

In discussing fractal dynamics, we emphasize the nested nature of fractal processes. Recent research suggests that cognitive processes are the result of multiply-nested systems. Behavioral nesting also has implications for how we think about team cognition.

The term "fractal" was coined to describe the recurring "fractured" geometry of nested structures over multiple scales of observation (Mandelbrot, 1977). If you magnify a fractal, it looks the same. This property, known as self-similarity, means that such a geometrical structure is scale invariant, that is, there is no intrinsic or preferred scale of observation. Fractals occur in natural structures (e.g., snowflakes, leaves), but they also occur

196 • *Theories of Team Cognition*

in behavioral processes (e.g., heart rhythms, free-market economies). Such processes are often described as nested, such that there is no inherent preferred level of analysis given that patterns are self-similar (or more accurately, self-affine; Eke, Herman, Kocsis, & Kozak, 2002). Thus fractal dynamics emerge not from independent components, but from interactions that pervade multiple time scales of system function.

Variability in simple and choice reaction time experiments has revealed latent fractal processes in people's responses in cognitive tasks (Gilden, Thornton, & Mallon, 1995). Thus, small variations are nested within larger variations, which are nested in even larger variations such that variation at the brain level is nested in variation at the body level, which is nested in variation at the task environment level, and so forth, making it improbable that any level can function independently of any another (Van Orden, Holden, & Turvey, 2003) and, further, that there is no preferred level of operation ("blueprints") of the cognitive system (cf. Gilden, 2001).

Fractal dynamics seem to be exhibited also by teams who must collaborate to formulate a plan, an instance of team cognition. For example, in teams collaborating to form evacuation plans, making decisions about small issues (e.g., cars versus boats) are temporally nested within decisions about larger issues (e.g., vehicles), which in turn are nested within even larger decisions (e.g., methods of evacuation; Gorman, Cooke, Amazeen, Hessler, & Rowe, 2009). An interesting aspect of team cognition, therefore, is that there does not need to be an intrinsic intent, or blueprint, on the part of team members to exhibit a multiply nested, fractal process. In team cognition, fractal dynamics result from simple team member interactions that are operating across multiple time scales.

Understandably, the fields of complexity, coordination dynamics, and fractals were not developed to understand team cognition. Similarly, ITC is not a theory of dynamics, but of team cognition. However, when viewed dynamically, team cognition shares many of the same features of complex, coordinated systems that operate across multiple, nested time scales. As an underpinning for ITC, dynamics are therefore one theoretical driver for new conceptualizations of team cognition in which components, literally team members, do not completely determine system behavior. In the next section, we explore the notion that perception, action, and cognition are specified by individual–environment interactions and, further, that team member–team member interaction is the interface for team cognition.

Assumption 2: Team Cognition Is Tied to Context

A tenant of ITC is that team cognition results from activity within a *team-environment system*. Teammates and their environment comprise a system that produces cognitive phenomena that cannot be attributed to any system constituent where a constituent can be a noncognitive task component. For example, teams can become skillful at a task, yet the process of acquiring the skill cannot be credited simply to an increase in teammates' task knowledge because the task, itself, is dynamic. Rather, the process of team skill acquisition is better attributed to the interactions among teammates when completing a changing, but similar, goal (Cooke, Kiekel, et al., 2001; Cooke, Shope, et al., 2001). Hence, we assert that team cognition is not static within the team or the sum of teammates' knowledge, but is instead *extracranial*—occurring in the interactions between teams and their task environments.

The assertion of extracranial cognitive activity is not novel. Andrew Clark (2003) claims that writing down information in a notebook is a way of extending cognitive activity beyond the skull, at least in a *weak embodied* sense (Chemero, 2009). For example, cognitive activities such as memory retrieval occur each time a shopper references an item from a list of things to purchase. Memory retrieval is a well-studied cognitive process, but the difference in this example is that the memory is *extracranially* retrieved from a written list rather than *intracranially* retrieved from items "stored" in the shopper's memory. The shopper's list serves as an external memory store outside of the shopper's skull, and retrieving an item from the list requires cognitive activity between the shopper and the list and is hence extracranial. Now, if the shopper's intracranial memory system was completely and utterly destroyed (as through a traumatic accident or disease), the shopper would have no way to process the list, and this memory system would fail; the shopper is (of course) an integral part of memory. However, if the list is lost, the memory system also fails. In the latter case, the memory system is clearly extended beyond the skull.

ITC posits that extracranial cognitive processing occurs in the context of individuals working as a team and helps to account for variance in team coordination and performance unaccounted for by aggregating individual-level knowledge measures. Alterman, Feinman, Introne, and Landsman's (2001) concept of a coordinating representation is aligned

198 • *Theories of Team Cognition*

with the idea of team cognition outside of the head. Theory and research on the importance of the coupling between individuals and their environments to cognitive processing is also regularly referred to in *ecological psychology*. In the following section, we cover some of the tenets of ecological psychology that help to provide the foundation for ITC.

Ecological Psychology and Gibson's Perspective on Perception

Ecological psychology is a systems approach to psychology that asserts the importance of studying the animal–environment system over studying the individual animal independent of its usual environmental constraints (Brunswik & Kamiya, 1953; Gibson, 1966). Let us use the human visual perceptual system as an example. Any basic cognitive psychology textbook provides the typical information-processing division between sensation and perception. Sensation results when light energy "strikes" the retina, and perception occurs across several steps (such as edge detection, memory retrievals, etc.), eventually becoming meaningful to the perceiver: The perceiver records an impoverished stimulus, and the stimulus must be processed and elaborated using stored representations from previous experiences to understand its meaning. In this case, vision and visual consciousness are indirect (Michaels & Carello, 1981).

James J. Gibson (1966, 1986) argued that theories based in indirect perception (representation) are flawed and that they have led the study of perception in the wrong direction. Gibson argued that perception is the dynamics of a *perception–action system*, and the process does not depend so heavily on the static (received) knowledge of the perceiver. Rather, perceivers act in their environment based on the changes of patterns of light, and the light patterns and their systematic changes provide information directly to the perceiver. An example of Gibson's *direct perception* is perceptual invariants attained through optic flow that provide immediate meaning about objects, such as their affordances (Gibson, 1986), or even the direction to move to catch a fly ball (McBeath, Shaffer, & Kaiser, 1995). Importantly, direct perception does not invoke the mediation of memories of past experiences or representations to make the visual experience meaningful.

So what does this all have to do with teams? ITC takes a similar perspective to team cognition as Gibson took to visual perception, and two primary distinctions between the ecological and information-processing approaches to understanding psychological phenomena should be pointed out because they provide important scaffolding for our theory of ITC.

First, an individual and his or her environment are a system for understanding cognitive activity in the ecological approach, whereas in the information-processing approach, the individual is isolated from his or her environment to study the internal "laws" of cognitive processing. In ITC, team cognitive activity is studied and measured as a teammate–environment system, rather than within each individual teammate. Hence, team cognition occurs when teammates interact with their environment, which can include other team members and tools for accomplishing their task and communicating with teammates. Other approaches to understanding team cognition implement an approach similar to the information-processing approach, by which teammate knowledge is measured as discrete overlapping or complementary representations within individual team members. Based on ITC, team cognition does not occur *within* team members and is not the sum of knowledge across team members, but rather, it is the result of interactions between team members and their continuous coupling to the task environment.

Second, the ecological perspective posits that animal–environment systems are complex systems, demonstrating overlap between the ecological perspective to psychology and the study of complex systems, described earlier. When considered from the ecological perspective, cognitive activity involves time and space (Michaels & Carello, 1981), whereas when considered from the information-processing perspective, time and space are typically divided into arbitrary symbolic units of information that must eventually be reunited ("binded") after the process has occurred. In ITC, team cognitive processing occurs across time frames greater than the individual without the requirement of discrete symbolic representations. For example, an important measure of team cognition based on ITC is the dynamic sending and receiving of task-relevant information, or *team coordination*. Although the shared cognition approach to understanding team cognition does explain some of the variance in team performance, the ecological approach to understanding team performance explains as much, if not more, of the variance (Cooke et al., 2007; Cooke, Kiekel, et al., 2001).

To summarize, the ecological approach to understanding cognition provides the theoretical foundation for ITC. Similar to the ecological approach, ITC asserts that interactions across the teammate–environment system

200 • *Theories of Team Cognition*

are integrated in team cognitive processes. Furthermore, adopting the ecological approach has led us to novel ways of measuring team cognition, such as team coordination, that focus on these interactions and are thus very different from measures used in the shared cognition approach to studying teams, such as shared mental models. ITC is not ecological psychology in the strict sense because ITC does not necessarily focus on cognitive activity as individual perception–action relations. Rather, ITC follows ecological psychology in a broader sense by studying the cognitive activity of team–environment systems. An assumption that is related to the ecological approach to studying teams is that team-level variables are the smallest (nonreducible) unit of analysis for studying team cognition, which is discussed in the following section.

Assumption 3: The Team Is the Preferred Unit of Analysis for Studying Team Cognition

The notion that cognition is extracranial has implications for the way in which we characterize the structure of teams. As mentioned in previous sections, we see teams as complex systems. Teams are also hierarchical entities. At the lowest level, teams are composed of individuals. At a higher level, individuals work as an integrated unit to accomplish tasks that are greater than any task that an individual can accomplish alone. At even higher levels, teams can interact with teams, where teams specialize in important aspects of a particular task. For example, many large companies have separate divisions for specialties such as human resources, manufacturing, and research and development. The hierarchical nature of teams leads to an important question: Which level of analysis is appropriate for measuring, testing, hypothesizing, and describing cognitive activities of teams? In this section, we focus on the influence of distributed cognition as a theoretical underpinning of the assumption that teams are complex systems and that team-level variables should be the unit of analysis where team cognition is concerned.

Distributed Cognition

As in ITC, distributed cognition places emphasis on cognition distributed across the components of a system, rather than the individuated cognitive processes at the component level. Thus, the level of interest is the system level. Unlike ITC, distributed cognition explains systems-level phenomena at both higher and lower levels of hierarchy than team cognition. Hutchins (2000) claims that cognition is distributed in three ways: (1) across people (where interaction is key), (2) across internal and external materials and environments, and (3) across time. As a result, distributed cognition is not only concerned with individual cognitive processes, but also with environmental factors and the role they play in cognition. The idea that cognition occurs "in the wild" comes from an interplay among the internal cognitive processes of individual actors but is also shaped by factors external to the actor such as culture, external artifacts, and other people. Indeed, the "moment of human practice" (Hutchins, 1995a, p. 372) is defined not only by the individual operator, but by a long history of practical knowledge handed down over generations of operators. According to the theory of distributed cognition, by focusing on the internal processes of an isolated practitioner, we are missing huge factors that play a part in cognition.

The distributed cognition approach has been applied in domains from rescue command (Artman & Garbis, 1998) to the design of functional technology (Kirsh, 2006), leading to a better understanding of "practical cognition." One of the most noted examples of the use of distributed cognition is the article by Hutchins (1995b), "How a Cockpit Remembers Its Speeds." In this article, Hutchins explores the cognitive activities performed by the cognitive system (cockpit) when the goal is adjusting critical aircraft equipment necessary for landing the aircraft. Hutchins uses the cockpit as the primary cognitive unit of analysis rather than the aircraft pilot. This cognitive system is made up of the pilots' external memory aids such as speed card booklets that give information about the relationships among aircraft weight, speed, and system status; communications between pilots for checking and crosschecking information; and the cognitive structures of the pilots themselves. Thus, cognition is examined as an interaction between the actors (pilots) and their environment.

The interactive theory of team cognition is influenced by some of the ideas set forth by distributed cognition. First, the idea that cognition is distributed across people is in line with ITC because we posit that cognition is not internal to any one team member. Individual team members are not the units of analysis; the level of interest is the team level. Second, by allowing cognition to reside outside the head of individuals and often in explicit communications, we are able to observe team cognition "in the wild," and emphasis is placed on teams as cognitive systems. As a result,

202 • *Theories of Team Cognition*

ITC theory focuses on the measurement of externalized team-level behaviors such as communication, process, and coordination as phenomenological team cognition. Third, the idea that cognition can be influenced by history and culture is important to ITC. The variance we see in the ways in which teams solve cognitive problems may be due to team histories or cultural practices that have emerged over time from the interplay among team members, and environmental and historical factors. It is the ability of history to influence team cognition that leads us to measure overt cognitive interactions (dynamically) over time.

At a glance, it may seem that ITC is merely distributed cognition applied to teams. Although ITC is influenced by some aspects of distributed cognition, there are other ways in which the two theories differ. For example, the theory of distributed cognition is rooted in traditional theories of cognition influenced by information-processing paradigms and uses the same concepts (e.g., representations, processes) and applies them to cognitive systems (Rogers, 2006). Essentially, in Hutchins' theory of distributed cognition, the system is treated as an information-processing unit. The information-processing theme is evident in the approach Hutchins (1995a) takes when describing the task of navigating a large sea vessel. The crew of a ship must engage in coordinated activities such as plotting navigation points. Hutchins approaches the analysis of this task as a system-level computational or information-processing activity. Essentially by moving the information-processing approach to a system level, Hutchins places emphasis on the coordination and interactions (processes) that transform representations of the system. Thus, a piece of information concerning the navigation of the ship can be taken from an external artifact such as a map, represented in the internal structure of a crew member, and communicated from one crew member to another, who then cross checks this information and transfers it to a chart that another crew member will use to steer the ship. This transformation of representations across media is analogous to the processing that takes place within an individual but, in this case, is observable at the system level.

ITC is influenced by the theory of distributed cognition in that teams are viewed as cognitive systems, whereby the cognitive activities of teams should be observed and measured at the team level (outside the heads of individual team members). ITC does not assert that team members receive inputs from the environment, represent those inputs, process them, and then output some team behavior. Instead, teams are viewed as cognitive systems whereby team cognition emerges through interactions of heterogeneous individuals. As such, measurement at the team level is a critical component to understanding team functioning. By merely focusing on the internal structure of team members and not taking overt behaviors into account, we are missing important information about the ability of teams to engage in cognitive activities.

CONCLUSION

ITC is aligned with a number of theories of cognition and behavior. Consistent with functionalism and dynamic complex systems, team cognition is an activity that unfolds over time. Likewise, team cognition is dynamically assembled in real time. This temporal unfolding can be understood using concepts of dynamical systems theory (Abraham & Shaw, 1992; Alligood, Sauer, & Yorke, 1996; Nicolis & Prigogine, 1989).

This perspective on team cognition has important implications for measurement. First, team cognition viewed as a static snapshot of team behavior would be impoverished. Instead, measures of team cognition should sample team process over time and use dynamical systems methods to understand the temporal patterns of teams. This assumption also has implications for how teams are trained. Conceptualizing team cognition as an activity suggests training and interventions that do not focus on transferring knowledge, but that instead center on methods for improving the interactions or team activity. For this reason, the ITC perspective would likely support team simulation, in which team interactions are practiced in real time, over classroom training.

Second, cognitive activity can occur outside of the head and is thus richly embedded in context. This assumption is inspired by direct perception and ecological psychology (Brunswik & Kamiya, 1953; Gibson, 1966), functionalism (James, 1890/1950), and distributed cognition (Hutchins, 1995a, 1995b, 2000). This assumption also has implications for measurement and intervention. When we are able to escape the bounds of the head and consider cognitive activity occurring in interactions with the world and other teammates, we are better able to observe cognition. If team cognition takes place through verbal communications (as it often does), then we can consider these communications as cognitive processing at the team level—analogous to individual cognitive processing—only observable. Also, considering cognition to occur outside of the head suggests

204 • *Theories of Team Cognition*

that training team cognition cannot be accomplished at the individual level and is best accomplished in the natural context or in a rich synthetic (simulated) environment.

Third, the idea that team cognition can (and must) be studied at the team level, in addition to being inspired by distributed cognition, is also inspired by others who talk about multilevel modeling (Kozlowski & Klein, 2000), time scales of human activity (Newell, 1990), and macrocognition (Klein, et al., 2003). Again, this assumption has explicit implications for measurement. Aggregation of individual-level measures would miss features of team cognition that emerge only through interaction. Thus, measurement at the team level needs to focus on team process and interactions. Interventions should also be designed that target this level, rather than the individual.

ITC is a relatively new perspective on team cognition. It addresses some of the limitations of the traditional shared cognition view in that it can deal with large and heterogeneous teams because it focuses on process, not knowledge. In addition, as described in this chapter, there is theoretical precedence in the study of cognition for such a perspective. Indeed, extracranial approaches to understanding cognition seem to be growing in popularity.

REFERENCES

Abraham, F. D., & Shaw, C. D. (1992). *Dynamics: The geometry of behavior.* Reading, MA: Addison-Wesley.

Alligood, K. T., Sauer, T. D., & Yorke, J. A. (1996). *Chaos: An introduction to dynamical systems theory.* New York, NY: Springer-Verlag.

Alterman, R., Feinman, A., Introne, J., & Landsman, S. (2001). Coordinating representations in computer-mediated joint activities. In *Proceedings of the 23rd Annual Conference of the Cognitive Science Society* (pp. 15–20). Mahwah, NJ: Lawrence Erlbaum Associates, Inc.

Artman, H., & Garbis, C. (1998). Situation awareness as distributed cognition. *Proceedings of the European Conference on Cognitive Ergonomics, Cognition and Co-operation,* 114–139.

Bak, P. (1996). *How nature works.* New York, NY: Springer-Verlag.

Bannon, L. J., & Bødker, S. (1991). Beyond the interface: Encountering artifacts in use. In J. M. Carroll (Ed.), *Psychology at the human-computer interface* (pp. 227–253). Cambridge, UK: Cambridge University Press.

Brunswick, E., & Kamiya, J. (1953). Ecological cue-validity of "proximity" and of other Gestalt factors. *The American Journal of Psychology, 66,* 20–32.

Chemero, A. (2009). *Radical embodied cognitive science.* Cambridge, MA: MIT Press.

Cheyne, J. A., & Tarulli, D. (1999). Dialogue, difference and the third voice in the zone of proximal development. *Theory & Psychology, 9*(1) 5–28.

Clark, A. (2003). *Natural born cyborgs: Minds, technologies, and the future of human intelligence*. Oxford, UK: Oxford University Press.

Collyer, S. C., & Malecki, G. S. (1998). Tactical decision making under stress: History and overview. In J. A. Cannon-Bowers & E. Salas (Eds.), *Decision making under stress: Implications for individual and team training* (pp. 3–15). Washington, DC: American Psychological Association.

Converse, S., Cannon-Bowers, J. A., & Salas, E. (1991). Team member shared mental models. *Proceedings of the 35th Human Factors Society Annual Meeting*, 1417–1421.

Cooke, N. J., & Gorman, J. C. (2009). Interaction-based measures of cognitive systems. *Journal of Cognitive Engineering and Decision Making, 3*, 27–46.

Cooke, N. J., Gorman, J. C., Duran, J., Myers, C. W., & Andrews, D. (in press). Retention of team coordination skill. In W. Arthur, E. Day, W. Bennett, & A. Portrey (Eds.), *Individual and team skill decay*. New York, NY: Routledge.

Cooke, N. J., Gorman, J. C., Duran, J. L., & Taylor, A. R. (2007). Team cognition in experienced command-and-control teams. *Journal of Experimental Psychology: Applied, Special Issue on Capturing Expertise across Domains, 13*, 146–157.

Cooke, N. J., Gorman, J. C., & Rowe, L. J. (2009). An ecological perspective on team cognition. In E. Salas, J. Goodwin, & C. S. Burke (Eds.), *Team effectiveness in complex organizations: Cross-disciplinary perspectives and approaches. SIOP Organizational Frontiers Series* (pp. 157–182). New York, NY: Taylor & Francis.

Cooke, N. J., Gorman, J. C., & Winner, J. L. (2007). Team cognition. In F. Durso, R. Nickerson, S. Dumais, S. Lewandowsky, & T. Perfect (Eds.), *Handbook of applied cognition* (2nd ed., pp. 239–268). Hoboken, NJ: Wiley.

Cooke, N. J., Kiekel, P. A., & Helm E. (2001). Measuring team knowledge during skill acquisition of a complex task. *International Journal of Cognitive Ergonomics: Special Section on Knowledge Acquisition, 5*, 297–315.

Cooke, N. J., Shope, S. M., & Kiekel, P. A. (2001). *Shared-knowledge and team performance: A cognitive engineering approach to measurement* (Technical Report, Grant No. F49620-98-1-0287). Wright-Patterson Air Force Base, OH: Air Force Office of Scientific Research.

Dixon, M. A., & Cunningham, G. B. (2006). Data aggregation in multilevel analysis: A review of conceptual and statistical issues. *Measurement in Physical Education and Exercise Science, 10*, 85–107.

Eke, A., Herman, P., Kocsis, L., & Kozak, L. R. (2002). Fractal characterization of complexity in temporal physiological signals. *Physiological Measurement, 23*, R1–R38.

Galantucci, B., & Sebanz, N. (2009). Joint action: Current perspectives. *Topics in Cognitive Science, 1*, 255–259.

Gibson, J. J. (1966). *The senses considered as perceptual systems*. Westport, CT: Greenwood.

Gibson, J. J. (1986). *The ecological approach to visual perception*. Hillside, NJ: Erlbaum.

Gigerenzer, G. (2002). From tools to theories: A heuristic of discovery. In *Adaptive thinking: Rationality in the real world* (pp. 3–26). Oxford, UK: Oxford University Press.

Gilden, D. L. (2001). Cognitive emissions of 1/f noise. *Psychological Review, 108*, 33–56.

Gilden, D. L., Thornton, T., & Mallon, M. W. (1995). 1/f noise in human cognition. *Science, 267*, 1837–1839.

Glenberg, A. M., Havas, D., Becker, R., & Rinck, M. (2005). Grounding language in bodily states: The case for emotion. In R. Zwaan & D. Pecher (Eds.), *The grounding of cognition: The role of perception and action in memory, language, and thinking*. Cambridge, UK: Cambridge University Press.

206 • *Theories of Team Cognition*

Goldberger, A. L., Amaral, L. A. N., Hausdorff, J. M., Ivanov, P. C., Peng, C.-K., & Stanley, H. E. (2002). Fractal dynamics in physiology: Alterations with disease and aging. *Proceedings of the National Academy of Sciences of the United States of America, 99*, 2466–2472.

Gorman, J. C. (2005). The concept of long memory for assessing the global effects of augmented team cognition. *Proceedings of the 11th International Conference on Human-Computer Interaction*, July 22–27, Las Vegas, NV.

Gorman, J. C. (2006). *Team coordination dynamics in cognitively demanding environments.* Unpublished doctoral dissertation, New Mexico State University, Las Cruces.

Gorman, J. C., Amazeen, P. G., & Cooke, N. J. (2010). Team coordination dynamics. *Nonlinear Dynamics, Psychology, and Life Sciences, 14*, 265–289.

Gorman, J. C., Cooke, N. J., Amazeen, P. G., Hessler, E. E., & Rowe, L. (2009). *Automatic tagging of macrocognitive collaborative processes through communication analysis* (Technical Report, Grant No. N00014-05-1-0625). Arlington, VA: Office of Naval Research.

Greeno, J. G. (1998). The situativity of knowing, learning, and research. *American Psychologist, 53*, 5–26.

Haken, H. (1977). *Synergetics: An introduction.* Berlin: Springer-Verlag.

Haken, H., Kelso, J. A. S., & Bunz, H. (1985). A theoretical model of phase transitions in human hand movements. *Biological Cybernetics, 51*, 347–356.

Hinsz, V. B. (1999). Group decision making with responses of a quantitative nature: The theory of social decision schemes for quantities. *Organizational Behavior and Human Decision Processes, 80*, 28–49.

Hutchins, E. (1995a). *Cognition in the wild.* Cambridge, MA: MIT Press.

Hutchins, E. (1995b). How a cockpit remembers its speeds. *Cognitive Science, 19*, 265–288.

Hutchins, E. (2000). Distributed cognition. In N. J. Smelser & P. B. Baltes (Eds.), *International encyclopedia of the social and behavioral sciences* (pp. 1–10). Oxford, UK: Pergamon.

Iberall, A. S. (1987). A physics for studies of civilization. In F. E. Yates (Ed.), *Self-organizing systems: The emergence of order* (pp. 521–540). New York, NY: Plenum Press.

James, W. (1950). *The principles of psychology* (Vol. 1). New York, NY: Dover. (Original work published in 1890).

Jirsa, V. K., & Kelso, J. A. S. (Eds.). (2004). *Coordination dynamics: Issues and trends.* Berlin: Springer-Verlag.

Juarrero, A. (1999). *Dynamics in action: Intentional behavior as a complex system.* Cambridge, MA: MIT Press.

Kelso, J. A. S. (1995). *Dynamic patterns: The self-organization of brain and behavior.* Boston, MA: MIT Press.

Kirsh, D. (2006). Distributed cognition: A methodological note. *Pragmatics & Cognition, 14*, 249–262.

Klein, G., Ross, K. G., Moon, B. M., Klein, D. E., Hoffman, R. R., & Hollnagel, E. (2003). Macrocognition. *IEEE Intelligent Systems, 18*, 81–84.

Kozlowski, S. W. J., & Klein, K. J. (2000). A multilevel approach to theory and research in organizations: Contextual, temporal, and emergent processes. In K. Klein & S. W. J. Kozlowski (Eds.), *Multilevel theory, research and methods in organizations: Foundations, extensions, and new directions* (pp. 3–90). San Francisco, CA: Jossey-Bass.

Kugler, P. N., & Turvey, M. T. (1987). *Information, natural law, and the self-assembly of rhythmic movement.* Hillsdale, NJ: Lawrence Erlbaum Associates, Inc.

Langan-Fox, J., Code, S., & Langfield-Smith, K. (2000). Team mental models: Techniques, methods, and analytic approaches. *Human Factors, 42*, 242–271.

Theoretical Underpinning of Interactive Team Cognition • 207

Leonard, H. B., & Howitt, A. M. (2006). Katrina as prelude: Preparing for and responding to Katrina-class disturbances in the United States—Testimony to U.S. Senate Committee, March 8, 2006. *Journal of Homeland Security and Emergency Management, 3*, 1–20.

Levesque, L. L., Wilson, J. M., & Wholey, D. R. (2001). Cognitive divergence and shared mental models in software development project teams. *Journal of Organization Behavior, 22*, 135–144.

Lorge, I., Fox, D., Davitz, J., & Brenner, M. (1958). A survey of studies contrasting the quality of group performance and individual performance, 1920–1957. *Psychological Bulletin, 55*, 337–372.

Mandelbrot, B. B. (1977). *Fractals, form, chance, and dimension.* San Francisco, CA: Freeman.

Mathieu, J. E., Goodwin, G. F., Heffner, T. S., Salas, E., & Cannon-Bowers, J. A. (2000). The influence of shared mental models on team process and performance. *Journal of Applied Psychology, 85*, 273–283.

McBeath, M. K., Shaffer, D. M., & Kaiser, M. K. (1995). How baseball outfielders determine where to run to catch fly balls. *Science, 268*, 569–573.

McFadden, R. D. (2009, January 15). Pilot is hailed after jetliner's icy plunge. *The New York Times*, p. A1.

Michaels, C. F., & Carello, C. (1981). *Direct perception.* Englewood Cliffs, NJ: Prentice-Hall.

Newell, A. (1990). *Unified theories of cognition.* Cambridge, MA: Harvard University Press.

Nicolis, G., & Prigogine, I. (1989). *Exploring complexity: An introduction.* New York, NY: W. H. Freeman.

Rogers, Y. (2006). Distributed cognition and communication. In K. Brown (Ed.), *Encyclopedia of language and linguistics* (pp. 181–202). Oxford, UK: Elsevier.

Salas, E., Dickinson, T. L., Converse, S. A., & Tannenbaum, S. I. (1992). Toward an understanding of team performance and training. In R. W. Swezey & E. Salas (Eds.), *Teams: Their training and performance* (pp. 3–29). Norwood, NJ: Ablex.

Schmidt, R. C., Bienvenu, M., Fitzpatrick, P. A., & Amazeen, P. G. (1998). A comparison of intra- and interpersonal interlimb coordination: Coordination breakdowns and coupling strength. *Journal of Experimental Psychology: Human Perception and Performance, 24*, 884–900.

Simon, H. A. (1999). *The sciences of the artificial* (3rd ed.). Cambridge, MA: MIT Press.

Skinner, J. E., Pratt, C. M., & Vybiral, T. (1993). A reduction in the correlation dimension of heartbeat intervals precedes imminent ventricular fibrillation in human subjects. *American Heart Journal, 125*, 731–743.

Tognoli, E., & Kelso, J. A. S. (2009). Brain coordination dynamics: True and false faces of phase synchrony and metastability. *Progress in Neurobiology, 87*, 31–40.

Van Orden, G. C., Holden, J. G., & Turvey, M. T. (2003). Self-organization of cognitive performance. *Journal of Experimental Psychology: General, 132*, 331–350.

Vygotsky, L. S. (1978). *Mind in society: The development of higher mental processes.* Cambridge, MA: Harvard University Press.

Weist, W. M., Porter, L. W., & Ghiselli, E. E. (1961). Relationships between individual proficiency and team performance efficiency. *Journal of Applied Psychology, 45*, 435–440.

Wertsch, J. V. (1991). A sociocultural approach to socially shared cognition. In L. B. Resnick, J. M. Levine, & S. D. Teaseley (Eds.), *Perspectives on socially shared cognition* (pp. 85–100). Washington, DC: American Psychological Association.

Wertsch, J. V. (1994). The primacy of mediated action in sociocultural studies. *Mind, Culture, and Activity: An International Journal, 1*, 202–208.

Wilson, M. (2002). Six views of embodied cognition. *Psychonomic Bulletin & Review, 9*, 625–636.

9

Articulating Collaborative Contributions to Activity Awareness

John M. Carroll, Marcela Borge,
Craig H. Ganoe, and Mary Beth Rosson

ACTIVITY AWARENESS

Groups engaged in collaborative activities of significant scope and duration must achieve and maintain *awareness* of diverse aspects of their shared activity in order to coordinate effectively. For example, they must verify mutual presence and attention, which is fairly straightforward in face-to-face interaction, but often subtle, difficult, and a continuing challenge in computer-mediated collaboration. Members need to know what tools and resources they have access to and also what tools and resources their counterparts can access. The availability of tools and resources may change throughout the course of an activity. The group must have an understanding of who among them might know potentially relevant information or know how to do something that might be critical to the collective endeavor. Members need to know something of their partners' attitudes and goals and of what their partners expect from them and of the activity. They need to know what criteria their partners will use to evaluate joint outcomes, the moment-to-moment focus of their attention and action during the collaborative work, and how the view of the shared plan and the work actually accomplished evolves over time. All of these intentional variables change constantly as the task context itself changes.

Awareness in collaborative situations is sometimes regarded as a relatively discrete achievement, such as awareness of a task context (situation awareness), of group consensus, or of a shared mental model. These

209

210 • *Theories of Team Cognition*

simplifications can be useful for somewhat scripted collaborative tasks, such as managing single-threaded processes or team training exercises. However, they do not address routine sources of complexity. In realistically complex tasks of significant scope and duration, the *current situation* is defined to a considerable extent by its history, which in turn is constantly reconstructed by the group and by its individual members. For instance, knowing how other group members respond to criticisms can have a profound effect on group discussion and argumentation. The current situation is defined also by continuous exogenous dynamics that present a constantly changing situation to the group. Indeed, if awareness were to be supported by discrete updates, it would require a continual torrent of information, which ipso facto could never be useful or even usable. A striking lesson from 20 years of research on computer-supported collaborative work (CSCW) is that people are actually quite poor at communicating their intentions with respect to goals and plans (Bannon, 1995; Suchman, 1994; Winograd, 1994).

Shared mental models are a popular way to think about the knowledge and skills that teams use to manage collective activity. But the notion of identical copies of knowledge used and maintained by team members to enable coordination is both exotic and cumbersome as a foundation for a joint endeavor. Team members who believe that they should hold exactly the same understanding of a current task might spend considerable time and effort verifying agreed-upon preconditions for action, making them less useful to their partners in action than members who have different perspectives and who could play different roles and take different team responsibilities. Moreover, too much literal shared understanding could entrain redundant capabilities, where a team is never better than its best member. Teams with homogeneous understandings are maximally vulnerable to groupthink and stagnant thinking. Analogous to arguments regarding natural selection, the more variation that exists in a team, in individual backgrounds, mind-sets, and strategic approaches, the better the chances for that team to adapt to new and novel situations (Chakravarthy, 1982). For realistic and complex one-of-kind situations, such as emergency response, information analysis, and software design, creativity, learning, and adaptation are critical to team performance. Theories of macrocognition must explicate the development and use of team knowledge in such circumstances. We are trying to articulate a sense of shared understanding among team members that is robust with respect to exogenous dynamics and that can, in principle, leverage collaboration to produce performance better than any team member.

In prior work, we introduced the concept of *activity awareness* as a programmatic analysis for the mutual awareness of partners sharing an activity of significant scope and duration (Carroll, Neale, Isenhour, Rosson, & McCrickard, 2003; Carroll, Rosson, Convertino, & Ganoe, 2006; Carroll, Rosson, Farooq, & Xiao, 2009). Activity awareness builds on, but transcends, synchronous awareness of where a partner's cursor is pointing, where the partner is looking, and other immediate features of a task situation. More importantly, it transcends the sharing of identical states of situation awareness or mental models. Indeed, we would argue that lower level and simpler aspects of awareness are appropriately conceptualized as mediated by shared mental models: All stakeholders in a joint activity must have the same understanding of primitive and objective situation properties, such as the document being edited, the key that was pressed, and the reference of a deictic. However, shared mental models are neither useful nor possible for intentional situation properties such as role-based interpretations and strategies, personal insights and perspectives, opportunistic problem solving derived from interactions with tools and other resources, value-based assessments drawing on personal histories, expectations and attributions about one's teammates, and so on.

In framing activity awareness, we appropriated the concept of *activity* from activity theory (Engeström, Miettinen, & Punamaki, 1999; Wertsch, 1981) to emphasize that collaborators need be aware of a whole, shared activity as complex, socially and culturally embedded endeavor, organized in dynamic hierarchies, and not merely aware of the synchronous and easily noticeable aspects of the activity. In this view, awareness is teleologically inseparable from collective regulation of a joint endeavor. Members need to be engaged with one another's interests, values, and possibly relevant knowledge and skills; initial and current goals and motivations; criteria for evaluating outcomes; and assessments of the status and trajectory of ongoing work. This engagement is continually negotiated and developed. We articulated this continual process of activity awareness into four facets (Table 9.1) that should be viewed as ongoing interaction protocols rather than static sources of knowledge. They are arenas of conceptual negotiation among members of a team. Ours is a developmental framework in the traditional sense of Piaget and Vygotsky: Higher

212 • *Theories of Team Cognition*

TABLE 9.1

Four Facets of Activity Awareness

Facet of Activity Awareness	Description
Common ground	**A communication protocol** for signaling and enhancing shared knowledge and beliefs
Communities of practice	**A coordination protocol** for developing and applying community-specific practices through enactment
Social capital	**A cooperation protocol** of resource exchanges that engender and sustain generalized reciprocity and trust
Human development	**A group regulation protocol** encouraging innovative decisions and approaches in open-system problem solving to evolve group capacities and performance

level facets are enabled by and resolve conflicts in lower level facets (for a more detailed discussion, see Carroll et al., 2006).

Most basically, activity awareness is achieved through the joint construction of *common ground*—shared knowledge and beliefs, mutually identified and agreed upon by members through a rich variety of linguistic signaling (Clark, 1996). Common ground is not merely having shared mental models (e.g., Mathieu, Heffner, Goodwin, Salas, & Cannon-Bowers, 2000); it is participating in a continuous regulatory protocol of testing and verifying conceptual alignment. Thus, an important part of common ground is signaling and acknowledging differences, in order to make it possible that differences among members can become resources to the group instead of risks. Common ground allows members to communicate more effectively by allowing elision of "given" information and emphasis on what is "new" (Clark & Haviland, 1977). It promotes group development through feelings of identification and belonging and through mutual trust and social support. Common ground helps people act together by helping them communicate about activity. In this sense, it is always critical to joint activity. However, joint activity also involves transcending explicit communication.

Communities of practice (CoPs) emerge from collaborative endeavors that are already creating common ground (Wenger, McDermott, & Snyder, 2002). The achievement of common ground makes it possible to develop a shared practice, that is, to articulate roles and responsibilities of members, including recruiting and socializing new members, and to codify standards of conduct and approaches to assessing performance.

Articulating Collaborative Contributions to Activity Awareness • 213

Shared practice is at least partly tacit knowledge (Duguid, 2005), conveyed through enactment and apprenticeship in activity contexts. Through participating together in work activity, such as planning and coordinating effort, giving and receiving advice, and evaluating joint outcomes (including diagnosing breakdowns), members continually learn, share, and refine core goals, values, and practices. These functions of CoPs constitute a facet of activity awareness. Note that higher order CoP achievements such as division of responsibility are enabled by common ground achievements such as identification and trust and, in turn, enable more complex and ambitious joint projects. Where common ground provides a lightweight and general foundation for collaboration, CoPs provide a richer and more narrowly scoped foundation.

Collaboration requires more than effective communication and shared practices. It requires shared values and motives (as in activity theory; Engeström et al., 1999) and a common framework for thinking about and managing social networks through time. Groups engaged in complex and sustained tasks inevitably experience stress; powerful social mechanisms must support sustained participation through effortful or divisive episodes. *Social capital* is created through the exchange of resources and support in a social network and the feelings and beliefs about generalized reciprocity that these exchanges engender in members (Coleman, 1988). Members' awareness of this overall framework of shared values and equitable treatment acts as an exception handling mechanism, preserving civility and performance in a group despite occasional conflicts.

When people plan, negotiate, and coordinate with others in open-ended endeavors over significant spans of time, when they solve problems that are ill defined and consequential, and when they stretch their own capabilities, they develop; that is, they come to experience and interact with the world in new ways. In activity theory, *human development* is a normal outcome of significant activity, but it is also profound in the sense that it qualitatively changes one's awareness of activity. As an individual develops, he or she becomes more able to understand, to reconcile, and to integrate different levels of performance and different approaches to problems by synthesizing zones of proximal development. The successive elaboration of personal perspectives further enhances each member's awareness of his or her own activity and creates myriad new ways to construct common ground, codify practices, and build social capital (Engeström, 2008).

214 • *Theories of Team Cognition*

A shorthand for activity awareness is a group's awareness and regulation of its own activity.

Activity awareness is fundamentally a dynamic process, not a state of knowledge. It involves monitoring and integrating many different kinds of information at different levels of analysis, such as events, tasks, goals, social interactions and their meanings, group values and norms, and more. It involves monitoring, integrating, and more or less continuingly learning about developing circumstances and the initiatives, reactions, and sense making of other people with respect to ongoing and anticipated courses of action. Activity awareness is not merely a matter of coordinating status information. It must be continually negotiated and constructed throughout the course of a collaborative interaction. It is a process that is constitutive of collaboration.

In this chapter, we address specific macrocognitive functions required for achieving and maintaining activity awareness in a small group. Our account articulates a set of specific collaborative competences as realms of regulation and control managed by individual team members. We describe how these regulatory processes contribute to activity awareness. Demonstrating competence requires the ability to monitor and regulate the thinking and behavioral processes that surround a task by using differing strategies to achieve preselected goals (Brown & Palincsar, 1985; Kuhn, Black, Keselman, & Kaplan, 2000; Schoenfeld, 1987; White, Shimoda, & Frederiksen, 1999). Teams can improve the quality of their interactions and their products by finding ways to systematize processes for monitoring and regulating collaborative activity and by developing better methods for team training and support. Software designers can also facilitate monitoring and regulating of these actions by designing technology that helps teams focus on these important processes while addressing problems arising from distributed contexts (non–face-to-face interactions).

Our argument proceeds as follows. In the next section, we summarize our ongoing experimental studies of activity awareness, emphasizing not only what we are learning but also the challenges introduced by an experimental laboratory research model. Following that, we outline a theory of collaborative competence and argue that collaborative competence should be seen as one of the core macrocognitive capacities that enables a CoP. The theory individuates four realms of regulation and control, and we argue that effective collaborations must succeed in these four realms; by forming and regulating these aspects of collaboration, groups will form and maintain shared practices, thereby supporting their activity awareness. In the final section, we discuss tools and activities we have been creating to support development of collaborative skills, and activity awareness more generally, in teams.

EMPIRICAL STUDIES OF ACTIVITY AWARENESS

Using activity theory (Engeström et al., 1999) and activity awareness (Carroll et al., 2006) as conceptual lenses, we have used experimental methods to investigate the dynamic processes of team formation and interaction (Carroll, Convertino, Rosson, & Ganoe, 2008; Convertino, Mentis, Bhambare, et al., 2008; Convertino, Mentis, Rosson, et al., 2008; Convertino, Mentis, Rosson, Slavkovic, & Carroll, 2009). Our first set of experiments focused on the protocol for assessing and contributing to common ground (Clark & Brennan, 1991). We studied three-person teams working on an emergency planning problem, where each team member was first trained for a particular role and gained expertise relevant to the problem (e.g., civil engineering). Using a variety of converging methods, we noted the ways in which shared understanding emerged, was reinforced, and contributed to shared decision making. Of particular interest was the distinction between *content* and *process* common ground: Most studies of common ground have worked with simpler tasks and have limited their attention to shared content (i.e., task-specific information), relying on over-learned communication processes (e.g., clarifying, checking). However, in our more complex setting, we documented the separate contributions of both forms of shared understanding—*what* the task is about and *how* we will manage our work with it (Convertino, Mentis, Bhambare, et al., 2008; Convertino, Mentis, Rosson, et al., 2008; Convertino et al., 2009).

Currently, we are conducting a related set of laboratory experiments where teams work together on information analysis scenarios. Although we are using similar methods in these studies, our specific focus is on the concept of *transactive memory* as an element of common ground (Nevo & Wand, 2005). Again, three-person teams work through an extended task, in this case a 4-hour crime-solving scenario. Each team member takes on the role of a different expert (records analyst, Web analyst, or interview analyst). The analysts have enough collective information to solve a series of fictitious laptop thefts (e.g., bank transactions, course schedules, online

216 • *Theories of Team Cognition*

interactions on Facebook and other sites, interview records). Together the team members share and build on one another's information to accomplish three tasks: (1) narrow down a list of 26 persons of interest to the eight most likely suspects (phase 1); (2) identify thieves for each of four thefts, along with their motives and accomplices (phase 2); and (3) predict the time, place, and thief for the next related crime (phase 3). In our analysis, we plan to explore relationships between levels of activity awareness in general, and shared understanding in particular, with levels of successful task completion. Methodologically, we are developing and refining measures for assessing shared understanding in a more distributed and dynamic fashion, that is, as a dynamic protocol that constructs and maintains shared information rather than as a singular mental model that is shared by all.

A challenge in scaling up the concept of awareness to collaborative activities of significant scope and duration is that some of the components' processes develop over time frames beyond the scale of a typical experiment. Our laboratory studies of emergency planning and information analysis involve 3 to 4 packed hours of problem solving, but the team experiences are still too brief to evoke the extended authentic negotiation, process innovation, and team learning involved in development of collaborative practices. The teams do not have the time to coalesce as CoPs. Therefore, we are exploring a more extended model of team interaction and learning within a project-based course in usability engineering; in this course, five to six advanced undergraduates form teams that work together for 15 weeks. In the balance of this chapter, we share the design research that we have been doing with learning activities and associated tools that are aimed at supporting activity awareness in these teams. We begin by detailing a theoretical framework for conceptualizing and supporting the development of team collaboration skills as an aspect of macrocognition that is a key element of activity awareness, and then describe in more detail the usability engineering teams and their collaborative activities.

THE RELATIONSHIP BETWEEN COLLABORATIVE COMPETENCE AND ACTIVITY AWARENESS

Macrocognition is a collection of mental processes that simultaneously simplify and complicate the study of human cognition and learning.

Warner and Letsky (2008) define macrocognition as "the internalized and externalized high-level mental processes employed by teams to create new knowledge during complex, one-of-a-kind, collaborative problem-solving" (p. 8). Thus, by definition, macrocognition brings cognition into the social realm by referring to a group of individuals who share common goals and work together to solve a problem. This sharing of goals and plans can be helpful to researchers because it provides them with a window into individuals' mental processes. As team members share, argue about, and build on information, researchers witness thought processes in action. However, collaborative problem solving is not as straightforward as some models of macrocognition might lead us to believe. The social dimension of macrocognition makes it far more intricate than individual problem solving; individuals must deal not only with the challenges inherent to the task, but also with the challenges that come from interacting with each other. With individual problem solving, researchers can infer correlations between ineffective or incorrect problem solving and particular thought processes. But in the case of macrocognition, the inferences are more difficult to make because failures in problem solving may arise from breakdowns in individual cognitive processes, group processes, or both.

The nature of the macrocognitive processes that a team follows can have important consequences on its development and performance as a team (Webb & Palincsar, 1996). For instance, some processes are known to promote learning and cognitive development. Conflict and controversy, central to Piagetian theories of cognitive development, can improve motivation, help people identify gaps in their own understanding, and facilitate deeper understanding (Brown & Palincsar, 1989; Engle & Conant, 2002; Johnson & Johnson, 1979; Piaget, 1976). As group members engage in argumentation, they defend their positions, provide rationale and evidence, look for more information, understand opposing points of view, and ultimately develop a deeper understanding of the concepts they discuss (Brown & Palincsar, 1989). Similar to conflict, the giving and receiving of help also provides individuals with opportunities to verbalize what they know or do not know and improve their understanding. Giving help encourages individuals to reorganize their thinking and provide information in a way that others will understand, helping them to clarify and identify gaps in their own understanding; receiving help can correct misconceptions and strengthen connections between already existing and evolving knowledge (Wittrock, 1990). Through mechanisms such as productive argumentation

218 • *Theories of Team Cognition*

and the giving and receiving of help, team members engage in the coconstruction of ideas. This process is at the very core of the Vygotskian theory of learning and development. As groups or pairs of individuals build on each other's ideas, they are able to produce and understand together what they cannot do alone (Brown & Palincsar, 1985; Forman & Cazdan, 1985; Vygotsky, 1978). It is thus surprising that the monitoring and regulation of these macrocognitive processes has received relatively little attention in education.

Similarities Between Macro- and Metacognition

Macrocognition shares many similarities with metacognition, and therefore, understanding its components and how they work to improve individual performance can help us to better understand how macrocognitive components such as collaborative competence may affect team outcomes. Metacognition is a vastly complicated term used to encompass a wide variety of theories about individual cognition and its various levels of analysis. The literature on it is quite extensive, but Brown (1984) and Schraw (1998) provide good reviews. For our purposes, we provide an extremely simplified breakdown of two of metacognition's major components: (1) knowledge about your own thinking and about an activity you are engaged in, and (2) regulation or control over your own cognitive and behavioral processes. Both of these components have been shown to affect individuals' learning and performance outcomes, but we will break the second one down further because it is most closely related to activity awareness.

There are many skills that have been associated with metacognitive regulation, but the most commonly cited are planning, monitoring, and evaluation (Schraw, 1998; White et al., 1999). Effective planning requires access to individual knowledge stores in order to understand the requirements of the activity and how best to satisfy objectives. An expert planner will use declarative, procedural, and conditional knowledge in order to select the best strategies for the task at hand (Bjork, 1994; Schraw, 1998). To effectively engage in regulatory activity, individuals have to be able to step back from the task, look at their activity as an object of thought, and evaluate the effectiveness of a strategy while they are working; this is often referred to as monitoring or online awareness. Online awareness helps individuals better assess a situation in order to evaluate and correct their strategies as necessary (for a review, see Schraw & Dennison, 1994).

Articulating Collaborative Contributions to Activity Awareness • 219

Turning now to macrocognition, we see these three components of metacognition—knowledge, regulation, and awareness—as similar in many ways to components of macrocognition, such as common ground, regulation or control of macrocognitive processes and behaviors, and activity awareness. Common ground is similar to the knowledge aspect of metacognition in that it encompasses the knowledge base one has of him- or herself, his or her group or organizations, and where, what, how, and in what ways knowledge is stored and shared. Macrocognitive regulation is quite similar to the type of regulation that an individual might have to enact in order to correct or prevent ineffective team strategies. Finally, we contend that just as awareness of one's individual activities is an essential aspect of metacognitive regulation, so too is activity awareness an essential component of macrocognitive regulation, as it will help the team to provide the most accurate evaluation of its current use of strategies, processes, products, and behaviors. Activity awareness and the development of macrocognitive skills (i.e., collaborative competence) work together much in the same way that that awareness of cognition and development of metacognitive skills work together—each helping the development of the other.

Developing Collaborative Competence

Although Vygotskian and Piagetian theory are often used to motivate collaborative interactions as a common element of educational and professional practice, little emphasis has been directed at teaching the skills needed for successful collaboration. Benefits from conflict and controversy, the giving and receiving of help, and the coconstruction of ideas all require individuals to feel comfortable enough to admit they do not understand an idea or to build on or criticize another's ideas. However, evidence suggests that many students are weak in the skills of critical evaluation that would lead them to identify misconceptions or erroneous solutions (Borge & Carroll, 2010; Driver, Newton, & Osborn, 2000; Nelson-Le Gall, 1981, 1985). Furthermore, many student teams lack the psychological safety (Edmondson, 1999) or perceived value of engaging in productive forms of argumentation (Metz, 2004; Webb & Palincsar, 1996). When a team is composed of individuals who lack the knowledge to understand the importance of such processes or the skill to perform such processes effectively, they will likely fail to reap the benefits associated

220 • *Theories of Team Cognition*

with collaborative problem-solving activities and fail to meet or exceed their individual capabilities (Barron, 2000, 2003).

Problems associated with collaborative processes can have profound effects on a team and often stem from an inability to monitor and regulate interactions (Barron, 2003; Borge & Carroll, 2010; West, 2007). Research on school-aged students working on complex mathematical activities has shown that even highly intelligent, capable teams can fail when interactions are not properly regulated (Barron, 2003). When students do not pay attention to aspects of communication or critical evaluation, they are likely to miss key bits of information necessary to correctly solve a problem and be completely unaware of each other's parallel activities (Barron, 2003; Borge, 2007). Another study, conducted by West (2007) and centering on collective cognition and entrepreneurial teams in the business world, found that improved performance was significantly associated with two team characteristics: differentiation (the variance in people's characteristics) and integration (the extent to which these differences can be used by a team as a resource). Having members with differing backgrounds, expertise, and so on can bring in a wider range of ideas and points of view, providing rich fodder for planning and problem solving. However, benefits of differentiation are dependent on the team's ability to walk a fine line between encouraging differences and integrating ideas. If there is too much differentiation, the group is unproductive; if there is too much integration, the team can fall subject to problems of groupthink. Once again, it comes back to issues of awareness, monitoring, and regulation.

Hogan (1999a) tried to improve collaborative interaction in school-age children by teaching them about collaborative activity and testing whether instruction could improve students' knowledge and practice of collaborative concepts and techniques. We refer to interventions of this sort as collaborative theory instruction: instructional activities aimed at teaching students about collaborative concepts and techniques. Hogan (1999a) embedded the instruction into a science unit where students collaborated on a project. The aim was to improve students' interactions by providing them with the tools necessary to maintain a well-run "social machine." However, Hogan's (1999a) findings were not as positive as expected. She found that collaborative theory instruction only improved students' awareness of the concepts and techniques associated with collaborative activity, but not students' ability to apply these concepts and techniques

Articulating Collaborative Contributions to Activity Awareness • 221

in real practice. In fact, she found no instances of students using these concepts and techniques to regulate their interactions.

We propose that if teams are to alter their macrocognitive processes, they must have mutual awareness of their objectives and how achievement of these goals imply different kinds of collaborative interactions. This knowledge can then bring about change: understand how current objectives agree or differ with shared goals for effective collaborative processes, identify problems that can interfere with these collaborative process goals, know differing strategies to correct or prevent these problems, and elaborate these with tactics to implement the strategies. The next step is to move from thought to action, to take this knowledge and practice applying it in context. In other words, being aware of what needs to be done is not enough; a team must be able to carry out its process-related objectives in real-world scenarios. This action-oriented process requires the regulatory aspect of metacognition: the control, the ability to select strategies and apply concepts. If the goal is to move from an understanding to an implementation of effective collaborative interactions, we need to connect mutual awareness to mutual regulation of shared tasks and processes. The ability to make this connection and apply it within a team environment is what we have termed *collaborative competence.*

Demonstrating competence, whether in mathematical problem solving (Schoenfeld, 1987), reading comprehension (Brown & Palincsar, 1985), scientific inquiry (Kuhn et al., 2000; White et al., 1999), or collaborative activity (Barron, 2003), requires an ability to monitor and regulate the thinking and behavioral processes that surround the task by using differing strategies to achieve preselected goals. Collaborative competence necessitates that collaborators understand the main goals of their interactions and are able to employ collective metacognitive and sociocognitive strategies to achieve these goals. In general, these strategies will correspond to verbalized interactions that a team can use to plan, monitor, reflect, and revise their group processes (metacognitive) in order to meet goals for communication, mediation of ideas, productivity, and joint planning (sociocognitive). People need explicit knowledge of task goals and strategies in order to monitor and control their performance (Boekaerts, 1996; Butler & Winne, 1995). Thus teams need to negotiate shared process and task goals and agree on differing strategies that they can use to prevent or correct problems before they occur.

222 • *Theories of Team Cognition*

Facilitating teams' negotiation of shared process and task goals requires careful structuring of collaborative activities so as to promote the use of collective metacognitive activities. Individual metacognitive activities can occur inside the head of one member and help that member to monitor and regulate his or her own performance. In this "individual" scenario, metacognitive awareness does not exist in the collaborative space. There is no shared understanding of process or task goals. Monitoring of group problems is not reciprocal and neither is process regulation. For metacognition to be collective, it must be verbalized and discussed by the group. Similar to Roschelle's (1992) claim that in order for knowledge convergence to occur meaning must be displayed, confirmed, and repaired by a group, we believe the same is true for process knowledge. Multiple team members must share awareness of problems or strategies, problems must be verbally identified when they occur, and the team must work together to use strategies to correct or prevent problems. When the activity or objective is to create effective collaborative processes, then the focus of collective metacognitive activities has to be on team process, not on tasks per se. Examples of such activities include team process planning (i.e., selecting process goals), team process regulation (i.e., using strategies to correct problems that counter process goals), and team process reflection (i.e., thinking about existing processes and the usefulness of strategies).

Articulating and Guiding Development of Collaboration Competence

Recently, researchers have been developing methods that guide students in focusing on process awareness and engaging in collective metacognitive activities; the methods rely on the modeling, scaffolding, coaching, and repeated practice that are characteristics of the cognitive apprenticeship teaching model (Collins, Brown, & Newman, 1991) that has been applied to domains such as mathematics, inquiry science, and reading comprehension (Brown & Campione, 1994; Brown & Palincsar, 1985; Schoenfeld, 1987). Researchers have also found the model useful in teaching collaborative competence (Borge, 2007; Borge & White, under review; White & Fredericksen, 2005). The model was applied by assigning beneficial sociocognitive roles to students and asking them to identify goals for their interactions, plan out strategies to prevent or correct problems, and then practice monitoring and regulating their set goals.

This sort of collaborative process instruction is known as collaborative competence instruction.

Following this approach, Borge (2007) found not only high frequencies of students regulating their interactions, but also significantly higher frequencies of students accepting or discussing such regulatory behaviors than dismissing or ignoring such behaviors. This was critical because collaborative activities operate within a group dynamic, which means that in order for regulation to work not only must someone propose a strategy or a goal for the team to focus on, but the team must also accept this proposal and use it. Despite these generally positive findings, questions remain as to which roles are necessary: What are the critical realms of regulation and control to which teams must attend? For instance, the Borge study also reported trends for teams to engage in parallel planning and decision making, where team members were unaware of others' comments or activities, even as they employed regulatory strategies. These are important considerations that need to be further explored and detailed.

Toward this aim, one aspect of our research on collaborative teams focuses on the social plane, where three elements of the team interact, and team members must figure out how to monitor and regulate each other's activity so as to learn from each other and be consistently successful problem solvers. These three elements are (1) the characteristics of the people who make up the team (e.g., expertise, personalities, cognitive styles, demographics); (2) the opportunities for and requirements placed on members (e.g., growth and experience, time demands, level of commitment); and (3) the resources available to the team (e.g., physical and digital tools) (McGrath, Arrow, & Berdahl, 2000). We contend that effective collaborative activity lies at the juncture of team process and these three elements, with the collaborative processes that take place between members as they learn about and deal with aspects of all three of these elements; this is where knowledge-building activity lives. These collaborative processes can be easily overlooked as a team focuses on finishing a task, prioritizing productivity over learning and evaluation (Borge & Carroll, 2010). Thus, we have argued that for problem-solving teams to continuously learn and be successful, they must pay attention to four realms of regulation and control: planning, communication, critical evaluation, and productivity. Each of these realms pushes team members to monitor and regulate interactions so as to promote processes associated with learning and cognitive development and further promote the development of activity awareness.

224 • *Theories of Team Cognition*

TABLE 9.2

Four Realms Contributing to Collaboration Competence

Planning: Developing a shared analysis of task goals that helps the team to select and focus on effective goals, work together in an equitable fashion, and plan activities and decisions jointly, with no one person controlling the team

Communication: Participating equally with other team members, contributing ideas, listening to and understanding each other, building on one another's ideas, and developing a shared understanding

Critical Evaluation: Considering differing points of view in a critical but constructive way, expressing and evaluating trade-offs, and reaching agreement about the best ideas or courses of action

Productivity: Monitoring the team's progress and the extent to which it does or does not meet deadlines; making adjustments in planning, communication, and critical evaluation to better meet deadlines; and producing high-quality work in a timely manner

Table 9.2 summarizes the four realms of collaborative skill, and we expand on them in the following paragraphs.

Planning is crucial because it encompasses developing an understanding of the explicit and implicit goals of the task, person variables, and resources that will enable a team to find the best possible strategies and tactics for action. A critical aspect of planning is organization, for example, ensuring that the group establishes organizational norms for collecting, integrating, and storing information. Team members should simultaneously build activity awareness when required to discuss collaborative process goals and objectives, select strategies, and employ tactics to implement, monitor, and control their group processes. These types of discussions can facilitate the development of a shared understanding of what the team will be doing, who will be responsible for differing aspects, in what order tasks will be accomplished, why it will be done as planned, where important information will be housed, and how they can access it.

Communication is obviously a necessary process in the coconstruction of ideas, as well as in the giving and receiving of help. However, to be effective, communication must fulfill specific objectives. Team members must ensure that they not only listen to who is speaking, but also are actually listening for understanding. In other words, they must make sure that they can summarize what another member has said from their own perspective and regulate activity accordingly when it is evident that team members are preoccupied or confused. These behaviors

Articulating Collaborative Contributions to Activity Awareness • 225

discourage parallel thinking, where team members work independently, constructing separate, unrelated ideas. Another important consideration is discouraging overdependence on leaders to communicate ideas and control information flow. This requires that a team pay attention to who is speaking and whether other team members are encouraged to contribute, in order to prevent dominant behaviors. In this way, the team increases the likelihood of integrating various forms of information and points of view.

Critical evaluation helps to ensure that team members pause to consider alternative solutions, evaluate options, and weigh these options to make effective decisions. Teams faced with time constraints can easily miss alternative options or better solutions as they rush to finish a task (Borge & Carroll, 2010). Schoenfeld (1987) analyzes this metacognitive deficiency with a comparison between naive and expert mathematical problem solvers. Naive problem solvers, those new to a task or field, were more likely than expert problem solvers to fall victim to linear forms of thinking, where they picked one strategy and soldiered on no matter how many dead ends they hit. In contrast, expert problem solvers alternated between selecting strategies, working on the problem, evaluating and changing strategies, and going back to the problem until it was successfully resolved. By requiring students to engage in critical evaluation of their own thinking processes and providing them with opportunities to "see" their own thinking processes, students were less likely to fall victim to ineffectual, linear forms of thinking. As an intervention, Schoenfeld (1987) shared his own (expert) thinking processes with students, by thinking aloud and verbalizing strategies while solving complex mathematical problems. He then coached students to focus on the strategies and processes they engaged in and to stop to evaluate them. Emphasizing these aspects of critical evaluation increased the likelihood that students would consider alternative strategies and solutions, evaluate their cognitive processes, and find the best solutions to complex problems.

Lastly, attention to the realm of *productivity* will encourage teams to continually balance critical evaluation with time constraints, pushing teams to find efficient ways to integrate ideas. Part of productivity is also being mindful of the quality of work the team is producing and ensuring that the team stops to implement the strategies they originally planned, forcing them to continually reflect on and revise team practices, interactions, responsibilities, and priorities.

226 • *Theories of Team Cognition*

Requiring team members to monitor and regulate all four realms as part of a collaborative task would increase team members' awareness of their emerging collaboration processes as they change and evolve during the course of their work, contributing to their overall activity awareness. However, attending to all four realms while simultaneously trying to accomplish a task may be overwhelming. One way to minimize the complexity and help teams manage all of the realms is to assign sociocognitive roles to team members, with one role for each of the four realms. The expectation is that each role requires a member to manage team interactions in a way that would help to fulfill the goals for that realm. Thus we have been specifying and guiding group members toward four roles that correspond to planning, communication, critical evaluation, and productivity.

In earlier work (Borge, 2007), we developed guides and activities to demystify collaborative processes for team members while providing them with concrete mechanisms for regulatory actions. More concretely, four guides were created to orient attention to and practice within the different realms of collaborative skill. Each guide presents the major process goals of that realm, problems that could interfere with process goals, strategies to correct or prevent these problems, and examples of tactics for carrying out strategies. The original work was conducted in the context of an elementary school classroom. Thus we have modified the guides to meet the needs of our current educational context (advanced undergraduates taking university courses; an excerpt from one guide for planning is shown in Figure 9.1). Similar modifications to these guides could be provided for a variety of educational settings or learning domains.

Assigning sociocognitive process–oriented roles to team members and supporting the roles with tools such as guides that include specific suggestions for action could prove extremely beneficial for teams. The roles are grounded in research literature and provide explicit objectives and strategies for preventing or correcting group processing problems. Having a clear understanding of all of the goals and subgoals of an activity, as well as mechanisms for correcting problems, is a critical part of successful self-regulation (Butler & Winne, 1995; Kuhn et al., 2000; Webb & Palincsar, 1996). We believe these roles could facilitate activity awareness with respect to CoPs, helping teams to select better approaches to activities and helping them monitor and regulate their interactions. Recurrent monitoring and regulating of interactions could increase the likelihood that a team

Articulating Collaborative Contributions to Activity Awareness • 227

Planning/organization goals and strategies

Coworker interactions (Teammates)

Goal: Take time to evaluate a task before starting it.

Problem: The team rushes to start working on the task without thinking about it.

Strategy: Take time to evaluate tasks and time constraints.
"Okay, we have 30 minutes to do three things. Does it make sense to give each 10 minutes, or do we think some are more complex than others?"

Problem: The team does tasks in order rather than prioritizing and assigning.

Strategy: Just because a team has three tasks listed, dosen't mean you need to do them in the order specified. Some tasks should be done first and others can be done simultaneously. In order to decide order, priority, and whether tasks can be assigned to subgroups, the team must spend a few moments discussing how much time, effort, and value each task has and think creatively about the best way to get it done.
"We have to interview our clients, collect information about the company, and then upload any artifacts to our case study. Well, we should not talk to clients before understanding their company or system so we should do that first—we can all research different areas. Then we should all come up with five important question and then we can select the best ones from that list. I think we should upload artifacts as we go; every time we find information on the company, take a screen shot and add it..."

Goal: Develop a joint game plan: strategically approach tasks as a team.

Problem: Meetings are disorganized and mismanaged.

Strategy: Prior to meeting send out an email asking members to suggest topics of discussion or tasks that need to be addressed during the meeting. Use this information to create an agenda for the meeting and email agenda to members.

FIGURE 9.1
Excerpt from collaboration competence guide (planning).

would be able to adapt to new problems as they emerge and resolve them before they corrupt the group's processes and products. Furthermore, giving each member a specific role may also help to distribute authority, so that each member becomes a valuable stakeholder in the team's processes. This could also reduce the probability that a priori social hierarchies will influence member participation.

We propose that team members who are assigned roles informed by theory and tested in practice will develop more effective collaborative practices than those who are simply left to develop their own social roles. Sociocognitive roles have been shown to naturally emerge "in the wild" (Hogan, 1999b). That is to say, that if left to their own devices, team members will develop their own sociocognitive roles, some helpful and

228 • *Theories of Team Cognition*

some detrimental to collaborative processes (i.e., promoter of reflection or promoter of distraction). But by focusing on desirable roles only, a set of assigned roles could be used over time to consistently promote positive behaviors, develop collaborative expertise, and facilitate productive, effective collaborative interactions. In the long run, the sociocognitive roles and supporting materials could potentially make a large contribution to the field of collaborative learning, assuming that use of this instructional method continues to show that teams can be taught to regulate and improve their collaborative interactions.

Although we have considered using materials like this to enhance the collaborative competence of the teams in our experimental studies of activity awareness, in the end, we felt the laboratory task context to be insufficient for the tactical learning of collaborative processes. Tactical learning requires repeated practice in order for participants to improve their problem-solving processes. Even a relatively toy-scale task such as the Missionary and Cannibals logic puzzle, can require more than three practice iterations (3.6 on average) for participants to improve their performance (Greeno, 1974). Getting teams to learn enough tactical knowledge to improve something as complex as group processes would likely require far more practice and longer lengths of time. A more appropriate context would be one where a team is expected to work together over a longer span of time on a complex, collaborative endeavor. A semester-long project, for example, could provide us with such an opportunity to implement and explore collaborative competence instruction and the development of technological tools to support it. We turn now to the work we have been carrying out in this more extended activity context.

SUPPORTING ACTIVITY AWARENESS IN COLLABORATIVE TEAMWORK

Our tool support for activity awareness originated in a participatory design project with science teachers, mentors, and middle school and high school students in Montgomery County, Virginia, that resulted in a "virtual school" environment for collaborative learning (Chin, Rosson, & Carroll, 1997). At that time (late 1990s), we had the goal of supporting synchronous collaboration in a virtual science lab, and our design attention was on situational and user interface widget awareness. Situational awareness can be roughly defined as "knowing what is going on around you" (Endsley, 2000, p. 4), while user interface widget awareness emphasizes what collaborators are currently doing in the system (e.g., where each person's cursor or mouse pointer currently is, what each of their viewports are displaying). However, subsequent analysis of students collaborating remotely using the virtual school software found that many long-term student collaboration breakdowns resulted from awareness problems less ephemeral than those addressed by situation awareness, namely awareness and coordination of team goals, plans to reach those goals, progress toward those goals, and criteria for assessing progress (Carroll et al., 2003). In these projects, the student teams would research a topic (e.g., bridge building), develop an understanding of related science concepts, and develop experiments to test their understanding (e.g., building a physical model). Teams consisted of students from classrooms at different schools, and the activity awareness issues were particularly problematic for distributed student teams that had minimal overlapping classroom time to use for synchronous sessions.

Awareness issues such as these motivated the design of Classroom BRIDGE, a collaborative software environment used by both distributed and same-place middle and high schools students on month-long or longer team science projects (Ganoe et al., 2003). This tool incorporates activity awareness support features that are integrated, incidental, and public: Awareness information is *integrated* into the system's primary information displays and functionality, it is collected *incidentally* (i.e., requiring no special action by users), and it is available *publicly* for everyone on the team to see. The shared workspace in Classroom BRIDGE includes timeline-based access to the content under development by a team. Instead of the hierarchical file structure commonplace on current desktop operating systems, students can access content using a timeline list view that emphasizes the order and intensity with which contributions are being made. Team members can quickly see which documents have been worked on recently, how often they have been used, and how they relate to upcoming deadlines. Classroom BRIDGE also includes a persistent chat that lets students see a history of their team discussions. Thus, although synchronous collaboration is still supported, students who cannot be in the same session can still review what has happened, follow up on discussions they missed, and so on. In our current design research, we are reusing many of the awareness concepts explored in Classroom BRIDGE, while also

230 • *Theories of Team Cognition*

investigating ways to provide more explicit support for the development of collaborative competence.

Simulating Real-World Collaboration Through Case-Based Learning

Our usability engineering course at Penn State relies a great deal on semester-long student design projects. To promote authentic learning, we introduce students to the Usability Case Studies (UCS) repository (http://ucs.ist.psu.edu/), which contains detailed design cases of software projects developed by companies and other organizations. Rich multimedia cases on the site document a history of user interface design and development for multiple design projects in industry, nonprofits, and academia. Materials from all phases of the usability engineering cycle (e.g., requirements gathering, interaction design, usability testing) are represented in the form of interviews, project documents, storyboards, screenshots of prototypes, and design rationale. The students carry out analysis activities using the case studies as resources; they also conduct their own design projects using the case studies as models of authentic practice.

Over the past few years, we have been experimenting with partially distributed team assignments in this course (see http://ist413.ist.psu.edu/). These assignments use case-based learning in which students analyze and apply ideas from the case library to their own design projects (Carroll & Rosson, 2005). The assignments also use distributed collaborative learning, where student teams are asked to work together outside of class using collaborative software over a period of several days to several weeks to develop a design analysis or prototype and a report describing their work. Our design research goal is not only to build collaborative software that can support the students' activities (e.g., continuing on from Classroom BRIDGE), but also to iteratively design the collaborative activities themselves, so as to best engage students in the real-world products and processes of usability engineering.

Each case study in the library contains concrete examples of the kinds of scenarios the teams will produce in their usability engineering projects. The cases are based on real-world examples so students can learn from real experiences. In this way, students can see the process as enacted by real practitioners and use these examples to guide their own scenario-based design projects. The cases introduce students to the "language" of usability practices in a meaningful, contextually authentic way. They also provide students with insights into expert thinking by allowing them to look at brainstorming artifacts and to "see" the process by which important decisions were made. By giving students the ability to see real practitioners engaged in real design and development tasks, we are providing students with not just technological tools, but cognitive tools to extend and expand their own understanding. However, herein is where the problem lies. They are provided with authentic examples via UCS but are missing the collaborative skills to use them properly.

From past iterations of our usability engineering course, we have found that students tend not to use the case studies in a fully collaborative fashion; they do not think deeply about the examples, discuss and critique their individual or shared inferences, or make connections between the cases and their own projects. For example, one collaborative homework assignment asked students to go through all of the cases and identify different aspects of the design process and draw out the underlying ideas, rationale, and approaches used by the cases:

> review the activity design, information design, and interaction design sections for a different case study in USC (Garden.com, TappedIn, PhoneWriter, PAWS, m-Banking, Virtual Science Fair).... You can certainly bring UI metaphors and other ideas into the discussion from other software you have used or know about, but at the least you should use all the ideas and approaches from the case studies...

If left to themselves, we have seen that many students let superficial differences detract from integration across cases. To do the assignment well, students should collaboratively analyze the different cases using more abstract concepts (i.e., how did they use their resources, what problems did they face, what was their design approach) and generalize their findings. However, we saw that irrelevant details would sometimes get in the way; for instance, a team working on a desktop website might totally ignore one case study because it was for a mobile device. This simplified their case-based learning task, but also reduced the richness of their analysis. Not all groups let these details derail them. For instance, at times, members tried to reject case content but were prevented from doing so by other team members who challenged their assumptions or forced them to reread instructions. These informal observations suggest that the activity provides opportunities for deeper learning, but that we may need to scaffold their collaborative processes.

The UCS repository is built on top of a database that allows access to the different types of content in each case (e.g., design artifacts, scenarios, design trade-offs). Taking advantage of these structures, we adapted the earlier Classroom BRIDGE workspace to serve as a front end to the UCS, allowing student teams to debate different parts of a case via comments (Xiao, Carroll, Clemson, & Rosson, 2008; see Figure 9.2). This design experiment helped us to see that allowing students to collaborate around individual pieces of content within a case is a powerful concept and that presenting materials that are already organized into pros and cons (the design trade-offs) provides a natural galvanizing function point for critical evaluation and discussion.

To promote critical thinking and develop a rich understanding of the real-world cases, team members must be challenged by their team and pushed to defend ideas or concepts. We are exploring other activities and tool features that might promote such behavior—for example, a case annotation activity in which students or field practitioners are asked to critically evaluate a case and point out trade-offs of decisions or identify

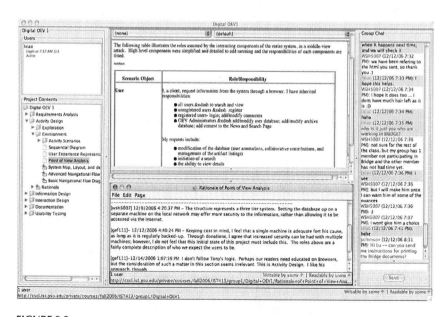

FIGURE 9.2
Workspace for reviewing and debating case study elements.

core concepts underlying particular implementations and explain why the cases evolved as they did. These annotated cases can also be archived in another section of the library. We are also investigating opportunities for documenting additional cases that highlight the critical role of collaborative skills in the life of a project. There are many real-world examples of organizational events that fail due to a lack of communication, critical evaluation, or planning. These cases can be used as a basis for reflective activities that push students to evaluate their own team's processes and functions. These reflective activities should incorporate the use of tools that encourage students and instructors to reflect on the case library, their activities, team processes, and other important aspects of the course. In this way, the instructor can have insights into students' thinking, and in addition, the students can have insights into the instructor's thinking.

Thus far, most of our work on collaborative case-based learning has focused on the importance of engaging with real-world content and in connecting what can be seen in a case study to what the team is trying to do in its own design project. One individual learning objective we are pursuing by employing authentic case-based materials and activities is that the team members will come to identify with and position themselves within the professional community of usability engineers (Carroll & Rosson, 2005). However, currently, we are addressing the group-level learning objective of promoting emergence of shared collaborative practices through the teamwork that the students engage in throughout this course. Articulating with respect to the construct of activity awareness, we want to develop activities, tools, and other interventions to make student teams more aware of their own collaborative activity and to help them develop and apply community practices in their own learning activities.

Toward Collaborative Activities That Promote a Community of Practice

We are currently designing a new workspace to support students' collaborative activities over the longer term, with the hope that this will enable emergence of a CoP. The students continue to do real-world projects with actual customers for their semester project, and one deliverable for these projects is a new usability engineering case; the workspace is used for developing and presenting this case.

In this new approach, the collaborative case-based learning activities have been integrated into the semester-long team projects. Now, relating the existing UCS case materials to the students' projects is integrated within each phase of the usability engineering process taught in the class. The new workspace design supports linking in these UCS Library resources. At a "checkpoint" at the midpoint of each phase, the instructor evaluates progress, but with respect to *both* product and process, particularly looking at how students incorporated what they have learned from the UCS Library. An early prototype of the new workspace appears in Figure 9.3 (Carroll, Borge, Ganoe, & Jiang, 2010; Jiang, Carroll, Borge, & Ganoe, 2010).

In previous instances of the course, the teams delivered written reports at the end of each phase, with a separate case study deliverable as part of the final project. Now, however, the ongoing development of a case study itself is a deliverable, and capture of the team's process is a graded part of the case. That is, team and team–customer communications, meeting notes, and so on have been defined as usability engineering *process artifacts* that are included with each team's case study. Each project team is paired with another project team that conducts a peer review during each phase of the usability engineering cycle. During in-class activities related to the project, the instructor and other faculty experts interact with the students about their projects. We anticipate that as students progress on the core

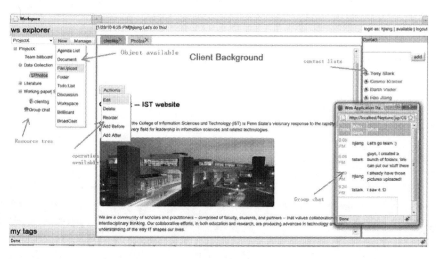

FIGURE 9.3
Workspace that integrates support for product and process.

course concepts through the long-term project, they will develop common ground over the "language" of usability engineering. The new workspace supports collaborative social tagging of content documents and artifacts, as well as linking to UCS Library content and other usability engineering resources on the Internet. Part of our approach is to both scaffold and evaluate how they communicate usability engineering as practice through the contents of the case study they develop.

We have not yet determined whether it will be important to define and assign explicit sociocognitive roles to team members, for instance focusing them on the four realms of planning, communication, critical thinking, and productivity. To some extent, these roles are conveyed implicitly through the current tools, in the form of features that enable agenda planning, social tagging for sharing and interconnecting ideas as they emerge, timelines for tracking progress, and so on. We also expect that our decision to collect and grade the process artifacts along with the products will motivate team members to monitor and regulate these processes on their own. However, we may discover that the tool's affordances are too subtle and that the teams need more direct guidance at times, perhaps in the form of in-class meetings where they role play or perhaps in asynchronous activities where they are asked to evaluate their own or another team's process artifacts, using one or another of these realms as a lens.

REFLECTIONS AND CONCLUSIONS

Much research on awareness has focused on relatively immediate or short-term phenomena, for example, one's awareness of who is "present" (social awareness; Dey & de Guzman, 2006), one's awareness of a collaborator's current focus of attention (gaze awareness; Ishii & Kobayashi, 1992), one's awareness of what a collaborator is pointing at or where a collaborator is working in a shared workspace (workspace awareness; Gutwin & Greenberg, 2002), or one's awareness of what a collaborator has recently done (action awareness; Begole, Rosson, & Shaffer, 1999). The totality of synchronous awareness is sometimes called situation awareness (Endsley, 2000). Immediate and short-term awareness phenomena are immensely important to effectively coordinating teamwork.

236 • *Theories of Team Cognition*

The programmatic construct of "activity awareness" articulates a set of conjectures about how these synchronous phenomena emerge and how they support larger scope, longer term collaborative capabilities and processes. We conceptualize this on analogy to individual cognition, where synchronous phenomena of perception and motor performance are both shaped by and help to shape larger scope, longer term capacities of learning and memory. Our objective is a more comprehensive and integrated account of awareness and coordination in collaborative activity. In this chapter, we explored how common ground and CoPs can emerge from teamwork, thereby enriching the shared understanding among team members that supports the processing and interpretation of synchronous awareness information.

During our virtual school research in public schools, we were able to identify breakdowns in activity awareness through video analysis (Carroll et al., 2003) and reproduce them in lab settings through the use of a confederate (Convertino, Neale, Hobby, Carroll, & Rosson, 2004). However, it is much easier to recognize when individual incidents of activity awareness problems occur than it is to measure at what level activity awareness exists between members of a team. We have begun to develop scales for team members to self-report activity awareness within the framework of the four facets (Convertino et al., 2004; working versions of the scales are at http://cscl.ist.psu.edu/public/projects/awareness/q.html). It may be possible to measure changes over time in how teams manage their process protocols. Through conversation content analysis, we have found that teams conducting information-sharing tasks will, over a few experimental sessions, shift from a pull-oriented approach (members asking for information from their teammates) for information sharing to a more efficient push-oriented approach (adding information to the discussion without direct prompting) (Convertino, Mentis, Rosson, et al., 2008). Although possibly task/domain specific, this may reflect a growing mutual understanding by the team as to what processes improve their performance. As part of our usability engineering course, we have developed rubrics for students to self-assess their collaborative competence through watching videos of their team at work. Similar assessments might also be conducted by domain experts at multiple points in time during long-term team activities to measure the evolution of a team's processes.

In response to our theoretical interest in larger scope awareness processes, we have expanded our empirical work to include classroom collaborative activities that take place over a semester rather than an afternoon. Like other researchers who study students' learning in classroom settings, we are interested in how to enhance student learning experiences, for example, understanding and leveraging the roles and impacts of collaborative work in problem-based learning (e.g., Brown & Campione, 1994; Brown & Palinacsar, 1985, 1989). More concretely, we are working to better articulate what collaboration is and how it can be taught and practiced in the classroom. At the same time, we have conceptualized the classroom as a research model for investigating team-based problem solving that takes place over significant spans of time. In our usability engineering course, teams of fourth-year students, most in their final college semester, work on realistic projects identifying requirements, developing designs and prototypes, and carrying out usability investigations for 14 weeks. This is a new way to think about classroom research, and for us, it is an opportunity to more systematically investigate relatively complex macrocognitive phenomena pertaining to activity awareness that we have observed in field studies.

We have been able to evoke common ground formation in experimental studies, but these studies involve sessions that last 3 to 4 hours. These are complex experimental models. Yet in these experimental models, we are probably only seeing the beginnings of teams initially negotiating and creating the most basic elements of common ground. Although we are continuing to pursue this kind of experimental model, we do not think it is likely that any 4-hour experimental procedure can be devised to systematically evoke the formation of CoPs or, indeed, any aspect of activity awareness beyond common ground formation. Thus, we need to identify research models that allow more systematic study of activity awareness, or we will be like the man who is looking for his car keys under the street light because that is where he can see the ground clearly but who knows that he dropped the keys across the street where it is dark. Studying only synchronous or nearly synchronous aspects of activity awareness can only provide an incomplete picture of how real teams functions in real activity contexts.

Thus far, our empirical studies and design research have focused on the macrocognitive protocols for communication and coordination (i.e., the activity awareness facets of common ground and CoPs; recall Table 9.1). However, in the longer term, we intend to expand the scope of our investigations to include the macrocognitive protocols for cooperation (social capital) and group regulation (human development). We

238 • *Theories of Team Cognition*

believe that teams collaborating on class projects may provide a setting for studying these higher level processes as well. For instance, at times, team members must adjust schedules and responsibilities in response to personal issues that arise for individual members; if we analyze the precursors and consequences of such events, we may find ways to operationalize and track the development of social capital. Similarly, we are beginning to explore the human development facet of activity awareness by considering how team leadership operates as a macrocognitive process in activity awareness.

We have articulated a rich framework for understanding the elements and dynamics of activity awareness as a requirement for effective collaboration. Our earlier studies of shorter term awareness phenomena provide a foundation for moving forward to investigate more challenging and long-term awareness processes. The frontier for us is cultivating research models that permit systematic analysis of the shared practices that enable activity awareness to emerge through continued negotiation and renegotiation of plans, actions, and reflections. By understanding the requirements of these more extended collaborative activities, we hope to design tools and materials that can not only can enhance activity awareness within the research model of an undergraduate course, but also prepare the students for more effective collaboration in the world.

ACKNOWLEDGMENTS

This research was supported by the Office of Naval Research (Grant Nos. N00014-0510549 and N00014-0910303), the U.S. National Science Foundation (Grant No. 0736440), and the Frymoyer Endowment.

REFERENCES

Bannon, L. (Ed.). (1995). Commentaries and a response in the Suchman-Winograd debate. *Computer-Supported Cooperative Work, 3,* 29–95.

Barron, B. (2000). Achieving coordination in collaborative problem-solving groups. *Journal of the Learning Sciences, 9,* 403–436.

Barron, B. (2003). When smart groups fail. *Journal of the Learning Sciences, 12,* 307–359.

Begole, J., Rosson, M. B., & Shaffer, C. A. (1999). Flexible collaboration transparency: Supporting worker independence in replicated application-sharing systems. *ACM Transactions on Computer-Human Interaction, 6,* 95–132.

Articulating Collaborative Contributions to Activity Awareness • 239

Bjork, R. A. (1994). Memory and metamemory considerations in the training of human beings. In J. Metcalf & A. P. Shimamura (Eds.), *Metacognition: Knowing about knowing*. Cambridge, MA: MIT Press.

Boekaerts, M. (1996). Self-regulated learning at the junction of cognition and motivation. *European Psychologist, 1*, 100–112.

Borge, M. (2007). Regulating social interactions: Developing a functional theory of collaboration. *Dissertation Abstracts International, 69-03*, 241.

Borge, M., & Carroll, J. (2010). *Using collaborative activity as a means to explore student performance and understanding.* Paper presented at the International Conference of the Learning Sciences, Chicago, IL.

Borge, M., & White, B. (under review). Collaborative competence: Instructional methodologies for tactical learning.

Brown, A. L. (1984). Metacognition, executive control, self-regulation and other more mysterious mechanisms. In F. E. Weinert & R. H. Kluwe (Eds.), *Metacognition, motivation, and learning* (pp. 60–108). Stuttgart, Germany: Kuhlhammer.

Brown, A. L., & Campione, J. C. (1994). Guided discovery in a community of learners. In K. McGilly (Ed.), *Classroom lessons: Integrating cognitive theory and classroom practice* (pp. 229–270). Cambridge, MA: MIT Press/Bradford.

Brown, A. L., & Palincsar, A. M. (1985). *Reciprocal teaching of comprehension strategies: A natural history of one program for enhancing learning.* Champaign, IL; Cambridge, MA: University of Illinois at Urbana-Champaign; Bolt Beranek and Newman Inc.

Brown, A. L., & Palincsar, A. M. (1989). Guided cooperative learning and individual knowledge acquisition. In L. B. Resnick (Ed.), *Knowing learning and instruction*. Mahwah, NJ: Lawrence Erlbaum Associates.

Butler, D. L., & Winne, P. H. (1995). Feedback and self-regulated learning: A theoretical synthesis. *Review of Educational Research, 65*, 245–281.

Carroll, J. M., Borge, M., Ganoe, C. H., & Jiang, H. (2010, April). *Distributed collaborative homeworks: Learning activity management and technology support.* Paper presented at the IEEE EDUCON-Education Engineering International Conference, Madrid, Spain.

Carroll J. M., Convertino G., Rosson M. B., & Ganoe C. H. (2008). Toward a conceptual model of common ground in teamwork. In M. P. Letsky, N. W. Warner, S. M. Fiore, & C. A. P. Smith, (Eds.), *Macrocognition in teams: Theories and methodologies* (pp. 87–106). Aldershot, UK: Ashgate Publishing.

Carroll, J. M., Neale, D. C., Isenhour, P. L., Rosson, M. B., & McCrickard, D. S. (2003). Notification and awareness: Synchronizing task-oriented collaborative activity. *International Journal of Human-Computer Studies, 58*, 605–632.

Carroll, J. M., & Rosson, M. B. (2005). A case library for teaching usability engineering: Design rationale, development, and classroom experience. *ACM Journal of Educational Resources in Computing, 5*, 1–22.

Carroll, J. M., Rosson, M. B., Convertino, G., & Ganoe, C. H. (2006). Awareness and teamwork in computer-supported collaborations. *Interacting with Computers, 18*, 21–46.

Carroll, J. M., Rosson, M. B., Farooq, U., & Xiao, L. (2009). Beyond being aware. *Information and Organizations, 19*, 162–185.

Chakravarthy, B. S. (1982). Adaptation: A promising metaphor for strategic management. *Academy of Management Review, 7*, 35–44.

240 • Theories of Team Cognition

Chin, J., Rosson, M. B., & Carroll, J. M. (1997). Participatory analysis: Shared development of requirements from scenarios. *Proceedings of the SIGCHI Conference on Human Factors in Computing Systems, CHI '97*, 162–169.

Clark, H. H. (1996). *Using language*. New York, NY: Cambridge University Press.

Clark, H. H., & Brennan, S. E. (1991). Grounding in communication. In L. B. Resnick, J. Levine, & S. D. Teasley (Eds.), *Perspectives on socially shared cognition* (127–149). Washington, DC: APA.

Clark, H. H., & Haviland, S. E. (1977). Comprehension and the given-new contract. In R. O. Freedle (Ed.), *Discourse production and comprehension* (pp. 1–40). Hillsdale, NJ: Erlbaum.

Coleman, J. C. (1988) Social capital in the creation of human capital. *American Journal of Sociology, 94*, S95–S120.

Collins, A., Brown, J. S., & Newman, S. E. (1991). Cognitive apprenticeship: Making things visible. *American Educator: The Professional Journal of the American Federation of Teachers, 15*, 6–11, 38–46.

Convertino, G., Mentis, H. M., Bhambare, P., Ferro, C., Carroll, J. M., & Rosson, M. B. (2008, May). Comparing media in emergency planning. *Proceedings of the 5th International ISCRAM Conference*, Washington, DC.

Convertino, G., Mentis, H. M., Rosson, M. B., Carroll, J. M., Slavkovic, A., & Ganoe, C. H. (2008). Articulating common ground in cooperative work: Content and process. In *Proceedings of the 26th Annual SIGCHI Conference on Human Factors in Computing Systems, Florence, Italy* (pp. 1637–1646). New York, NY: ACM Press.

Convertino, G., Mentis, H. M., Rosson, M. B., Slavkovic, A., & Carroll, J. M. (2009). Supporting content and process common ground in computer-supported teamwork. In *Proceedings of ACM Conference on Human Factors in Computing Systems, CHI 2009* (pp. 2339–2348). New York, NY: ACM Press.

Convertino, G., Neale, D. C., Hobby, L., Carroll, J. M., & Rosson, M. B. (2004). A laboratory method for studying activity awareness. In *Proceedings of the Third Nordic Conference on Human-Computer Interaction* (pp. 313–322). Tampere, Finland: ACM.

Dey, A. K., & de Guzman, E. (2006). From awareness to connectedness: The design and deployment of presence displays. In R. Grinter, T. Rodden, P. Aoki, E. Cutrell, R. Jeffries, & G. Olson (Eds.), *Proceedings of the SIGCHI Conference on Human Factors in Computing Systems* (pp. 899–908). New York, NY: ACM Press.

Driver, R., Newton, P., & Osborne, J. (2000). Establishing the norms of scientific argumentation in classrooms. *Science Education, 84*, 287–312.

Duguid, P. (2005). The art of knowing: Social and tacit dimensions of knowledge and the limits of the community of practice. *Information Society, 21*, 109–118.

Edmondson, A. (1999). Psychological safety and learning behavior in work teams. *Administrative Science Quarterly, 44*, 350–383.

Endsley, M. R. (2000). Theoretical underpinnings of situation awareness: A critical review. In M. R. Endsley & D. J. Garland (Eds.), *Situation awareness analysis and measurement*. Mahwah, NJ: LEA.

Engeström, Y. (2008). Enriching activity theory without shortcuts. *Interacting with Computers, 20*, 256–259.

Engeström, Y., Miettinen, R., & Punamaki, R.-L. (Eds.). (1999). *Perspectives on activity theory*. Cambridge, UK: Cambridge University Press.

Engle, R. A., & Conant, F. R. (2002). Guiding principles for fostering productive disciplinary engagement: Explaining an emergent argument in a community of learners classroom. *Cognition and Instruction, 20*, 399–483.

Forman, E., & Cazdan, C. (1985). Exploring Vygotskian perspectives in education. In J. V. Wertsch (Ed.), *Culture, communication, and cognition: Vygotskian perspectives* (pp. 323–347). New York, NY: Cambridge University Press.

Ganoe, C. H., Somervell, J. P., Neale, D. C., Isenhour, P. L., Carroll, J. M., Rosson, M. B., et al. (2003). Classroom BRIDGE: Using collaborative public and desktop timelines to support activity awareness. In *ACM UIST 2003: Conference on User Interface Software and Tools* (pp. 21–30). New York, NY: ACM.

Greeno, J. (1974). Hobbits and orcs: Acquisition of a sequential concept. *Cognitive Psychology, 6*, 270–292.

Gutwin, C., & Greenberg, S. (2002). A descriptive framework of workspace awareness for real-time groupware. *Computer Supported Cooperative Work, 11*, 411–446.

Hogan, K. (1999a). Thinking aloud together: A test of an intervention to foster students' collaborative scientific reasoning. *Journal of Research in Science Teaching, 36*, 1085–1109.

Hogan, K. (1999b). Sociocognitive roles in science group discourse. *International Journal of Science Education, 21*, 855–882.

Ishii, H., & Kobayashi, M. (1992). ClearBoard: A seamless medium for shared drawing and conversation with eye contact. In P. Bauersfeld, J. Bennett, & G. Lynch (Eds.), *Proceedings of the SIGCHI Conference on Human Factors in Computing Systems* (pp. 525–532). New York, NY: ACM Press.

Jiang, H., Carroll, J. M., Borge, M., & Ganoe, C. H. (2010, July). *Supporting partially distributed, case-based learning in an advanced undergraduate course in usability engineering.* Paper presented at iCALT 2010: 10th IEEE International Conference on Advanced Learning Technologies, Sousse, Tunisia.

Johnson, R. T., & Johnson, D. W. (1979). Cooperative learning, powerful sciencing. *Science and Children, 17*, 26–27.

Kuhn, D., Black, J., Keselman, A., & Kaplan, D. (2000). The development of cognitive skills to support inquiry learning. *Cognition and Instruction, 18*, 495–523.

Mathieu, J. E., Heffner, T. S., Goodwin, G. F., Salas, E., & Cannon-Bowers, J. A. (2000). The influence of shared mental models on team process and performance. *Journal of Applied Psychology, 85*, 273–283.

McGrath, J. E., Arrow, H., & Berdahl, J. L. (2000). The study of groups: Past, present, and future. *Personality and Social Psychology Review, 4*, 95–105.

Metz, K. E. (2004). The knowledge-building enterprises in science and elementary school classrooms: Analysis of problematic differences and strategic leverage points. In L. B. Flick & N. G. Lederman (Eds.), *Scientific inquiry and the nature of science: Implications for teaching, learning, and teacher education.* Dordrecht, the Netherlands: Kluwe Publishers.

Nelson-Le Gall, S. (1981). Help-seeking: An understudied problem-solving skill in children. *Developmental Review, 1*, 224–246.

Nelson-Le Gall, S. (1985). Help-seeking behavior in learning. In E. V. Gordon (Ed.), *Review of research in education* (Vol. 12, pp. 55–90). Washington, DC: American Educational Research Association.

Nevo, D., & Wand, Y. (2005). Organizational memory systems: A transactive memory approach. *Decision Support Systems, 39*, 549–562.

Piaget, J. (1976). *The grasp of consciousness: Action and concept in the young child.* Cambridge, MA: Harvard University Press.

Roschelle, J. (1992). Learning by collaborating: Convergent conceptual change. *Journal of the Learning Sciences, 2*, 235–276.

242 • *Theories of Team Cognition*

Schoenfeld, A. H. (1987). What's all the fuss about metacognition? In A. H. Schoenfeld (Ed.), *Cognitive science and mathematics education* (pp. 189–215). Hillsdale, NJ: Lawrence Erlbaum Associates.

Schraw, G. (1998). Promoting general metacognitive awareness. *Instructional Science, 26,* 113–125.

Schraw, G., & Dennison, R. (1994). Assessing metacognitive awareness. *Contemporary Educational Psychology, 19,* 460–475.

Suchman, L. A. (1994). Do categories have politics? *Computer-Supported Cooperative Work, 2,* 177–190.

Vygotsky, L. S. (1978). Interaction between learning and development. In M. Cole, V. John-Steiner, S. Scribner, & E. Souberman (Eds.), *Mind in society: The development of higher psychological processes* (pp. 79–91). Cambridge, MA: Harvard University Press.

Warner, N., & Letsky, M. (2008). Empirical model of team collaboration focus on macrocognition. In M. Letsky, N. Warner, S. Fiore, & C. Smith (Eds.), *Macrocognition in teams: Theories and methodologies* (pp. 15–33). Burlington, VT: Ashgate Publishing Company.

Webb, N., & Palincsar, A. S. (1996). Group processes in the classroom. In D. C. Berliner & R. C. Calfee (Eds.), *Handbook of educational psychology* (pp. 841–873). New York, NY: Simon & Schuster Macmillan.

Wenger, E., McDermott, R., & Snyder, W. M. (2002). *Cultivating communities of practice: A guide to managing knowledge.* Cambridge, MA: Harvard Business School Press.

Wertsch, J. V. (Ed.). (1981). *The concept of activity in Soviet psychology.* Armonk, NY: M.E. Sharp Inc.

West, G. P. (2007). Collective cognition: When entrepreneurial teams, not individuals, make decisions. *Entrepreneurship Theory and Practice, 31,* 77–102.

White, B. Y., & Frederiksen, J. R. (2005). Theoretical framework and approach for fostering metacognitive development. *Educational Psychologist, 40,* 211–223.

White, B. Y., Frederiksen, J. R., & Collins, A. (2009). The interplay of scientific inquiry and metacognition: More than a marriage of convenience. In D. Hacker, J. Dunlosky, & A. Graesser (Eds.), *Handbook of metacognition in education* (pp. 175–205). New York, NY: Routledge.

White, B. Y., Shimoda, T., & Frederiksen, J. R. (1999). Enabling students to construct theories of collaborative inquiry and reflective learning: Computer support for metacognitive development. *International Journal of Artificial Intelligence in Education Computers as Cognitive Tools, Volume Two: No More Walls, 10,* 151–182.

Winograd, T. (1994). Categories, disciplines, and social coordination. *Computer Supported Cooperative Work, 2,* 191–197.

Wittrock, M. (1990). Generative processes of comprehension. *Educational Psychologist, 24,* 345–376.

Xiao, L., Carroll, J. M., Clemson, P., & Rosson, M. B. (2008). Support of case-based authentic learning activities: A collaborative case commenting tool and a collaborative case builder. In *Proceedings of the 42nd Hawaii International Conference on System Sciences.* Kona, HI: IEEE.

Section IV

Cognitive and Computer Science Perspectives

10

Combinations of Contributions for Sharing Cognitions in Teams

Verlin B. Hinsz and Jared L. Ladbury

Teams in organizations are ubiquitous (Cohen & Bailey, 1997; Devine, Clayton, Philips, Dunford, & Melner, 1999) and important for organizational functioning (Sundstrom, McIntyre, Halfhill, & Richards, 2000). Teams appear at all levels of an organization—from top management teams to sales groups to accounting teams—to such an extent that new hires who do not have the necessary skills to work in teams can struggle in the workplace (Ellis, Bell, Ployhart, Hollenbeck, & Ilgen, 2005; Hollenbeck, DeRue, & Guzzo, 2004). Teams work to accomplish the goals of the organization and are expected to function at a higher level than individuals working alone (Letsky, Warner, Fiore, & Smith, 2008). All in all, teams have become an ever-present and necessary component of organizational life.

Part of working in teams involves sharing cognitions. By sharing cognitions we are referring to the processes that team members engage in to develop a collective understanding regarding aspects of their interaction and the tasks assigned to them. Once the processes have occurred, we can refer to the collective understanding as shared cognitions. Methods by which cognitions can become shared can include collectively processing the information available, understanding how shared resources will be used, and developing knowledge of the skills and abilities each team member possesses. Sharing cognition is a critical component of what allows teams to accomplish their goals.

Sharing cognition is a cornerstone of why teams are believed to outperform individuals on important tasks. For example, a potential advantage of having a team make a hiring decision as opposed to an individual is that a team has the possibility of remembering and processing much more information than an individual. If all team members

245

246 • *Theories of Team Cognition*

could remember unique information and then bring each unique piece of information up for discussion, the potential exists for the team to gather much more information and thus make a much better decision than that of a single individual. In this way, the team sharing cognitions during discussion could rely on a much larger pool of information than an individual working alone could remember and process. Without sharing cognitions, teams would find interaction and task performance markedly more difficult.

An interesting feature of teams is their interdependence with regard to task performance. If one team member fails to share critical information at the appropriate time, an entire venture can fail. Many tasks in modern organizations are cognitive in nature, such as deciding where a new plant will be located, advocating that research and development efforts should commence for a life-saving drug, and interpreting information from an applicant file for a potential hiring decision. Thus, sharing cognition in teams is important if teams are to complete the tasks assigned to them (Hinsz, Wallace, & Ladbury, 2009; Kozlowski & Bell, 2003). The frequent sharing of cognition in teams not only allows teams to complete tasks, but also helps to improve team effectiveness (DeChurch & Mesmer-Magnus, 2010; Kozlowski & Ilgen, 2006).

This chapter and this book attempt to address the theoretical perspectives that can be brought to bear on sharing cognition in teams. We offer a perspective based on the general approach of considering information processing in teams (Hinsz, 2001; Hinsz, Tindale, & Vollrath, 1997). In particular, we describe the theory of combinations of contributions and use the theory to elucidate various features of sharing cognition in teams that follow from the combinations-of-contributions theory approach. To provide some background for understanding the implications of combinations-of-contributions theory, we will begin by highlighting some traditional views of teams that attempt to explain team interaction.

A FRAMEWORK FOR TEAM FUNCTIONING

For the purposes of this chapter, we define teams as two or more team members who interact interdependently on a task to achieve a common goal. These teams often anticipate future interactions and have a history of previous interaction. Members of teams also generally share an identity as a team. In many teams, the members serve specific roles, which reflect how the member is to behave and contribute so as to attain desirable goals (cf. Hinsz et al., 2009). Research in team performance encompasses a number of different areas, but we will restrict ourselves to a particular set of approaches and perspectives we have been following for some time. These approaches tend to be multidisciplinary and are built on a variety of influences but tend to focus around the topic of information processing in teams.

One of the traditional perspectives to team action and performance is known as the I-P-O framework. The I-P-O framework provides a perspective for thinking about the inputs (I), processes (P), and outcomes (O) associated with team action and performance (Hackman & Morris, 1975; Ilgen, Hollenbeck, Johnson, & Jundt, 2005; McGrath, 1964). The basic premise of the framework is that inputs contribute to team processes, which in turn lead to important team outcomes. Figure 10.1 presents an overview of the I-P-O framework we will discuss.

The I-P-O framework suggests that three categories of inputs contribute to the outcomes of team processes: member characteristics, team characteristics, and task characteristics. Member characteristics refer to those factors that influence team outcomes derived from characteristics the team members bring with them to the team interaction such as cognitive ability (Devine & Philips, 2001). Team characteristics refer to those particular aspects of the team that influence the outcomes of the team interaction

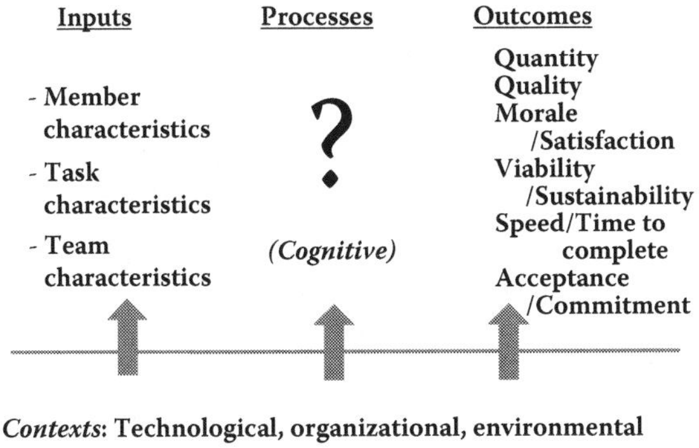

Inputs	Processes	Outcomes
- Member characteristics	**?**	Quantity Quality Morale /Satisfaction
- Task characteristics		Viability /Sustainability Speed/Time to complete
- Team characteristics	*(Cognitive)*	Acceptance /Commitment

Contexts: Technological, organizational, environmental

FIGURE 10.1

An illustration of the input-process-outcome (I-P-O) model of team interaction and performance.

248 • *Theories of Team Cognition*

such as their history, leadership structure, and norms for interaction (Hackman & Morris, 1975). The task characteristics are those features of the task that relate to the team performance outcomes such as whether the task is unitary or divisible (Steiner, 1972) or whether it involves generation or evaluation (McGrath, 1984). Because traditionally productivity was the primary measure of team outcomes, the task characteristics accounted for about 80% of the variance in team outcomes (McGrath & Altman, 1966). Task characteristics influence the team outcomes because they define what resources (e.g., member characteristics) need to be brought to bear on the task for differences in performance to emerge. Certain tasks require the team to be organized in a specific fashion and the skills members bring to the task components to be orchestrated in a certain order for the task to be completed successfully (Hackman, 1990).

The member, team, and task inputs categorize the primary variables that have been found to influence team outcomes. However, different inputs influence the team outcomes in differential ways. We take a multidimensional view of the outcomes of the task. Traditionally, productivity on the task in terms of quantity (e.g., number of widgets constructed) was the critical outcome. However, other outcomes may be important beyond quantity. Hackman (1987) suggests that one could consider the quantity and quality of performance to be one outcome of the team interaction. That is, did the team performance outcome meet the expectations of the organization or agency that requested the performance? In a case such as the architectural design of a building, quality of production may outweigh the number of drawings a firm can produce in the evaluation by a potential client. Morale or satisfaction of the team members can also be considered an important outcome (e.g., the Hawthorne studies; Roethlisberger & Dickson, 1939). By keeping team morale high, the team may be more motivated to complete additional tasks with high quality in the future. In all of these cases, team productivity may remain constant; however, each of the other outcomes has the potential to generate additional positive results for the team and the organization.

Hackman (1987) suggested that additional outcomes need to be considered for teams. The viability of the team to survive and be sustained into the future can be an important outcome because extensive organizational resources are often invested into a team. If the team disintegrates and members no longer want to work together after completing a single task, the team may be seen as a failure even if the task assigned to the team was completed successfully. Understanding the processes that lead to disharmony may be important so that other teams will be viable after an initial task performance period.

It is important to recognize that the inputs and outcomes of team interaction occur in a specific context. Contextual factors also have an influence on the inputs, the outcomes, and the processes of team interaction. Many researchers have argued that contextual factors play important roles in team interaction and performance results. In particular, the organizational factors, such as the reward structure in place and the resources the organization provides its members, influence the nature of the team interaction and performance (Hackman, 1987). The environment external to the team and organization also influence the nature of team interaction and performance. For example, substantial research has show how uncertainty, rapid change, and competition are all environmental influences that can influence team interaction and performance (Marks, Mathieu, & Zaccaro, 2001). In the past decades, the technological context of the team interaction and performance has also received considerable attention in terms of technological support for collaborative work (Galegher, Kraut, & Egido, 1990). Extensive research has examined the impact of technology on team interaction and performance (e.g., Galegher et al., 1990; McGrath & Hollingshead, 1994; McNeese, Salas, & Endsley, 2001). By understanding the contextual factors that influence team interaction, we are better able to predict team performance on tasks that are quite complex. However, how teams go about improving their performance remains a question of some debate (Weingart, 1997).

The major unresolved issue in the I-P-O framework is the processes that transform the inputs into outcomes. Many different approaches to identifying these processes have been proposed and examined in the past decades (e.g., interaction process analysis; Bales, 1950), but no clear organized set of processes have emerged that fully explain the processes by which particular inputs result in a set of outcomes. Consequently, it is not surprising that the cognitive processes by which the informational inputs of team members lead to outcomes of cognitive task performance are not well conceptualized. Yet, we do offer one approach for considering shared cognition in teams as part of those processes, that is, the perspective of teams as information processors (Hinsz et al., 1997).

The basic premise of the teams-as-information-processors perspective is that teams process information according to a set of phases much

250 • *Theories of Team Cognition*

as individuals do (Hinsz, 2001). For any cognitive task, teams must attend to the important information; bring it into a collective processing space; and encode, store, and then retrieve the information for later use. Thus, team cognitive processes might be thought of as parallel to the cognitive processes of team members. Accordingly, research efforts are required that test this premise to discover the degree to which individual and team processing of information follow the same patterns. The important aspects of the processes teams face when confronting a cognitive task are the sharing of information and cognitive processing that happens in the team. The perspective of teams as information processors follows the tradition of considering the nature of how team member (cognitive) inputs can be combined to produce collective (cognitive) outcomes.

A SOCIAL COMBINATION APPROACH TO TEAMS

One way of considering the processes whereby inputs are transformed into outcomes in teams is that of the social combination approach (Baron & Kerr, 2003). The social combination approach argues that although the processes might not be directly observed, it is possible to construct plausible hypotheses of the processes by which inputs are transformed into outcomes. In research, it has been found that a number of different plausible hypotheses can be generated based on prior theory, research, and knowledge of the nature of the team interaction. These plausible hypotheses are then stated in terms of formal combinatorial processes (i.e., models) for how inputs are transformed into outcomes. Research studies can then be conducted in which the outcomes are assessed and are predicted by inputs that are observed or constructed through manipulation. The plausible models are then applied to the inputs to determine how well the model predictions can account for the observed outcomes.

A number of types of social combinatorial models have been developed and applied (e.g., Anderson & Graesser, 1976; Crott, Zuber, & Schermer, 1986; Penrod & Hastie, 1981). However, the models associated with social decision schemes theory (Davis, 1973) are elegant exemplars (Davis, 1996; Hinsz, 1999; Kerr, 1981; Laughlin, 1980, 1996; Stasser & Davis, 1981). These social combinatorial approaches lay the groundwork for considering how the cognitive processes of team interaction transform the inputs into the outcomes of team cognitive task performance.

Social combinatorial models like those associated with social decision schemes theory offer an important perspective on team interaction by providing researchers with a method for combining individual member inputs, which can then be translated into team outcomes. Additional perspectives have been developed to specify exactly which combinatorial rule is most appropriate for predicting team outcomes given the task the team faces (Davis, 1982; Hinsz, 1999; Laughlin & Ellis, 1986; Laughlin & Hollingshead, 1995). This research has resulted in an extensive knowledge of the settings and situational contexts that make a particular combinatorial rule a better fit to observed data. Our approach takes a more general perspective that attempts to make a priori predictions regarding the best way for teams to combine their particular inputs to arrive at positive outcomes.

COMBINATIONS OF CONTRIBUTIONS

The social combination approach can be seen in the theory of combinations of contributions we offer for considering sharing cognition in teams. According to the theory of combinations of contributions, the outcomes of team interaction on a task can be predicted based on two components: the contributions and the combinations. The contributions refer to the critical inputs that team members bring with them to the task situations. For cognitive task performance, contributions would include cognitive skills, task-relevant knowledge and abilities, memories, information integration capabilities, and processing goals. The combinations refer to the aggregation principle by which these contributions are combined to lead to the team outcomes. Combinations would include those strategies by which the information is pooled, shared, and integrated (e.g., averaging, most able member). From an I-P-O perspective, contributions would be the inputs that are critical for team process to occur, and combinations are the strategies the team uses to translate inputs into outcomes. Importantly, contributions and combinations must relate directly to the cognitive processes involved in how team inputs result in team outcomes on a cognitive task. Figure 10.2 illustrates one way that the theory of combinations of contributions can be integrated within the I-P-O framework.

252 • *Theories of Team Cognition*

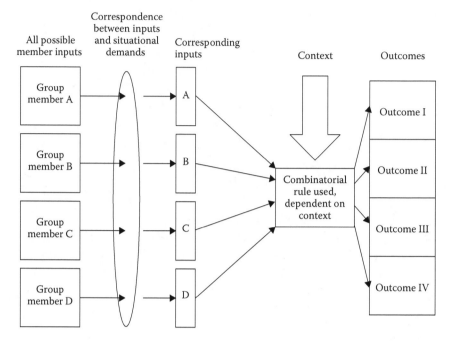

FIGURE 10.2
An illustration of the theory of combinations of contributions integrated within the input-process-outcome (I-P-O) framework. (Copyright © 2010 by Verlin B. Hinsz. Reprinted with permission.)

Combinations-of-contributions theory offers a unique outlook on team processes from the I-P-O framework because it emphasizes both the inputs team members bring to the task and the strategies by which those inputs are combined. However, the theory goes beyond the statement of the role of combinations and contributions to provide principles by which both the combinations and contributions operate. The principles of correspondence and context help to establish the specific methods by which contributions and combinations influence team outcomes, respectively.

For contributions, the principle of correspondence applies in that the contributions that are expected to influence outcomes are those that correspond along the critical dimensions upon which the outcomes are evaluated. If one is measuring an outcome such as problem solutions, one must evaluate team members based on inputs that relate to problem solutions such as domain knowledge and problem-solving skills (Laughlin, 1980). In addition, the contributions that are more proximal (i.e., relevant to the task) will be more influential in the prediction of team outcomes compared with inputs that are more distal. This is because proximal inputs correspond more directly with specific tasks demands. Problem-solving skills will be more predictive of the development of problem solutions than general measures of distal variables (e.g., personality). This is not to say that distal inputs will have no effect, but simply that selecting inputs for study should be given careful consideration with regard to how well they correspond to the task being performed and the outcomes being evaluated.

With regard to the combinations, the principle of context notes that the combinatorial rule that operates on the inputs to predict the outcomes depends greatly on the context. One of the truths that can be said about teams, team interaction, and team performance is that *teams are context situated and context sensitive* (Levine, Resnick, & Higgins, 1993; Tindale, Kameda, & Hinsz, 2003). Variations in the context in which the team operates have important influences on the combinatorial process whereby the team will combine inputs to produce team outcomes. Teams are so context sensitive that the same combinatorial rule may not even apply for the same task if other variations in the context are present.

Teams always exist in a context, and teams are sensitive to this context. Consequently, the combinatorial rule that summarizes the processes by which inputs are transformed into outcomes is dependent on the context. Research has demonstrated that there are systematic patterns in the ways in which changes in context influence the combinatorial rule that appears to arise (e.g., Davis, 1982; Hinsz et al., 1997; Laughlin, 1980). Such changes in context can include whether or not the task contains a demonstrably correct answer, the size of the team, and team member motivations to complete the task (Laughlin & Hollingshead, 1995). Further examinations of the potential for particular elements of context to moderate the combinatorial rule used by teams is fruitful research because other systematic patterns may be uncovered. The principle of context helps to demonstrate how changes in the context can change the combinatorial rule that best summarizes the process by which team outcomes arise.

The components and principles of the combinations-of-contributions theory provide a conceptual basis for informing our general understanding of the sharing of cognition in teams. The theory establishes that we must examine the contributions the team members bring with them to the task and the strategies by which those contributions are combined into a collective team outcome. Additionally, the theory states that the inputs must correspond to critical task dimensions. Also, the context within

254 • *Theories of Team Cognition*

which the team is working will be a major contributing factor to the manner by which inputs are combined. If inputs do not correspond to the task, they cannot be reasonably expected to predict the team outcome. If the context changes for the team, the combinatorial rule may change as well. This theory forces researchers and individuals in applied settings to be cognizant of, and adapt to, changes in the correspondence between team member contributions to the task and the context within which the team is functioning.

To illustrate these notions regarding the features of the theory of combinations of contributions, we present Table 10.1, which provides a summary of the components and principles of the theory with particular references to cognitive examples of the components and illustrative literatures relating to the components. To illustrate further implications of the theory, we will next describe two research topics to show how the theory of combinations of contributions can organize research regarding an understanding of sharing cognition in teams. In particular, we will describe research dealing with information sharing and shared mental models to show how combinations-of-contributions theory can further our understanding of team phenomena related to these examples of sharing cognition in teams.

INFORMATION SHARING IN TEAMS

One of the great potentials for interacting teams is that they can bring different ideas, perspectives, and information of their members together

TABLE 10.1

The Components and Principles Associated with the Theory of Combinations of Contributions

	Component	
	Contribution	**Combination**
Cognitive examples of components	Memories; problem solution; bias	Pooling; partially shared; averaging
Applicable principle	Correspondence	Context
Examples of principle	Proximal versus distal influence	Judgmental versus intellectual task
Illustrative literature	Team composition	Group decision rules

to address a common problem (Hinsz et al., 1997). Because a team is likely to have much more information than any one member, teams can potentially use all this information to solve the problem or address the issue at hand. Consequently, teams have the potential to greatly exceed the performance of individuals. One example of this is when critical information is distributed among the team members and a discussion will bring all this critical information out for consideration as the team confronts a problem (Stasser & Titus, 1985, 1987). However, the research literature on information sharing in teams suggests that this potential is rarely achieved (Brodbeck, Kerschreiter, Mojzisch, & Schulz-Hardt, 2007; Stasser & Titus, 2003). Instead, team members often spend much of their time discussing shared information and fail to pool their unique knowledge to arrive at the best decision. Research demonstrates that specific processes and information sharing biases lead to critical information not coming to light during discussion (Brodbeck et al., 2007; Gigone & Hastie, 1993; Reimer, Kuendig, Hoffrage, Park, & Hinsz, 2007; Stasser & Titus, 1985).

The information sampling bias is one such bias. Groups are often biased to discuss particular information based on how that information is distributed among group members. Specifically, information that different members already know or have (i.e., shared information) is discussed more frequently than unshared or uniquely held information. That is, the information sampling bias is that unshared information is proportionally less likely to be brought up in discussion than shared information. Empirical work and meta-analyses have shown this effect to be particularly robust (Brodbeck et al., 2007; Mesmer-Magnus & DeChurch, 2009; Stasser & Titus, 2003). The information sampling bias occurs even when group members are made aware that the information is differentially distributed (Wittenbaum & Stasser, 1996) or when group members are shown to have differential expertise regarding the task (Stasser, Stewart, & Wittenbaum, 1995).

An informative way to understand this bias toward discussing shared information was initially discussed by Stasser and Titus (1987). They proposed the collective information sampling model based on the binomial expansion. This formal model specifies that the probability that a piece of information will be discussed in a team, P_D, is a function of the probability of a team member bringing that information up during the team discussion, p_d, and the number of team members who could bring the piece of

256 • *Theories of Team Cognition*

information up during discussion, r, because they share knowledge of that piece of information. Formally, P_D is expressed as equal to $1 - (1 - p_d)^r$.

There are a number of compelling aspects of the collective information sampling model. Primary among them is that the model is extremely powerful in predicting the likelihood of a piece of information being discussed in a group (Stasser & Titus, 1985, 1987). Second, the research seems to indicate that little appears to influence the likelihood of a piece of information being discussed other than the variables for which there are parameters in the collective information sampling model. The collective information sampling model indicates that only the number of individuals that share the information and the probability of an individual bringing the information up for team discussion will influence the probability of the information coming up during discussion. Thus, changes to the group such as role assignment, leadership structure, or personality characteristics should only modify P_D insofar as they make it more or less likely that an individual will bring up a piece of information for team discussion (i.e., impact p_d) or change the number of individuals that share the information (i.e., impact r).

Although little seems to change the likelihood of information being shared within the collective information sampling model, research has uncovered situations that violate assumptions of the model such as when team members have knowledge of different expertise and when team members differ in status. Nevertheless, teams show the same bias for discussing shared information (Wittenbaum & Stasser, 1996). Wittenbaum, Hubbell, and Zuckerman (1999) describe a mutual enhancement model that proposes a motivational explanation for discussing more shared information in groups compared with unshared information. Mutual enhancement states that by discussing information that is shared within the group, both the communicator and the receiver of the information feel validated and competent within the task environment. By discussing shared information, both participants in the discussion demonstrate that they know and can recognize information that is relevant to the discussion, thus establishing competency. Discussing shared information is then reinforced by the receiver with verbal conformation and other nonverbal cues displaying interest such as leaning in or nodding. Thus, the repeated rewards associated with discussing shared information create motivational reasons for interaction participants to focus on shared information.

Motivation may also play a critical role in information exchange due to the way unique information is contributed during discussion (Dennis, 1997). Unique information is often presented in the context of a large amount of shared information. Team members may have a large amount of positive information regarding one alternative that is shared among the team and a single piece of unique information regarding another alternative that is unshared. In such a case, team members may choose to prefer the alternative supported by the shared information and only contribute the information that supports their initial decision (Stasser & Titus, 1985). This effect has been termed preference consistency and represents an important reason for discussing shared information (Greitmeyer & Schulz-Hardt, 2003).

Ultimately, research on information sampling demonstrates a clear effect of teams tending to discuss more shared compared with unshared information. This tendency can result in positive decisions being made if the shared information directs the team to the most appropriate alternative. However, there are situations in which unique information distributed among team members points to a different and more beneficial alternative than the information the team members share. In such situations, it would be advantageous to understand the factors that promote the contribution and processing of unshared information. Research on the hidden profile effect has attempted to establish the conditions under which unshared information will be discussed within a team, which is expected to lead to superior decision making.

Much of the research on information sharing in teams has focused on the hidden profile problem (Brodbeck et al., 2007; Stasser & Titus, 2003). In this context, information is distributed among team members in such a way that much information is shared among the team members. However, critical information needed to reach a quality team response is unshared and uniquely held by the team members. If the team members shared the critical pieces of information, then a quality outcome is likely. For example, if all members of a team are presented with all the information, then the team almost always reaches the high-quality response. However, when the critical information is unshared and distributed among the team members, success is often absent. As illustrated in Table 10.2, imagine that a six-person team is presented with information in such a fashion so that all members receive five pieces of shared information from a set of six pieces of information (A1, A2, A3, A4, A5, or A6) and one piece of unshared or unique information from a separate set of six pieces of information (B1,

258 • *Theories of Team Cognition*

TABLE 10.2

Hypothetical Distribution of Shared and Unshared Information in a Six-Person Team that Illustrates a Hidden Profile

Information Unit for Team Member	Team Member					
	I	II	III	IV	V	VI
1	A1	A2	A3	A4	A5	A6
2	**B2**	A3	A4	A5	A6	A1
3	A3	**B4**	A5	A6	A1	A2
4	A4	A5	**B6**	**B1**	A2	A3
5	A5	A6	A1	A2	**B3**	A4
6	A6	A1	A2	A3	A4	**B5**

Note: The A information units are each shared among five team members, and the B information units are unshared among the team members.

B2, B3, B4, B5, or B6). If the B information pieces are critical for an appropriate team response, then given the information sampling model, it is highly unlikely that the team would respond appropriately. This is because the collective information sampling model indicates the probability of the team discussing any individual item in the B set is very low simply because the information is unshared ($r = 1$). Comparatively, the probability of the team discussing any or all pieces of information in the A set is high due to the fact that five members of the team share that information ($r = 5$).

This research on information sharing and, in particular, on the hidden profile illustrates how the theory of combinations of contributions can organize our understanding of the related literature. The contributions that team members bring to the hidden profile are the shared and unshared information that they hold. Additionally, research suggests that the collective information sampling model is a robust description of the combination of those shared and unshared pieces of information. The collective information sampling model is a model of the combination of these contributions. The p_d are the member contributions, and the collective information sampling model describes how the information is combined.

The research also shows that correspondence is important. Within the combinations-of-contributions framework, individual contributions must correspond to the task the team is attempting to complete. Issues of correspondence can be thought of in two different ways within the hidden profile problem, through the characteristics of the team members and the relevance of the information they possess. Recall in the collective information sampling model that the parameters of interest are p_d and r. Thus, characteristics of the individual that lead the team members to bring up their information (e.g., better memory) will influence how likely it will be for an individual team member to bring forth the information he or she holds and, consequently, how likely the team is to discuss that piece of information. In this way, team member characteristics must correspond to the task of discussion. Without the willingness or ability to discuss information with the team, p_d drops to a level at which it is unlikely that this team will discuss any unique information that this particular team member may possess.

The second way that correspondence is important to the hidden profile problem is in the relationship between the information and the task. Information that corresponds to the task will be more beneficial to team members attempting to solve a hidden profile than information that is irrelevant or tangential to the task. If the critical information for resolving a hidden profile is unique to particular team members, the hidden profile may be much more difficult to solve compared with one in which the corresponding information is shared among team members. Thus, both the distribution of information and whether or not that information is critical to completing the task must be considered when examining the hidden profile problem. Therefore, we would expect that teams that have critical information shared among them would be more likely to arrive at the "correct" solution when completing the hidden profile problem than teams that have critical information unshared.

The implications of combinations-of-contributions theory for research on the hidden profile effect are compelling, but the theory itself is applicable to many different aspects of information sharing in teams. The example of the hidden profile demonstrating the utility of the collective information sampling model shows that once the combinatorial rule is known, the likelihood of a single piece of information being shared is clearly predictable. In addition, we can consider the contribution each member brings to the task and correspondence of both that team member with the task and the team member's contribution with the anticipated outcome. In a similar fashion, we can also consider how the perspectives, cognitive representations, or frameworks that team members bring with them to the task can influence team performance. This is reflected in the literature on mental models in teams (Klimoski & Mohammed, 1994). We next show how combinations-of-contributions theory helps us

260 • *Theories of Team Cognition*

understand the nature of shared cognition in teams for the case of shared mental models.

SHARED MENTAL MODELS AS SHARED COGNITION IN TEAMS

Mental models describe an individual's beliefs and expectations regarding interaction with a system (Hinsz, 1995). The system may be the individual's interaction partners, the task to be accomplished, the method by which the task will be accomplished, the technology with which team members must interact to complete the task, or many others. In our view of mental models, *beliefs* are the critical concept when thinking about the structure and functioning of mental models. By conceptualizing mental models as beliefs, mental models can be assessed using any system of measuring beliefs. This is important because one of the historical problems of mental models is their specification and assessment (Hinsz, 1995).

Mental models represent a single individual's beliefs or expectations regarding a system. However, for some aspects of functioning, we must have an understanding of not only the system as we see it, but how our interaction partners perceive and interact with the system as well. By having a shared understanding of the system, a team may be able to execute behaviors that would be impossible to perform without shared knowledge. For example, imagine a basketball player wishes to execute a "no-look pass" in which the player passes the ball to a teammate without looking at that teammate so as not to signal to the defense where the pass is going. Both passer and receiver need to share expectations for the pass to be completed successfully. They must share an understanding that such a maneuver is possible and will be beneficial to the team and of the context of the game in which it is most likely to occur. They must share knowledge of where each of them is on the court. The passer must know where the receiver is expected to be so that the ball is thrown to the correct position, and the receiver must know where the passer is expected to be so that the receiver can properly prepare to receive the ball and set up for the impending shot. Research on the phenomenon of shared mental models has been reviewed extensively, and we need not explore it fully here (for reviews, see DeChurch & Mesmer-Magnus, 2010; Salas & Cannon-Bowers, 2001). However, a brief review of this literature is necessary to understand how combinations-of-contributions theory can enhance our understanding of shared mental models.

Early literature demonstrated the utility of shared mental models by demonstrating that team performance can be predicted, in part, by the degree to which mental models are shared among team members (DeChurch & Mesmer-Magnus, 2010). Greater overlap in mental models was associated with improved team functioning and performance. Shared mental models came to be viewed as an important aspect of team functioning (Cannon-Bowers & Salas, 2001).

Additional research into shared mental models showed the necessity of specifying the type of mental model that must be shared to achieve the desired outcome (Cannon-Bowers, Salas, & Converse, 1993). As noted earlier, a number of mental models can exist for a single task. Mental models can be associated with the task, the person's interaction partners, the technology to be used, and so on. By measuring different types of mental models, researchers were able to discern that some mental models were necessary for improved team performance, whereas others were unrelated to task performance (Mathieu, Heffner, Goodwin, Salas, & Cannon-Bowers, 2000).

The literature on shared mental models demonstrates both the effect of shared mental models and the necessity to specify how shared mental models are expected to impact team performance. Research on shared mental models often aims to test one conceptual hypothesis—that is, that the sharedness of mental models among team members enhances team interaction and performance, or what would be considered outcomes in the I-P-O framework. Studies often test a conceptual hypothesis that the more the mental model is shared among team members, the more effective the team interaction and performance. However, this hypothesis is often misspecified in the literature.

Testing the sharedness of mental models among team members and relating that sharedness to outcomes fails to appreciate the importance of the accuracy or appropriateness of mental models. In the original literature on mental models that one finds in the cognitive and human factors literatures (Gentner & Stevens, 1983; Johnson-Laird, 1983; Rouse & Morris, 1986), the focus was on individuals and how accurate or appropriate the mental model was for performing the task effectively.

262 • *Theories of Team Cognition*

However, with the consideration of shared mental models, the accuracy and appropriateness of mental models has sometimes been overlooked. As noted in the theory of combinations of contributions, correspondence of contributions is important. In the case of mental models, a team member has to have accurate or appropriate beliefs for the task performance to improve.

Based on combinations-of-contributions theory, the proper hypothesis for the relationship between shared mental models and team performance is that accuracy and appropriateness of the mental models in the team influence team performance. The degree to which these member mental models are shared moderates this relationship. If the team members share an inappropriate mental model, they may agree on how to perform the task together, but they will do so incorrectly. Therefore, team performance is enhanced when team members have mental models that correspond to the appropriate way to accomplish the task. The efficiency and agreement about how to act will be improved to the degree they share appropriate mental models, and task performance will improve as a result. Meta-analysis shows that when the shared mental model hypothesis is specified correctly, the relationship between shared mental models in teams and interaction and performance is quite strong and stable (DeChurch & Mesmer-Magnus, 2010). In much of the research, the sharedness and the accuracy of mental models are confounded. Sometimes accuracy is not assessed but is assumed. By establishing how well the shared mental models correspond with task demands, we may develop a much clearer understanding of the relationship between shared mental models and team performance.

The theory of combinations of contributions also raises a question about how to conceptualize "shared" mental models. That is, how do researchers combine member mental models (as contributions) to represent the team mental model? Research has used a variety of aggregation measures (e.g., within-group correlation $[r_{wg}]$, intraclass correlation [ICC]; Bliese, 2000). However, other aggregation rules might be just as useful. A disjunctive aggregation rule would suggest that if one member of the team has an appropriate mental model, then team interaction and performance will improve. Alternatively, a conjunctive aggregation rule would propose that all members of the team have to share an appropriate mental model for team performance and interaction to improve. As specified by the theory of combinations of contributions, the combinatorial rule that would be applied is dependent on the context. One could see that for specific tasks, disjunctive or conjunctive aggregation strategies might apply. Merely using the agreement (e.g., r_{wg}, ICC) among members of a team may not aggregate the mental models appropriately, so the prediction of team interaction and performance would fall short of its potential. In essence, researchers need to understand a context to be able to state which degree of sharedness of mental models (fully shared, completely redundant, partially shared, complementary, or compatible) is needed for team interaction and performance to be affected by the member mental models. So, what is the combinatorial rule that should be applied to aggregate member mental models (e.g., disjunctive, conjunctive, complementary, similarity)? The theory of combinations of contributions suggests that it will vary as a function of the context. There are many ways to combine member mental models, but if done appropriately, researchers will have a better conception of how the team mental model predicts team interaction and performance.

Our definition of mental models relies on beliefs as the core component of mental models. As we defined mental models, it is clear that member beliefs and expectations are what are expected to influence team outcomes. Our reflection on team member beliefs and expectations has led us to consider them to play a larger role on team functioning. We can see that member beliefs and expectations can be expressed individually (e.g., skills needed to excel on the task), interpersonally (e.g., stereotypes of members of social groups), and at the level of teams (e.g., our team has these attributes). Teammate attributes lead to beliefs and expectations we could consider stereotypes when they are shared among team members. Members of a team may share a particular belief regarding the abilities of another teammate. These shared beliefs may then impact what that team member is expected to accomplish or the role that this particular team member is expected to take on while in the team. Notice that in this case, the principle of correspondence must be applied at the level of expectation as well as the level of outcomes. If a particular person is assigned a particular role based on the expectations and beliefs of other team members, those team members' expectations must correspond to the actual abilities of the team member being assigned a role, and the team member's actual abilities must correspond to the outcome of interest. If either of these correspondence points is incorrect, the team member and potentially the entire team may not achieve the desired outcome.

264 • *Theories of Team Cognition*

In addition to stereotypes, other factors may be influenced by the interplay between team member expectations and team member behaviors. When one team member acts consistently with regard to another member's beliefs and expectations, self-fulfilling prophecies and behavioral confirmation may result. In addition, cross-level effects can occur between mental models at different levels. Individual expectations influence expectations about teammates, which in turn influence social relations. Within this conceptualization, interpersonal awareness becomes a construct similar to situational awareness. In addition, beliefs and expectations about whether or not the team has the personnel necessary to respond to task demands could influence a team-level assessment of whether or not the task can be completed. There are also expectations and beliefs about the task environment that can influence situation awareness and thus impact task performance independent of beliefs regarding interpersonal interactions.

The literature regarding shared mental models can present contradictory findings. However, the addition of combinations-of-contributions theory represents an important step in specifying shared mental models, both in their correspondence to the task and the context in which they occur. The correspondence aspect of combinations-of-contributions theory aids our understanding by demonstrating that the member mental models under consideration (i.e., contributions) need to be accurate and appropriate for the task outcomes being considered. The context for which the member mental models are applied will also influence the combinatorial rule of sharedness with which team member mental models are specified for predicting team performance. Consequently, the theory of combinations of contributions provides a conceptual basis for a better understanding of the relationship between shared mental models and team outcomes.

COMBINATIONS OF CONTRIBUTIONS AND SHARING COGNITIONS IN TEAMS

Shared mental models and information sharing in teams represent two areas of study relevant to the application of combinations-of-contributions theory. By establishing the contributions each team member brings with them to the team interaction, how those contributions correspond to the task, the context in which the team will perform their task, and how the context will affect the combinatorial rule that is most effective at predicting how the team will integrate their contributions, one can develop an effective conceptualization of team functioning. In some cases, the combinatorial rule may have few parameters, as in the collective information sampling model. In others, the aggregation principle may be more complex, as with individuals having mental models for multiple aspects of the task they must accomplish, but potentially only needing to share a subset of that information to be successful. An example of this type of team would be a manufacturing assembly line. Each team member holds a unique mental model regarding his or her specific task. The only information that would need to be shared is information directly task relevant to that specific member as well as information about the ultimate goal. In this case, defining the combinatorial rule would require assessing the unique information from all members along the line, summing that information, and accounting for the small amounts of information that are shared among neighboring stations. Such an aggregation principle would be much more complex but would still follow the basic principles of combinations-of-contributions theory.

The theory of combinations of contributions views teams processing information in much the same manner as individuals; however, team members must share that information to reach their greatest potential. By sharing cognitions, teams are potentially better able to capitalize on the greater memory capacity, processing power, and information aggregation that forming a team allows. Combinations-of-contributions theory defines the problem of combining information in teams and stipulates the conditions necessary for the combination of contributions to produce the desired outcomes. In this regard, the theory of combinations of contributions is directly applicable to conditions of sharing cognitions in teams.

The contributions of team members are highly important to any task situation. Team members are expected to bring certain personal resources with them into the team interaction. In a task with cognitive components, such resources could be information, memory capacity, cognitive representations, or the effectiveness of a number of cognitive functions. However, the contributions must correspond to the outcome of interest. If the information a team member possesses is irrelevant, or the cognitive abilities brought by the member do not correspond to task demands, the contribution cannot be expected to relate to the outcome of interest. As a consequence, the correspondence of the resources team members bring

266 • *Theories of Team Cognition*

to the interaction and task as contributions helps determine whether the team will succeed or fail to achieve its potential on the task.

The combinations or aggregation strategies of the contributions also play a pivotal role in determining team performance on a cognitive task. How the team combines its members' contributions is critical to how well they perform on a task in a collective outcome environment. Combining the correct contributions in the most appropriate way can lead to increased performance on the task and potentially optimal outcomes. When considering combining contributions, the context is critical. Each situation the team encounters occurs within a particular context. The team must adjust to this context if it hopes to use each member's contributions optimally. Our understanding of how cognitions are effectively combined for team performance will be enhanced to the degree that research uncovers the systematic ways in which contexts influence the combinatorial strategies of information processing in teams.

We have shown how the theory of combinations of contributions can help explorations of information sharing in teams and mental models in teams. By defining what each team member brings to the team and how well those contributions correspond to the task environment, establishing how the team will combine member inputs to reach a collective outcome, and paying particular attention to the context in which the team operates, we can advance our understanding of shared cognition in teams. Moreover, combinations-of-contributions theory provides a conceptual framework that can aid in the broader understanding of how sharing cognition in teams influences team interaction and performance.

ACKNOWLEDGMENT

Preparation of this chapter was supported by a grant to V.B.H. from the National Science Foundation (BCS – 0721796).

REFERENCES

Anderson, N. H., & Graesser, C. C. (1976). An information integration analysis of attitude change in group decision. *Journal of Personality and Social Psychology, 34,* 210–222.

Bales, R. F. (1950). *Interaction process analysis: A method for the study of small groups.* Cambridge, MA: Addison-Wesley.

Combinations of Contributions for Sharing Cognitions in Teams • 267

Baron, R. S., & Kerr, N. L. (2003). *Group process, group decision, group action*. New York: Open University Press.

Bliese, P. D. (2000). Within-group agreement, non-independence, and reliability: Implications for data aggregation and analysis. In K. Klein & S. W. J. Kozlowski (Eds.), *Multilevel theory, research, and methods in organizations: Foundations, extensions, and new directions* (pp. 349–381). San Francisco, CA: Jossey-Bass.

Brodbeck, F. C., Kerschreiter, R., Mojzisch, A., & Schulz-Hardt, S. (2007). Group decision making under conditions of distributed knowledge: The information asymmetries model. *Academy of Management Review, 32*, 459–479.

Cannon-Bowers, J. A., & Salas, E. (2001). Reflections on shared cognition. *Journal of Organizational Behavior, 22*, 195–202.

Cannon-Bowers, J. A., Salas, E., & Converse, S. (1993). Shared mental models in expert team decision making. In N. J. Castellan (Ed.), *Individual and group decision making* (pp. 221–246). Hillsdale, NJ: Lawrence Erlbaum Associates.

Cohen, S. G., & Bailey, D. E. (1997). What makes teams work: Group effectiveness research from the shop floor to the executive suite. *Journal of Management, 23*, 239–290.

Crott, H. W., Zuber, J. A., & Schermer, T. (1986). Social decision schemes and choice shift: An analysis of group decisions among bets. *Journal of Experimental Social Psychology, 22*, 1–21.

Davis, J. H. (1973). Group decision and social interaction: A theory of social decision schemes. *Psychological Review, 80*, 97–125.

Davis, J. H. (1982). Social interaction as a combinatorial process in group decision. In H. Brandstatter, J. H. Davis, & G. Stocker-Kreichgauer (Ed.), *Group decision making* (pp. 27–58). London, UK: Academic Press.

Davis, J. H. (1996). Group decision making and quantitative judgments: A consensus model. In E. Witte & J. H. Davis (Eds.), *Understanding group behavior: Consensual action by small groups* (Vol. 1, pp. 35–59). Hillsdale, NJ: Erlbaum.

DeChurch, L. A., & Mesmer-Magnus, J. R. (2010). The cognitive underpinnings of effective teamwork: A meta-analysis. *Journal of Applied Psychology, 95*, 32–53.

Dennis, A. R. (1997). Information exchange and use in small group decision making. *Small Group Research, 27*, 532–550.

Devine, D. J., Clayton, L. D., Philips, J. L., Dunford, B. B., & Melner, S. B. (1999). Teams in organizations: Prevalence, characteristics, and effectiveness. *Small Group Research, 30*, 678–711.

Devine, D. J., & Philips, J. L. (2001). Do smarter teams do better: A meta-analysis of cognitive ability and team performance. *Small Group Research, 32*, 507–532.

Ellis, A. P. J., Bell, B. S., Ployhart, R. E., Hollenbeck, J. R., & Ilgen, D. R. (2005). An evaluation of generic teamwork skills training with action teams: Effects on cognitive and skill based outcomes. *Personnel Psychology, 58*, 641–672.

Galegher, J., Kraut, R. E., & Egido, C. (1990). *Intellectual teamwork: Social and technological foundations of cooperative work*. Hillsdale, NJ: Lawrence Erlbaum Associates.

Gentner, D., & Stevens, A. L. (1983). *Mental models*. Hillsdale, NJ: Lawrence Erlbaum Associates.

Gigone, D., & Hastie, R. (1993). The common knowledge effect: Information sharing and group judgment. *Journal of Personality and Social Psychology, 65*, 959–974.

Greitemeyer, T., & Schulz-Hardt, S. (2003). Preference-consistent evaluation of information in the hidden profile paradigm: Beyond group-level explanations for the dominance of shared information in group decisions. *Journal of Personality and Social Psychology, 84*, 322–339.

268 • *Theories of Team Cognition*

Hackman, J. R. (1987). The design of work teams. In J. Lorsch (Ed.), *Handbook of organizational behavior* (pp. 315–342). Englewood Cliffs, NJ: Prentice-Hall.

Hackman, J. R. (1990). *Groups that work and those that don't: Creating conditions for effective team work.* San Francisco, CA: Jossey-Bass.

Hackman, J. R., & Morris, C. G. (1975). Group tasks, group interaction process, and group performance effectiveness: A review and proposed integration. *Advances in Experimental Social Psychology, 8*, 45–99.

Hinsz, V. B. (1995). Mental models of groups as social systems: Considerations of specification and assessment. *Small Group Research, 26*, 200–233.

Hinsz, V. B. (1999). Group decision making with responses of a quantitative nature: The theory of social decision schemes for quantities. *Organizational Behavior and Human Decision Processes, 80*, 28–49.

Hinsz, V. B. (2001). A groups-as-information-processors perspective for technological support of intellectual teamwork. In M. McNeese, E. Salas, & M. Endsley (Eds.), *New trends in cooperative activities: Understanding system dynamics in complex environments* (pp. 22–45). Santa Monica, CA: Human Factors and Ergonomic Society.

Hinsz, V. B., Tindale, R. S., & Vollrath, D. A. (1997). The emerging conceptualization of groups as information processors. *Psychological Bulletin, 121*, 43–64.

Hinsz, V. B., Wallace, D. M., & Ladbury, J. L. (2009). Team performance in dynamic task environments. In G. P. Hodgkinson & J. K. Ford (Eds.), *International review of industrial and organizational psychology* (Vol. 24, pp. 183–216). New York, NY: Wiley.

Hollenbeck, J. R., DeRue, D. S., & Guzzo, R. (2004). Bridging the gap between I/O research and HR practice: Improving team composition, team training and team task design. *Human Resource Management, 43*, 353–366.

Ilgen, D. R., Hollenbeck, J. R., Johnson, M., & Jundt, D. (2005). Teams in organizations: From input-process-output models to IMOI models. *Annual Review of Psychology, 56*, 517–543.

Johnson-Laird, P. N. (1983). *Mental models.* Cambridge, UK: Cambridge University Press.

Kerr, N. L. (1981). Social transition schemes: Charting the group's road to agreement. *Journal of Personality and Social Psychology, 41*, 684–702.

Klimoski, R., & Mohammed, S. (1994). Team mental model: Construct or metaphor? *Journal of Management, 20*, 403–437.

Kozlowski, S. W. J., & Bell, B. S. (2003). Work groups and teams in organizations. In W. C. Borman, D. R. Ilgen, & R. J. Klimoski (Eds.), *Handbook of psychology: Industrial and organizational psychology* (Vol. 12, pp. 333–375). London, UK: Wiley.

Kozlowski, S. W. J., & Ilgen, D. R. (2006). Enhancing the effectiveness of work groups and teams. *Psychological Science in the Public Interest, 7*, 77–123.

Laughlin, P. R. (1980). Social combination processes of cooperative problem-solving groups on verbal intellective tasks. In M. Fishbein (Ed.), *Progress in social psychology* (pp. 127–155). Hillsdale, NJ: Lawrence Erlbaum Associates.

Laughlin, P. R. (1996). Group decision making and collective induction. In E. H. Witte & J. H. Davis (Eds.), *Understanding group behavior, Vol. 1: Consensual action by small groups* (pp. 61–80). Hillsdale, NJ: Lawrence Erlbaum Associates.

Laughlin, P. R., & Ellis, A. L. (1986). Demonstrability and social combination processes on mathematical intellective tasks. *Journal of Experimental Social Psychology, 22*, 177–189.

Combinations of Contributions for Sharing Cognitions in Teams • 269

Laughlin, P. R., & Hollingshead, A. B. (1995). A theory of collective induction. *Organizational Behavior and Human Decision Processes, 61*, 94–107.

Letsky, M. P., Warner, N. W., Fiore, S. M., & Smith, C. A. P. (Eds.). (2008). *Macrocognition in teams: Theories and methodologies.* Burlington, VT: Ashgate.

Levine, J. M., Resnick, L. B., & Higgins, E. T. (1993). Social foundations of cognition. *Annual Review of Psychology, 44*, 585–612.

Marks, M. A., Mathieu, J. E., & Zaccaro, S. J. (2001). A conceptual framework and taxonomy of team processes. *Academy of Management Review, 26*, 356–376.

Mathieu, J. E., Heffner, T. S., Goodwin, G. F., Salas, E., & Cannon-Bowers, J. A. (2000). The influence of shared mental models on team process and performance. *Journal of Applied Psychology, 85*, 273–283.

McGrath, J. E. (1964). *Social psychology: A brief introduction.* New York, NY: Holt, Rinehart & Winston.

McGrath, J. E. (1984). *Groups: Interaction and performance.* Englewood Cliffs, NJ: Prentice-Hall.

McGrath, J. E., & Altman, I. (1966). *Small group research: A synthesis and critique of the field.* New York, NY: Holt, Rinehart, & Winston.

McGrath, J. E., & Hollingshead, A. B. (1994). *Groups interacting with technology: Ideas, evidence, issues, and an agenda.* Thousand Oaks, CA: Sage Publications.

McNeese, M., Salas, E., & Endsley, M. (Eds.). (2001). *New trends in cooperative activities: Understanding system dynamics in complex environments.* Santa Monica, CA: Human Factors and Ergonomics Society.

Mesmer-Magnus, J. R., & DeChurch, L. A. (2009). Information sharing and team performance: A meta-analysis. *Journal of Applied Psychology, 94*, 535–546.

Penrod, S. D., & Hastie, R. (1981). A computer simulation of jury decision making. *Psychological Review, 87*, 133–159.

Reimer, T., Kuendig, S., Hoffrage, U., Park, E. S., & Hinsz, V. B. (2007). Effects of the information environment on group discussions and decisions in the hidden-profile paradigm. *Communication Monographs, 74*, 1–28.

Roethlisberger, F. J., & Dickson, W. J. (1939). *Management and the worker.* Cambridge, MA: Harvard University Press.

Rouse, W. B., & Morris, N. M. (1986). On looking into the black box: Prospects and limits in the search for mental models. *Psychological Bulletin, 100*, 349–363.

Salas, E., & Cannon-Bowers, J. A. (Eds.). (2001). Shared cognition [Special issue]. *Journal of Organizational Behavior, 22*(2).

Stasser, G., & Davis, J. H. (1981). Group decision making and social influence: A social interaction sequence model. *Psychological Review, 88*, 523–551.

Stasser, G., Stewart, D. D., & Wittenbaum, G. M. (1995). Expert roles and information exchange during discussion: The importance of knowing who knows what. *Journal of Experimental Social Psychology, 31*, 244–265.

Stasser, G., & Titus, W. (1985). Pooling of unshared information in group decision making: Biased information sampling during discussion. *Journal of Personality and Social Psychology, 48*, 1467–1478.

Stasser, G., & Titus, W. (1987). Effects of information load and percentage of shared information on the dissemination of unshared information during group discussion. *Journal of Personality and Social Psychology, 53*, 81–93.

Stasser, G., & Titus, W. (2003). Hidden profiles: A brief history. *Psychological Inquiry, 14*, 304–313.

Steiner, I. D. (1972). *Group process and productivity.* New York, NY: Academic Press.

270 • *Theories of Team Cognition*

Sundstrom, E., McIntyre, M., Halfhill, T., & Richards, H. (2000). Work groups: From the Hawthorne Studies to the work teams of the 1990s and beyond. *Group Dynamics: Theory, Research, and Practice, 4*, 44–67.

Tindale, R. S., Kameda, T., & Hinsz, V. B. (2003). Group decision making. In M. A. Hogg & J. Cooper (Eds.), *Handbook of social psychology* (pp. 381–403). Thousand Oaks, CA: Sage Publications.

Vroom, V. H. (1969). Industrial social psychology. In G. Lindzey & E. Aronson (Eds.), *Handbook of social psychology* (Vol. 5, 2nd ed., pp. 196–268). Reading, MA: Addison-Wesley.

Weingart, L. R. (1997). How did they do that? The ways and means of studying group process. *Research in Organizational Behavior, 19*, 189–239.

Wittenbaum, G. M., Hubbell, A. P., & Zuckerman, C. (1999). Mutual enhancement: Toward an understanding of the collective preference for shared information. *Journal of Personality and Social Psychology, 77*, 967–978.

Wittenbaum, G. M., & Stasser, G. (1996). Management of information in small groups. In J. L. Nye & A. M. Brower (Eds.), *What's social about social cognition? Research on socially shared cognition in small groups* (pp. 3–28). Thousand Oaks, CA: Sage Publications.

11

Considering the Influence of Task Complexity on Macrocognitive Team Processes

Rebecca Lyons, Heather Lum, Stephen M. Fiore, Eduardo Salas, Norman Warner, and Michael P. Letsky

In many contexts, teams are capable of solving complex problems that are well beyond the capacity of any one individual team member (Salas, Cannon-Bowers, & Johnston, 1997; Salas, Rosen, Burke, & Goodwin, 2009). However, not all teams are successful, and failures often come at high costs. Identifying factors that distinguish successful and unsuccessful team collaboration has thus been a consistent and highly relevant topic of team research.

Through efforts to understand what makes teams successful, much has been learned about the components of effective teamwork when it comes to behavioral coordination (e.g., Cannon-Bowers & Salas, 1997; Cannon-Bowers, Tannenbaum, Salas, & Volpe, 1995; Marks, Mathieu, & Zaccaro, 2001; Salas et al., 2009). However, problem-solving performance in high-stakes, time-sensitive environments necessitates processes beyond behavioral coordination. Specifically, the problem solving required for performance in these complex, novel situations is thought to involve internalized and externalized high-level processes used by teams to create knowledge. This complex collaborative cognition is referred to as macrocognition in teams (Letsky, Warner, Fiore, & Smith, 2008). As a relatively new concept, empirical literature directly addressing macrocognition in teams is still lacking.

Following on current theory in *team cognition* (Salas & Fiore, 2004) and recent work on *macrocognition in teams* (Fiore, Elias, Salas, Warner, & Letsky, 2010; Fiore, Rosen, et al., 2010; Fiore, Smith-Jentsch, Salas, Warner, & Letsky, 2010; Letsky et al., 2008), we discuss *task*

271

272 • *Theories of Team Cognition*

complexity as a factor that may help us develop a better understanding of collaborative problem solving. In this chapter, we first briefly define macrocognition in teams and summarize some of its major processes. We then discuss how to operationalize task complexity in the context of macrocognition in teams. We describe representative samples of the research that has empirically examined this construct and conclude with a discussion of the implications for macrocognition. In short, our goal with this chapter is to extend our extant theorizing on macrocognition in teams and discuss task complexity as a factor that may help extend the field's understanding of collaborative problem solving.

MACROCOGNITION IN TEAMS

The concept of macrocognition initially emerged from the need to understand how cognition occurs in complex environments. In cognitive engineering, researchers were studying naturalistic environments and argued that, in such settings, cognitive processes emerge in different ways when compared to laboratory settings (Cacciabue & Hollnagel, 1995). They noted that macrocognition involved "the role of cognition in realistic tasks, that is, in interacting with the environment. Macrocognition only rarely looks at phenomena that take place exclusively within the human mind or without overt interaction. It is thus more concerned with human performance under actual working conditions than with controlled experiments" (Cacciabue & Hollnagel, 1995, p. 57). Following on this work, Klein et al. (2003) theorized that contextually bound complex cognitive processes (e.g., sensemaking, uncertainty management) form the core of macrocognition.

More recently, *collaborative* aspects of problem solving and high-level cognitive processes during teamwork have been addressed in studies of macrocognition (Warner & Letsky, 2008). Here, macrocognition is defined as "the internalized and externalized high-level mental processes employed by teams to create new knowledge during complex, one-of-a-kind, collaborative problem solving" (Letsky, Warner, Fiore, Rosen, & Salas, 2007, p. 7). In the macrocognition in teams view, "high-level"

Influence of Task Complexity on Macrocognitive Team Processes • 273

involves combining, visualizing, and aggregating information to resolve ambiguity in support of the discovery of new knowledge and relationships. This is argued to be a result of the dynamic and complex nature of the task as well as the inherent properties of team interaction that emerge during collaborative problem solving. Letsky et al. (2007) further identify four collaboration stages that arise during problem solving: knowledge construction, collaborative team problem solving, team consensuses, and outcome evaluation and revision. This conceptualization of macrocognition in teams forms the foundation for our exploration of how task complexity may impact these processes. We next briefly review the processes argued to unfold across these stages (for more details, see Fiore, Rosen, et al., 2010).

Processes Involved in Macrocognition in Teams

In studying macrocognition in team dynamic problem solving, we ultimately desire to know what processes are involved. Fiore, Rosen, et al. (2010) proposed that there are five major macrocognitive processes related to collaborative problem solving: individual knowledge building, team knowledge building, internalized team knowledge, externalized knowledge, and team problem-solving outcomes (Figure 11.1).

Individual knowledge building involves the cognitive or behavioral actions an individual takes in order to build personal knowledge. The actions may include efforts by an individual to gather information and to piece this information into a mental model of the problem. An individual may also use his or her knowledge to create a physical product of some form; that is, a type of cognitive artifact such as a diagram or table that represents important aspects of the task.

Team knowledge building, the second primary macrocognitive process, focuses on actions that take place between several individuals. Team knowledge-building processes emerge as team members begin to share information in order to develop a reservoir of knowledge held at the team level. Interindividual actions of relevance under the general process of team knowledge building include team information exchange, team knowledge sharing, solution generation, solution evaluation, and negotiation.

Internalized knowledge is the knowledge possessed by an individual that may or may not be distinct from the knowledge held by other team

274 • Theories of Team Cognition

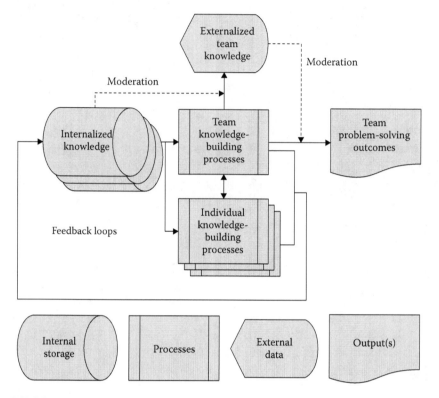

FIGURE 11.1
Model for research on macrocognition in teams (note that multiple overlapping symbols indicate representations for multiple team members). (From Fiore, S. M., Rosen, M. A., Smith-Jentsch, K. A., Salas, E., Letsky, M., & Warner, N. *Hum. Factors*, 52, 2010. With permission.)

members. Team members may hold uniquely held information that is related to their specific area of expertise. This allows the team member to add to the overall knowledge available to the team. *Externalized team knowledge* relates to knowledge that team members have agreed upon in the course of their collaboration.

Team problem-solving outcomes refer to the effectiveness of a selected solution (i.e., was the tasked problem appropriately solved?). The quality of the outcome may be related to the number of objectives met or the degree to which the team met various goals (e.g., time). Thus, our conceptualization of macrocognition in teams emphasizes knowledge building, assumed to occur through collaboration.

TASK COMPLEXITY

Within this broader theoretical context, we next argue that we need a clearer explication of how task factors impact this collaborative process. Macrocognition in teams is intrinsically linked to the task environment (e.g., the characteristics of the task will in part dictate the processes and the effectiveness of team processes used to perform the task). Consequently, a formal understanding of macrocognitive tasks is a critical need both for developing laboratory-based experimentation that captures the robustness of real-world tasks and for leveraging experimental findings into practical interventions (e.g., training, system and task design) to support macrocognition in organizational contexts.

In short, critical to our overall goal of improving collaboration is an understanding of how the nature of the task interacts with team problem solving. To some degree, the specific characteristics of a task will dictate the processes that are relevant to performance of the task. In this section, we follow on our earlier work (Lum, Fiore, Rosen, & Salas, 2008) and summarize the empirical literature addressing task complexity in complex problem solving. The objective of this review is to isolate several of the primary ways in which specific features of task complexity have been demonstrated to influence behaviors, cognitions, and outcomes related to complex problem solving. Our discussion of the task complexity literature will broadly be based around the outcomes affected by task complexity.

Task Complexity and Information Seeking and Use

In a public administration setting, Byström and Järvelin (1995) analyzed work diaries to examine the effects of task complexity on information seeking and the effectiveness of information use. Complexity was conceived as the *a priori determinability* of a task (i.e., preknown structure of inputs and results). From this study, they concluded that in information seeking, complex information is required for more complex tasks and that additional domain and problem-solving information are required. In addition, task complexity was observed to moderate the use of information sources. Specifically, participants accessed a greater number of sources when addressing complex tasks and disparately used available

276 • *Theories of Team Cognition*

sources. As complexity increased, participants reported greater sharing of general-purpose sources and decreased use of problem and fact-oriented sources.

Task Complexity and Task Strategies Used

Although numerous studies have examined the direct effects of task complexity factors on performance outcomes, why these effects are observed has less commonly been examined.

Toward this need, several studies have examined the influence of task complexity characteristics on team strategy. As a primary example, Saavedra, Earley, and Van Dyne (1993) tested a model based on their previously proposed theory of complex interdependence. Saavedra et al. (1993) reported a positive correlation between complex interdependence and team performance, both in terms of quantity and quality. This relationship was partially mediated by the task strategy used. This suggests that the interdependence factors comprising complex interdependence (i.e., task, goal, and feedback interdependence) should inform the strategies used to complete the task. Individuals given specific goals have similarly been observed to perform at a higher quality level and complete work more quickly, depending on the complexity of the task (Mone & Shalley, 1995). These benefits to performance are at least partially attributable to the task strategy used. It was observed that over multiple performance periods, task strategy was modified more by teams performing complex tasks.

Task Complexity and Team Engagement

The complexity of a task can also influence the time and effort team members invest in the collaborative problem-solving process, as demonstrated in terms of both physical (Latané, Williams, & Harkins, 1979) and cognitive tasks (Harkins & Petty, 1982). Social loafing is a well-documented concept in social psychology that suggests that when individuals perform as part of a group, they put in less effort than if they were to perform alone or told that their personal performance could be monitored within the group. Although individuals' physical engagement is not necessarily relevant to collaborative problem-solving tasks, understanding individuals' cognitive contributions is critical. Building on Latané et al.'s (1979) studies of physically demanding tasks, Harkins and Petty (1982) manipulated task complexity in terms of the cognitive difficulty of a brainstorming task. Participants were asked to generate as many possible alternative uses as they could for either a knife (low difficulty) or a detached doorknob (high difficulty). Results indicated that the negative effects of social loafing on performance were reduced for the higher complexity condition.

Task Complexity and Team Performance

Software redesign was the context through which the role of task and team familiarity was examined along with variations in complexity (Espinosa, Slaughter, Kraut, & Herbsleb, 2007). Software development and testing require a unique blend of individual and team cognition in that the nature of the tasks has varying periods of interdependence. Archival data of software development teams were analyzed, with task complexity measured through task size and structural complexity. Task size in this particular study was defined as the number of thousands of lines of software instructions. Structural complexity was defined as characteristics that make software difficult to change and understand and was measured as the number of software modules impacted by a request for modification to the code. Espinosa et al. (2007) found that task familiarity helped reduce task completion time more strongly for tasks with lower structural complexity. Perhaps most importantly for understanding collaborative problem solving, an interesting differential effect of task and team familiarity is seen. Espinosa et al. (2007) found that familiarity with a task is beneficial for tasks lower in complexity, but it has less of an effect as complexity increases. Furthermore, the benefit of task familiarity is particularly prominent when team familiarity is low, whereas when task familiarity is low, there is a benefit of team familiarity.

Task Complexity and Technology Use

Others have examined the degree to which technology use impacts collaboration. Technological support systems are increasingly used to facilitate teamwork in distributed work teams. However, the implementation of such technologies is not equally effective across tasks types. Specifically, the complexity of a task, defined in terms of teammate interdependence, has been demonstrated to differentially influence group performance

278 • *Theories of Team Cognition*

depending on the mode through which team members interact (Straus & McGrath, 1994). Computer-mediated teams and face-to-face teams performing various tasks (idea generation, intellective, or judgment tasks) were observed to perform similarly in terms of the quality of their work; however, computer-mediated teams were significantly less productive, with greater task complexity (manipulated via increases in task interdependence) increasing this disparity.

Task Complexity and Team Diversity

Diversity of a team's members also appears to influence the degree to which the complexity of a task influences performance. Higgs, Plewnia, and Ploch (2005) demonstrated that for complex tasks, teams with greater role diversity performed more effectively than less diverse teams; however, for straightforward tasks, team member diversity appeared to hinder team performance.

Task Complexity and Cognitive Fit

Task complexity research has also considered the interaction of task characteristics and individual differences (e.g., experience, cognitive capabilities) and concepts of fit. Specific to the complexity of problem-solving tasks, Vessey (1991) proposed that problem-solving processes best contribute to effective and efficient problem-solving performance when individuals possess accurate mental representation of a problem space. Initial support for this paradigm was demonstrated through an analysis of the literature on information acquisition tasks that also incorporated individual information evaluation. Information acquisition was broken down into tasks where information was obtained either through spatial (i.e., graphs) or symbolic (i.e., tables) formats. Results support the benefits of cognitive fit, both in terms of the quality of problem solving and time. In terms of task complexity, this work suggests that the features of a task may dictate the use of different cognitive aids in problem solving.

Task Complexity and Decision Making

Expanding on Vessey's (1991) cognitive fit theory, Speier (2006) added a second, more direct indicator of task complexity (i.e., number of information

Influence of Task Complexity on Macrocognitive Team Processes • 279

cues required to solve a problem). By examining the interaction of this task complexity measure with the presentation format of information (i.e., spatial versus symbolic), they found that information format was differentially related to task complexity. More specifically, for both simple and complex spatial tasks, information presented in spatial formats (i.e., graphs) contributed to faster, more accurate decision making. Compared with symbolic formats, spatial formats also reduced decision time for simple symbolic tasks. Accuracy and decision time did not differ for complex symbolic tasks. Interestingly, confidence ratings of decision makers did not necessarily align with performance outcomes. For both complex symbolic tasks and simple spatial tasks, decision makers reported greater confidence in their decision when using tables versus graphs; however, tables were only more beneficial in decision making for the complex symbolic tasks. Presenting information through tables for simple spatial tasks thus appears to provide users with false confidence in their responses.

Summary

To summarize across these studies, first, the most significant findings from research in cognitive fit suggest that spatial formats result in better decision accuracy, as well as faster decision time for most tasks. With regard to task complexity, evidence suggested that "decision-makers using analytical processes consciously or subconsciously traded-off accuracy to ease the cognitive load associated with the symbolic task" (Speier, 2006, p. 1127). Second, such findings have implications in complex situations where information is shared during a macrocognitive task within a team setting. Furthermore, the findings suggest that, within a macrocognitive setting, where processes such as knowledge building and integration are key, the presentation of information may be important in simplistic tasks but less relevant as the tasks get more complex. Third, findings indicate that decision makers rely more heavily on perceptual processes in complex tasks and that symbolic formats allowed for faster decision time for analytic processing. In short, the results of these studies can enhance our understanding of the circumstances under which different cognitive artifacts can most effectively be used. Furthermore, the insights on the differential benefits of varied information formats could be applied in knowledge object development, by generating knowledge objects that are best suited to match the problem context.

280 • *Theories of Team Cognition*

We next discuss in more detail how these findings can be used to augment theory and research for macrocognition in teams.

IMPLICATIONS OF TASK COMPLEXITY FOR MACROCOGNITION IN TEAMS

Looking across the literature, a number of implications for understanding task complexity in the context of macrocognition are evident. To help advance theory and guide future empirical examinations of macrocognition in teams, we now focus on integrating the findings from the task complexity literature with the previously addressed processes of macrocognition in teams. Propositions are provided regarding the manner in which variations in task complexity might affect the macrocognitive team processes within team collaboration (see Tables 11.1 to 11.5).

Implications for Individual Knowledge-Building Processes

A foundational element in the process of team problem solving is the development of individual knowledge through information gathering. Individuals must further be able to make sense of this information and piece it together in a manner that helps conceptualize the task. Theory has suggested that the most relevant macrocognitive team processes are those related to individual knowledge building.

The task complexity literature indicates several potential implications for the individual knowledge-building processes. The subprocess of individual information gathering involves determining what information is needed and identifying information sources. The task complexity literature suggests that the specific demands of a task determine the precise information required for successful task performance. It has been demonstrated that information content, sources, and timing of information search are each influenced by the features of a task. Beyond the content of information sought by an individual, the complexity of a task may also influence the strategies used in the information-search process. For example, Byström and Järvelin (1995) present evidence that the degree to which the structure of a task is made evident prior to task performance (i.e., a priori determinability) influences the strategies used in the information-search process. Additionally, the complexity features of task size and task

Influence of Task Complexity on Macrocognitive Team Processes • 281

familiarly are likely to interact in their influence on the information-search process. More complex tasks tend to require more information, which may inherently increase the anticipated use of information-gathering processes; however, familiarity with a task implies some level of preexisting knowledge and increased awareness of information requirements, thus minimizing information-gathering demands. The familiarity of a problem also holds implications for the process of individual information synthesis. An individual with an existing mental frame of the problem has the advantage of adding new information to an existing structure, which may enhance the speed and accuracy of synthesis, assuming the original mental structure was accurate.

In terms of the individual knowledge-building processes, information obtained by an individual may be externalized in the development of knowledge objects. The intention of knowledge objects is to support the individual in their understanding of the task. The task complexity literature suggests that the process of knowledge-object development should target different forms of knowledge objects based on the type of information presented by a problem. A better understanding of the manner in which the knowledge-object processes support the problem-solving process may guide individuals in the creation of knowledge objects of optimal utility. Based on our review of the literature, we have distilled a set of propositions that relate task complexity to individual knowledge building (Propositions 1 to 3 in Table 11.1).

TABLE 11.1

Propositions for the Influence of Task Complexity on Individual Knowledge-Building Processes

---

Propositions

Proposition 1: The individual knowledge-building process of information gathering will be influenced in terms of the quantity of information demands, the sources through which information is sought, and the time allocated to this process by task complexity features such as a priori determinability, task size, and task familiarity, which change the scope or difficulty of the problem.

Proposition 2: The individual knowledge-building process of individual information synthesis will be related to the structural complexity and familiarity of a problem, with novel, difficult information requiring the most effort toward synthesis.

Proposition 3: The individual knowledge-building process of knowledge-object development will more strongly contribute to solution option generation and the selection of an effective problem solution when the form of the knowledge object is complementary to the characteristics of the problem solution.

---

282 • *Theories of Team Cognition*

Implications for Team Knowledge-Building Processes

The extent to which team members contribute to team knowledge-building processes, such as exchanging information, generating and sharing solution options for consideration, and participating in the evaluation and discussions of solution alternatives, can greatly contribute to the effectiveness of a team's problem-solving efforts. For example, the exchange of information between team members provides access to a greater quantity of knowledge and contributes to the generation of team solution options that otherwise would not have been proposed. To promote the effectiveness of these macrocognitive processes and/or develop systems to support their performance, we must first understand the factors that may promote or inhibit their effectiveness.

Leveraging from the complexity literature, it will be beneficial for researchers of macrocognition in teams to understand the relationship between task complexity and social loafing. As previously discussed, Harkins and Petty (1982) successfully reduced the occurrence of social loafing for groups performing difficult brainstorming tasks compared with groups performing easy tasks. This finding is particularly applicable to the macrocognitive process of team solution option generation because it involves individuals' contributions to the identification of solutions. Furthermore, in terms of the stages of collaborative team problem solving, the requirement for a team solution option generation process will be most heavily required in the problem model development stage where individuals participate in the generation of possible solutions to a problem. In essence, this is a brainstorming activity. Thus, we infer that social loafing of team members performing problem-solving tasks will respond similarly to changes in task complexity. Based on the task complexity literature, Propositions 4 to 8 in Table 11.2 address how task complexity may relate to team knowledge building.

Implications for Internalized Team Knowledge

An important and dynamic aspect of team performance involves the sharing of the team members' unique knowledge. Within the context of teamwork, sharing unique knowledge involves the transfer of relevant information that is held by one teammate to another. Furthermore, the knowledge that is transferred should also be relevant to the goal or mission

Influence of Task Complexity on Macrocognitive Team Processes • 283

TABLE 11.2

Propositions for the Influence of Task Complexity on Team Knowledge-Building Processes

Propositions
Proposition 4: The team knowledge-building process of team information exchange will be most required when a priori determinability is low, thus increasing the need for task clarification.
Proposition 5: The team knowledge-building process of knowledge sharing is essential when task interdependence is high and team members start with different knowledge sets.
Proposition 6: The team knowledge-building process of solution option generation will be more participative for tasks that are cognitively demanding.
Proposition 7: The team knowledge-building process of team evaluation and negotiation of alternatives will be hindered with structurally complex tasks with multiple potential courses of action.
Proposition 8: The team knowledge-building process of team process and plan regulation will be facilitated by familiar, modest tasks of limited ambiguity. For more structurally complex tasks, the task interdependence of team members will inform the optimal team strategy for problem solving.

of interest. If this is accomplished properly, a level of internal team knowledge similarity may develop and lead to a better developed mental model of the problem (cf. Fiore & Schooler, 2004). From these findings, we have distilled a set of propositions that relate task complexity to internalized team knowledge (Propositions 9 to 10 in Table 11.3).

Implications for Externalized Team Knowledge

Important to the overall aspect of team knowledge is the amount of information internalized along with the external information being shared. This knowledge sharing and transfer is a process by which team members pass their individual understanding to other team members. This

TABLE 11.3

Propositions for the Influence of Task Complexity on Internalized Team Knowledge Processes

Propositions
Proposition 9: The internalized team knowledge process of team knowledge similarity will become more important when task interdependence is high and challenged by a lack of a priori determinability.
Proposition 10: The internalized team knowledge process of team knowledge resources will be most important when tasks require high task interdependence.

284 • *Theories of Team Cognition*

process is measured in terms of both the number of exchanges between team members and the quality of the information that is passed (Letsky et al., 2007).

One critical part of team knowledge building is the overt recognition of patterns in the data and information by team members and in the identification and projection of trends. Pattern recognition can be seen as the perceptual processes used to identify the constellation of cues indicative of some environment or event, whereas trend analysis is a form of pattern recognition that unfolds over time (Letsky et al., 2007). In addition to this, uncertainty reduction is a theory that describes factors that may influence exchange of information and communication in an attempt to reduce uncertainty in a situation. Proponents of this theory (e.g., Gudykunst & Nishida, 1984) believe that attitude and cultural similarity may be factors that decrease uncertainty between two teammates because it reduces the need for large numbers of alternative explanations for someone's behavior. In this context, task complexity will alter the degree to which patterns can be discerned as well as the ease with which uncertainty can be reduced in the problem environment. Building on these findings, we have distilled a set of propositions that relate task complexity to externalized team knowledge (Propositions 11 to 13 in Table 11.4).

Implications for Team Problem-Solving Outcomes

Through team knowledge-building processes, the team comes to a shared understanding of the problem, the goals, and the rules for

TABLE 11.4

Propositions for the Influence of Task Complexity on Externalized Team Knowledge Processes

Propositions
Proposition 11: The externalized team knowledge process of cue–strategy associations will be relevant primarily for tasks with high interdependence requirements and cognitive difficulty.
Proposition 12: The externalized team knowledge processes of pattern recognition and trend analysis will be more demanding for larger tasks of structural complexity.
Proposition 13: When faced with a task of a priori determinability, the externalized team knowledge process of uncertainty resolution may ensure teams come to collective consensus regarding key problem variables and may help teams compensate for lack of initial task certainty.

Influence of Task Complexity on Macrocognitive Team Processes • 285

TABLE 11.5

Propositions for the Influence of Task Complexity on Team Problem-Solving Outcomes

Propositions

Proposition 14: The quality of a team's plan (problem-solving solution) is contingent upon an accurate cognitive representation of the task problem and will be moderated by task complexity.

Proposition 15: The efficiency of team problem solving will be facilitated by familiar, modest tasks of limited ambiguity, assuming an accurate cognitive representation of the task problem. Communication mode may also modify the efficiency of reaching problem solutions, particularly when task interdependence is high.

Proposition 16: Efficiency of plan execution will be most influenced by the task size, structural complexity of a task, and task familiarity.

solution. These processes roughly correspond to traditional cognitive views of a problem space with an initial position, a goal position, and a set of operators that may be used to solve the problem (Letsky et al., 2007). Additionally, as the team conceptualizes the problem at hand, it is important to know which team members possess which pieces of information. Information that is held by all members of the team is referred to as congruent knowledge. However, in some cases, each team member may hold different *pieces of the puzzle*, known as complementary knowledge. This will affect the quality of the team's plan depending on the type of knowledge that is held by each team member and the team as a whole. After information has been collected, the team generates a set of possible solutions. Often, many possibilities are generated so that the team may have alternatives should it decide that a solution is no longer viable. In Table 11.5, Propositions 14 to 16 describe how various task complexity features may influence the process of solution generation and team problem solving outcomes.

CONCLUSIONS

Across the studies discussed in this chapter, we see some important implications for understanding complexity in the context of macrocognition in teams. From this, we have provided notional propositions to consider for a programmatic study of macrocognition in teams. Critical to supporting the design and development of systems and methods for

286 • *Theories of Team Cognition*

collaboration is an understanding of how the nature of the task interacts with problem-solving environments. Therefore, we suggest that research on macrocognition in teams examines tasks varying in complexity (i.e., differing amounts of variables and levels of interaction; Wood, 1986) and structure (well or ill defined; Campbell, 1988) and how these interact at the individual and team level when engaged in collaborative problem solving.

First, from the practical standpoint, research across a variety of contextually grounded factors would support understanding and improving operational performance. For example, such research can provide a fuller understanding of the extensibility of tools, and methods developed to support collaboration can be determined. From the theoretical standpoint, research on macrocognition would benefit from further integration of concepts such as task complexity and structure—concepts that have arisen out of the cognitive and organizational sciences. For example, such research can shed light on how knowledge integration, recognized as a critical component of collaborative problem solving (cf. Fiore, Cuevas, Scielzo, & Salas, 2002), varies dependent on the task. This research will inform the principles that articulate how variations of task complexity differentially influence the effectiveness of problem-solving processes across collaborative environments. In sum, such research can lead to a better understanding of how task complexity impacts macrocognition in teams in particular, and collaboration in general.

In this chapter, we have briefly reviewed findings on task complexity in the empirical research literature to glean their implications for understanding macrocognition in teams. Our objective is to begin outlining how variations of the task produce differences at the individual and team level and impact macrocognitive processes. Our overarching goal is to provide the foundation on which principles of collaborative problem solving can be derived. We suggest that only by investigating collaboration within differing task contexts will we be able to determine how macrocognitive processes unfold in one-of-a-kind problem-solving settings. Through analyses of knowledge construction, collaboration, consensus, and evaluation in problem-solving environments, we will be better able to investigate the potential interaction between the complexity of the task and macrocognitive processes.

ACKNOWLEDGMENT

This research was supported by the Office of Naval Research (ONR) Collaboration and Knowledge Interoperability Program and ONR Multidisciplinary University Research Initiative Grant No. N000140610446 (Dr. Michael P. Letsky, Program Manager).

REFERENCES

Byström, K., & Järvelin, K. (1995). Task complexity affects information seeking and use. *Information Processing & Management, 31*, 191–213.

Cacciabue, P. C., & Hollnagel, E. (1995). Simulation of cognition: Applications. In J. M. Hoc, P. C. Cacciabue, & E. Hollnagel (Eds.), *Expertise and technology: Issues in cognition and human-computer cooperation* (pp. 55–74). Hillsdale, NJ: LEA.

Campbell, D. J. (1988). Task complexity: A review and analysis. *Academy of Management Review, 13*, 40–52.

Cannon-Bowers, J. A., & Salas, E. (1997). Teamwork competencies: The interaction of team member knowledge, skills, and attitudes. In H. F. O'Neil, Jr. (Ed.), *Workforce decision making* (pp. 221–246). Hillsdale, NJ: Erlbaum.

Cannon-Bowers, J. A., Tannenbaum, S. I., Salas, E., & Volpe, C. E. (1995). Defining competencies and establishing team training requirements. In R. Guzzo & E. Salas (Eds.), *Team effectiveness and decision making in organizations* (pp. 333–380). San Francisco, CA: Jossey-Bass.

Espinosa, J., Slaughter, S., Kraut, R., & Herbsleb, J. (2007). Familiarity, complexity, and team performance in geographically distributed software development. *Organization Science, 18*, 613–630.

Fiore, S. M., Cuevas, H. M., Scielzo, S., & Salas, E. (2002). Training individuals for distributed teams: Problem solving assessment for distributed mission research. *Computers in Human Behavior, 18*, 125–140.

Fiore, S. M., Elias, J., Salas, E., Warner, N., & Letsky, M. (2010). From data, to information, to knowledge: Measuring knowledge building in the context of collaborative cognition. In E. Patterson & C. Miller (Eds.), *Macrocognition metrics and scenarios: Design and evaluation for real-world teams* (pp. 179–200). London, UK: Ashgate Publishing.

Fiore, S. M., Rosen, M. A., Smith-Jentsch, K. A., Salas, E., Letsky, M., & Warner, N. (2010). Toward an understanding of macrocognition in teams: Predicting processes in complex collaborative contexts. *Human Factors, 52*, 203–224.

Fiore, S. M., & Schooler, J. W. (2004). Process mapping and shared cognition: Teamwork and the development of shared problem models. In E. Salas & S. M. Fiore (Eds.), *Team cognition. Understanding the factors that drive process and performance* (pp. 133–152). Washington, DC: American Psychological Association.

Fiore, S. M., Smith-Jentsch, K. A., Salas, E., Warner, N., & Letsky, M. (2010). Toward an understanding of macrocognition in teams: Developing and defining complex collaborative processes and products. *Theoretical Issues in Ergonomic Science, 11*, 250–271.

Gudykunst, W. B., & Nishida, T. (1984). Individual and cultural influences on uncertainty reduction. *Communication Monographs, 51*, 23–36.

288 • *Theories of Team Cognition*

Harkins, S. G., & Petty, R. E. (1982). Effects of task difficulty and task uniqueness on social loafing. *Journal of Personality and Social Psychology, 43*, 1214–1229.

Higgs, M., Plewnia, U., & Ploch, J. (2005). Influence of team composition and task complexity on team performance. *Team Performance Management, 11*, 227–250.

Klein, G., Ross, K. G., Moon, B. M., Klein, D. E., Hoffman, R. R., & Hollnagel, E. (2003). Macrocognition. *IEEE Intelligent Systems, 18*, 81–85.

Latané, B., Williams, K., & Harkins, S. (1979). Many hands make light the work: The causes and consequences of social loafing. *Journal of Personality and Social Psychology, 37*, 822–832.

Letsky, M., Warner, N., Fiore, S. M., Rosen, M. A., & Salas, E. (2007). Macrocognition in complex team problem solving. *Proceedings of the 12th International Command and Control Research and Technology Symposium*. Washington, DC: U.S. Department of Defense Command and Control Research Program.

Letsky, M., Warner, N., Fiore, S. M., & Smith, C. (Eds.). (2008). *Macrocognition in teams: Theories and methodologies*. London, UK: Ashgate Publishers.

Lum, H. C., Fiore, S. M., Rosen, M. A., & Salas, E. (2008). Complexity in collaboration: Developing an understanding of macrocognition in teams through examination of task complexity. Poster session presented at the meeting of Human Factors and Ergonomics Society, New York, NY.

Marks, M. A., Mathieu, J. E., & Zaccaro, S. J. (2001). A temporally based framework and taxonomy of team processes. *Academy of Management Review, 26*, 356–376.

Mone, M. A., & Shalley, C. E. (1995). Effects of task complexity and goal specificity on change in strategy and performance over time. *Human Performance, 8*, 243–252.

Saavedra, R., Earley, P. C., & Van Dyne, L. (1993). Complex interdependence in task-performing groups. *Journal of Applied Psychology, 78*, 61–72.

Salas, E., Cannon-Bowers, J. A., & Johnston, J. H. (1997). How can you turn a team of experts into an expert team? Emerging training strategies. In C. E. Zsambok & G. Klein (Eds.), *Naturalistic decision making* (pp. 359–370). Mahwah, NJ: Lawrence Erlbaum Associates.

Salas, E., & Fiore, S. M. (Eds.). (2004). *Team cognition*. Washington, DC: American Psychological Association.

Salas, E., Rosen, M. A., Burke, C. S., & Goodwin, G. F. (2009). The wisdom of collectives in organizations: An update of the teamwork competencies. In E. Salas, G. F. Goodwin, & C. S. Burke (Eds.), *Team effectiveness in complex organizations: Cross-disciplinary perspectives and approaches* (pp. 39–82). New York, NY: Taylor & Francis Group.

Speier, C. (2006). The influence of information presentation formats on complex task decision-making performance. *International Journal of Human-Computer Studies, 64*, 1115–1131.

Straus, S. G., & McGrath, J. E. (1994). Does the medium matter? The interaction of task type and technology on group performance and member reactions. *Journal of Applied Psychology, 79*, 87–97.

Vessey, I. (1991). Cognitive fit: A theory-based analysis of the graphs versus tables literature. *Decision Sciences, 22*, 219–240.

Warner, N., & Letsky, M. (2008). Empirical model of team collaboration focus on macrocognition. In M. Letsky, N. Warner, S. Fiore, & C. Smith (Eds.), *Macrocognition in teams* (pp. 15–33). London, UK: Ashgate.

Wood, R. E. (1986). Task complexity: Definition of the construct. *Organizational Behavior and Human Decision Processes, 37*, 60–82.

12

Team Knowledge: Dimensional Structure and Network Representation

J. Alberto Espinosa and Mark A. Clark

Researchers have described team knowledge in a variety of ways—using more than 20 different terms, according to one count (Cannon-Bowers & Salas, 2001)—and have operationalized its measurement into an overall team knowledge score, whether shared (e.g., through schema similarity; Rentsch & Klimoski, 2001), aggregated as team-level information (e.g., Faraj & Sproull, 2000; Levesque, Wilson, & Wholey, 2001; Lewis, 2003; Mathieu, Goodwin, Heffner, Salas, & Cannon-Bowers, 2000), or distributed across teams (cf. Cooke, Salas, Kiekel, & Bell, 2004). Although this approach has been useful for connecting various aspects of team knowledge content to antecedents and broad outcomes such as team performance (Cooke et al., 2003; Cramton, 2001; Faraj & Sproull, 2000; Nelson & Cooprider, 1996; Rentsch & Hall, 1994), it has not helped us understand how this knowledge is organized within the team. Researchers and managers are thus stymied from understanding how such outcomes are differentially influenced by the dynamics of team interaction, such as whether knowledge resides in cliques or certain clusters of individuals; the specific location of given content domains, especially in larger teams; and what this knowledge represents (e.g., transactive memory, shared mental models, team awareness). In this chapter, we suggest a method to capture how team knowledge is held, representing and measuring team knowledge as a network of dyads in order to yield a more detailed depiction that accounts for both its structure and content. Such representations are useful to both researchers and practitioners to pinpoint performance variance and allocate knowledge resources appropriately to a task.

Central to this representation is the notion that team knowledge is more than simply content, but actually is a function of who in the team possesses which node of knowledge and how this knowledge is structured

289

290 • *Theories of Team Cognition*

across members. This in turn influences team interaction and performance. Accordingly, we refer to team knowledge content as the pool of knowledge available to the team, including how it is relevant to a particular domain and its related task outcome (cf. Schultz, 2001), whereas team knowledge structure is the manner in which knowledge is held, organized, or distributed among members, influencing its readiness to apply to *decisions and actions* (Davenport, De Long, & Beers, 1998). Content includes knowledge about both task and team characteristics (Klimoski & Mohammed, 1994), and structural complexity escalates with team size, as potential patterns of interaction increase when more team members interact. Our approach suggests that team knowledge can be represented using certain fundamental dimensions (e.g., sharedness, durability), which can be used to represent various popular knowledge constructs (e.g., shared mental models, team awareness). We describe this multidimensional view of team knowledge using concepts from the extant literature before illustrating our analytical approach.

Our approach uses social network analysis methods, helping account for the various types and configurations of team knowledge that may result from combinations of knowledge content and the manner in which it is differentially held across team members. Similarly to its use in describing complex social network relations in systems of social actors (Carley & Krackhardt, 1996), network analysis can represent multiple knowledge domains of each team member as nodes in a team knowledge system (Scott, 1991; Wasserman & Faust, 1994). The link between any two member nodes (knowledge domains of given members) depicts the knowledge relationship between the members, such as whether knowledge is shared in some domains but not others. When all linkages relevant to a given research question are included, the result is a team knowledge network with multiple knowledge metrics (e.g., densities, centralities, isolates, structure, cliques) that more completely describes knowledge relationships among members. Not incidentally, this network can be depicted visually, simplifying the identification of knowledge configurations for teams of increasing size and complexity.

A strength of a network analytic approach is that knowledge distribution can be analyzed at the individual, dyadic, subgroup, or overall level, which helps identify the location of knowledge centralities (e.g., which members share more knowledge with others) and deficits (e.g., knowledge isolates who share little task knowledge with others) that can substantially influence the team's ability to carry out certain tasks, even if the aggregate knowledge of the remaining members is relatively high (Tziner & Eden, 1985). For example, some research has shown that the most central members in a group attain higher performance levels (Ahuja, Galletta, & Carley 2003) and provide more useful knowledge to their peers (Wasko & Faraj, 2005) for certain tasks. Centrally knowledgeable members can act as hubs through which most knowledge is exchanged, thus influencing how the team coordinates and processes information, even if the overall aggregate knowledge of other team members is low, which underscores the importance of understanding how knowledge is structured in a team. Finally, team-level depictions will specify these lower level structures (isolates, dyads, and subgroups), as well as the overall availability of relevant knowledge that has been shown to relate to team performance outcomes (cf. Cooke et al., 2004; Faraj & Sproull, 2000). This multilevel depiction may be especially useful as teams become larger, with more complex knowledge distributions.

In this chapter, we first describe how various forms of team knowledge can be represented in terms of a few basic underlying dimensions. We then discuss our proposed approach—network analysis—to represent and measure team knowledge, including computational and visual examples. We conclude with final discussion and implications.

BASIC UNDERLYING DIMENSIONS OF TEAM KNOWLEDGE

The literature on team knowledge includes various representations and measures (Cannon-Bowers & Salas, 2001), giving researchers a wide selection of constructs to fit the needs of their specific inquiry. At the same time, the variety of constructs blurs our understanding of team knowledge and makes it difficult to compare and validate empirical findings across studies. We argue that these various perspectives of team knowledge can be reconciled by taking a multidimensional perspective, formulating these various constructs from more basic dimensions of team knowledge content and structure. Once again, we are not proposing specific dimensions, but we are simply arguing that these dimensions exist. We start by suggesting some general dimensions that are applicable to any

292 • *Theories of Team Cognition*

form of team knowledge (i.e., *sharedness, domain, durability,* and *type*) to illustrate our concepts but recognize that other dimensions exist and that further research is needed to identify a comprehensive set of team knowledge dimensions.

Sharedness: Individual Versus Shared

This dimension considers how knowledge is distributed and organized across members within the team—that is, how a team member's knowledge interrelates with other members' knowledge (i.e., how much knowledge similarity or overlap there is among members). Although it is accepted that knowledge can be held individually or collectively (Nonaka, 1994), team knowledge has typically been characterized as knowledge shared between members. We believe, however, that team knowledge should be thought of structurally as the combination of both components: the individual knowledge possessed by each team member that is not possessed by other members, which is important for specialization in transactive memory systems (Lewis, 2003), and the knowledge that is shared among members, which is important to coordinate and integrate task activities. Although both types of knowledge are important, individual unshared knowledge can be most beneficial to the team when others have some understanding of what this knowledge is and are able to access it when they need it (cf. Faraj & Sproull, 2000).

Although individual knowledge is important for performance in individual tasks, the team cognition literature suggests that shared knowledge is important to coordinate the activities in these individual tasks so that the respective dependencies among these activities are effectively handled. The individual unshared knowledge possessed by experts, combined with the shared knowledge that exists among members, creates holistic team knowledge structures that are different and more complex than the aggregation of the parts (Cooke et al., 2003). Shared knowledge provides a common knowledge base through which team interaction can occur, which enables team members to tap into expert knowledge sources in the team (Alavi & Leidner, 2001). It helps members synchronize their actions based on accurate expectations about what others in the team are likely to do (Wittenbaum & Stasser, 1996). How much knowledge two members share will influence how much they interact and how much further knowledge they exchange (Carley, 1986), how effectively they communicate (Cramton, 2001), and how well they coordinate (Cannon-Bowers, Salas, & Converse, 1993; Klimoski & Mohammed, 1994). The knowledge that team members share helps create team knowledge structures that are different and more complex than the aggregation of the parts (Cooke et al., 2003), which enables members to synchronize their actions based on accurate expectations about what others in the team are likely to do (Wittenbaum & Stasser, 1996).

The shared portion of team knowledge has been characterized in a number of ways. Shared mental models (i.e., organized knowledge that team members share about the task and each other, acquired by working, interacting, and training together) help members form accurate explanations and expectations about task activities (Cannon-Bowers et al., 1993; Klimoski & Mohammed, 1994; Kraiger & Wenzel, 1997). Mutual knowledge is knowledge that team members share and know that they share it; it improves common ground among team members and makes their communication more effective (Clark & Carlson, 1982; Clark & Marshal, 1981; Cramton, 2001; Fussell & Krauss, 1992; Krauss & Fussell, 1990). Shared knowledge is an understanding among team members of the technologies and processes that affect their mutual performance (Nelson & Cooprider, 1996), which provides members with the ability to access knowledge sources in the team and apply them effectively when necessary (Alavi & Leidner, 2001). Finally, transactive memory—knowledge of who knows what in the team—helps teams determine who to contact when they need to access others' individual knowledge and to assign task responsibilities to the appropriate specialists (Wegner, 1986, 1995).

Domain: Taskwork Versus Teamwork

The knowledge domain can include knowledge about various aspects of the task itself (i.e., taskwork) and about various aspects of team members (i.e., teamwork; Cooke, Salas, Cannon-Bowers, & Stout, 2000; Klimoski & Mohammed, 1994; Rentsch & Hall, 1994). This classification is also consistent with the research literature on familiarity suggesting two main types of familiarity for working teams: task familiarity and team familiarity (Gruenfeld, Mannix, Williams, & Neale, 1996; Harrison, Mohammed, McGrath, Florey, & Vanderstoep, 2003; Littlepage, Robison, & Reddington, 1997). Furthermore, taskwork and teamwork knowledge can be decomposed into further subdomains, as applicable for the task

294 • *Theories of Team Cognition*

itself. For example, a management team may require task knowledge of financial, marketing, and production issues. Teamwork knowledge may also include various things such as knowing who has which expertise (i.e., transactive memory; Faraj & Sproull, 2000; Lewis, 2003; Wegner, 1995) and awareness of who is around when needed (Boyer, Handel, & Herbsleb, 1998), among other things.

Durability: Long Lasting Versus Fleeting

This dimension describes knowledge content but also has structural implications, because it refers to how particular knowledge will be relevant for the task (rather than how long ago the knowledge was acquired). The team cognition literature often discusses either durable or fleeting knowledge, but studies rarely include both, despite their distinct natures (Cooke et al., 2003, 2004). Durable knowledge—acquired through experience with a task domain and by interacting and training with other team members—is relevant to the task over long periods of time up to the entire duration of the task (e.g., knowledge of a programming language when coding new software). Representations of this include team mental models (e.g., Cannon-Bowers et al., 1993; Carley, 1997; Klimoski & Mohammed, 1994; Kraiger & Wenzel, 1997; Mathieu et al., 2000; Stout, Cannon-Bowers, & Salas, 1999), schema similarity (Rentsch & Hall, 1994; Rentsch & Klimoski, 2001), shared knowledge (Nelson & Cooprider, 1996), and transactive memory (Wegner, 1986, 1995).

Although durable knowledge is most important for carrying out the task competently, team members also need fleeting knowledge, which is more immediately relevant for specific task situations. One important property of fleeting knowledge is that its relevance diminishes or disappears when the situation ends. For example, an airplane pilot must be attentive to specific instrument readings and weather conditions at a given time during the flight, but once on the ground, such information is no longer relevant and can therefore be forgotten. In a team context, situation awareness can be defined as understanding how events in the task environment, such as the activities of other team members at a given point in time, affect the future of the task and one's own current activities (cf. Dourish & Bly, 1992; Endsley, 1995). Thus, team members should not only have situational awareness to carry out their task responsibilities, but also team situation awareness to work effectively as a coordinated unit (Wellens, 1993).

Type: Content or Structure

This dimension distinguishes the specific knowledge available in the team (i.e., content) from how this knowledge is organized and distributed within the team (i.e., structure). We distinguish team knowledge structure from its individual counterpart in the cognitive literature (e.g., Cooke et al., 2003; Mathieu et al., 2000; Rentsch & Klimoski, 2001), which refers to internal knowledge organization and how various task activities relate to one another. Thus, a particular type of knowledge may describe the individual or relational attributes of the knowledge of its members. Prior seminal research has applied the concept of individual and relational attributes to describe other aspects of teamwork and member interaction dynamics (Barley, 1986, 1990). The type dimension illustrated here is an extension of this concept in which knowledge is viewed as a network of content nodes, one for each team member, with every pair of nodes connected with links describing their respective knowledge relationships.

Investigating all possible content and structure dimensions of team knowledge, and the extent to which these dimensions are orthogonal, is beyond the scope of this chapter. We call for further research in this area to either identify a more substantiated set of team knowledge dimensions or determine that various sets of dimensions are possible depending on the area of inquiry. Nevertheless, Figure 12.1 illustrates how several popular team knowledge constructs can be described in terms of the four dimensions we have illustrated. We now discuss the use of social network methods to represent and measure team knowledge.

A NETWORK ANALYTIC APPROACH TO TEAM KNOWLEDGE REPRESENTATION

We offer network analysis as a method for capturing team knowledge across multiple dimensions, with each node representing a team member's knowledge content in a particular domain, whereas links among these nodes represent various knowledge structures among members, dyads, and subgroups (Carley, 1997). Our approach involves four steps: (1) identifying the team knowledge dimensions applicable to the particular research study; (2) measuring all relevant knowledge dimensions for

296 • *Theories of Team Cognition*

Sharedness	Domain	Durability	Aspect	
			Content	**Structure**
Individual	Taskwork	Long-term	Task knowledge	Mental model of the task
		Fleeting	Situation awareness	
	Teamwork	Long-term	Transactive memory	Mental model of the team
		Fleeting		
Relational	Taskwork	Long-term	Shared task knowledge	Shared mental model of the task
		Fleeting	Shared task awareness	
	Teamwork	Long-term	Shared team knowledge	Shared mental model of the team
		Fleeting	Team awareness	

FIGURE 12.1

Popular team knowledge constructs and their basic dimensions.

each team member (i.e., for each network node) and for every dyad in the team (i.e., for each network link); (3) incorporating all the node and link measures into sociomatrices (i.e., matrices with each cell representing the knowledge relationship between two members of a dyad) and sociograms (i.e., network diagrams representing all nodes and links); and (4) applying the relevant network analysis tools from the rich set of methods available to compute and visually represent useful network analysis metrics (e.g., centralities, isolation, cliques, clusters, structure).

Using this network analytic approach, all individual and relational measures of knowledge can be represented as a multidimensional *sociomatrix* (Scott, 1991; Wasserman & Faust, 1994). If only one dimension of team knowledge needs to be represented, the sociomatrix will only contain one row and one column for each member. So, cell i,j (off-diagonal) will contain a value corresponding to the knowledge relationship (e.g., shared knowledge) between members i and j. One useful property of a sociomatrix is that it can represent not only relational attributes, but also individual attributes. For example, cell i,i (diagonal) will contain a value corresponding to the individual knowledge attribute (e.g., amount of knowledge in a particular domain) for member i. Therefore, a sociomatrix can be used to represent one content dimension of team knowledge along with one structure or relational dimension, provided that these dimensions are conceptually related. We illustrate this concept in Figure 12.2 (for simplicity of illustration, all of the matrix elements are normalized to a 0 to 1 scale).

If the knowledge relationship between i and j is the same as the knowledge shared by j and i, the shared knowledge matrix is *symmetrical* with respect to the diagonal. For example, shared knowledge is considered to be symmetrical because the knowledge shared by i and j is identical to the knowledge shared by j and i. However, a particular knowledge relationship can be *asymmetrical*. For example, how much i knows about j's expertise on a particular domain may be different from how much j knows about i's expertise. As illustrated in Figure 12.2, if we want to represent knowledge of who knows what in the team using a sociomatrix, the diagonal elements would be null (i.e., not relevant) or, alternatively, 1 (i.e., one knows 100% what one knows). The off-diagonal elements x_{ij} would contain how much member i knows about j in a particular aspect or task domain. Because this value is different than how much member j knows about i, the matrix

Shared knowledge (cutoff = 0.5)					
Mbr	1	2	3	4	5	6
1	0.37	0.37	0.33	0.37	0.37	0.37
2	0.37	0.57	0.43	0.46	0.57	0.56
3	0.33	0.43	0.56	0.33	0.56	0.54
4	0.37	0.46	0.33	0.52	0.51	0.48
5	0.37	0.57	0.56	0.51	0.91	0.84
6	0.37	0.56	0.54	0.48	0.84	0.84

Symmetric sociomatrix

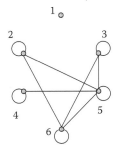

Dichotomized-undirected sociogram

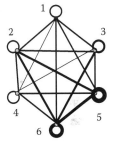

Valued-undirected sociogram

Knowledge of who knows what					
Mbr	1	2	3	4	5	6
1		0.10	0.20	0.20	0.30	0.10
2	0.20		0.00	0.46	0.57	0.56
3	0.60	0.43		0.33	0.56	0.54
4	0.37	0.46	0.33		0.51	0.48
5	0.60	0.30	0.20	0.30		0.80
6	0.60	0.80	0.60	0.90	0.80	

Asymmetric sociomatrix

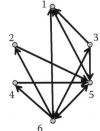

Dichotomized-directed sociogram

FIGURE 12.2

An illustration of sociomatrices and sociograms. For simplicity of illustration, all of the matrix elements are normalized to a 0 to 1 scale.

298 • *Theories of Team Cognition*

is not symmetrical with respect to the diagonal (i.e., $x_{ij} \pm x_{ji}$). The sociomatrix relationship is generally interpreted as row → column when the matrix is asymmetrical. For example, member 1's knowledge about member 6 is 0.1, whereas member 6's knowledge about member 1 is 0.6; thus, member 6 knows more about member 1 than member 1 knows about member 6. Another advantage of sociomatrices is that they can represent more than one dimension at a time by superimposing multiple layers of matrices, one for each dimension or knowledge domain being considered. For example, a sociomatrix representing individual task knowledge, shared knowledge, and knowledge of who knows what can be composed by superimposing the two sociomatrices illustrated in Figure 12.2.

A *sociogram* is the visual representation of a sociomatrix. As illustrated in Figure 12.2, each member is depicted as a node in this graph, and the relationship between any two members (e.g., their shared knowledge) is represented as a link between the two nodes. The link connecting members i and j represents the knowledge relationship between these two members and is equivalent to the value x_{ij} in the respective sociomatrix. Individual attributes from the diagonal elements of the respective sociomatrix are represented as recursive relationships or as a circular link from a node to itself, as illustrated in the shared knowledge sociogram in Figure 12.2.

Sociograms can also be *valued* or *dichotomized*. In a valued graph, all dyads are connected, and the line densities are proportional to the value of the relationship value x_{ij}. However, valued graphs can be somewhat confusing, especially when representing large teams, because each node needs to connect to every other node. Figure 12.2 shows one valued graph containing many links of various densities. A valued graph for a team of n members would have $n(n-1)/2$ lines of various densities, which is not very informative. Instead, such tightly packed populations are often represented using *dichotomous* graphs, in which a link is drawn only if the relationship value exceeds a certain threshold amount deemed important. For example, in Figure 12.2, we used the midpoint of the scale as a cutoff point to illustrate the sociograms. The respective dichotomized sociogram includes a line for every relationship in which $x_{ij} \geq 0.5$ (bold-faced figures).

Sociograms can also be *directed* or *undirected*. A sociogram is undirected if the sociomatrix is symmetrical with respect to the diagonal, that is if $x_{ij} = x_{ji}$, so the relationship links between nodes do not need arrows in their visual representation, as in the shared knowledge example in Figure 12.2. In contrast, a sociogram is directed if the sociomatrix is asymmetrical with respect to the diagonal ($x_{ij} \neq x_{ji}$), so the relationship links between nodes need arrows in their visual representation, as in the example about who knows what in Figure 12.2. The arrow is generally drawn in the direction of the relationship. For example, member 3 knows the expertise of member 1 but not the other way around.

Network analytic tools such as sociograms and sociomatrices are ideally suited to represent and analyze multiple dyadic relationships in a group. In particular, they allow the researcher to aggregate either individual or dyadic relationship attributes, if appropriate, to reproduce some of the existing aggregate or collective measures of team knowledge. At the same time, because the representation and measures we propose are based on individual and dyadic measures of various dimensions, network analysis methods allow us to retain the structural detail that makes up the knowledge in the team. This is particularly important for larger teams for which it is important to understand relationships such as who talks to whom, who shares knowledge with whom, and who knows what others know. Also, the measures that can be derived from such a representation are based on basic, computationally simple network analysis methods that include useful information, such as "slices" (all relationships for dyad or clique of interest), members' knowledge centralities, and the presence of knowledge clusters.

For example, there are two 3-member cliques (3-5-6 and 2-5-6) for the knowledge domains of interest in Figure 12.2. Taking a slice for these two cliques and jointly analyzing their individual knowledge, shared knowledge, and transactive memory reveals interesting insights into this team. For instance, members 5 and 6 are in both cliques and are also the most knowledgeable members of the team. Member 5 has a higher "degree" of centrality (i.e., more links than other members) and is the most knowledgeable member of the team. Interestingly, member 6 is highly knowledgeable, shares knowledge with three other members, and knows the expertise of every member, but only member 5 knows what this member knows. In contrast, everybody knows what member 5 knows, but this member does not know what other members know, except for member 6. Such interesting insights into the team's knowledge structure are not possible with pure aggregate measures only.

By way of example, in the next section, we will formulate measures for one content dimension (i.e., task knowledge) and one structure

300 • *Theories of Team Cognition*

dimension (i.e., sharedness), both of which are popular dimensions in the team knowledge literature (space limitations preclude examination of further dimensions, but their analysis follows a similar pattern). We also detail a preliminary validation of the derived measure. We then discuss how this measure can be used for another structure dimension of interest—shared knowledge of the team, which is similar to concepts such as directory structure (Anand, Manz, & Glick, 1998), transactive memory (Wegner, 1986), and expertise coordination (Faraj & Sproull, 2000). We then discuss how similar measures can be developed for other dimensions of team knowledge, including useful measures such as knowledge distribution, knowledge isolates, and knowledge cliques, and how network analysis methods can be used to provide visual representations of team knowledge using network diagrams. We then briefly compare network analysis to commonly used team knowledge measures and offer concluding remarks.

NETWORK ANALYSIS OF TEAM KNOWLEDGE: AN ILLUSTRATION MEASURING SHAREDNESS AND TASK KNOWLEDGE

Because a team's shared task knowledge is a function of the task knowledge shared by every dyad in the team (Klimoski & Mohammed, 1994), we begin by measuring shared task knowledge at the dyad level and then discuss how to incorporate all dyadic measures into a network model representing the knowledge of the entire team. We then describe our measurement approach.

The individual knowledge content pool in the team can be represented as a knowledge matrix $K_{(NxT)}$ with one row for each of the N team members and one column for each of the T task-relevant knowledge domains, with elements k_{it} representing the amount of knowledge that member i has with respect to task domain t. For example, in a software task, T would represent the number of areas that a software developer would need to know to do the job competently (e.g., software programming language used, application domain, software tools available, software libraries available) or knowledge about team process techniques that may be useful in completing the task (e.g., communication styles, decision modes). This is referred to as an *incidence* matrix in network analysis terminology, because it represents people's relations to matters such as knowledge areas, professions, or other associations (Scott, 1991).

Similarly, the shared task knowledge for the team in one particular task domain t can be represented in a sociomatrix $STK_{t(NxN)}$ containing one row and one column for each team member. The element stk_{tij} of this *sociomatrix* represents the task knowledge shared by members i and j with respect to task domain t. The diagonal cells stk_{tii} in this matrix can either contain the amount of knowledge of member i in task domain t or can be left blank if individual knowledge is not of interest. The values in each cell stk_{tij} can be computed in a number of ways, and the computation will differ depending on whether the cell is in the diagonal or off-diagonal. The diagonal elements (i,i) for each task domain t would simply contain these ratings in that domain. The off-diagonal element (i,j) for each task domain t can be computed using any knowledge or schema similarity metric such as within-team agreement rating (James, Demaree, & Wolf, 1984), correlation, and quadratic assignment procedure (QAP) correlation (Hubert, 1987), which have been used in team cognition studies (Cooke et al., 2003; Levesque et al., 2001; Mathieu et al., 2000; Rentsch & Klimoski, 2001). Alternatively, other methods quantifying the amount of knowledge overlap or knowledge distance (i.e., reverse similarity) can be used.

The advantage of representing shared task knowledge using this network analysis approach is that the respective matrices and measures can then be decomposed to any level of detail desired. For example, instead of aggregating the STK_t matrices into an overall matrix STK, the team's shared task knowledge can be modeled as a three-dimensional matrix $STK_{(TxNxN)}$, with elements stk_{tij} representing the task knowledge shared by members i and j with respect to task domain t. Measures can then be obtained for the shared task knowledge for the whole team (i.e., aggregate), for any dyad (i.e., a matrix "slice" across all task domains), and for any task domain (i.e., one layer of the matrix). This multidimensional sociomatrix can also be used to compute metrics that describe shared task knowledge structure in the team (e.g., centralized, dispersed) and allows us to use powerful network analytic methods to do things such as computing key network attributes (e.g., densities, centralities), identifying relationship patterns (e.g., cliques, clusters, subgroups, isolates, gaps), performing network-based statistical analysis, and providing visual representations using sociograms.

302 • Theories of Team Cognition

The example in Figure 12.3 illustrates this computation and visual representation for a team of $N = 6$ members based on $T = 3$ task knowledge areas: financial management, production, and marketing. The links in the sociogram were drawn using a cutoff value of 4, which is the midpoint of the 1 to 7 rating scale used. We can see that the $STK_{FINANCE}$ matrix is very sparse, with only members 5 and 6 sharing substantial task knowledge in

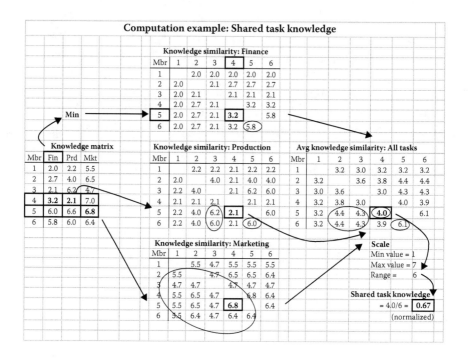

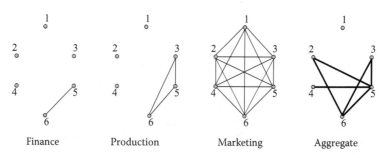

FIGURE 12.3
Illustration of computation and visual representation of shared task knowledge.

this area, reducing the likelihood of full group discussions about finance. The $STK_{PRODUCTION}$ matrix shows a fair amount of task knowledge shared by some members but not by others. In contrast, the $STK_{MARKETING}$ matrix represents a fully connected network, evident of substantial shared marketing knowledge, providing a common ground for marketing discussions. We can also see that on the aggregate STK matrix that member 1 is a knowledge isolate, whereas members 5 and 6 have the highest amounts of shared task knowledge with other members in all task areas and on the aggregate. This could be valuable information, for example, when analyzing decision flow or team leadership factors.

A similar method can be used to represent other aspects of team knowledge, such as shared knowledge of the team. Although knowing who knows what in the team is important (Faraj & Sproull, 2000; Liang, Moreland, & Argote, 1995; Wegner, 1995), recent transactive memory research suggests that this knowledge is more effective when members have a shared understanding of what team members know (Brandon & Hollingshead, 2004; Lewis, 2003) because it allows team members to make more effective task assignments that integrate this expertise. Therefore, a representation and measure for shared knowledge of the team can be constructed in a similar fashion to the shared task knowledge variable, but using knowledge similarity members have about each other, rather than about the task. Members' beliefs can be elicited by asking questions about one another. As suggested in the team cognition literature (Cooke et al., 2003, 2004), the questions asked about members should relate to important characteristics about these members, relevant to the task as uncovered during the task analysis. For example, in a given software task, team members will need to know each other's knowledge about software languages, software development processes, software tools, application domain, and how different members interact, or other process issues. Responses to such task-specific questions can then be compared between pairs of member to evaluate their similarity.

In sum, network analysis tools such as sociograms and matrices can be applied to the measurement of team knowledge so as to account for multiple content and structure dimensions. Furthermore, dyadic knowledge can be aggregated into team-level knowledge depictions without sacrificing valuable information about the distribution of the knowledge in individual members and subgroups. In the following section, we conduct a preliminary validation of these network analysis tools through a set of

304 • *Theories of Team Cognition*

teams that combine their members' knowledge to complete a management simulation task.

PRELIMINARY EMPIRICAL PROOF OF CONCEPT

As part of a related study, we did some preliminary analysis to evaluate whether our proposed method of conceptualizing team knowledge using various individual and relational knowledge dimensions using social network analysis methods was feasible. We collected data from 57 student teams working in a graduate-level management simulation course in which each team managed a simulated firm. We constructed two shared task knowledge measures using the method described in the previous two sections using responses to peer ratings of each other's knowledge in specific task domains (i.e., financial, production, and marketing management of the team's simulated companies). We used survey methods to evaluate two coordination variables: task coordination (i.e., the extent to which team members felt that their task activities were well coordinated) and strategy coordination (i.e., the extent to which their individual functional strategies, such as operations, finance, or marketing, were well coordinated). Overall, we found strong positive and significant correlation ($p < .001$) of shared task knowledge with both strategy coordination and task coordination, suggesting that shared task knowledge is generally important in the aggregate. We then entered network variables that describe how this task knowledge is distributed in the team, and the effect of shared task knowledge became nonsignificant in both coordination models; degree of knowledge isolation became significant in the task coordination model (negatively related), whereas team knowledge centrality became significant in the strategy coordination model (centrality of members being positively related to strategy coordination). Similarly, the proportion of task cliques became a significant (negatively related) predictor of team cohesion, such that fewer cliques made a more cohesive team. These results suggest that some of the effects of shared team knowledge may be more appropriately accounted for by isolates, cliques, and centrality, rather than simply aggregate shared knowledge.

These findings, demonstrating that understanding how teams hold and use knowledge must go beyond simple aggregate or mean knowledge levels, are important to both researchers and practitioners working with teams. Without accounting for pockets of knowledge, researchers attempting to find relationships among team knowledge resources and coordination outcomes may find their effect masked by the aggregate measures (e.g., sum or mean knowledge levels). Isolated pockets of knowledge may be detrimental to task coordination, centrally knowledgeable members may help to coordinate firm strategies, and shared task knowledge with a minimal number of cliques may be good for team cohesion. Firms and team managers can use this information to staff and train their teams, optimizing levels of shared knowledge across team members.

Although we only provide a brief illustration, we can speculate how our approach may be used to represent and measure other dimensions. For example, the measures discussed to this point are suitable for relatively durable knowledge. However, more fleeting knowledge like team situation awareness (only relevant for particular situations) requires additional matrices for each relevant slice of awareness (e.g., task awareness, presence awareness) at both individual (i.e., content) and shared (i.e., structure) levels. Although relatively durable knowledge can use recall-based elicitation methods (e.g., surveys), more fleeting awareness knowledge requires more dynamic methods, such as asking a participant questions during task execution (Cooke et al., 2000).

NETWORK ANALYSIS AND CURRENT APPROACHES TO TEAM KNOWLEDGE REPRESENTATION AND MEASUREMENT

The value of the network analysis approach can be further understood in the context of extant team knowledge measures. In this section, we briefly overview several measures that have been used to represent team cognition, shared knowledge, and transactive memory, discussing their relative contributions and relationships. In general, although these methods are useful for measuring specific aspects of team knowledge, they focus primarily on dyadic and aggregate measures. Our approach builds on these measures by providing a multidimensional perspective that can include multiple dimensions of team knowledge content and structure for all members and dyads as a decomposable knowledge network. Because network analysis allows measures to be aggregated or kept in a smaller unit, it

306 • *Theories of Team Cognition*

can reproduce existing measures or be represented through network tools such as sociomatrices, isolates, and centralities.

Shared knowledge has been represented through a variety of measures, including textual analysis, task important ratings, quadratic assignment, and within-team agreement. Textual analysis (Carley, 1997) builds cognitive maps through identification of word sequences commonly used by team members that are drawn from work documents, memos, electronic mail, discussion boards, interview transcripts, and other available written materials. This method is particularly useful for archival research. In another study with student teams working on software projects, Levesque et al. (2001) used similarity metrics to measure shared knowledge using within-team agreement ratings (James et al., 1984) on responses to a number of task-related questions. Related to shared knowledge is the concept of schema similarity, which focuses on similarity of knowledge structures among team members, rather than similarity of the content of that knowledge (Cooke et al., 2003, 2004). This has been measured by compiling networks of members who similarly rate the importance of a list of team tasks, such that individual networks for each task activity are represented as nodes and task relationships are represented by links among these nodes.

Numerically, these networks can be represented as squared matrices, with the nodes or task activities listed in both the row and column headings and the respective cells containing the value of the relationship between the task activities in the respective row and column. The shared schema metrics for any given dyad are then computed using a metric measuring the similarity between the individual schema networks of the two dyad members. The shared schema value for the entire team is then computed as an aggregation or average of all dyad shared schema measures. The dyad similarity metrics are computed in a number of ways. For example, one study used QAP correlation (Mathieu et al., 2000) to measure schema similarity through correlating two square matrices (Hubert, 1987). The resulting QAP correlation value is the same as a Pearson correlation value between all the corresponding elements of the two matrices, but QAP reports a nonparametric method to estimate the statistical significance value (i.e., p value) because the relationship values in the matrix cells are not always independent. This method is useful for network data and can also be used in multivariate regression analysis (Krackhardt, 1987, 1988).

Similarly, Cooke et al. (2003) used task-relatedness matrices to compute taskwork schema agreement in a simulated task involving helicopter missions, using the proportion of identical links between the task-relatedness networks of the two dyad members rather than QAP correlation. They also computed teamwork schema agreement by asking members which types of information had to be exchanged among three different types of crew member roles and then computing the proportion of identical responses among team members. Once again, these task-relatedness networks and matrices are useful to represent the individual knowledge structure of each team member, and the QAP correlation method is an excellent way of calculating a similarity metric between the respective knowledge structures of every dyad in the team. Our proposed approach extends methods like the ones we just described by representing every member's individual knowledge along with every dyad's knowledge relationship in a network or sociomatrix for the entire team.

Several measures have also been proposed for transactive memory. The review by Lewis (2003) concluded that transactive memory can be measured by evaluating team members' agreement about who knows what in the team, which is a form of shared knowledge about teamwork, and proposed an aggregate measure that incorporates knowledge specialization, credibility, and coordination. Similarly, Brandon and Hollingshead (2004) suggested using dimensions of accuracy, sharedness, and validation to measure transactive memory effectiveness. Faraj and Sproull (2000) measured the similar concept of expertise coordination (i.e., the ability to find expertise in a team and use it when needed). Although these are useful measures to evaluate the transactive memory of a team as a whole, our approach can be used to capture how this transactive memory is organized within the team. For example, some members may have very high knowledge of other members' areas of expertise, whereas others may have specialized knowledge only; yet others may have both or neither, which can make a difference in how the team performs.

Network analysis can successfully represent shared knowledge and transactive memory, whether as single dimensions or in greater detail as part of aggregated knowledge matrices and sociograms. For instance, specialization is a dimension of knowledge content of each member, whereas credibility and knowledge similarity are structural dimensions at the dyadic or aggregated levels. Without network analysis, measures of sharedness and transactive memory provide an incomplete picture of a team's knowledge distribution, especially as teams get larger. This knowledge

308 • *Theories of Team Cognition*

organization may be a critical factor in team performance, particularly when certain team members have roles that may be more critical to team success than others. Furthermore, network analysis sociomatrices can be multidimensional, representing multiple aspects of team knowledge with a single multidimensional matrix and the corresponding layers of sociograms. This network representation also enables the extraction of a slice to analyze a particular dyad or clique of interest across all dimensions (Wasserman & Faust, 1994).

CONCLUDING REMARKS

Although they advanced considerably in recent years, current team knowledge measurements do not depict how knowledge is distributed in a team, which becomes more important as teams become larger and subgroups hold specialized expertise. In this chapter, we offer a method to capture both the structure and content of team knowledge, yielding representations useful to both researchers and practitioners in pinpointing performance variance and allocating knowledge resources. This contribution (a) builds on strengths of current measures; (b) is computationally simple in the sense that no specialized statistical or network analysis software is necessary; (c) can be used at the highest aggregate level or at detail sublevels (members, dyads, or cliques), allowing analysis of slices across multiple dimensions of interest; (d) contains individual knowledge attributes that describe content dimensions and relational attributes that describe structural dimensions, thus providing a more complete picture of the team's knowledge; (e) allows the computation and visual representation of various dimensions of team knowledge and how this knowledge is distributed in the team; and (f) provides a richer explanation of how the distribution of knowledge within a team influences performance and its antecedents. Our preliminary evidence suggests that viewing team knowledge from a network perspective adds explanatory power—having isolates may not be good for task coordination; having centrally knowledgeable members may help coordinate firm strategies; and shared task knowledge may be good for team cohesion, provided that there are not many cliques in the team. We have also developed and validated a measure for shared task knowledge and transactive memory, suggesting a method for their visual representation. Future work may build on these proposed measures in order to conduct sound research on this important topic.

The primary utility of the network analytic approach is that the added knowledge metrics can be used to more accurately depict the distribution of knowledge within a team, including multiple domains as a coherent set. In practice, this more detailed depiction is accomplished by decomposing team knowledge into more granular levels of structure. Network analysis tools can be useful in gaining even further insights into team knowledge distribution. For example, as referred to previously, we computed a *knowledge isolation index* from the shared task knowledge networks to measure the presence of knowledge isolates in the team. For each team, we counted the number of members who did not share task knowledge with any member in each task domain. We used the overall shared task knowledge average for all teams as the cutoff value. In other words, a team member was considered a finance isolate if his or her shared knowledge in the finance task domain with each of the other members was below average, and the same rule applied for the production and marketing task areas. The number of isolates in each team was then averaged across all task domains.

So, for example, a team with an isolate average of 1 indicates that, on average, there is one isolate in the team. This could mean that there is one isolate in each of the three task areas, three isolates in a single task area, or anywhere in between. This measure could then be divided by the number of team members to obtain a normalized index value ranging from 0 to 1, such that a value of 0 indicates no isolates whatsoever (i.e., all shared task knowledge networks in all three task areas are fully connected) and a value of 1 indicates that all members are isolates in all task areas (i.e., there is no shared task knowledge in the team). The next step would be to compute a correlation value of this index with the other measures used in the validation analysis. In our previous example, for instance, we found that the isolation index is negatively correlated to team performance, task coordination, and strategy coordination. Although further multivariate analysis is needed to test knowledge isolates in given contexts, these preliminary results suggest that network analysis metrics can be useful in understanding which aspects of team knowledge drive performance.

Separately or together, these tools extend the ability of network analysis to depict knowledge distribution in teams, potentially increasing our understanding of how such knowledge is related to team antecedents and consequences. Researchers may choose the tools most appropriate for their research

310 • *Theories of Team Cognition*

questions, just as they choose relevant dimensions to include as slices of the multidimensional sociomatrix. Managers working with teams can share the benefits of this approach using this more detailed understanding to staff, train, and deploy their teams. Overall, the network analysis approach offers practical flexibility while maintaining an ability to credibly represent multidimensional team knowledge content and structure, providing both researchers and practitioners with an additional set of tools to understand team performance and to inform decisions about team resource distribution.

REFERENCES

Ahuja, M. K., Galletta, D. F., & Carley, K. (2003). Individual centrality and performance in virtual R&D groups: An empirical study. *Management Science, 49*, 21–38.

Alavi, M., & Leidner, D. E. (2001). Knowledge management and knowledge management systems: Conceptual foundations and research issues. *MIS Quarterly, 25*, 107–136.

Anand, V., Clark, M. A., & Zellmer-Bruhn, M. (2003). Team knowledge structures: Matching task to information environment. *Journal of Managerial Issues, 5*, 15–31.

Anand, V., Manz, C. C., & Glick, W. H. (1998). An organizational memory approach to information management. *Academy of Management Review, 23*, 796–809.

Barley, S. (1986). Technology as an occasion for structuring: Evidence from observations of CT scanners and the social order of radiology departments. *Administrative Science Quarterly, 31*, 78–108.

Barley, S. (1990). The alignment of technology and structure through roles and networks. *Administrative Science Quarterly, 35*, 61–103.

Boyer, D. G., Handel, M. J., & Herbsleb, J. D. (1998). Virtual community presence awareness. *ACM SIGGROUIP Bulletin, 19*, 11–14.

Brandon, D. P., & Hollingshead, A. (2004). Transactive memory systems in organizations: Matching tasks, expertise, and people. *Organization Science, 15*, 633–644.

Cannon-Bowers, J. A., & Salas, E. (2001). Reflections on shared cognition. *Journal of Organizational Behavior, 22*, 195–202.

Cannon-Bowers, J. A., Salas, E., & Converse, S. (1993). Shared mental models in expert team decision-making. In J. Castellan (Ed.), *Individual and group decision-making: Current issues* (pp. 221–246). Hillsdale, NJ: Lawrence Erlbaum Associates, Inc.

Carley, K. (1986). An approach for relating social structure to cognitive structure. *Journal of Mathematical Sociology, 12*, 137–189.

Carley, K. (1997). Extracting team mental models through textual analysis. *Journal of Organizational Behavior, 18*, 533–558.

Carley, K., & Krackhardt, D. (1996). Cognitive inconsistencies and non-symmetric friendship. *Social Networks, 18*, 1–27.

Clark, H., & Carlson, T. (1982). Speech acts and hearers' beliefs. In N. V. Smith (Ed.), *Mutual knowledge* (pp. 1–36). New York, NY: Academic Press.

Clark, H., & Marshal, C. (1981). Definite reference and mutual knowledge. In A. K. Joshi, I. Sag, & B. Webber (Eds.), *Elements of discourse and understanding* (pp. 10–63). New York, NY: Cambridge University Press.

Cooke, N. J., Kiekel, P. A., Salas, E., Stout, R. J., Bowers, C., & Cannon-Bowers, J. A. (2003). Measuring team knowledge: A window to the cognitive underpinnings of team performance. *Group Dynamics: Theory, Research and Practice, 7,* 179–199.

Cooke, N. J., Salas, E., Cannon-Bowers, J. A., & Stout, R. J. (2000). Measuring team knowledge. *Human Factors, 42,* 151–173.

Cooke, N. J., Salas, E., Kiekel, P. A., & Bell, B. (2004). Advances in measuring team cognition. In E. Salas & S. M. Fiore (Eds.), *Team cognition: Understanding the factors that drive process and performance* (pp. 83–106). Washington, DC: American Psychological Association.

Cramton, C. D. (2001). The mutual knowledge problem and its consequences for dispersed collaboration. *Organization Science, 12,* 346–371.

Davenport, T. H., De Long, D. W., & Beers, M. C. (1998). Successful knowledge management projects. *Sloan Management Review, 39,* 43–57.

Dourish, P., & Bly, S. (1992, May). *Portholes: Supporting awareness in a distributed work group.* Paper presented at the ACM Conference on Human Factors in Computing Systems (INTERCHI), Monterrey, CA.

Endsley, M. (1995). Toward a theory of situation awareness in dynamic systems. *Human Factors, 37,* 65–84.

Faraj, S., & Sproull, L. (2000). Coordinating expertise in software development teams. *Management Science, 46,* 1554–1568.

Fussell, S., & Krauss, R. (1992). Coordination of knowledge in communication: Effects of speakers' assumptions about what other know. *Journal of Personality and Social Psychology, 62,* 378–391.

Ghiselli, E. E., Campbell, J. P., & Zedeck, S. (1981). *Measurement theory for the behavioral sciences.* San Francisco, CA: W. H. Freeman.

Gruenfeld, D. H., Mannix, E. A., Williams, K. Y., & Neale, M. A. (1996). Group composition and decision making: How member familiarity and information distribution affect process and performance. *Organizational Behavior and Human Decision Processes, 67,* 1–15.

Harrison, D. A., Mohammed, S., McGrath, J. E., Florey, A. T., & Vanderstoep, S. W. (2003). Time matters in team performance: Effects of member familiarity, entrainment, and task discontinuity on speed and quality. *Personnel Psychology, 56,* 633–669.

Hubert, L. (1987). *Assignment methods in combinatorial data analysis.* New York, NY: Dekker.

James, L. R., Demaree, R. G., & Wolf, G. (1984). Estimating within-group interrater reliability with and without response bias. *Journal of Applied Psychology, 69,* 85–98.

Klimoski, R. J., & Mohammed, S. (1994). Team mental model: Construct or metaphor. *Journal of Management, 20,* 403–437.

Krackhardt, D. (1987). QAP partialling as a test of spuriousness. *Social Networks, 9,* 171–186.

Krackhardt, D. (1988). Predicting with networks: Nonparametric multiple regression analysis of dyadic data. *Social Networks, 10,* 359–381.

Kraiger, K., & Wenzel, L. (1997). Conceptual development and empirical evaluation of measures of shared mental models as indicators of team effectiveness. In M. Brannick, E. Salas, & C. Prince (Eds.), *Team performance assessment and measurement* (pp. 63–84). Mahwah, NJ: Lawrence Erlbaum Associates.

Krauss, R., & Fussell, S. (1990). Mutual knowledge and communicative effectiveness. In J. Galegher, R. E. Kraut, & C. Egido (Eds.), *Intellectual teamwork: Social and technological foundations of cooperative work* (pp. 111–146). Hillsdale, NJ: Lawrence Erlbaum.

312 • Theories of Team Cognition

Levesque, L. L., Wilson, J. M., & Wholey, D. R. (2001). Cognitive divergence and shared mental models in software development project teams. *Journal of Organizational Behavior, 22*, 135–144.

Lewis, K. (2003). Measuring transactive memory systems in the field: Scale development and validation. *Journal of Applied Psychology, 88*, 587–604.

Liang, D., Moreland, R., & Argote, L. (1995). Group versus individual training and group performance: The mediating role of transactive memory. *Personality and Social Psychology Bulletin, 21*, 384–393.

Littlepage, G., Robison, W., & Reddington, K. (1997). Effects of task experience and group experience on group performance, member ability, and recognition of expertise. *Organizational Behavior and Human Decision Processes, 69*, 133–147.

Mathieu, J., Goodwin, G. F., Heffner, T. S., Salas, E., & Cannon-Bowers, J. A. (2000). The influence of shared mental models on team process and performance. *Journal of Applied Psychology, 85*, 273–283.

Nelson, K. M., & Cooprider, J. G. (1996). The contribution of shared knowledge to IS group performance. *MIS Quarterly, 20*, 409–432.

Nonaka, I. (1994). A dynamic theory of organizational knowledge creation. *Organization Science, 5*, 14–37.

Rentsch, J. R., & Hall, R. J. (1994). Members of great teams think alike: A model of the effectiveness and schema similarity among team members. In M. M. Beyerlein & D. A. Johnson (Eds.), *Advances in interdisciplinary studies of work teams: Theories of self-managing work teams* (Vol. 1, pp. 223–261). Greenwich, CT: JAI Press.

Rentsch, J. R., & Klimoski, R. J. (2001). Why do great minds think alike? Antecedents of team member schema agreement. *Journal of Organizational Behavior, 22*, 107–120.

Schultz, M. (2001). The uncertain relevance of newness: Organizational learning and knowledge flows. *Academy of Management Journal, 44*, 661–681.

Scott, J. (1991). *Social network analysis: A handbook.* Thousand Oaks, CA: Sage Publications.

Stout, J. A., Cannon-Bowers, J., & Salas, E. (1999). Planning, shared mental models, and coordinated performance: An empirical link is established. *Human Factors, 41*, 61–71.

Tziner, A., & Eden, D. (1985). Effects of crew composition on crew performance: Does the whole equal the sum of its parts? *Journal of Applied Psychology, 70*, 85–93.

Wasko, M., & Faraj, S. (2005). Why should I share? Examining social capital and knowledge contribution in electronic networks of practice. *MIS Quarterly, 29*, 35–57.

Wasserman, S., & Faust, K. (1994). *Social network analysis: Methods and applications.* Cambridge, UK: Cambridge University Press.

Wegner, D. (1986). Transactive memory: A contemporary analysis of the group mind. In B. Mullen & G. Goethals (Eds.), *Theories of group behavior* (pp. 185–205). New York, NY: Springer-Verlag.

Wegner, D. (1995). A computer network model of human transactive memory. *Social Cognition, 13*, 319–339.

Wellens, R. (1993). Group situation awareness and distributed decision-making: From military to civilian applications. In J. Castellan (Ed.), *Individual and group decision-making: Current issues* (pp. 267–291). Hillsdale, NJ: Lawrence Erlbaum Associates.

Wittenbaum, G. M., & Stasser, G. (1996). Management of information in small groups. In J. L. Nye & A. M. Brower (Eds.), *What's social about social cognition?* (pp. 3–27). Thousand Oaks, CA: Sage Publications.

13

Intelligent Agents as Teammates

Gita Sukthankar, Randall Shumaker, and Michael Lewis

INTRODUCTION

Team behavior has almost exclusively been studied as involving humans interacting in tasks that require collective action to achieve success. Long a feature in science fiction, it recently has become technologically possible to create artificial entities that can serve as members of teams, as opposed to simply being automated systems operated by human team members. In the computing and robotics literature, such entities are called *software agents*. The term *embodied agent* is often used to describe physical robots in order to differentiate them from purely software agents; however, for the purposes of this chapter, we will use *agent* to refer to both because we intend to argue that some form of embodiment, virtual or physical, is an important element in establishing and maintaining membership in a team. The term *intelligent agent* is probably overly generous for describing the cognitive performance possible within the next decade, but implicit in the proposed elevation of status to teammate is the assumption that agents are capable of serving a role within the team that would otherwise have to be served by a human. This does not imply that human-level cognitive capability is feasible, required, or even desired, only that serving as a team member implies a different kind of interaction and collaboration with human team members than is expected of other forms of automation. If the agent must exhaustively consider interactions between its actions and the past and future actions of all other team members, achieving good teamwork becomes a computationally intensive problem. For the purpose of this survey, we limit our discussion of agents to pieces of software that (a) are autonomous, defined as capable of functioning independently for a significant length of time, (b) proactively act in anticipation of future

313

314 • *Theories of Team Cognition*

events, and (c) are capable of self-reflection about their and their teammates' abilities. In this chapter, we will review research on multiagent systems, mixed initiative control, and agent interaction within human teams to evaluate the technological outlook, potential, and research directions for developing agents to serve as genuine team members.

AGENT-ONLY TEAMS

The study of human teams provides key insights about facilitating teamwork yet lacks the detailed computational models required to create a synthetic agent with teamwork skills. Theoretical work from the artificial intelligence (AI) community on agent teamwork (Grosz & Kraus, 2003; Tambe, 1997) establishes the following desiderata for agent teams. First, the agents need to share the goals they want to achieve, share an overall plan that they follow together, and, to some degree, share knowledge of the environment (situation awareness) in which they are operating. Second, the agents need to share the intention to execute the plan to reach the common goal. Third, the agents must be aware of their capabilities and how they can fulfill roles required by the team high-level plan. Fourth, agents should be able to monitor their own progress toward the team goal and monitor teammates' activities and team joint intentions (Cohen & Levesque, 1991). Using these basic teamwork ideas, many systems have been successfully implemented using a variety of computational mechanisms, including teams supporting human collaboration (Chalupsky et al., 2001), teams for disaster response (Nair, Tambe, & Marsella, 2003), and teams for manufacturing (Sycara, Sadeh-Koniecpol, Roth, & Fox, 1990).

Guaranteeing Coordination

In addition to identifying suitable roles for agents to play in human teams, to implement a software system, appropriate coordination and communication mechanisms must be selected. For some domains, simple prearranged coordination schemes, such as the locker room agreement (Stone & Veloso, 1999) in which the teams execute preselected plans after observing an environmental trigger, are adequate. Although this coordination

Intelligent Agents as Teammates • 315

model has been successful in the RoboCup domain, the locker room agreement breaks down when there is ambiguity about what has been observed. For instance, what happens when one agent believes that the trigger has occurred but another agent missed seeing it? STEAM (Shell for TEAMwork) (Tambe, 1997; Tambe et al., 1999) was designed to address this problem; the agents explicitly reason about goal commitment, information sharing, and selective communication. This framework incorporates prior work by Cohen and Levesque (1990) on logical reasoning about agent intention and goal abandonment. Having agents capable of reasoning about fellow agents' intentions makes the coordination process more reliable because the agents are able to reason about sensor and coordination failures. By giving all team members proxies imbued with this reasoning capability, it is possible to include agents, robots, and humans in a single team (Scerri et al., 2003). Other formalisms such as SharedPlans (Grosz & Kraus, 2003) have been employed successfully in building collaborative interface agents to reason about human intentions.

The RETSINA agent architecture (Sycara, Paolucci, Giampapa, & van Velsen, 2003) instantiates reasoning mechanisms based on Shared-Plans to:

1. Identify relevant recipients of critical information and forward information to them
2. Track task interdependencies among different team members
3. Recognize and report conflicts and constraint violations
4. Propose solutions to resolve conflicts
5. Monitor team performance

RETSINA agents are an implementation of the Anti-Air Warfare Team Observation Measure (ATOM) model of teamwork proposed by Smith-Jentsch, Johnson, and Payne (1998). The ATOM model postulates that, besides their individual competence in domain-specific tasks, team members in high-performance teams must have domain-independent team expertise that is composed of four different categories: information exchange, communication, supporting behavior, and team initiative/ leadership. The performance of teams, especially in tightly coupled tasks, is believed to be highly dependent on these interpersonal skills.

To be an effective team member, besides doing its own task well, an agent must be able to receive tasks and goals from other team members, be able

316 • *Theories of Team Cognition*

to communicate the results of its own problem-solving activities to appropriate participants, monitor team activity, and delegate tasks to other team members. A prerequisite for an agent to perform effective task delegation is to know (a) which tasks and actions it can perform itself, (b) which of its goals entail actions that can be performed by others, and (c) who can perform a given task. The RETSINA agent architecture (Sycara, Decker, Pannu, Williamson, & Zeng, 1996) includes a communication module that allows agents to send messages, a declarative representation of agent goals, and planning mechanisms for fulfilling these goals. Therefore, an agent is aware of the objectives it can plan for and the tasks it can perform. In addition, the planning mechanism allows an agent to reason about actions that it cannot perform itself and should be delegated to other agents.

Dealing With Dynamic Environments

Dynamic environments offer the following additional challenges to agent teamwork: (a) The environment is open, and the team constitution could vary dynamically through addition, substitution, or deletion of teammates; (b) team members are heterogeneous (having different or partially overlapping capabilities); (c) team members share domain-independent teamwork models; (d) individual and team replanning is necessary while supporting team goals and commitments; and (e) any team member can initiate team goals.

In forming a team to execute a mission, team members with different capabilities might be required. The location and availability of potential teammates is not necessarily known at any given point in time. Moreover, during a mission, teams may have to be reconfigured due to loss—total or partial—of team member capabilities (e.g., a robot loses one of its sensors) or the necessity of adding team members to the team. Automated support for addition, substitution, or deletion of team members requires extensions to current teamwork models: (a) development of robust schemes for agents to find others with required capabilities (i.e., agent discovery); (b) development of robust algorithms for briefing new team members so as to make them aware of the mission and current plans of the team; and (c) individual role adjustment and (re)negotiation of already existing plans due to the presence of the new (substitutable) teammate. One potential coordination mechanism that addresses many of these issues is capability-based coordination, in which all the agents advertise their capabilities with a matchmaking agent that can match agents to roles (Sycara et al., 2003). After a team has been formed (or reconfigured through capability-based coordination), team members must monitor teammates' activities in order to pursue and maintain coherent team activity, team goals, and commitments. Once team goals have been formulated, team members perform domain-specific planning, information gathering, and execution according to their expertise while maintaining team goals. An agent's planning must take into consideration temporal constraints and deadlines, as well as resource constraints and decision trade-offs.

Team Planning

Theoretical work on team behavior (Cohen & Levesque, 1991; Grosz & Kraus, 1996) stresses that the agents need to share the goals they want to achieve, the plan that they follow together, and knowledge of the environment in which they are operating. In addition, they need to share the commitment to execute the plan to reach the common goal. Furthermore, team members must be aware of their capabilities and how they can fulfill roles required by the team high-level plan and should be able to monitor their own progress toward the team goal and monitor teammates' activities and team joint intentions. The theoretical work and the operationalization of these representational and inferential abilities constitute a generic model of teamwork. System implementation of team coordination (Tambe, 1997) has resulted in the creation of an agent wrapper (Pynadath & Tambe, 2002) that implements a generic model of teamwork. An instance of such a wrapper can be associated with any agent in the multiagent system and used to coordinate the agent's activity with team activity. Teamwork wrappers can be used to wrap nonsocial agents to enable them to become team oriented.

However, human–agent teams require additional functionality not provided by agent-only models such as capability-based coordination and team-oriented planning. These extensions are discussed in the following sections.

Making Agents Proactive

Any agent can generate a team goal, thus becoming a team initiator. Becoming a team initiator requires the ability to perceive and assess events

318 • *Theories of Team Cognition*

as meriting initiation of team-formation activities. The team initiator must be able to generate a skeletal team plan, determine the initiator's own roles (by matching his or her capability to plan requirements), and find additional teammates through capability-based coordination. The team initiator is also responsible for checking that the collective capabilities of the newly formed team cover all requirements of the team goal.

Current models of teamwork are agnostic with respect to agent attitudes but implicitly assume a general cooperative attitude on the part of individuals that make them willing to engage in teamwork. Experimental work on human high-performance teams (Salas, Prince, Baker, & Shrestha, 1995), with numerous human military subjects in time-stressed and dangerous scenarios, has demonstrated that attitudes of team help are important factors in achieving high performance. Currently, there is no theoretical framework that specifies how such agent attitudes can be expressed, whether it is possible to incorporate such attitudes into current teamwork theories (e.g., joint intentions or SharedPlans), or what additional activities such attitudes entail during teamwork.

One consequence of agents' attitude of proactive assistance is a clearly increased need for team monitoring. In prior work, monitoring teammates' activities was done so as to maintain joint intentions during plan execution. Therefore, monitoring was done (Tambe, 1997) to ascertain (a) team role nonperformance (e.g., a team member no longer performs a team role), or (b) whether some new event necessitates team goal dissolution (e.g., realizing that the team goal has already been achieved). When developing schemes for tracking intentions of heterogeneous human–agent teams and dealing with the issue of appropriate levels of information granularity for such communications, additional monitoring must be done as a result of the proactive assistance agent attitude. Agents should volunteer to get information that is perceived to be useful to a teammate or the team as a whole. Moreover, agents should send warnings if they perceive a teammate to be in danger (e.g., Agent A warns Robot B of impending ceiling collapse in B's vicinity). Additional monitoring mechanisms, such as time-outs and temporal- and location-based checkpoints that are established during briefing, may also be useful. Time-outs are used to infer failure of an agent to continue performing its role (e.g., if it has not responded to some warning message).

In large dynamic environments, detailed monitoring of individual and team activity via plan recognition is not possible because the agents' activities are not directly perceivable by others most of the time. Hence, it is assumed that agents communicate and monitor one another's activities via Agent Communication Languages such as Foundation for Intelligent Physical Agents (FIPA) or Knowledge Query Manipulation Language (KQML). The content of the communication can be expressed in a declarative language (e.g., Extensible Markup Language [XML] or DARPA Agent Markup Language [DAML]). Agents communicate significant events (e.g., a new victim may have been heard), events pertaining to their own ability to continue performing their role (e.g., I lost my vision sensor), and requests for help (e.g., can someone who is nearby come help me lift this rubble?). These types of communication potentially generate new team subgoals (e.g., establish a team subgoal to get the newly heard victim to safety) and possibly the formation of subteams. The sender or the receiver of the message can initiate the new team subgoal.

HUMAN–AGENT TEAMWORK

Researchers desire to make agents an integral part of teams (Christoffersen & Woods, 2004); however, this desire has not yet been fully realized. Teaming with agents is also distinct from operating them or tasking groups of agents to perform some function. Currently, fielded robots and agent-based decision support systems almost exclusively operate in command mode, with an operator directly monitoring and controlling the system. Significant research has been conducted studying control functionality for robots and decision systems to improve the performance of human teams supported by agents; primarily robots because these are the systems most actively in use (Fincannon, Keebler, Jentsch, & Evans, 2008; Ososky, Evans, Keebler, & Jentsch, 2007; Parasuraman, Cosenzo, & De Visser, 2009). This research deals with operation of multiple robots by a small number of operators and coordination of vehicles and systems between human operators. Barnes, Cosenzo, Jentsch, Chen, and McDermott (2006) also explore this in the context of virtual worlds. Although this is important work and helps inform important agent teaming issues, the teamwork is among humans, with agents acting as extensions of the human operator rather than directly as team members. The conceptual leap needed for true human–agent teaming is the move to working with agent systems rather

320 • *Theories of Team Cognition*

than operating agents. This conceptual change is more than technological; even more significant are issues of human trust in agents, team integrity with nonhuman members, and new concepts for span of control for agents. Sycara and Lewis (2004) identified three primary roles played by agents interacting with humans:

1. Agents supporting individual team members in completion of their own tasks: These agents often function as personal assistant agents and are assigned to specific team members (Chalupsky et al., 2001). Task-specific agents used by multiple team members (e.g., Chen & Sycara, 1998) also belong in this category.
2. Agents supporting the team as a whole: Rather than focusing on task completion activities, these agents directly facilitate teamwork by aiding communication, coordination among human agents, and focus of attention. The experimental results summarized in Sycara and Lewis (2004) indicate that this might be the most effective aiding strategy for agents in hybrid teams.
3. Agents assuming the role of an equal team member: These agents are expected to function as "virtual humans" within the organization, capable of the same reasoning and tasks as their human teammates (Traum, Rickel, Gratch, & Marsella, 2003). This is the hardest role for a software agent to assume because it is difficult to create a software agent that is as effective as a human at both task performance and teamwork skills.

RESEARCH CHALLENGES

Creating shared understanding between human and agent teammates is the biggest challenge facing developers of mixed-initiative human–agent organizations. The limiting factor in most human–agent interactions is the user's ability and willingness to spend time communicating with the agent in a manner that both humans and agents understand, rather than the agent's computational power and bandwidth (Sycara & Lewis, 2004). Horvitz (1999) formulates the problem of mixed-initiative user interaction as a process of managing uncertainties—managing uncertainties that agents may have about users' goals and focus of attention and

Intelligent Agents as Teammates • 321

uncertainties that users have about agent plans and status. Regardless of the agents' roles, creating agent understanding of user intent and making agents' results intelligible to a human are problems that must be addressed by any mixed-initiative system, whether the agents reduce uncertainty through communication, inference, or a mixture of the two. In addition, protecting users from unauthorized agent interactions is always a concern in any application of agent technology.

Adjustable autonomy, the agent's ability to dynamically vary its own autonomy according to the situation, is an important facet of developing agent systems that interact with humans (Scerri, Pynadath, & Tambe, 2001, 2002). Agents with adjustable autonomy reason about transfer-of-control decisions and may assume control when the human is unwilling or unable to do a task. In many domains, the human teammates possess greater task expertise than the software agents, but less time; with adjustable autonomy, the human's time is reserved for the most important decisions, while agent members of the team deal with the less essential tasks. Scerri et al. (2001) demonstrated the use of Markov decision processes to calculate an optimal multiple transfer-of-control policy for calendar scheduling user interface agents. Having agents with adjustable autonomy is beneficial to agent teams. For example, a robot may ask a software agent for help in disambiguating its position, a software agent may relinquish control to a human to get advice concerning the choice between two decision-making alternatives, or a human may relinquish control to a robot in searching for victims. However, many interesting research problems remain, such as how control can be relinquished in ways that do not cause difficulties to the team, how to maintain team commitments, and how to support large-scale interactions with many agents.

There are additional issues specific to the role assumed by the agent. Agents that support individual human team members face the following challenges: (a) modeling user preferences, and (b) considering the status of the user's attention in timing services (Horvitz, 1999). Agents aiding teams (Lenox, 2000; Lenox, Hahn, Lewis, Payne, & Sycara, 2000; Lenox, Roberts, & Lewis, 1997; Lenox et al., 1998) face an additional set of problems: (a) identifying information that needs to be passed to other team members before being asked, (b) automatically prioritizing tasks for the human team members, and (c) maintaining shared task information in a way that is useful for the human users. Agents assuming the role of equal team members (Fan, Sun, McNeese, & Yen, 2005; Fan, Sun, Sun,

322 • *Theories of Team Cognition*

McNeese, & Yen, 2006; Traum et al., 2003) must additionally be able to do the following: (a) competently execute their role in the team, (b) critique team errors, and (c) independently suggest alternate courses of action.

Human–agent teams have been used in a variety of applications, including command and control scenarios (Burstein & Diller, 2004; Xu, Volz, Miller, & Plymale, 2003), disaster rescue simulations (Schurr, Marecki, Scerri, Lewis, & Tambe, 2005), team training in virtual environments (Traum et al., 2003), and personal information management (Chalupsky et al., 2001). Because these applications have widely different requirements, the generality of the models and results between domains is questionable. The following distinctions are instructive:

- How many humans and agents are there in the team? Are the agents supporting a team of humans, or is it a team of agents supporting one user?
- How much interdependency is there between agents and humans? Can the humans perform the task without the agents?
- Are the agents capable of unsolicited activity, or do they merely respond to the commands of the user?

Agents Supporting Team Members

In this class of applications, the software agents aid a single human in completing his or her tasks and do not directly interact with other human team members. Two organizational structures are most commonly found in these types of human–agent teams. In the first structure, each human is supported by a single agent proxy. Agent proxies interact with other agents to accomplish the human's tasks. In the second structure, each human is supported by a team of agents that work to accomplish the single human's directives. Often there are no other humans involved in the task, and the only "teamwork" involved is between the software agents. Examples of this type of agent system are agents assisting humans in allocating disaster rescue resources (Schurr et al., 2005) or conducting a noncombat evacuation operation (NEO) (Giampapa, Paolucci, & Sycara, 2000). In the NEO scenario, the agents eavesdropped on human conversations to determine proactively what kind of assistance humans could use and engaged in capability-based coordination to identify agents that could supply the needed information.

Agents Acting as Team Members

Instead of merely assisting human team members, the software agents can assume equal roles in the team, sometimes replacing missing human team members. It can be challenging to develop software agents of comparable competency with human performers unless the task is relatively simple. Agents often serve this role in training simulation applications by acting as team members or tutors for the human trainees. Rickel and Johnson (2002) developed a training simulator to teach human boat crews to correctly respond to nautical problems, using STEVE, a SOAR-based agent with a graphical embodiment. The Mission Rehearsal Environment (Traum et al., 2003) is a command training simulation that contains multiple *virtual humans* who serve as subordinates to the human commander trainee. The human must negotiate with the agents to get them to agree to the correct course of action. It is uncommon in human–robot applications to have robots acting as team members, rather than supporters; however, limited examples of human–robot teamwork are starting to emerge in the Segway RoboCup division, where each soccer team is composed of a Segway-riding human paired with a robotically controlled Segway (Argall, Gu, Browning, & Veloso, 2006).

Agents Supporting Human Teams

In this class of applications, the agents facilitate teamwork between humans involved in a group task by aiding communication, coordination, and focus of attention. In certain applications, this has shown to be more effective than having the agents directly aid in task completion. For the TANDEM target identification control and command task, Sycara and Lewis (2004) examined different ways of deploying agents to support multiperson teams. Different agent-aiding strategies were experimentally evaluated within the context of a group target identification task, including (a) supporting the individual by maintaining a common visual space, (b) supporting communication among team members by automatically passing information to the relevant team member, and (c) supporting task prioritization and coordination by maintaining a shared checklist. The two team-aiding strategies (supporting communication and task prioritization) improved team performance significantly more than supporting team members with their individual tasks. Aiding teamwork also requires

324 • *Theories of Team Cognition*

less domain knowledge than task aiding, which makes the agents potentially reusable across domains.

Human–Robot Teams

Recently there has been increasing interest in the problem of creating effective human–robot interfaces (Atherton, Harding, & Goodrich, 2006; Harris, Banerjee, & Rudnicky, 2005; Lewis, Tastan, & Sukthankar, 2010; Nielsen, Goodrich, & Crandall, 2003; Squire, Trafton, & Parasuraman, 2006; Stubbs, Hinds, & Wettergreen, 2006; Wang, Lewis, & Scerri, 2006). A significant amount of research is currently being focused on social robots, with particular emphasis on evoking and recognizing social cues in human–robot interaction (Breazeal, Takanishi, & Kobayashi, 2008). This highly anthropomorphic approach is appropriate for exploring basic human–agent interaction concepts, and much has been learned that will enable constructing agent teammates, but translating highly anthropomorphic agents to the field may be problematic at this stage of development. Informal interaction with Army personnel indicates limited usefulness of detailed anthropomorphic means of communication, such as face displays, and a general aversion to this approach in robots. Laboratory research supports this notion (Sims et al., 2005) while reinforcing the observation that humans have a predisposition to anthropomorphize mechanical objects. An important finding is that people who interact with robots consistently are more comfortable if there is a clear distinction between the agents and humans. Matching form with actual capability is likely to be an important factor in agent acceptance and effective membership in a team. For a variety of practical reasons already mentioned, there can be too much anthropomorphism in the design of agents. Unfortunately, little of this theoretically interesting and successful laboratory work has moved to real-world applications of the kind we envision. This issue requires careful attention in attempting to make human–agent teaming a reality. An alternative to anthropomorphism for teaming agents is a simplified agent personification that could be termed biomorphic, in that it takes advantage of the tendency noted previously for humans to attribute capabilities based on form, but does not seek to directly replicate human features. In this approach, we seek to exploit existing physical features of robots and to create appropriate embodiments for software agents that reinforce accurate human assessment of agent capability and state, reinforce the human mental model of the agent, and facilitate natural human communication modalities.

Human–Agent Interaction

We suggest that three important facets of human–agent interaction are (a) mutual predictability of teammates (Sycara & Lewis, 2004), (b) team knowledge (shared understanding), and (c) mutual adaptation. Mutual predictability means that parties must make their actions sufficiently predictable to the teammates to make coordination effective and also try to form some estimate of many features of the team activity (e.g., how long it will take a teammate to perform an action). Team knowledge refers to the pertinent mutual knowledge, beliefs, and assumptions that support the interdependent actions and the construction or following of plans to fulfill the team goals. Team knowledge (shared understanding/shared knowledge) can exist before the team is formed (through previous experiences) or must be formed, maintained, and repaired after the team has started its collaboration. The ability to be directed and mutual adaptation are key components of teamwork because they express the interdependencies of team activity. If the way one player performs an activity has no effect on another, then the two players work in parallel but do not coordinate. Additionally, the agent designers must consider using multimodal interaction or modifying the agent persona to enhance communication between the humans and agents.

Multimodal Interaction

Speech, gesture, and posture are important human–agent communication channels for the kind of dynamic and interactive team activities envisioned as likely near-term to midterm applications; however, agent–agent communication and, to some degree, human–agent communication can take advantage of technical adjuncts not usually available to human teammates. To facilitate agent assimilation within a team, at a minimum, the agent should be able to interpret, appropriately respond to, and generate, in some form, standard arm and hand gestures. This does not necessarily have to be done entirely visually. Research in communicating with agents using accelerometer-based input devices was successful in sending standard Army Field Manual hand and arm signals when direct observation

326 • *Theories of Team Cognition*

was not possible (Chen & Sharlin, 2008; Varcholik & Barber, 2008). This method of communication provides redundant gesture information, visual and electronic, significantly improving classification reliability, while at the same time being low cost. Perhaps most interesting, it opens the possibility of reliable human–agent gestural communication beyond the line of sight. The complement of this has also been demonstrated using vibrotactile belts or vests as signaling devices to humans. This gestural–tactile modality has been investigated for human team member communication; two authors in particular (Merlo et al., 2006; Prewett et al., 2006) describe the effectiveness of this modality for reliably providing information over a distance, with the added benefit of reducing the problem of spatial translation due to body orientation and position. Agents can readily become bidirectional participants using this communication modality as an adjunct to direct visual observation.

Excellent research work in multimodal communication for agents has been done in laboratory environments, primarily focusing on the use of speech and gesture interfaces in the context of collaboration. William Kennedy and a research team at the Navy Center for Applied Research in Artificial Intelligence (NCARAI) (Kennedy et al., 2007) considered the reconnaissance element of intelligence, surveillance, and reconnaissance (ISR) as a practical team task in which to explore covert communication along with the spatial reasoning and perspective-taking elements needed for effective cooperation. The physical environment was a simplified version of a team covert surveillance task but was adequate for exploring issues in interpretation of simple speech and gesture-based interaction at a level of complexity comparable to that of the shepherd–sheepdog example. This research highlighted the need for multiple internal situation representations, ranging from engineering-oriented metric position information from sensors and map-oriented navigation data to the qualitative and cognitively plausible representations needed for effective verbal and gestural dialog with humans. A related study at NCARAI (Trafton et al., 2005) explored the issue of perspective taking as a crucial element in human–agent interaction in the context of a shared task and further addressed the importance of mapping between cognitively inspired and engineering-oriented internal models. The two research projects described support the technical feasibility of limited-context, limited-vocabulary multimodal interaction that human–agent team behavior will require with some important caveats, including dealing with noise and corrupted signals, multiple humans and agents communicating where there may be differing simultaneous contexts, and the importance of appropriate internal models.

Agent Persona

Much of the research discussed so far was conducted with little attention to the physical form of the agent. Although this factor was not important for exploring many of the underlying issues in human–agent interaction that are required for teaming, it will be a concern when implementing physical agents that can operate within a team. This issue goes beyond agents in the form of robots, where physical form is clearly an issue; we contend that even purely software agents will need some sort of appropriate physical representation to most effectively work with humans as a teammate and be perceived as able to effectively perform tasks within the team. Creating an appropriate agent persona will clearly enhance acceptance and support a crucial aspect of agent incorporation within teams—trust and confidence among team members, human or otherwise.

Turing's test for AI entails engaging a human observer in a text-based dialog with a computer such that the human is unable to distinguish whether the interaction is with a human or a computer. Relatively simple programs such as ELIZA (Weizenbaum, 1966) came surprisingly close to reaching this criterion at least for short periods of time. For this early attempt, however, this was not so much due to technical merit as the fact that humans seem to have a strong predisposition to attribute anthropomorphic characteristics to machines, as a number of studies have shown (Ellis et al., 2005; Powers & Kiesler, 2006; Sims et al., 2005). The likelihood of success in developing agents that can serve as members of human teams is enhanced by this predisposition, but there is substantial argument against constructing agents that could be confused with humans, not the least of which is that the level of cognitive performance that we can expect to achieve within the foreseeable future will be far from comparable to human performance. Although it might be tempting to provide the most human-like external appearance and behavior that we can achieve, this would likely create performance expectations that are far beyond those which we are likely to be able to achieve within a decade or two. Because effective teamwork requires sophisticated models of tasks, other agents, and the team's roles, goals, and plans, as well as the

328 • *Theories of Team Cognition*

ability to communicate effectively, agents must possess these capabilities, preferably in a form readily compatible with the human equivalent, but not necessarily in the form of a cognitive model. Much of the research in human–agent social interaction has taken an anthropomorphic approach, replicating facial features, gestures, and other biologically inspired features. Excellent examples of this include Honda's Asimo and the National Aeronautics and Space Administration (NASA)'s Robonaut (Ambrose et al., 2000). In both cases, significant effort went into replicating human-like external features, such as a face, and providing human-like means for locomotion (Asimo) and manipulation (Robonaut and Asimo). Both also use good speech generation and some level of verbal dialog capability, although cognitive performance is substantially below the level that external appearance would suggest.

Team Knowledge

Team knowledge is critical to understanding team performance because it explains how members of effective teams interact with one another (Cannon-Bowers & Salas, 2001). It does not refer to a unitary concept; instead, it refers to different types of knowledge that need to be shared in effective teams. Teams build knowledge about specific tasks (both declarative and procedural task-specific knowledge), items related to tasks (e.g., expectations of how teams operate), characteristics of teammates (e.g., strengths, preferences, weaknesses, tendencies), and attitudes and beliefs of teammates (Cannon-Bowers, Tannenbaum, Salas, & Volpe, 1995). Knowledge of the strengths and weaknesses of teammates and their attitudes and beliefs can be generalized across a variety of tasks. Knowledge that is task related can be used across similar tasks.

Team knowledge and shared understanding need to be formed between humans and agents despite the presence of multiple representations. As Cooke, Salas, Cannon-Bowers, and Stout (2000) point out, members of human teams have both shared and unshared knowledge of the team's task and state. Agents are likely to have varying levels of intelligibility to other members of their team because the tasks and conditions they are responding to will be known to different extents by other team members. One of the ways to address this is through customization of the agent communication for each team member based on the agent's estimation of what the human teammate knows. Another way is to always give human team members the maximum amount of information the agent considers relevant but without customization. Team knowledge implies that the agents will have a clear idea of important features of the team composition. For agents to perform as full-fledged team members, they must have a clear model of team goals, team membership, member capabilities, and member roles in procedurally defined tasks.

Mutual Predictability

Mutual predictability, as well as team knowledge, entails knowledge transfer between team members. It enables teammates to communicate and coordinate in a meaningful manner. Humans represent most knowledge implicitly in their brains. This knowledge needs to be represented in some explicit manner for other teammates to understand it. The introduction of agents into teams creates impediments to mutual predictability. The greatest impediment to agents assisting human users lies in communicating their intent and making results intelligible to them (Lewis, 1998). To this end, representation schemes that are declarative and intelligible both by humans and agents are most useful. Research on knowledge representation within agents is primarily based on logic-based formalisms (Brachman & Levesque, 1984). High-level messaging languages such as KQML contain message types intelligible both to agents and humans (e.g., inform, tell, ask) and have been used in systems such as RETSINA for successful human–agent collaboration. Different forms of communication (e.g., text, pictures, menus) might vary in effectiveness as carriers of knowledge transfer between teammates, both human and agent.

Mutual Adaptation

Mutual adaptation is defined by how team members alter their roles to fulfill team requirements. Researchers acknowledge that the most effective agents will need to change their level of initiative, or exhibit adjustable autonomy, in response to the situation to be most effective (Horvitz, 1999; Scerri et al., 2002). For agents to appropriately exercise initiative, they must have a clear model of the team's goals, member roles, and team procedures. Agents can execute transfer-of-control strategies (Scerri et al., 2001), which specify a sequence of changes of autonomy level when the human is occupied and cannot make timely decisions, but such strategies

330 • *Theories of Team Cognition*

must be designed to fit within human expectations, rather than violating them. An important research question is whether teams perform better when agents have a constant but potentially suboptimal level of autonomy or when agents constantly adjust to the team's context.

Communication

Underpinning team knowledge, mutual predictability, and mutual adaptation is clear and effective communication. Because we are designing and building agents rather than training them individually, the task of creating agent equivalents for mental models can be considered separately from communication, easing the requirements for high-level natural language capability. Additionally, we can readily replicate such models among agents once these models are created and can even provide dynamic model updating among agents if desired. Dynamically maintaining agent internal models during team efforts, however, must rely to a significant degree on the ability to generate and understand the implicit and explicit communication naturally used between human team members. Although agents may be able to use technical modalities among themselves that are unavailable to human team members, to the degree technically feasible, we should seek to provide the capability for agents to effectively use human communication modalities.

Ideally, human–agent intrateam communication would be able to directly exploit the modalities and conventions used by human team members (e.g., speech, gesture, postural cues, and perhaps some degree of affect recognition), rather than requiring specialized control stations and the need for extensive operator training and attention to controlling an agent. As a practical matter though, there will almost certainly be a control station operated by a designated agent handler to deal with maintenance, database update, and other operational issues. If intrateam communication required such a control station for every team member to communicate with an agent, team behavior would be significantly negatively impacted, so the objective is to seek to minimize specialized interfaces for most purposes The operating environments where human–agent teams will most likely need to operate for most useful applications require that the speech, gesture, and other signaling modalities used must cope with background noise, need for silence, varying accents, simultaneous speakers in the background, visual occlusion,

Application of Human–Robot Teamwork

In this section, we present a case study describing the development of an intelligent user interface to facilitate human–robot teamwork that we built and evaluated at the Intelligent Agents Lab at University of Central Florida. The effectiveness of a human–robot team can be enhanced in a variety of ways, including improving task allocation across entities with different capabilities (Koes, Nourbakhsh, & Sycara, 2006), using adjustable autonomy to improve the timing of agent intervention (Scerri et al., 2003; Sierhuis et al., 2003), and building explicit models of user distraction (Fan & Yen, 2007; Lewis et al., 2010). However, in some cases, tasking (which entity should perform the task) and timing (when should the agents/robots act autonomously) are relatively straightforward to compute. The barrier to adjustable autonomy in a human–robot system can be selecting effective actions during time segments when the robot is acting autonomously. This is a problem for all autonomous systems operating in uncertain environments, yet human–robot systems have options that are unavailable to normal robots. A common solution is to decrease the time period of autonomous operation and increase the amount of user intervention, but in cases where the task is complicated and the user's workload is already high, this approach threatens to degrade the overall system performance. We propose an alternate approach in which the agents and robots leverage information about what the user is doing and has recently done to decide their future course of action. We demonstrate our approach on a multirobot manipulation task that is both difficult to perform autonomously due to sensor limitations and challenging for human teleoperation because of the higher degrees of freedom.

In our multirobot manipulation task, the user directs a team of two mobile robots to lift objects using an arm and gripper for transport to a goal location. The environment contains a heterogeneous selection of objects, some of which can be transported by a single robot and others that require both robots to lift. Figure 13.1(a) shows a picture of the team of robots cooperatively moving an object that cannot be carried by a single robot; Figure 13.1(b) shows the same robots manipulating different objects in close proximity, clearing obstacles in parallel. Such tasks are versions of

332 • *Theories of Team Cognition*

FIGURE 13.1
(a) Two robots cooperate to lift a box. One robot is teleoperated, while the other moves autonomously to mirror the user's intentions. The user can seamlessly switch robots during such maneuvers. (b) Robots cooperate to clear the environment of objects in parallel and deposit them in the goal location.

the multirobot foraging problem that has been successfully addressed by decentralized task allocation algorithms (Goldberg et al., 2003) but with the additional complication that grasp planning and manipulation must be executed by the human due to sensor limitations. Like cooperative box pushing (Kalra, Ferguson, & Stentz, 2005), multirobot manipulation requires tight coordination between robots, but the task is additionally difficult because a poor grasp from either of the robots will lead to the object being dropped. Augmenting the robots with manipulation capabilities increases the number of potential usage cases for a multirobot system. For instance, a number of urban search and rescue (USAR) systems have been demonstrated that can map buildings and locate victims in areas of poor visibility and rough terrain (Wang et al., 2006). Adding manipulation to the robots could enable them to move rubble, drop items, and provide rudimentary medical assistance to the victims. The RoboCup Rescue competition has recently been extended to award points for manipulation tasks. The RoboCup@Home

Intelligent Agents as Teammates • 333

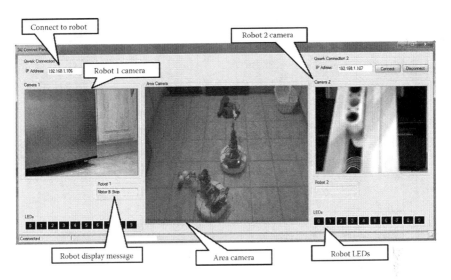

FIGURE 13.2
The Intelligent Agent Interface is designed to enable the user to seamlessly switch teleoperation across multiple robots. The IAI supports a cooperative mode where the agent supports the user's active robot by mirroring its intentions.

competition, which aims to develop domestic service robots, also includes manipulation of household objects such as doors, kitchen utensils, and glasses. A set of standardized tests is used to evaluate the robot's abilities and performance in a realistic home environment setting.

To address the problem of creating an effective human–agent–robot team capable of executing challenging multirobot manipulation tasks, we developed the Intelligent Agent Interface (IAI; Figure 13.2), which adjusts its autonomy based on the user's workload. In addition to automatically identifying user distraction, the IAI leverages prior commands that the user has issued to one robot to determine a course of action of the second robot. To enable the human to simultaneously control multiple robots, the interface allows robots to be placed in a **search** mode, where the robot continues moving in the specified direction, while hunting for objects and avoiding obstacles. IAI monitors each of the robots and identifies robots that are ignored by the operator through measuring time latencies. It then assumes control of the unattended robot and cedes control if the user sends the robot an explicit teleoperation command. The IAI provides the user with two important new cooperative functions: autonomous positioning of the second robot (**locate ally**) and a **mirror** mode in which the second robot simultaneously executes a modified version of the commands that the user has issued to the actively controlled

334 • *Theories of Team Cognition*

robot. When the user requests help to move a large object, these cooperative functions enable the robot to autonomously move to the appropriate location and cooperatively lift the object and drive in tandem to the goal.

Robots have the following modes of operation:

Search: The robots wander the area searching for objects.

Help: A robot enters this mode if the human operator calls for help or when the teleoperated robot is near an object too large to be moved by an individual robot.

Pickup: The robot detects an object and requests that the human teleoperate the arm.

Transport: The robot transports an object held by the gripper to the goal.

Locate ally: The unmanaged robot autonomously moves to a position near the teleoperated robot based on command history.

Mirror: The robot mimics the commands executed by the teleoperated robot to simultaneously lift an object and transport it to the goal location.

In a typical usage scenario, the IAI moves the unattended robot around the environment in search of objects to be moved (clutter). At the start of the mission, the region is roughly partitioned into two areas of responsibility for exploration. Given this partition, each robot independently searches its assigned space. The robot's current state is displayed on the user interface for the benefit of the human operator. When the user needs help manipulating an awkward object, the second robot can be called using the gamepad controller. The **help** function can also be automatically activated by the IAI system, based on the other robot's proximity to large objects. Once in the **help** mode, the robot executes the **locate ally** behavior.

IAI maintains a history of both robots' navigational movements and uses dead reckoning to determine the teleoperated robot's position. Each robot has a cliff sensor, which when activated indicates that a robot has been forcibly moved. If that occurs, the IAI system notifies the user to reorient the robot by driving it to its initial starting position. If the user is not actively soliciting help, the unmanaged robot typically moves into the **search** mode; once the robot detects an object, it notifies the user that it needs help with manipulation. After the object has been lifted by the user, the robot transports it to the goal. The aim of the IAI system is to smoothly transition between the unmanaged robot rendering help to the user and asking for help with the manipulation section of the task. The human operator can also opt to put the other robot into **mirror** mode. In this mode, the unmanaged robot intercepts the commands given to the teleoperated robot and attempts to duplicate them in its own frame of reference. This mode is essential for reducing the workload of the operator during cooperative manipulation, when two robots are required to lift the object. By combining the **help, locate ally**, and **mirror** modes, the robot can autonomously detect when its help is needed, move to the correct position, and copy the teleoperated robot's actions with minimal intervention from the operator.

The baseline system, designated as manual operation, consisted of a standard teleoperation setup where the human operator controls all aspects of the robot's motion using the Xbox 360 controller. The user interface is only used to display camera viewpoints, and the robots never attempt to act autonomously. In our proposed approach, the user has access to the additional commands **help** and **mirror** through the controller. The IAI automatically detects lack of robot activity and triggers the **search** mode to hunt for objects with the unmanaged robot. When an object too large for a single robot is detected, the IAI system autonomously positions the robot and waits for the user to activate the mirror. We measured task performance using two metrics: (a) the time required to complete the task, and (b) the number of times objects were dropped during the scenario. We saw that in the majority of runs, IAI significantly accelerated the human operator's progress. We attribute this to the fact that the robot controlled by the IAI continues to assist the human operator, while the teleoperation condition forces the user to inefficiently multitask between robots. In addition, the number of average drops was lower with IAI in all three scenarios. In general, IAI results in fewer drops because the mirror mode enables the user and agent to coordinate grasping and movement, whereas in manual mode, the user risks dropping the object as a robot is moved during two-handed manipulation tasks.

Adding manipulation capabilities to a robot team widens its scope of usage tremendously at the cost of increasing the complexity of the planning problem. By off-loading the manipulation aspects of the task to the human operator, we can tackle more complicated tasks without adding additional sensors to the robot. Rather than increasing the workload of the human user, we propose an alternate approach in which the robots

336 • *Theories of Team Cognition*

leverage information from commands that the user is executing to decide their future course of action. We illustrate how this approach can be used to create cooperative behaviors such as mirroring and locate ally; together, the robots can coordinate to lift and transport items that are too awkward to be manipulated by a single robot. In the user study, our mixed-initiative user interface (IAI) showed statistically significant improvements in the time required to perform foraging scenarios and the number of dropped items. Users were able to master the interface quickly and reported a high amount of user satisfaction. This case study shows how effective user interface design can be used to improve mutual predictability between humans and robots. Within the constraints of the scenario, the robots are able to accurate predict the human's intentions well enough to function autonomously for limited periods of time.

CONCLUSIONS

It is important to establish reasonable expectations for team-oriented agents. The development time frame we will consider is approximately 10 years; extrapolating beyond this would likely put us more into the realm of science fiction than is appropriate. Within this time frame, the prospect for achieving anything approaching human-level performance in agents for any of the critical elements of team behavior we require is not good. For setting more practical objectives for agent performance, consider a well-known case of human and nonhuman agent team behavior: shepherds and sheepdogs. We believe this model is a good exemplar for many reasons, not least of which is that the tasks performed by this human–agent team have direct civil and military team analogs, such as searching, convoying, perimeter protection, area patrol, and crowd management. An important element of such teaming that we also should seek to emulate is that the number and ratio of human and agent team members may vary, with the team members adjusting to available team resources within the context of the team mission. This requires every element of macrocognition as previously defined. Furthermore, the shepherd–sheepdog example is a working example of entities with differing cognitive, physical performance, and communication capabilities collaborating on shared missions in dynamic environments.

Intelligent Agents as Teammates • 337

Organizationally, the shepherd–sheepdog example is similar to what we expect will be the case for most human–agent team applications; a human specifies, monitors, and controls overall execution of the mission. There are, of course, some circumstance even in the example given where the agent might need to act or deviate from a plan without direct communications but within the framework of the assigned mission. Because agents are expected to display initiative in executing their element of tasks, mechanisms for planning and validation against mission objectives are required. Examples where this is important include dealing appropriately with contingencies, adjusting dynamically with humans and other agents while executing assigned tasks, and communicating mission-relevant events within the team. The types of direct communication used effectively within the shepherd–sheepdog team are verbal and nonverbal sounds, as well as gestures, postures, and perhaps affect. Such communication is often bidirectional: dogs are skilled at recognizing direct commands and nonverbal cues from humans and can generate many signals that humans can readily comprehend. This nonverbal communication is surprisingly rich: Dogs can express understanding, nonconcurrence, noncomprehension, and even concern. They can also get humans' and other agents' attention and signal mission-relevant information using combinations of various modalities.

The elevation of agents to teammate status has important practical and psychological implications, with the burden of adapting to human team dynamics, standards of performance, and interaction falling primarily on agents, with perhaps some small accommodation on the part of human team members. In short, human team behavior sets the conditions to which agents must accommodate, and creating agent analogs to human cognitive processes and communication modalities is the technical challenge for agent designers.

There has been significant progress in AI research over five decades; however, we should not expect to achieve human levels of cognitive capability in agents for a long time, despite prediction of a computing singularity by an important AI researcher, Raymond Kurzweil (2006). There has also been quite good progress in the sort of natural language understanding and gesture recognition that would facilitate full team membership; Sofge et al. (2004) and Trafton et al. (2005) explicitly examine this issue. However, almost exclusively, this has been accomplished in the context of the first category proposed by Sycara and Lewis (2004)—agents

338 • *Theories of Team Cognition*

supporting individual team members in completion of their own tasks. Moreover, these efforts, although successful and useful, were conducted in benign environments and in limited problem-solving contexts. In short, full team membership is perhaps too technically challenging at this time and, in any event, would precipitate significant social and pragmatic complications within the team structure. For many useful purposes, however, full team membership is unnecessary, and there have been many successful demonstrations of human–agent teams in which the agents only possessed limited cognitive capabilities.

Salas, Dickinson, Converse, and Tannenbaum (1992) characterize human teams as "a distinguishable set of two or more people who interact dynamically, interdependently, and adaptively towards a common and valued goal/objective/mission" (p. 4). Researchers desire to make agents an integral part of teams (Christoffersen & Woods, 2004); however, this desire has not yet been fully realized. Current software agents currently lack the dynamism and adaptivity in Salas et al.'s (1992) description of human teams and are more capable of supporting human teamwork skills than executing them autonomously. There has been tremendous progress in constructing some of the necessary components necessary to build an agent team member, most notably in the areas of planning, coordination, and multimodal interfaces. The problems of building team knowledge, mutual predictability, and adaptability remain formidable challenges barring the formation of effective human–agent teams. However, in the near term, it is possible to create an effective social-computational system composed of human and agent teammates that bolster each other's weaknesses to form a team in which the whole is greater than the sum of the parts.

ACKNOWLEDGMENTS

The authors would like to thank Katia Sycara and Bennie Lewis. This research was partially supported by National Science Foundation Award No. IIS-0845159.

REFERENCES

Ambrose, R., Aldridge, H., Askew, R. S., Burridge, R., Bluethmann, W., Diftler, M., et al. (2000). Robonaut: NASA's space humanoid. *IEEE Intelligent Systems, 15*, 57–63.

Argall, B., Gu, Y., Browning, B., & Veloso, M. (2006, March). The first Segway soccer experience: Towards peer-to-peer human robot teams. *Proceedings of the First Annual Conference on Human-Robot Interactions.*

Atherton, J., Harding, B., & Goodrich, M. (2006). Coordinating a multi-agent team using a multiple perspective interface paradigm. *Proceedings of the AAAI 2006 Spring Symposium: To Boldly Go Where No Human-Robot Team Has Gone Before*, 47–51.

Barnes, M. J., Cosenzo, K. A., Jentsch, F., Chen, J. Y. C., & McDermott, P. (2006). Understanding soldier robot teams in virtual environments. In *Virtual media for military applications* (pp. 10-1–10-14). Meeting Proceedings RTO-MP HRM-136, Paper 10. Neuilly-sur-Seine, France: RTO.

Brachman, R., & Levesque, H. (1984). *Knowledge representation and reasoning.* Burlington, MA: Morgan Kaufmann.

Breazeal, C., Takanishi, A., & Kobayashi, T. (2008). Social robots that interact with people. In B. Siciliano & O. Khatib (Eds.), *Springer handbook of robotics* (pp. 1349–1369). New York, NY: Springer.

Burstein, M., & Diller, D. (2004). A framework for dynamic information flow in mixed-initiative human/agent organizations. *Applied Intelligence, 20*, 283–298.

Cannon-Bowers, J., & Salas, E. (2001). Reflections on shared cognition. *Journal of Organizational Behavior, 22*, 195–202.

Cannon-Bowers, J., Tannenbaum, S., Salas, E., & Volpe, C. (1995). Defining team competencies: Implications for training requirements and strategies. In R. Guzzo & E. Salas (Eds.), *Team effectiveness and decision making in organizations.* San Francisco, CA: Jossey-Bass.

Chalupsky, H., Gil, Y., Knoblock, C., Lerman, K., Oh, J., Pyndath, D., et al. (2001). Electric elves: Applying agent technology to support human organizations. *Proceedings of the Innovative Applications of Artificial Intelligence Conference*, 51–58.

Chen, G., & Sharlin, E. (2008). Exploring the use of tangible user interfaces for human-robot interaction: A comparative study. *Proceedings of the 26th Annual SIGCHI Conference on Human Factors in Computing Systems*, 121–130.

Chen, L., & Sycara, K. (1998). Webmate: A personal agent for browsing and searching. *Proceedings of the Second International Conference on Autonomous Agents*, 132–139.

Christoffersen, K., & Woods, D. (2004). How to make automated systems team players. In E. Salas (Ed.), *Advances in human performance and cognitive engineering research* (Vol. 2, pp. 1–12). Bingley, UK: Emerald Group Publishing Limited.

Cohen, P., & Levesque, H. (1990). Intention is choice with commitment. *Artificial Intelligence, 42*, 213–261.

Cohen, P., & Levesque, H. (1991). Teamwork. *Nous, 25*, 487–512.

Cooke, N., & Gorman, J. (2007). Assessment of team cognition. In P. Karwowski (Ed.), *International encyclopedia of ergonomics and human factors.* New York, NY: Taylor & Francis.

Cooke, N., Gorman, J., Pedersen, M., & Bell, B. (2007). Distributed mission environments: Effects of geographic distribution on team cognition, process, and performance. In S. Fiore & E. Salas (Eds.), *Towards a science of distributed learning and training.* Washington, DC: American Psychological Association.

Cooke, N., Salas, E., Cannon-Bowers, J., & Stout, R. (2000). Measuring team knowledge. *Human Factors, 42*, 151–175.

340 • *Theories of Team Cognition*

Ellis, L., Sims, V., Chin, M., Pepe, A., Owens, C., Dolezal, M., et al. (2005). Those a-maze-ing robots: Attributions of ability based on form, not behavior. *Proceedings of the Human Factors and Ergonomics Society 49th Annual Meeting*, 598–681.

Fan, X., Sun, S., McNeese, M., & Yen, J. (2005). Extending the recognition-primed decision model to support human-agent collaboration. *Proceedings of International Conference on Autonomous Agents and Multiagent Systems*, 945–952.

Fan, X., Sun, B., Sun, S., McNeese, M., & Yen, J. (2006). RPD-enabled agents teaming with humans for multi-context decision making. *Proceedings of International Conference on Autonomous Agents and Multiagent Systems*, 34–41.

Fan, X., & Yen, J. (2007). Realistic cognitive load modeling for enhancing shared mental models in human-agent collaboration. *Proceedings of the International Conference on Autonomous Agents and Multiagent Systems*, 383–390.

Fincannon, T., Keebler, J. R., Jentsch, F. G., & Evans, A. W. III (2008). Target identification support and location support among teams of unmanned system operators. *Proceedings of the 26th National Army Science Conference*, Orlando, FL.

Fiore, S., Salas, E., Cuevas, H., & Bowers, C. (2003). Distributed coordination space: Toward a theory of distributed team process and performance. *Theoretical Issues in Ergonomic Science, 4*, 340–363.

Fiore, S., & Schooler, J. (2004). Process mapping and shared cognition: Teamwork and the development of shared problem models. In E. Salas & S. Fiore (Eds.), *Team cognition: Understanding the factors that drive process and performance*. Washington, DC: American Psychological Association.

Friedkin, N. (1998). *A structural theory of social influence*. Cambridge, UK: Cambridge University Press.

Giampapa, J., Paolucci, M., & Sycara, K. (2000). Agent interoperation across multiagent boundaries. *Proceedings of the Fourth International Conference on Autonomous Agents*, 179–186.

Goldberg, D., Cicirello, V., Dias, M., Simmons, R., Smith, S., & Stentz, A. (2003). Market-based multi-robot planning in a distributed layered architecture. In A. C. Shultz, L. E. Parker, & F. E. Schneider (Eds.), *Multi-robot systems: From swarms to intelligent automata: Proceedings from the International Workshop on Multi-Robot Systems* (Vol. 2, pp. 27–38). Philadelphia, PA: Kluwer Academic Publishers.

Grosz, B., & Kraus, S. (1996). Collaborative plans for complex group action. *Artificial Intelligence, 86*, 269–357.

Grosz, B., & Kraus, S. (2003). The evolution of SharedPlans. In A. Rao & M. Wooldridge (Eds.), *Foundations and theories of rational agency* (pp. 227–262). Philadelphia, PA: Kluwer Academic.

Harris, T., Banerjee, S., & Rudnicky, A. (2005). Heterogeneous multi-robot dialogues for search tasks. *Proceedings of the AAAI Spring Symposium Intelligence*.

Horvitz, E. (1999). Principles of mixed-initiative user interfaces. *Proceedings of the SIGCHI Conference on Human Factors in Computing Systems*, 159–166.

Kalra, N., Ferguson, D., & Stentz, A. (2005). Hoplites: A market-based framework for planned tight coordination in multirobot teams. *Proceedings of the International Conference on Robotics and Automation*, 1170–1177.

Kennedy, W. G., Bugajska, M. D., Marge, M., Adams, W., Fransen, B. R., Perzanowski, D., et al. (2007). Spatial representation and reasoning for human-robot collaboration. In *Proceedings of the Twenty-Second Conference on Artificial Intelligence* (pp. 1554–1559). Vancouver, Canada: AAAI Press.

Koes, M., Nourbakhsh, I., & Sycara, S. (2006). Constraint optimization coordination architecture for search and rescue robotics. *Proceedings of the IEEE International Conference on Robotics and Automation*, 3977–3982.

Kurzweil, R. (2006). *The singularity is near: When humans transcend biology*. New York, NY: Penguin.

Lenox, T. (2000). *Supporting teamwork using software agents in human-agent teams*. Unpublished doctoral thesis, Westminster College, New Wilmington, PA.

Lenox, T., Hahn, S., Lewis, M., Payne, T., & Sycara, K. (2000). Agent-based aiding for individual and team planning tasks. *Proceedings of IEA 2000/HFES 2000 Congress*.

Lenox, T., Lewis, M., Roth, E., Shern, R., Roberts, L., Rafalski, T., et al. (1998). Support of teamwork in human-agent teams. In *Proceedings of IEEE International Conference on Systems, Man, and Cybernetics*, 1341–1346.

Lenox, T., Roberts, L., & Lewis, M. (1997). Human-agent interaction in a target identification task. *Proceedings of IEEE International Conference on Systems, Man, and Cybernetics*, 2702–2706.

Lewis, M. (1998). Designing for human-agent interaction. *AI Magazine, 19*, 67–78.

Lewis, B., Tastan, B., & Sukthankar, G. (2010). Agent assistance for multi-robot control. *Proceedings of Autonomous Agents and Multiagent Systems*.

Merlo, J. L., Terrence, P. L, Stafford, S., Gilson, R., Hancock, P. A., Redden, E. S., et al. (2006). Communicating through the use of vibrotactile displays for dismounted and mounted soldiers. *Proceedings of the 25th Annual Army Science Conference*, Orlando, FL.

Nair, R., Tambe, M., & Marsella, S. (2003). Role allocation and reallocation in multiagent teams: Towards a practical analysis. *Proceedings of the Second International Joint Conference on Autonomous Agents and Multiagent Systems*.

Nielsen, C., Goodrich, M., & Crandall, J. (2003). Experiments in human-robot teams. In A. Schulz & L. Parker (Eds.), *Multirobot teams: From swarms to intelligent automata*. Philadelphia, PA: Kluwer Academic.

Ososky, S., Evans, A. W. III, Keebler, J. R., & Jentsch, F. (2007). Using scale simulation and virtual environments to study human-robot teams. In D. D. Schmorrow, D. M. Nicholson, J. M. Drexler, & L. M. Reeves (Eds.), *Foundations of augmented cognition* (4th ed., pp. 183–189). New York, NY: Springer.

Parasuraman, R., Cosenzo, K., & De Visser, E. (2009). Adaptive automation for human supervision of multiple uninhabited vehicles: Effects on change detection, situation awareness, and mental workload. *Military Psychology, 21*, 270–297.

Powers, A., & Kiesler, S. (2006). The advisor robot: Tracing people's mental model from a robot's physical attributes. In *Proceedings of the 2006 ACM Conference on Human-Robot Interaction* (pp. 218–225). New York, NY: Association for Computing Machinery.

Prewett, M. S., Yang, L., Stilson, F. R. B., Gray, A. A., Coovert, M. D., & Burke, J. (2006). The benefits of multi modal information: A meta-analysis comparing visual and visual-tactile feedback. *Proceedings of the 8th International Conference on Mulitmodal Interfaces*, 333–338.

Pynadath, D., & Tambe, M. (2002). An automated teamwork infrastructure for heterogeneous software agents and humans. *Journal of Autonomous Agents and Multi-Agent Systems (JAAMAS): Special Issue on Infrastructure and Requirements for Building Research Grade Multi-Agent Systems, 7*, 71–100.

Rickel, J., & Johnson, W. L. (2002) Extending virtual humans to support team training in virtual reality. In G. Lakemeyer & B. Nebel (Eds.), *Exploring artificial intelligence in the new millennium*. Burlington, MA: Morgan Kaufmann Publishers.

342 • *Theories of Team Cognition*

Salas, E., Dickinson, T., Converse, S., & Tannenbaum, S. (1992). Towards an understanding of team performance and training. In R. Swezey & E. Salas (Eds.), *Teams: Their training and performance* (pp. 3–29). Norwood, NJ: Ablex.

Salas, E., & Fiore, S. (Eds.). (2004). *Team cognition: Understanding the factors that drive process and performance.* Washington, DC: American Psychological Association.

Salas, E., Prince, C., Baker, D. P., & Shrestha, L. (1995). Situation awareness in team performance: Implications for measurement and training. *Human Factors, 37,* 123–136.

Scerri, P., Pynadath, D., Johnson, L., Rosenbloom, P., Schurr, N., & Tambe, M. (2003). A prototype infrastructure for distributed robot-agent-person teams. *Proceedings of International Conference on Autonomous Agents and Multiagent Systems.*

Scerri, P., Pynadath, D., & Tambe, M. (2001). Adjustable autonomy in real-world multi-agent environments. *Proceedings of the International Conference on Autonomous Agents,* 300–307.

Scerri, P., Pynadath, D., & Tambe, M. (2002). Towards adjustable autonomy for the real world. *Journal of Artificial Intelligence Research, 17,* 171–228.

Schurr, N., Marecki, J., Scerri, P., Lewis, P., & Tambe, M. (2005). The DEFACTO system: Training tool for incident commanders. *Proceedings of the 17th Innovative Applications of Artificial Intelligence Conference.*

Sierhuis, M., Bradshaw, J. M., Acquisti, A., van Hoof, R., Jeffers, R., & Uszok, A. (2003). Human-agent teamwork and adjustable autonomy in practice. *Proceedings of the International Symposium on Artificial Intelligence, Robotics and Automation in Space.*

Sims, V., Chin, M., Sushil, D., Barber, D., Ballion, T., Clark, B., et al. (2005). Anthropomorphism of robotic forms: A response to affordances? *Proceedings of the 49th Annual Meeting Human Factors and Ergonomics Society,* 602–605.

Smith-Jentsch, K., Johnson, J., & Payne, S. (1998). Measuring team-related expertise in complex environments. In J. Cannon-Bowers & E. Salas (Eds.), *Decision making under stress: Implications for individual and team training.* Washington, DC: American Psychological Association.

Sofge, D., Trafton, G., Cassimatis, N., Perzanowski, D., Bugajska, M., Adams, W., et al. (2004). Human-robot collaboration and cognition with an autonomous mobile robot. In F. Groen, N. Amato, A. Bonarini, E. Yoshida, & B. Kröse (Eds.), *Proceedings of the 8th Conference on Intelligent Autonomous Systems (IAS-8)* (pp. 80–87). Amsterdam: IOS Press.

Squire, P., Trafton, G., & Parasuraman, R. (2006). Human control of multiple unmanned vehicles: Effects of interface type on execution and task switching times. *Proceedings of the First Annual Conference on Human-Robot Interactions.*

Stasser, G., Stewart, D., & Wittenbaum, G. (1995). Expert roles and information exchange during discussion: The importance of knowing who knows what. *Journal of Experimental Social Psychology, 31,* 244–265.

Stone, P., & Veloso, M. (1999). Task decomposition, dynamic role assignment, and low-bandwidth communication for real-time strategic teamwork. *Artificial Intelligence, 110,* 241–273.

Stubbs, K., Hinds, P., & Wettergreen, D. (2006). Challenges to grounding in human-robot interaction: Sources of errors and miscommunications in remote exploration robotics. *Proceedings of the First Annual Conference on Human-Robot Interactions.*

Sycara, K., Decker, K., Pannu, A., Williamson, M., & Zeng, D. (1996). Distributed intelligent agents. *IEEE Expert Intelligent Systems and Their Applications, 2,* 36–46.

Sycara, K., & Lewis, M. (2004). Integrating agents into human teams. In E. Salas & S. Fiore (Eds.), *Team cognition: Understanding the factors that drive process and performance.* Washington, DC: American Psychological Association.

Sycara, K., Paolucci, M., Giampapa, J., & van Velsen, M. (2003). The RETSINA multiagent infrastructure. *Autonomous Agents and Multi-agent Systems, 7,* 29–48.

Sycara, K., Sadeh-Koniecpol, N., Roth, S., & Fox, M. (1990). An investigation into distributed constraint-directed factory scheduling. *Proceedings of the Sixth IEEE Conference on AI Applications.*

Tambe, M. (1997). Towards flexible teamwork. *Journal of AI Research, 7,* 83–124.

Tambe, M., Shen, W., Mataric, M., Goldberg, D., Modi, P., Qiu, Z., et al. (1999) Teamwork in cyberspace: Using TEAMCORE to make agents team-ready. *Proceedings of AAAI Spring Symposium on Agents in Cyberspace.*

Trafton, J. G., Cassimatis, N. L., Bugajska, M. D., Brock, D. P., Mintz, F. E., & Schultz, A. C. (2005). Enabling effective human-robot interaction using perspective-taking in robots. *IEEE Transactions on Systems Man Cybernetics, 35,* 460–470.

Traum, D., Rickel, J., Gratch, J., & Marsella, S. (2003). Negotiation over tasks in hybrid human-agent teams for simulation-based training. *Proceedings of International Conference on Autonomous Agents and Multiagent Systems (AAMAS).*

Varcholik, P., & Barber, D. (2008). Interactions and training with unmanned systems and the Nintendo Wiimote. *Proceedings of the Interservice Industry Training, Simulation and Education Conference (IITSEC),* Orlando, FL.

Wang, J., Lewis, M., & Scerri, P. (2006). Cooperating robots for search and rescue. *Proceedings of International Conference on Autonomous Agents and Multi-agent Systems (AAMAS).*

Weizenbaum, J. (1966). ELIZA: A computer program for the study of natural language communication between man and machine. *Communications of the Association for Computing Machinery, 9,* 36–45.

Xu, D., Volz, R., Miller, M., & Plymale, J. (2003). Human-agent teamwork for distributed team training. *Proceedings of the 15th IEEE International Conference on Tools with Artificial Intelligence.*

14

Looking at Macrocognition Through a Multimethodological Lens

Michael D. McNeese and Mark S. Pfaff

INTRODUCTION

Since the 1980s, our research groups have actively pursued different angles of team cognition, studied multiple theoretical perspectives of teamwork as emergent within complex environments, observed how teamwork is constrained by context and environment, and developed and tested new intelligent decision aids to improve performance in various ways. This work is structured using two windows of opportunity: (1) research completed prior to 2000 at the Air Force Research Laboratory, Human Engineering Division, Wright-Patterson Air Force Base, Ohio, during which time the first author, Michael D. McNeese, worked as a senior scientist and director of the *Collaborative Systems Technology Laboratory*; and (2) research subsequently conducted at the College of Information Sciences and Technology, The Pennsylvania State University, University Park, Pennsylvania, during which time both authors were part of the *MINDS (Multidisciplinary Initiatives in Naturalistic Decision Systems) Group*. The objective of this chapter is to provide the reader with an interdisciplinary viewpoint of the human, social, and technological significance of teams and team performance within the purview of macrocognition.

Certainly much has been reviewed and published on many aspects of teamwork during this period. The specific intent of this chapter is to provide one view of the meshing of information, technology, work, people, and context in a rough historical pattern through the personal experiences of the authors. So where does one begin? At the beginning, of course.

345

346 • *Theories of Team Cognition*

BACKGROUND OF THE LIVING LABORATORY PERSPECTIVE

Beginning Primitives

Around 1977, McNeese's initial directions and interests in teamwork gravitated toward the integrative aspects of social psychological constructs (e.g., personal space) and environmentally- and ecologically-based design of settings. This interest developed into a research project that determined how different settings within the domain of a university influenced personal space behaviors. The methodological approach of this research used ethnographical analysis of the way people were influenced by the social presence of "others." Clearly this would not be called teamwork by standard definitions used today. *Teamwork* is the "dynamic, simultaneous, and recursive enactment of process mechanisms which inhibit or contribute to team performance or performance outcomes" (Salas, Stagl, Burke, & Goodman, 2007, p. 190). However, there are some basic notions—say primitives—that drove this beginning research. First, there was the idea of *social actors* influencing the behavior of other social actors. This meant that when people were around other people in given situations, their behavior might be altered. Second, the cause for altered behavior in a university setting focused on how different environmental designs (e.g., libraries, student unions) influenced peoples' behavior when the *presence* of the setting was upon them. Thus began an early career with interests in people, design, action, and influences at the social level. This research was conceptually related to the work of Robert Barker and others (see Barker, 1968) and was typically indexed with other work termed *architectural psychology* or *environmental psychology* (Heimstra & McFarling, 1978). Inherent in this early research was the desire to consider the role of ecology, context, and design as related to principles of social interaction. As often cited from William Mace, the request, "Ask not what is inside your head but what your head is inside of," states the case for an ecological imperative (Mace, 1977, p. 43). This early research emphasized how cognition and action are afforded through contextual variants.

Another primitive in this initial research was that of observing dynamic social interaction as it emerged in real-world situations (today, often referred to as situated cognition or distributed cognition; see Brown,

Collins, & Duguid, 1989; Lave & Wenger, 1991). Although we have examined many theoretical positions and parameters during the years, the distributed and situated cognition approaches have been the most pervasive in our work, sustaining a philosophy that successfully integrates ecology with cognitive systems and team activities. This presents an interdisciplinary understanding of teamwork and how to support teamwork through innovation of systems. This framing might best be captured by Lave's explanation, "Cognition observed in everyday practice is distributed, stretched over, not divided, among mind, body, activity, and culturally organized settings" (Lave, 1988, p. 1). The book *New Trends in Cooperative Activities: System Dynamics in Complex Environments* (McNeese, Salas, & Endsley, 2001) has exemplified this broad, integrative approach. The goal of this chapter is to look at how our work in shared cognitive systems research has evolved from historical work at the U.S. Air Force (USAF) to contemporary cases of distributed cognition, while using a Living Laboratory research framework.

Macrocognition

In recent years, the notion of team cognition has received increased attention in the team literature, and various categories have been investigated, including team mental models, transactive memory, and collective learning (e.g., McNeese, Brewer, Jones, & Connors, 2006; McNeese & Rentsch, 2001; Mohammed & Dumville, 2001). Recently, Letsky, Warner, Fiore, Rosen, and Salas (2007) have discussed macrocognition as a form of team cognition operating in problem-solving teams. Specifically, they define macrocognition as the "internalized and externalized high-level mental processes employed by teams to create new knowledge during complex, one-of-a-kind, collaborative problem solving" (Letsky et al., 2007, p. 7). Through the conceptual and empirical efforts of Letsky and his colleagues over the past several years, a model of team collaboration has evolved describing 14 macrocognitive processes across four independent dynamic stages (knowledge construction, collaborative team problem solving, team consensus and outcome, and evaluation and revision).

Although much of our long history of work in team cognition (beginning from McNeese & Brown, 1986; Snyder & McNeese, 1987) connotes both consistency and similarity to the work of Letsky, Warner, Fiore,

348 • *Theories of Team Cognition*

and Smith (2008), it has developed from different primitives. Therein, some contrasts can be drawn. Much of what is presented in this chapter targets ideas that point to the meaning of macrocognition as a nexus for spawning new research studies, developing distributed cognitive support systems, and understanding specific fields of practice. McNeese (1986) used the terms *macrocognition* and *macroawareness* to emphasize that when intelligent systems are designed to support humans, cognition needs to be appreciated and understood in the larger sense-surround it takes place in. More specifically, even though cognitive processes are situated in the head, they are also informed by the environment, technological affordances, and other human actors. Although our original use of the term *macrocognition* emphasized the individual construction of cognition, the transactions and adaptation with the environment to pursue emerging intentions, and the salience of the sense-surround, our present definition has evolved to include two specific theoretical constructs: *perceptual anchors* and *team cognition*. Perceptual anchors tie macrocognitive factors to the ideas of direct perception and how levels of macrocognition are both perceived and understood through repeated pickups of information to construct cognition on-the-fly in context (see McNeese, 2000; Young & McNeese, 1995). This construct is historically related to ecological work previously identified but is also grounded in Bransford's ideas (Bransford & Stein, 1993) about how meaning is constructed through perceptual differentiation as a person contrasts and compares various events and experiences as they pursue emerging intentions. This construct has been enabled in our research programs through provision of accessible video streams, interface visualizations, virtual environments, or geographic mapping of information that assimilates macrocognitive processes with the problems or issues at hand in individual or team work.

When cognition is expanded to the team context, new social dynamics are present that create collaborative aspects of work. Macrocognition hence embodies the context cognition takes when enacted through teamwork, with shared meanings being constructed through joint understanding of situations, circumstances, and events. A significant strand of our work often involves the abstraction, consolidation, access, and recall of these joint constructions in terms of team mental models, team schema (McNeese & Rentsch, 2001; McNeese, Rentsch, & Perusich, 2000), or concept maps (Brewer & McNeese, 2004). The macrocognitive viewpoint is pervasive in almost all of the research reported in this chapter as a general overlay that expresses our theoretical stance in both cognitive science and teamwork.

Living Laboratory Framework

Since the 1980s, the research involving macrocognition, teamwork, social interaction, and real-world situations can be framed through the use of the Living Laboratory framework shown in Figure 14.1 (McNeese, 1996; McNeese, Brewer, et al., 2006). This perspective has been used to conceptually model the objectives and interdisciplinary research initiatives that have been put forward to integrate cognitive science and teamwork understanding. Although our initial exposure to research and development in teamwork and team performance was not cast in this frame, that work contributed to the emergence of this perspective. The "living" component of this framework is a referent to the idea that teams interact with complexity through emergent actions, often as dynamic, living systems constrained by the context they live in. A basic explanation of the Living Laboratory can start from the relationships among theory, problems, and practice. The basic premise within this framework is that problems that are noticed, found, identified, and explored (Bransford & Stein, 1993) can become the basis for research from top-down theoretical and bottom-up practical positions. Problems often emerge in context within a field of practice, and although specific to given situations, they can be informed by theoretical principles and assertions. Problems can be framed and solved

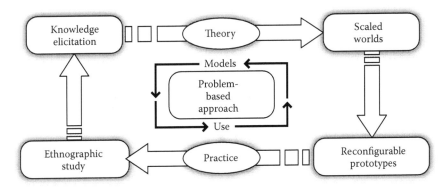

FIGURE 14.1
The contemporary Living Laboratory framework.

350 • *Theories of Team Cognition*

from many perspectives and hence serve as anchors for understanding the world of teamwork.

The activities on the left side of the Living Laboratory in Figure 14.1 tend to have a logical relationship that exists between them in how knowledge elicitation can actively inform what a researcher observes in ethnographic sessions. Elicitation of knowledge is important for acquiring a user's perspective, understanding, or explanation of his or her experiences, cases, and lessons. Just like ethnography, elicitation may come in different forms or techniques, depending on the nature of the research. Knowledge may be obtained from novices or experts and used in different ways to inform scenarios within scaled-world simulations or to become the basis for prototyped designs. Knowing the why, what, and how of people's expertise can become the basis upon which design affordances are implemented. The activities on the right side of the framework represent another logical relationship as they focus on translating knowledge into designs. Although this side deals with people too, it has a distinct relation with technology, as new, emerging technologies are used to build innovations into simulations and introduce new design affordances within prototypes. Part of the Living Laboratory expectation is to produce use-centered technologies that, through repeated tests in a scaled world, represent seasoned designs, which when applied to the field of practice produce real differences in performance. Scaled-world simulations try to bring attributes and processes that exist in real-world situations into the lab but on a "lab-sized world" to study. Simulations like this show what could happen in real-world events and aim to be entirely realistic to the extent they can be practical or safe. Simulations themselves may be vehicles for experts to provide opinions and knowledge about given cases, scenarios, or designs. Hence they can function in the role of a knowledge elicitation exercise and further refine knowledge elicited, albeit in different ways. Simulations have become the means by which we carry out specific experimental designs that test independent variables in realistic and meaningful conditions and scenarios that demonstrate many of the problems extant in a living world of work that teams encounter.

In many ways, *designs via prototypes* allow us to express previous Living Laboratory activity outcomes in a highly tangible fashion and provide an interface, system, or tool that exhibits characteristics of expert knowledge, represents a theoretical view, and/or addresses a challenging problem. We prefer to have prototypes that can first be housed in our simulations

Looking at Macrocognition Through a Multimethodological Lens • 351

for refinement and testing prior to design interventions in practice. Prototypes contain conceptualizations directly distilled from ethnography, knowledge elicitation, theory, and simulation. They signal an attempt to influence team performance through a distinct means. Whether they are effective is an empirical question that needs to be assessed within specified contexts and constraints. Designs evolve via research activities with end-users or study participants and hence represent an accumulated whole. Prototypes can incorporate the latest state-of-the-art technologies and represent various degrees of sophistication.

The four activities of the Living Laboratory can work interchangeably or in succession, depending on the needs of the researcher. Knowledge elicitation, ethnography, simulation, and design have been arranged to provide for a maximally evolved understanding of the nexus of information, technology, people, and context within team performance.

HISTORICAL PRECEDENCE OF TEAMWORK RESEARCH IN MILITARY OPERATIONS

Warfare is often defined as acts of opposition between convening forces. Opposition can involve the weakening or breakdown in the opposing force's power or will. Strategies and tactics are introduced to facilitate breakdowns sooner. The strategies and tactics involve highly complex missions consisting of weapons, support systems, and various resources all of which require logistical movements in constrained conditions. Within missions there are many forms of systems supporting other systems. Warfare creates complexity which has components that are ill-defined, dynamic, changing, unanticipated, and fluidic. Mission plans change as a function of (a) threats induced by the enemy, (b) what is known or not known about opposing forces (i.e., intelligence), (c) consideration of environmental instabilities (e.g., terrain, weather, night operations), and (d) remaining resources and supplies, to mention a few factors that are traded-off as solutions are imparted. Warfare, however, is highly enabled and constrained by humans working together at various levels of an operation. Humans form teams which in turn are combined to form larger entities (e.g., battalions). Teamwork is everywhere as battle management plans are carried out by many teams in differing contexts. As mentioned, warfare occurs when opposing forces engage in battle. A team's performance is the measure of its progress and effectiveness as engaged in a targeted mission. However, team

352 • *Theories of Team Cognition*

performance in the grander scheme relates to how a team's effort is beneficial in defeating the threat. Hence, success in warfare is invariably related to how well humans function in teams and this effort is entwined within the overall system of systems campaign to subdue opposing force activities. (McNeese, 1998, p. 161)

When McNeese began employment at the USAF Medical Research Laboratory, his primary research responsibility was to study cognitive processes involved in Command, Control, and Communications (C^3), in particular teamwork, technologies, and processes related to C^3. This chapter is designed to review these topics at two distinct phases: (1) critical research that evolved from the historical precedence of the North American Aerospace Defense Command (NORAD) C^3 work, and more recently, (2) contemporary research that engages emergency crisis management and shared cognitive systems. Although this occurred in the 1980s, the seminal activities inherent in the Living Laboratory view provided the framework to address research problems in teamwork and teamwork supported by cognitive aids.

Pre-2000 Historical Case: The NORAD Human Factors Initiative

During the mid-1980s, one of the USAF research lab's projects was to improve the NORAD site as well as other C^3 work at differing command posts. The NORAD work was initiated through the C^3 Operator Performance Engineering (COPE) program. This was a prominent program that was set up to assess and evaluate state-of-the-art technologies to use in improving NORAD performance (individual and team) and developing decision-making scenarios. From this case, we can see how the Living Laboratory framework can be used to make sense of disparate research elements. Because much of the emphasis in the NORAD facility focused on large group displays to improve team performance, these provide a logical beginning. In fact, the field of practice itself in this case is highly intertwined with the problem state. The problem state included not really understanding what the relevant *use* of this emerging technology was in the course of operations. Stated another way, it was not really clear how displays were useful for teamwork. This is an excellent example of technologies being developed simply because they could

Looking at Macrocognition Through a Multimethodological Lens • 353

(techno-centricity), but users in practice were unsure of what advantages they really provided. Therein, the core of our research focus was to determine (a) how team performance developed in NORAD, (b) how the large group display might enhance this performance, and (c) how the built and contextual environments influence use of the technology and team performance.

The *reconfigurable prototype design and technology* element of the Living Laboratory hence became the first focal point. One could think of this as the objective of determining the social impacts of technology on team performance. This begins the utilization of theories that underline small group productivity within a set context (e.g., Hackman & Morris, 1975; Roby, 1968), wherein technology persists as a strong element of that context. The state-of-the-art technologies that were applicable at the time were the use of large group displays in command posts and then, in the later 1980s, the use of video teleconferencing technologies. What we discovered was that use of these kinds of technologies is inextricably coupled with social interaction, information sharing, and other elements of practice that coincide in the context. This discovery in essence afforded an understanding that "cognition in the wild" (Hutchins, 1995, p. 370) and other theories providing a strong contexualistic overture to cognition (e.g., situated cognition, distributed cognition) could form the focus required for a comprehensive understanding of the NORAD field of practice. The social impacts of technology objectives necessarily ascended to theoretical points of view within the Living Laboratory in order to take a comprehensive view of what was going on in a complex context.

The laboratory purchased an advanced large group display that was deemed most useful wherein it was tested for luminance, display, and human factors prior to being enlisted in experimental studies (McNeese & Katz, 1987). Various people on our investigation team observed and interviewed operators during trips to the NORAD command, therein implementing the ethnographical and knowledge elicitation elements of the Living Laboratory. As we began to look at the real-world practice, a deeper understanding of problems, use, and practice was derived. This would be the case throughout our research into the 1990s in various domains beyond the NORAD field of practice. This coincides with our first study investigating personal space impacts within environments and places ecological constraints as highly important within the Living Laboratory framework.

354 • *Theories of Team Cognition*

One should note that this worldview aligns with other systems-level approaches that emphasize the necessity of ecological–contextualistic impetus in real work, including approaches that are both more distant (Gibson, 1979; Tolman & Brunswick, 1935) and more recent, such as cognitive engineering (Rasmussen, Pejtersen, & Goodstein, 1994), situated cognition (Lave & Wenger, 1991), and contextualism (Hoffman & Nead, 1983). In fact, the real-world practice provided a kind of "ground truth" that theoretical perspectives could be compared against. This was especially true in McNeese's own theoretical ideas about situated cognition, problem solving, and the necessity of perceptual anchors to uncover meaning in teamwork (McNeese, 2000). Perceptually anchored interfaces would allow users to see a visualization of complex phenomena, hence allowing a more direct perceptual basis for exploring problems and reasoning about solutions. Within complex contexts, these types of interfaces provide a common operational picture (McNeese, Pfaff, et al., 2006) for teams sharing information and developing joint solutions. Out of real *problems*, as defined by various users within different functions or roles, came the basis for thinking about causality, explanation (i.e., the limitations and constraints embedded in the work context whether it emerged from human, technological, and/or spatial–logistical factors), and outcomes. By analyzing this basis in depth, experimenters could generate relevant hypotheses for experimentation, test designs of new innovative technologies that would remove problematic limitations, adapt performance in positive ways, and devise scenarios useful for incorporation within scaled worlds. Therein, the reflectivity from practice to problems to theory and back again provided impetus for imagination and creation that allowed the work to go far beyond the given problem.

The information from these reflections formulated additional problem states and facilitated further study of newer computer-based interaction techniques such as speech recognition, computer workstation design, and environmental factors such as noise and lighting. However, the main focus was the intersection of social and cognitive psychology and large-scaled displays as they affected team performance (McNeese & Brown, 1986). As we started to look at this intersection, we reviewed a number of theoretical positions and frameworks that could inform experiments wherein the use of displays (both small and large in size) and the distributed location of team members might influence performance. Many of the theoretical positions were referential to basic ideas underlying social interaction and became

Looking at Macrocognition Through a Multimethodological Lens • 355

the basis for more exploration of contemporary theories. For example, in the paper by McNeese and Brown (1986), these theories were reviewed as potentially applicable to the work in team decision making. As the NORAD initiative began to propagate across these Living Laboratory elements, some of the first studies implemented began to assess the differences between collocated versus distributed teamwork and look at the role of technologies to support cognitive understanding, situation awareness, and decision analysis. All of this resulted in what we might now call "concurrent spiraling," where mutual informative activities in the Living Laboratory approach result in innovation in theory, simulation, and technology expansions.

This demonstrates the holistic, integrative aspects of using this kind of framework wherein exploration and discovery represent core values that propel both science and technology for a given domain of interest. The spinoffs with respect to *technology* itself sustained laboratory specialization beyond large group displays into ventures such as collaborative technologies, computer-supported cooperative work, video teleconferencing, virtual interfaces, data walls, unified surfaces, and affective computing for teamwork, to name a few (McNeese, Pfaff, et al., 2006). However, the *scaled-world simulation* component of the work became the bedrock that congealed other elements together to produce explication of theories, different types of technological advancements, design guidelines, additional knowledge elicitation, and so on. These vectors were the nerve center for work that still exists today, albeit in different forms, venues, and applications (see the section on contemporary cases later in this chapter). The early NORAD initiative became the basis for several unique scaled-world simulations that enabled technology integration and development as well as the application and testing of team decision-making theories and hypotheses. The theory and hypotheses often drove the experiments, but the simulation made it possible to bring elements of practice into the lab to examine. By examining results and using them as evaluative feedback for improvement of theory and technology, scaled worlds became much of the heart of our work, as they still are today.

Scaled-World Simulation

Scaled-world development became one of the best outcomes of initially getting involved with the NORAD project because it laid the foundation for the Team Resource Allocation Problem (TRAP) simulation (Brown & Leupp, 1985; Kimble & McNeese, 1987; Wilson, McNeese, &

356 • *Theories of Team Cognition*

Brown, 1987), which began investigations into small-group productivity theory and provided a theoretical basis for several different collaborative work simulations developed from 1983 to 2000 that enabled research to expand significantly across *team situation awareness* (C³ Interactive Task for Identifying Emerging Situations [CITIES]; Wellens & Ergener, 1988), *distributed decision making* (DDD; Kleinman, Pattipati, Luh, & Serfaty, 1992; McNeese et al., 2000), *collective induction* (Jasper; Cognition and Technology Group at Vanderbilt, 1992; McNeese, 2000) and *affective collaborative computing* (Hudlicka, 2003; Hudlicka & McNeese, 2002). As mentioned, this provided much of the foundation for continuing to make scaled worlds prominent parts of the Living Laboratory approach, which continued for contemporary cases inclusive of newer simulation environments while at Pennsylvania State University, including NeoCITIES (McNeese et al., 2005) and Three-Block Challenge (Fan et al., 2005). Table 14.1 provides a summary of this research as it relates to theory, technology, application domains, and models.

TABLE 14.1

Scaled-World Simulations at U.S. Air Force Human Engineering Division I (1983–2000)

Scaled World	Context	Theory	Model	Contribution
TRAP	NORAD C³	Integrating information theory, distributed team decision making	Math	Human factors considerations for large group displays
CITIES	Crisis management integrating fire and police teams	Information richness, psychological distance, team situation awareness	Expert systems	Effects of communication bandwidth on distributed decision making
Jasper[a]	Crisis planning and response	Analogical transfer, perceptual anchors, collective induction	Problem-space objects	Impact of sociocognitive factors on cooperative learning
DDD[b]	AWACS air crew battle management	Team mental models, fuzzy set theory in team decision making	Fuzzy cognitive maps	Teamwork aids for mediating information and supporting shared mental models

[a] Adapted from Cognition and Technology Group at Vanderbilt (1997).
[b] Adapted from Aptima, Inc.

Looking at Macrocognition Through a Multimethodological Lens • 357

The use of the Living Laboratory framework produced other concurrent spirals that resulted in new methodological and representational formats enabling both the study of teamwork and possibilities for collaborative understanding among teams. The foremost example of this was work adapted from conceptualization and graphical–semantic knowledge as revealed through concept mapping (Nosek & McNeese, 1997). Although our lab initially used concept maps to acquire knowledge from fighter pilots and apply this knowledge in the design of interfaces (McNeese et al., 1990), we eventually adapted concept mapping for use with teams (McNeese, Zaff, Brown, Citera, & Wellens, 1992). Additional work in this area was done with fuzzy cognitive maps, which were also applied in complex team operations with another simulation involving Scud missile defense developed by Perusich and McNeese (2006). We subsequently have used the fuzzy cognitive maps knowledge representation as the basis for a team decision aid (Jones, Jefferson, Connors, McNeese, & Obieta, 2005).

In summary, the NORAD initiative resulted in a wide flurry of activities that advanced teamwork and team performance in various ways, many of which were unexpected and led to new theoretical ideas and measures and technological outputs. The problems within the collaborative context of NORAD became seeds that developed broadly across many interdisciplinary junctures and continue to be facile in contemporary team research. At this point, the chapter will take a look at more contemporary work that continues previous strands of research.

CONTEMPORARY ADVANCEMENT OF MACROCOGNITION AND TEAM RESEARCH

The historical case of the NORAD human factors initiative, along with subsequent team performance research at the USAF Research Laboratory, provided foundations and specializations of research that have impacted and continue to inform current contemporary team research cases that intersect information, technology, theory, and context, albeit through new passages. Similar to the historical case, current research may be viewed through the Living Laboratory lens, as contemporary work seems to be fueled by the scaled-world simulation and the power of contextual fields of

358 • *Theories of Team Cognition*

practice. We have strengthened the left corridor of the Living Laboratory by enhancing interviews, ethnography, and cognitive walkthrough work to help in the development of scaled-world scenarios and tasks and seed ideas for technological innovation. The ecological underpinnings and situated elements of the environment continue to be strongly emphasized as being highly influential in determining emerging team activities and awareness. One difference is that for certain studies, the emphasis may not be on developing a new simulation but rather on adapting scenarios to fit a client–server architecture that provides interfaces and resources to create new applications as necessary. Although this approach may not fit every opportunity that exists, it does provide leverage and enablement in contexts that involve collaboration, team resource allocation, and execution. It is also worth emphasizing that the simulation technology and flexible programming environment have facilitated scaled-world adaption much more quickly than during the 1990s, affording the development and insertion of decision aids, interfaces, and experimental measures in a much more effective orchestration.

Table 14.2 provides newer areas of focus (since McNeese has been on the faculty at Pennsylvania State University) that show the evolution from previous historical strands. A review of the contemporary case reveals that the primary driving impetus is the context of *emergency crisis management*. This has been fueled by three factors: (1) the collaborative activities and tragic events associated with the September 11, 2001, terrorist attack, along with other recent disasters and terrorist acts that have since occurred; (2) the high connectivity between C^3, command posts, crisis management, terrorism, intelligence analyst work, and subsequent emphasis on this kind of research by the Department of Homeland Security and other agencies; and (3) continuation of previous work history in battle management and decision aids (McNeese et al., 2000), knowledge management (Nosek & McNeese, 1997), and knowledge elicitation/integration (McNeese, Zaff, Citera, Brown, & Whitaker, 1995; Zaff, McNeese, & Snyder, 1993). When these factors are combined together, the desire and ability to pursue work in emergency crisis management seems like a natural evolution. One should note though that we have continued specific C^3 work, with the research involving the development and use of the R-CAST agent architecture as an intelligent support system for decision making and information seeking in Army C^3 (Fan et al., 2009).

TABLE 14.2
The Contemporary Case of Scaled-World Simulations

Scaled World	Context	Theory	Model	Contribution
Jasper II[a]	Crisis planning and response	Analogical transfer, perceptual anchors, distributed cognition, hidden knowledge profiles	Problem-space objects	Utility of perceptual anchors in overcoming hidden knowledge profiles
NeoCITIES	Geocollaborative crisis management of teams	Perceptual anchors, distributed cognition, team situation awareness, hidden knowledge, temporal team mental models	Scoring model	Multiple perspectives on team behaviors, group decision making, and system design for complex collaboration
Three-Block Challenge	Army C[3]I	Recognition-primed decision making, human–agent collaboration	Artificial intelligence model	Effectiveness of recognition-primed decision–enabled agents for information sharing in complex situations

[a] Adapted from Cognition and Technology Group at Vanderbilt (1997).

Using the Living Laboratory framework to capture progressions in research activity, much of the current focus in teamwork is predicated on problems dealing with the changing sense of events in crises and situations. Types of problems typically experienced by teams in real-world contexts include extreme time pressure; information overloading; unattained levels of interdependency; poor establishment of common ground; shared work that is full of tensions, emotions, conflicts, and stress; multiethnic teamwork bound by cultural beliefs; hidden knowledge that is often not communicated; and multiorganization constraints that decrease motivation, to name a few. Our research has dealt with specific fields of practice, particularly emergency medicine, hurricane crisis management, image analyst work, intelligence analyst work, collaborative police operations, 911 call centers, emergency operations centers, tsunami disaster management, and homeland security preparations and exercises at local, state, and national levels (McNeese, Pfaff, et al., 2006). Many of these domains depend on the necessity of having command posts, using distributed mobile operations, establishing team situation awareness, creating a common operational picture, engaging in team resource allocation, information seeking, and making interdependent decisions that affect team members in different ways. The ethnography and knowledge elicitation components of the Living Laboratory have been in play to help researchers understand much of the constraints and technological factors that intersect work. We have continued work with previous methods (e.g., concept mapping) but developed new temporal and procedural variations as well (Brewer & McNeese, 2004; Glantz, 2006).

Although one can draw an indirect connection among these domains and fields of practice, the research mentioned in the historical case also provided some distinct direct points of transference for current research. This is evidenced by examining the scaled-world simulation component of the Living Laboratory, particularly for the CITIES simulation. The simulation directly examines distributed cognition and situation awareness within crisis scenarios wherein teams must assess problem situations before constructing joint, interdependent solution paths. Because we were already working in crisis management, in addition to C^3, it was an easy transition to extend the CITIES simulation to a new platform for supporting more complex team structures and richer user interactions. This became the NeoCITIES simulation.

NeoCITIES is a computer-based, scaled-world simulation that mimics several aspects of distributed emergency crisis management work and can emulate several different kinds of events through active design of scenarios representative of real-world situations. It extends the original CITIES task (Wellens & Ergener, 1988). NeoCITIES participants engage in data gathering, analysis, coordination, and communication activities, which can range from moderate in pace and complexity to overloaded and time pressured, requiring divided attention and frequent task switching. The group consists of a team of teams: three dyads in which each member has a distinct role. This experimental framework provides a holistic assessment of distributed macrocognitive processes through collection of real-time performance data, such as timeliness and accuracy of responses to events or detection of emerging patterns (Jones, 2006), tool use patterns that also branch into usability data on the tools and affordances provided (Balakrishnan, Pfaff, McNeese, &

Looking at Macrocognition Through a Multimethodological Lens • 361

Adibhatla, 2009), and analysis of the team's communications during the simulation (Pfaff, 2009). Furthermore, this framework provides an opportunity to explore the impact of training methods on team mental models and performance (Hamilton, 2009) and interventions to manage information overload (Hellar, 2009). Details of the underlying fieldwork (Terrell, McNeese, & Jefferson, 2004), technical development (McNeese et al., 2005), and game play of NeoCITIES (Jones, 2006) have already been published. NeoCITIES has advanced the exploration and testing of theories involving team situation awareness, information sharing, team mental models, perceptual anchors, and mood induction. It has been particularly adaptive and specifically allows for team and task interdependency and cognition situated in the context of scenario-driven events and promotes shared teamwork to solve integrated problems. Because the studies that have been conducted are specifically designed to look at teams interacting through distributed means, NeoCITIES is necessarily a vehicle for studying various orchestrations of distributed cognition.

In addition to the use of NeoCITIES, we constructed a new simulation architecture (R-CAST Three-Block Challenge) for the U.S. Army that emulates C^3 team interdependence while encountering multicontext team decision making within urban warfare scenarios. Fan et al. (2009) used the information and knowledge obtained from users, operators, and analysts familiar with various contextual variations, critical incidents, and unusual circumstances to design simulated scenarios that were more realistic with respect to context, situation, and team cognition. This research case is especially innovative because it is an example of the use of intelligent agents as teammates to assist in information seeking and decision making when information overload may cause stressful situations, in particular when team members must consider multiple contexts simultaneously. This genre of research continues the confluence of intelligent systems as one means of addressing cognitive and coordination constraints where teams are apt to require adaptive flexibility to solve problems.

Table 14.2 reveals that the current research, theory, and technologies appear to be more highly integrated across simulations. It is also true that the theory and technology assessment may be transferable across simulation platforms (e.g., the use of intelligent agents within both NeoCITIES and Three-Block Challenge), which helps to inform overall theoretical

362 • *Theories of Team Cognition*

perspectives regarding multihuman, multiagent problem solving. One can also see that *distributed cognition, situation awareness, team mental models, perceptually anchored cooperative learning,* and *naturalistic decision making* provide the theoretical substrates of current distributed shared cognition systems research. These theoretical views are a small subset of contemporary team research in general, but they define the niche our research group is working within. Conceptually, this niche has inroads that lead to computer-supported cooperative work (CSCW), human–computer interaction, and artificial intelligence. Emphasis continues to be placed on the ecological considerations and the context-aware character of team performance. Furthermore, the Three-Block Challenge research shows the necessity of being able to consider multiple entwined contexts during the course of decision making, underlining the idea that highly functioning teams need to have the means for flexible control, along with adaptive exchange of information, as situations rapidly change state.

Having said all of this, there are two *major changes* in the direction of team performance research in contrast to earlier historical cases that should be highlighted. First, almost all of our simulations and reconfigurable designs now place emphasis on the role of geospatial and geotemporal aspects of context as team decision making evolves. This places a new understanding on what context is and how it figures into designing systems that support distributed work. Interactive maps within interfaces, geographic information systems with three-dimensional maps (Balakrishnan et al., 2009), and new transactive memory systems (Adibhatla, Shapiro, McNeese, & Balakrishnan, 2009) provide visual-spatial representations of time, distance, speed, tracks, and rates in relation to locales, space, sites, places, buildings, artifacts, or events. These tools can reflect a lot of logistical, practical, and useful information when teams engage in problem solving. The continuing development of the NeoCITIES simulation is geared toward active use of such entities within the overall group interface.

Second, research involving NeoCITIES, Jasper, and Jasper II (an advanced orchestration of the Jasper task that provides a collaborative infrastructure for distributed, shared cognition as an overlay on top of the Jasper video) over the last several years has investigated distributed cognition and management of knowledge among team members especially when there is *hidden knowledge* that a given team member possesses (or discovers). This spans along the lines of earlier research involving hidden knowledge from Stasser and colleagues (see Stasser & Titus, 2003) that suggests people do not always share unique knowledge, but frequently discuss only knowledge considered to be common or shared. When situations demand integration of hidden or unique knowledge to produce the best solutions, keeping knowledge hidden can result in team performance deficits. Hidden knowledge within NeoCITIES is accomplished when (a) a member is given knowledge that is unique to his or her role but is useful to share for overall problem-decision space, and (b) during the course of problem solving, a member is supplied with information that was previously hidden that, if used, could alter problem solving, decision making, and resource allocations. For example, with NeoCITIES, we have introduced sets of cues (that are distributed across members or roles) that progressively show indications of terrorist activities approaching a college campus (e.g., an early cue might be that a known terrorist is spotted at an area airport). One of the things that can be measured then is how quickly a team (or team of teams) can develop a common operational picture and act on this new knowledge based on the number of cues introduced, the temporal frequency of the cues, and how the amount of cues are distributed across the team. This activity represents joint pattern recognition but requires communication and coordination of resources as well, so it introduces multiple elements of complexity. An example of hidden knowledge experiments is used within the Jasper task (see Jefferson, Ferzandi, & McNeese, 2004).

We have experimentally assessed and evaluated many theoretical foundations of distributed cognition, but have also used these theoretical approaches to ground the development of collaborative technologies and intelligent systems within the scaled-world simulations. Although there is not enough space to go into all of these studies and developments, we will select one example, "Effects of Mood and Stress on Group Communication and Performance in a Simulated Task Environment" (Pfaff, 2008). This was a dissertation project that examined the impact and interactions among some of the psychological factors especially relevant to teams working in technologically complex environments, as provided by the NeoCITIES scenario. The next section of this chapter is designed to provide the reader with a more specific look at current research that exemplifies a shared cognitive systems approach within the NeoCITIES scaled world.

364 • *Theories of Team Cognition*

AN EXAMPLE OF CURRENT MACROCOGNITION RESEARCH IN THE LIVING LABORATORY

The third full study using the NeoCITIES simulation was more theoretical in nature than the first two, which focused more on validating the scaled world and the aids and affordances embedded within it. This study, conducted by the second author, Mark Pfaff, delved deeply in the area of decision making under stress to explore possible mediating or moderating relationships between stress and mood among team members. Here, the software was extended to integrate psychological manipulations and measures that induced controlled mood and stress states and administered psychological assessments of the participants at specific times during the simulation.

Armed with a data set of baseline performance parameters from the preceding two studies, we arranged to use six-person teams from an undergraduate course on human–computer interaction for a semester-long series of experimental sessions to determine the effects of mood and stress on team cognition in this simulated task environment (Pfaff, 2008; Pfaff & McNeese, 2010). By employing stable teams over the course of several weeks, we were better able to approximate the emergent dynamics of real teams. This is something that is difficult to create in one-shot studies of "team" behavior, because an ad hoc group of people is not necessarily a *team* with common goals, mutual accountability, and a shared history (Brannick & Prince, 1997).

Over the course of several weeks, these teams went through multiple NeoCITIES simulations. Counterbalanced happy and sad mood inductions were applied with the presence or absence of two different stressors: time pressure and performance pressure. Data were collected from multiple sources, including text chat messages within and between dyads, time-stamped resource allocation actions, errors, and per-dyad performance scores based on how successfully their events were resolved. Pre- and posttask assessments of mood and stress states were recorded from individual self-reported surveys.

Results indicated that time pressure and performance pressure stressors each interacted differently with changes in mood. Under conditions of high time pressure, a *mediating* relationship was found showing that this stressor diminished performance not directly, but by increasing negative

Looking at Macrocognition Through a Multimethodological Lens • 365

affect, which then led to a decline in dyad performance. However, the motivating effect of the performance pressure stressor was *moderated* by affect. Teams in the sad mood condition showed no response to increased performance pressure, whereas those in the happy mood were propelled to significantly higher levels of task performance. Text chat logs revealed that mood and stress altered team communication behaviors in ways that significantly impacted team perspective and information sharing (Pfaff, 2009).

In summary, the NeoCITIES simulation affords two essential factors for successful research on team cognition. The first is an engaging real-time user experience for both novice users and domain experts. The second is a thorough methodology for precisely controlling task conditions and recording meaningful data at nearly every level of user engagement, from individual user interface actions to the swarm of messages and interactions flowing between team members.

CONCLUSIONS AND FUTURE WORK

As we continue exploring elements of the Living Laboratory using unique fields of practice, we are coming to understand team cognition in differing ways. One of the difficult aspects of this learning is the integration element, wherein the design of new technologies reflects iterative learning and holds the promise to make cognition more fluent while affording distributed work practice. As we reflect on our work in team performance, there are some lessons learned worth mentioning. The following areas have all been noted in other venues, but their joint and mutual effects on research perhaps necessitate more control or awareness.

First, what is demanded in the research paradigm is important for team performance. Moderators we found salient include:

- Required levels of interdependence of team members: We first noted that the information sharing and reasoning required in the TRAP scaled world developed strong interdependence among team members. We have tried to keep this element active across our simulations to underline this necessary element of team cognition.

- Salient information representation and information display: Again, this was first noticed in TRAP and continues to specify many subtleties of technology prototypes and simulation design. Elements of perceptual interfaces, transactive memory, and fuzzy cognitive maps trace their preeminence to this basic concern that is important not only for theory and simulations but also for fields of practice.
- Task complexity (multistep solutions, ill-defined emergent context): One of the troubles we discovered early on was that many experimental results were for "toy problems" that did not have complex, emerging elements in them. In turn, findings were often of little value when scaled up to real-world contexts. This provided determination to create scaled worlds that could simulate wicked problems that mimicked real-world contexts that would afford broader generalizations. As a result, most of our simulations are developed with experts to make the scaled world as realistic as possible.
- Degree of training necessary for complex scenarios: Because a lot of team cognition is especially predicated on the level of learning assimilated and the degree of training provided, it is no surprise that training is a primary factor in many of the experiments that have taken place. This places much value on conducting pilot studies that assess the thresholds of learning that are required before participants can be involved in the actual experiment. This is just as important when considering a new interface, decision aid, or technology because it is a unique aspect of the social impacts of a technology.

Second, multiple measures for various sociocognitive factors are important to capture. Methods that have been effective include protocol analysis, speech acts (frequency and duration), speed–accuracy trade-offs, problem space analysis, and complex task outcome scores.

Lastly, there are significant conceptual differences between team cognition, team situation awareness, and team performance. For example:

- An increase in team situation awareness does not necessarily mean an increase in performance.
- Individual differences do count in teams and can influence results across different tasks.

- Collaborative technologies help teams, but beware of trade-offs related to group process. Individuals working alone use such technologies differently than face-to-face teams do together.
- Theoretical positions need more focus and respect for the role of context.

Currently our work focuses on leveraging new group interfaces that allow teams to have greater understanding of all the constraints that they have to assess and act on within a set time–space continuum (interfaces that actively afford perceiving and learning emerging contexts). Coincident with the crisis management focus are the elements of contextual stress, anxiety, and moods that can enhance or detract from team performance. The recent research example described earlier specifically looks at these topics within the NeoCITIES simulation while also considering individual differences in team members. Although we will continue with lab studies, an alternate goal is using the university campus as a Living Laboratory for testing distributed teams in scenarios that use mobile personal digital assistants, distributed cognition that develops over time with observation, and adaptive group interfaces designed for various roles across multiple strategic locations. Within these real-world scenarios, we can observe natural constraints and barriers to how a common operational picture develops and what types of collaborative technology work are needed to respond to planning, intervention, or operational readiness. Certainly such contexts are extreme examples of how the psychological and affective elements of crisis management need to be integrated with the technical and infrastructural elements to equate to success. Implementation of this research is under consideration for various realistic scenarios that involve potential terrorist or natural disaster plots. This gives a new, broader definition to applying the Living Laboratory but places context at the heart of teamwork as it should be.

REFERENCES

Adibhatla, V., Shapiro, A., McNeese, M. D., & Balakrishnan, B. (2009). Design and development of a transactive memory system prototype for geocollaborative crisis management. In *Proceedings of the 53rd Annual Meeting of the Human Factors and Ergonomics Society* (pp. 389–393). Santa Monica, CA: Human Factors and Ergonomics Society.

368 • *Theories of Team Cognition*

Balakrishnan, B., Pfaff, M. S., McNeese, M. D., & Adibhatla, V. (2009). NeoCITIES Geo-tools: Assessing impact of perceptual anchoring and spatially annotated chat on geo collaboration. In *Proceedings of the 53rd Annual Meeting of the Human Factors and Ergonomics Society* (pp. 294–298). Santa Monica, CA: Human Factors and Ergonomics Society.

Barker, R. G. (1968). *Ecological psychology: Concepts and methods for studying the environment of human behavior.* Palo Alto, CA: Stanford University Press.

Brannick, M. T., & Prince, C. (1997). An overview of team performance and measurement. In M. T. Brannick, E. Salas, & C. Prince (Eds.), *Team performance assessment and measurement: Theory, methods, and applications* (pp. 3–16). Mahwah, NJ: Lawrence Erlbaum Associates.

Bransford, J. D., & Stein, B. S. (1993). *The ideal problem solver: A guide for improving thinking, learning, and creativity* (2nd ed.). New York, NY: Freeman & Co.

Brewer, I., & McNeese, M. D. (2004). Expanding concept mapping to address spatio-temporal dimensionality. *Proceedings of the First International Conference on Concept Mapping. Concept Maps: Theory, Methodology, Technology, 1,* 101–107.

Brown, C. E., & Leupp, D. G. (1985). *Team performance with large and small screen displays* (Publication No. AAMRL-TR-85-033). Wright-Patterson Air Force Base, OH: Armstrong Aerospace Medical Research Laboratory.

Brown, J. S., Collins, A., & Duguid, P. (1989). Situated cognition and the culture of learning. *Educational Researcher, 18,* 32–42.

Cognition and Technology Group at Vanderbilt. (1992). The Jasper series as an example of anchored instruction: Theory, program description, and assessment data. *Educational Psychologist, 27,* 2–10.

Cognition and Technology Group at Vanderbilt. (1997). *The Jasper Project: Lessons in curriculum, instruction, assessment, and professional development.* Mahwah, NJ: Lawrence Erlbaum Associates.

Fan, X., McNeese, M. D., Sun, B., Hanratty, T., Allender, L., & Yen, J. (2009). Human-agent collaboration for time-stressed multi-context decision making. *IEEE Transactions on Systems, Man, and Cybernetics, Part A, 40,* 306–320.

Fan, X., Sun, S., Sun, B., Airy, G., McNeese, M., Yen, J., et al. (2005). Collaborative RPD-enabled agents assisting the three-block challenge in command and control in complex and urban terrain. *Proceedings of the Conference on Behavior Representation in Modeling and Simulation (BRIMS),* 113–123.

Gibson, J. J. (1979). *The ecological approach to visual perception.* Boston, MA: Houghton Mifflin.

Glantz, E. J. (2006). *Challenges supporting cognitive activities in dynamic work environments: Application to police domain.* Unpublished doctoral dissertation, The Pennsylvania State University, University Park.

Hackman, J. R., & Morris, C. G. (1975). Group tasks, group interaction process, and group performance effectiveness: A review and proposed integration. In L. L. Beckowitz (Ed.), *Advances in experimental social psychology* (Vol. 8, pp. 47–101). New York, NY: Academic Press.

Hamilton, K. (2009). *The effect of team training strategies on team mental model formation and team performance under routine and non-routine environmental conditions.* Doctoral dissertation, The Pennsylvania State University, University Park. Retrieved June 1, 2010, from http://gradworks.umi.com/33/80/3380911.html

Heimstra, N. W., & McFarling, F. H. (1978). *Environmental psychology* (2nd ed.). Monterey, CA: Brooks/Cole Publishing Company.

Looking at Macrocognition Through a Multimethodological Lens • 369

Hellar, D. B. (2009). *An investigation of data overload in team-based distributed cognition systems.* Doctoral dissertation, The Pennsylvania State University, University Park. Retrieved June 1, 2010, from http://gradworks.umi.com/33/80/3380915.html

Hoffman, R. R., & Nead, J. M. (1983). General contextualism, ecological science and cognitive research. *The Journal of Mind and Behavior, 4,* 507–559.

Hudlicka, E. (2003). To feel or not to feel: The role of affect in human-computer interaction. *International Journal of Human-Computer Studies, 59,* 1–32.

Hudlicka, E., & McNeese, M. D. (2002). User affective and belief states: Assessment and user interface adaptation. *Journal of User Modeling and User Adapted Interaction, 12,* 1–47.

Hutchins, E. (1995). *Cognition in the wild.* Cambridge, MA: MIT Press.

Jefferson, T., Jr., Ferzandi, L., & McNeese, M. D. (2004). Impact of hidden profiles on distributed cognition in spatially distributed decision-making teams. In *Proceedings of the 48th Annual Meeting of the Human Factors and Ergonomics Society.* Santa Monica CA: Human Factors and Ergonomics Society.

Jones, R. E. T. (2006). *The development of an emergency crisis management simulation to assess the impact a fuzzy cognitive map decision-aid has on team cognition and team decision-making.* Doctoral dissertation, The Pennsylvania State University, University Park. Retrieved August 24, 2007, from http://gradworks.umi.com/32/31/3231841.html

Jones, R. E. T., Jefferson, T., Jr., Connors, E. S., McNeese, M. D., & Obieta, J. F. (2005). *Exploring fuzzy cognitive maps for use in a crisis-management simulation.* Paper presented at the Conference on Behavior Representation in Modeling and Simulation, Universal City, CA.

Kimble, C., & McNeese, M. D. (1987). *Emergent leadership and team effectiveness on a team resource allocation task* (Publication No. AAMRL-87-TR-064). Wright-Patterson Air Force Base, OH: Armstrong Aerospace Medical Research Laboratory.

Kleinman, D., Pattipati, K., Luh, P., & Serfaty, D. (1992). Mathematical models of team performance: A distributed decision-making approach. In R. Swezey & E. Salas (Eds.), *Teams: Their training and performance* (pp. 177–218). Norwood, NJ: Ablex Publishing Corporation.

Lave, J. (1988). *Cognition in practice: Mind, mathematics, and culture in everyday life.* Cambridge, UK: Cambridge University Press.

Lave, J., & Wenger, E. (1991). *Situated learning: Legitimate peripheral participation.* Cambridge, UK: Cambridge University Press.

Letsky, M., Warner, N., Fiore, S. M., Rosen, M., & Salas, E. (2007). *Macrocognition in complex team problem solving.* Paper presented at the 12th International Command and Control Research Symposium, Newport, RI.

Letsky, M., Warner, N., Fiore, S. M., & Smith, C. (Eds.). (2008). *Macrocognition in teams.* London, UK: Ashgate Publishers.

Mace, W. M. (1977). James J. Gibson's strategy for perceiving: Ask not what's inside your head, but what your head's inside of. In R. Shaw & J. Bransford (Eds.), *Perceiving, acting, and knowing: Towards an ecological psychology* (pp. 43–65). Hillsdale, NJ: Lawrence Erlbaum Associates.

McNeese, M. D. (1986). Humane intelligence: A human factors perspective for developing intelligent cockpits. *IEEE Aerospace and Electronic Systems, 1,* 6–12.

McNeese, M. D. (1996). Collaborative systems research: Establishing ecological approaches through the living laboratory. In *Proceedings of the 40th Annual Meeting of the Human Factors Society* (pp. 767–771). Santa Monica, CA: Human Factors Society.

370 • *Theories of Team Cognition*

McNeese, M. D. (1998). Teamwork, team performance, and team interfaces: Historical precedence and application significance of the research at the USAF Fitts Human Engineering Division. In *Proceedings of the IEEE International Symposium on Technology and Society* (pp. 161–166). South Bend, IN: IEEE Society on Social Implications of Technology.

McNeese, M. D. (2000). Socio-cognitive factors in the acquisition and transfer of knowledge. *International Journal of Cognition, Technology, and Work, 2,* 164–177.

McNeese, M. D., Bains, P., Brewer, I., Brown, C. E., Connors, E. S., Jefferson, T., et al. (2005). The NeoCITIES simulation: Understanding the design and methodology used in a team emergency management simulation. In *Proceedings of the Human Factors and Ergonomics Society 49th Annual Meeting* (pp. 591–594). Santa Monica, CA: Human Factors Society.

McNeese, M. D., Brewer, I., Jones, R. E. T., & Connors, E. S. (2006). Supporting knowledge management in emergency crisis management: Envisioned designs for collaborative work. In J. Yen & R. L. Popp (Eds.), *Emergent information technologies and enabling policies for counter-terrorism* (pp. 255–280). Hoboken, NJ: Wiley-IEEE Press.

McNeese, M. D., & Brown, C. E. (1986). *Large group displays and team performance: An evaluation and projection of guidelines, research, and technologies* (Publication No. AAMRL-TR-86-035). Wright-Patterson Air Force Base, OH: Armstrong Aerospace Medical Research Laboratory.

McNeese, M. D., & Katz, L. (1987). Legibility evaluation of a large screen display system under medium ambient illumination. *Proceedings of the Society for Information Display, 28,* 59–65.

McNeese, M. D., Pfaff, M. S., Connors, E. S., Obieta, J., Terrell, I. S., & Friedenberg, M. A. (2006). Multiple vantage points of the common operational picture: Supporting complex teamwork. In *Proceedings of the 50th Annual Meeting of the Human Factors and Ergonomics Society* (pp. 467–471). Santa Monica, CA: Human Factors Society.

McNeese, M. D., & Rentsch, J. R. (2001). Social and cognitive considerations of teamwork. In M. D. McNeese, E. Salas, & M. Endsley (Eds.), *New trends in cooperative activities: System dynamics in complex environments* (pp. 96–113). Santa Monica, CA: Human Factors and Ergonomics Society Press.

McNeese, M. D., Rentsch, J. R., & Perusich, K. (2000). Modeling, measuring, and mediating teamwork: The use of fuzzy cognitive maps and team member schema similarity to enhance BMC³I decision making. In *IEEE International Conference on Systems, Man, and Cybernetics* (pp. 1081–1086). New York, NY: Institute of Electrical and Electronic Engineers.

McNeese, M. D., Salas, E., & Endsley, M. (Eds.). (2001). *New trends in cooperative activities: System dynamics in complex environments.* Santa Monica, CA: Human Factors and Ergonomics Society Press.

McNeese, M. D., Zaff, B. S., Citera, M., Brown, C. E., & Wellens, R. (1992). The role of a group-centered approach in the development of computer-supported collaborative design technologies. In *Proceedings of the 36th Annual Meeting of the Human Factors and Ergonomics Society* (pp. 867–871). Santa Monica, CA: Human Factors Society.

McNeese, M. D., Zaff, B. S., Citera, M., Brown, C. E., & Whitaker, R. (1995). AKADAM: Eliciting user knowledge to support participatory ergonomics. *International Journal of Industrial Ergonomics, 15,* 345–363.

McNeese, M. D., Zaff, B. S., Peio, K. J., Snyder, D. E., Duncan, J. C., & McFarren, M. R. (1990). *An advanced knowledge and design acquisition methodology: Application for the pilots associate* (Publication No. AAMRL-TR-90-060). Wright-Patterson Air Force Base, OH: Armstrong Aerospace Medical Research Laboratory.

Mohammed, S., & Dumville, B. C. (2001). Team mental models in a team knowledge framework: Expanding theory and measurement across disciplinary boundaries. *Journal of Organizational Behavior, 22*, 89–106.

Nosek, J., & McNeese, M. D. (1997). Augmenting group sensemaking in ill-defined, emerging situations. *Information Technology and People, 10*, 241–252.

Perusich, K. A., & McNeese, M. D. (2006). Using fuzzy cognitive maps for knowledge management in a conflict environment. *IEEE Systems, Man and Cybernetics, 3*, 810–821.

Pfaff, M. S. (2008). *Effects of mood and stress on group communication and performance in a simulated task environment.* Doctoral dissertation, The Pennsylvania State University, University Park. Retrieved December 16, 2008, from http://gradworks.umi.com/33/25/3325967.html

Pfaff, M. S. (2009). Emotional conversations in command and control: The impact of mood and stress on computer-mediated team communication behaviors. In *Proceedings of the 53rd Annual Meeting of the Human Factors and Ergonomics Society* (pp. 414–418). Santa Monica, CA: Human Factors Society.

Pfaff, M. S., & McNeese, M. D. (2010). Effects of mood and stress on distributed team cognition. *Theoretical Issues in Ergonomics Science, 11*, 321–339.

Rasmussen, J., Pejtersen, A. M., & Goodstein, L. P. (1994). *Cognitive systems engineering.* New York, NY: Wiley.

Roby, T. B. (1968). *Small group performance.* Chicago, IL: Rand McNally.

Salas, E., Stagl, K. C., Burke, C. S., & Goodwin, G. F. (2007). Fostering team effectiveness in organizations: Toward an integrative theoretical framework of team performance. In R. A. Dienstbier (Series Ed.) & B. Shuart, W. Spaulding, & J. Poland (Vol. Eds.), *Modeling complex systems: Vol. 52. Current theory and research in motivation* (pp. 185–243). Lincoln, NE: University of Nebraska Press.

Snyder, D. E., & McNeese, M. D. (1987). *Conflict resolution in cooperative systems* (Publication No. AAMRL-TR-87-066). Wright-Patterson Air Force Base, OH: Armstrong Aerospace Medical Research Laboratory.

Stasser, G., & Titus, W. (2003). Hidden profiles: A brief history. *Psychological Inquiry, 3–4*, 302–311.

Terrell, I. S., McNeese, M. D., & Jefferson, T. (2004). Exploring cognitive work within a 911 dispatch center: Using complementary knowledge elicitation techniques. In *Proceedings of the 48th Annual Meeting of the Human Factors and Ergonomics Society* (pp. 605–609). Santa Monica, CA: Human Factors Society.

Tolman, E. C., & Brunswik, E. (1935). The organism and the causal texture of the environment. *Psychological Review, 42*, 43–77.

Wellens, A. R., & Ergener, D. (1988). The C.I.T.I.E.S. game: A computer-based situation assessment task for studying distributed decision making. *Simulation & Games, 19*, 304–327.

Wilson, D., McNeese, M. D., & Brown, C. E. (1987). Team performance of a dynamic resource allocation task: Comparison of shared versus isolated work setting. In *Proceedings of the 31st Annual Meeting of the Human Factors Society* (pp. 1345–1349). Santa Monica, CA: Human Factors Society.

Young, M. F., & McNeese, M. D. (1995). A situated cognition approach to problem solving with implications for computer-based learning and assessment. In G. Salvendy & M. Smith (Eds.), *Human-computer interaction: Software and hardware interfaces* (Vol. II, pp. 825–830). Amsterdam, the Netherlands: Elsevier Science Publ. B.V.

Zaff, B. S., McNeese, M. D., & Snyder, D. E. (1993). Capturing multiple perspectives: A user-centered approach to knowledge acquisition. *Knowledge Acquisition, 5*, 79–116.

15

Gaining Insight Into Team Processes on Cognitive Tasks With Member Expectations and the Social Relations Model

Jared L. Ladbury and Verlin B. Hinsz

Collaboration in teams is quite remarkable. If we think about how a set of alternatives is discussed by a team facing a decision, coming to consensus about one alternative is quite complex (Hinsz, 1999). Imagine a couple attempting to select a movie to attend. Whether or not a particular film is brought up as a possible alternative depends on a large number of factors. Does the person suggesting the movie believe the movie will be good or bad? Does that person expect his or her partner would enjoy that movie? Has the person's partner enjoyed other movies of that genre or reacted positively to previews? Does the person suggesting the movie possess some unique knowledge about the partner that may indicate the partner would go against expectations and enjoy the movie? All this information can influence whether or not a particular movie is even presented as an alternative, let alone selected and eventually attended. Expanding the number of alternatives, the number of decisions to be made, or the number of team members involved adds increasing complexity to the question. Understanding how a team of investment bankers chooses a set of stocks to maximize profitability for their clients adds multiple levels of complexity. Yet, the effectiveness of the collaboration and actions of this team is a critical question for its clients.

In many cases of team research, the processes teams use to achieve their outcomes are seen as somewhat of a *black box* (Hackman & Morris, 1975). Processes are often difficult to measure and potentially even more difficult to quantify (Weingart, 1997, 2006). This poses a problem to researchers

374 • *Theories of Team Cognition*

who seek to understand the antecedents and consequences of the processes of teams. However, a coherent and comprehensive method is necessary for studying the processes of teams so that an understanding of team effectiveness can be achieved. In particular, if the processes of teams can be quantified, then a richer understanding may result (Ilgen & Hulin, 2000). Being able to quantify process would allow researchers to understand both the team member qualities that lead to specific processes and the processes that lead to beneficial and harmful outcomes. This chapter proposes that team processes can be inferred by establishing to what degree and in what way expectations are shared among team members. Team member expectations regarding the task and interactions are proposed as an important quality of team members performing tasks that lead to team processes. Team processes based on these expectations are proposed to lead to team outcomes in predictable ways.

We propose a conceptualization of team functioning that examines the role of shared and unshared team member expectations that lead to team interaction outcomes. For the purposes of this conceptualization, expectations are defined broadly as beliefs. In particular, the beliefs of interest will concern other team members, their potential behavior, or the nature of their interactions with others. Expectations can have a powerful effect on team interactions and functioning (DeChurch & Mesmer-Magnus, 2010a). Accurate expectations can allow a team to coordinate actions without the need for explicit communication (tacit coordination; Rico, Sanchez-Manzanares, Gil, & Gibson, 2008). Other expectations could also alter the pattern of interaction within the team in both positive and negative ways. We develop our conceptualization from this perspective of the cognitive beliefs that team members have about their team, its interactions, and outcomes. This chapter will explore the relationships among team member expectations, processes associated with team interaction, and the outcomes of the team interaction. The theoretical conceptualization we propose also involves the quantification of the processes used by teams that lead to the final outcome.

TEAM MEMBER QUALITIES

A large literature exists that considers the qualities that team members bring with them to the interaction that are also associated with team functioning. These team member qualities are generally easy to measure, are often easily recognizable to everyone in the team, and can have moderate to large effects on team performance (Bell, 2007). Organizations are often interested in the best combination of particular abilities or skill sets to assign to a project because of the importance placed on these qualities by conventional wisdom and research literature (Hackman, 1987). As a result of the importance placed on inputs as indicators of future outcomes, much research has focused on the capability of individual and team inputs to predict team outcomes (Levine & Moreland, 1990).

One research arena for team member qualities considers the relationship between workgroup diversity and outcomes such as productivity and solution quality. By examining the impact of the distribution of team member qualities, in this case diversity within the team, we can understand how a quality impacts an important team outcome such as production. Some research shows a curvilinear relationship between diversity and positive outcomes (Pellid, Eisenhardt, & Xin, 1999; Watson, Kumar, & Michaelsen, 1993), although such effects are found to a greater extent in laboratory studies than for intact workgroups (Williams & O'Reilly, 1998). Specifically, heterogeneous teams often underperform homogenous teams during the initial stages of a laboratory task. However, given enough time, heterogeneous teams make up for the early losses and, by the end of the task, outperform homogenous teams. Such results are often interpreted as demonstrating the need for a common structure to develop in which the norms of communication and interaction are firmly established before highly effective interactions can occur. Once the set of norms is established in a heterogeneous team, the team members use their diverse backgrounds and skill sets to construct new and potentially novel solutions to the problem.

The effects of diversity in teams offer an important window into the factors that can impact team outcomes. Some interpretations state that a shared understanding must develop through communication with individuals with diverse backgrounds before desirable outcomes are produced (Ancona & Caldwell, 1992). Team structure and norms for communication provide the basis upon which successful team interactions can be built. However, what is important about team structure that makes it essential for the development of useful outcomes?

We propose that the structure-reflecting processes of a team are perceived by team members. The knowledge team members acquire about

376 • *Theories of Team Cognition*

the structure of their teams may be represented as a set of beliefs about how the structure influences team interactions, the antecedent conditions of those interactions, and the consequences of those interactions. Because team members develop those beliefs about the team structure and associated processes, they also hold expectations about the role of team structure for the interactions and actions of the team. Team members use expectations to predict the course of events that will happen within the team interaction. They also use expectations to understand concepts such as team norms and to assign roles to the best possible team member for the task (Steiner, 1976). Accurate expectations allow team members to correctly predict what other team members are doing, what they will do in the future, and in what way the actions of all team members are interdependent. Without accurate expectations of how the team functions, team members may not understand how to best complete the task or how to generate positive social relations within the team. If, on the other hand, team members hold accurate expectations regarding how best to contribute to beneficial outcomes within the team, team members can act in ways that not only fulfill their own roles but also allow them to assist other team members.

Although the importance of team member expectations is frequently described in the literature on team functioning (DeChurch & Mesmer-Magnus, 2010a; Hinsz, 1995, 2004), exactly how team member expectations lead to outcomes is a challenging question. One theoretical framework states that team members have particular qualities that can be collectively referred to as inputs. Inputs may be personality factors the team member has or could be more task relevant, such as knowledge of how to complete a particular task. Once the team has been formed, team members must somehow combine their inputs. Combining inputs requires some team processes. Team processes are then expected to predict team outcomes (the input-process-outcome [I-P-O] framework; McGrath, 1964).

INFERRING PROCESSES OF INTERACTING TEAMS

Process is often the focus, either explicitly stated or implied, of research on teams. There is much speculation regarding the processes that occur within a team that will transform team member qualities into the desired outputs. However, the link between process and team outcomes is less understood than might be expected given the importance placed on process within conceptual models (e.g., the I-P-O framework; Ilgen, Hollenbeck, Johnson, & Jundt, 2005). Part of the reason may be that *process* has been defined broadly and applied liberally to a variety of different conceptual methods (Kozlowski & Bell, 2003). Some researchers have gone so far as to support abandoning the term process all together (Kozlowski & Ilgen, 2006) and instead focusing on moderators of the relationship between inputs and outcomes (Ilgen et al., 2005).

So what can be done with the concept of process? Although it is true that process is difficult to assess, it is possible to infer process (Weingart, 1997). Rather than directly measuring a team interaction process, which could be disruptive to the interaction process, one can observe a large number of team interactions and use an outcome or distribution of outcomes to estimate the process. Inferring process is advantageous because it requires less assessment than direct measurement. However, inferring process, just as with assessing process, requires a conceptual framework that specifies the processes of interest for the desired outcomes.

Some team-related research traditions have attempted to infer process based on measurements of inputs and outcomes. For example, social decision scheme (SDS) theory (Davis, 1973) was conceived as an attempt to infer a decision process based on the distribution of individual preferences before the interaction and the decisions reached as a function of the interaction (Stasser, 1999). In some social decision schemes research, each member of the group is asked to respond individually to a question or problem that has a fixed number of alternatives. These member responses are used to establish the distribution of preferences for each alternative within the group. The group then convenes, discusses the issue, and selects one answer to be the group's response. By examining the pattern of responding of a sample of groups, one can infer how the groups generally arrived at their final decisions. For example, if one finds that a group solves a word problem correctly as long as one group member initially prefers the correct answer (i.e., truth-wins; Laughlin & Ellis, 1986), one could infer that the correct group members were able to persuade the incorrect group members that their preferred alternative was correct. This is one example in which the contents of the *black box* of process can be inferred.

378 • *Theories of Team Cognition*

Another example of inferring the black box of team process is through the use of shared mental models (Cannon-Bowers, Salas, & Converse, 1993). When interacting, individuals often have different beliefs regarding how the team should be structured, the status of each particular member, the methods for going about making a decision, and so on. The extent to which information regarding how the team will function is shared among individuals comprises one example of a shared mental model (Hinsz, 2004). Shared mental models are primarily concerned with expectations and predictions. If a basketball player can predict with reasonable certainty where each teammate will be on the court at a particular time, maneuvers such as a "no-look pass" can be executed that would not be possible otherwise. Both the ball passer and pass receiver need to share information regarding what the other person is doing for the pass to be successful. The passer needs to be able to predict with reasonable accuracy where the receiver will be on the court since the passer will not look at the receiver. The pass receiver needs to be aware that the possibility of a pass exists and must have an understanding of where the passer expects the receiver to be should the pass be executed. By having this shared understanding, the two teammates are able to potentially catch the defense off guard and score a basket.

Shared mental models can have a number of interrelated facets. Depending on the task, shared knowledge on a particular facet can potentially offset problems that could occur if complete information is not shared (Cannon-Bowers & Salas, 2001). These four components include (1) knowledge of the equipment used to complete the task, (2) knowledge of the task itself and what the team must do to accomplish that task, (3) knowledge about teammates and the inputs they may bring to the situation, and (4) knowledge about how the team is expected to interact with one another (Cannon-Bowers et al., 1993; Hinsz, 1995; Mathieu, Heffner, Goodwin, Salas, & Cannon-Bowers, 2000). The degree to which each of these facets is shared is expected to impact team outcomes. The impact on team outcomes is expected to be stronger in teams that have time or communication restraints placed on them (Cannon-Bowers et al., 1993). If team members have an accurate shared mental model, they will be able to predict with reasonable certainty what their teammates will do, the resources each of the team members will need to accomplish their tasks, and how team members are expected to interact with one another. Knowing this information allows the team to act without the need for additional discussion. Being able to predict how the team will function allows the team members to continue fulfilling their roles even though communication may be at a minimum.

Shared mental models demonstrate process by their ability to summarize what has occurred during an interaction process. By discussing, acting, and interacting in a team, individuals share information. After sharing a large enough amount of information, team members begin to develop the knowledge necessary to compose a mental model. If the mental model is adequately assessed and represented, it should be possible to infer what information was shared and how much it was shared.

The problem with inferring process from mental models is largely one of measurement (DeChurch & Mesmer-Magnus, 2010b; Hinsz, 1995; Klimoski & Mohammad, 1994). It is difficult to assess exactly what information has been shared, how extensively the information has been shared, and how information sharing translates into shared mental models within a team. However, this is not to say that it is impossible to understand how information is shared within a team. Research that examines patterns of information sharing and how it relates to team functioning is exemplified by research on uncovering the best solution when there is a hidden profile (Mesmer-Magnus & DeChurch, 2009; Reimer, Kuendig, Hoffrage, Park, & Hinsz, 2007; Stasser & Titus, 2003). Groups and teams tend to focus on information that is already shared among the members when discussing issues of relevance (Stasser & Titus, 1987). If information that is already shared among team members is preferentially discussed within the team, there may be little opportunity for a complete shared mental model to form. This may reduce the team's ability to add to the mental model of team functioning and leave the team with a less than complete understanding of the task and how each team member is working to complete it. Thus, even though the information may be shared among team members, there is no guarantee that they have shared information relevant to the task or that their shared information is accurate (Cooke, Salas, Cannon-Bowers, & Stout, 2000). Consequently, because of the bias toward discussing shared information in groups and teams, the team may not have the knowledge needed to respond appropriately in a critical situation. Such an effect demonstrates how information sharing can influence how effective and ineffective teams might function. If properly conceptualized and assessed, shared mental models may provide a conceptual basis for

380 • *Theories of Team Cognition*

understanding how the processes of information exchange in teams influence team outcomes.

As this example of information sharing and shared mental models illustrates, inferences about processes may be our best method of understanding what is happening within the context of team interactions. Social decision scheme theory and shared mental models are two ways in which process can be inferred, but there are other methods that could also shed some light on team processes. Of particular interest is the potential for social relations model/modeling (SRM; Kenny, 1994; Kenny & La Voie, 1984) to illuminate portions of process that would not have been available without the aid of SRM (Rentsch & Woehr, 2004).

The power of the SRM to study effects in teams has been examined in important ways. Rentsch and Woehr (2004) support the claim that a component of SRM can be used as a quantitative index of team member schema similarity (see Rentsch & Hall, 1994, for more discussion of team member schema similarity). They argue that the extent to which team members agree with one another regarding qualities of the other team members (i.e., all team members agree that Sally is good at performing behavior X and Jim is good at performing behavior Y) represents team member schema similarity. The importance of consensus within teams regarding the team's functioning is well documented (Mesmer-Magnus & DeChurch, 2009). The SRM provides a means for calculating the degree of consensus in a team, which provides a leap forward for research in teams and understanding how expectations influence team functioning. However, consensus is not the only index of team functioning calculated with the SRM. The SRM provides multiple indices of underlying processes that may also impact team functioning. In this fashion, the SRM provides a means of inferring team process that can enlighten us regarding how teams complete tasks.

The SRM assumes that all social interactions can be described in terms of the variance among judgments that team members make about all members in the interaction. The model begins by having each member of a team make a quantifiable judgment regarding other members of the team. Judgments are then analyzed to determine the effect of the person making the judgment, the person being judged, and any idiosyncratic relationships on the overall judgment. Once these effects are calculated for each team member, the variance in the effects is calculated to arrive at team-level indices of how the team arrived at their judgments. These indices help us to infer more about the process the team is using and also understand how those processes are leading to the outcomes that are observed.

Assessment of the variance components allows for a more stringent test of the mediating link between inputs and outcomes suggested by the I-P-O framework because the variance components are normally distributed numerical observations reflecting underlying processes. This allows the researcher to use a regression framework to assess any links between the variance components representing process and any group-level outcomes the researcher believes are influenced by process. In addition, SRM can be used to calculate the relationship between an individual difference variable and a participant's perceptions of the other group members. Notice that this sequence results in a change in the level of analysis. It begins with individual differences and a single participant's expectations. The individual expectations of a number of different group members are then combined into a group-level understanding of process, which can then be related to group outcomes. To fully test the mediating links suggested by the I-P-O model, a between-subjects manipulation at the individual level can be used. This ensures all calculations are made at the group level of analysis and allows for a stringent test of mediation.

What should be most evident from our discussion of process is that process is challenging to both define and measure. Many conceptual approaches exist that attempt to infer process, but no single method has yet emerged that satisfactorily infers process and allows for a stringent test of the meditational relationship of inputs, processes, and outcomes, with inputs affecting outcomes only as a result of the team processes that occur. As discussed later, the SRM offers a new method to both infer process and test some of the assumptions of the I-P-O framework. However, the potential of the SRM has yet to be fully realized in this regard.

SOCIAL RELATIONS MODEL

SRM is a statistical method used to disentangle the interdependencies associated with dyadic data—that is, data in which the responses of two or more individuals are nonindependent or share a common element (Kenny, Kashy, & Cook, 2006). It was initially proposed by Kenny and La Voie (1984) to overcome a particular problem associated with person

382 • *Theories of Team Cognition*

perception. Perceptions of two individuals interacting with one another are not independent. Person A's ratings of persons B, C, and D will be dependent on how person A generally rates people. Ratings of person B by persons A, C, and D will all be dependent on how person B is generally seen by others (Kenny, 1994; Kenny et al., 2006). Because the data are interdependent, the assumptions of statistical tests used to test hypotheses are often violated.

In response to this, the SRM was developed. SRM is an extension of generalizability theory (Cronbach, Gleser, Nanda, & Rajaratnam, 1972) that takes judgments associated with a social interaction and partitions them into effects associated with the actor (who does the perceiving), the partner (who is being perceived), and the relationship of the actor and partner, which represents any unique information the actor and partner may have about each other. If only one set of judgments is made, the relationship component also contains any error that exists within the measurements.

This partitioning of the variance in the judgments into components is important because of an interesting problem associated with team interaction. When one person is interacting with a team, that individual is both perceiving and being perceived by the team (Kenny, 1994). In addition, that individual is usually aware of being perceived by other members of the team. This awareness may cause the person to interact differently within the team and to have different opinions about the team and its members and cause other team members to have different opinions and actions toward the individual. SRM allows one to assess the effect person A may have on person B *independent* of the effect person B has on person A and any unique aspects that may be associated with their relationship.

To calculate the necessary variance components, one begins by asking all members of a team to give their perceptions of each interaction partner. The most common method is to use rating scales completed in a round-robin style. For example, imagine that a researcher predicts that the beliefs members have about their interaction partners' dispositions (e.g., agreeableness) will improve collaborative performance on a given task. To test this hypothesis, all members of the team complete a measure of agreeableness. The members of the team are also asked to rate each member of the team on agreeableness. Every team member's perceptions of every other team member's agreeableness results in a large data matrix. When properly analyzed with SRM methods, these data can establish the degree to which all the aspects of social perception influenced the ratings of agreeableness.

Gaining Insight Into Team Processes on Cognitive Tasks • 383

Potentially, team members may rate each member of the team similarly, perhaps using beliefs about their own agreeableness as a starting point and slightly adjusting their perceptions of others' agreeableness from that anchor point. Or, team members may display an ability to gain consensus on other team members' agreeableness. Consensus among the members may cause the team to expect a particular team member to be particularly disagreeable, which may change how the team members interact with that individual and substantially influence team performance on the task.

The variance components associated with actor, partner, and relationship effects within SRM represent how team members are perceiving and interacting with one another. When quantified, the variance components are characterized as indices, with each index having a unique meaning within the model and representing a different aspect of team process. Table 15.1 demonstrates how SRM components can be used to statistically quantify the manner in which information may be shared among team members. The top part of Table 15.1 represents a team that displays maximum actor variance. Note that team members have little agreement regarding partner

TABLE 15.1

Representation of Team Data and Its Effects on
Social Relations Model Indices

Team Generating a Large Actor Variance			
	Ratees		
Raters	#1	#2	#3	#4
#1		50	50	50
#2	35		35	35
#3	20	20		20
#4	1	1	1	

Team Generating a Large Partner Variance			
	Ratees		
Raters	#1	#2	#3	#4
#1		20	35	50
#2	1		35	50
#3	1	20		50
#4	1	20	35	

Note: Numbers within the cells represent a numerical assessment made by the rater about the ratee ranging from 1 to 50.

384 • *Theories of Team Cognition*

qualities but are consistent across partners with their ratings. Actor effects assess the extent to which one person tends to see all their interaction partners as similar. The bottom part of Table 15.1 represents a team that displays maximum partner variance. This team shows a large amount of agreement for the interaction partners but shows little consistency within an individual rater. Partner effects demonstrate the extent to which an interaction partner is seen similarly by all interaction partners.

SRM also provides a method for performing supplemental analyses using the information obtained from the judgments among the team members. In particular, using the variance components associated with the actor, partner, and relationship effects, additional indices can be calculated that provide a clearer understanding of the interaction process that may have occurred within the team (see Table 15.2 for a list of SRM components).

TABLE 15.2

Primary Variance Components of the Social Relations Model

Name	Description
Actor	Tendency for team members doing the rating to rate other team members similarly
Partner	Tendency for team members to be rated similarly by all other team members
Relationship	Tendency for team members to use unique information unrelated to actor and partner variance when rating other team members
Other Indices Within the Social Relations Model	
Assumed similarity	Tendency for the team member to believe that all team members will respond as they respond. Represented by the correlation between self-ratings and the team member's actor effect.
Self–other agreement	Tendency for team member A to agree with other team members regarding the rating of team member A. Represented by the correlation between self-ratings and the team member's partner effect.
Generalized reciprocity	Tendency for team members that rate other team members highly to be rated highly by their team members (e.g., Jon is rated by his team members as trustworthy because he believes all his team members are trustworthy). Represented by the correlation between the team member's actor and partner effect.
Dyadic reciprocity	Tendency for team member B to rate team member A highly because team member A rated team member B highly (e.g., Patty trusts Jon because Jon trusts Patty). Represented by the correlation between two individuals' relationship effects.

These secondary analyses can include the extent to which the team member demonstrates agreement with other team members and the extent to which the team members' expectations of others are related to their expectations for themselves. The SRM allows researchers to obtain a wealth of information associated with a team interaction by taking a large matrix of data and partitioning the matrix into meaningful variance components.

SRM is an important tool that team researchers can use to answer interesting questions. For example, when the extent and pattern of shared information is part of an important theoretical question, SRM can be used to summarize the processes associated with expectations regarding information sharing. Table 15.1 demonstrates how the variances components represent different patterns of information sharing. However, to effectively use the SRM method, the questions must be theoretically driven with specific predictions regarding how the components in the SRM are expected to fit within the larger conceptualization of the team interaction. One theoretical framework that can help drive predictions is the I-P-O framework (McGrath, 1964) in which individual inputs, such as shared and unshared cognitions, lead to team processes, summarized by the SRM indices, which in turn lead to team-level outcomes.

All of the SRM indices are essentially summary measures for expectations and perceptions about what occurs during a team interaction process. For example, imagine that team members are performing a complicated, interdependent, and time-sensitive task. Each member of the team has some degree of confidence that every other member of the team knows their role within the team and is able to complete their portion of the task. By establishing the degree to which each team member believes their interaction partners are competent and able to perform the task, SRM variances may be able to index the extent to which team members believe one among them needs special attention. This situation would be demonstrated by a large partner variance for that team. Alternatively, the set of judgments summarized by an index might represent the extent to which one person within the team believes the rest of the team incapable of completing the task and believes that he or she needs to perform all possible roles. Such expectations may lead to those team members failing to focus on their own roles to the detriment of the entire team. This situation would be demonstrated by a large actor variance in which the nondelegating team member would believe all other team members' abilities to be similar and low.

386 • *Theories of Team Cognition*

Each of the secondary indices (see Table 15.2) also yields important information regarding how teams function and arrive at particular outcomes. Self–other agreement can be used to establish whether the expectations a team member has for him- or herself are similar to the expectations the other team members hold for that person. Assumed reciprocity demonstrates that team members use their own expectations as a guide when forming expectations about their partners. General reciprocity represents the extent to which a team member's expectations result in similar expectations from other team members. For example, one may expect that team members who trust their teammates more are also trusted by their teammates more. Dyadic reciprocity can take this same notion to a dyadic level in which teammate B trusts teammate A because teammate A trusts teammate B (Kenny et al., 2006). All of the SRM components taken together represent a rich combination of data that can allow researchers to infer the team processes that are occurring within the team.

By applying the SRM to teams, the potential exists to address the difficult problem of quantifying aspects of the team interaction processes. For example, imagine a team of basketball players. We could ask each player to rate every other player on various abilities such as shooting, passing, and leadership. The extent that these cognitions are shared and the pattern of how those cognitions are shared can be numerically established using SRM. Various important outcome measures would then be established such as points per game and wins, which could then be predicted using the SRM indices. Thus, we can infer how teams were able to arrive at their outcomes and attempt to relate the outcomes to potentially influential inputs. In this fashion, the indices derived from the SRM would summarize underlying processes of team interaction and functioning that influence the degree to which the team is more or less effective in terms of specified outcomes of interest.

THE PREDICTION OF TEAM OUTCOMES FROM SRM INDICES

When studying the effects of team interaction on team performance, the qualities of the resulting outcomes are often the greatest concern, particularly in applied settings (Hackman, 1987, 1992). Employers will want to know the benefits that would result from implementing a new team-building procedure if one is attempting to convince those employers that a team-building training exercise is important for the continued competitiveness of their business (Klein et al., 2009). Demonstrating that teams that received team-building training arrived at higher quality solutions in less time than teams that did not receive the training would be of great interest to organizations interested in implementing the training (see Salas et al., 2008, for recent meta-analysis of the effectiveness of team building).

Outcomes are multifaceted. Outcomes can include task-related outcomes such as the number of solutions offered for a problem or the quality of those solutions. Outcomes could also focus on the social aspects of an interaction such as how long the team spent discussing irrelevant information or the degree to which team members would like to work with one another in the future. The outcome of interest is essentially determined by the task and the theoretical or applied question. Indeed, McGrath (1984) estimates that 80% of the variance in team outcomes is task dependent. Different outcomes can be more or less important depending on the task the team faces. Because there are multiple outcomes that can indicate team performance, and given that the team's task determines to a large extent which outcomes will be more or less relevant, it is important to review outcomes that have historically been important in research and to understand the context in which each one becomes relevant. In the process, this discussion of team outcomes provides a basis for describing how the SRM approach can help explain how processes summarized by the SRM indices may predict the different outcomes.

Quantity

For more than 100 years, researchers have been concerned with the quantity of team production (McGrath & Altman, 1966). Tasks that tend to focus on quantity include knowledge or correct answers generated by a team and assembly line work (e.g., the classic Hawthorne studies; Roethlisberger & Dickson, 1939). In both cases, increasing the amount of output accomplished is of primary importance. As work becomes increasingly collaborative and team oriented (Kozlowski & Bell, 2003), research has continued to focus on productivity in teams. One aspect related to collaboration and productivity is social loafing—the tendency for individuals to exert less

388 • *Theories of Team Cognition*

effort when their efforts are pooled (Latané, Williams, & Harkins, 1979). Interestingly, interventions that reduce social loafing also tend to increase team performance (Kozlowski & Bell, 2003). Such interventions can generally be said to influence team processes and include having a team of close friends rather than strangers complete the task, making it easier to identify individual contributions, and providing clear performance standards.

The amount of goods produced is one method to demonstrate social loafing in teams. However, social loafing occurs with cognitive tasks as well (Weldon & Gargano, 1987). Some research has chosen to focus on knowledge and correct solutions reached by teams. Models of team productivity tend to assume that there is a maximum level of productivity that a team can achieve. Moreover, as team size increases, there is a negatively accelerating function of increases in productivity. More team members allow for more potential resources to be brought to the task but also increase the likelihood that process losses will occur (Steiner, 1972). Empirical research shows that as teams become larger, they tend to arrive at more correct answers but take more time to do so (Bray, Kerr, & Atkin, 1978). In cases of productivity and knowledge generation, there are trade-offs that occur when adding additional team members. With product generation, adding additional team members may not result in more being achieved because of coordination loses that inevitably occur in large teams.

The trade-offs associated with production quantity could indicate that multiple processes are occurring within the team and that there is an optimum level at which each process needs to occur to generate maximum performance. In the SRM framework, a team may require an accurate understanding of how many units each person is able to produce, which would be indicated by greater partner variance. However, it is also possible that team members may produce more if they simply assume that everyone is producing a similar amount of units. Within SRM, this would be indicated by larger actor variance. Thus, indices derived from the SRM approach can be seen as related to the quantity of outcomes produced.

Quality

The quality or accuracy of the performance of a team is an important outcome as well. Research focusing on brainstorming demonstrates that quality can be just as important an outcome as quantity (Paulus & Brown, 2007). When examining both quantity and quality of outcomes in a brainstorming task, Vroom, Grant, and Cotton (1969) demonstrated that forming a team for the task can have beneficial or detrimental effects depending on the phase of the task in which the team interacts. If a team is brought together and asked to brainstorm solutions, they tend to generate fewer ideas per person than individuals working alone (Paulus & Brown, 2007). However, teams are better able to evaluate the quality of solutions. Similarly, when given a number of potential solutions generated during the brainstorming session, teams are better able to determine the best solution. Thus, team interaction sometimes hinders quantity of production but can improve the evaluation of quality.

When brainstorming in teams, some team members may become more concerned with how their ideas will be evaluated (Camacho & Paulus, 1995). When that is the case, team members that do not hold such self-evaluation concerns may actually produce the most quality solutions. Not holding these self-evaluation concerns would be represented by a near zero correlation between what the team members think is a good idea and what the team members believe the team will think is a good idea. Within SRM, this correlation is often referred to as metaperception. If one is unaware of what the team believes is a good idea, the notion of evaluation may be less important within that team. Team members may thus behave as though they are alone, even if they are working with the team. Consequently, indices derived from the SRM can be used to predict a number of outcomes related to the quality of outcomes produced by teams.

Team Sustainability

Team researchers have often been concerned with the more social aspects of team interaction. Society expects that some groups, such as families, should remain together. A primary metric of success or failure of a family is the ability of the group members to continue interacting with one another. Other teams, such as military aircraft or construction crews, must complete tasks together over long periods of time. If they remain together, they are expected to become a more effective and efficient team. Thus, team sustainability has been proposed as being another important outcome of team interactions (Hackman, 1987). Although sustainability has been placed in models of effective team experience, there have been few studies that attempt to improve team sustainability (Kozlowski & Ilgen, 2006).

390 • *Theories of Team Cognition*

Whether or not a team is sustainable may have a great deal to do with member perceptions. In particular, team members may seek to remain in teams in which they are accurately perceived. Accurate expectations may facilitate the team in relating to one another. For example, if team members know what each member is capable of contributing to the team, team members may not suffer the feelings of frustration associated with coworkers expecting too much or too little from a team member. Within SRM, greater accuracy with regard to expectations would be demonstrated by greater partner variance within the model. Consequently, if a team has greater partner variance, it would be predicted that team members would have less negative affect regarding working in their team and be more willing to continue working with the team in the future.

Summary

As can be seen from this discussion, outcomes are multifaceted, and it is important to treat them as such. When attempting to study outcomes of team interaction, one must begin with a theoretical grounding and understand how the team's task could relate to the outcome of interest. One must also be concerned with the nature of the inputs one measures when attempting to relate those inputs to outcomes. The large number of possible inputs implies that not all inputs will relate to the same outcome. The task and the inputs and outcomes of interest must be carefully selected to be able to address the questions of interest regarding team performance. It is also important to have a theoretical understanding of how the processes one proposes will affect outcomes to be able to obtain predictable results using SRM indices. In some situations, actor variance may increase performance, whereas in others, it may decrease performance. SRM is an important tool for obtaining predictable results. To obtain those results, researchers will need to clearly specify how the pattern of data represented by the SRM indices is expected to relate to the potential outcomes.

THE SRM APPLIED TO SHARED COGNITION IN TEAMS

The SRM has proven to be a useful tool for evaluating many aspects of social interaction. Some of these applications include perceptions and

Gaining Insight Into Team Processes on Cognitive Tasks • 391

attainment of status within a team (Anderson & Kilduff, 2009), levels of transference within group therapy (Markin & Kivlighan, 2008), and trust within a group (Bergman, Small, Bergman, & Rentsch, 2010). Applying the SRM has led to the detection of important and interesting findings not revealed by popular modeling techniques (e.g., analysis of variance). Anderson, Srivastava, Beer, Spataro, and Chatman (2006) asked team members to assess their own status within the team, the status of the other team members, and how much they liked each team member. They found that the team members who were most liked by the rest of the team were the team members who had the most agreement among actor and partner perceptions related to team status. This finding indicates that liking within the team was related to being accurate with regard to one's status within the team. Those who perceived their status as being higher or lower than what the other team members perceived were not as well liked within the team. By using the SRM to assess both the actor and partner affects associated with perceived status, the researchers were able to uncover a team process (perception of status differences among team members) that showed differential outcomes (increased liking and cohesion).

The basic I-P-O framework implies that inputs have an effect on outcomes mediated by the effects of process. The SRM allows one to examine the effects of expectations and infer some of the processes that occurred within the team. One can establish the degree to which members agree on status within the team, the methods for completing the task, and the competencies that team members brought to the task. Using SRM, we can assess the processes that may have occurred within the team. In doing so, we can relate the inputs to the process and the process to the outcomes that occur when the team completes the task (Figure 15.1).

Rentsch and Woehr (2004) propose using the partner effect as a general index of team member schema similarity. Team member schema similarity refers to information organized and structured in similar ways across team members (Rentsch & Hall, 1994). They argue that because partner variance is concerned with agreement within the team, it should be a reasonable measure of the amount of information that is shared among the team. Because a primary component of shared mental models is that all members of the team should have a basic shared understanding of the task and how to accomplish their goal, they conclude that variance associated with the partner effect is an important index that should

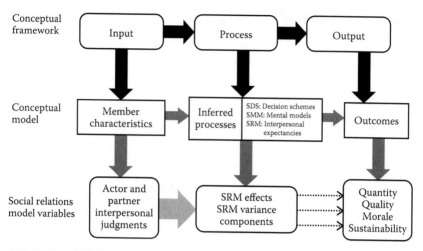

FIGURE 15.1
The conceptual framework, conceptual model, and the variables that represent an interpersonal expectations approach to the team interaction process.

be considered in team research. Their conceptualization represents an important step forward regarding research in teams using the SRM. Certainly, the degree to which information is shared within a group has been shown to be a powerful indicator of team performance (Mesmer-Magnus & DeChurch, 2009). Teams that have more shared information have shown increased performance across a number of task environments (Mesmer-Magnus & DeChurch, 2009). However, the amount of shared information may not be the only critical factor when examining team performance. Other aspects of the interaction such as when and with whom the information is shared could potentially affect the team's success or failure on the task.

The methods associated with the SRM allow us to go beyond the idea of shared information to examine the impact of information that is unshared as well as information that is believed to be shared but is actually not. SRM is a powerful tool when analyzing team interactions because it is context independent and does not require us to focus on one particular variable that is believed to be important (e.g., shared information). Although we may be most interested in the amount of shared information, the possibility exists that a degree of uniqueness of information may be beneficial (Reimer, Reimer, & Hinsz, 2010). For instance, research on transactive memory

Gaining Insight Into Team Processes on Cognitive Tasks • 393

demonstrates that group members attending to and remembering unique aspects of a problem can greatly improve the information-processing capacity and efficiency of the group as a whole (Littlepage, Hollingshead, Drake, & Littlepage, 2008). For effective transactive memory, the information itself would not be completely shared among the individual members. All that would need to be shared is a knowledge that a distribution of the information is occurring, an understanding of which information each team member is responsible for remembering, and an agreement that each team member will take responsibility for the information assigned them. It is also possible that each team member holding unique information could have benefits for team functioning. For outcomes such as time to complete the task, it may be beneficial for team members to hold unique information about their role in completing the task.

In a similar vein, a large actor effect associated with a particular team would show a tendency for the team members to treat all interaction partners similarly. Perhaps treating all interaction partners similarly could lead to less concern with the structural or relationship elements associated with the team interaction. Consequently, teams with large actor effects may complete tasks more quickly and have fewer process losses associated with explicitly deciding how the team will complete its task.

It is also important to consider the degree to which different indices associated with the SRM may impact different types of outcomes. One can consider a large number of potential effects associated with the SRM components and different outcomes (see Table 15.2 for a summary of the different SRM indices described in this section). We will focus primarily on the outcomes of solution quality, speed with which the task is completed, team morale and satisfaction with the outcome, and sustainability of the team. For the illustrative examples, we will focus on a team decision-making situation, although this is just one of the types of interaction amenable to an SRM analysis.

Quality of solution is of primary importance because a poor decision can be costly. To attain quality decisions, a team first needs a stable foundation from which to work. This would involve all team members knowing their roles, the norms of the team, and the constraints under which the team operates for making the decision. Such processes would be represented by a pattern of large partner variance among the team members, indicating that team members hold a consensus regarding how the team functions. Teams need this consensus because all members are assigned

394 • *Theories of Team Cognition*

roles. If all team members have the same perception about the competencies of each individual team member, they are more likely to accurately gauge that team member's abilities and place that member in a role that corresponds to the person's capabilities.

Finally, poor decisions are often made if the team removes possibilities for dissension (Janis, 1982). Thus, quality decisions are more likely to result when team members feel that dissension is tolerated and necessary. The possibility for dissension will be marked by small actor variance and low assumed reciprocity. Recall that actor variance represents the tendency for team members to view all other team members similarly and that assumed reciprocity represents the correlation between a team member's self-evaluation and that team member's evaluation of all other team members. Teams that are high in these two attributes may view their team members as a homogenous set. These beliefs may, in turn, reduce the tendency for team members to seek dissenting opinions or even cause the belief that a dissenting opinion is absent within the team. Reducing assumed reciprocity may facilitate dissension because individuals will be able to recognize and appreciate the discrepancy between what they believe and what other team members believe.

The speed with which the decision is made is another important outcome associated with team decisions. Decisions must often be made quickly, and decision-making teams that can make decisions quickly are highly valued. The indices associated with speed of decision will differ depending on whether or not the team has a history of interaction. Teams that make decisions quickly without a history of interaction will be marked by large actor variance and high assumed reciprocity. Large actor variance is preferred because it increases the use of default or assumed structures for team interaction. Assumed reciprocity is also important because all team members will want to feel they are on the same page with the rest of the team. If they believe this, dissension will be minimized and decisions will be quicker. Teams that make quick decisions but have a history of interaction are expected to have a much different pattern of SRM indices. Rather than needing to develop a structure for their interaction, they will have a structure in place that has been tested through repeated interactions. This will result in lower actor variance and larger partner variance. The proposed relationships would follow a speed–accuracy trade-off in newly formed teams. Recall that we expect that actor variance would be positively related to speed of

Gaining Insight Into Team Processes on Cognitive Tasks • 395

completing the task but negatively associated with quality or accuracy. However, the SRM analysis also leaves open the possibility that increased partner variance could also allow speed of task completion to increase without an associated detriment to accuracy. A result of this kind would demonstrate that teams whose members develop a shared and accurate perception of all team members (a large partner variance within SRM) would outperform teams that fail to do so. It is also predictable that teams with large partner variance would outperform teams with small partner variance; however, this would depend on the size of the team's actor variance. Teams with large partner variances should outperform teams (a) with small partner variances but large actor variances on accuracy tasks, and (b) with small partner variances and small actor variances on speed tasks. The complexity of the predictions indicates how the SRM approach can help researchers comprehend the richness of relationships in interacting teams.

Team morale and satisfaction with the decision are other important outcomes that should be associated with an expected pattern of interpersonal indices. Morale will increase with accurate perception and the ability to place the best individual within the proper role. In the case of the indices, the pattern will be one of high partner variance and high reciprocity. These relationships would exist because satisfaction is a function of being placed in a situation that uses each team member's unique abilities in important and useful ways (Harrison, Newman, & Roth, 2006). Team member consensus regarding which team member would best fill a particular role will result in more team members being placed in roles that take advantage of their unique skill sets. Large partner variance would indicate that a number of individuals agree that each team member would be best at filling one role and not another role. Each individual will be viewed accurately, which will lead to placement in roles that better suit the team member's talents, which should also increase satisfaction with the overall experience. The net effect will be greater satisfaction with the team, the task, and the final team solution.

As these examples illustrate, applying the SRM to predict team outcomes can result in the test of a large number of potential hypotheses. The SRM is an important tool that can add to our understanding of team process and functioning because of its focus on the interdependence associated with team member judgments. The SRM also has the benefit of the assessments of team interaction occurring independent of context. Indeed, the SRM

AREAS OF TEAM AND SMALL GROUP RESEARCH OPEN TO INVESTIGATION USING SRM

A number of research areas are amenable for research using an SRM approach. We have already touched on some, such as perceptions and attainment of status in teams (Anderson & Kilduff, 2009; Anderson et al., 2006). There are other areas for which an SRM approach can inform current research, particularly if SRM is coupled with the I-P-O framework.

Research on diversity in teams could be enhanced using the SRM method. Previous research has shown that diverse teams have poorer performance at the beginning of the task but can overcome early difficulties to be just as or more effective than comparable nondiverse teams (Pellid et al., 1999). The initial poor performance is often explained in terms of the team needing to develop common ground, expectations for communication, and so on, before effective interaction can begin. SRM offers a means for testing this prediction directly. By having team members rate the social climate of their team at multiple points during their interactions, one could test whether or not diverse teams gain greater consensus regarding how team members are expected to behave and if this greater consensus leads to more effective team outcomes.

The impact of cultural diversity on team functioning could also be used to answer questions in more applied contexts. Interactions among culturally diverse individuals are an increasing reality for members of modern organizations. For example, multinational coalitions are becoming the norm in some military endeavors (Sutton & Pierce, 2003). From laboratory research on teams, we might expect that multinational coalitions would have initial difficulties when working together. However, it might also be the case that nations train their military members in the norms of communication, levels of specificity, and so on, with sufficient similarity that two soldiers from culturally diverse backgrounds may not have the initial task difficulties that other multicultural teams may have.

Another realm that could benefit from using SRM to investigate team process is social dilemma research. Social dilemmas are situations in which individual team members must make a choice between cooperating or competing with their fellow team members. Rewards are structured such that an individual team member receives the most rewards if that team member competes and all other team members cooperate. However, the team as a whole receives the most rewards if all team members cooperate. Thus, a conflict is created between what is best for the team as a whole and what is best for each individual team member. SRM analyses can be useful because an individual's decision is based on how that person expects the other team members will behave. Thus, consensus with regard to expectations of whether or not the other team members will compete may lead to the most positive benefits for the team. This effect should occur because teams that agree on the tendencies of their team members to compete or cooperate should be more likely to predict when a teammate will compete and attempt to compensate for competitive behavior.

These examples highlight just a few areas suitable for the SRM approach. Each represents an area for which important research findings are likely to result with further consideration from the SRM perspective. In each of these areas, SRM helps to illuminate the nature of the interaction by assessing expectations that can then be related to important team outcomes.

CONCLUSIONS

All of the variance components associated with the SRM can be used to construct indices of interaction processes that occur within a team. Each of these indices can be expected to mediate the relationship between specific inputs and specific outcomes of team interactions in relation to the I-P-O framework. The SRM approach captures a summary of the team process that occurred rather than the process itself. The indices derived from the SRM allow for the quantification of process as well as making specific predictions regarding how inputs relate to processes and the processes relate to outcomes. Application of the SRM conceptualization allows a specific test of the mediation implied by the I-P-O framework that previously was not possible using more common analytic techniques (e.g., interaction process analysis; Bales, 1970).

A beneficial feature of the social relations approach is that the aggregation problem associated with studying teams and their members is better resolved than with other methods. In the social relations method, individual scores are combined into variance components that exist at the team level. A single score is computed for each team, which can then be easily related to team outcomes. Because the indices derived from SRM are generic to team interactions, they are not conditioned by the context in which the team exists. Rather, the indices provide a means of understanding how team interaction patterns, team tasks, and context influence team processes. With regard to shared cognition in teams, these SRM-based indices provide numerical assessments of a variety of the ways information in a team in used. We have shown how the SRM-based indices reflect the extent to which information is shared within the team and the pattern of information sharing in teams.

Using the variance components generated by the SRM, we can infer team process and relate the indices to individual inputs and team outcomes. This SRM approach can significantly improve our ability to test the predictions of the I-P-O framework and also demonstrate that specific inputs lead to specific outcomes. By understanding the effects inputs and processes have on team outcomes, we may be able to offer strategies for improving team performance. The strategies derived from SRM-based inferred processes should be applicable to investment bankers choosing stocks, diplomatic envoys attempting to slow nuclear proliferation, and couples selecting a movie they can watch as a couple.

REFERENCES

Ancona, D. G., & Caldwell, D. F. (1992). Demography and design: Predictors of new product team performance. *Organizational Science, 3*, 321–341.

Anderson, C., & Kilduff, G. J. (2009). Why do dominant personalities attain influence in face-to-face groups? The competence-signaling effects of trait dominance. *Journal of Personality and Social Psychology, 96*, 491–503.

Anderson, C., Srivastava, S., Beer, J. S., Spataro, S. E., & Chatman, J. A. (2006). Knowing your place: Self-perceptions of status in face-to-face groups. *Journal of Personality and Social Psychology, 91*, 1094–1110.

Bales, R. F. (1970). *Personality and interpersonal behavior*. New York, NY: Holt, Rinehart, & Winston.

Bell, S. (2007). Deep-level composition variables as predictors of team performance: A meta-analysis. *Journal of Applied Psychology, 92*, 595–615.

Bergman, J. Z., Small, E. E., Bergman, S. M., & Rentsch, J. R. (2010, April). *Trust in temporary teams: It's about the trustor*. Paper presented at the 25th Annual Meeting of the Society for Industrial and Organizational Psychology, Atlanta, GA.

Bray, R. M., Kerr, N. L., & Atkin, R. S. (1978). Effects of group size, problem difficulty, and sex on group performance and member reactions. *Journal of Personality and Social Psychology, 36*, 1224–1240.

Camacho, L. M., & Paulus, P. B. (1995). The role of social anxiousness in group brainstorming. *Journal of Personality and Social Psychology, 68*, 1071–1080.

Cannon-Bowers, J. A., & Salas, E. (2001). Reflections on shared cognition. *Journal of Organizational Behavior, 22*, 195–202.

Cannon-Bowers, J. A., Salas, E., & Converse, S. (1993). Shared mental models in expert team decision making. In N. J. Castellan (Ed.), *Individual and group decision making* (pp. 221–246). Hillsdale, NJ: Lawrence Erlbaum Associates.

Cooke, N. J., Salas, E., Cannon-Bowers, J. A., & Stout, R. (2000). Measuring team knowledge. *Human Factors, 42*, 151–173.

Cronbach, L. J., Gleser, G. C., Nanda, H., & Rajaratnam, N. (1972). *The dependability of behavioral measurements: Theory of generalizability of scores and profiles*. New York, NY: Wiley.

Davis, J. H. (1973). Group decision and social interaction: A theory of social decision schemes. *Psychological Review, 80*, 97–125.

DeChurch, L. A., & Mesmer-Magnus, J. R. (2010a). The cognitive underpinnings of effective teamwork: A meta-analysis. *Journal of Applied Psychology, 95*, 32–53.

DeChurch, L. A., & Mesmer-Magnus, J. R. (2010b). Measuring shared team mental models: A meta-analysis. *Group Dynamics, 14*, 1–14.

Hackman, J. R. (1987). The design of work teams. In J. W. Lorsch (Ed.), *Handbook of organizational behavior* (pp. 315–342). Englewood Cliffs, NJ: Prentice-Hall.

Hackman, J. R. (1992). Group influences on individuals in organizations. In M. D. Dunnette & L. M. Hough (Eds.), *Handbooks of industrial and organizational psychology* (Vol. 3, 2nd ed., pp. 199–267). Palo Alto, CA: Consulting Psychologists Press

Hackman, J. R., & Morris, C. G. (1975). Group tasks, group interaction process, and group performance effectiveness: A review and proposed integration. *Advances in Experimental Social Psychology, 8*, 45–99.

Harrison, D. A., Newman, D. A., & Roth, P. L. (2006). How important are job attitudes? Meta-analytic comparisons of integrative behavioral outcomes and time sequences. *Academy of Management Journal, 49*, 320–325.

Hinsz, V. B. (1995). Mental models of groups as social systems: Considerations of specification and assessment. *Small Group Research, 26*, 200–233.

Hinsz, V. B. (1999). Group decision making with responses of a quantitative nature: The theory of social decision schemes for quantities. *Organizational Behavior and Human Decision Processes, 80*, 28–49.

Hinsz, V. B. (2004). Metacognition and mental models in groups: An illustration with metamemory of group recognition memory. In E. Salas & S. Fiore (Eds.), *Team cognition: Understanding the factors that drive process and performance* (pp. 33–58). Washington, DC: American Psychological Association.

Ilgen, D. R., Hollenbeck, J. R., Johnson, M., & Jundt, D. (2005). Teams in organizations: From input-process-output models to IMOI models. *Annual Review of Psychology, 56*, 517–543.

Ilgen, D. R., & Hulin, C. L. (2000). *Computational modeling of behavior in organizations: The third scientific discipline*. Washington, DC: American Psychological Association.

Janis, I. (1982). *Groupthink* (2nd ed.). Boston, MA: Houghton-Mifflin.

Kenny, D. A. (1994). *Interpersonal perception: A social relations analysis*. New York, NY: Guilford Press.

400 • *Theories of Team Cognition*

Kenny, D. A., Kashy, D. A., & Cook, W. L. (2006). *Dyadic data analysis*. New York, NY: Guilford Press.

Kenny, D. A., & La Voie, L. (1984). The social relations model. In L. Berkowitz (Ed.), *Advances in experimental social psychology* (Vol. 18, pp. 142–182). Orlando, FL: Academic Press.

Klein, C., DiazGrandos, D., Salas, E., Le, H., Burke, C. S., Lyons, R., et al. (2009). Does team building work? *Small Group Research, 40*, 181–222.

Klimoski, R., & Mohammed, S. (1994). Team mental model: Construct or metaphor? *Journal of Management, 20*, 403–437.

Kozlowski, S. W. J., & Bell, B. S. (2003). Work groups and teams in organizations. In W. C. Borman, D. R. Ilgen, & R. J. Klimoski (Eds.), *Handbook of psychology: Industrial and organizational psychology* (Vol. 12, pp. 333–375). London, UK: Wiley.

Kozlowski, S. W. J., & Ilgen, D. R. (2006). Enhancing the effectiveness of work groups and teams. *Psychological Science in the Public Interest, 7*, 77–123.

Latané, B., Williams, K., & Harkins, S. (1979). Many hands make light the work: The causes and consequences of social loafing. *Journal of Personality and Social Psychology, 37*, 822–832.

Laughlin, P. R., & Ellis, A. L. (1986). Demonstrability and social combination processes on mathematical intellective tasks. *Journal of Experimental Social Psychology, 22*, 177–189.

Levine, J. M., & Moreland, R. L. (1990). Progress in small-group research. *Annual Review of Psychology, 41*, 585–634.

Littlepage, G. E., Hollingshead, A. B., Drake, L. R., & Littlepage, A. M. (2008). Transactive memory and performance in work groups: Specificity, communication, ability differences, and work allocation. *Group Dynamics: Theory, Research, and Practice, 12*, 223–241.

Markin, R. D., & Kivlighan, D. M. (2008). Central relationship teams in group psychotherapy: A social relations model analysis of transference. *Group Dynamics: Theory, Research, & Practice, 12*, 290–306.

Mathieu, J. E., Heffner, T. S., Goodwin, G. F., Salas, E., & Cannon-Bowers, J. A. (2000). The influence of shared mental models on team process and performance. *Journal of Applied Psychology, 85*, 273–283.

McGrath, J. E. (1964). *Social psychology: A brief introduction*. New York, NY: Holt, Rinehart & Winston.

McGrath, J. E. (1984). *Groups: Interaction and performance*. Englewood Cliffs, NJ: Prentice-Hall.

McGrath, J. E., & Altman, I. (1966). *Small group research: A synthesis and critique of the field*. Oxford, UK: Holt, Rinehart, & Winston.

Mesmer-Magnus, J. R., & DeChurch, L. A. (2009). Information sharing and team performance: A meta-analysis. *Journal of Applied Psychology, 94*, 535–546.

Paulus, P. B., & Brown, V. R. (2007). Toward more creative and innovative group idea generation: A cognitive-social-motivational perspective of brainstorming. *Social and Personality Psychology Compass, 1*, 248–265.

Pellid, L. H., Eisenhardt, K. M., & Xin, K. R. (1999). Exploring the black box: An analysis of work group diversity, conflict, and performance. *Administrative Science Quarterly, 44*, 1–28.

Reimer, T., Kuendig, S., Hoffrage, U., Park, E., & Hinsz, V. (2007). Effects of the information environment on group discussions and decision in the hidden-profile paradigm. *Communication Monographs, 74*, 1–28.

Reimer, T., Reimer, A., & Hinsz, V. B. (2010). Naïve groups can solve the hidden-profile problem. *Human Communication Research, 36*, 440–464.

Rentsch, J. R., & Hall, R. J. (1994). Members of great teams think alike: A model of team effectiveness and schema similarity among team members. *Advances in Interdisciplinary Studies of Work Teams, 1*, 223–262.

Rentsch, J. R., & Woehr, D. J. (2004). Quantifying congruence in cognition: Social relations modeling and team member schema similarity. In E. Salas & S. M. Fiore (Eds.), *Team cognition: Understanding the factors that drive process and performance* (pp. 11–31). Washington, DC: American Psychological Association.

Rico, R., Sanchez-Manzanares, M., Gil, F., & Gibson, C. (2008). Team implicit coordination processes: A team knowledge-based approach. *Academy of Management Review, 33*, 163–184.

Roethlisberger, F. J., & Dickson, W. J. (1939). *Management and the worker*. Cambridge, MA: Harvard University Press.

Salas, E., DiazGranados, D., Klein, C., Burke, C. S., Stagl, K. C., Goodwin, G. F., et al. (2008). Does team training improve team performance? A meta-analysis. *Human Factors, 50*, 903–933.

Stasser, G. (1999). A primer of social decision scheme theory: Models of group influence, competitive model-testing, and prospective modeling. *Organizational Behavior and Human Decision Processes, 80*, 3–20.

Stasser, G., & Titus, W. (1987). Effects of information load and percentage of shared information on the dissemination of unshared information during group discussion. *Journal of Personality and Social Psychology, 53*, 81–93.

Stasser, G., & Titus, W. (2003). Hidden profiles: A brief history. *Psychological Inquiry, 14*, 304–313.

Steiner, I. D. (1972). *Group process and productivity*. New York, NY: Academic Press.

Steiner, I. D. (1976). Task-performing groups. In J. W. Thibaut, J. T. Spence, & R. C. Carson (Eds.), *Contemporary topics in social psychology* (pp. 393–422). Morristown, NJ: General Learning Press.

Sutton, J. L., & Pierce, L. G. (2003). *A framework for understanding cultural diversity in cognition and teamwork*. Paper presented at the 8th International Command and Control Research and Technology Symposium.

Vroom, V. H., Grant, L. D., & Cotton, T. S. (1969). The consequences of social interaction in group problem solving. *Organizational Behavior and Human Performance, 4*, 77–95.

Watson, W. E., Kumar, K., & Michaelsen, L. K. (1993). Cultural diversity's impact on interaction process and performance: Comparing homogenous and diverse task groups. *Academy of Management Journal, 36*, 590–602.

Weingart, L. R. (1997). How did they do that? The ways and means of studying group process. *Research in Organizational Behavior, 19*, 189–239.

Weingart, L. R. (2006). Impact of group goals, task component complexity, effort, and planning on group performance. In J. M. Levine & R. L. Moreland (Eds.), *Small groups* (pp. 309–325). New York, NY: Psychology Press.

Weldon, E., & Gargano, G. M. (1985). Cognitive effort in additive task groups: The effects of shared responsibility on the quality of multiattribute judgments. *Organizational Behavior and Human Decision Processes, 36*, 348–361.

Williams, K. Y., & O'Reilly, C. A. (1998). Demography and diversity in organizations: A review of 40 years of research. *Research in Organizational Behavior, 20*, 77–104.

Section V

Social Psychology, Communication, and Developmental Perspectives

16

Team Cognition and the Accountabilities of the Tool Pass

Timothy Koschmann, Gary Dunnington, and Michael Kim

TOWARD A "SCIENCE OF TEAMS"

The title of this book, *Theories of Team Cognition: Cross-Disciplinary Perspectives*, hints at a broader agenda, one both rich with promise and fraught with potential troubles. Teamwork lies at the nexus of a variety of disciplinary interests. Cognitive and social psychology, organization science, human factors research, and communication studies, to name a few, all have scholarly interests related to the functioning of groups and teams. Given this convergence of interest, it would seem mutually advantageous to find ways of sharing insights across fields. The current volume seeks to engender just such a conversation. It endeavors to do so by trying to articulate the assumptions and "theoretical drivers" that motivate and undergird research within these disciplines. It represents a first step toward advancing this kind of conversation within an area of study that already has an overabundance of ways of formulating its topic, for example, distributed cognition (Hutchins, 2006), group cognition (Stahl, 2006), macrocognition (Cacciabue & Hollnagel, 1995; Klein et al., 2003; Letsky & Warner, 2008), socially shared cognition (Cannon-Bowers & Salas, 2001; Resnick, Levine, & Teasley, 1991), team learning (Senge, 1990), and team cognition (Salas & Fiore, 2004). By creating a taxonomy of theoretical models and seeking to identify areas of overlap between them, it is hoped that progress can be made toward integrating basic findings related to the performance of teams.

In this way, the book addresses a larger agenda, one intended to eventually lead to a "science of teams," a science that would enable us to make

405

406 • *Theories of Team Cognition*

positive recommendations regarding how teams should function. This would require establishing an agreed upon theoretical vocabulary and set of measurement methods. Taken for granted within this larger enterprise is a shared allegiance to a way of conducting research that entails (a) formulating an abstract model of what counts as the phenomenon of interest, (b) constructing operational means of measurement, and (c) using these measures to test hypotheses about how the matter, so construed, might be done better. The disciplines currently participating in the conversation on teamwork (i.e., cognitive and social psychology, management science, communication studies) all have a strong psychological orientation. However, as we expand the circle of participation wider and reach out to other disciplines, some problems begin to emerge. It becomes apparent that this strategy of beginning from a base of theoretical constructions is not one that is universally embraced across the human sciences. Indeed, some social scientists reject this kind of approach categorically and on principle. We will examine one critique of formal theorizing in the social sciences and point out its relevance to the task of constructing a science of teams. We offer a sample of an alternative form of analysis and suggest a framework for what might be termed a "hybrid" approach to studying teams.

GARFINKEL'S CRITIQUE OF THE PARSONIAN THEORY OF ACTION

As a discipline, sociology is centrally concerned with explicating the basis of society and social structure. It addresses the classical Hobbesian question of how it happens that our interaction with others is, for the most part, orderly. A historically important position on this question was that developed by Talcott Parsons. The state of the discipline in the early part of the 20th century, as Parsons described it, resembled the contemporary literature on teamwork. He reported "there are as many systems of sociological theory as there are sociologists" and lamented "there is no common basis" (Parsons, 1937, p. 774). Parsons sought to rectify this. His ambition was to develop not only a unifying theoretical base for sociology, but also one that would serve for all the "sciences of action" (p. 769)—economics, political science, and psychology. In a volume that profoundly shaped sociological inquiry for half a century, Parsons

Team Cognition and the Accountabilities of the Tool Pass • 407

surveyed the writings of four prominent social theorists of the previous century and proposed a unified framework for studying social action.* His approach was based on the study of "the elementary unit act" (p. 768). By his account, this unit act could be analyzed in terms of four more fundamental components:

> (1) [The act] implies an agent, *an actor* [italics added]. (2) For purposes of definition, the act must have *an end* [italics added], a future state of affairs toward which the process of action is oriented. (3) It must be initiated in *a situation* [italics added] of which the trends of development differ in one or more important respects from the state of affairs to which the action is oriented, the end. The situation is in turn analyzable into two elements: those over which the actor has no control, that is which he cannot alter, or prevent from being altered, in conformity with his end, and those over which he has such control. The former may be termed *the conditions* [italics added] of action, the latter *the means* [italics added]. Finally, (4) there is inherent in the conception of this unit, in its analytical uses, a certain mode of relationship between these elements. That is, in the choice of alternatives, there is a "normative orientation" of action. Within the area of control of the actor, the means employed cannot, in general, be conceived either as chosen at random or as dependent exclusively on the conditions of action, but must in some sense be subject to the influence of *an independent, determinate selective factor* [italics added], a knowledge of which is necessary to the understanding of the concrete course of action. (Parsons, 1937, pp. 44–45)

Parsons believed a science of human action could be constructed on the basis of an analysis of this sort.

By including subjective elements such as perceived "ends," "normative orientations," and choice among alternatives, Parsons sought to incorporate the perspective of the actor into his model. It was to be a model whereby action was not strictly determined by environmental conditions but reflected some form of choice on the part of the actor. Thus, Parsons titled his approach "the voluntaristic theory of action" (Parsons, 1937, p. 62). The actor's choices in this model, however, are guided by socially accepted norms of conduct. Parsons defined an *end* as, "a future state of

---

* Parsons' (1937) book, *The Structure of Social Action*, examined and sought to integrate the writings of Alfred Marshall, Vilfredo Pareto, Émile Durkheim, and Max Weber. Durkheim and Weber are foundational theorists in sociology. The other two, Marshall and Pareto, were polymaths, also known for their contributions in economics and social philosophy.

408 • *Theories of Team Cognition*

affairs to which action is oriented by virtue of the fact that it is deemed desirable by the actor(s)" (p. 75). A *norm*, therefore, "is a verbal description of the concrete course of action thus regarded as desirable, combined with an injunction to make certain future actions conform to this course" (p. 75). Action, from the observer's perspective, is made meaningful in the light of such norms, although Parsons' model does not require that the agent necessarily be mindful of these socially prescribed norms when acting. Parsons endeavored to construct a means of studying action, one that could still meet the standards of an empirical science and provide a basis for prediction. His approach was thorough and elegant. As an effort to unify existing social theory, it was a tour de force.

Harold Garfinkel, one of Parsons' students, had certain reservations with regard to the program put forward by his mentor. The Parsonian "theory of action," in Garfinkel's view, was curiously detached from the practicalities of what people actually do. Garfinkel (1952, p. 58) charged that the Parsonian actor inhabits "a world-by-definition" and explained: "This world is populated *not with persons but with puppets* [italics added]. These puppets are creatures of [the theorist's] own design: ideal types." Garfinkel protested, however, that actors are not "judgmental dopes" (p. 259)—they are not simply following rules or complying with normative standards. The model advanced by Parsons, he argued, fails to engage the forms of practical reasoning actually employed by actors within their social arrangements. Social order, for Garfinkel, is an actor's achievement and something that needs to be investigated within his or her vernacular world. He argued that any situation can "be viewed as self-organizing with respect to the intelligible character of its own appearances as either representations of or as evidences-of-a-social-order" (Garfinkel, 1967, p. 33). In place of Parsons' hypothesized action frame, we find a proposal to look instead at how members themselves actually produce their social settings as understandable. "The argument that meaning requires order, and the empirical elaboration of how this is achieved through sequential devices and reflexive attention, are Garfinkel's unique contribution to social theory" (Rawls, 2008, p. 703).

Garfinkel overturned Parsons' program of system building and replaced it with an empirical one devoted to describing the processes through which actors themselves construct meaningful worlds. He directs our attention to how actors produce their actions as sensible and competent. Button and Sharrock (1998) write:

Team Cognition and the Accountabilities of the Tool Pass • 409

> The design of social actions so that others can make sense of them is an indispensible feature of social action, for unless it is possible for people to recognize "ordinary social facts," they would not be capable of mutually adjusting their conduct with respect to one another in commonplace settings. (p. 75)

These kinds of design and recognition, it should be noted, are also prerequisites to any form of teamwork.

Social settings are organized in particular ways. Garfinkel noted, "Any setting organizes its activities to make its properties as an organized environment of practical activities detectable, countable, recordable, reportable, tell-a-story-aboutable, analyzable—in short, *accountable*" (Garfinkel, 1967, p. 33, italics in original). Garfinkel located the key to addressing the Hobbesian problem of social order in participants' practical reasoning, specifically their methods of accounting for their own actions. This notion, the notion of accountability, is one of fundamental importance to his approach to doing sociology. Actions "are not only done, they are done so that they can be seen to have been done" (Button & Sharrock, 1998, p. 75, italics in original). Participants' actions are produced in ways that make them recognizable for what they are, and in producing the actions in just that way, members offer an account of what they are doing. When Garfinkel speaks of accountability, therefore, he is concerned with "the ways in which actions are *organized*: that is, put together as publicly observable, reportable occurrences" (Button & Sharrock, 1998, p. 75, italics in original).

Actions are accountable in the ways in which they document or give an account of themselves. However, they are accountable in another way, as well. In ordinary parlance, we use the term *accountable* in the sense of being responsible to one another. This usage has a normative character. As Garfinkel (1967) explained:

> In exactly the way that persons are members to organized affairs, they are engaged in serious and practical work of detecting, demonstrating, persuading through displays in the ordinary occasions of their interactions the appearances of consistent, coherent, clear, chosen, planful arrangements. (p. 34)

Members are obliged to produce their actions in ways that will appear sensible to others. Actions are accountable, therefore, both in the sense of offering an account of themselves and in the sense that they are obliged to be performed one particular way and not another.

410 • *Theories of Team Cognition*

We have methods for producing our actions as sensible and accountable. As Garfinkel (1967) expressed it, "In exactly the ways in which a setting is organized, it *consists* of methods whereby its members are provided with accounts of the setting as countable, storyable, proverbial, comparable, picturable, representable—i.e., accountable events" (p. 34). Heritage (1984) describes Garfinkel's approach as a "cognitive-moral" (p. 120) one. It leads to a different form of sociological analysis:

> Garfinkel consequently turns the problem of social order into a concern with how people organize social actions so that others can make sense of them, so that each person involved in an interaction can identify the actions being performed by others—and thus comprehend the relationship of the actions to the complex of activity under whose auspices they are done, and whose implementation they comprise. (Button & Sharrock, 1998, p. 75)

Agents' orientations to their own actions held little relevance to Parsons' analytic framework, but for Garfinkel, accounts are not only important as material for analysis, but also play a critical role in the creation and maintenance of the social organization itself (Heritage, 1984). Garfinkel proposed the name *ethnomethodology* for this approach to doing sociology, one that focuses on the details of how participants accountably produce their actions as sensible. It begins from his policy that they have methods for doing so. The task for sociology, from Garfinkel's perspective, is one of explicating what these methods might be.

THE ACCOUNTABILITIES OF THE TOOL PASS

To illustrate how an ethnomethodologically informed analysis of team cognition might proceed, we offer a concrete example. We focus here on the forms of accountability made visible in a simple act, the passing of a tool from a scrub nurse to a surgeon during the course of a surgical procedure.[*] It would be hard to find a setting more deeply steeped in regulation

---

[*] Garfinkel and Livingston (2003) use formatted queues as an everyday example of a methodically ordered social activity. Heritage (1984, Chapter 5) uses the example of a greeting exchange. Note that issuing a greeting and forming a queue are not methods, as we use the term here, but instead depend on an array of more fundamental methods for recognizing that a greeting has been issued, for displaying that one is standing in a line, and so on. The same is true for tool passes.

Team Cognition and the Accountabilities of the Tool Pass • 411

and accountability than the operating theatre. We look here at two examples of tool passing and show how they might be analyzed in terms of how participants offer accounts of what they are doing through their actions.

Excerpt 1 provides an abbreviated transcript from an observed operation.[*] The transcribed fragment comes from a "keyhole" surgical procedure. This means that rather than laying the patient open, the operative procedure was carried out using instruments inserted through small "ports" in the patient's side. As seen in Figure 16.1, the surgeon and the scrub nurse were positioned on opposite sides of the operating table. Video monitors were placed across the table from each, enabling them to view the interior space of the patient's body.[†] In the excerpted fragment, the surgeon extracted a tool from the patient's body while issuing a request for a "clip applier." His request took the form of a specifying expression and an adverb ("please"). To satisfy the request, his respondent must resolve the referring expression. Sanchez Svensson (2005) noted that there is no standardized nomenclature for surgical instruments. Naming conventions may vary from hospital to hospital and from surgeon to surgeon. The tools of surgery may be known by a variety of names based on function, the inventor of the instrument, the place where it was invented, and so on.

|00:11:45;16| S: ⌈((*withdraws tool held in right hand from port and sets it aside on patient*))
|00:11:45;16| S: ⌊**A clip applier please.**
|00:11:46;13| N: ((*selects tool from table*))
|00:11:47;05| N: ((*extends tool handle toward surgeon*))
|00:11:48;03| S: ⌈((*extends right hand toward nurse*))
|00:11:48;03| S: ⌊((*shifts gaze down*))
|00:11:48;14| N: ⌈((*places tool in surgeon's hand*))
|00:11:48;14| S: ⌊((*receives requested instrument*))
|00:11:50;12| S: ((*inserts tool in port*))

EXCERPT 1 (#99-001)

---

[*] The transcripts are prepared using the notational conventions of Conversation Analysis (Jefferson, 2004). Spoken speech is presented in bold face to set it off from the other action descriptions. Square brackets mark actions that temporally co-occur. The column to the left contains time code marking the onset of the action appearing in that line.

The recording analyzed here comes from the Southern Illinois University Surgical Education Video Archive. This is a collection of videotaped surgeries gathered over a decade at two teaching hospitals affiliated with the medical school. Further information about the video archive can be found at http://www.siumed.edu/call/index.html.

[†] See Mondada (2003) and Koschmann, LeBaron, Goodwin, and Feltovich (2011) for a more elaborate discussion of visualization in endoscopic surgeries.

412 • *Theories of Team Cognition*

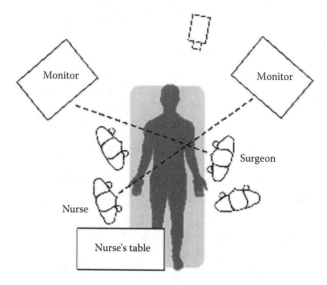

FIGURE 16.1
Layout of the surgical workspace showing the relative positions of the surgeon and the scrub nurse to each other and to their respective video monitors.

Tool changes occur frequently during the conduct of a surgical procedure, and small inefficiencies would accumulate over the course of the operation. In this case, only 5 seconds elapsed from the moment that the first tool was withdrawn from the patient's body to the time when the second was placed into service. The process was executed swiftly and with great economy of motion.

Safety and sterility are also important considerations in this setting. Instruments must be handled in ways that avoid contamination. Surgeons often wear two pairs of gloves, reducing sensitivity. Therefore, care must be taken to avoid dropping tools. Many of the instruments are sharp and must be handed off in ways that avoid injury to the parties involved. Furthermore, every instrument (e.g., scalpel, cautery, scissors, forceps) is designed to be held in a specific way. It falls to the passer to position the tool in the hand of the surgeon so that it can be placed into use without need for reorientation or examination.* In this case, the

---

* There is clearly more to it than this. See Sanchez Svensson, Heath, and Luff (2007) for a detailed description of how a particular instrument might be passed in different ways depending on the task at hand.

Team Cognition and the Accountabilities of the Tool Pass • 413

instrument is almost 50 cm in length with a long, thin shaft, a working tip, and a pistol grip on the other end. The nurse lifted the tool from the end of the shaft, the part that would eventually be inserted into the patient's body, and placed the pistol grip into the surgeon's outstretched hand.

The choreography of this tool pass resembles that of a handshake. The surgeon's hand and the tool arrive at the same instant meeting in a place midway between the two parties. This level of coordination requires careful monitoring of the progress of the ongoing procedure on the part of the scrub nurse and anticipation of what will be done next. Sanchez Svensson (2005) described the situation as follows:

> The smooth accomplishment of the passing of instruments is not simply a matter of constantly attending to what others are doing; attentiveness and "sensitivity to" others' conduct is embedded in an understanding of the routine ways of conducting procedures and using particular instruments. It is not that the passing of an instrument is an instant response to a request, but an anticipated and organized accomplishment in and through the developing course of the participant's activities. (p. 176)

We might say that timeliness and accuracy are accountable matters with respect to the tool pass, but how would we know that this was the case? One way that this could be demonstrated would be by describing instances in which participants' expectations were violated. Excerpt 2 contains a transcript of a second tool pass from the same operation. As in Excerpt 1, a request was issued simultaneous with the withdrawal of a tool from the patient's body signaling the initiation of a tool pass cycle. The surgeon extended his hand to receive the requested tool, but instead of delivering a tool, the nurse asked him to repeat his request. After the surgeon did so, the nurse placed the requested tool in his outstretched hand, and the operative procedure went on.

In this case, the choreography of the tool pass seems disrupted. The surgeon's hand arrived, but there was nothing there to meet it. Just as an unreciprocated invitation to shake hands is an accountable matter, a failure to produce a requested tool is also an accountable event. Although she had already selected a tool from the table following the request, the nurse did not make it available to the surgeon (Figure 16.2). The surgeon's shift of gaze toward the nurse inquired into the problem. By not passing the instrument in her hand, the nurse performed an accountable action, one

|00:09:08;06| S: ⌈((withdraws instrument held in right hand from port and sets it aside))
|00:09:08;06| S: ⌊**Could I have a Maryland please?**
|00:09:10;10| S: ⌈((extends right hand across table toward nurse))
|00:09:10;10| N: ⌊((lifts clip applier from tool table))
|00:09:10;15| N: **Pardon?**
|00:09:10;18| S: ((looks to scrub nurse))
|00:09:10;26| S: **Mary⌈land.**
|00:09:11;04| S: ⌊((returns eyes to video monitor))
|00:09:12;06| N: ((replaces clip applier on table))
|00:09:13;08| N: ((selects requested instrument from tool table))
|00:09:13;14| S: ((directs gaze toward arriving tool))
|00:09:14;15| N: ⌈((places tool in surgeon's hand))
|00:09:14;15| S: ⌊((receives requested instrument))
|00:09:16;17| S: ((inserts tool in port))

EXCERPT 2 (#99-001)

that constituted a withholding. But why would she withhold it? Because it was the wrong tool, of course! Or, more precisely, because she was uncertain that the object in her hand matched the surgeon's specification. Her withholding announced this uncertainty.

The surgeon's shift in gaze revealed an expectation violated. By continuing to hold his hand out, he marked that his request remained open and

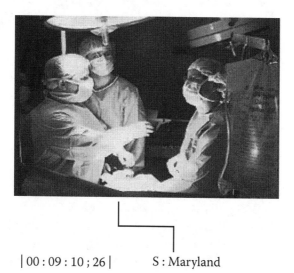

| 00 : 09 : 10 ; 26 | S : Maryland

FIGURE 16.2
The surgeon extends his hand and looks to the scrub nurse. The scrub nurse holds a clip applier in her right hand.

Team Cognition and the Accountabilities of the Tool Pass • 415

unsatisfied. He displayed his orientation to timeliness and held the nurse accountable for the delay. The nurse's withholding of the tool also displayed an expectation violated. At the stage in the procedure in which this exchange occurred, the work consisted of doing blunt dissection and applying clips to vessels that are about to be divided.* A routine sequence of instruments, therefore, might be as follows: blunt-tipped forceps, clip applier, followed by a scissors. Although the tool requested by the surgeon is commonly used within the procedure, it falls outside of this typical sequence, and therefore, its use would be harder to anticipate. The nurse's withholding of the tool within her hand displayed her accountable orientation to producing the *correct* tool. The nurse and surgeon made their orientation to timeliness and accuracy visible to each other and, in so doing, rendered it visible to us as well.

The actions of both parties stand as an account of how the they viewed their work, how they understood what they were doing together, and who they were. They did these things in the way they did not *because* they were nurses and surgeons; instead, the participants presented themselves recognizably and accountably *as* nurses and surgeons by doing these things in just the way that they did.

A HYBRID APPROACH TO STUDYING TEAMWORK

We have sketched out an example of how an ethnomethodologically informed analysis of teamwork might be done. By directing attention to the accountable methods through which members of the team produced their actions, Garfinkel offers us a different way to theorize our topic. Rawls (2003) writes:

> Garfinkel has opened the way for a new sort of theorizing.... There is no reason, in principle, why theorists cannot be faithful to the phenomena; no reason why they have to proceed in generic terms. Garfinkel has shown us the possibility of empirical theorizing and it is in these terms that I was to refer to Garfinkel as one of the great social theorists of the twentieth century. (p. 145)

---

* See Koschmann et al. (2011) for a more detailed description of this particular operative procedure.

416 • *Theories of Team Cognition*

Built into Garfinkel's "empirical theoretic" approach is an entirely different treatment of shared cognition.

Cannon-Bowers and Salas (2001) wrote, "the concept of shared cognition can help us to explain what separates effective from ineffective teams by suggesting that in effective teams, members have similar or compatible knowledge, and that they use this knowledge to guide their (coordinated) behavior" (p. 196). A variety of names have been attached to the forms of knowledge underlying team performance, including teamwork competency (Cannon-Bowers & Salas, 1997), team knowledge (Cooke, Salas, Cannon-Bowers, & Stout, 2000), team mental models (Mohammed & Dumville, 2001), team situational awareness (Salas, Fiore, Cannon-Bowers, & Stout, 2001), and transactive memory (Brandon & Hollingshead, 2004). These different formulations reflect different theoretical orientations and would seem to suggest that there might be a variety of different kinds of knowledge relevant to the work of teams. Whatever the nature of the knowledge, however, there seems to be widespread agreement that some form of knowledge sharing is essential to coordinated action.

Garfinkel (1952) wrote:

> The big question is not whether actors understand each other or not. The fact is that they do understand each other, that they *will* understand each other but the catch is that they will understand each other regardless of how they *would* be understood. ... The big question for the "problem of understanding" is thus the question of describing the conditions under which men do in fact perceive each other in the ways that they do. (pp. 367–368, italics in original)

Rather than attempting to codify what knowledge is shared, Garfinkel focuses on the organizational details of how the sharing gets done. As Schegloff (1991) recounted:

> what seemed programmatically promising to Garfinkel was a procedural sense of common or shared, a set of practices by which actions and stances could be predicated on and displayed as oriented to "knowledge held in common"—knowledge that might thereby be reconfirmed, modified, and expanded. (pp. 151–152)

The eponymous methods studied by ethnomethodologists are the procedures whereby shared understandings are created, negotiated, and sustained.

Team Cognition and the Accountabilities of the Tool Pass • 417

The question that motivates this book concerns how might we begin to rigorously and scientifically study the work of teams. Teams have been defined as

> a distinguishable set of two or more people who interact dynamically, interdependently, and adaptively toward a common and valued goal/object/mission, who have each been assigned specific roles or functions to perform, and who have a limited life span of membership. (Salas, Dickinson, Converse, & Tannebaum, 1992, p. 4)

Left unasked, however, is how it is that teams constitute themselves as teams in the first place. How would we begin to investigate such a matter? In a recent paper, Rawls (2008) described what ethnomethodologically informed "hybrid studies of work" might contribute to organizational studies. Her recommendations, however, apply with equal force to the study of teams. Drawing on Garfinkel's writings, Rawls describes how not only teams, but all social groups are constituted. Rawls (2008) notes that Garfinkel

> proposes that situated actors, engaged in constructing a sequential order of meaning, constitute a group only when, and only for as long as, the sequential character of the interaction in which they are currently engaged requires of them collectively a mutual commitment to constitutive properties of the situation. (p. 707)

This was quite evident in the two instances of tool passing that we examined earlier. The nurse and surgeon displayed a mutual orientation to the accountabilities of the task at hand.

Hybrid studies of work focus on just how a local sense of orderliness is produced. This is seen, not in a study of abstracted features, but rather in the study of how participants make visible the accountable aspects of their concerted activity. Rawls (2008) writes that a "focus on detail in habits and routines does not look for order, nor treat meaning, intelligibility or mutual action as a matter of order" (p. 706). Rawls continues: "The workers are pictured as managing to enact just the right routines at the just the right time, and the question of how they know when or what is not problematized" (p. 706). We need to look beyond such features to the ordering accountabilities that lie behind. Rawls proposes the following:

> What is required for the study of how this order is jointly made is a method that preserves the contingencies of its local production, those sequential

418 • *Theories of Team Cognition*

details oriented toward by workers in doing their work and a theory treating these contingencies themselves, not the routines and habits an observer might see "sedimenting" from them, as essential. (p. 706)

When any specific case is reduced to a count-able within an externally imposed theoretical category, we risk losing our grasp of the ordering properties of the setting of production, its local contingencies, and its observable accountabilities. This is the basis for Garfinkel's methodological prescription that cases be studied in their practical details. He "is interested in how—just how—contingencies are rendered as recognizable objects using shared methods that exhibit an immediate order that *can* be seen in each single case" (Rawls, 2008, p. 704). To begin to understand the work of teams from an actor's perspective, we need to start collecting study-able instances of just what we are taking teamwork to be and augment them with carefully constructed analyses designed to document the vernacular methods by which the participants carry out their work. The enterprise is *empirically grounded*, not only in the sense that it directly studies teamwork as a naturally occurring phenomenon, but also because it retains a record of the circumstances under which each analyzed instance arose (much as we have done here with the tool pass examples). This enables the reader of an account to reconstruct the analyzed event and thereby evaluate the adequacy of its analysis.[*]

Teams become teams in the ways that members locally manage the accountabilities and contingencies that shape their work. To develop a grasp of the "just whatness" of teamwork, it needs to be studied as a "thing-in-its-details" (Garfinkel & Livingston, 2003, p. 23). This represents a proposal for an "incommensurable, asymmetric, and alternate" (Garfinkel, 2002, p. 192) approach to building a science of teams.

REFERENCES

Brandon, D. P., & Hollingshead, A. B. (2004). Transactive memory systems in organizations: Matching tasks, expertise and people. *Organization Science, 15*, 633–644.

Button, G., & Sharrock, W. (1998). The organizational accountability of technological work. *Social Studies of Science, 28*, 73–102.

---

[*] This opens into a broader discussion of the "validity" of an analysis, which we will not pursue here. Interested readers might consult Seedhouse (2005).

Cacciabue, P. C., & Hollnagel, E. (1995). Simulation of cognition. In J.-M. Hoc, P. C. Cacciabue & E. Hollnagel (Eds.), *Expertise and technology: Cognition and human-computer cooperation* (pp. 55–74). Hillsdale, NJ: Lawrence Erlbaum Associates.

Cannon-Bowers, J. A., & Salas, E. (1997). Teamwork competencies: The interaction of team member knowledge skills and attitudes. In O. F. O'Neil (Ed.), *Workforce readiness: Competencies and assessment* (pp. 151–174). Hillsdale, NJ: Lawrence Erlbaum Associates.

Cannon-Bowers, J. A., & Salas, E. (2001). Reflections on shared cognition. *Journal of Organizational Behavior, 22*, 195–202.

Cooke, N., Salas, E., Cannon-Bowers, J. A., & Stout, R. (2000). Measuring team knowledge. *Human Factors, 42*, 151–173.

Garfinkel, H. (1952). *The perception of the other: A study in social order.* Unpublished doctoral dissertation, Harvard University, Cambridge, MA.

Garfinkel, H. (1967). *Studies in ethnomethodology.* Englewood Cliffs, NJ: Prentice-Hall.

Garfinkel, H. (2002). *Ethnomethodology's program: Working out Durkheim's aphorism.* Lanham, MD: Rowman & Littlefield.

Garfinkel, H., & Livingston, E. (2003). Phenomenal field properties of order in formatted queues and their neglected standing in the current situation of inquiry. *Visual Studies, 18*, 21–28.

Heritage, J. (1984). *Garfinkel and ethnomethodology.* Cambridge, UK: Polity Press.

Hutchins, E. (2006). The distributed cognition perspective on human interaction. In N. J. Enfield & S. Levinson (Eds.), *Roots of human sociality: Culture, cognition and interaction* (pp. 375–398). New York, NY: Berg.

Jefferson, G. (2004). Glossary of transcript symbols with an introduction. In G. Lerner (Ed.), *Conversation analysis: Studies from the first generation* (pp. 13–31). Amsterdam, the Netherlands: John Benjamins Publishing.

Klein, G., Ross, K. G., Moon, B. M., Klein, D. E., Hoffman, R. R., & Hollnagel, E. (2003). Macrocognition. *IEEE Intelligent Systems, 18*, 81–84.

Koschmann, T., LeBaron, C., Goodwin, C., & Feltovich, P. (2011). "Can you see the cystic artery yet?" A simple matter of trust. *Journal of Pragmatics, 43*, 475–488.

Letsky, M., & Warner, N. W. (2008). Macrocognition in teams. In M. Letsky, N. W. Warner, S. M. Fiore, & C. A. P. Smith (Eds.), *Macrocognition in teams* (pp. 1–14). Burlington, VT: Ashgate Publishing.

Mohammed, S., & Dumville, B. C. (2001). Team mental models in a team knowledge framework: Expanding theory and measurement across disciplinary boundaries. *Journal of Organizational Behavior, 22*, 89–106.

Mondada, L. (2003). Working with video: How surgeons produce video records of their actions. *Visual Studies, 18*, 59–73.

Parsons, T. (1937). *The structure of social action: A study in social theory with special reference to a group of recent European writers.* New York, NY: McGraw-Hill.

Rawls, A. W. (2003). Harold Garfinkel. In G. Ritzer (Ed.), *The Blackwell companion to major contemporary social theorists* (pp. 122–153). Oxford, UK: Blackwell.

Rawls, A. W. (2008). Garfinkel, ethnomethodology and workplace studies. *Organization Studies, 29*, 701–732.

Resnick, L. B., Levine, J. M., & Teasley, S. D. (Eds.). (1991). *Perspectives on socially shared cognition.* Washington, DC: American Psychological Association.

Salas, E., Dickinson, T. L., Converse, S. A., & Tannebaum, S. I. (1992). Toward an understanding of team performance and training. In R. W. Swezey & E. Salas (Eds.), *Teams: Their training and performance* (pp. 3–29). Norwood, NJ: Ablex.

420 • *Theories of Team Cognition*

Salas, E., & Fiore, S. M. (Eds.). (2004). *Team cognition: Understanding the factors that drive process and performance*. Washington, DC: American Psychological Association.

Salas, E., Fiore, S. M., Cannon-Bowers, J. A., & Stout, R. (2001). Team situational awareness: Cue recognition training. In M. McNeese, E. Salas, & M. R. Endsley (Eds.), *New trends in cooperative activities: Understanding system dynamics in complex environments* (pp. 169–190). Santa Monica, CA: Human Factors and Ergonomics Society.

Sanchez Svensson, M. (2005). *Configuring awareness: Work, interaction and collaboration in operating theatres*. Unpublished doctoral dissertation, Kings College, University of London, London, UK.

Sanchez Svensson, M., Heath, C., & Luff, P. (2007). Instrumental action: The timely exchange of implements during surgical operations. In L. Bannon, I. Wagner, C. Gutwin, R. Harper, & K. Schmidt (Eds.), *Proceedings of the 10th European Conference on Computer-Supported Work* (pp. 41–60). London, UK: Springer.

Schegloff, E. (1991). Conversation analysis and socially shared cognition. In L. Resnick, J. Levine, & S. Teasley (Eds.), *Perspectives on socially shared cognition* (pp. 150–171). Washington, DC: American Psychological Association.

Schegloff, E. (1996). Confirming allusions: Towards an empirical account of action. *American Journal of Sociology, 104*, 161–216.

Seedhouse, P. (2005). Conversation analysis as research methodology. In K. Richards & P. Seedhouse (Eds.), *Applying conversation analysis* (pp. 251–266). New York, NY: Palgrave.

Senge, P. (1990). *The fifth discipline: The art and practice of the learning organization*. New York, NY: Doubleday.

Stahl, G. (2006). *Group cognition: Computer support for building collaborative knowledge*. Cambridge, MA: MIT Press.

17

Transactive Memory Theory and Teams: Past, Present, and Future

*Andrea B. Hollingshead, Naina Gupta,
Kay Yoon, and David P. Brandon*

Most individuals have a specific role to play on their teams. Some roles are formally assigned such as manager or supervisor, positions on a football team, or tasks on an assembly line. Others emerge through interaction such as "interpersonal conflict expert," "social planner," or "technology problem solver." Roles serve as a way of delegating responsibility for different aspects of the team's tasks. Although teams may have similar role structures, team cognition about members' roles can vary greatly across teams because each individual comes with different knowledge, motivation, experiences, skill sets, and ability levels. One explanation for the ubiquitous finding that team performance often improves over time is that experienced teams are able to make better use of each individual's expertise (Liang, Moreland, & Argote, 1995).

Transactive memory systems theory is a theory about how people in relationships, groups or teams (we use these two terms interchangeably), and organizations learn "who knows what" and use that knowledge to decide "who will do what," resulting in more efficient and effective individual and collective performance (Hollingshead, 2010a). Transactive memory explains how people in collectives learn, store, use, and coordinate their knowledge to accomplish individual, group, and organizational goals (Hollingshead, 2009). Transactive memory theory can be used to describe three components of team cognition: (1) its structure and organization; (2) the processes underlying its development and change; and (3) its content.

A fundamental premise of transactive memory theory is that other people can serve as external memory aids. Groups of interdependent

421

422 • *Theories of Team Cognition*

individuals, by dividing responsibility for different knowledge areas and using one another as external storage devices, can create a memory system that holds much more information than any one of those individuals could retain alone. The immediate benefit to group members is an eased cognitive workload due to the division of labor—members can share the burden for remembering information that is relevant for their group and can ask other members for information based on their areas of responsibility (Hollingshead, 2000). Evidence of transactive memory systems has been found in a variety of relationships and groups, including married couples, dating couples, families, friends, coworkers, and project teams in both organizational and laboratory settings (e.g., Argote, 1999; Argote, Ingram, Levine, & Moreland, 2000; Faraj & Sproull, 2000; Hollingshead, 1998a, 1998b, 2000, 2001; Lewis, Lange, & Gillis, 2005; Liang et al., 1995; Moreland & Myaskovsky, 2000).

This chapter begins with an overview of the origins of transactive memory followed by a discussion of the theoretical extensions that have been made since the mid-1980s by group and team researchers. We focus only on those theoretical extensions that are relevant to cognition in work teams and do not address those about couples in close relationships (for review, see Hollingshead & Brandon, 2003). We conclude with a theoretical integration, a critique, and future research directions. One important assumption that underlies transactive memory systems theory is that, taken together, members have sufficient knowledge, skills (broadly defined, so this includes learning and information retrieval skills), resources, and motivation to perform group tasks.

ORIGINAL THEORETICAL FORMULATIONS

Transactive memory theory has its roots in social and cognitive psychology. In the mid-1980s, Wegner, Giuliano, and Hertel (1985) set out to discover conceptual clarity in an area of inquiry they described as "dangerous territory... something of a black hole"—the notion of "group mind" (p. 253). These authors noted that previous conceptions of group mind were abundant (at various levels of sophistication), but all basically drew an analogy between the individual mind and a social system, using terms such as "collective conscious versus unconscious" and "mind of the crowd" (p. 254) to describe within-group similarities and the tendency of groups to act as units. The danger in using such notions, according to Wegner et al., was that the group mind did not actually reside anywhere and there was no way to communicate with the group mind in an observable fashion, which led some theorists to rather exotic explanations, such as telepathy and magic, to explain group mind phenomena.

The major errors in the group mind concept arose from the emphasis on shared mental processes of group members as a defining quality and the tendency to ignore communication processes among group members. To address these concerns, Wegner and his colleagues developed transactive memory theory (Wegner et al., 1985; Wegner, 1987, 1995).

Escape From the Group Mind: Transactive Memory Theory

Wegner et al. (1985) proposed a theory of group memory that emphasized cognitive interdependence in "intimate dyads" (people in very close interpersonal relationships) or the tendency of intimates to think differently when with their partner than when alone. Termed "transactive memory," the theory focused on how information enters dyads and then is organized and used by those dyads. Constructing the system involved building individual memory systems, but those systems are linked together by interaction. A two-component definition of transactive memory was composed of "(1) an organized store of knowledge that is contained entirely in the individual memory systems of the group members and (2) a set of knowledge-relevant transactive processes that occur among group members" (Wegner et al., 1985, p. 256). More simply put, transactive memory is what you know, what I know, what we know, and how we get that knowledge from one another. Thus, it is a property of a group and not traceable to any of the individuals alone. In subsequent work, Wegner (1987, 1995) expanded the theory beyond dyads and elaborated the processes, structures, and outcomes associated with the development of transactive memory systems.

Processes of Transactive Memory: Encoding, Storage, and Retrieval

Wegner et al. (1985) proposed three central processes of transactive memory: how information gets into the system, how it stays there, and how it is later used or, in transactive memory terminology, encoding, storage

424 • *Theories of Team Cognition*

and modification, and retrieval. Encoding information, or getting data into the transactive memory system, is a process of individual dyad members encountering information and then discussing it in ways that inform each member about what the other knows. For example, talking about a dish at a dinner party and what the recipe may involve will encode that information into the dyadic transactive memory system. Such chats about information may also change that information from fact to idiosyncratic interpretation or vice versa, as perception drives conversation and perception is not always exact (that wasn't cilantro in the recipe, it was Italian parsley!).

Once stored, memories may be altered to a degree by communication or the need to make the information communicable, for example, simplifying facts or removing inconsistencies to make a story easier to repeat or to reconcile it with new, related information. At retrieval, dyad members communicate to retrieve information one or both has stored. Retrieval may involve a "do you remember that recipe…" kind of process called interactive cueing where partners interact to retrieve some piece of information. Information may again be altered by the communication process, but group members working together to recall information may still be more effective than individual recall.

Wegner (1995) compared transactive memory to computer system memory and human groups to computer networks having shared directories describing the distribution of expertise. Expertise is defined in the transactive memory literature to broadly include the know-what, know-how, and know-why of a knowledge domain (Quinn, Anderson, & Finkelstein, 1996).

Necessary to maintain such a system are processes of directory updating, information allocation, and retrieval coordination. As applied to transactive memory systems, directories are metamemories about what others know. Directories are created from multiple sources of information about group member expertise. Updating of directories is ongoing, moving from any crude notions of expertise to more accurate representations, and may be difficult if a particular directory structure becomes entrenched in group members.

Information allocation is described as "the procedure whereby individual memories are fashioned into a differentiated group memory that is useful to the group" (Wegner, 1995, p. 332). If ideally executed, information allocation will direct data to the group member with the internal directory structure best suited to store that particular kind of information.

Some drawbacks to allocation are that some group members may eventually forget useful areas of information or progressive differentiation may occur, where small differences in memory structures may become magnified over time (although such differentiation may also be natural and useful to the group).

Retrieval coordination refers to using the directories one has of one's own information and the directories representing information held by others to reach a particular item—that is, knowing if one has some piece of information or knowing that someone else does. Although such knowledge requires group agreement about the distribution of expertise among its members, ultimately individuals must update their directories to make retrieval coordination effective.

Structures of Transactive Memory

How memory is organized in a transactive memory system is also described in initial formulation by Wegner et al. (1985). Transactive memory makes use of three kinds of information group members have about each other's knowledge: higher order information (broad categories of a topic), lower order information (data falling within a higher order category), and location information (where information may be found). For example, the higher order category of "recipes" could contain dishes containing the lower order information "cilantro" and then be stored in the location of dyad member "Giada."

Transactive memory systems have both differentiated and integrated structures. Differentiated knowledge structures involve information that is distributed across individuals: "A differentiated transactive memory occurs when different items of information are stored in different individual memory stores but the individuals know the general labels and locations of the items they do not hold personally" (Wegner, 1987, p. 204). In contrast, integrated knowledge structures involve information that is common to all members: "An integrated transactive memory occurs when the same items of information are held in different individual memory stores and the individuals are aware of the overlap because they share label and location information as well" (Wegner, 1987, p. 204). Differentiation can also lead to a second form of integration as new information is generated when two disparate items are considered jointly by groups and are tied together by a new common label.

426 • *Theories of Team Cognition*

How labels and locations are distributed in dyads and other groups is described using the terms "differentiation" (recognizing others' areas of expertise, or what you know and what I know) and "integration" (shared knowledge, or what we both know). Wegner et al. (1985) suggest that dyad members who know each other's higher-order categories have a better chance to access related lower-order information and create an efficient transactive memory system. Effective couples will develop an efficient balance between integrated and differentiated structures. For example, although both parents may share common information about their children, June may know more about their culinary preferences, while Ward knows more about their need for moral training, and each will rely on the other for information about those subjects.

Wegner (1987) extended transactive memory beyond intimate dyads and applied the concepts of differentiation and integration to organizations and other contexts. Organizations where members must carry out similar functions will be best served by highly integrated transactive memory systems (e.g., a group of salesman selling the same products), whereas differentiated memory systems are useful to organizations where tasks are more specialized (e.g., a building contractor supplying expertise in architecture, plumbing, electrical, and carpentry areas). Ultimately, however, the transactive memory system in an organization should service task structure, with differentiation and integration varying among organizational groups as needed.

Content of Transactive Memory

In groups, a transactive memory system starts developing as soon as individuals learn about one another's areas of expertise. Attributions of expertise arise from areas such as demographics (men know about cars), known personal expertise (over time, a group learns that one member is an expert on phrenology), or circumstantial knowledge responsibility (the first person who mentions an upcoming tax law change is viewed by the group as an expert on that topic from then on). Ideally, a group fleshes out expertise well enough that no information passes through without being claimed by a group expert. Furthermore, for transactive memory to be fully effective, group members must take responsibility for information in their areas of expertise, and group discussions must occur to provide all group members with labels as to where needed information lies among their membership.

As was the case with intimate dyads, transactive retrieval processes in groups may not only produce elaborated integrations of existing information, but also generate new integrations of information into the system.

The most detailed description of expertise categories that fuel transactive memory development is provided in Wegner (1995). Notions of expertise are created from multiple sources of information, or "entries": Default entries are based on surface observations (e.g., demographic stereotypes), negotiated entries (e.g., assignment of responsibility for a task by an employer), expertise entries (e.g., a scholarly degree), and access entries (attributing expertise based on first, repeated, or recent exposure to information). Updating notions of expertise is ongoing, moving from any crude initial default entries to more accurate representations, and is often difficult if a particular directory structure becomes entrenched in group members. The development of transactive memory systems is thus depicted as an evolution of perceptions of expertise, driven by transactive processes that in turn create a dynamic framework for the storage and utilization of knowledge distributed across group members.

More recently, theory and research have examined how surface observations based on demographic stereotypes can affect the development of transactive memory. There is some evidence that stereotyping may give rise to a self-reinforcing cycle where tasks are assigned according to stereotypical notions about expertise (Fraidin & Hollingshead, 2005; Hollingshead & Fraidin, 2003). Stereotypes begin the cycle by influencing the development of convergent expectations about who is likely to know most about different knowledge areas. *Convergent expectations* occur when members have similar predictions about how others will behave and serve as a basis of tacit coordination (Schelling, 1960). Convergent expectations based on stereotypes then lead to stereotypical task assignments, and those assignments lead members to learn stereotypical knowledge. The improvement in stereotypical knowledge justifies future stereotypical task assignments because members, in fact, become experts in areas consistent with stereotypes that they may not have had previously. For example, a team composed of white Americans may judge an Asian member to be better at math based on a cultural stereotype about Asians. The Asian member may also think she is better at math than her teammates based on the same cultural stereotype. Thus, the group forms a convergent expectation that the Asian member knows more about math and, as a result, is assigned math-related tasks. This can happen regardless of whether the Asian partner

428 • *Theories of Team Cognition*

actually knows more about math than other members and without communication (cf. Fraidin & Hollingshead, 2005). Communication may serve to reinforce rather than reduce the effects of stereotypes in demographically diverse groups (Yoon & Hollingshead, 2010).

Outcomes of Transactive Memory

Task performance has been the most studied outcome of transactive memory. Researchers have demonstrated that both differentiated and integrated knowledge structures in transactive memory systems can have positive effects on task performance depending on the nature of the group task (Gupta & Hollingshead, 2010). Most studies of transactive memory have investigated the effects of a differentiated transactive memory system on task performance across a variety of different teams both in the laboratory and in the field (Austin, 2003; Hollingshead, 1998a, 1998b; Lewis, 2003; Liang et al., 1995; Moreland, Argote, & Krishnan, 1996; Wegner, Erber, & Raymond, 1991). A general finding across settings is that members of experienced groups often perform their tasks more quickly and accurately than newly formed groups because of their differentiated transactive memory system. In addition to a reduced and shared cognitive load for members, recognized experts tend to have relatively more influence on decisions related to their assigned areas of expertise (Hollingshead, 1998b). A differentiated transactive memory may trigger "task representations" that emphasize discussion of all specialized information (van Ginkel & van Knippenberg, 2009). In other words, group members' understanding of the task is influenced by their awareness about the specialized knowledge distribution in the group. It is important to note that in all studies that demonstrated positive effects of a differentiated transactive memory system, the task reward structure encouraged specialization: Members received higher payoffs if they divided responsibility for different parts of the task among members (Hollingshead, 2001).

However, there are boundary conditions regarding the positive effects of differentiated transactive memory on task performance. One performance disadvantage of a differentiated transactive memory system is that groups have no backup. Thus, if the designated expert fails to recall relevant information, that information is irretrievable by the group (Wegner, 1987). When the task or an imposed process interferes with the group's natural transactive memory system, task performance suffers (Hollingshead, 1998a; Wegner et al., 1991). Task or membership volatility also attenuates the positive relation between differentiated transactive memory and task performance (Ren, Carley, & Argote, 2006). Information can slip through the system when members leave the group (Wegner, 1987). Social stereotypes can be reinforced when members' knowledge assignments are consistent with those stereotypes (Yoon & Hollingshead, 2010). Boredom and limited opportunities for learning and for personal growth may sometimes result when group members have tightly constrained areas of expertise. In contrast, an integrated transactive memory may be beneficial for task performance under some circumstances, such as when members need to help or substitute for one another (Gupta & Hollingshead, 2010; Wegner, 1987) or the group recognizes more serious negative group consequences for omitted than for redundant information (Hollingshead, Brandon, Yoon, & Gupta, 2010).

Affective and motivational outcomes such as liking, trust, commitment, satisfaction, cohesion, and effort have been understudied. Although there is evidence that transactive memory is positively associated with relationship satisfaction (Wegner et al., 1985), the direction of the causal relationship is not clear. We will return to this topic in the section "Current and Future Research Directions."

Summary

In a sense, the term transactive "memory" is a misnomer, because it is about more than learning, storing, and remembering information; it is also about knowledge transmission and knowledge generation, which involve communication. A depiction of transactive memory theory is provided in Figure 17.1. Moving from left to right, the figure begins with the prerequisites for development. At the very least, transactive memory development requires membership in a group (dyad or larger), some shared tasks or goals to make group membership and transactive memory meaningful, the opportunity to interact, and some starting point for notions of expertise. With those influences in place, there is the opportunity for transactive memory phases (encoding, storage, and retrieval) to take place and, thus, to develop needed structures of labels, locations, differentiation, and integration. From the group's use of transactive memory, both positive and negative consequences may result. Figure 17.1 is meant to depict a

430 • *Theories of Team Cognition*

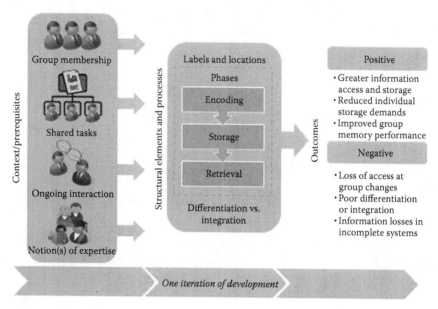

FIGURE 17.1
Depiction of original transactive memory theory.

single iteration of transactive memory development; it is assumed that over the history of a group, different parts of the model will go through many iterations. For instance, interaction may inject new information into the system, or group membership changes may require an update of expertise assignments.

The contribution of transactive memory theory, as stated across three texts (Wegner, 1987, 1995; Wegner et al., 1985), is an elaborated, detailed framework for understanding knowledge storage and exchange in groups that is applicable across a range of group characteristics and contexts and with defined processes for how information is placed and retrieved. In addition, the theory provides a dynamic picture of how such phenomena originate and change over time, allowing for an explanation of how shared memory varies within and across groups.

At a conceptual level, the statement of theory and related empirical study results provide support for the larger conceptual notion of cognitive interdependence. At a practical level, transactive memory has provided groundwork not only for establishing effective work groups, but also for preventing valuable knowledge loss when those groups disband. We now move to theoretical extensions that apply to work teams.

THEORETICAL EXTENSIONS

Extending Transactive Memory Theory to Organizational Settings

Several researchers working within the organizational context (simulated and/or actual) have pushed the boundaries of transactive memory theory beyond the initial conceptualization. Studies by Liang et al. (1995) and Moreland and colleagues (Moreland, 1999; Moreland et al., 1996; Moreland, Argote, & Krishnan, 1998) first provided direct evidence of transactive memory in teams in a series of laboratory experiments. Subsequently, studies by Lewis (2003, 2004), Austin (2003), Faraj and Sproull (2000), and Rau (2005) provided evidence of transactive memory and its positive effects on performance in field studies involving a range of teams, including business consulting teams, retail teams, software development teams, and top management teams.

Liang et al. (1995) and Moreland et al. (1996, 1998) showed that teams performing a radio assembly task manifested behaviors indicating a strong transactive memory: specialization, credibility, and coordination. As team members gain an understanding of their colleagues' relative expertise, they develop knowledge that is different but complementary (specialization). However, this occurs only if they trust that those colleagues will remember information in their areas of relative expertise (credibility). Task coordination (ability of team members to coordinate their work efficiently) occurs as members develop high levels of specialization and credibility leading to high team performance. Thus, a strong transactive memory is evidenced by the display of high levels of all three behaviors. Drawing on these manifestations by laboratory teams, Lewis (2003) provided conceptual and empirical evidence that the three elements (specialization, credibility, and task coordination) do indeed reflect transactive memory in ongoing teams as well. The development of a general (as opposed to task-specific) scale of transactive memory (Lewis, 2003) has facilitated more field research on transactive memory in teams.

These behavioral measures correlate with the direct measures of transactive memory such as accuracy and agreement about members' knowledge of "who knows what" (Moreland et al., 1998). However, there has also been further thought on the completeness of these direct measures in

432 • *Theories of Team Cognition*

capturing transactive memory. According to Brandon and Hollingshead (2004), transactive memory functions best when individual mental models are (a) accurate in their representations of expertise, (b) shared across group members, and (c) validated (i.e., group members' actions meet members' expectations about their areas of expertise and responsibility). Task performance will be best in groups when tasks are assigned to members based on their relative expertise, when members share the same mental models regarding members' expertise, and when recognized experts are willing and able to contribute their knowledge to the group (Brandon & Hollingshead, 2004). When all these factors are high, the group has a convergent transactive memory system (Brandon & Hollingshead, 2004).

There are three broad directions in which the transactive memory theory has been extended: emergence and development, content, and dynamics of transactive memory.

Emergence and Development of Transactive Memory

A transactive memory system emerges when workgroup members become aware of the knowledge held by their peers. The early conceptualization of transactive memory development suggested that long-term interaction (social in the case of couples) was necessary for transactive memory to fully develop. However, work in organizational settings presents two modifications: Interaction does not need to be long term and is not necessary for the development of transactive memory. First, preliminary task-related interactions can create a transactive memory. Research by Liang et al. (1995) and Moreland et al. (1996, 1998) showed that training team members together (i.e., providing a shared task experience) can create transactive memory systems. This is because group training results in group members acquiring a shared conceptualization of the task and its subtasks and in group members specializing in subtasks according to their abilities and interests. Group members declare their expertise early on in performing the group task (Rulke & Rau, 2000). Other task-related interactions regarding setting team goals, allocating roles to the different team members, and scheduling activities can also help in transactive memory emergence (Lewis, 2004; Prichard & Ashleigh, 2007).

However, although preliminary interactions can help create a transactive memory, Lewis (2004) has shown that the communication medium (face to face or technology mediated) used in the interactions is crucial.

Frequent face-to-face communication helped in transactive memory emergence, but technology-mediated communication has an information suppression effect (Lewis, 2004). In fact, technology-mediated communication in the later phase of transactive memory (i.e., when members retrieve information and use the transactive memory) was also ineffective (Lewis, 2004). Group members inhibited by the lack of nonverbal cues do not clarify their answers or proactively seek information about the task as much as they would if they were face to face.

Second, interactions may not be necessary for initial transactive memory to further develop (Hollingshead, 2000; Lewis, 2004; Moreland & Myaskovsky, 2000). A transactive memory system develops when group members are given feedback about the other group members' performance on the skills required by the task (Moreland & Myaskovsky, 2000). Although group members acquire information about each other's expertise in a manner different from that of interacting group members, they use the information in a similar manner—to allocate roles and coordinate their actions efficiently. Furthermore, transactive memory develops when group members become aware that the group will consist of experts in different knowledge domains and thus have a differentiated distribution of expertise (Hollingshead, 2000; Lewis, 2004). This awareness suggests to group members that they have unique knowledge that is complementary to that of the others, leading to their taking responsibility for some areas of expertise and relying on others for other areas. Thus, the group forms a preliminary template of expertise–person links or an initial transactive memory before the members start interacting. However, it is to be noted that when it comes to expertise evaluations, interactions might assume more importance.

Thus, whether group members become aware of the distribution of expertise through observation or information, it is perceived cognitive interdependence that is the prerequisite for the development of transactive memory, as it motivates members to attend to what other members know in the group and to begin developing a conceptual map regarding "who knows what." Without it, a transactive memory system is not likely to develop. Perceived cognitive interdependence occurs when members perceive that each member's outcomes are dependent on the knowledge or information held by other members of the group (Hollingshead, 2001). It can be stimulated by different group reward structures, divisible task structures, a general need for cognitive simplicity, a close relationship, or

434 • *Theories of Team Cognition*

some combination of these factors. Perceptions of cognitive interdependence are more important than the reality of it, although they are likely to be positively associated.

Content of Transactive Memory

As originally formulated, transactive memory theory (Wegner, 1987) indicated that group members use one another as storehouses of information and assign information based on notions of relative expertise. The resulting system of labels (i.e., areas of knowledge) and locations (i.e., people) provides the group with access to a large body of knowledge while at the same time reducing the cognitive load for remembering information across group members. Two theoretical extensions are provided by Brandon and Hollingshead (2004) and Austin (2003).

First, Brandon and Hollingshead (2004) extended Wegner's (1987) initial conceptualization by adding task to labels and locations as a defining element of the cognitive representation of the system. That is, task is viewed as a macro-organizing feature defining the overall structure of transactive memory and as a micro-element defining the connections between expertise and people, in the form of task–expertise–person (TEP) units. The addition of TEP units to transactive memory theory evolves from a general view that task perceptions are fundamental to the transactive memory system. Understanding that the task of building a home requires areas of expertise, such as architectural design, plumbing, and so on, helps the construction team identify the subtasks, the expertise or information needed for each subtask, and the responsible person. Furthermore, the perceived structure of the task will likely define the major labels and locations of the transactive memory system; for example, architecture, plumbing, electrical, and carpentry will likely be the top-level hierarchical labels for expertise.

Second, Austin (2003) expanded the focus from shared distribution of task-related expertise to include shared knowledge of the social relationships with persons outside the group. Knowledge contained in a group at one point in time for a single task may soon be irrelevant as the group assignment changes shape or is enlarged. To bring in the requisite new knowledge, groups can acquire the knowledge themselves, recruit a person with the new knowledge, or rely on knowledge holders outside the group to share their knowledge. The most efficient way of bringing in the knowledge of persons outside the group is by means of group member social networks. Hence the incorporation of social networks is important given the reality of challenges facing ongoing teams. Moreover, network recognition (an individual's perception of the network of social relationships among a group of people) or "who knows who" provides the group members with access to an even larger body of knowledge (Ho & Wong, 2009).

Dynamics of Transactive Memory

The dynamic nature of the transactive memory is discussed with reference to intact teams (Brandon & Hollingshead, 2004), changing tasks (Lewis et al., 2005; Ren et al., 2006), and changing team membership (Lewis, Belliveau, Herndon, & Keller, 2007; Moreland et al., 1998) at the organizational or multiple levels (Anand, Manz, & Glick, 1998; Jackson & Klobas, 2008; Moreland & Argote, 2003; Nevo & Wand, 2005; Peltokorpi, 2004).

Brandon and Hollingshead (2004) argued that transactive memory evolves from three iterative, independently operating, but reciprocally influential cyclical processes: (1) satisfaction of conditions leading to perceived cognitive interdependence among group members, (2) TEP unit and individual mental model development, and (3) shared mental model development (i.e., reconciling perceptions across group members; Figure 17.2). At the beginning of transactive memory development, groups are likely to proceed linearly through the model; however, the model is dynamic and can be nonlinear. Group activities at later points in the model may induce changes in all three processes.

Brandon and Hollingshead (2004) describe TEP units as constructed via an ongoing, iterative process of three related cycles: *construction*, *evaluation*, and *utilization*. In the *construction* cycle, full or partial TEP units evolve from each member's notions about task, expertise, and people. Once constructed, full or partial TEP units do not represent certainty, but rather hypotheses a group member has about the distribution of task-relevant information within the group. Wegner (1995) states that one quality of transactive memory systems is the modification of crude notions of expertise via group communication to more refined and accurate conceptions, which suggests a dynamic quality to TEP units. Thus, in the second cycle of TEP development, hypothesized full TEP units,

436 • *Theories of Team Cognition*

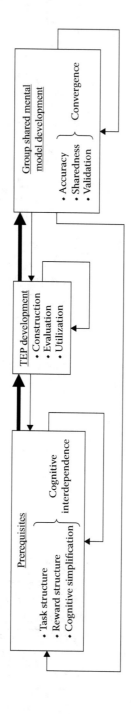

FIGURE 17.2
Development of transactive memory in organizations. (Reprinted from Brandon, D. P., & Hollingshead, A. B., *Organization Science*, 15, 2004. With permission.)

components of TEP units, or partial TEP units are tested, confirmed, and/or revised using available information in the *evaluation* phase. After the construction and evaluation cycles are satisfied, group members make use of TEP units for transactive memory tasks in the utilization cycle, such as requesting or passing along information. Results from the utilization feed back to the earlier cycles for further TEP development, as needed. Over time, ongoing iterations of TEP development cycles will produce more accurate representations of who knows what about the group task.

A transactive memory can also transfer over different tasks (Lewis et al., 2005; Ren et al., 2006) or tasks with rapidly changing elements (Akgun, Byrne, Keskin, Lynn, & Imamoglu, 2005; Dayan & Di Benedetto, 2009). Lewis et al. (2005) showed that when group members gain experience at similar tasks, they are able to derive basic principles of the task domain. Hence, they form an abstract conceptualization of the task domain and are able to transfer their learning to other tasks in a similar task domain. A developed transactive memory has a positive effect on tasks beyond the task for which it was developed. Using a computational model to run virtual experiments, Ren et al. (2006) showed that a transactive memory is more beneficial when there are rapid changes in tasks than when the task was stable. Possibly the same reasons explain the usefulness of transactive memory for new product development teams performing nonroutine (less repetitive elements) tasks (Akgun et al., 2005; Dayan & Di Benedetto, 2009).

However, there is less conceptual evidence for transfer of transactive memory with changing membership. Stability in team membership is important for a strong transactive memory (Akgun et al., 2005; Lewis et al., 2005), and member turnover can have negative effects on transactive memory development (Moreland et al., 1998). Lewis et al. (2007) explain the negative effects by showing that when there are changes in membership, group members, including those who are new to the group, continue to use the same mental map of expertise–member links. The reliance on the old transactive memory structure can render ineffective the transactive processes in the group if the newcomer's expertise is not a complete match to that of the member the newcomer replaces.

Lastly, although early conceptualizations of transactive memory focused on couples or workgroups, some later perspectives focused on large groups or organizations. Some researchers describe organizational transactive memory as a multilevel system consisting of individual, group, and systemic memories; others describe it at the systemic or organizational level (Anand et al., 1998; Jackson & Klobas, 2008; Nevo & Wand, 2005; Peltokorpi, 2004). Either way, the organizational transactive memory is conceptualized as a facilitator in searching for the right knowledge resources, integrating the knowledge from different parts of the organization, and applying the knowledge to the problem at hand. It would be cognitively challenging for members of an organization to store information about all the expertise–person links. Hence, this body of research has developed around technology, organizational rules (Kieser & Koch, 2002), and knowledge network attributes (Garner, 2006) that can help organizations create metadirectories of knowledge about all employees. These metadirectories help organizational members to direct incoming knowledge to the right person and to retrieve knowledge from the organizational memory efficiently when needed.

The extension of group transactive memory theory to organization transactive memory has its challenges (Moreland & Argote, 2003; Ren et al., 2006). Ren et al. (2006) showed that a transactive memory was more beneficial in terms of quality of performance at the small group level but more beneficial in terms of speed of performance at the large group level. To explain this discrepancy, they identified two mechanisms through which transactive memory affects performance: ease in searching for knowledge and ease in task coordination. The former mechanism benefits performance quality, whereas the latter benefits performance speed.

In addition, Moreland and Argote (2003) theorized that dynamic organizations (characterized by changing team membership) can have weaker transactive memory at the team level and stronger transactive memory at the organizational level. The rotation of personnel through different teams makes it difficult to plug the gaps of knowledge resulting from a person leaving as well as to learn and evaluate the knowledge of newcomers. However, rotated personnel also have awareness about "who knows what" with respect to a larger number of people. They can also draw on a larger social network to locate expertise within the organization. It is often important to note that in organizations, departmental units and cross-functional teams may have areas of expertise associated with them as well as the individuals that compose them.

Transactive Memory Theory and Teams • 439

Summary

Transactive memory research in organizational settings has made theoretical contributions in three areas: development of transactive memory, content of transactive memory, and dynamics of transactive memory. First, transactive memory develops in newly formed groups as members gain knowledge about others' expertise (through observation or information). Second, the conceptualization of content in the individual memory systems that compose the team's transactive memory is expanded from individual expertise to include social relationships and from expertise-person links to TEP links. Third, transactive memory theory is extended to reflect dynamic processes in organizations—changes in expertise, tasks, membership, and the coexistence of multiple transactive memories.

Communication-Based Extensions to Transactive Memory Theory

Important theoretical insights on the nature of team transactive memory have also been made by communication scholars who study the patterns of knowledge allocation, sharing, and retrieval among members in the system (Hollingshead & Brandon, 2003).

Transactive Memory as a Public Good

Fulk, Monge, Yuan, and colleagues differentiate between connective and communal knowledge systems (Fulk, Flanagin, Kalman, Monge, & Ryan, 1996; Fulk, Heino, Flanagin, Monge, & Bar 2004; Yuan, Fulk, & Monge, 2007). A connective system is the person-to-person knowledge system where knowledge resides in the heads of people. To access connective systems effectively, members must have an accurate sense of "who knows what." Most of the research on transactive memory has explored connective systems, but the notion of a communal knowledge system certainly applies as well.

In contrast, a communal knowledge system is the generalized exchange between members of the system and a common knowledge repository (Fulk et al., 2004). It is not necessary to know "who knows what" to make use of the knowledge in a communal transactive memory system. A variety of technology-mediated information repositories such as corporate intranets, expertise databases, and expert reference systems allow

440 • *Theories of Team Cognition*

organizational teams to externalize the storage of knowledge resources that team members hold (Hollingshead, Fulk, & Monge, 2002). The externalization of information outside human minds presents different processes for directory updating, information allocation, and information retrieval (Yuan et al., 2007).

Because knowledge is located and available in a common storage system, team members may be able to retrieve needed information without direct interaction with experts, although information about the connective system may be available. For example, a staff directory, an expert directory search system, and/or an office procedures handbook may provide information about each member's expertise, role, and responsibilities in the system. Once this repository system is accurately established, directory updating and information retrieval may be more straightforward and time efficient than human systems. This expands information access for users by allowing access to information on demand: any amount at any time (Yuan et al., 2007). However, information retrieval through nonhuman repositories may be limited in the type of information people can access and retrieve. Tacit knowledge is not easily communicated via technologies and may require direct interaction with the expert for more complete and accurate information retrieval (Child & Shumate, 2007).

One of the most critical boundary conditions under which communal knowledge systems can operate effectively in nonhuman agents is the information holders' will and motivation to externalize what they know and actively use what others contribute to the repository (Fulk et al., 2004; Hollingshead et al., 2002; Yuan et al., 2007; Yuan, Fulk, et al., 2005). Without reaching a critical mass of participation, the knowledge system will be incomplete or not up to date and not useful to members in the system.

Thus, the functionality provided by knowledge repositories can be viewed as a public good (Hardin, 1982). The knowledge is accessible to all members of the collective and is not diminished for other members when one member consumes it (Fulk et al., 2004). Because of this nonexcludable and nonrival nature of knowledge repositories, nonparticipation and free riding are the biggest obstacles in creating and maintaining communal systems. Considering the value (e.g., the amount and usefulness of knowledge available in the system) and the cost (e.g., time and energy to contribute and retrieve information), nonparticipation and/or free riding are least likely to occur when individual members minimize costs incurred from knowledge contribution (Fulk et al., 2004; Hollingshead et al., 2002). Researchers have identified that rewards for contribution, penalties for non-contribution, individuals' identification with the collective (Hollingshead et al., 2002), and cooperative influence from other members (perception of how much others contribute; Yuan et al., 2007) tend to motivate individual members to contribute to the communal knowledge system. As such, communal knowledge systems are subject to some of the same incentives and disincentives toward participation as other types of public goods.

When team members do not foresee individual benefits from sharing what they know and/or anticipate costs exceeding the benefits of knowledge sharing, they are less likely to contribute to the collective knowledge system (Fulk et al., 2004; Yuan, Fulk, et al., 2005). The perceived value of individual participation and perceptions of costs and benefits are also influenced by other team members' level of contribution (Yuan, Fulk, et al., 2005). Reciprocity is an important driver of individual contributions. Team members are more likely to contribute to and retrieve from a communal knowledge system when they perceive other members to do the same (Yuan, Fulk, et al., 2005) and when they envision how their knowledge might be beneficial to future team members (Kalman, Monge, Fulk, & Heino, 2002).

A communal knowledge system can become self-sustaining once it reaches a critical point in its development. This state occurs when the costs for participation by other individuals are outweighed by the benefits those individuals can acquire from access to the system (Fulk, Monge, & Hollingshead, 2005).

Communication Network Approach

Recently, a body of research on transactive memory theory has emerged that treats the transactive memory system as a collection of individuals in a social network. This approach treats transactive memory as a multilevel system, which is a macrolevel cognitive representation of knowledge that emerges from micro-interactions among nodes in the system (Yuan, Fulk, Monge, & Contractor, 2010). This approach delineates individual- and group-level processes in the development of the transactive memory system and examines how the individual- and group-level processes feed each other (e.g., Yuan, Monge, & Fulk, 2005). Much of the research from this approach has been conducted in field settings with a wide variety of teams.

442 • *Theories of Team Cognition*

Similar to Wegner's (1995) conceptualization of the transactive memory system as a computer network, the network perspective focuses on the nature and the structure of ties that team members form with one another and among individual transactive memory systems. Such ties are a direct manifestation of communication among members and allow researchers to examine how communication plays a role in the emergence, development, and maintenance of the transactive memory system. The network approach makes unique contributions to transactive memory theory by examining direct and indirect links between team members and how the attributes of both individuals and the network affect the ways in which people share information in teams.

Individual-Level Variables

Variables at the individual level include what team members know (content of expertise), how they evaluate what self and others know (perception of expertise), and how individual motivations affect information sharing. These individual-level characteristics determine who creates communication links with whom in the transactive memory system and the extent to which information is shared through these communication links. Research from this perspective examines whether communication ties exist between experts and nonexperts in certain knowledge domains and how the perception of others' expertise determines the creation of such ties. Expert members are often at the center of a network because multiple nonexpert members seek information from the expert in specific knowledge areas (Palazzolo, 2005). However, when one perceives multiple members to be experts in a domain or when one has inaccurate perceptions of others' expertise, the centrality of communication links to experts may disappear. Instead, communication ties will be made to multiple members who may or may not be experts. In those cases, the accuracy of information retrieval will suffer (Palazzolo, 2005). Social motives (going to someone who I like or with whom I feel comfortable) may override accuracy motives (going to the person who knows most), which can lead to less effective information transmission (Contractor & Monge, 2002; Palazzolo, 2005).

Group-Level Variables

One of the most important contributions that the network perspective has made to the transactive memory systems theory is its attention to group-level characteristics. Compared to other research on the transactive memory system that examined small teams (2 to 5 members), this line of work has examined larger teams (up to 15 to 20 members). Group-level characteristics include (a) network attributes such as communication density (the extent to which people communicate with one another in a network), network structure (patterns of relationships), and network size (the number of people in a network), and (b) group-level processes such as directory development and task interdependence at the group level. These group-level variables derive from the relations and interactions among people and not directly from individual characteristics (Wasserman & Faust, 1994).

Network attributes have been theorized to influence transactive memory system in terms of all three core processes: directory updating, information allocation, and information retrieval. Communication density of a network represents the amount of communication among team members. A highly dense communication network is more likely than a lean communication network to accurately identify its team members' areas of expertise and, in turn, more accurately allocate to and retrieve from the person who has the domain expertise pertaining to any new information (Palazzolo, 2005; Palazzolo, Serb, She, Su, & Contractor, 2006; Yuan et al., 2010). Network size negatively affects the amount of communication, which leads to inaccuracy in expertise recognition and information allocation (Palazzolo et al., 2006). Decentralized networks, where hierarchy is minimal and communication density is high, are more likely to facilitate more information exchange among members than centralized networks, which is positively associated with accuracy (Rulke & Galaskiewicz, 2000).

The network perspective differentiates group-level processes from individual-level processes. In particular, directory development and task interdependence at the group level are recognized as constructs distinct from those at the individual level (Yuan et al., 2010). Although the development of expertise directories and the perceptions of task interdependence start at the individual level, group-level directory development and task interdependence are not the mere convergence of individual-level characteristics but higher order constructs that emerge from individual actions. The theoretical contribution of this multilevel approach is particularly significant because compared with most research that examined individual-level variables only, the multilevel approach identifies both individual- and group-level influences on how teams can maximize information exchange in their transactive memory systems.

Summary

The key theoretical contributions that communication-based approaches have made to transactive memory theory are as follows: (a) the application of public goods theory to consider what motivates individuals to contribute their knowledge to a shared repository that can function as a transactive memory system; (b) the extension of transactive memory systems to consider nonhuman as well as human agents; and (c) a multilevel approach that examines the relations between group-level, network-level, and individual-level factors in the development of transactive memory systems (Figure 17.3).

THEORETICAL INTEGRATION

The journey started by Wegner et al. (1985) into the transactive memory of intimate couples has since taken many paths, exploring application of the concepts to such areas as other types of groups, more refined notions

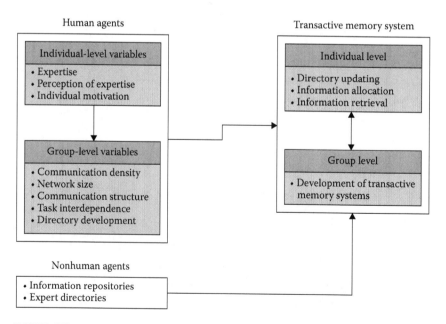

FIGURE 17.3
Communication-based approaches and transactive memory.

of expertise, how transactive memory relates to work issues and structures in organizations, and how transactive memory interacts with technology. Along the way, theorists and researchers have elaborated on the mental structures that organize transactive memory and have identified endogenous and exogenous variables, both social and technological, that facilitate the development and functioning of the shared memory structures guiding transactive memory (Hollingshead, 2010b). Thus, a team's transactive memory can be viewed as a sociotechnical system: a complex of interactions among people and technology relating to tasks and other goal-directed behavior in the workplace that are most effective when the social and technological elements "fit" together (cf. Pasmore, 1988).

Figure 17.4 presents a general description of the influences on development of shared memory structures (depicted in the center of the figure) in transactive memory systems. Represented in the outer layer of the figure are major prerequisites and sources of information needed for transactive memory development. Because transactive memory is associated with groups, membership in some type of group, from dyads to organizations, is required; attributes of the group, such as a size or diversity, will have an influence on the ultimate shape of the transactive memory system.

Notions of expertise, arising from various expertise entries identified by the theory, are also essential to developing transactive memory, as is communication among group members and other external information sources. In all groups, but particularly in organizations, the influences of network attributes on interaction will influence how transactive memory develops and is accessed. The breakdown of the group task will define important areas of expertise, and feedback from the task is essential to refining notions of expertise. In addition, like all group phenomena (and in particular for work groups), technology will influence transactive memory, not only in how modern technology influences communication, but also via nonhuman agents serving as sources of information.

The purpose in placing all these influences in the same layer is to indicate the rich interaction that can happen among them as people use a variety of sources of information to update directories (Wegner, 1995). For example, upon receiving assignment to a new case via a conference call, four detectives decide to break up the case into four areas of assignment (i.e., task structure) based on their own areas of expertise (i.e., negotiated entries): Bosley will manage home base and communications (i.e., network structure), with Jill, Kelly, and Sabrina going undercover to become experts on

446 • *Theories of Team Cognition*

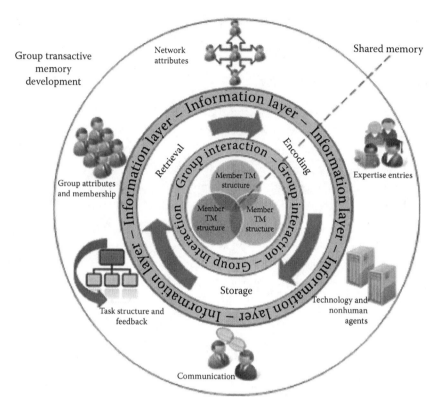

FIGURE 17.4
Transactive memory theory as a sociotechnical system. TM = transactive memory.

various suspects in the case. After Kelly exits the group, new group member Kris steps in, talks with Bosley (i.e., communication), and reads notes the other detectives have left on the computer system (i.e., technology and nonhuman agents) to catch up on the case.

The result of the direct and indirect influences of the factors presented in the first layer is to produce information, represented as the "information layer" in Figure 17.4. Essentially this is an extension of the Wegner et al. (1985) definition of communication as the transfer of information, and the descriptions of sources and influences on information from transactive memory researchers, into a notion of a general pool of information available for use in transactive memory processes.

The third layer of Figure 17.4 represents the encoding, storage, and retrieval phases that take place in the individual minds of group members. The phases are depicted as dynamic and ongoing, because it is rare to find that the information layer has grown static. Furthermore, the act of retrieval is likely to inform encoding by verifying or calling into question existing entries or providing new information to be encoded. Group interaction is placed as the fourth layer of the model, because it is the strongest influence on the formation of shared memory (represented by the center of the Venn diagram of overlapping group member transactive memory structures). The influence of group interaction on developing shared memory structures is emphasized not only in works on transactive memory by Wegner and colleagues, but also research on mental models that points to communication as essential to forming shared representations (cf. Salas, Sims, & Burke, 2005).

CURRENT AND FUTURE RESEARCH DIRECTIONS

In this chapter, we focused on transactive memory as a theory of team cognition. Many new and promising avenues of research have arisen that will lead to future theoretical extensions. Some of that research is moving beyond cognition and linking transactive memory research with other psychological processes. One notable omission from much of transactive memory theory is the impact of affect and emotion on the transactive memory system. For example, how are the processes of directory updating, information allocation, and retrieval coordination affected when members like versus dislike others in their group? In a paper that begins to unpack the complex relations between cognition and affect, Huang (2009) posits that positive affect can influence all three dimensions of transactive memory effectiveness: accuracy, sharedness, and validation.

Studies by Ellis (2006), Pearsall, Ellis, and Stein (2009), and Zhang, Hempel, Han, and Tjosvold (2007) have begun to expand notions of motivation in transactive memory. Their findings suggest that transactive memory can function only when members are motivated and engaged in the team. A group climate supporting innovation enhances motivation (Zhang et al., 2007), and acute stress inhibits motivation (Ellis, 2006). In addition, information sharing behaviors in transactive memory systems can be strategic because having expertise in a particular domain that no one else has can be viewed as a source of power (cf. Wittenbaum, Hollingshead, & Botero, 2004). Research has also begun examining not just the benefits of transactive memory but also the sources, processes, and outcomes of transactive memory errors (Hollingshead et al., 2010). More theory and research are needed on the error correction process: How does the team self-correct when knowledge responsibilities become unbalanced in the team?

Studies of transactive memory are expanding across a wide variety of organizational contexts that will inspire future theory building. In particular, there have been a number of studies of teams performing in high-pressure environments, such as air-traffic control teams (Smith-Jentsch, Kraiger, Cannon-Bowers, & Salas, 2009), medical teams (Tschan et al., 2009), medical trauma centers (Faraj & Xiao, 2006), anesthesia teams (Michinov, Olivier-Chiron, Rusch, & Chiron, 2008), and orthopedic surgical teams (Reagans, Argote, & Brooks, 2005). The findings from these studies demonstrate that experience working together increases team learning and improves team performance. Smith-Jentsch et al. (2009) have shown that shared consensus on relative strengths and weaknesses in teams with overlapping expertise is likely to increase the requesting and accepting of backup by members. Tschan et al. (2009) demonstrated that teams can often suffer from an illusion of transactive memory where members assume that members holding important information would communicate it to the team. Faraj and Xiao (2006) produced evidence that expertise coordination may be essential to manage and apply diverse expertise, but suggest that other types of coordination might be needed to respond to unexpected developments.

The influence of communication medium on transactive memory development is a challenge for virtual teams (Alavi & Tiwana, 2002; Cordery & Soo, 2008). Effective transactive memory development using only technology-mediated communication required a high frequency of communication and took longer to develop (Kanawattanachai & Yoo, 2007). Many researchers (and organizations) are exploring other sorts of technology-based solutions. For example, Allan, Korolis, and Griffith (2009) described the effective use of wikis and other technologies as support for transactive memory in a highly innovative and dynamic team—the NASA Ames Intelligent Robotics Group. Future theorizing on transactive memory should consider how Web 2.0 and 3.0 applications are influencing and will influence transactive memory systems in the future. For example, automated agents in today's digital systems are increasingly becoming "smarter" by being more (a) adaptive, (b) specialized, and

(c) proactive. Research should also continue to explore the utilization of communal transactive memory to accelerate connective transactive memory development in teams, and vice versa, as technology evolves (cf. Fulk et al., 1996).

Future conceptual development is needed to move transactive memory theory beyond knowledge sharing in close relationships, work groups, and organizations where group membership is known, where members perceive cognitive interdependence, and where they have shared goals. One such example is emergent response groups of local citizens (and victims), relief organizations, local governments, and volunteers that emerge to provide disaster relief (Majchrzak, Javenpaa, & Hollingshead, 2007). These groups are often characterized by unstable task definitions and assignments; pursuit of multiple, conflicting, and changing purposes and perspectives; fleeting and sometimes unclear group membership; geographically distributed, diverse, and unfamiliar members; and voluntary member participation often based on urgent personal needs (Drabek & McEntire, 2003). However, emergent response groups are able to function (and succeed) with relatively little expertise and specialization, little knowledge of other members' capabilities, and few, if any, agreed-upon cues about how to encode, store, and retrieve each member's knowledge.

Majchrzak et al. (2007) suggested several extensions are needed to transactive memory theory so that it can be applied to emergent response groups and other ad hoc temporary groups. First, task-relevant expertise is often not present, so any knowledge of relationships, tools, or tasks plus an ability and willingness to act on that knowledge may serve as the basis of task assignment and specialization. That is, both capability and motivation, in addition to the domain knowledge typically examined by transactive memory systems theory, are required. Second, expertise credibility in emergent response groups may be less important for coordination than being able to constantly create and recreate trust through actions. Finally, knowledge coordination in an emergent response group will need to occur without shared mental models of who knows what and who will do what. Based on past experiences with emergencies either as observers or participants, members may have individual mental models about how people should behave in emergency situations and about roles they and others may play (Faraj & Xiao 2006; Moreland & Argote, 2003), as well as about routines (Feldman & Pentland, 2003) for

450 • *Theories of Team Cognition*

performing in an emergency situation. They will need to evolve mechanisms for coordination. They may coordinate face to face with dialogue or through intermediaries, either human or a Web site. They may quickly evolve a routine, may constantly negotiate actions, or may adopt a set of parallel actions.

Moving Toward Theory-Based Interventions

One goal of group theory is to guide the development of interventions to improve group functioning. Our theoretical review suggests that a developed transactive memory system is often beneficial for team performance and that interventions should be designed to accelerate the formation of transactive memory. Previous research has identified several factors that facilitate development of transactive memory: cognitive interdependence (Wegner et al., 1985), task interdependence (Yuan et al., 2010), team rewards that encourage specialization (Hollingshead, 2001), information about team members' expertise (Moreland & Myaskovsky, 2000) and/or opportunities for task-related team communication (cf. Hollingshead, 1998a), and an engaging work environment that supports innovation (Zhang et al., 2004.) These interventions are not likely to work for every team.

Thinking about transactive memory as a sociotechnical system requires an analysis of how teams' social relations, their task, their technologies (both for communication and for production), and their workplace might influence the effectiveness of various interventions on the development of transactive memory. In the not too distant future, recommender systems may move beyond identifying experts to suggesting online communication, database, and other tools teams may need based on historical profiles of team members, their previous communication patterns, their task, and their reward structure. Future work should develop specific guidelines for extending theoretical constructs of transactive memory into teamwork intervention strategies.

REFERENCES

Akgun, A. E., Byrne, J., Keskin, H., Lynn, G. S., & Imamoglu, S. Z. (2005). Knowledge networks in new product development projects: A transactive memory perspective. *Information & Management, 42*, 1105–1120.

Alavi, M., & Tiwana, A. (2002). Knowledge integration in virtual teams: The potential role of KMS. *Journal of American Society for Information Science and Technology, 53,* 1029–1037.

Allan, M. B., Korolis, A. A., & Griffith, T. L. (2009). Reaching for the moon: Expanding transactive memory's reach with wikis and tagging. *International Journal of Knowledge Management, 5,* 51–63.

Anand, V., Manz, C. C., & Glick, W. H. (1998). An organizational memory to information management. *Academy of Management Review, 23,* 796–809.

Argote, L. (1999). *Organizational learning: Creating, retaining and transferring knowledge.* Norwell, MA: Kluwer Academic Publishers.

Argote, L., Ingram, P., Levine, J. M., & Moreland, R. L. (2000). Knowledge transfer in organizations: Learning from the experience of others. *Organizational Behavior and Human Decision Processes, 82,* 1–8.

Austin, J. R. (2003). Transactive memory in organizational groups: The effects of content, consensus, specialization, and accuracy on group performance. *Journal of Applied Psychology, 88,* 866–878.

Brandon, D. P., & Hollingshead, A. B. (2004). Transactive memory systems in organizations: Matching tasks, expertise, and people. *Organization Science, 15,* 633–644.

Child, J. T., & Shumate, M. (2007). The impact of communal knowledge repositories and people-based knowledge management on perceptions of team effectiveness. *Management Communication Quarterly, 21,* 29–54.

Contractor, N. S., & Monge, P. R. (2002). Managing knowledge networks. *Management Communication Quarterly, 16,* 249–258.

Cordery, J. L., & Soo, C. (2008). Overcoming impediments to virtual team effectiveness. *Human Factors and Ergonomics in Manufacturing, 18,* 487–500.

Dayan, M., & Di Benedetto, C. A. (2009). Antecedents and consequences of teamwork quality in new product development projects: An empirical investigation. *European Journal of Innovation Management, 12,* 129–155.

Drabek, T. E., & McEntire, D. A. (2003). Emergent phenomena and the sociology of disaster: Lessons, trends and opportunities from the research literature. *Disaster Prevention and Management, 12,* 97–112.

Ellis, A. P. J. (2006). System breakdown: The role of mental models and transactive memory in the relationship between acute stress and team performance. *Academy of Management Journal, 49,* 576–589.

Faraj, S., & Sproull, L. (2000). Coordinating expertise in software development teams. *Management Science, 46,* 1554–1568.

Faraj, S., & Xiao, Y. (2006). Coordination in fast-response organizations. *Management Science, 52,* 1155–1169.

Feldman, M. S., & Pentland, B. T. (2003). Reconceptualizing organizational routines as a source of flexibility and change. *Administrative Science Quarterly, 48,* 94–118.

Fraidin, S. N., & Hollingshead, A. B. (2005). "I know what I'm doing": The impact of gender stereotypes about expertise on task assignments in groups. In M. Neale, E. Mannix, & M. Thomas-Hunt (Eds.), *Research on managing groups and teams* (Vol. 7, pp. 121–142). Greenwich, CT: JAI Press.

Fulk, J., Flanagin, A., Kalman, M., Monge, P., & Ryan, T. (1996). Connective and communal public goods in interactive communication systems. *Communication Theory, 6,* 60–87.

Fulk, J., Heino, R., Flanagin, A. J., Monge, P. R., & Bar, F. (2004). A test of the individual action model for organizational information commons. *Organization Science, 15,* 569–585.

452 • *Theories of Team Cognition*

Fulk, J., Monge, P. R., & Hollingshead, A. B. (2005). Knowledge resource sharing in dispersed multinational teams: Three theoretical lenses. In D. Shapiro, J. Cheng, & M. Von Glinow (Eds.), *Managing multinational work teams: Theory advancement and global application* (pp. 159–189). London, UK: Elsevier/JAI.

Garner, J. (2006). It's not what you know: A transactive memory analysis of knowledge networks at NASA. *Journal of Technical Writing and Communication, 36,* 329–351.

Gupta, N., & Hollingshead, A. B. (2010). Integrated vs. differentiated transactive memory effectiveness: It depends on the task. *Group Dynamics: Theory, Research, and Practice, 14,* 384–398.

Hardin, R. (1982). *Collective action.* Baltimore, MD: Johns Hopkins University Press.

Ho, V. T., & Wong, S. S. (2009). Knowing who knows what and who knows whom: Expertise recognition, network recognition, and individual work performance. *Journal of Occupational and Organizational Psychology, 82,* 147–158.

Hollingshead, A. B. (1998a). Communication, learning, and retrieval in transactive memory systems. *Journal of Experimental Social Psychology, 34,* 423–442.

Hollingshead, A. B. (1998b). Retrieval processes in transactive memory systems. *Journal of Personality and Social Psychology, 74,* 659–671.

Hollingshead, A. B. (2000). Perceptions of expertise and transactive memory in work relationships. *Group Processes and Intergroup Relations, 3,* 257–267.

Hollingshead, A. B. (2001). Cognitive interdependence and convergent expectations in transactive memory. *Journal of Personality and Social Psychology, 81,* 1080–1089.

Hollingshead, A. B. (2009). Transactive memory. In J. Levine & M. Hogg (Eds.), *Encyclopedia of group processes and intergroup relations* (pp. 931–933). Thousand Oaks, CA: Sage.

Hollingshead, A. B. (2010a). Transactive memory. In J. Levine & M. Hogg (Eds.), *Encyclopedia of group processes and intergroup relations.* Thousand Oaks, CA: Sage.

Hollingshead, A. B. (2010b). Communication, coordinated action, and focal points in groups: From dating couples to emergency responders. In C. R. Agnew, D. E. Carlston, W. G. Graziano, & J. R. Kelly (Eds.), *Then a miracle occurs: Focusing on behavior in social psychological theory and research* (pp. 391–410). New York, NY: Oxford University Press.

Hollingshead, A. B., & Brandon, D. P. (2003). Potential benefits of communication in transactive memory systems. *Human Communication Research, 29,* 607–615.

Hollingshead, A. B., Brandon, D. P., Yoon, K., & Gupta, N. (2010). Communication and knowledge-sharing errors in groups: A transactive memory perspective. In H. Canary & R. McPhee (Eds.), *Communication and organizational knowledge: Contemporary issues for theory and practice.* New York, NY: Taylor Francis/Routledge.

Hollingshead, A. B., & Fraidin, S. N. (2003). Gender stereotypes and assumptions about expertise in transactive memory. *Journal of Experimental Social Psychology, 39,* 355–363.

Hollingshead, A. B., Fulk, J., & Monge, P. (2002). Fostering Intranet knowledge sharing: An integration of transactive memory and public goods approaches. In P. Hinds & S. Kiesler (Eds.), *Distributed work: New research on working across distance using technology* (pp. 335–355). Cambridge, MA: MIT Press.

Huang, M. (2009). Conceptual framework of the effects of positive affect and affective relationships on group knowledge networks. *Small Group Research, 40,* 323–346.

Jackson, P., & Klobas, J. (2008). Transactive memory systems in organizations: Implications for knowledge directories. *Decision Support Systems, 44,* 409–424.

Kalman, M., Monge, P., Fulk, J., & Heino, R. (2002). Motivations to resolve communication dilemmas in database-mediated collaboration. *Communication Research, 2,* 125–154.

Kanawattanachai, P., & Yoo, Y. (2007). The impact of knowledge coordination on virtual team performance over time. *MIS Quarterly, 31,* 783–808.

Kieser, A., & Koch, U. (2002). Organizational learning through rule adaptation: From the behavioral theory to transactive organizational learning. In M. Augier & J. G. March (Eds.), *The economics of choice, change, and organization: Essays in memory of Richard M. Cyert* (pp. 237–249). Cheltenham, UK: Elgar.

Lewis, K. (2003). Measuring transactive memory systems in the field: Scale development and validation. *Journal of Applied Psychology, 88,* 587–604.

Lewis, K. (2004). Knowledge and performance in knowledge-worker teams: A longitudinal study of transactive memory systems. *Management Science, 50,* 1519–1533.

Lewis, K., Belliveau, M., Herndon, B., & Keller, J. (2007). Group cognition, membership change, and performance: Investigating the benefits and detriments of collective knowledge. *Organizational Behavior and Human Decision Processes, 103,* 159–178.

Lewis, K., Lange, D., & Gillis, L. (2005). Transactive memory systems, learning and learning transfer. *Organization Science, 16,* 581–598.

Liang, D. W., Moreland, R., & Argote, L. (1995). Group versus individual training and group performance: The mediating role of transactive memory. *Personality and Social Psychology Bulletin, 21,* 384–393.

Majchrzak, A., Jarvenpaa, S. L., & Hollingshead, A. B. (2007). Coordinating expertise among emergent groups responding to disasters. *Organization Science, 18,* 147–161.

Michinov, E., Olivier-Chiron, E., Rusch, E., & Chiron, B. (2008). Influence of transactive memory on perceived performance, job satisfaction and identification in anaesthesia team. *British Journal of Anaesthesia, 100,* 327–332.

Moreland, R. L. (1999). Transactive memory: Learning who knows what in work groups and organizations. In L. Thompson, D. Messick, & J. Levine (Eds.), *Sharing knowledge in organizations* (pp. 3–31). Hillsdale, NJ: Lawrence Erlbaum.

Moreland, R. L., & Argote, L. L. (2003). Transactive memory in dynamic organizations. In R. S. Peterson & E. A. Mannix (Eds.), *Leading and managing people in the dynamic organization* (pp. 135–162). Mahwah, NJ: Lawrence Erlbaum Associates, Inc.

Moreland, R. L., Argote, L. L., & Krishnan, R. (1996). Socially shared cognition at work: Transactive memory and group performance. In J. L. Nye & A. M. Brower (Eds.), *What's social about social cognition? Research on socially shared cognition in small groups* (pp. 57–84). Thousand Oaks, CA: Sage.

Moreland, R. L., Argote, L. L., & Krishnan, R. (1998). Training people to work in groups. In R. S. Tindale, J. Edwards, E. J. Posavac, F. B. Bryant, Y. Suarez-Balcazar, E. Henderson-King, et al. (Eds.), *Theory and research on small groups* (pp. 37–60). New York, NY: Plenum Press.

Moreland, R. L., & Myaskovsky, L. (2000). Exploring the performance benefits of group training: Transactive memory or improved communication? *Organizational Behavior and Human Decision Processes, 82,* 117–133.

Nevo, D., & Wand, Y. (2005). Organizational memory information systems: A transactive memory approach. *Decision Support Systems, 39,* 549–562.

Palazzolo, E. T. (2005). Organizing for information retrieval in transactive memory systems. *Communication Research, 32,* 726–762.

454 • *Theories of Team Cognition*

Palazzolo, E. T., Serb, D. A., She, Y., Su, C., & Contractor, N. (2006). Coevolution of communication and knowledge networks in transactive memory systems: Using computational models for theoretical development. *Communication Theory, 16*, 223–250.

Pasmore, W. A. (1988). *Designing effective organizations. The sociotechnical systems perspective.* New York, NY: John Wiley & Sons.

Pearsall, M. J., Ellis, A. P. J., & Stein, J. H. (2009). Coping with challenge and hindrance stressors in teams: Behavioral, cognitive, and affective outcomes. *Organizational Behavior and Human Decision Processes, 109*, 18–28.

Peltokorpi, V. (2004). Transactive memory directories in small work units. *Personnel Review, 33*, 446–467.

Prichard, J. S., & Ashleigh, M. J. (2007). The effects of team-skills training on transactive memory and performance. *Small Group Research, 38*, 696–726.

Quinn, J. B., Anderson, P., & Finkelstein, S. (1996.) Making the most of the best. *Harvard Business Review, 74*, 71–80.

Rau, D. (2005). The influence of relationship conflict and trust on transactive memory: Performance relation in top management teams. *Small Group Research, 36*, 746–771.

Reagans, R., Argote, L., & Brooks, D. (2005). Individual experience and experience working together: Predicting learning rates from knowing who knows what and knowing how to work together. *Management Science, 51*, 869–881.

Ren, Y., Carley, K. M., & Argote, L. (2006). The contingent effects of transactive memory: When is it more beneficial to know what others know. *Management Science, 52*, 671–682.

Rulke, D. L., & Galaskiewicz, J. (2000). Distribution of knowledge, group network structure, and group performance. *Management Science, 46*, 612–625.

Rulke, D. L., & Rau, D. (2000). Investigating the encoding process of transactive memory development in group training. *Group and Organizational Management, 25*, 373–396.

Salas, E., Sims, D. E., & Burke, C. S. (2005). Is there a "big five" in teamwork? *Small Group Research, 36*, 555–599.

Schelling, T. C. (1960). *The strategy of conflict.* Cambridge, MA: Harvard University Press.

Smith-Jentsch, K. A., Kraiger, K., Cannon-Bowers, J. A., & Salas, E. (2009). Do familiar teammates request and accept more backup? Transactive memory in air traffic control. *Human Factors, 51*, 181–192.

Staggers, N., & Norcio, A. F. (1993). Mental models: Concepts for human-computer interaction research. *International Journal of Man-Machine Studies, 38*, 587–605.

Tschan, F., Semmer, N. K., Gurtner, A., Bizzari, L., Spychiger, M., Breuer, M., et al. (2009). Explicit reasoning, confirmation bias, and illusory transactive memory: A simulation study of group medical decision making. *Small Group Research, 40*, 271–300.

van Ginkel, W. P., & van Knippenberg, D. (2009). Knowledge about the distribution of information and group decision making: When and why does it work? *Organizational Behavior and Human Decision Processes, 108*, 218–229.

Wasserman, S., & Faust, K. (1994). *Social network analysis: Methods and applications.* Cambridge, UK: Cambridge University Press.

Wegner, D. M. (1987). Transactive memory: A contemporary analysis of the group mind. In B. Mullen & G. R. Goethals (Eds.), *Theories of group behavior* (pp. 185–205). New York, NY: Springer-Verlag.

Wegner, D. M. (1995). A computer network model of human transactive memory. *Social Cognition, 13*, 319–339.

Wegner, D. M., Erber, R., & Raymond, P. (1991). Transactive memory in close relationships. *Journal of Personality and Social Psychology, 61*, 923–929.

Wegner, D. M., Giuliano, T., & Hertel, P. T. (1985). Cognitive interdependence in close relationships. In W. J. Ickes (Ed.), *Compatible and incompatible relationships* (pp. 253–276). New York, NY: Springer-Verlag.

Wittenbaum, G. M., Hollingshead, A. B., & Botero, I. C. (2004). Cooperative to motivated information sharing in groups: Moving beyond the hidden profile paradigm. *Communication Monographs, 71*, 286–310.

Yoon, K., & Hollingshead, A. B. (2010). Cultural stereotyping, convergent expectations, and performance in cross-cultural collaborations. *Social Psychological and Personality Science, 1*, 160–167.

Yuan, Y. C., Fulk, J., & Monge, P. R. (2007). Access to information in connective and communal transactive memory systems. *Communication Research, 34*, 131–155.

Yuan, Y. C., Fulk, J., Monge, P. R., & Contractor, N. (2010). Expertise directory development, shared task-interdependence, and strength of communication network ties as multilevel predictors of expertise exchange in transactive memory work group systems. *Communication Research, 37*, 20–47.

Yuan, Y. C., Fulk, J., Shumate, M., Monge, P. R., Bryant, J. A., & Matsaganis, M. (2005). Individual participation in organizational information commons: The impact of team level social influence and technology-specific competence. *Human Communication Research, 31*, 212–240.

Yuan, Y. C., Monge, P. R., & Fulk, J. (2005). Social capital and transactive memory systems in work groups: A multilevel approach. In K. M. Weaver (Ed.), *Best papers proceedings of the 65th Annual Meeting of the Academy of Management* (pp. C1–C6). Briarcliff Manor, NY: Academy of Management.

Zhang, Z., Hempel, P., Han, Y., & Tjosvold, D. (2007). Transactive memory links work team characteristics and performance. *Journal of Applied Psychology, 92*, 1722–1730.

18

Team Cognition, Communication, and Sharing

Marshall Scott Poole

A common denominator in theories of team cognition is that they presume team members share something, be it a mental model of taskwork or teamwork, a common set of categories, knowledge about members' tendencies and skills, or schema. As Klimoski and Mohammed (1994) and Cannon-Bowers and Salas (2001) note, exactly what is meant by "share" differs across theories.

Sharing is a complex, multidimensional phenomenon that is also central to the study of communication. Communication, after all, is concerned with exchanging information and establishing common meanings, that is, with sharing. This chapter will focus on the various meanings that sharing can have, drawing on the literature in communication and psychology, and will advance a model of sharing as co-orientation of perspectives that suggests several different levels at which cognitions might be shared, articulating additional dimensions of sharing.

PREVIOUS WORK ON SHARED COGNITION

Cannon-Bowers and Salas (2001) summarized work on shared cognition in terms of what is shared and what is meant by shared. In response to the first question of what must be shared, they suggested four general categories: (1) knowledge specific to a particular task (e.g., how to take apart an engine), (2) knowledge related to the task (e.g., knowledge about how engines generally operate; knowledge about teamwork), (3) knowledge of other team members (e.g., their general tendencies, attitudes, values), and (4) shared attitudes and beliefs (e.g., that doing work well is important; that hard work is its own reward).

457

458 • *Theories of Team Cognition*

In answer to the second question regarding what is meant by shared, Cannon-Bowers and Salas (2001) also propose four broad categories:

1. *Shared or overlapping*: When two or more members must have some common knowledge but not redundant knowledge (e.g., surgeon and nurse, who know about operations but have different knowledge bases). In this case, there is a "knowledge base associated with the task and ... a portion of that knowledge base must be common to members" (p. 198).
2. *Similar or identical*: When members must have exactly the same knowledge (e.g., common attitudes about the value of feedback for teamwork).
3. *Compatible or complementary*: When members may not share or have similar knowledge, but their knowledge must lead team members to draw similar expectations for performance. An example would be a multidisciplinary team in which members have specialized expertise and that expertise enables them to have "accurate expectations for themselves, their teammates, and the task to guide behavior" (p. 198).
4. *Distributed*: When knowledge is shared in the sense that it is distributed among members, each of whom has a special expertise or role in the team. This enables the team to have adequate coverage of the knowledge required for the task.

As Cannon-Bowers and Salas (2001) put it, "in any given team, some knowledge will have to be shared, other knowledge similar, and yet other knowledge distributed or complementary" (p. 199).

Langan-Fox (2003) defines sharedness in terms of congruence, the degree of similarity of the mental models among team members, and consensus, the degree to which members have discussed and recognize agreement on a common model. Along a similar line, advocating a phenomenological approach to the notion of sharing, Klimoski and Mohammed (1994) argue that sharing implies not only some level of commonality, but also

> some level of awareness by and among group members regarding how they interpret tasks, situations, and events ... and that each member be aware of the level of awareness of other group members regarding the similarities and differences of their mutual thought processes. (p. 422)

This adds another layer of awareness above and beyond the knowledge itself.

In a discussion of socially shared meaning, Thompson and Fine (1999, p. 280), who acknowledge Higgins for the suggestion, note that the term "shared" can have three meanings. First, shared can mean "divided up into portions," that is, distributed among members of the social unit. Second, shared can mean "'experienced' or 'held in common.'" This refers to common knowledge, such as overlapping cognitive representations, shared schemata, or common experience. Third, shared can mean "partaking in an agreement." They note that this relates to the notion of consensus or acceptance and includes "taking the perspective of others,... establishing an agreement as to what is being said or understood,... consensual validation and consensual representation, shared recognition of social meaning,... collective construction of socially agreed meaning," and a number of other things (p. 280).

This third sense of sharing differs from the notions of shared discussed in previously referenced works, because it carries with it the implication that there is no static thing (e.g., knowledge, attitudes, beliefs, schemas) that is shared or distributed, but that what is shared is being constructed as parties interact. This is a much more fluid and dynamic notion of sharing than the concept of shared mental model implies. It suggests that sharing is a process and that what is shared is intersubjectively constructed among parties. It is, however, consistent with the notion of team cognition.

Klimoski and Mohammed's (1994) phenomenological approach to sharing recognizes the importance of reflexivity in interaction, while Thompson and Fine's (1999) third interpretation of sharing implicates its processual nature. Reflexivity and process have long been theorized and studied by scholars of communication, and it is to the body of work that conceptualizes sharing as a reflexive process that we now turn.

CO-ORIENTATION: SHARED COGNITION IN A HALL OF MIRRORS

Co-orientation refers to the different levels on which interpersonal perception occurs and offers a useful model of the various types of sharing that can occur in teams. The notion of co-orientation refers to the mutual

460 • *Theories of Team Cognition*

orientation of individuals in a group toward an object (e.g., knowledge, belief, attitude) and can be traced back to the interactionist social psychology of John Dewey and George Herbert Mead. An early model of co-orientation was Newcomb's (1953) ABX model. As Scheff (1967) observes, "Implicit in the coorientation approach is a social-systemic model of consensus rather than an individual-systemic model as assumed in the definition of consensus as the sum of individual agreement with X" (p. 34). Co-orientation allows for cases in which there is actually not agreement, but individual members believe there is (pluralistic ignorance), an important situation that can explain blunders and misdiagnoses based on team mental models.

A framework for modeling and measuring co-orientation was developed by Laing, Phillipson, and Lee (1966). It has been applied in studies of mass communication by McLeod and Chaffee (1973) and interpersonal communication by Sillars and Scott (1983). Kenny (1988) demonstrated some affinities between co-orientation levels and various types of social relations in his model.

Several levels of co-orientation can be distinguished based on Laing et al. (1966). The model assumes that actors A and B orient toward a common object, belief, attitude, or state, X. Given this, the following levels can be defined:

- *Agreement of A and B* can be assessed through assessing the correspondence between A(X) and B(X). For example, A and B may agree (or disagree) that rapid, honest feedback is an important component of teamwork.
- *A's understanding of B* can be assessed by assessing the correspondence between A's B(X) and B(X). For example A may accurately understand that B thinks that rapid, honest feedback is an important component of teamwork. Accuracy here refers to correct understanding of B by A.
- *A's recognition of B's understanding of A* can be assessed by assessing the correspondence between A's B's A(X) and B's A(X). For instance, A may recognize correctly (or incorrectly) that B understands that A thinks that rapid, honest feedback is an important component of teamwork.
- *A's perception of agreement with B* can be assessed by assessing the correspondence between A's B(X) and A(X). For example, A may

Team Cognition, Communication, and Sharing • 461

perceive that B's belief that rapid, honest feedback is an important component of teamwork agrees with A's belief about feedback as well.

- *A's perception of B's understanding of A* can be assessed by assessing the correspondence between A's B's A(X) and A(X). For example, A may believe that rapid, honest feedback is an important component of teamwork and also believe that B knows that A holds this belief, thus perceiving that B understands him or her.

Recognition of understanding and perception of agreement are meta-level constructs, whereas perception of understanding is a meta-metalevel construct. Both of these represent reflexivity of understanding.

Another meta-metalevel perception is *A's realization of B's understanding of A*, which can be assessed by assessing the correspondence between A's perception of B's understanding of A [represented by the correspondence between A's B's A(X) and A(X)] and the actual B's A(X). Actor A can feel understood correctly, feel understood incorrectly, feel misunderstood correctly, or feel misunderstood incorrectly.

The co-orientation model is formulated in terms of dyads, but it can be generalized to teams or larger groups (Scheff, 1967). Stryker (1962) and Kenny (1988) both developed analysis of variance (ANOVA)–like models that can sort out some of the components of co-orientation.

Scheff (1967) developed a model of consensus for societies and social groups that is useful for conceptualizing sharing in teams. He traced sharing up three levels in the co-orientation hierarchy, as shown in Table 18.1. As Table 18.1 indicates, it is possible for teammates to have a shared model, but misunderstand that they do (pluralistic ignorance), and also realize that they misunderstand (realized pluralistic ignorance).

Communication tends to generate co-orientation. Studies have shown that it does not necessarily produce agreement or shared belief, but that it does increase understanding and accuracy between partners (Miller, Nunnally, & Wackman, 1975). Feedback and closed-loop communication also tend to increase accuracy and understanding. As members train together and go through scenarios, talking them through, they come to know each other and their tendencies and capabilities. At a certain point, sufficient co-orientation is achieved so that members no longer need to communicate as they act, although communication and reflection after action help to reorient members to one another. The more experience team

462 • *Theories of Team Cognition*

TABLE 18.1

States of Co-orientation in a Group or Collective

Co-orientation State	Members Agree With X	Members Understand Degree of Agreement/ Disagreement	Members Realize Degree of Understanding
Consensus (second degree)	Yes	Yes	Yes
Consensus (first degree)	Yes	Yes	No
Realized pluralistic ignorance	Yes	No	Yes
Pluralistic ignorance	Yes	No	No
Dissensus (first degree)	No	Yes	Yes
Dissensus (second degree)	No	Yes	No
Realized false consensus	No	No	Yes
False consensus	No	No	No

members have with one another, the higher their level of co-orientation is likely to be. When members who do not know each other well have to work together (e.g., as an airline crew), verbal and nonverbal communication serves to signal that they have shared understandings of the work and their roles, thus generating co-orientation.

CO-ORIENTATION, TEAM COGNITION, AND PERFORMANCE

Team Functioning

What are the implications of co-orientation for team cognition and functioning? First, we should distinguish three elements of team functioning: performance per se, error detection (i.e., determining the causes of performance decrements), and learning. Based on the co-orientation model, we can make some predictions.

If we take the traditional foci of shared cognition, knowledge about the task, knowledge about other members, and common attitudes and values, then the implications are fairly clear for performance. For complex tasks, task knowledge should be distributed among members, so for this type of knowledge, rows 3 and 7 in Table 18.1 are most likely to lead to high levels of performance, with row 3, in which there is a realization of the distribution among members, having the greatest likelihood of effective performance.

Team Cognition, Communication, and Sharing • 463

A team in which members share common attitudes and values, understand that they do, and realize that they understand they do (row 1 in Table 18.1) is most likely to have high levels of performance, and it seems unlikely that failing to realize they share (row 5) will result in decrements in performance. In terms of knowledge of other members, teams in which members agree on this knowledge, understand that they agree, and realize that they understand their agreement (row 1) are most likely to react effectively. Teams in which there is disagreement in knowledge of other members, misunderstanding of this disagreement, and failure to realize the misunderstanding (row 8) are much more likely to react in an unpredictable and uncoordinated fashion.

Almost the opposite is likely to be the case for error detection. Teams in rows 1 and 5 (Table 18.1) will have a common theory and approach to their work, and this uniformity is likely to make them less effective at recognizing errors in diagnosis or response than teams in which there is more disagreement on models and approaches (rows 3 and 7). Moreover, to the degree to which the members understand they disagree and realize this, they are more likely to attend to alternative views and detect errors.

Learning, too, is likely to occur more when there is realization of disagreement among members about their performance and the factors that promote it. Disagreement and realization thereof are likely to foster debate and discussion, which lead to learning. However, as Cannon and Edmondson (2001) found, sharing beliefs about how to deal with failure is also important to group learning.

Team Identity, Identification, and Affect

Although these direct effects on team functioning are significant, coorientation studies suggest that there may be even more important impacts on another construct that has not received as much attention among scholars of teamwork and team cognition, namely team identity and its impact on performance and effectiveness.

Laing et al. (1966) observed that people construct and recognize their identities through coming to understand how others see them. As they note, "Self-identity ('I' looking at 'me') is constituted not only by our looking at ourselves, but also by our looking at others looking at us and our reconstitution and alteration of these views of the others about us" (p. 5). Hence, processes of co-orientation are fundamental to the constitution

464 • *Theories of Team Cognition*

and sustenance of individual and dyadic identity. How might this be extended to apply to groups and teams?

Donald T. Campbell (1958) argued that groups are real entities insofar as they are perceived as such and that such perceptions are more likely when gestalt principles of perceptual organization apply to a collection of individuals. Hence, when we see a group of individuals who are proximate, similar, and have a common fate, we are more likely to perceive the individuals as a group. However, this does not address the important problem of whether the set of individuals perceive themselves to be a group. This perception should be mediated by co-orientation, the extent to which team members recognize their shared beliefs and understandings.

When team members see their beliefs, attitudes, and behaviors mirrored in other members, these beliefs, attitudes, and behaviors are validated and reinforced, creating a self-reinforcing feedback loop that strengthens not only their adherence but also their confidence that others will adhere. A team whose members recognize that they understand each other correctly not only will be capable of acting as a unit, but also will feel that they can anticipate one another's actions and their effects. Members will perceive the team to have an identity that they can participate in. This, in turn, will make the members more confident in the team, enhancing its collective self-efficacy.

The converse is also likely to be true. When members either understand that they disagree or misunderstand their agreement, this creates uncertainty about how the team should act, which creates a self-reinforcing feedback loop that weakens their confidence in others and increases uncertainty. In this type of team, members are unlikely to perceive team identity and hence are less likely to identify with the team. This should reduce member sense of collective self-efficacy.

It also seems likely that in teams with high degrees of co-orientation, there will be affective identification with the team over and above cognitive identification. Emotional investment in other members and in the unit as a whole—what Van der Vegt and Bunderson (2005) call collective team identification—derives from the bonds between members who feel understood and valued by other members. These affective bonds provide an additional source of motivation to engage in important teamwork behaviors such as backing each other up and compensating for problems. They also add an additional layer of esprit de corps to the unit that should enhance its functioning.

Finally, teams in which members have a high degree of realization also will not have to "think" or communicate as much as those with lower degrees of realization, which should lower their mental workload overall. Bowers, Braun, and Morgan (1997) summarized evidence that the need to communicate and coordinate with each other significantly increased flight crews' ratings of overall workload, stress, and effort.

Promoting Co-orientation

Effective co-orientation—defined as agreement among members on beliefs and attitudes critical for effective teamwork and taskwork, correct understanding of one another, accurate recognition of understanding, accurate perceptions of agreement and understanding, and correct realization of understanding—is clearly desirable in teams. So the next logical step is to consider how to promote it. At least five factors, one structural and four communication related, contribute to effective co-orientation.

The first factor that contributes to effective co-orientation is *stability of team membership*. The longer members are together, the more likely they are to build co-orientation through direct interaction, through observation of one another, and through information gleaned from third parties. Members who work together over longer periods of time are more likely to develop accurate transactive memory systems (see Chapter 17, this volume) and shared mental models (Rentsch & Klimoski, 2001), as well as knowledge about one another's attitudes and habitual tendencies. Turnover, however, puts members in the position of having to start over again with the newcomer. It is important to note that here we are referring to stability of membership, not stability of structure. If anything, some changes in structure, such as shifting roles, will increase co-orientation because members will experience others' perspectives.

Closed-loop communication, a cornerstone of the team effectiveness literature, is a second process that promotes effective co-orientation. In closed-loop communication (McIntyre & Salas, 1995; Salas, Sims, & Burke, 2005), members follow up with other members to make sure that a message was received and acknowledge receipt of messages to their senders. Members also clarify with receivers that the message is understood as intended. Closed-loop communication can contribute to at least two levels of co-orientation. It can help to clarify whether there is agreement between members in the loop and also may surface disagreements that need to be

466 • *Theories of Team Cognition*

discussed. In addition, it may contribute to understanding when members compare the meanings they have extracted from exchanges and to recognition of understanding.

As we have noted, understanding and recognition may be correct or incorrect. Agreement, understanding, and recognition of understanding are more likely to be correct if closed-loop communication is done properly. A perfunctory response, such as a simple "roger" or "I got you," is unlikely to close the loop adequately. One way to ensure the loop is closed well is to use "active listening," in which the receiver focuses a significant portion of attention on the sender, filters out distractions, listens for detail, asks questions for clarification, and repeats the gist of the sender's message (and in some cases, the exact message) (Nichols & Stevens, 1957). Ideally, both parties to the exchange would use active listening. Given the cognitive load imposed by active listening, it is more likely to be feasible in low-stress situations than in complex and dynamic situations. For situations with higher levels of stress, effective closed-loop communication requires preparation among members through training and practice.

Closed-loop communication by itself is likely to be more effective in promoting the lower levels of co-orientation. Higher levels of co-orientation, such as correct perceptions of understanding and realization of understanding or misunderstanding, require more intensive communication and thus are less likely to be correlated with closed-loop communication.

Training is a third promoter of co-orientation. Training offers members the opportunity to test whether there is agreement, understanding, recognition, and perception of agreement and understanding and to bring themselves into alignment. If a proper set of skills, knowledge, attitudes, and competencies is defined (Cannon-Bowers, Tannenbaum, Salas, & Volpe, 1995), members can practice, and from practice, co-orientation grows.

Although there is little explicit research on training and co-orientation, it seems likely that several characteristics of training will help develop co-orientation most effectively. To promote the types of discussion that enhance co-orientation, training should not focus solely on drilling and practice, but should also focus on mutual feedback and discussion among members. This enables members to assess one another and to compare perspectives, at least tacitly. If explicit reflection and review are included in training, problems with co-orientation are likely to be identified, and reflection and review should increase at all levels. This is particularly likely if the review and debriefing focus on how the group engaged in its task rather than simply emphasizing success or failure (Van den Bosch & Riemersma, 2004). The more physically and psychologically realistic the training, the more effectively co-orientation developed during training is likely to transfer (Kozlowski & DeShon, 2004). Training that explicitly focuses on the development of shared vocabulary and mental models is likely to be especially effective at enhancing co-orientation.

Training offers team members opportunities to reflect that they may not have in the press of real situations. Through training, co-orientation can be developed prior to actual engagement; "preengineering" co-orientation enables the team to be effective when there is neither time nor space for developing agreement, understanding, recognition, or realization.

Metacommunication is a third process that promotes co-orientation. Metacommunication is communication about the process of communication itself. Members engage in metacommunication, for example, when they talk about a how a misunderstanding occurred and what they could do to avoid such a misunderstanding in the future. Metacommunication can focus on the messages themselves, on the nature of the interaction between the parties, or on the context in which communication occurs.

Metacommunication that focuses on the messages themselves consists of discussion about the meaning of terms, aspects of the message that foster misunderstandings, and how messages can be crafted more effectively. It also focuses on assumptions the sender and receiver might be making about the knowledge one another has.

Metacommunication regarding the interaction among the parties deals with (a) mechanics of transmission, (b) actions that frame the process of communication, and (c) communication style. Transmission mechanics refer to the physical properties of the communication, such as volume and speed of talking. Metacommunication about these mechanics may address problems or may deal with improvements. It is also sometimes necessary to metacommunicate about actions that frame the message-exchange process. One party may, for example, turn away right after conveying a message, preventing the other from closing the loop. Metacommunication can help members understand how to frame their interactions. Communication style refers to "the way one verbally and paraverbally

468 • *Theories of Team Cognition*

interacts to signal how literal meaning should be taken, interpreted, filtered, or understood" (Norton, 1978, p. 99). Dimensions underlying style include dominance–submissiveness, dramatic–understated, open–closed, precise–imprecise, and attentive–inattentive (Rubin, Palmgreen, & Sypher, 2009). Metacommunication about style negotiates preferred styles within the team.

Metacommunication about context focuses on how the environment, task, and other external factors influence communication. If the team is going to be in a very noisy environment, for example, members may work out a system of hand signals.

Metacommunication promotes higher levels of co-orientation because it gives members an opportunity to explore whether their recognitions, perceptions, and realizations are correct and to align them. Metacommunication requires team members to focus their attention on something other than the task at hand, and this is not particularly easy to do when the group is preoccupied by its work. Metacommunication is best conducted in a separate session and is an important part of training. After-action reviews are another context in which metacommunication is both appropriate and useful.

Finally, creation of a constructive climate in which there is psychological safety to make and correct errors, trust, and open communication among members provides a supportive context for the effects of the preceding four factors. There is a large and robust body of research on group and organizational climate that shows how an open climate that fosters trust, shared power, and group cohesiveness fosters information sharing, reflection, and the types of interaction that enhance co-orientation (Folger, Poole, & Stutman, 2009). In a particularly germane study, Edmondson, Bohmer, and Pisano (2001) found that group learning was promoted by a climate of psychological safety, "a shared belief that well-intentioned interpersonal risks will not be punished" (p. 688).

The real-world conditions under which teams function are not always conducive to a constructive climate. Sometimes a single error can be fatal. Constructive climates are most useful when teams are in training and when they are under lower stress conditions. Fostering a constructive climate during periods of team development, along with an awareness among members of when errors are not permissible would provide an ideal balance for development of co-orientation and the utilization of co-orientation to promote effective team performance.

CONCLUSION

This chapter has argued that what is shared in team cognition can be conceptualized in terms of co-orientation around behaviors, attitudes, and beliefs. It has presented the co-orientation model as a way of capturing the reflexive nature of shared cognition. Although achieving high levels of co-orientation can be linked to performance, error detection, and learning in teams, an even more important outcome is that co-orientation is related to the collective identity of the team. Both cognitive and affective identification can occur with the team, and each carries particular motivations for members.

REFERENCES

Bowers, C. A., Braun, C. C., & Morgan, B. B. (1997). Team workload: Its meaning and measurement. In M. T. Brannick, E. Salas, & C. Prince (Eds.), *Team performance assessment and measurement* (pp. 85–108). Mahwah, NJ: LEA.

Campbell, D. T. (1958). Common fate, similarity, and other indices of the status of aggregates of persons as social entities. *Behavioral Science, 3*, 14–25.

Cannon, M. D., & Edmondson, A. C. (2001). Confronting failure: Antecedents and consequences of shared beliefs about failure in organizational work groups. *Journal of Organizational Behavior, 22*, 161–177.

Cannon-Bowers, J. A., & Salas, E. (2001). Reflections on shared cognition. *Journal of Organizational Behavior, 22*, 195–202.

Cannon-Bowers, J. A., Tannenbaum, S. I., Salas, E., & Volpe, C. E. (1995). Defining competencies and establishing team training requirements. In R. A. Guzzo, E. Salas, and Associates (Eds.), *Team effectiveness and decision making in organizations* (pp. 333–380). San Francisco, CA: Jossey-Bass.

Edmondson, A. E., Bohmer, R. M., & Pisano, G. P. (2001). Disrupted routines: Team learning and new technology implementation in hospitals. *Administrative Science Quarterly, 46*, 685–716.

Folger, J. P., Poole, M. S., & Stutman, R. (2009). *Working through conflict* (6th ed.). New York, NY: Pearson.

Kenny, D. A. (1988). Interpersonal perception: A social relations analysis. *Journal of Social and Personal Relationships, 5*, 247–261.

Klimoski, R., & Mohammed, S. (1994). Team mental model: Construct or metaphor? *Journal of Management, 20*, 403–437.

Kozlowski, S. W. J., & DeShon, R. J. (2004). A psychological fidelity approach to simulation based training: Theory, research, and principles. In S. Shiflett, L. Elliot, E. Salas, & M. Coovert (Eds.), *Scaled worlds: Development, validation, applications* (pp. 76–99). Aldershot, UK: Ashgate.

Laing, R. D., Phillipson, H., & Lee, A. R. (1966). *Interpersonal perception*. New York, NY: Harper and Row.

470 • *Theories of Team Cognition*

Langan-Fox, J. (2003). Skill acquisition and the development of a team mental model. In M. A. West, D. Tjosvold, & K. G. Smith (Eds.), *International handbook of organizational teamwork and cooperative working* (pp. 321–359). London, UK: Wiley.

McIntyre, R. M., & Salas, E. (1995). Measuring and managing for team performance: Emerging principles from complex environments. In R. A. Guzzo & E. Salas (Eds.), *Team effectiveness and decision making in organizations* (pp. 9–45). San Francisco, CA: Jossey-Bass.

McLeod, J., & Chaffee, S. H. (1973). Interpersonal approaches to communication research. *American Behavioral Scientist, 16,* 467–500.

Miller, S., Nunnally, E., & Wackman, D. (1975). *Alive and aware: Improving communication in relationships.* Minneapolis, MN: Interpersonal Communication Programs.

Newcomb, T. M. (1953). An approach to the study of communicative acts. *Psychological Review, 60,* 393–404.

Nichols, R. G., & Stevens, L. A. (1957). *Are you listening?* New York, NY: McGraw-Hill.

Norton, R. W. (1978). Foundation of a communicator style construct. *Human Communication Research, 4,* 99–112.

Rentsch, J. R., & Klimoski, R. J. (2001). Why do "great minds" think alike? Antecedents of team member schema agreement. *Journal of Organizational Behavior, 22,* 107–120.

Rubin, R. B., Palmgreen, P., & Sypher, H. E. (2009). *Communication research measures: A sourcebook.* New York, NY: Routledge.

Salas, E., Sims, D. E., & Burke, C. S. (2005). Is there a "big five" in teamwork? *Small Group Research, 36,* 555–559.

Scheff, T. (1967). Toward a sociological model of consensus. *American Sociological Review, 32,* 32–46.

Sillars, A. L., & Scott, M. D. (1983). Interpersonal perception between intimates. *Human Communication Research, 10,* 153–176.

Stryker, S. (1962). Conditions for accurate role-taking: A test of Mead's theory. In A. Rose (Ed.), *Human behavior and social processes* (pp. 41–62). Boston, MA: Houghton Mifflin.

Thompson, L., & Fine, G. A. (1999). Socially shared cognition, affect and behavior: A review and integration. *Personality and Social Psychology Review, 3,* 278–302.

Van den Bosch, K., & Riemersma, J. (2004). Reflections on scenario-based training in tactical command. In S. Shiflett, L. Elliot, E. Salas, & M. Coovert (Eds.), *Scaled worlds: Development, validation, applications* (pp. 1–21). Aldershot, UK: Ashgate.

Van der Vegt, G. R., & Bunderson, J. S. (2005). Learning and performance in interdisciplinary teams: The importance of collective team identification. *Academy of Management Journal, 48,* 532–547.

Watzlawick, P., Beavin, J. H., & Jackson, D. D. (1967). *Pragmatics of human communication.* New York, NY: Norton.

19

Team Cognition, Communication, and Message Interdependence

Stephenson J. Beck and Joann Keyton

MESSAGE INTERDEPENDENCE AND TEAM COGNITION

Teamwork is an incredible phenomenon. Importantly, teamwork requires interdependence among group members to achieve a superordinate goal. But interdependence among members, specifically the interdependence they portray through messages in interaction, is not well understood. Because no group member can predict what another group member might say (or perfectly predict his or her own contribution; cf. Warner, Letsky, & Cowen, 2005), "the flow of communication can follow virtually any path" (p. 270). Teamwork is always a partially improvised, flexible dialogue among individuals. It is this property of conversation in teams that leads to new ideas, information sharing, and problem solving.

In previous research, teamwork has been characterized as an adaptation process, one that can be seen in a team's coordination, cooperation, and communication (Salas & Cannon-Bowers, 2000). This adaptation is a complex, multifaceted game that group members play with the hope of moving toward the accomplishment of a certain purpose. Teamwork is based on a shared understanding of factors and information pertinent to the group's goal, the relationships among members, and knowledge of how communicative processes work. Together, this shared understanding, which we label here as team cognition, is the foundation, process, and outcome of team interaction. As is evident by this definition, team cognition is a difficult construct to capture methodologically; however, a communicative approach accounts for much of the complexity of team cognition, specifically when considering message interdependence.

471

472 • *Theories of Team Cognition*

In this chapter, we first define communication, emphasizing the interdependent nature of team interaction. Second, we define team cognition, highlighting the difference between team cognition and shared team cognition. Next, we present nine propositions that underlie a communicative approach to understanding team cognition in terms of its foundation, process, and outcome. Next, we demonstrate the nine propositions through an analysis of jury interaction data. We conclude by examining the implications of using a communicative approach to team cognition, emphasizing methodological difficulties that arise when analyzing team interaction.

DEFINING COMMUNICATION

Communication is the process of symbol production, reception, and usage; conveyance and reception of messages; and the meanings that develop from those messages (Keyton, Beck, & Asbury, 2010). Communication scholars focus on interaction; apart from its interaction, a group fails to exist. Thus, interaction is more than a tool; it is what makes a group a group (Frey, 1994). Through their interaction, individuals (a) acknowledge themselves as group members; (b) develop, share, and commit to goals specific to the group; and (c) create task and relational interdependencies. Members' subjective meanings (Delia, 1977) are a joint production of group members' expressed messages. Thus, meanings are socially constructed within a context, composed of the situation and environment of a group in a specific time, place, and location, and both facilitate and constrain the messages produced, interpreted by, and acted upon by group members.

Because communication is both symbolic and socially created, messages and meanings are only interpretable as interdependent sequences of group and team talk (Keyton et al., 2010). Talk here is defined to include all forms of message transmission including verbal and nonverbal communication, as well as electronic media. The sequential nature of interaction is essential to understanding process, necessitating research methodologies inclusive of the sequential flow of group talk. Such research methodologies are then able to consider how messages are interdependent in accomplishing processes and outcomes.

Team Cognition, Communication, and Message Interdependence • 473

Thus, communication, or interaction, can be described as the symbols or messages that are negotiated into meaning by team members (Blumer, 1969). Communication is not transmitted or exchanged; rather, it is *talked* into meaning by team members who simultaneously engage sender and receiver roles. By maintaining both roles, team members' messages are interdependent in that they depend on messages preceding and influence messages following their own statements. If talk is not reflective of message interdependence, interactions will become topically, sequentially, and conversationally incoherent. Group members may struggle to know how to proceed or become confused and doubt that group members have sufficient team cognition upon which to base interaction.

In addition, message interdependence creates added meaning that would otherwise not exist if messages were separate and isolated. For example, following are two hypothetical interactions using the same messages. The order of the messages changes the flow and meaning of the conversation.

Example 1

Sally: I bet everyone loved the meeting yesterday.
Tim: No, are you serious? Didn't like it that much.
Sally: Did you talk to David about Mark's comments after the meeting?

Example 2

Sally: I bet everyone loved the meeting yesterday.
Tim: Did you talk to David about Mark's comments after the meeting?
Sally: No, are you serious?
Tim: Didn't like it that much.

In the first example, Tim disagrees with Sally's statement and states that he did not like the meeting. In the second example, it appears that David did not like the meeting, and Tim's feelings of the meeting are unknown. Message interdependence, specifically the sequence of messages and which members spoke them, changes the meaning of the conversation.

In a team, the sender role is more prominent because it is easier for observers to identify who is speaking. However, the receiver role, which is enacted simultaneously by all other team members, can be more influential because receivers can accept, reject, or further negotiate what a single message or sequence of messages means. This is an especially important point because the overwhelming majority of team members listen more

474 • *Theories of Team Cognition*

than they speak simply due to logistics. In teams, the communication process becomes complicated because there are always multiple receivers who may or may not respond to the sender's message. For example, team member A says, "Do you agree that we should move ahead as we planned?" Team member B responds, "Sure, we all agree." But this simple exchange hides several important elements. First, team member A's message is ambiguous. What does *moving ahead as planned* invoke for team member A, B, C, or D? Because only team member B responds, there is a presumption that members C and D also agree. Is their silence passive agreement? If they are agreeing, is their agreement on exactly the same issue? Or do they remain silent because they conclude it is not worth the trouble to once again contest member A's view of their activity? Or perhaps they are not even paying attention.

Team communication is further complicated in that communication serves multiple functions. Group researchers have long identified both task and relational message functions (e.g., Bales, 1950; Benne & Sheats, 1948; Watzlawick, Beavin, & Jackson, 1967), among others (e.g., identity goals; Clark & Delia 1979). Furthermore, these task and relational identifications can be applied to all messages of the group, therein providing a baseline for analyzing team cognition across other team processes, such as conflict management, leadership, and decision making. In sum, message interdependence is the emergent structure created by team members in their talk or conversation; in turn, a team's conversational sequences are foundational to the team processes identified by Marks, Mathieu, and Zaccaro (2001). That is, team members perform these transition, action, and interpersonal processes by talking them into being.

DEFINING MACROCOGNITION

Macrocognition has been associated (although loosely) with communication. In cognitive science, communication is required to move cognition from the level of a single unit of analysis to the team (Bara, 1995). In cognitive engineering, Cacciabue and Hollnagel (1995) used macrocognition to describe how cognition emerges, especially in regard to demands of natural environments (see also Klein et al., 2003). From this earlier position, macrocognition has been adopted in the study of collaborative contexts, as Warner et al. (2005) argue that macrocognition encompasses both internalized and externalized processes occurring during team interaction. Thus, talk or conversation among team members is presumed.

More recently, Letsky, Warner, Fiore, Rosen, and Salas (2007) defined macrocognition as "internalized and externalized high-level mental processes employed by teams to create new knowledge during complex, one-of-a-kind, collaborative problem solving" (p. 7). It is this definition that we work with in this chapter, as we argue that ambiguity cannot be resolved and new knowledge cannot be developed among team members without interaction among them. Whereas the internalized processes are not expressed through writing or speaking and cannot be directly observed or operationalized, externalized processes *can be* observed and measured. Communication between and among team members would constitute externalized macrocognitive processes because it can be directly observed by both team members and others. Moreover, decision making, sensemaking, planning, adaptation, problem detection, and coordination are social and symbolic activities we believe teams can only accomplish if team members talk with one another (Keyton et al., 2010). Indeed, Keyton et al. (2010) argue that "communication is evidence of cognitive activity" (p. 273).

In this chapter, we use two terms that refer to macrocognition. Team cognition is used when referring to the collective understanding group members have of a certain topic or issue and is based primarily on group interaction. Shared cognition or shared team cognition is used where specifically referring to an assessment of the amount of similarity or overlap within team cognition. Thus, team cognition focuses on group member perceptions of group understanding, and shared team cognition focuses on an assessment of the similarity of group understanding.

DISSECTING TEAM COGNITION

In line with the efforts of this book, we take a nuanced view of team cognition and examine its relationship to communication in three ways: foundational, processual, and outcome. In addition, we specifically consider

476 • *Theories of Team Cognition*

and emphasize how this relationship is influenced by message interdependence. The propositions set forth are founded on assumptions of a communicative research perspective. Although we do not assume our proposition list to be exhaustive, we do believe those proposed here are central to understanding the relationship between team cognition and communication. We begin with a foundational view because it underlies the entire communicative process.

Foundation

First, conversation in any type of group is based on team cognition brought into the group by its members. Perhaps these pre-event cognitions are perceptions and assumptions about the formal roles of group members or presumed cognitive similarity based on demographics, such as sex, race, ethnicity, or other status characteristics. Even if team members do not know one another well, there is still team cognition about how groups work in general and how that template applies to group interaction (e.g., Galanes, 2003; Sunwolf & Seibold, 1998). Or, there may be team cognition based on the type of task a group is performing. In these instances, team cognition about people, groups, and tasks creates a foundation for the team. Despite the foundation of shared meaning, team members are probably not aware of the number of cognitive structures they share or the degree to which they share them.

For communication among team members to begin and then move forward, some type of opening act must occur, and others must follow— otherwise a conversation does not ensue. These opening messages can be verbal, nonverbal, or both. For example, eye contact between team members may initiate conversation in the meeting. Using electronic media, one team member would have to initiate a personal or system-generated communication for the team meeting to begin. If team members gather for a meeting but do not say any words to one another until the meeting starts, it would be assumed that something is wrong. Normally, some sort of small talk would initiate conversation. Also, many individuals smack their lips (or open their mouth to speak) or change their seating position (i.e., lean forward) before speaking, as an indication that they want the attention of the team members. Initial messages create a starting point for message interdependence to take place (i.e., the second message is influenced by the first message). Understanding such nuances of opening conversation

Team Cognition, Communication, and Message Interdependence • 477

is a function of shared understanding or team cognition about how teams communicate.

Similarly, it would be deemed inappropriate for team members to start a meeting by screaming at one another. Again, such messages would indicate that something is wrong with the team. According to Berger (1977), people have mental structures and steps that help them plan their interactions with each other. These goal-directed actions can be either specific domain knowledge or general domain knowledge. It is the latter that is important here, and in many ways is similar to the transportable team competencies identified by Cannon-Bowers, Tannenbaum, Salas, and Volpe (1995). Thus, people (based on their experiences or the vicarious experiences of others) create and maintain a universal team cognition about expectations for team member interaction, and subsequent message interdependence, at meetings. These expectations are present at initial meetings between group members and at subsequent meetings as norms develop (Sigman, 1984). In either case, team members have a shared understanding about what is generally considered appropriate or inappropriate in team interaction and how one should conduct himself or herself in relation to others in interaction.

Of course, there may be differences in what some consider to be appropriate, especially because individuals evaluate their communication differently than others evaluate it (Hullman, 2007). A blunt, direct comment can be interpreted as helpful by one team member and harsh by another. The manifestation of these differences influences individual members' perceptions of a team's shared understanding. Even though members may be aware that their views of group discussion are different than other members' views, this realization itself becomes a component of the ever-evolving team cognition.

Due to these complexities, the foundational aspect of team cognition is difficult to identify and articulate. Whether the presumptions team members make about one another (on any dimension or characteristic) are true or not, they move forward with their actions and communication *as if* they are true. Thus, shared team cognition refers to the perceived similarity of understanding group members have about a certain issue, implicitly assuming that individuals have their own potentially different perceptions of the team's cognition. Even though differences are present, team members often communicate as if team cognition was completely shared. Otherwise, coordinated, interdependent

478 • *Theories of Team Cognition*

interaction would cease to exist. Propositions 1 through 3 formalize these positions:

> Proposition 1: Team cognition is the foundation for a team's understanding of how to talk appropriately.
> Proposition 2: Team cognition may be perceived differently by each team member.
> Proposition 3: Each team member communicates based on his or her perception of team cognition.

Process

As the team is communicating, shared cognition is developed from the interdependent interactions of team members. The degree to which team members develop greater sharedness of team cognition can be based on many elements of the team's interaction. For example, the combination of who talks, for how long, and on what topic influences the degree to which team cognition is shared. The degree to which members are given opportunities to discuss, ask questions, and share information and opinions will also influence the degree of shared team cognition. The degree of relational talk interspersed with task and procedural talk will influence the degree of shared team cognition. Additionally, how group members negotiate between conflicting individual and group goals (Wittenbaum, Hollingshead, & Botero, 2004) can influence the degree of shared team cognition. For example, a group member may withhold valuable information from the group in order to make another member look bad, thus accomplishing a personal goal but frustrating the group goal. Alternately, a team leader speaking for long periods of time followed by "yes, sir" from the other team members may give the illusion of shared cognition. And indeed, they may have shared cognition, if such an interaction leads to similar perceptions of how group members understand an issue.

Often, a team member comes to a social interaction event (e.g., meeting) with a perspective that makes him or her valuable to the group. This perspective, in addition to individual characteristics such as knowledge, experience, and mood, will influence the way each member interprets team interaction. Inevitably, each person will have a unique perspective. Team members attempt to bridge these differences (or create shared team cognition) through interaction. Messages reveal many things about the perspective of an individual; messages act as a piece of evidence to be interpreted. For example, if a team member (Jim) says, "That wasn't my assignment," then it is possible that team members will interpret the message in any of several ways. First, the content of the message appears straightforward, in that Jim provided an appropriate response to a request for information. Second, team members may interpret this as Jim worrying about responsibility for an assignment, possibly revealing insecurity about his work. Third, Jim's statement can also be interpreted as passing the responsibility or blame to someone else. Thus, team members could interpret this statement in a variety of ways.

The potential for one statement to be interpreted differently by group members but still remain a central foundation for interaction is displayed in the language convergence/meaning divergence theory of Dougherty, Kramer, Klatzke, and Rogers (2009). Dougherty et al. (2009) demonstrate how common labels become helpful in interaction while allowing members to have differing interpretations. Furthermore, they argue that the "combined analysis of convergence and divergence [is] where the illusion of shared meaning becomes apparent" (p. 36).

In addition, Eisenberg (1984) points out that the potential for a common message to have different meanings for groups or organizations can be a strategic advantage for speakers. For example, a chief executive officer (CEO) may use ambiguous words so that organizational members opposing each other can interpret the message as consistent with their ways of thinking. This allows both of them to be supportive of the CEO's message but for different reasons, and the unarticulated differences may give the illusion of consensus within the organization.

Essentially, then, team cognition from a communication perspective focuses on the degree of shared understanding that team members *express*. For team cognition to exist, individual understandings must at least be congruent with one another (Cronin & Weingart, 2007). In other words, perceptions of team cognition create a foundation for interaction, but it is the expression of those perceptions through interdependent messages (i.e., process) that allows team members to evaluate whether their perceptions are compatible. Doing so acknowledges that individuals will interpret the same messages in a group meeting differently, but that enough overlap is present for subsequent action to be taken by group members. Thus, the interaction process influences team cognition, which becomes the foundation of future interaction processes.

480 • *Theories of Team Cognition*

How do teams take these divergent interpretations and maintain a conversation toward a specific goal? Even though each individual's understanding of messages can be different and is evolving throughout interaction, the assumption of a certain level of shared understanding remains. For example, in the earlier example, Jim's comment would likely not cause meeting interaction to stop in order to discuss the different meanings of his statement. Most likely, it would focus on the individual who is responsible for the assignment or the interpretation that appears most explicit from the message. The other different interpretations of the message probably will not be dealt with immediately or at all; thus, they do not influence the flow of conversation. Although messages in interaction are interdependent, team members can choose which interpretation to base their next message on. Thus, all speakers have a say in the flow of conversation. Again, the first interpretation mentioned in the previous Jim example will probably be the basis for the next messages. Interpretations that are workplace oriented (e.g., "He is ducking responsibility"), personally oriented (e.g., "I can't stand that guy"; "Good job avoiding that trap"), or processually oriented (e.g., "He is just slowing this meeting down") may be held by team members but not immediately and explicitly articulated in conversation. However, if Jim continues to make these statements about every project, other team members may start to believe that he is ineffective, unproductive, or irresponsible. Evidence of team cognition may be shown in future interaction by team members as they avoid Jim's comments or have a negative predisposition toward anything Jim says.

To further complicate things, team member do not all receive the same messages. Group composition can fluctuate across meetings due to absences and visitors (Keyton, Ford, & Smith, 2008; Putnam & Stohl, 1990; Stohl & Putnam, 1999). Obviously, absences prevent all members from receiving the same messages. Visitors can change group dynamics and climate, leading members to interpret messages differently. If a member is absent from a meeting or not paying attention, changes in the evolution of shared cognition in the team, at least as perceived by other members, may diverge from those not attending. Because not all members speak at the same time, the majority of team members' group-centered action is listening. Listening is a high-energy activity and is often not conducted with the same energy and care as when an individual speaks. All listening is not equal; team members could be listening only to hear if their name is mentioned. In addition, other distractions, such as side conversations between two team members or checking electronic devices, may prevent messages from reaching all team members.

Importantly, this moves beyond simply verbal communication. As a team member speaks, other members are giving off nonverbal cues. All team members are simultaneously communicating. A majority of this communication may go unnoticed. Although peripheral vision allows for seeing multiple members at the same time, many nonverbal messages may be seen by only a few members, and some nonverbal messages may not be seen at all. Some nonverbal communication could be interpreted as a message, whereas others are not. For example, if a team member is sitting upright, steadily tapping her pen loudly against the table, and staring at the clock, many individuals would perceive this as someone who wants the meeting to end. Some would even say she is explicitly stating it. However, there may be individuals who are not aware or do not recognize her actions as a message and figure that she is simply listening to the meeting.

An individual's perception of team cognition becomes the starting point for communication. For example, if a group member feels like the group is "against him," he may respond defensively. It could be true that the group does feel he deserves the blame, but that is not as important to his message creation as *his perception* of what others think. His messages will be based on his perception of team cognition. It is important to emphasize that a team member may have a completely different perception from the rest of the team. Propositions 4 through 7 formalize these positions about the process of team cognition:

Proposition 4: Team cognition is reflected in and created by interaction.

Proposition 5: Team members' individual perceptions drive team conversation to reveal, hide, or negotiate team cognition.

Proposition 6: Team members simultaneously navigate multiple orientations (i.e., task, relational, procedural) when creating team cognition.

Proposition 7: Silence and nonverbals can be implicitly or explicitly used by the sender and viewed by other team members as communicating a message.

482 • *Theories of Team Cognition*

Outcome

Team cognition can also be operationalized as the degree of shared meaning team members believe they walk away with. As an outcome, team cognition may be information about decisions or other tasks, new or modified understandings about the context in which the information was shared, the task itself, or relationships among team members. Clearly, one of the outcomes of the communication process is the team cognition foundation for future interaction. Thus, the three different aspects this chapter has focused on (foundation, process, and outcome) are all inputs and outputs for each other.

Can fully shared team cognition be achieved? This is not likely because individual team members bring individual preferences and perspectives to the team. Furthermore, team members may not be motivated to speak, or they may strategically speak for multiple personal goals at the expense of group goals (Hollingshead, Jacobsohn, & Beck, 2007). But greater shared team cognition is likely to be dependent on the degree to which the interaction-based creation of team cognition is encouraged and facilitated. Team member analysis of the interaction as a whole, specifically recognizing the interdependent messages that created holistic meaning, leads to team cognition outcomes. It will also be influenced by team member awareness of the differing perceptions other members hold of team cognition.

How can we evaluate the amount, level, or degree of team cognition? This is especially difficult to answer because a 10% overlap in team cognition may be highly functional in one circumstance and a 90% overlap may be highly dysfunctional in another. Clearly the use of percentages to illustrate this point oversimplifies team cognition, but it does portray the context-dependent nature of determining team cognition effectiveness. For example, a team may make a decision in regard to whom they should hire out of three candidates. Two of the candidates are below par, and no one wants to hire them. For the third candidate, there are a variety of different perspectives. Team member A thinks she is very qualified for the job. Team member B does not think she is very qualified, but thinks she is easy to work with, which he highly values. Team member C is pretty apathetic about the whole process, as long as they do not hire the two bad candidates. Team member D thinks she is attractive. They all come together with little discussion and decide to hire the third

Team Cognition, Communication, and Message Interdependence • 483

candidate. The group was in agreement that the first two candidates were not qualified for the job, and thus, we can assume they have a high level of shared team cognition. However, they all had different views of why the third candidate should be hired; in fact, they used different criteria to make their decisions. But because they did not discuss these differences in depth and because they all agreed on the outcome, it appears that a lower level of shared team cognition was necessary to make their decision. Propositions 8 and 9 formalize our positions on outcomes:

> Proposition 8: Interaction leads to team cognition that is often not consistent across team members. However, a certain amount of shared team cognition exists.
> Proposition 9: Different levels of shared team cognition will be effective in different situations.

DEMONSTRATING THREE COMMUNICATIVE ASPECTS OF TEAM COGNITION

In line with the efforts of this book, we explore the cognitive processes of macrocognition in the complex, dynamic, and emerging interaction of team members. Of particular interest are ad hoc, rapidly formed teams that must deal with difficult short-term situations. These types of teams are more likely to work within ill-defined, even chaotic, time-pressured situations in which decision consequences are high and the creation of shared team cognition difficult.

Juries are one type of team that shares these characteristics. A jury is a type of problem-solving team formed with zero history to deliberate on complex information. There is no correct answer; communication is unrestricted and naturally occurring. Moreover, a jury can only return a guilty verdict or sentencing decision when sufficient shared team cognition about their task and the facts of the case is achieved. Thus, a jury must simultaneous manage decisions about their intermember relations, procedures for decision making, and how to use details presented by conflicting sides in their information processing. Jury decisions are not simple and are not necessarily sequential. Juries are also not rehearsed and scripted the way in which court proceedings are (i.e., questioning of witnesses, summation

484 • *Theories of Team Cognition*

to jury). Finally, jury decisions are conceptual and conflictual (McGrath, 1984). We use transcripts of a jury that must decide (a) if the defendant is guilty, (b) if the specification of mass murder is met, and (c) the sentencing penalty if guilt is found.

To further illustrate the way communication and team cognition are related, examples of the nine propositions will be shown and discussed. Due to the complexity of team cognition and difficulty in finding natural examples that portray each proposition individually, examples will illustrate the interdependent and overlapping nature of the propositions.

The data used for our illustrations derive from the murder case *State of Ohio v. Mark Ducic* (2005). In the trial phase, Ducic, a drug dealer and past felon, was convicted of two counts of premeditated murder. The data used here come from the sentencing phase, where jurors are trying to decide among several sentences, from 25 years in prison with the possibility of parole to the death penalty (which necessitates a unanimous decision). The judge has provided a set of instructions, which detail that the jury must weigh aggravating and mitigating factors in making their decision. Initially, and as shown in the following excerpts[*], the jurors ran into problems with the definition of mitigating factors. In Excerpt 1, Juror 7 first lays out her belief as to whether drugs played a role in the defendant's choices. Before she is finished speaking, Juror 1 interrupts and agrees with the previous statement. Juror 7 continues. Although Juror 1 had already agreed with the statement, his next statements suggest he thinks Juror 7 is moving past the issue at hand. Jurors 7 and 12 show that they believe they are talking about mitigating factors, and at this point, Juror 1 realizes that his interpretation of mitigating factors is different from the others.

Excerpt 1

Juror 7   And what we're saying is that it bears... it bears on the sentence that the drugs are involved... that he might, if not for drugs, he might have made a better choice. He might have made a better choice and at this point in this discussion...

Juror 1   I couldn't agree with you more.

Juror 7   ... in this point in this discussion I'm not... I'm not gonna cave to send this man off to get strapped on a damn gurney somewhere...

---

[*] Excerpts taken from transcript of jury deliberations provided by the court upon request.

Team Cognition, Communication, and Message Interdependence • 485

Juror 1   We're not anywhere near that right now. We're talking about factors that are mitigating.

Juror 7   We all know what we're talkin' about.

Juror 12   I'm with you.

Juror 1   No. That's not what I'm talkin' about at all. I'm talking about mitigating factors.

Shortly after the above excerpt, jurors broke for dinner. Upon returning, and now that the confusion involving mitigating factors was obvious, jurors take turns defining mitigating. In Excerpt 2, Juror 1 attempts to define mitigating factors by offering a definition and two examples. Juror 8 follows up by disagreeing with Juror 1 and offering her own perspective. Jurors 1 and 8 exchange messages, before an exasperated Juror 4 suggests getting a dictionary.

Excerpt 2

Juror 1   I'd like to just read one more thing and then give you a couple examples of the way I see it, and please help me here. Mitigating factors are factors that lessen the moral culpability of the defendant. So they lessen the moral blend. Okay? So, what does that mean, lessen the moral culpability? Who wants to take a stab at that so I'm on the right page here? Lessen the moral culpability. Here's what I think it means, okay? I think a good example of mitigating would be if a lifelong alcoholic quit doing alcohol and went to AA. That's a mitigating factor. It lessens his moral blend. It offsets what he has been doing up until that point. Let me just finish my...

Okay. A mitigating circumstances for a drug addict would be a drug addict that stopped doing drugs and went to Al-anon, so you can give him credit for his action that offsets his doing drugs. It would be like a murderer that got religion. He got religion. He got religious. He understood the, the wrongness, for lack of a better word, of his behavior. He is remorseful. That's mitigating to me. Now, I want somebody please help me with this, cause I need to understand this. Go head. Mitigating.

Juror 8   I think mitigating is different from what you think. I think it is a factor that helps you to soften or decrease the actual, [inaudible] keep use the same word to explain it, the blame or what

486 • *Theories of Team Cognition*

have you. In your case, you ... I think I would come to that conclusion that you have if I blamed the victim ... and I think that a mitigating circumstance in the case example you gave is the giving up of the drug abuse. I think it's a factor, like for example whether he stops taking the drug ... I mean the mitigating factor is that he can't stop taking the drug. Not that he goes to AA.

Juror 1   He can't stop taking the drugs. How is that he can't ... I don't understand.

Juror 8   If you're physiologically dependent on them, at the time ...

Juror 1   You're an addict. So, an addict ... being an addict is being a mitigating circumstance?

Juror 8   I didn't say that.

Juror 1   Okay. Help me.

Juror 4   We need a dictionary.

Jurors attempted to debate the sentencing issue without resolving their definitional troubles. In Excerpt 3, five jurors are disagreeing about what are considered mitigating factors. Several of them try to make their opinions known; others are making comments that are not directly related to the conversation; and some comments are completely ignored.

Excerpt 3

Juror 8   Well, I was gonna confer with you and, um, for a change ... we have our different understandings of what mitigating is and until we come to a common ground on it we're going to be spinning our wheels.

Juror 2   Mhm. Right. In trouble. Yup.

Juror 12   Everybody can give their thought on the factors ... the mitigation factors, but we don't have a common ground for what a mitigation is so everyone can say, well I disagree with this or I disagree with that.

Juror 1   I, I ... are you finished? Margaret?

Juror 8   I'm finished.

Juror 1   I have to summarily disagree with the two of your comments about the drugs. The fact that he is doing drugs. Unless I misunderstood you, the fact that he was doing drugs is a mitigating circumstance. Now, that was about twenty minutes ago, something like that? Maybe I didn't hear you correctly ...

Juror 7	That he was a drug addict.
Juror 12	You can add me to that…
Juror 1	That fact that he… that's a mitigating circumstance?
Juror 7	Yes.
Juror 12	You can add me to their [inaudible – all speaking].
Juror 1	Help me with this.
Juror 7	I'm not condoning what the man did…
Juror 1	I'm not talking about value judgments. How is that a mitigating factor?
Juror 7	I don't think that all his faculties are there while he is under the influence of drugs? I don't think that… He might not…
Juror 1	Who doesn't agree with that?
Juror 7	… he might not…
Juror 1	Lessen moral culpability. That doesn't mean that his moral… does that make him less culpable?
Juror 1	Standards, morals of the society.
Juror 12	He has no standards when he is on drugs.
Juror 2	Are you gonna excuse a drunker driver from killing your kid?
Juror 7	This is why I think that.
Juror 12	He still did it. Yeah.
Juror 8	I have a definition.
Juror 7	Because the man might not do what he did if he was not involved in this circle or involved in drug addiction.

Analyzing Excerpts in Relation to Propositions

Evidence of the nine propositions is portrayed throughout the three selected excerpts. The first three propositions focus on the foundational aspect of team cognition in relation to communication. Proposition 1 states that team cognition is the foundation for a team's understanding of how to talk appropriately. The three excerpts demonstrate several examples of Proposition 1, including tolerance for disagreements and interruptions and agreement on legitimate subject matter. When disagreement or interruptions take place in the excerpts, conversation does not cease. Instead, members continue to speak accordingly. In other contexts, disagreements and interruptions would be considered inappropriate. Despite the differences upon which this interaction is predicated, jurors have a general idea of what is appropriate and acceptable in conversation. Reactions to

488 • *Theories of Team Cognition*

inappropriate behavior in groups often demonstrate the differences in team cognition among group members.

Proposition 2 states that team cognition may be perceived differently by each team member. In Excerpt 1, Juror 1 indicates that interpretations diverge. Jurors 7 and 12 had just agreed that everyone was on the same page in terms of discussion, but Juror 1 sees differences. Interestingly, the three jurors seem to be consistent in terms of the importance of the issue, but Jurors 7 and 12 think the discussion is focused on mitigating factors, and although Juror 1 agrees with the overall point, he does not believe it falls within the realm of mitigating factors. The perceptual differences become manifest through interaction; up until this point, jurors believe that team cognition is shared. Differences in interpretation are multidimensional, in that individuals can agree and disagree using whatever criteria they deem appropriate. Thus, evidence of a team cognition foundation is present (Proposition 1), while still allowing for multiple interpretations (Proposition 2).

Extending from Proposition 2, Proposition 3 states that each team member communicates based on his or her perception of team cognition. Because Juror 12 (Excerpt 1) believes that everyone is talking about the same thing and is on the same page, she comments that she is "with" the other two jurors, suggesting she sees a high level of shared team cognition. Juror 1 sees differences in how members are interpreting the current level of team cognition in relation to mitigating factors, and his messages are indicative of this.

Again, the demonstration of the first three propositions is dependent on the interdependence of messages. Juror 1's difference in perception is only made manifest through the comments of Jurors 7 and 12. He initially thinks everyone is on the same page, but the other jurors' comments make the differences in team cognition clear to him. However, the messages of Jurors 7 and 12 also indicate that they did not see any differences, and their messages are clearly in response to Juror 1's initial messages. Thus, message interdependence brings out the different perceptions of messages.

As can be expected, propositions involving the process aspect of team cognition's relationship to communication flow directly from the foundational aspect. Proposition 4 states that team cognition is reflected in and created by interaction. As shown in the previous paragraph, messages reflect individual perceptions of team cognition, and these messages become data upon which other group members can adapt their perceptions of team cognition; these conversational moves demonstrate a juror's utilization of message interdependence. Excerpt 2 shows another example of a juror making explicit the differences in team cognition among members. After Juror 1 has attempted to define mitigating factors, Juror 8 states that she understands the definition of mitigating differently. It can be assumed that this difference came to light when Juror 1 described his definition in the previous speaking turn. These two examples show specific, explicit instances where team cognition and individual perceptions of team cognition were reflected in and created by interaction; implicit instances exist as well, although they are more subtle and may not be as observable as explicit instances.

Related to Proposition 4, Proposition 5 states that team members' individual perceptions drive team conversation to reveal, hide, or negotiate team cognition. This is based on the presumption that some members may be aware of differences, whereas others may not. Messages in interaction are where such differences are played out.

Again, Excerpt 1 is a good example of this. The three jurors agree with one another at some point in the conversation, but by the end of the excerpt, they realize that there are differences in their meanings. Juror 1's initial statement suggests that he sees the issue similarly to Juror 7, but by the end of the interaction, he realizes that his understanding of mitigating factors is different from the others. Ironically, the statement that illustrated this difference was when Juror 7 said that they all knew what they were talking about. This revealed to Juror 1 that the others thought they were discussing mitigating factors, when he did not see it that way. They had conducted their conversation up to that point under the assumption that they understood things similarly, but through interaction, the differences became known. Subsequently, Juror 1's next statements in both Excerpts 1 and 2 show his efforts to negotiate the jury's team cognition.

Proposition 6 states that team members simultaneously navigate multiple goal orientations (i.e., task, relational, procedural) when creating team cognition. This is evidenced several times throughout Excerpt 2. After Juror 8 denies what Juror 1 said about her, Juror 8 says, "Okay. Help me." The way this is phrased, in a relational, submissive manner, may diffuse any tension caused by the competitive nature of the definitional debate. In addition, Juror 4 suggests an alternative approach, alleviating a need to have a back-and-forth debate on the topic. Similarly, in Excerpt 1, Juror 12 stated, "I'm with you." This could have easily been stated in task-oriented terms (e.g., I agree with the idea), but the personal

490 • *Theories of Team Cognition*

nature suggests that relational and maintenance goals are simultaneously being accomplished with the jury's task goals. Due to the multifunctional nature of messages, communication can be strategically adapted to accomplish multiple individual and group goals simultaneously (Hollingshead et al., 2007).

Proposition 7 states that silence and nonverbals can be implicitly or explicitly used by the sender and viewed by other team members as communicating a message. Video recordings of the jury deliberations show a variety of ways that nonverbals are used to convey messages. Verbal and nonverbal messages are interpreted simultaneously; however, sometimes verbals and nonverbals may contradict one another. When verbal and nonverbal channels of communications are inconsistent, group members may suspect deception (Burgoon, 1980, 1985). Clearly it is difficult to convey this proposition using only transcripts, but it should be noticed that not all jury members are actively engaged in the conversation. Silence is difficult to interpret; when someone does not participate, are they silently consenting or dissenting with the majority? Interestingly, voting patterns showed that jurors who spoke less during deliberations voted toward a more lenient sentence than the more vocal jurors. This suggests that jurors who do not speak may have opinions that differ from the rest and should not be excluded from team cognition research.

Both the foundational and process aspects of team cognition are directly related to how communication affects team cognition outcomes. Proposition 8 states that team cognition, which stems from interaction, is not consistent across all team members, but a core similarity of cognition is needed. Excerpt 3 shows an example of this in that the conversation (a) goes in several directions, (b) is completely dependent on previous comments for which direction it takes, and yet, (c) still manages to take place. There is general core knowledge about what the topic is, even if there are clear differences in perception as well. But without this core knowledge, the conversation would fall apart.

Proposition 9 states that different levels of shared team cognition will be effective in different situations. Clearly from Excerpt 3, the amount of team cognition similar across all jurors is small or at least unknown or not explicitly clear. At the end of the excerpt, Juror 8 suggests a new definition of mitigation, which is ignored and somewhat out of place from the rest of the conversation. In addition, the first three jurors who speak say in essence the same thing but perhaps felt the need to speak

Team Cognition, Communication, and Message Interdependence • 491

because of the confusion in what others were saying. Perhaps they simply were not listening. The jurors' inability to have a common understanding of the subject matter, specifically their definition of mitigating factors, has prevented them from effectively resolving the matter. A higher level of shared team cognition is needed for a successful outcome in this context.

CONCLUSION

The nine propositions detailed in this chapter articulate the relationship between team cognition and communication. Central to this relationship is the interdependent nature of messages. This interdependence is played out in foundation-, processual-, and outcome-level aspects of interaction. These cyclical aspects feed into one another. The outcomes of group interaction become the foundation for future interaction; in addition, process is an outcome in and of itself.

Importantly, a communicative perspective of team cognition provides a point of analysis to better understand team cognition. Messages are evidence of team cognition. This overcomes many of the limitations to which self-report methodologies succumb, such as participant bias or validity and reliability issues associated with survey instrumentation. Perhaps combining currently used macrocognition methodologies with those used in communication analysis will provide stronger multiple-method approaches to our understanding of group process and outcomes (see Beck & Keyton, 2009, for a multiple-method example). Pairing cognitive measures with team member messages can provide us with a more thorough and complete understanding of team interaction.

However, before moving forward on analysis of team cognition from a communicative perspective, it is important to recognize the difficulties associated with such an approach. Poole, Keyton, and Frey (1999) have pointed to five difficulties unique to group communication methodologies. First is the concept of synergy, or the notion that group process can create more than the original sum of the parts. This is often essential in accomplishing superordinate goals (Keyton, 2006). The opposite can also be true; in ineffective groups, task and relational problems can lead groups to produce less than the sum of its individual members. Capturing these

492 • *Theories of Team Cognition*

additional dynamics is difficult but essential to understanding message interdependence.

Second, group constructs are difficult to capture because they are often multidimensional and account for the involvement of multiple group members and the subsequent number of relationships present in groups. No matter what, certain dimensions of understanding may be missing from data collection, which can hamper efforts to examine team cognition. Third, a group's permeable and fluid boundaries can lead to many member composition changes across group activities. Accounting for this bona fide group dimension is difficult across longitudinal studies (Putnam & Stohl, 1990) and, as discussed earlier, complicates attempts to understand a team's shared meaning at any point in time.

Fourth, group behavior is difficult to capture in general. For example, group members often interact strategically, trying to accomplish individual and group goals (Hollingshead et al., 2007; Wittenbaum et al., 2004). Trying to account for the various strategic components of interaction can be problematic. A focus on strategy may require neglecting another aspect of communication. This problem is true for all methodologies; focusing on one message dimension often means neglecting another, and this is problematic due to the variety of possible ways to convey shared meaning to others. Last, group constructs are often systemic of other constructs embedded in the organization (Poole et al., 1999). This makes it difficult to account solely for group-specific behavior.

In conclusion, a communicative perspective of team cognition provides a more developed understanding of how team members rely on message interdependence to develop and maintain team cognition. This chapter also qualitatively demonstrates how the interdependence of messages provides evidence of team cognition. Despite the difficulties associated with this approach, considering team cognition from a communicative perspective enables researchers to base their claims on evidence manifest in interaction.

REFERENCES

Bales, R. F. (1950). *Interaction process analysis.* Cambridge, MA: Addison-Wesley.
Bara, B. G. (1995). *Cognitive science: A developmental approach to the simulation of the mind.* Hillsdale, NJ: Lawrence Erlbaum.

Beck, S. J., & Keyton, J. (2009). Perceiving strategic meeting interaction. *Small Group Research, 40*, 223–246. doi: 10.1177/1046496408330084

Benne, K., & Sheats, P. (1948). Functional roles of group members. *Journal of Social Issues, 4*, 41–49.

Berger, C. R. (1977). *Planning strategic interaction: Attaining goals through communicative action.* Mahwah, NJ: Lawrence Erlbaum.

Blumer, H. (1969). *Symbolic interactionism: Perspective and method.* Berkeley, CA: University of California Press.

Burgoon, J. K. (1980). Nonverbal communication research in the 1970s: An overview. In D. Nimmo (Ed.), *Communication yearbook 4* (pp. 179-197). New Brunswick, NJ: Transaction.

Burgoon, J. K. (1985). Nonverbal signals. In M. L. Knapp & G. R. Millers (Eds.), *Handbook of interpersonal communication* (pp. 349–353). Beverly Hills, CA: Sage.

Cacciabue, P. C., & Hollnagel, E. (1995). Simulation of cognition: Applications. In J. M. Hoc, P. C. Cacciabue, & E. Hollnagel (Eds.), *Expertise and technology: Cognition and human-computer cooperation* (pp. 55–73). Hillsdale, NJ: Lawrence Erlbaum.

Cannon-Bowers, J. A., Tannenbaum, S. I., Salas, E., & Volpe, C. E. (1995). Defining competencies and establishing team training requirements. In R. A. Guzzo, E. Salas, & associates (Eds.), *Team effectiveness and decision making in organizations* (pp. 333–380). San Francisco, CA: Jossey-Bass.

Clark, R. A., & Delia, J. G. (1979). Topoi and rhetorical competence. *Quarterly Journal of Speech, 65*, 187–206. doi:10.1080/00335637909383470

Cronin, M. A., & Weingart, L. R. (2007). Representational gaps, information processing, and conflict in functionally diverse teams. *Academy of Management Review, 23*, 761–773.

Delia, J. G. (1977). Constructivism and the study of human communication. *Quarterly Journal of Speech, 63*, 66–83. doi:1080/00335637709383368

Dougherty, D. S., Kramer, M. W., Klatzke, S. R., & Rogers, T. K. K. (2009). Language convergence and meaning divergence: A meaning centered communication theory. *Communication Monographs, 76*, 20–46. doi:10.1080/03637750802378799

Eisenberg, E. M. (1984). Ambiguity as strategy in organizational communication. *Communication Monographs, 51*, 227–242. doi:10.1080/03637758409390197

Frey, L. R. (1994). The call of the field: Studying communication in natural groups. In L. R. Frey (Ed.), *Group communication in context: Studies of natural groups* (pp. ix–xiv). Hillsdale, NJ: Lawrence Erlbaum.

Galanes, G. J. (2003). In their own words: An exploratory study of bona fide group leaders. *Small Group Research, 34*, 741–770. doi: 10.1177/1046496403257649

Hollingshead, A. B., Jacobsohn, G. C., & Beck, S. J. (2007). Motives and goals in context: A strategic analysis of information-sharing groups. In K. Fiedler (Ed.), *Social communication* (pp. 257–280). New York, NY: Psychology Press.

Hullman, G. W. (2007). Communicative adaptability scale: Evaluating its use as an "other-report" measure. *Communication Reports, 20*, 51–74. doi:10.1080/0893421 0701643693

Keyton, J. (2006). *Communicating in groups: Building relationships for group effectiveness.* New York, NY: Oxford University Press.

Keyton, J., Beck, S. J., & Asbury, M. A. (2010). Macrocognition: A communication perspective. *Theoretical Issues in Ergonomics Science, 11*, 272–286.

Keyton, J., Ford, D. J., & Smith, F. L. (2008). A meso-level communicative model of interorganizational collaboration. *Communication Theory, 18*, 376–406. doi:10.1111/j.1468-2885.2008.00327.x

494 • *Theories of Team Cognition*

Klein, G. K., Ross, K. G., Moon, B. M., Klein, D. E., Hoffman, R. R., & Hollnagel, E. (2003). Macrocognition. *IEEE Intelligent Systems, 18*, 81–84. doi:10.1109/MIS.2003.1200735

Letsky, M., Warner, N., Fiore, S. M., Rosen, M. A., & Salas, E. (2007). *Macrocognition in complex team problem solving.* Paper presented at the 11th International Command and Control Research and Technology Symposium (ICCRTS), Cambridge, UK.

Marks, M. A., Mathieu, J. E., & Zaccaro, S. J. (2001). A temporally based framework and taxonomy of team processes. *Academy of Management Review, 26*, 356–376.

McGrath, J. E. (1984). *Groups: Interaction and performance.* Englewood Cliffs, NJ: Prentice-Hall.

Poole, M. S., Keyton, J., & Frey, L. R. (1999). Group communication methodology: Issues and considerations. In L. R. Frey, D. S. Gouran, & M. S. Poole (Eds.), *The handbook of group communication theory and research* (pp. 92–112). Thousand Oaks, CA: Sage.

Putnam, L. L., & Stohl, C. (1990). Bona fide groups: A reconceptualization of groups in context. *Communication Studies, 41*, 248–265.

Salas, E., & Cannon-Browers, J. A. (2000). The anatomy of team training. In S. Tobias & D. Fletcher (Eds.), *Training and retraining: A handbook for businesses, industry, government, and military* (pp. 312–335). Farmington Hills, MI: Macmillan.

Sigman, S. J. (1984). Talk and interaction strategy in a task-oriented group. *Small Group Behavior, 15*, 33–51. doi: 10.1177/104649648401500102

State of Ohio v. Mark Ducic, 162 Ohio App.3d 721, 2005-Ohio-4291 (2005).

Stohl, C., & Putnam, L. L. (1999). Group communication in context: Implications for the study of bona fide groups. In L. R. Frey (Ed.), *Group communication in context: Studies of natural groups.* Hillsdale, NJ: Lawrence Erlbaum.

Sunwolf, & Seibold, D. R. (1998). Jurors' intuitive rules for deliberation: A structurational approach to communication in jury decision making. *Communication Monographs, 65*, 282–306. doi:10.1080/03637759809376455

Warner, N., Letsky, M., & Cowen, M. (2005). Cognitive model of team collaboration: Macro-cognitive focus. *Proceedings of Human Factors and Ergonomics Society Annual Meeting,* 269–273.

Watzlawick, P., Beavin, J., & Jackson, D. (1967). *Pragmatics of human communication: A study of interactional patterns, pathologies, and paradoxes.* New York, NY: Norton.

Wittenbaum, G. M., Hollingshead, A. B., & Botero, I. C. (2004). From cooperative to motivated information sharing in groups: Moving beyond the hidden profile paradigm. *Communication Monographs, 71*, 286–310. doi:10.1080/0363452042000299894

20

Team Reason: Between Team Cognition and Societal Knowledge

Peter Musaeus

INTRODUCTION

High-reliability teams have high levels of training, and their members come from different disciplines, such as medicine, nursing, or military science. Team reason, therefore, is likely to bear the mark of a formal knowledge repertoire or tool kit. This knowledge is associated with a socially valued social practice that embodies a range of cultural traditions that can be classified as, for instance, natural scientific, legal, religious, or artistic and that might influence how the team reasons. Thus, how the team makes sense of the dynamic environment depends on how the team reasons with tools and ideas formed within cultural traditions developed through societal history. Cultural-historical practices form, as argued in social philosophy for centuries (Hegel, 1807/1977), the backdrop for reason; in other words, there is an inherent, deep-seated sociality behind any kind of cognition and reason. Therefore, individual cognition, macrocognition, and team cognition are social phenomena, not primarily because knowledge is shared and can be made public but because team cognition is unthinkable without social practices such as natural science or art that provide means for team members to think and reason with. Thus, what members of society take to be rational, that is to say, mediated by societal institutions and with goals, norms, and underlying assumptions amenable to critical scrutiny, might shape what a high-reliability team takes to be worth pursuing. Thus, the notion of team reason aims to describe how societal institutions validate and shape knowledge, goals, tools, and ideas relevant to high-reliability team problem solving.

495

496 • *Theories of Team Cognition*

This chapter explores an important tension in team and macrocognitive research between long-term knowledge and short-term knowledge. Short-term knowledge can be understood as fleeting knowledge associated with team situational awareness (Cooke, Salas, Kiekel, & Bell, 2004). This short-term knowledge might be conceived as a type of team cognition in the here and now, for instance, in regard to team coordination, workspace awareness, or up-to-the-moment understanding (Fiore, Rosen, Salas, Burke, & Jentsch, 2008, p. 157). However, team cognition also draws from the notion of long-term knowledge conceived as team cognitive structures, such as mental models and "knowledge of the nature and causes of the problem" (Fiore et al., 2008, p. 153) referring to problems related to the situation. Orasanu and Fischer (1992, p. 189) argued that although professional teams clearly have shared background knowledge, as also argued earlier in terms of scientific knowledge, the fact that accidents and errors occur illustrates the need for something in addition to shared background knowledge—a shared team understanding of the current situation.

However, errors do not occur because teams have a shared knowledge background, and they do not disappear regardless of the number of shared team models a team might have, because the models could be wrong. An ethnographic video study by Xiao and Moss (2001) on trauma resuscitation teams found that the teams were characterized by a high degree of shared responsibility to prevent failures. The teams practiced a checks and balances system where team members were expected to register and speak out loud the vital signs of the patient. This verbalization served to create shared team task awareness, but in order for such a system of mutual group checking to function, the team must share an idea about what knowledge is, what signs are worth communicating, and why they are doing this. Thus, team reason is a precondition for a checks and balances system. In sum, there is a fundamental problem in claiming that teams rely on representations of the here and now and then trying to discern this from shared background knowledge. It seems unfortunate to want to make a split between short- and long-term knowledge because fleeting knowledge does not logically count as a comprehensive understanding of knowledge and cognition (Hegel, 1807/1977) but as merely futile attempts to capture the here and now. The problem is, briefly put, that any shared situation model must assume and explain many heres and many nows, which it claims not to necessitate.

In light of the vexed problem of accounting for knowledge in team cognition, this chapter will revisit the notion that high-reliability teams faced with ill-structured problems strive to grasp first the here and now, second the shared situation, and third the nature of the problem by modeling it through cultural tools. The third idea can be called striving for a universal conceptualization, referring to knowledge that transcends and explains the meaning of the problem or task and not only the particular situational awareness. The ability of the understanding of the team to transcend the here and now of the situation relies, as mentioned earlier, on team members' scientific, artistic, legal, or other forms of knowledge. Such knowledge is not primarily private knowledge in the team but is a process that emerges in relation to the given social practices and norms that the team is part of and coproduces through its activity. In sum, the knowledge requirements involved in team coordination in high-reliability and dynamic environments involve both understanding the here and now and more stable enactments of knowledge (referred to as long-term knowledge). Thus, the team's formal knowledge interweaves with the team's situational understanding and thus hypothetically patterns team cognitive functions such as sensemaking, situational awareness, and transactive memory.

This chapter draws on sociocultural theory (Hedegaard, 2002; Hegel, 1807/1977; Lave, 1988; Vygotsky, 1934/1986) to make a conceptual distinction between team reason and team cognition. This chapter develops a model of team reason and argues that team reason is concomitant to team cognition. Team reason describes processes of team cognition, in which team activity is patterned by societal knowledge or cultural tool kits, here defined as relations that "mediate thought and place their stamp on our representations of reality" (Bruner, 1991, p. 3) and "what our culture knows for us in the form of the structure" (Hutchins, 1996, p. 316). In short, team reason focuses on actions for which the team ponders its knowledge base and its norms for making evaluations. Notions of both team reason and team cognition describe the complex coordination of teamwork, social relationships, and team tasks in a social practice. Specifically, the notion of team reason entails the following:

1. *Societal knowledge.* This refers to members who actively engage with cultural-historically organized knowledge repertoires through verbal team communication or nonverbal means such as constructing scientific diagrams and gesturing. This gives a double focus on tools

498 • *Theories of Team Cognition*

and ideas that originate outside the team but that are appropriated and enacted by the team.

2. *Moral identity.* This refers to ways the team members think and talk about what they are committed to, including what counts as true knowledge. For instance, the team takes falsification to be a valid scientific method but not religious experience. What the team takes to be valid, true, and good knowledge speaks to their moral identity. When teams consider their norms for making evaluations, they are defining who they are. In other words, how team members think rationally about knowledge begs a number of normative questions about what is right and wrong.

A stronger focus is needed on the move from societal knowledge or social practice to the team's appropriation of knowledge as team cognitive functions. This calls for a stronger research focus on the knowledge base involved. For example, in medical cognition, the following statement has been made previously: "Traditional accounts of medical reasoning described the diagnostic process in a way that is independent of the underlying structure of the domain knowledge" (Patel, Arocha, & Zhang, 2005, p. 730). The point is that team reason is not the sole property of the individual team members nor is team cognition the sole property of the team. However, the notion of team reason requires first, that reason derives from institutions and societal knowledge and second, that reason is associated with epistemological and moral identity questions.

Organization of Argument

This chapter proposes an analytic distinction between team cognition and team reason. Both team cognition and team reason are emergent team phenomena and are contingent on social relations that pertain to the team, task, work organizations, and short- and long-term knowledge. However, in the case of team reason, this is explicated as knowledge bases or societal knowledge. This is illustrated in Figure 20.1, which shows that team reason and team cognition are horizontally related and that team reason mediates between team cognition and societal knowledge.

The purpose of this chapter is to conceive of team cognition in broader terms by investigating the institutional influences on team cognition. This chapter investigates knowledge and norms of knowledge, part of what in

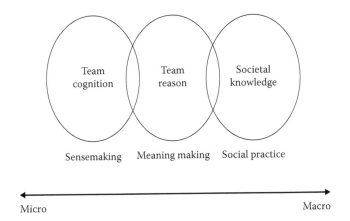

FIGURE 20.1
Team reason at mesolevel.

team cognitive research is dubbed long-term knowledge, but here is tied to the institutional order and societal knowledge potentially patterning team cognition. The argument is that team participation, in social (e.g., scientific, artistic, legal) practice, patterns how the team reasons and what knowledge the team holds as rational. A theoretical model is developed of the relations between team, organization, institution, and state/government in relation to team cognition, team reason, and societal reason. This model is tentatively illustrated with the example of medical teams. Finally, it is argued that team reason is amenable to empirical study and that analyzing processes of team reason should be seen as a necessary supplement to the research field of team cognition.

Relevance

Team reason is relevant to investigate for four reasons:

1. Societal knowledge and norms about what is socially valued and sanctioned are underresearched areas in team cognitive and macrocognitive research.
2. The notion of team reason provides a way to conceive of team members' tool use, problem framing, the origin and limits of team members' knowledge, and appropriation from repertoires of knowledge, including professional standards and norms. This is relevant in order to arrive at a critical understanding of the processes that make team

500 • *Theories of Team Cognition*

cognition possible at an institutional level (i.e., understanding the knowledge base and tools of high-reliability organizations).

3. The notion of team reason is a way to bring team cognitive and macrocognitive research into contact with broader strands of social theory, including, for instance, sociocultural and educational theory.

4. A focus on the cultural traditions and institutional patterns of team cognition is relevant to create cross-fertilization between team cognitive research and organizational research.

In conclusion, whether it is concomitant to team cognition, as argued in this chapter, or a rational aspect already incorporated in the notion of team cognition (as shared background knowledge, mentioned earlier), team reason is an important theme in team cognition research. It is important to understand team life as a sociocultural achievement where goals, tools, and ideas are produced, not only by the individual team, but also by teams' cultural traditions and social practices.

OVERVIEW AND DEFINITIONS: SITUATING TEAM REASON

The Sociocultural Tradition and Social Practice

Team reason is not a well-defined term in the organizational or team cognitive literature. As mentioned earlier, the notion derives from Hegel's antidualistic philosophy that was the source of early and influential social theoretical approaches to the notion of group mind (Wegner, 1987, p. 185). Arguably, the same line of thought influenced Vygotsky's (1934/1986) argument around the beginning of the 1930s that thought, speech, and concepts derive from the social realm of human activity and societal practice. According to this sociocultural line of thinking, a team reasons well if the institutions in which the team participates (e.g., organizations or scientific educational communities with which the team identifies) are good and rational. This means that they are perceived to have ends that the team members can see the rationale behind. Reason refers to the joint or communal cognition about human cooperation and human life. Reason refers to what we as human beings, who are societal beings, hold to be true and take to be reasonable about knowledge, social institutions, and about being at home in the world. This view has, for instance, been influential in inspiring cognition in practice (Lave, 1988), situated cognition (Hutchins, 1996), and the situated focus on participation in social practice. Social practice refers to the cultural-historical context that gives meaning to what team members do at work, including what is said, documented, and codified, as well as "all the implicit relations, tacit conventions, subtle cues, untold rules of thumb, recognizable intuitions, specific perceptions, well-tuned sensitivities, embodied understandings, underlying assumptions and shared world views" (Wenger, 1998, p. 47). Arguably, the above research traditions form a sociocultural and interdisciplinary approach developed mainly with inspiration from psychology, philosophy, ethnography, education, linguistics, literary theory, and anthropology. According to a sociocultural perspective, to understand team cognition, it is necessary to look at team participation in social practice because the team's cognitive activity is shaped by histories and mediated by tools and ideas.

Team Macrocognition and the Practice Turn

At first glance, it seems, from the previous discussion, as if there is a clash between the sociocultural tradition and the pragmatic concerns in macrocognitive research interested in team achievement and performance rather than "the detailed theoretical accounts of how cognition takes place in the human mind" (Cacciabue & Hollnagel, 1995, p. 57). How to create functional cognitive systems and functional team cognition is an important aim, but it should not stand in opposition to asking questions about the context and content of the knowledge and truth claims of the teams studied. Macrocognitive research points to the value in not being constrained by the hard question about mechanisms (the underlying mental processes involved in team cognition) and pushes toward the what: the team product or team achievement of work relating to cognitive functions. The point is that important headway has recently been made to bridge this gap. Contemporary team cognitive approaches aim to develop a non-Cartesian, nondualistic approach to work and to cognition as social activity (Cooke, Gorman, & Rowe, 2009). This can be interpreted as part of a general "practice turn" in the social sciences (Schatzki, 2001), which, in the present context of team research, represents a turn from cognitive structures of knowledge (Cannon-Bowers, Salas, & Converse, 1993; Klimoski & Mohammed, 1994) to team participation in social practice.

502 • *Theories of Team Cognition*

Metacognition

Metacognition can be understood as control of cognition and knowledge of one's cognition (Flavell, 1979). Research on team cognition and related research have used the notion of metacognition to denote cognitive learning strategies that enhance learning and that can been extended to team decision making. Orasanu and Fischer (1992, p. 189) extended elements of individual metacognition to account for the team's shared situation model specified in terms of a clearly specified goal, accurate interpretation of the goal, strategies to reach it, and continuous monitoring of progress. Along this line, a study by Entin, Serfaty, and Deckert (1994) on shared mental models in tactical military teams found that periodic situation updates about uncertain, unreliable, or conflicting information could develop a shared metacognitive model. It is fair to say that metacognition has been a relevant term in studies on team cognition. However, because metacognition is not defined in terms of, and does not explicitly relate to, societal knowledge, social practice, or cultural tools, metacognition is not synonymous with team reason. To conclude, because the notion of metacognition does not readily focus on work sites, tools, institutional order, societal knowledge, and what in a cultural tradition counts as rational reason, as distinct from cognition, this chapter will use the term team reason and not team metacognition.

In summary, team reason is a notion that describes the knowledge base (beyond the here and now), also called the repertoire of ideas or societal knowledge, constituting rational team cognitive processes. Thus, in terms of rationality, team cognition probably covers more processes than team reason; however, team reason is broader in terms of the emphasis on institutional knowledge. Concerns with knowledge, morals, and culture have not yet been a major concern in team cognitive and macrocognitive research, perhaps out of fear that this would merely lead to futile philosophizing rather than pragmatic guidance to the applied fields studied. This chapter aims to bring a focus on how normative team evaluations bear on team cognition. The point is that team knowledge and what this knowledge says about the team need to be explored more in terms of the spoken and unspoken norms team members jointly believe in and reflect upon. How do teams come to take some things about the world (task and team inclusive) to be true? What counts as knowledge to a team? Team theories of knowledge and norms are important considerations for team cognitive research.

A THEORETICAL MODEL OF TEAM REASON

The themes outlined previously attempted to situate team reason in the landscape of team cognition. The argument proposed is that team reason is an intermediate phenomenon between team cognition and societal knowledge. This section develops the argument that the framework is intended to open an avenue for team cognitive research in the direction of institutional orderings or patterns of knowledge to improve understanding of team phenomena and to give a broader conception of team cognitive processes to encompass both epistemological and moral claims about what is valid knowledge. This model, depicted in Figure 20.2, suggests that team cognitive functions (sensemaking, situational awareness, transactive memory, or other macrocognitive functions) are situated at the team level, whereas team reason pertains to extrateam activities and relates to societal knowledge.

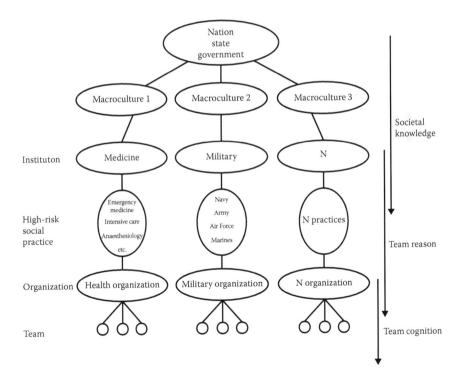

FIGURE 20.2
Levels of analysis.

504 • *Theories of Team Cognition*

The Model

The framework depicts team reason as an intermediate between societal knowledge and team cognition. The model is inspired by Hedegaard's (2004) model of cultural identity distinguishing between three levels: state, institution, and person. Figure 20.2 distinguishes between four levels: (1) governmental body/national state, (2) institutions, (3) organizations, and (4) team.

As Figure 20.2 suggests, the argument is that team cognition is about team members' joint sensemaking at the team–organizational level, whereas team reason is about meaning making on the team–organizational–institutional axis. This distinction between sense and meaning is inspired by Leontiev's (1978) distinction between personal sense and objective meaning but is applied to teams. The notion of sensemaking emphasizes the active involvement that teams have in striving to comprehend complex environments: "Sensemaking is about the ways people generate what they interpret" (Weick, 1995, p. 13), which means to act or wait and see what a person says before knowing what to think (Weick, 1988). In actual social practice, as discussed later in terms of observing team reason, team reason is concomitant to team cognition. For example, an emergency medical team might measure the patient's vital signs; talking about these measurements, indeed the very measuring, is an example of reason or knowing what (scientific) knowledge these tools can yield. However, team reason is not about dynamic assessment (as in team cognition), not about the here and now or depending on who is on the job, what their level of training and expertise is, or how the tasks are coordinated. The medical resuscitation team, for instance, relies on monitoring tools (such as electrocardiogram tracing, blood pressure readings, and saturation readings), which when interpreted, aid the team in detecting problems and coordinating responses, and in so doing, the team reasons about what is right or wrong.

In summary, team reason describes sensemaking specifically about knowledge base, what norms are implicit in the team's work tasks, which normative and evaluative standards the team has adopted, and what this says about the team. Team reason draws from the objective, codified knowledge associated with science(s); from narratives; and potentially from any socially valued social practice (such as art, law, or religion).

Societal Knowledge

Societal knowledge is defined as sociocultural webs of significance (Bruner, 1986) in institutions such as the health system, the military system, the family, or the police force. These webs refer to the cultural-historically organized ways for teams to arrange what they take to be knowledge and how they make claims about this knowledge and their performance. Societal knowledge is not merely a passive pool of propositions and values but a field charged with meanings (i.e., ideas and tangible tools) that a team can appropriate. Societal knowledge is defined as "collective knowledge within different institutions" and "[e]xplicit or shared knowledge of community ... practices" (Hedegaard, 2002, p. 23). What, more precisely, is collective or societal knowledge? The knowledge held as valuable (good or useful) by society and its cultural traditions and institutions can be called societal knowledge. This knowledge is, as mentioned earlier, mediated by institutions such as work organizations or scientific (educational) institutions. Thus, when a team uses logical reasoning to solve a problem, diagnose a patient, or prescribe the right treatment, the team members do not reinvent logic or medicine; instead, they appropriate already established knowledge repertoires. Team reason comes into play when a team appropriates societal knowledge, which is knowledge organized through tools and ideas, for instance, documents, technologies, guidelines, and protocols such as the Advanced Trauma Life Support program, developed in one cultural context (the United States) but adopted in several other cultural contexts (Driscoll & Wardrope, 2005). Team reason is about what counts as right knowledge and what norms to follow as a team. For instance, in medical practice, diagnostic tools enable the practitioner to solve medical problems of pathology. Medical texts (books and journals) are taken as resources that the team members consult during dynamic teamwork or through debriefings. These tools, which develop the medical work activity, carry with them particular cultures, historical remains from their development (Hutchins, 1996). The use of tools and ideas is an accumulation and transmission of social knowledge that influences team behavior beyond concrete tool use by influencing how the team reasons.

The object of study in investigating team reason (and the societal knowledge relevant to a particular team) is not primarily the team's knowledge understood as the team members' knowledge as a whole, but rather the symbol excavation or the archeology of knowledge of society (Foucault, 1972). Societal

506 • *Theories of Team Cognition*

knowledge is the study of epistemological culture, scientific institutions, and power (Foucault, 1972). Team reason is concerned with the accomplishments of a given cultural history—the produced artifacts, truths, and artistic products; in short, everything venerated by a culture and its communities, institutions, and teams; a culture's historical and societal achievements.

Society is a historical notion often argued to have emerged in the 19th century (Rabinow, 1992, p. 7). Therefore, the study of team reason needs to engage in a type of knowledge archaeology (Foucault, 1972) that is both a historical and experimental study, for instance using document analysis to dig out what a given work culture hides. For example, it has been noted that the high degree of division of labor in health care creates various ecologies of different kinds of knowledge (Anspach, 1987), where medical and nursing knowledge complement each other but where knowledge can be distributed unevenly and, hence, power is also distributed unevenly. To repeat, medical teamwork may be viewed as a practical accomplishment that emerges despite the fact that medical team members often have unequal power or status (Anspach, 1987). It is a simplification to think that there is a uniform logic behind team reason or that scientific knowledge is a coherent system of thought. Medical professionals, for instance, make inferences with a complex organization built on several sciences, including surgery, biochemistry, psychology, and sociology (Patel et al., 2005, p. 734). It follows that team cognition is a paradoxical notion that aims to describe on the one hand, a system whose behavior is about the haphazard, random situational awareness in the here and now and, on the other hand, abstractly toward long-term knowledge. Rational team behavior is not well described as expressing either short- or long-term knowledge. Team behavior follows norms and knowledge that are historically developed and when conceived as team reason are amenable to empirical study, as argued in the section "Observing and Measuring Team Reason."

Team Reason and Team Cognition

Processes of team reason are concomitant to processes of team cognition, but team reason refers to appropriation of societal knowledge and team communication about this knowledge base in a professional social practice. Thus, studying team reason (in the context of team cognitive phenomena with high-reliability teams facing ill-structured problems in dynamic environments) includes studying team cognitive functions and supporting cognitive processes, such as shared awareness, transactive memory, and sensemaking. However, the focus is on the momentary cognitive strategies of a particular team in relation to knowledge and strategies, which are approved indirectly or directly by an organization or institution thus aiding the individual to structure the problem. Mediating tools (e.g., diagnostic instruments in medical teams) are both historical and cultural events as well as complex processes appropriated by team members, but it remains to be proven how societal knowledge is useful in the dynamic environment that the team faces. As argued earlier, the point is that the fleeting knowledge of situational awareness (Cooke et al., 2004) actually means talking about something that takes place in a historical context because social practice is, as mentioned in the Introduction, defined in terms of historical, documented, codified knowledge and shared world views as well as the tacit, implicit conventions of the team.

Team reason presumes a cultural organization that influences how and what teams think about in the form of either paradigmatic knowledge or narrative knowledge. Paradigmatic knowledge "seeks to transcend the particular by higher and higher reaching for abstraction" (Bruner, 1986, p. 13). For instance, the medical team draws on medical research, and they use the tools vested to them by their profession and by science. This represents societal knowledge pertaining to more than just the medical profession. The team members justify their team's knowledge with reference to a system of propositions and procedures for falsifying knowledge, and their profession has ways of ensuring that team members have been socialized into the norms of the profession, such as through the Hippocratic Oath, as discussed later.

Storytelling and narratives in organizations and education have been described as particularly powerful sources of meaning-making activity (Bruner, 2004). Narratives have been argued to be an important kind of cognition used, for instance, by physicians and nurses to understand patient stories (Benner, 1991). Stories are understood as contextually rich anecdotes about difficult problem solving and have been shown to be ways for technicians, in the form of metaphorical war stories, to convey and store knowledge (Orr, 1996). In analogy, narrative knowledge could be hypothesized to be used by teams to engage in story sharing, based on narrative schemes borrowed from cultural tool kits (Bruner, 1986). Team members might use narrative knowledge to link past events with future events or interpret events and thus form new ways of understanding the

508 • *Theories of Team Cognition*

task (or the team) in the process. The idea that narratives play an important role in team cognition is not new, although there is, as noted by Fiore, McDaniel, and Jentsch (2009), a lack of empirical team studies on how teams use literary forms to cognize and express their identity. Societal knowledge, in the form of paradigmatic knowledge or narrative knowledge, is appropriated by teams as a condition for performing acts of team reason. Both paradigmatic and narrative knowledge are rational types of knowledge depending on what is considered adaptive and rational in the given social practice that the team participates in.

AN ILLUSTRATION OF THE MODEL

To illustrate the difference between team cognition and team reason, take as an example a medical team, such as an emergency medicine (EM) team or the more specialized trauma resuscitation team. An EM team aims to provide relief and treatment to one or more patients who have suffered high-impact accidents. Hospital operations of the team include work in the operating room or intensive care unit and require adaptive team role coordination in order to perform dynamic tasks such as triaging and diagnosis. EM team performance might hypothetically be predicted by team cognition, such as the team's situational and shared awareness, sensemaking, shared mental models, and transactive memory (Cooke et al., 2004). At the same time, team members draw from a societal knowledge when they use tools or communicate about moral identities.

Some ethnographic studies on high-reliability medical team cognition provide transcripts about team member communication concerning concrete diagnostic tools (e.g., computed tomography, x-ray), but not concerning how the team members reason about these tools (Sarcevic, Marsic, Lesk, & Burd, 2008; Xiao & Moss, 2001). This could be explained with reference to the argument that reasoning is implicit in tool use (Hutchins, 1996). There are two alternative explanations: Either team reason is rare in high-reliability teams under time pressure, or empirical studies have not focused on team reason, but only on team cognition. In both cases, it is no surprise that there is a lack of studies directly describing team reason.

An indirect account of team reason is described in an ethnographic study conducted by Yun, Faraj, Xiao, and Sims (2003) on team leadership and coordination in trauma resuscitation teams. The study found that the attending surgeon assumed a teaching role toward the residents. An attending surgeon, quoted in Yun et al. (2003), said the following about the residents:

> they will come up and say "I'm gonna do this." My first question is "why" and the way I go with this is "what are your choices, why do you, if you have four choices why do you pick that?" I think it's the better way to do it ... because what I want to teach them is the way of thinking ... I want you to consider a problem, find what the problem is. (p. 203)

The recalled incident is about the resident being summoned to think about a problem and give explicit reasons about his or her choice of action. The incident is part of the communication in the bay during resuscitation. The incident is not, as could perhaps be expected, part of reflective team learning such as debriefing, which would not necessarily qualify as falling under the topic of team cognition or team reason. This example suggests that reason is at play even in high-reliability environments and stressful situations. The example illustrates team reason to the extent that team members were jointly probing for an explanation, strived to synthesize their observations into an accurate task description, and in this process, drew explicitly on medical knowledge.

Reasoning about and acting out norms is an example of team reason. There are several norms at play in medical teamwork, most notably the Hippocratic Oath, which is sworn by doctors upon graduation to act in the patient's best interest, do no harm, and help those in need (Dickstein, Erlen, & Erlen, 1991). A medical team that follows the Hippocratic Oath reflectively commits to its norms, and this type of team reason is not abstract, but a concrete and defining characteristic of what it means to be a medical team: a team that obeys norms about the patient's best interest. Obviously, there is more to a medical team's identity, such as the epistemological aspect of the team using medical reasoning (Patel et al., 2005) or nursing reasoning, which are both scientific reasoning and normative reasoning about caregiving (Benner, 1991).

The previous example from Yun et al. (2003) suggests that team reason contains both an epistemological aspect and normative or moral aspect, and both can be hypothesized to be defining characteristics of what it means to be a high-reliability team. However, there is no sharp division between these two aspects of team reason. In other words, the team is not engaged in either efficient problem solving or ethical action. A medical

510 • *Theories of Team Cognition*

team is always, whether in decision making or treatment, faced with a question that is at the same time technical and moral: What is the right and good course of action with respect to the situation of the patient? Pellegrino, a physician, writes about the physician's decision making: "To be technically right a decision must be objective; to be good it must be compassionate. It is in the fusion of these opposing attitudes that the end of clinical medicine is fulfilled" (Pellegrino, 1987, p. 208). Team reason occurs when norms of what is right and good are reflected upon by the medical team.

For example, if the medical team is engaged in scientific reasoning about diagnosis, team communication might be concerned with measuring physiological parameters of the patient, whereas the narratological mode is reflected in talk and acts about patient history (i.e., a story with a plot, theme, hero, and problems to be overcome). Members of an EM team are expected to understand how to use scientific measurement tools, and as such, they draw from a natural scientific discourse about, for instance, hypothesis testing as part of what constitutes scientific reasoning (Dunbar & Fugelsang, 2005). This illustrates that team reason occurs at an institutional level. However, it is seen at the team level at the same time in acts of diagnosing, problem solving, probing, or administering medicine.

In sum, team reason occurs on the backdrop of the conceptual and technological tools vested to the team by society to solve societal problems, such as relating to health, technological, or religious demands. Scientific knowledge engages participants in scientific activities such as experimentation, problem solving, and causal reasoning (Dunbar & Fugelsang, 2005, p. 705). Team reason occurs when the team takes stock of a formal discipline, the sanctioned body of knowledge. A medical team might measure and record changes in the patient's physiological state through three kinds of cues: technological, perceptual/observational, and interactional (interacting with the patient) (Anspach, 1987). Team members share and create stories or cooperate to model things and make their reasoning explicit to each other. There is no evidence, and, in fact, it is theoretically unlikely, that in the heat of battle, such as during an operation, the nurse-anesthetist and resident anesthesiologists engage in lengthy epistemological or moral conversations about what constitutes knowledge or what counts as right and reasonable. This reflects a limited understanding about these issues. Team reason is not about the length of conversations, formal epistemology, or moral studies; instead, it is about verbal and nonverbal actions relating to societal knowledge and norms, including what the team members say they are or ought to be. For example, the EM team engages in team reason if it converses about medical and nursing science to use cues (technological, perceptual, or interactive) in order to assess patients and ameliorate their ailments. This counts as team reason because what they do is rational, as judged from the point of view of medical and nursing standards and practices.

Observing and Measuring Team Reason

It is generally agreed that team cognition can be studied empirically by a variety of data elicitation techniques (Cooke et al., 2004). Because team reason is, as argued in this chapter, concomitant to team cognition, processes of team reason could probably be studied with these techniques. However, the question is how team cognition and team reason are discerned in empirical investigations. Taking the example of verbal team communication, team reason would emerge in communication in which the team was trying to figure out what counts as knowledge, what reasons team members give for their planned actions, and what is considered right and wrong. Hypothetically, it would also be possible that the team enacts narrative knowledge or morality through subtle nonverbal cues such as hand gesturing to show approval or disapproval of proposed courses of action concerning the good of the patient.

Observing and measuring how teams engage in team reason is probably vested with the same problem as studying any kind of organizational behavior: The researcher risks inferring more than is warranted by the observation. The researcher can infer from team communication or behavior that the team enacts certain routines, but the researcher cannot readily know whether these are deliberate actions on behalf of the team members or organizational enactments of routines (Mehan, 1984). Does the EM team use team reason just because the team communication is about medical paradigmatic knowledge, or would it make more sense just to call this "team communication" without implying the implied macro-order entailed by the notion of reason? This chapter argues that team reason is a fruitful notion and helps to distinguish the team's deliberate action in communication to draw upon societal knowledge and modes of reasoning that are not particular to the single team but universal across a given culture of teams.

512 • *Theories of Team Cognition*

It is not a new idea to incorporate "culture" into a metric relating to team behavior. This has been done, for instance, in the field of patient safety. Safety culture can be seen not only in artifacts (e.g., manuals, procedures, protocols), but also at the level of safety culture referring to the employee's belief that safety is important and depends on his or her own participation to create and follow the organization's safety standards (Helmreich & Merritt, 1998, p. 133). Concretely, therefore, the study of team reason could borrow inspiration from the metrics on degrees to which an organization has developed a safety culture (Sexton et al., 2006). The degree to which an organization possesses a culture of safety is measurable in principle, although the notion of culture seems elusive at first glance. By analogy, the degree to which a given high-risk work culture and its teams reflect and critically scrutinize knowledge (and claims about what is real and worthwhile) could be studied. Therefore, team reason is not a tacit phenomenon elusive to empirical scrutiny. Team reason and team cognition are arguably empirical phenomena amenable to observation and data elicitation; however, they are also concepts used by a research community to order various team phenomena and derive at principles of pragmatic interest, as in macrocognitive research (Cacciabue & Hollnagel, 1995), and to influence actual team performance.

This chapter has argued that processes of team reason describe teams that jointly use knowledge as either paradigmatic or narrative and solve problems with the use of cultural tool kits. Cultural ways of solving problems through tool use is a team activity imbued with history. Therefore, team cognition should be studied as cultural-historical relations that depend on the development of, for instance, health care institutions in order to formulate team reason about what the team (constituted by team members) takes to be true and effective. This raises a need for document analysis: historical analysis combined with empirical studies of teams struggling to make sense of ill-structured environments. In particular, empirical studies on team reason could focus on situations in which teams use tools and ideas that are sanctioned by institutions, whether this includes physical/tangible objects such as mock-ups, scientific diagrams, and pictures, or ideal/intangible objects that the team members share through dialogue or experiments.

Thus, the study of team reason should probably include document analysis to study canonical knowledge and the archeology of knowledge and history of social practice pertaining to the phenomenon of study, as argued earlier. Given that society is a historical notion and societal knowledge is not amenable to objective observation (Rabinow, 1992, p. 7), there is no valid way to measure a cultural tool kit objectively. Therefore, the study of team reason is amenable to objective study, including observation of team behavior, but this should go hand in hand with document analysis inspired by knowledge archaeology (Foucault, 1972). Furthermore, a metric of team reason could query the situations in which teams reason about norms of conduct, the nature of the team's knowledge, the customs, and the institutional logic as inferred, for example, from documents pertaining to the given social practice or organization that pattern team member behavior. A methodology is needed that captures both the cognitive strategies that enable complex team cognition in dynamic environments and the questions about which cultural tool kits influence task knowledge and enable problem solving in these environments. Why is knowledge distributed the way it is, for instance in relation to power and hierarchy at work? What do team members' attitudes and beliefs (Cannon-Bowers & Salas, 2001) say about their team identity? Work is needed to clarify how teams appropriate knowledge from social practices in specific situations and how they negotiate what they hold to be valuable, true, or good.

CONCLUSION

The phenomenon of team reason describes the institutional and social order about team members' beliefs, goals, knowledge, and evaluations about what is right and rational, or put another way, whether a proposed course of team action is effective, safe, incorrect, or unethical. Team reason is concomitant to team cognition and stresses both the epistemic question of what knowledge is used to perform macrocognitive acts in teams and the normative question of what is reasonable and good for the team in the particular context of work. This chapter took an interdisciplinary approach to team cognition, drawing on sociocultural theory. Team reason tries to capture those aspects of team cognitive behavior that have a bearing on institutional knowledge and cultural traditions, but future studies are needed. Studies could examine the institutions that commission high-reliability teams, formulate their missions, and educate and

514 • *Theories of Team Cognition*

train team members. Future studies could also focus on team members' actions, actions of socialized persons who communicate with and within cultural repertoires or tool kits, societal knowledge structures, and norms about what is right and wrong.

In conclusion, team reason represents a sociocultural perspective on the burgeoning interdisciplinary cognitive engineering and organizational research field of team cognition. Research into team reason is needed in this context to answer how teams justify their reasoning and how the teams come to appropriate societal knowledge and norms about what the teams take for granted. Team reason can be expressed as paradigmatic or narrative knowledge and represents team cognition from the point of view of rational institutional discourse. Elaborating on team reason might mean that team cognition can encompass questions about knowledge, attitude, moral commitments, and motives. Ultimately, team reason provides a way for teams to critically examine the knowledge and social practices that they create and are created by.

REFERENCES

Anspach, R. (1987). Prognostic conflict in life-and-death decisions: The organization as an ecology of knowledge. *Journal of Health and Social Behaviour, 28,* 215–231.

Benner, P. (1991). The role of experience, narrative and community in skilled ethical comportment. *Advances in Nursing Science, 14,* 1–21.

Bruner, J. (1986). *Actual minds, possible worlds.* Cambridge, MA: Harvard University Press.

Bruner, J. (1991). The narrative construction of reality. *Critical Inquiry, 18,* 1–21.

Cacciabue, P. C., & Hollnagel, E. (1995). Simulation of cognition: Applications. In J. M. Hoc, P. C. Cacciabue, & E. Hollnagel (Eds.), *Expertise and technology: Cognition and human-computer cooperation* (pp. 55–74). Hillsdale, NJ: Lawrence Erlbaum Associates.

Cannon-Bowers, J. A., & Salas, E. (2001). Reflections on shared cognition. *Journal of Organizational Behavior, 22,* 195–202.

Cannon-Bowers, J. A., Salas, E., & Converse, S. A. (1993). Shared mental models in expert team decision making. In N. J. Castellan, Jr. (Ed.), *Current issues in individual and group decision making* (pp. 221–246). Hillsdale, NJ: Erlbaum.

Cooke, N. J., Gorman, J. C., & Rowe, L. J. (2009). An ecological perspective on team cognition. In E. Salas, J. Goodwin, & C. S. Burke (Eds.), *Team effectiveness in complex organizations: Cross-disciplinary perspectives and approaches* (pp. 157–182). Mahwah, NJ: Lawrence Erlbaum.

Cooke, N. J., Salas, E., Kiekel, P. A., & Bell, B. (2004). Advances in measuring team cognition. In E. Salas & S. M. Fiore (Eds.), *Team cognition: Understanding the factors that drive process and performance* (pp. 83–106). Washington, DC: American Psychological Association.

Dickstein, E., Erlen, J., & Erlen, J. A. (1991). Ethical principles contained in currently professed medical oaths. *Academic Medicine, 66,* 622–624.

Driscoll, P., & Wardrope, J. (2005). ATLS: Past, present, and future. *Emergency Medical Journal, 22,* 2–3.

Dunbar, K., & Fugelsang, J. (2005). Scientific thinking and reasoning. In K. Holyoak (Ed.), *Cambridge handbook of thinking & reasoning* (pp. 705–725). Cambridge, UK: Cambridge University Press.

Entin, E. E., Serfaty, D., & Deckert, J. C. (1994). *Team adaptation and coordination training* (Technical Rep. No. 648-1). Burlington, MA: Alphatech, Inc.

Fiore, S. M., McDaniel, R., & Jentsch, F. (2009). Narrative-based collaboration systems for distributed teams: Nine research questions for information managers. *Information Systems Management, 26,* 28–38.

Fiore, S. M., Rosen, M., Salas, E., Burke, S., & Jentsch, F. (2008). Processes in complex team problem solving: Parsing and defining the theoretical problem space. In M. Letsky, N. Warner, S. M. Fiore, & C. Smith (Eds.), *Macrocognition in teams* (pp. 143–163). London, UK: Ashgate.

Flavell, J. (1979). Metacognition and cognitive monitoring: A new area of psychological inquiry. *American Psychologist, 34,* 906–911.

Foucault, M. (1972). *The archaeology of knowledge* (A. Sheridan-Smith, Trans.). New York, NY: Harper & Row Publishers.

Hedegaard, M. (2002). *Learning and child development. A cultural-historical study.* Aarhus, Denmark: Aarhus University Press.

Hedegaard, M. (2004). A cultural-historical approach to learning in classrooms. *Outlines: Critical Social Studies, 6,* 21–34.

Hegel, G. W. F. (1977). *Phenomenology of spirit.* Oxford, UK: Oxford University Press. (Original work published in 1807)

Helmreich, R. L., & Merritt, A. C. (1998). Organizational culture. In R. L. Helmreich & A. C. Merritt (Eds.), *Culture at work in aviation and medicine* (pp. 107–174). Brookfield, VT: Ashgate.

Hutchins, E. (1996). *Cognition in the wild.* Cambridge, MA: The MIT Press.

Klimoski, R., & Mohammed S. (1994). Team mental model: Construct or metaphor? *Journal of Management, 20,* 403–437.

Lave, J. (1988). *Cognition in practice: Mind, mathematics and culture in everyday life.* Cambridge, UK: Cambridge University Press.

Leontiev, A. N. (1978). *Activity, consciousness, personality.* Englewood Cliffs, NJ: Prentice Hall.

Mehan, H. (1984). Institutional decisionmaking. In B. Rogoff & J. Lave (Eds.), *Everyday cognition: Its development in social context.* Cambridge, MA: Harvard University Press.

Orasanu, J. M., & Fischer, U. (1992). Team cognition in the cockpit: Linguistic control of shared problem solving. In *Proceedings of the 14th Annual Conference of the Cognitive Science Society* (pp. 189–194). Hillsdale, NJ: Erlbaum.

Orr, J. (1996). *Talking about machines: An ethnography of a modern job.* Ithaca, NY: ILP Press.

Patel, V. L., Arocha, J. F., & Zhang, J. (2005). Thinking and reasoning in medicine. In K. J. Holyoak & R. G. Morrison (Eds.), *The Cambridge handbook of thinking and reasoning* (Vol. XIV, pp. 727–750, 858). New York, NY: Cambridge University Press.

Pellegrino, E. D. (1987). The anatomy of clinical-ethical judgments in perinatology and neonatology: A substantive and procedural framework. *Seminars in Perinatology, 11,* 202–209.

516 • *Theories of Team Cognition*

Rabinow, P. (1992). Studies in the anthropology of reason. *Anthropology Today, 8,* 7–10.

Sarcevic, A., Marsic, I., Lesk, M. E., & Burd, R. S. (2008). Transactive memory in trauma resuscitation. In *Proceedings CSCW 2008* (pp. 215–224). New York, NY: ACM Press.

Schatzki, T. R. (2001). Introduction: Practice theory. In T. R. Schatzki, K. K. Cetina, & E. von Savigny (Eds.), *The practice turn in contemporary theory* (pp. 1–14). London, UK: Routledge.

Sexton, J. B., Helmreich, R. L., Neilands, T. B., Rowan, K., Vella, K., Boyden, J., et al. (2006). The safety attitudes questionnaire: Psychometric properties, benchmarking data, and emerging research. *BMC Health Services Research, 6,* 44.

Vygotsky, L. S. (1986). *Thought and language.* Cambridge, MA: MIT Press. (Original work published 1934)

Wegner, D. M. (1987). Transactive memory: A contemporary analysis of the group mind. In B. Mullen & G. R. Goethals (Eds.), *Theories of group behavior* (pp. 185–208). New York, NY: Springer-Verlag.

Weick, K. E. (1988). Enacted sensemaking in crisis situations. *Journal of Management Studies, 25,* 305–317.

Weick, K. E. (1995). *Sensemaking in organizations.* Thousand Oaks, CA: Sage.

Wenger, E. (1998). *Communities of practice: Learning, meaning and identity.* Cambridge, UK: Cambridge University Press.

Xiao, Y., & Moss, J. (2001). Practices of high reliability teams: Observations in trauma resuscitation. In *Proceedings of the Human Factors and Ergonomics Society 45th Annual Meeting* (pp. 395–399). Santa Monica, CA: Human Factors and Ergonomics Society.

Yun, S., Faraj, S., Xiao, Y., & Sims, H. P., Jr. (2003). Team leadership and coordination in trauma resuscitation. In M. M. Beyerlein, D. A. Johnson, & S. T. Beyerlein (Eds.), *Team-based organizing* (pp. 189–214). Amsterdam, the Netherlands: JAI.

21

Group Cognition in Online Teams

Gerry Stahl and Carolyn Penstein Rosé

This chapter represents a disciplinary perspective from computer-supported collaborative learning (CSCL), an interdisciplinary field concerned with leveraging technology for education and with analyzing cognitive processes such as learning and meaning making in small groups of students (Stahl, Koschmann, & Suthers, 2006). *Group cognition* is a theory developed to support CSCL research by describing how collaborative groups of students could achieve cognitive accomplishments together and how that could benefit the individual learning of the participants (Stahl, 2006). It is important to note that although it may very well be the case that a group of students working together manage to solve problems faster than any of them may have been able to do alone, the most important benefits to group cognition are the potential for genuinely innovative solutions that go beyond the expertise of any individual in the group, the deeper understanding that is achieved through the interaction as part of that creative process, and the lasting impact of that deep understanding that the students take with them when they move on from that interaction, which they may then carry with them as a new resource into subsequent group problem-solving scenarios. Group cognition can then be seen as what transforms groups into factories for the creation of new knowledge.

The types of problems that have been the focus of exploration within the group cognition paradigm have not been routine, well-structured problems where every participant can know exactly what his or her piece of the puzzle is up front in such a way that the team can function as a well-oiled machine. Many critical group tasks do not fit into well-known and practiced protocols—for example, low-resource circumstances that may occur in disaster situations, where standard solutions are not an option. In acknowledgement of this, the focus within the group cognition research

518 • *Theories of Team Cognition*

has been on problems that offer groups the opportunity to explore creatively how those problems can be approached from a variety of perspectives, where the groups are encouraged to explore unique perspectives. The processes that are the concern of group cognition research have not primarily been those that are related to efficiency of problem solving (as in some other chapters in this volume). Rather, the focus has been on the pivotal moments when a creative spark or a process of collaborative knowledge building occurs through interaction. Our fascination has been with identifying the conditions under which these moments of inspiration are triggered, with the goal of facilitating this process of group innovation and collaborative knowledge creation.

In this collaboratively written chapter, we consider insights from group cognition in light of synergistic ideas from other subcommunities within CSCL. Within the field of CSCL, the topic of what makes group discussions productive for learning has been explored—with a similar focus and similar findings, perhaps with subtle distinctions—under different names, such as *transactivity* (Azmitia & Montgomery, 1993; Berkowitz & Gibbs, 1983; di Lisi & Golbeck, 1999; Teasley, 1997), *uptake* (Suthers, 2006), *social modes of coconstruction* (Weinberger & Fischer, 2006), and *productive agency* (Schwartz, 1998). Despite differences in orientation between the subcommunities where these frameworks have originated, the conversational behaviors that have been identified as valuable are quite similar. Specifically, these different frameworks universally value explicit articulation of reasoning and making connections between instances of articulated reasoning. For example, Schwartz (1998) and de Lisi and Golbeck (1999) make similar arguments for the significance of these behaviors from the Vygotskian and Piagetian theoretical frameworks, respectively. The idea of transactivity as a property of a conversational contribution originates from a Piagetian framework and requires that a contribution contain an explicit reasoning display and encode an acknowledgement of a previous explicit reasoning display. However, note that when Schwartz describes from a Vygotskian framework the kind of mental scaffolding that collaborating peers offer one another, he describes it in terms of one student using words that serve as a starting place for the other student's reasoning and construction of knowledge. This implies explicit displays of reasoning, so that the reasoning can be known by the partner and then built upon by that partner. Thus, the process is similar to what we describe for the production of transactive contributions. In both cases, a transactive analysis would say that mental models are articulated, shared, mutually examined, and potentially integrated.

The theory of group cognition has been explored primarily using data from the Virtual Math Teams (VMT) Project (documented in Stahl, 2009a). Although much of the analysis of VMT data takes the form of detailed case studies conducted manually (often in group data sessions), the VMT Project and CSCL generally are also interested in the use of software algorithms to aid in the analysis of online discourse (Kang et al., 2008; Rosé et al., 2007, 2008) or collaborative recorded speech (Gweon, Kumar, & Rosé, 2009), especially with the promise that effective facilitation of collaborating groups can eventually be automated (Chaudhuri, Kumar, Howley, & Rosé, 2009; Cui, Chaudhuri, Kumar, Gweon, & Rosé, 2009; Kumar, Ai, & Rosé, 2010; Kumar, Rosé, Wang, Joshi, & Robinson, 2007). Some of this automatic analysis work has focused explicitly on properties such as transactivity (Joshi & Rosé, 2007; Rosé et al., 2008), whereas other work has focused on lower level conversational processes that can be seen as building blocks that enable the recognition of transactivity (Ai, Kumar, Nagasunder, & Rosé, 2010; Wang & Rosé, 2007, 2010) or more general-purpose text-mining techniques related to making fine-grained stylistic distinctions (Arora, Joshi, & Rosé, 2009; Joshi & Rosé, 2009; Mayfield & Rosé, 2010). As part of this effort, we have worked to transcend the theoretical underpinnings of frameworks such as transactivity to think more about a linguistic-level lens through which to view the data that might serve as a form of *interlingua*, or intermediate representation, that would make it more natural to bridge between different theoretical frameworks (Howley, Mayfield, & Rosé, in press). This objective of working toward a linguistic-level lens that is close to being theory neutral with respect to learning science theories is particularly key for our collaboration because of the way that the group cognition framework does not make the same assumptions about mental models and cognitive processes as do many of the previously mentioned other frameworks.

Group cognition is a postcognitive theory, like some of the theories presented in other chapters of this volume. Postcognitivism is a tradition characterized by situated, nondualistic, practice-based approaches, as described by Musaeus (see Chapter 20, this volume). Cognitivism—which tends to retain theoretical remnants of the Cartesian dualism of the mental and physical worlds—originally arose through the critique of behaviorism, with the argument that human responses to stimuli in the world

520 • *Theories of Team Cognition*

are mediated by cognitive activity in the mind of the human agent. This argument was particularly strong in considerations of linguistic behavior (Chomsky, 1959). More recently, postcognitivist theories have argued that cognitive activity can span multiple people (as well as artifacts), such as when knowledge develops through a sequence of utterances by different people and the emergent knowledge cannot be attributed to any one person or assumed to be an expression of any individual's prior mental representations (e.g., Bereiter, 2002, p. 283).

In his seminal statement of postcognitivist theory, Hutchins (1996) pointed to group cognitive phenomena: "The group performing the cognitive task may have cognitive properties that differ from the cognitive properties of any individual" (p. 176). "The cognitive properties of groups are produced by interaction between structures internal to individuals and structures external to individuals" (p. 262). However, rather than focusing on these group phenomena themselves, Hutchins usually analyzes sociotechnical systems and the cognitive role of highly developed artifacts (e.g., airplane cockpits, ship navigation tools). In focusing on the cultural level—characteristically for a cultural anthropologist—he does not often analyze the cognitive meaning making of the group itself.

Group cognition theory explicitly focuses on these interpersonal phenomena and investigates data in which one can observe the development of cognitive achievements in the interactions of small groups of people, often in online collaborative settings, where interactions can be automatically logged. By interaction, we mean the discourse that takes place in the group. Thus, what Beck and Keyton (see Chapter 19, this volume) write concerning macrocognition or team cognition applies to group cognition, namely that it is communicatively based and can be tracked in team members' interdependent messages. Group cognition is fundamentally a linguistic (speech or text) process, rather than a psychological (mental) one, as mentioned earlier. Thus, unlike the theory of transactivity described earlier, this postcognitive approach does not assume cognitive constructs such as mental models, internal representations, or retrievable stores of personal knowledge. In the online setting of VMT, cognition is analyzed by looking closely at the ways in which meaning is built up through the interplay of text postings, graphical constructions, and algebraic formulations (Çakir, Zemel, & Stahl, 2009). Methodologically, our case studies of group cognition use a form of interaction analysis (Jordan & Henderson, 1995) adapted from conversation analysis (Sacks, 1962/1995) to the CSCL context (Stahl, 2009a, p. 47). In our ongoing collaboration, we are exploring ways of extending these approaches in light of linguistic frameworks such as systemic functional linguistics (Christie, 1999; Martin & Rose, 2003; Martin & White, 2005).

The title of this chapter already reflects a tension that permeates this book as a whole (see Chapter 16, this volume)—the tension between the human sciences and the natural sciences, between *understanding* team cognition (e.g., with microanalysis of situated case studies) and *explaining* it (e.g., modeling, confirming general hypotheses, formulating laws, and specifying predictive causal relations). Group cognition in online teams involves both humans and computers, both highly situated collaborative interactions and programmed computer support. Therefore, our methodology includes both microanalysis of group discourse in unique case studies and the automated coding of the discourse log for statistical hypothesis testing.

The field of CSCL is particularly interested in the ways small groups can build knowledge together thanks to communication and support from networking technology. We hope that CSCL environments can be designed that make it possible for and encourage groups to think and learn collaboratively. In our research, we, along with our colleagues, look at logs of student groups chatting and drawing about mathematics in order to see if they build on each other's ideas to achieve more than they would individually. How do they understand each other and build shared language and a joint problem focus? What kinds of problems of understanding do they run into, and how do they overcome those? How do they accomplish intersubjective meaning making; interpersonal trains of thought; shared understandings of diagrams; joint problem conceptualizations; common references; coordination of problem-solving efforts; planning, deducing, designing, and describing; and problem solving, explaining, defining, generalizing, representing, remembering, and reflecting as a group? What can we say about the general methods that small groups use to learn and think as groups? How can we support and encourage this better with software support for social awareness, social networking, simulations, visualizations, and communication; with intelligent software agents; with pedagogical scaffolds and guidance; with training and mentoring; with access to digital resources; and with new theories of learning and thinking? To answer these complex questions, we must look carefully at the details of discourse in CSCL groups and develop innovative tools (both analytic and automated) and theories (of cognition by individuals, small groups, and discourse communities).

522 • *Theories of Team Cognition*

VIEWS OF LEARNING AND THINKING

The learning sciences view learning as involving meaning making by the learners (Stahl et al., 2006). Students who just passively accept instruction without thinking about it and coming to understand it in their own way of making sense of things will be wasting everyone's time. Why? Because they will not be able to *use* the new knowledge or to *explain* it. Of course, this construction of meaning takes place over time: Someone can learn something one day and make sense of it later, when they try to use it in different circumstances and to explain their use to other people and to themselves. But if they never integrate what they have learned into their own thinking and acting—by applying it where appropriate and talking about it clearly—then they will not have really learned. What sociologists like Bernstein, as presented in Hasan's (1999) overview, know about social interactions and contribute to our understanding of the significance of group cognition is the way participants internalize the resources that evolve within one interactional context and then recontextualize them in new and radically different contexts they find themselves in later. In this way, the new knowledge that is created, or the new or enhanced knowledge-building skills that are appropriated, can replicate and spread contagiously. It is this magic that, for instance, makes seemingly inconsequential interactions between mothers and children while cleaning the oven play a key role in a child's preparation for schooling (Cloran, 1999). It is precisely because of the tremendous impact the results of these interactions can have going forward that the local sacrifice that may occur in terms of efficiency of the interaction can be viewed as a small price to pay when one considers the long-term cost–benefit ratio and the profound impact of one transformational experience of group cognition.

Vygotsky (1930/1978) made an even stronger argument. He showed for the major forms of human psychological functioning that the individual capabilities were derived from interpersonal experiences:

> An interpersonal process is transformed into an intrapersonal one. Every function in the child's cultural development appears twice: first, on the social level and later, on the individual level; first *between* people (*interpsychological*), and then *inside* the child. This applies equally to voluntary attention, to logical memory, and to the formation of concepts. All the higher functions originate as actual relations between human individuals. (p. 57, italics in original)

Although all functions of individual cognition are derived from group cognition, the reverse is not true. As Hutchins (1996) demonstrated with his example of the bridge of a large Navy ship, not all group cognition can be internalized by an individual: "The distribution of knowledge described [in the book] is a property of the navigation team, and there are processes that are enabled by that distribution that can never be internalized by a single individual" (p. 284). Whether or not specific skills and knowledge can be mastered by individuals or only by teams, the learning of those skills or knowledge seems to rely heavily and essentially on group cognition. That is why we try to promote and to study group cognition.

What we, as learning scientists, have learned about learning and thinking in recent decades in the West is influenced by what philosophers before us said. For instance, most Western philosophers until the middle of the 1900s thought that knowledge could be expressed by propositions, sentences, or explicit statements. If that were true, then the learning of knowledge could, indeed, consist simply of students individually hearing or reading the right sentences and remembering them.

But Ludwig Wittgenstein's book, *Philosophical Investigations*, published in 1953, questioned this view of learning and thinking. It looked at math as a prime example. Mathematical knowledge can be seen as a set of procedures, algorithms, or rules. Wittgenstein asked how one can learn to follow a mathematical rule (Wittgenstein, 1944/1956, Part VI; Wittgenstein 1953, §185-243, esp. §201). For instance, if someone shows you how to count by fours by saying, "4, 8, 12, 16," how do you know how to go on? Is there a rule for applying the rule of counting by fours? (Such as, "Take the last number and add four to it.") And if so, how do you learn to apply that rule? By another rule? Eventually, you need to know how to do something that is not based on following a propositional rule—like counting and naming numbers and recognizing which numbers are larger. The use of explicit rules must be somehow grounded in other kinds of knowledge. These other kinds include the tacit knowledge of how to behave as a human being in our culture: how to speak, count, ask questions, generalize, put different ideas together, apply knowledge from one situation to another context, and so on. *And these are the kinds of things that one initially learns socially, in small groups or in child-parent dyads.* Wittgenstein's question brought the logical view of knowledge as explicit propositions into a paradox: If knowledge involves knowing rules, then it must involve knowing how to use rules, which is itself *not* a rule.

524 • *Theories of Team Cognition*

Wittgenstein was an unusual philosopher because he said that problems like this one could not be solved by contemplation, but rather by looking at how people actually do things. He said, "Don't think, look!" (Wittgenstein, 1953, §66). In studying group cognition, we try to follow Wittgenstein's advice. We try to view how small groups of people actually *do* things. Our focus is on understanding how the group magic occurs concretely in interaction.

A perspective on cognition is a particular way of viewing it. Rather than telling you what our *views* or ideas are about learning and thinking in CSCL groups, we will show you how we *view* or observe learning and thinking in CSCL groups. The term "view" has this double meaning: It means both viewing by looking at something with one's eyes and also viewing in the metaphorical sense of thinking about something from a conceptual perspective. Although Wittgenstein himself did not actually look at empirical examples of how people follow rules in math, we can. By carefully setting up a CSCL session, we can produce data that allow us to view groups of students learning how to follow math rules and thinking about the math rules. This is what we do to view learning and thinking in CSCL groups. It is the basic approach of the science of group cognition (see Stahl, 2009b, for a discussion of the scientific methodology).

The work of our research teams and other colleagues involves looking closely at some rich examples of student groups learning and thinking about math. We would like to share a brief excerpt from one of these examples and talk about how we go about viewing the learning and thinking of this group of students. In particular, how do they construct their group cognition through collaborative meaning-making activities?

In this chapter, we will look at the meaning-making work of a group of students, analyzing their language-based interaction at multiple levels: the overall *event*, a specific hour-long *session* of the 2-week event, a discussion *theme* that arose, a discourse *move* that triggered that theme, a pivotal *interchange*, a single *utterance*, and a particular *reference* in the utterance. By looking at the linguistic connections, we can see how the syntax, semantics, and pragmatics weave a network of meaningful references that accomplishes a set of cognitive achievements. On the one hand, we can see the linguistic elements of the log and their structure of temporal and hierarchical relationships as accomplishing group cognition by, at each moment, constraining the next utterance as situated in the context of event, session, theme, discourse moves, eliciting adjacency pairs, preceding utterances, and network of references. On the other hand, human actors creatively design accountable responses (see Chapter 16, this volume) within the constraining situation defined by these contextual elements. That is, among the constraints on the actors is the requirement that their linguistic actions make sense in the ongoing discourse and that they reveal their meaning and relevance in their linguistic design. Although people often design their utterances to convey the impression that they are the result of psychological processes (change of mental state, expression of internal reflections), we can analyze the group cognition in terms of the linguistic effects of the observable words and drawing actions, without making any assumptions about individual mental representations. The individual students are active as linguistic processors—interpreting and designing the utterances—but the larger mathematical and cognitive accomplishments are achieved through the group discourse, which exists in the computer displays, observable by the students and—even years later—by analysts. As Koschmann, Dunnington, and Kim suggest in Chapter 16 of this volume, we can see and make explicit how teams become teams in the ways that they manifest the contingencies and accountabilities of their unique situation, using conventional linguistic structures as resources.

THE EVENT: VMT SPRING FEST 2006 TEAM B

Here, we will be talking about an online event that occurred in 2006. The interaction is preserved in a computer log, which can be replayed by researchers. Three students, each probably about 16 years old, were assigned to be Team B, and they met with a facilitator in an online chat environment on May 9, 10, 16, and 18, in 2006, for about an hour in the late afternoon each day. The participants were distributed across three time zones in the United States. The event was part of the VMT research project. Neither the students nor we know anything more about each other's personal characteristics or background.

The topic for this event was to explore a pattern of sticks forming a stair-step arrangement of squares (Figure 21.1) and then to explore similar patterns chosen by the students themselves. The VMT online environment consisted primarily of a synchronous chat window and a shared

526 • Theories of Team Cognition

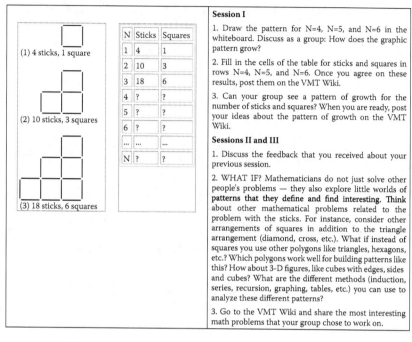

FIGURE 21.1
Topic for VMT Spring Fest 2006.

whiteboard. At the end of each session, the students were supposed to post their findings on a wiki, shared with other teams participating in the Spring Fest. Between sessions, the facilitator posted feedback to the students in a textbox on the whiteboard.

THE SESSION: SESSION 3, MAY 16, 7:00 P.M.

Let's look at an excerpt from the end of the third session. The three students had already solved the original problem of the stair-step pattern of squares. They had also made up their own problem involving three-dimensional pyramids. Now they turned to look at the problem that Team C had described on the wiki after session 2. Team B is looking at an algebraic expression that the other team of students had derived for a diamond pattern of squares. They start to draw the pattern in their whiteboard (Figure 21.2) and chat as a team about the problem of this new pattern.

Group Cognition in Online Teams • 527

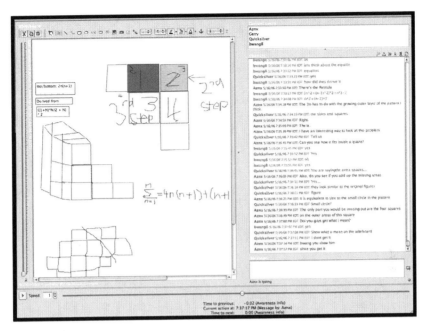

FIGURE 21.2
The VMT Replayer showing the VMT online environment.

THE THEME: "I HAVE AN INTERESTING WAY TO LOOK AT THIS PROBLEM"

One of the students, Aznx, begins to make a proposal on how to "look" at their problem. First, he announces, "I have an interesting way to look at this problem." Note that he uses the word "look" in the same double meaning of "view" that was mentioned earlier. As we will see, he means he has a new way to think about the problem mathematically—and that involves a way of observing a visual image of the problem. The group does its thinking both by typing text and algebraic expressions in the chat window and by simultaneously drawing and viewing diagrams or geometric constructions of the problem in the shared whiteboard (see Çakir et al., 2009, for an analysis of the coordination by the group of their text, symbols, and drawings).

Aznx's announcement opens an opportunity for the group to discuss a way of looking at the problem. In fact, the group takes up the offer that is implicit in Aznx's statement, and the students spend the next 8 minutes

528 • *Theories of Team Cognition*

trying to each understand it. As it turns out, they will work on this view of the problem for the rest of this session and most of their final session.

A VMT chat session can generally be analyzed as a series of themes or discussion topics. Often, themes come and go, and different themes overlap, with one wrapping up while another gets started. Researchers can identify the boundaries of a theme: when a new theme opens and an old one closes (Zemel, Xhafa, & Çakir, 2009).

In this case, the group has been talking about how the diamond pattern grows as a geometric figure for a couple of minutes, and then they discuss Team C's algebraic expression for a couple of minutes. As those themes get played out and there is a pause in the chat, Aznx makes a move to open a new theme for the group.

A MOVE: SHOWING HOW TO VIEW THE PROBLEM

Aznx's announcement that he has a perspective to share with the group is a way of introducing a new theme, a "preannouncement" (Schegloff, 2007, pp. 37–44; Terasaki, 2004). Conversations often flow by new contributions picking up on something that was already being discussed. Online text chat tends to be more open than face-to-face talking; chat does not follow the strict turn-taking rules of conversation. However, it is still common to do some extra work to change themes even in chat. In a sense, Aznx is asking permission from the group to start a new theme. Quicksilver responds encouragingly right away by saying, "Tell us" (Figure 21.3).

Actually, Aznx already starts typing his proposal before he gets Quicksilver's response, but it is not posted until afterward. The next step in his proposal is: "Can you see how it fits inside a square?" Here, he structures his contribution as a question, which elicits a response from the other members of the team. Note that he uses the term "see" in his proposal with the same double meaning as the term "look" in his prior announcement. As we shall see (in both senses), the group tries to work out and comprehend Aznx's proposal both conceptually and visually.

Both Bwang and Quicksilver respond to Aznx's proposal with "Yes." However, both modify this response. Bwang starts to type something else

line	date	start	post	delay		
919	5/16/06	19:35:26	19:35:36	0:00:06	Aznx	I have an interesting way to look at this problem.
920	5/16/06	19:35:41	19:35:42	0:00:03	Quicksilver	Tell us
921	5/16/06	19:35:38	19:35:45	0:00:00	Aznx	Can you see how it fits inside a square?
922	5/16/06	19:35:45	19:35:45	0:00:07	Bwang	yes
	5/16/06	19:35:49	19:35:52	0:00:00	Bwang	[user erased message]
923	5/16/06	19:35:51	19:35:52	0:00:01	Quicksilver	Yes
924	5/16/06	19:35:52	19:35:53	0:00:02	Bwang	oh
925	5/16/06	19:35:55	19:35:55	0:00:06	Bwang	yes
926	5/16/06	19:35:53	19:36:01	0:00:04	Quicksilver	You are sayingthe extra spaces...
927	5/16/06	19:35:58	19:36:05	0:00:06	Aznx	Also, do you see if you add up the missing areas

FIGURE 21.3
The move to introduce Aznx's new way of looking at the group's problem.

but erases it; then he posts two messages: "oh" and "yes." This suggests some hesitation in responding to the proposal immediately. Quicksilver follows his initial positive response with, "You are sayingthe extra spaces ...." He is asking for more clarification of the proposal. While Quicksilver is typing his request for clarification, Aznx is typing an expansion of his initial proposal: "Also, do you see if you add up the missing areas."

The analysis of interaction moves is central to the science of group cognition. This is the level of granularity of many typical group cognitive actions. Discourse moves are ways in which small online groups get their work done. They often follow conventional patterns—speech genres (Bakhtin, 1986) or member methods (Garfinkel, 1967)—which makes them much easier for participants to understand. Researchers can also look for these patterns to help them understand what the group is doing.

In this case, a new theme is being opened, one that will provide direction for the rest of this group's event together. This move is an example of one way in which a group can establish a shared understanding of a diagram or select a joint problem conceptualization (depending on how we take the terms "look" and "see"). Other moves that we often see in VMT logs are, for instance, defining shared references, coordinating problem-solving efforts, planning, deducing, designing, describing, solving, explaining, defining, generalizing, representing, remembering, and reflecting as a group.

530 • *Theories of Team Cognition*

A PAIR: QUESTION/RESPONSE: "CAN YOU SEE HOW IT FITS INSIDE A SQUARE?"/"YES"

In conversation analysis, one typically looks for "adjacency pairs" (Duranti, 1998; Sacks, 1962/1995; Schegloff, 2007). A prototypical adjacency pair is question/answer. Aznx's offering of a question—"Can you see how it fits inside a square?"—followed by Bwang's and Quicksilver's responses—"yes," "Yes"—illustrate this structure for the simplest ("preferred") case: One person poses a yes/no question, and the others respond with an affirmative answer.

Response structures are often more complicated than this. Text chat differs from talk in that people can be typing comments at the same time; they do not have to take turns and wait until one person stops talking and relinquishes the floor. They will not miss what the other person is saying, because unlike with talk, the message remains observable for a while. The disadvantage is that one does not observe how people put together their messages, with pauses, restarts, corrections, visual cues, intonations, and personal characteristics. Although it is possible to wait when you see the notification indicating that someone else is typing, people often type simultaneously, so that the two normal parts of an adjacency pair may be separated by other postings. For example, Quicksilver's question (line 926 in Figure 21.3) separated Aznx's continuation of his line 921 posting in line 927, because 926 appeared before 927, although 927 was typed without seeing 926. So in chat, we might call these "response pairs" rather than "adjacency pairs." Although they may be less sequentially *adjacent* than in talk, they are still direct *responses* of one posting to another.

Because the sequencing in online chat texting is less tightly controlled than in face-to-face talk, response pairs are likely to become entangled in the longer sequences of group moves. This may result in the common problem of "chat confusion" (Fuks, Pimentel, & Pereira de Lucena, 2006; Herring, 1999). It can also complicate the job of the researcher. In particular, it makes the task of automated analysis more complicated. In convoluted chat logs, it is essential to work out the response structure (threading) before trying to determine the meaning making. The meaning making still involves participants interacting through the construction of response pairs, but in chat, people have to recreate the ties among these pairs. Realizing this, the group members design their postings to be read in ways that make the response pair or threading structure apparent, as we will see (Zemel et al., 2009).

AN UTTERANCE: QUESTION: "CAN YOU SEE HOW IT FITS INSIDE A SQUARE?"

In his posting—"Can you see how it fits inside a square?"—Aznx is comparing the relatively complicated diamond shape to a simple square. This is a nice strategy for solving the group's problem. The group can easily compute the number of stick squares that fill a large square area. For instance, if there are five little squares across the width of a square area (and therefore, five along the height), then there will be 5^2, or 25, little squares in the area. In general, if there are N little squares across the width, there will be N^2 to fill the area. This is a strategy of simplifying the problem to a simple or already known situation—and then perhaps having to account for some differences. So Aznx's posting seems to be relevant to thinking about the math problem conceptually.

At the same time, Aznx poses his proposal in visual or graphical terms as one of "seeing" how one shape "fits inside" of the other. The group has been looking at diagrams of squares in different patterns, both a drawing by Team C in their wiki posting and Team B's own drawings in their whiteboard. So Aznx's proposal suggests visualizing a possible modification to one of the diamond drawings, enclosing it in a square figure (see the white diamond pattern enclosed in the gray square in Figure 21.4). He is asking the others if they can visualize this also, so that the group can use this to simplify and solve their problem with the diamond.

Aznx presents his proposal about rethinking the problem as a question about visualizing the diagram. The group has been working in the VMT environment, going back and forth between text in the chat and drawings in the whiteboard. They have started with problems presented graphically and have discussed these graphical problems in their text chat. They have shared different ways of viewing the relationships within the drawings, and they have gradually developed symbolic algebraic ways of expressing general relationships about patterns in these drawings, working out these symbolic expressions in the chat and then storing them more persistently in the whiteboard.

532 • *Theories of Team Cognition*

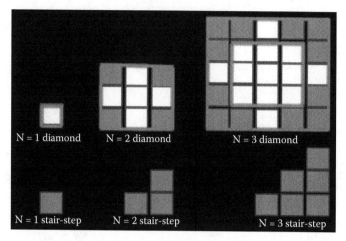

FIGURE 21.4
White diamond patterns and gray stair-step patterns.

We have been calling Aznx's chat posting a "problem-solving math proposal" (Stahl, 2006, Chapter 21). However, it is presented in the grammatical form of a *question*. Aznx did not simply state a proposal like, "I think we should enclose the diamond in a square, calculate the size of the square, and then subtract the missing areas." Rather, he first announced that he had "an interesting way to look at this problem" and then explained his way of looking by asking if the others could "see how it fits inside a square." Presenting a proposal calls on the others to accept the proposal and to start to work on it. Of course, the others can reject the proposal, ask for clarifications about it, make a counterproposal, or ignore the proposal.

However, Aznx's utterance is not a full proposal that the others must accept or reject. It is another preliminary step. It asks the others if they can visualize something. It puts this to them as a question. If they say yes, then Aznx can proceed to make his proposal—or perhaps the others will see the implications of his interesting way to look at the problem and propose the strategy without Aznx having to advocate it, explain it, and defend it. If they say no—that they cannot see how it fits inside a square—then he can explain his view further so they will be better prepared to accept his proposal.

Aznx's chat posting avoids articulating a complete proposal; by starting the conversation about the visualization, it involves the others in articulating the proposal *collaboratively*. In fact, in the subsequent discussion, the others do "see" the strategy that is implicit in Aznx's interesting view of the problem, and they do help to articulate the strategy and then pursue it. By designing his proposal as this preliminary question about viewing the problem, Aznx succeeds in directing the group problem solving in a certain direction without his having to fully work out a detailed, explicit proposal. Aznx does not seem to be presenting a solution that he has worked out in his head. Rather, he is presenting his "interesting idea" for an approach to solving the problem so that the group will proceed to use the idea and work as a group to try to solve the problem with this approach.

A REFERENCE: "IT"

Aznx's question is ambiguous at a purely syntactic level. It asks the others, "Can you see how *it* fits inside a square?" To what does the term "it" refer? People use pronouns like "it" rather than lengthy explicit noun phrases when the reference is clear from the context. This situates the utterance in its context—it's meaning cannot be gathered from the utterance considered in isolation. Often, "it" will reference something that was recently referred to in a previous contribution that the new utterance is building on. For instance, "it" could refer to something mentioned in Aznx's previous utterance, "I have an interesting way to look at this problem." But to say that it refers to "this problem" does not make complete sense. The *problem* does not fit inside a square.

However, a minute earlier, when the group was discussing Team C's equations, Aznx said about part of an equation, "The 3n has to do with the growing outer layer of the pattern I think." He was referencing different aspects of the growth of the diamond pattern, particularly its "outer layer." So when he announces that he has an interesting way to view the problem, it is reasonable to assume that his new way of looking may be closely related to the observation that he had just reported about the outer layer of the diamond pattern. Because everyone in the group was following the flow of the discussion, Aznx could refer to the topic of the outer layer of the diamond pattern in the shorthand of the pronoun "it." When he typed, "Can you see how it fits inside a square?" he could assume that the readers of this posting would understand that he was referring to how some aspect of the diamond pattern can be seen as fitting inside of some square shape.

534 • *Theories of Team Cognition*

Although the reference to some aspect of the diamond pattern is relatively clear, the details are not clear about just what aspect of the diamond is to be visualized or focused on visually, where a square is to be constructed, and how the diamond fits inside the square. At this point, only a rather confusing image of a diamond pattern is visible on the whiteboard (see Figure 21.2). To *make sense* of "it," everyone has to follow the flow of discussion and the way in which the math topic is being developed as a "joint problem space" that is being understood and visualized by the whole group.

Bwang and Quicksilver both respond initially to Aznx's question with "Yes." However, as we saw, Bwang indicates some hesitancy in his response, and Quicksilver asks for further clarification. Aznx and Quicksilver discuss what they see when they fit a diamond pattern inside a square. Quicksilver notes that the "extra spaces" (shaded gray in Figure 21.4) look similar to the stair-step pattern that the team worked on previously. But Aznx goes on to talk about the four squares on the outer areas of the square, confusing Quicksilver. That is, as they each try to work out the details of Aznx's view, they display that they are not *seeing* things quite the same way. They have not yet achieved an adequate shared understanding or shared view.

Quicksilver suggests that Aznx show what he means on the whiteboard, so the ambiguity of his proposal can be resolved. Rather than drawing it himself, Aznx asks Bwang to do a drawing, since Bwang said he could see what Aznx was talking about. Bwang has in the past shown himself to be skilled at making drawings on the whiteboard, whereas Aznx has not tried to draw much.

Bwang draws a clear diagram on the whiteboard for the diamond pattern when $N = 2$ (Figure 21.5). As soon as Bwang completes his drawing, he makes explicit the problem-solving proposal that is implicit in Aznx's way of viewing the problem or the pattern: "We just have to find the whole square and minus the four corners." His drawing has made this process visible. He drew the diamond pattern with white squares and then filled in a large square that the diamond fits into by adding gray squares. The gray squares fill in symmetrical spaces in the four corners of the diamond pattern. The group can now look at this together in the shared whiteboard, providing a shared view of the matter to the group.

The group then discusses the view of the diamond pattern fitting into an enclosing square. They eventually realize that some of their observations are only true for the diamond pattern at a certain stage, such as $N = 2$.

Group Cognition in Online Teams • 535

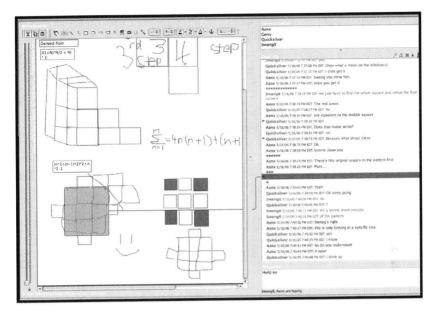

FIGURE 21.5
Bwang has drawn the white diamond for $N = 2$ with gray squares filling in the corners of an enclosing square. Quicksilver is pointing to a diamond pattern for $N = 3$, also redrawn lower on the whiteboard.

So Bwang then draws the pattern for $N = 3$. Here it starts to become visible to the group that the gray squares in each corner follow the stair-step pattern (Figure 21.6).

The group has realized that viewing a graphical image of a mathematical pattern can be helpful in thinking about the pattern. They treat the whiteboard as a shared, viewable image of aspects of the joint problem space of their collaborative work. Viewing this image and pointing out elements of it ground their chat discourse.

However, the image drawn by Bwang captures just one particular stage in the pattern, one value of N. They then start to look at images for different values of N or different stages in the growing pattern. They count the number of gray squares in a corner as N increases and notice that it goes: 0, 1, 3, 6 (see Figure 21.4). This pattern is familiar to them from their earlier analysis of the stair-step pattern. They call this sequence "triangular numbers," from Pascal's triangle, which is often useful in combinatorics math problems. They know that this sequence can be generated by Gauss's formula for the sum of the consecutive integers from 1 to N: $(N + 1)N/2$.

536 • *Theories of Team Cognition*

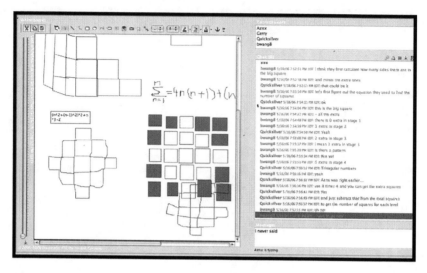

FIGURE 21.6
Bwang expanded his drawing to make the diamond for *N* = 3. Note that the gray corners are now stair-step patterns.

Unfortunately, at that point, Bwang has to leave the group. But when they return in session 4, they will quickly put together the simple formula for the enclosing square minus this formula for the number of squares in each of the four corners to solve their problem.

VIEWING THE LEARNING AND THINKING

Let us pause now from all these details about the case study of three students in a VMT session and talk about how we view learning and thinking in CSCL groups. We have tried to demonstrate how we view learning and thinking in CSCL groups by *viewing* how a group of three students engaged in collaborative thinking and learning processes within an online environment for drawing and chatting.

We went through several levels of analysis of the group discourse (Figure 21.7). We started by mentioning the overall context of the *event*. This was an online event in which Team B, consisting of three students, met in the VMT environment to discuss patterns of squares formed by sticks. We then focused on the smaller *session* unit, looking at Team B's third session, in which they considered a pattern that another group, Group C,

Event:	VMT Spring Fest 2006, Team B
Session:	Session 3, May 16, 7:00 pm
Theme:	"I have an interesting way to look at this problem"
Move:	Show how to view
Pair:	"Can you see how it fits inside a square?" "Yes"
Utterance:	"Can you see how it fits inside a square?"
Reference:	"It," diamond pattern

FIGURE 21.7
Levels of analysis of online group discourse.

had analyzed. Within this session, we identified one of several *themes* of discussion in that session, namely the one involving Aznx's "interesting way to look at this problem."

Aznx introduced the theme by initiating a group problem-solving *move*. Namely, he got the group to view the problem in a certain way, as a diamond enclosed in a square. We saw how the group ended up drawing images in their shared whiteboard of diamond patterns enclosed in squares. Aznx introduced this group move in a subtle way; he did not simply come out and say, "We should analyze this pattern as partially filling an enclosing square." Rather, he first announced that he had an interesting view, involving the others in his approach to make it a group problem-solving process. Then he asked if the others could view the problem in a certain way. He did this through a question/answer response *pair*: He asked a question, which elicited a yes-or-no response from the others. By eliciting the response, he oriented the others to looking at the diagram in the whiteboard in a certain way—namely in the way that his question implicitly proposed. A set of lines on the whiteboard are not immediately meaningful—they must be seen (interpreted) *as* something (Heidegger, 1927/1996, §32; Wittgenstein, 1953, §II xi).

Aznx's formulation of his question looks like a simple *utterance* in question format, but it entails selection from a number of different ways of picturing the relationships among the diamond pattern, the enclosing square, and the empty corners. To begin with, one must decide what the *reference* to "it" is doing.

Indexical references like the pronoun "it" are ubiquitous in online text chat—and unavoidable according to Garfinkel (1967). They require the reader to understand or reconstruct the implicit threading or response structure of the chat. The difficulty of doing this often leads to confusions,

538 • *Theories of Team Cognition*

which require the participants to spend time clarifying the content and structure of their discussion. For instance, in our example of the move of seeing the diamond in the square, the group had to engage in a couple minutes of chatting and drawing to coconstruct a shared understanding of the problem.

Issues of shared understanding can be analyzed as linguistic problems of reference. In other words, to view learning and thinking in CSCL groups, we do not try to figure out what is going on in the heads of the students; rather, we try to figure out what is going on in their chat postings and their drawing actions. This is what we call the group's *interaction*. In VMT, the interaction of the VMT consists of sequences of chat postings and drawing actions.

Our first step in figuring out what is going on in the chat postings and drawing actions is generally to try to analyze the sequencing of these by reconstructing their response structure—what previous action each new action is responding to and what kinds of action it is eliciting, what it is opening up an interaction space for, or what kinds of responses it is making relevant as next postings. Often, this leads to some kind of threading diagram (Çakir, Xhafa, & Zhou, 2009), uptake graph (Suthers, Dwyer, Medina, & Vatrapu, 2010), or interaction model (Wee & Looi, 2009). This represents graphically a basic structure of the meaning-making sequencing. Then we try to understand what problem-solving work is being accomplished at each point in the sequence. This involves looking at different levels of granularity, such as the event, session, theme, move, pair, utterance, and reference. Understanding the meaning that the group is coconstructing in their interaction generally involves going back and forth through these different levels and integrating partial interpretations from the different levels (Gadamer, 1960/1988).

Through this process, we can gradually view the learning and thinking that takes place in the CSCL group. This learning and thinking is not something that takes place primarily in the minds of the individual participants (although the individuals in the group are each continuously using their linguistic skills to understand what is going on and to respond to it with their postings and drawings). Rather, when there is an intense collaborative process taking place in the online environment, the thinking and learning takes place in the visible text and graphical interactions.

According to the theory of group cognition, thinking in a CSCL collaborative interaction does not take place in the way we usually think of thinking. Thoughts, or cognitive processes, do not take place by neurons connecting and firing in a brain; they take place by text postings and drawings referring to each other and building on each other, in the spirit of the idea of transactivity introduced earlier. We will look more at how this takes place in a minute. Similarly, learning does not take place the way we learned about learning. It is not a change in the amount of knowledge stored in a brain. Rather, it is a matter of knowledge artifacts being gradually refined through sequences of text postings and graphical drawings that are interrelated and that explicate each other. The knowledge artifacts may be statements about a problem the group is working on, as viewed from a new perspective that the group has developed. The knowledge artifact might be a drawing, such as Bwang's in Figure 21.6, or an algebraic formula that sums up the group's analysis of pattern growth.

CONSTRUCTING THE JOINT PROBLEM SPACE

When one studies logs of VMT, one sees that the teams spend a lot of time and effort constructing shared understanding about references in their postings. The reason that teams and other small groups devote so much time and energy to resolving confusing references is that the network of references that they build up together plays an essential role in their group learning and thinking. In the theory of CSCL, there is considerable emphasis on the idea of "common ground" (Clark & Brennan, 1991) and "joint problem space" (Teasley & Roschelle, 1993). A group establishes common ground largely by reaching a shared understanding of how references work in their discourse. As it interacts over time, a group coconstructs a network of references that can become quite complex.

The "shared understanding" that is built up is akin to the notion of *coorientation*, which "refers to the mutual orientation of individuals in a group toward an object (e.g., knowledge, belief, attitude) and can be traced back to the interactionist social psychology of John Dewey and George Herbert Mead" (Poole, Chapter 18, this volume). Psycholinguistic metaphors of comparing stored mental representations are unnecessary and can be misleading, reducing all knowledge to individual mental possessions. Team members share a world centered on their task; they orient as a group to the objects that populate that world, such as Aznx's proposals,

540 • *Theories of Team Cognition*

Bwang's drawings, and Quicksilver's queries. *Because they share a common world*—which they coconstitute largely through their discourse, mediated by the larger common social, cultural, and historical horizons of their world—*they coconstruct a shared understanding.*

The shared network of references defines the context or *situation* in which the group discourse continues to take place (Heidegger, 1927/1996, §18). Aznx's reference to "it" that we looked at contributed to a network of meaning that the group built up continuously through their interaction. This network included images of sticks in various patterns (such as diamonds at stage $N = 2$ and $N = 3$), the relationships of the patterns (such as a diamond enclosed in a square with stair-step empty corners), concepts referred to by technical terms (such as "triangular numbers" or "summation"), and symbols representing mathematical operations (such as equations for number of squares in a pattern).

As a group builds up its network of shared references, it can use more shortcut references (symbols, names, pronouns) to point to things without creating confusion. People can use deictic references to point to things in the network, such as "this formula," "the second equation," or "it." In linguistic terms, the shared network of references provides a background for referring to things, a so-called "indexical ground of deictic reference" (Hanks, 1992).

In problem-solving terms, the network of references forms a joint problem space, a shared view of the topic that the group is addressing (Sarmiento & Stahl, 2008). For Team B, the joint problem space starts in their first session with the stair-step pattern and the chart of the number of sticks and squares for each stage of this pattern as presented in the topic description for the event (see Figure 21.1). By the middle of session 3, it includes the diamond pattern and the view of "it" enclosed in a square, forming empty corners. It also includes triangular numbers and their associated formula, as well as several other equations from Team C and from Team B's own work. The team's interaction (the text postings and drawings) gradually creates this joint problem space and is (reflexively) situated within it. The work and utterances of the team can only be understood (by the participants and by us as researchers) through an ongoing understanding of the joint problem space as a network of meaningful reference.

Achievements of group cognition are not automatic, and they can be quite fragile. They require work not only to construct shared understandings, but also to maintain the understanding of knowledge artifacts and to transfer their meaning to changing situations. After Bwang left the third session, Aznx and Quicksilver tried to review the group's accomplishments. They become confused about various equations and unsure of their ability to explain what the group has figured out. They ended the session with Quicksilver saying, "then let's pick it up next time when Bwang can explain it." This ends one session and projects what will happen in a future session. When the group meets for its fourth session, Aznx and Quicksilver do eventually get together with Bwang to review the derivation of the equation based on the view of the problem that Aznx introduced in the theme we just considered. The discussion in session 4 refers back to the group's work in session 3 and also to Team C's work in session 2. But it does this in ways that are situated in Team B's session 4 context (Sarmiento-Klapper, 2009). The team members and the memories they bring with them from the past are reconstituted in the new group situation and made relevant to the current themes, problem space, and available resources.

FORMING GROUPS AND COCONSTRUCTING KNOWLEDGE ARTIFACTS

At the beginning of session 1, the students were not part of a particularly effective group or team. They did not build much on each other's contributions and were hesitant to make proposals, ask each other to undertake tasks, produce permanent drawings, or manipulate mathematical symbols. That all changed dramatically in the course of their four-session event. By the end, they had many graphical, narrative, and symbolic representations or expressions related to their mathematical topic. They worked effectively together and solved their problems well. Problem-solving methods that one person introduced were later proposed and used by the other group members.

You may be wondering if each of the students learned mathematics. An interesting thing about looking closely at what really went on in this event is that what we traditionally consider to be the math content actually plays a relatively minor role in the group's problem solving. Yes, content is brought in: For examples, the students talk about triangular numbers,

542 • *Theories of Team Cognition*

and they apply the formula for summing consecutive integers. Often, this math content is brought in quickly through proposals by individuals. It is then discussed through responses to the proposal that check that everyone understands the math content and agrees on its applicability. However, the bulk of the hard work is not accessing the traditional math content, but selecting, adapting, integrating, visualizing, sharing, explaining, testing, refining, building on, and summarizing sequences of group response pairs. These proposals and discussions reference not only math content, but also various related resources that the group has coconstructed or made relevant.

The learning and thinking of the group takes place through the group's discourse, as a temporally unfolding multilevel structure of response/adjacency pairs interwoven into larger sequences of group moves, problem-solving themes, and sessions of events. The group learns about the mathematics of its topic by building and exploring an increasingly rich joint problem space. It thinks about the mathematical relationships and patterns by following sequences of proposals, raising and responding to various kinds of questions, and engaging in other sorts of interactional moves. Some of this gets summarized in persistent knowledge artifacts such as drawings, concepts, equations, solution statements, and textual arguments. The building of the joint problem space generally requires a lot of work involving resolving references and coconstructing a shared network of meaning.

The math skills—like following certain procedures to do long division or to transform symbols—are not where the deep learning takes place and real knowledge is involved. Rather, the ability to sustain progressive inquiry through methods of group interaction is the real goal. This ability makes use of the math content and skills as resources for answering questions and coming up with new proposals. Learning math is primarily a process of becoming a participant in the discourse community of people conversant in mathematics. Learning math collaboratively involves engaging in linguistic methods of shared meaning making—and other semiotic practices like geometric construction and algebraic symbolization. These are the tacit foundations of mathematics, the abilities needed in order to follow the rules of explicit math procedures.

If you wonder how to view learning and thinking in CSCL groups as an example of team cognition, follow Wittgenstein's advice: "Don't think, look!" Our colleagues and we have tried to do this by looking at the work of VMT in the way we have just described. We have been amazed to discover that collaborative learning and group cognition are a lot different than people traditionally thought.

LOOKING FORWARD: TOWARD ENHANCING TRANSACTIVE INTERACTIONS WITH AUTOMATIC FACILITATION

In this chapter, we have described the group cognition framework in relation to work in other subcommunities within the broader CSCL community, where similar conversational processes have been examined from different perspectives, with different styles. Although group cognition has not typically been investigated through categorical coding aided by automatic text processing technology, as has been done frequently within the transactivity tradition (Ai, Sionti, Wang, & Rosé, 2010; Joshi & Rosé, 2007; Rosé et al., 2008), the advantage of approaching the analysis that way is that it enables the possibility of automatic monitoring as well as automatic triggering of support.

There have already been quite a few successful studies of student groups benefitting from the support of automatically triggered conversational agents that enrich the interaction between students (Chaudhuri et al., 2009; Cui et al., 2009; Kumar & Rosé, 2010; Kumar et al., 2007; Wang et al., 2007), many of which used a version of the VMT environment augmented with this form of dynamic collaborative learning support (Cui et al., 2009; Kumar & Rosé, 2009). For example, early evaluations measured the extent to which students learned more in conditions when automatic support was offered in the environment compared with conditions where it was not (Kumar et al., 2007; Wang et al., 2007). These early studies showed that insertion of a support agent into the environment increased pre- to posttest learning gains by about one standard deviation, which is a full letter grade. Subsequent studies compared alternative versions of this form of automatic support. These evaluations showed additional increases in effectiveness as we successively refined the design of the support. For example, Chaudhuri et al. (2009) showed that students learned more when the support agents allowed the students to put off discussion with the

544 • *Theories of Team Cognition*

support agents until they were ready to give it their full attention. Kumar et al. (2010) showed that students learned more when the support agents engaged in social behavior in addition to just offering cognitive support.

Encouraged by these early successes, which we celebrate, we are continuing to push forward with this intellectual and technical integration of group cognition analysis using manual and automated methods. For example, we acknowledge that much of the richness of the type of thick description presented in this chapter is lost when the analysis is reduced to a sequence of a small number of labels, tags, or codes. Furthermore, we acknowledge that even with perfect knowledge of where pivotal moments in collaboration are occurring or not occurring, this analysis is not the same thing as having the wisdom to know when to intervene or not and how to guide the conversation effectively. These recognitions do not leave us discouraged, however. Instead, they convince us of the great potential that our collaboration holds. With this in mind, then, in our current work, we are striving for a deeper intellectual integration of these different analytical traditions in order to create a yet more powerful form of dynamic collaboration support that will eventually make the power of group cognition as ubiquitous as the World Wide Web.

REFERENCES

Ai, H., Kumar, R., Nagasunder, A., & Rosé, C. P. (2010). Exploring the effectiveness of social capabilities and goal alignment in computer supported collaborative learning. In V. Aleven, J. Kay, & J. Mostow. (Eds.) *Proceedings of the 10th International Conference on Intelligence Tutoring Systems*, June, Pittsburgh, PA.

Ai, H., Sionti, M., Wang, Y. C., & Rosé, C. P. (2010). Finding transactive contributions in whole group classroom discussions. In K. Gomez, L. Lyons, & J. Radinsky (Eds.), *Learning in the disciplines: Proceedings of the International Conference of the Learning Sciences*, Vol. 1, Full Papers. Chicago, IL: International Society of the Learning Sciences.

Arora, S., Joshi, M., & Rosé, C. P. (2009). Identifying types of claims in online customer reviews. In *Proceedings of Human Language Technologies: The 2009 Annual Conference of the North American Chapter of the Association for Computational Linguistics* (pp. 37–40). Stroudsburg, PA: Association for Computational Linguistics.

Azmitia, M., & Montgomery, R. (1993). Friendship, transactive dialogues, and the development of scientific reasoning. *Social Development, 2,* 202–221.

Bakhtin, M. (1986). *Speech genres and other late essays* (V. McGee, Trans.). Austin, TX: University of Texas Press.

Bereiter, C. (2002). *Education and mind in the knowledge age.* Hillsdale, NJ: Lawrence Erlbaum Associates.

Group Cognition in Online Teams • 545

Berkowitz, M., & Gibbs, J. (1983). Measuring the developmental features of moral discussion. *Merrill-Palmer Quarterly, 29*, 399–410.

Çakir, M. P., Xhafa, F., & Zhou, N. (2009). Thread-based analysis of patterns in VMT. In G. Stahl (Ed.), *Studying virtual math teams* (pp. 359–371). New York, NY: Springer.

Çakir, M. P., Zemel, A., & Stahl, G. (2009). The joint organization of interaction within a multimodal CSCL medium. *International Journal of Computer-Supported Collaborative Learning, 4*, 115–149.

Chaudhuri, S., Kumar, R., Howley, I., & Rosé, C. P. (2009). Engaging collaborative learners with helping agents. *Proceedings of Artificial Intelligence in Education.*

Chomsky, N. (1959). Review of verbal behavior, by B. F. Skinner. *Language, 35*, 26–57.

Christie, F. (Ed.). (1999). *Pedagogy and the shaping of consciousness: Linguistic and social processes.* London, UK: Cassell.

Clark, H., & Brennan, S. (1991). Grounding in communication. In L. Resnick, J. Levine, & S. Teasley (Eds.), *Perspectives on socially-shared cognition* (pp. 127–149). Washington, DC: APA.

Cloran, C. (1999). Contexts for learning. In F. Christie (Ed.), *Pedagogy and the shaping of consciousness: Linguistics and social processes.* New York, NY: Continuum.

Cui, Y., Chaudhuri, S., Kumar, R., Gweon, G., & Rosé, C. P. (2009). Helping agents in VMT. In G. Stahl (Ed.), *Studying virtual math teams.* New York, NY: Springer.

de Lisi, R., & Golbeck, S. L. (1999). Implications of the Piagetian theory for peer learning. In A. M. O'Donnell & A. King (Eds.), *Cognitive perspectives on peer learning* (pp. 3–37). Hillsdale, NJ: Lawrence Erlbaum Associates.

Duranti, A. (1998). *Linguistic anthropology.* Cambridge, UK: Cambridge University Press.

Fuks, H., Pimentel, M., & Pereira de Lucena, C. (2006). R-u-typing-2-me? Evolving a chat tool to increase understanding in learning activities. *International Journal of Computer-Supported Collaborative Learning, 1*, 117–142.

Gadamer, H.-G. (1988). *Truth and method.* New York, NY: Crossroads. (Original work published in 1960)

Garfinkel, H. (1967). *Studies in ethnomethodology.* Englewood Cliffs, NJ: Prentice-Hall.

Gweon, G., Kumar, R., & Rosé, C. P. (2009). Towards automatic assessment for project based learning groups. *Proceedings of Artificial Intelligence in Education.*

Hanks, W. (1992). The indexical ground of deictic reference. In A. Duranti & C. Goodwin (Eds.), *Rethinking context: Language as an interactive phenomenon* (pp. 43–76). Cambridge, UK: Cambridge University Press.

Hasan, R. (1999). Society, language and the mind: The meta-dialogism of Basil Bernstein's theory. In F. Christie (Ed.), *Pedagogy and the shaping of consciousness: Linguistics and social processes.* New York, NY: Continuum.

Heidegger, M. (1996). *Being and time: A translation of Sein und Zeit* (J. Stambaugh, Trans.). Albany, NY: SUNY Press. (Original work published in 1927)

Herring, S. (1999). Interactional coherence in CMC. *Journal of Computer Mediated Communication, 4*, doi: 10.1111/j.1083-6101.1999.tb00106.x

Howley, I., Mayfield, E., & Rosé, C. P. (in press). Linguistic analysis methods for studying small groups. In C. Hmelo-Silver, A. M. O'Donnell, C. A. Chinn, & C. Chan (Eds.), *International handbook of collaborative learning.* New York, NY: Taylor & Francis.

Hutchins, E. (1996). *Cognition in the wild.* Cambridge, MA: MIT Press.

Jordan, B., & Henderson, A. (1995). Interaction analysis: Foundations and practice. *Journal of the Learning Sciences, 4*, 39–103.

546 • *Theories of Team Cognition*

Joshi, M., & Rosé, C. P. (2007). Using transactivity in conversation summarization in educational dialog. *Proceedings of the SLaTE Workshop on Speech and Language Technology in Education.*

Joshi, M., & Rosé, C. P. (2009). Generalizing dependency features for opinion mining. *Proceedings of the Association for Computational Linguistics.*

Kang, M., Chaudhuri, S., Kumar, R., Wang, Y., Rosé, E., Cui, Y., et al. (2008). Supporting the guide on the SIDE. *Proceedings of Intelligent Tutoring Systems (ITS '08).*

Kumar, R., Ai, H., & Rosé, C. P. (2010). Choosing optimal levels of social interaction: Towards creating human-like conversational tutors. In V. Aleven, J. Kay, & J. Mostow (Eds.), *Proceedings of the 10th International Conference on Intelligence Tutoring Systems,* June, Pittsburgh, PA.

Kumar, R., & Rosé, C. P. (2009). Building conversational agents with Basilica, *Proceedings of the North American Chapter of the Association for Computational Linguistics,* 5–8.

Kumar, R., & Rosé, C. P. (2010). Engaging learning groups using social interaction strategies. In *Proceedings of the 11th Annual Conference of the North American Chapter of the Association for Computational Linguistics,* June, Los Angeles, CA.

Kumar, R., Rosé, C. P., Wang, Y. C., Joshi, M., & Robinson, A. (2007). Tutorial dialogue as adaptive collaborative learning support. *Proceeding of the 2007 Conference on Artificial Intelligence in Education,* 383–390.

Martin, J. R., & Rose, D. (2003). *Working with discourse: Meaning beyond the clause.* New York, NY: Continuum.

Martin, J. R., & White, P. R. (2005). *The language of evaluation: Appraisal in English.* Basingstoke, UK: Palgrave.

Mayfield, E., & Rosé, C. P. (2010). Using feature construction to avoid large feature spaces in text classification. *Genetic and Evolutionary Computation Conference - GECCO,* 1299–1306.

Rosé, C. P., Gweon, G., Arguello, J., Finger, S., Smailagic, A., & Siewiorek, D. (2007). Towards an interactive assessment framework for engineering design learning. *Proceedings of ASME 2007 International Design Engineering Technical Conferences & Computers and Information in Engineering Conference.*

Rosé, C. P., Wang, Y. C., Cui, Y., Arguello, J., Stegmann, K., Weinberger, A., et al. (2008). Analyzing collaborative learning processes automatically: Exploiting the advances of computational linguistics in computer-supported collaborative learning. *International Journal of Computer Supported Collaborative Learning, 3,* 237–271.

Sacks, H. (1995). *Lectures on conversation.* Oxford, UK: Blackwell. (Original work published in 1962)

Sarmiento, J., & Stahl, G. (2008). *Extending the joint problem space: Time and sequence as essential features of knowledge building.* Paper presented at the International Conference of the Learning Sciences (ICLS 2008), Utrecht, the Netherlands.

Sarmiento-Klapper, J. W. (2009). *Bridging mechanisms in team-based online problem solving: Continuity in building collaborative knowledge.* Unpublished doctoral dissertation, College of Information Science and Technology, Drexel University, Philadelphia, PA.

Schegloff, E. A. (2007). *Sequence organization in interaction: A primer in conversation analysis.* Cambridge, UK: Cambridge University Press.

Schwartz, D. (1998). The productive agency that drives collaborative learning. In P. Dillenbourg (Ed.), *Collaborative learning: Cognitive and computational approaches.* New York, NY: Elsevier Science/Permagon.

Stahl, G. (2006). *Group cognition: Computer support for building collaborative knowledge.* Cambridge, MA: MIT Press.

Stahl, G. (2009a). *Studying virtual math teams.* New York, NY: Springer.

Stahl, G. (2009b). Toward a science of group cognition. In G. Stahl (Ed.), *Studying virtual math teams* (pp. 555–579). New York, NY: Springer.

Stahl, G., Koschmann, T., & Suthers, D. (2006). Computer-supported collaborative learning: An historical perspective. In R. K. Sawyer (Ed.), *Cambridge handbook of the learning sciences* (pp. 409–426). Cambridge, UK: Cambridge University Press.

Suthers, D. D. (2006). Technology affordances for inter-subjective meaning making: A research agenda for CSCL. *International Journal of Computer Supported Collaborative Learning, 1,* 315–337.

Suthers, D. D., Dwyer, N., Medina, R., & Vatrapu, R. (2010). A framework for conceptualizing, representing and analyzing distributed interaction. *International Journal of Computer-Supported Collaborative Learning, 5,* 5–44.

Teasley, S. D. (1997). Talking about reasoning: How important is the peer in peer collaboration? In L. B. Resnick, R. Säljö, C. Pontecorvo, & B. Burge (Eds.), *Discourse, tools and reasoning: Essays on situated cognition* (pp. 364–384). New York, NY: Springer.

Teasley, S. D., & Roschelle, J. (1993). Constructing a joint problem space: The computer as a tool for sharing knowledge. In S. P. Lajoie & S. J. Derry (Eds.), *Computers as cognitive tools* (pp. 229–258). Mahwah, NJ: Lawrence Erlbaum Associates, Inc.

Terasaki, A. K. (2004). Pre-announcement sequences in conversation. In G. Lerner (Ed.), *Conversation analysis: Studies from the first generation* (pp. 171–224). Philadelphia, PA: John Benjamins

Vygotsky, L. (1978). *Mind in society.* Cambridge, MA: Harvard University Press. (Original work published in 1930)

Wang, H. C., & Rosé, C. P. (2007). Supporting collaborative idea generation: A closer look using statistical process analysis techniques. *Proceedings of Artificial Intelligence in Education.*

Wang, H. C., & Rosé, C. P. (2010). Making conversational structure explicit: Identification of initiation-response pairs in online discussion. *Human Language Technologies: The 2010 Annual Conference of the North American Chapter of the Association for Computational Linguistics,* 673–676.

Wang, H. C., Rosé, C. P., Cui, Y., Chang, C. Y., Huang, C. C., & Li, T. Y. (2007). Thinking hard together: The long and short of collaborative idea generation for scientific inquiry. *Proceedings of Computer Supported Collaborative Learning.*

Weinberger, A., & Fischer, F. (2006). A framework to analyze argumentative knowledge construction in computer supported collaborative learning. *Computers & Education, 46,* 71–95.

Wee, J. D., & Looi, C.-K. (2009). A model for analyzing math knowledge building in VMT. In G. Stahl (Ed.), *Studying virtual math teams* (pp. 475–497). New York, NY: Springer.

Wittgenstein, L. (1953). *Philosophical investigations.* New York, NY: Macmillan.

Wittgenstein, L. (1956). *Remarks on the foundations of mathematics.* Cambridge, MA: MIT Press. (Original work published in 1944)

Zemel, A., Xhafa, F., & Çakir, M. P. (2009). Combining coding and conversation analysis of VMT chats. In G. Stahl (Ed.), *Studying virtual math teams* (pp. 421–450). New York, NY: Springer.

22

Facilitating Effective Mental Model Convergence: The Interplay Among the Team's Task, Mental Model Content, Communication Flow, and Media

Sara A. McComb and Deanna M. Kennedy

When tasks are complex, a team of individuals, rather than the individuals by themselves, may be more capable of achieving a successful outcome. However, the team's performance may in part depend on whether the members are able to come together on a cognitive level by forming shared mental models (Klimoski & Mohammed, 1994; Kraiger & Wenzel, 1997). Mental models are repositories of knowledge held in the mind of individual team members that influence behaviors and enable the team to complete its task objectives (Mathieu, Heffner, Goodwin, Salas, & Cannon-Bowers, 2000). As information is shared among teammates, the mental models of team members may become similar, or converge, which brings the members together at the team level (McComb, 2007). The convergence of mental models has, through empirical research, been linked to team performance (e.g., Carley, Diesner, Reminga, & Tsvetovat, 2007; Cooke, Salas, Kiekel, & Bell, 2004). Understanding the dynamics of the convergence process, however, is still a limited but growing area and one that may be key to improving team outcomes.

Several studies have linked shared mental models (i.e., the result of the mental model convergence process) to team performance and other outcome measures (McComb, 2008). In many cases, the relationship is positive (e.g., Edwards, Day, Arthur, & Bell, 2006; Gurtner, Tschan, Semmer, & Nägele, 2007). In other cases, however, the relationship with team performance has not been positive (e.g., McComb & Vozdolska,

550 • *Theories of Team Cognition*

2007). Indeed, converged mental models can, at times, work against the team's performance when they create behaviors and actions that are contrary to the team's objectives. For instance, McComb and Vozdolska (2007) found that cooperation mental models negatively related to performance. They suggest that the team members may become overconfident in their assessment of cooperation, creating groupthink around the task processes. Such negative outcomes could also be the result of team members converging on mental model content that is erroneous (e.g., inaccurate situation assessments) or captures detrimental team functioning that exists among team members (e.g., high levels of conflict). Thus, understanding the content comprising mental models and examining how it evolves during the convergence process may help us better anticipate how mental model convergence will impact team outcomes. One approach for observing mental model content and the convergence process is through team communication.

Recently, Kennedy and McComb (2010) drew a theoretical link between the mental model convergence process and team communication. They suggest that as team members exchange information, their internal mental models change and often converge. Moreover, the communication behaviors and practices used by the team members provide a means of viewing the mental model convergence process as it unfolds during team collaboration. Yet, research also suggests that the team's task may influence the communication practices followed by the team (Cooke, Gorman, & Kiekel, 2008; Poole, 1978). Hence, we extend Kennedy and McComb's (2010) research by examining the interplay between the team's task and communication. Our purpose is to develop a taxonomy that highlights how specific communicated content, delivered in a particular manner and via certain media, may facilitate effective mental model convergence across various types of tasks.

Our chapter begins with a brief review of the connection between mental model convergence and communication. Second, we examine two aspects of team communication that may be influenced by the task on which the team is working, namely the flow of information and the media through which communication transpires. Third, we discuss the link between the team's task and the content being exchanged. Next, we amalgamate the various pieces presented into a taxonomy that prescribes specific communication practices depending on the team's task. Finally, we offer implications for research and practice.

MENTAL MODEL CONVERGENCE AND COMMUNICATION

The mental model convergence process has been conceptualized as an iterative three-phase process. It involves orienting team members to the problem space that requires information sharing, differentiating the external information received during orientation from the team members' existing mental model content, and integrating the new information into their internalized mental models (McComb, 2007). When team members orient themselves to the team and its task, they become purposeful in sharing information about their own knowledge by externalizing it in a way to be received by their teammates. The external information is sorted cognitively by each team member, and similarities or differences with their existing mental models are identified (e.g., Newell & Simon, 1972; Schroder, Driver, & Streufert, 1967). The sorted information supports, changes, or appends the team members' currently held mental models. As team members integrate this new information into their existing mental models, more similar mental models emerge across the team members (McComb, 2007). In this way, when people work together in teams, the process of sharing information may change the mental models of all the members (Hinsz, Tindale, & Vollrath, 1997).

An explicit way information is shared among team members is through communication. As such, communication provides a window into the cognitive processes of the team (Cooke et al., 2008). Taking this relationship into account, the connection among team communication, information processing, and mental models has been presented in a framework by Kennedy and McComb (2010). Specifically, they use the Shannon and Weaver (1949) model of information transmission with the addition of a feedback loop to represent the way information about mental model content is communicated among team members during the convergence process. The transmission model indicates that information derives from a source and is transmitted via a channel where it may be affected by internal/external noise. The noise-filtered information is then received and ultimately reaches its destination. In terms of the mental model convergence process, Kennedy and McComb (2010) suggest that during the orientation phase of the convergence process, information contained in a team member's mental model (i.e., the source) is transmitted

552 • *Theories of Team Cognition*

through communication where noise (e.g., clatter in the environment or discrepancies from personal interpretation) may be encountered. In the differentiation phase, the received information is compared to the team members' extant mental model content and then integrated into the members' mental model(s) (i.e., the destination). As a result, the content of teammates' mental models may be affected such that members' mental models become similar over time.

As described earlier, communication plays an important role in the mental model convergence process. Although the differentiation and integration phases of the convergence process are concerned with internal cognitive processing, the orientation phase may be different. Kennedy and McComb's (2010) framework suggests that during the orientation phase, communication is used to externalize information purposeful in bringing mental model content out into the environment for other team members to receive. As a result, from an examination of this communication, the mental model convergence process may be surmised. In other words, communication may be considered an explicit representation of underlying implicit cognitive processes because it allows us to observe what mental model content is being discussed and how the convergence process is progressing.

COMMUNICATION DECONSTRUCTED

Kennedy and McComb (2010) treat communication as a black box that facilitates the mental model convergence process. However, communication has many facets. Moreover, the manner in which teams communicate may be dependent on the task they are undertaking (Cooke et al., 2008; Poole, 1978). Thus, we examine two aspects of communication that may be useful in deconstructing the information exchange occurring among team members and, more importantly, that may assist us in identifying the most effective means of exchanging information for different types of tasks. First, we address communication flow, the manner in which information is conveyed. In particular, we suggest that the information required for various types of tasks may benefit from conversations that are focused, diffuse, or some combination of both. Second, we examine media used to communicate, specifically face to face and computer mediation, because exchanges via these media may be more (or less) useful in completing different task types.

Communication Flow

The dynamics of communication flow may impart information about underlying team cognitive processes (Cooke et al., 2008). Specifically, the flow of communication may suggest how the mental model convergence process unfolds as team members exchange mental model content among themselves. Two ways that team communication may unfold are through focused or diffused information exchange.

Focused communication, a product of the communication convergence process described by Dennis and Valacich (1999), involves the narrowing in on a common understanding of the information being exchanged and the acknowledgement by all individuals that this understanding has been reached. As the team works toward consensus (i.e., convergence), feedback and responsive information are often communicated to show understanding or agreement (Murthy & Kerr, 2003). When focused communication is undertaken by teams, the mental model convergence process may be conceptualized as a composition-based emergence process (Kozlowski & Klein, 2000) where the end products are shared mental models that have similar content across team members.

In contrast, diffused communication results from what Dennis and Valacich (1999) describe as the conveyance process of communication. That is, individuals are purposeful in disseminating diverse information and adding to the variety of sources. Communication in this way may be concerned with increasing the information about alternatives through a discussion of many topic areas (VanGundy, 1988). Because this divergent type of communication does not require all of the team members to agree on the meaning of each topic, it may increase the number and scope of alternatives discussed (Murthy & Kerr, 2003). At the cognitive level, a compilation-based emergence process may best represent the mental model convergence process, and the end products may be compatible mental models composed of "different knowledge across individuals that forms a congruent whole" (Kozlowski & Klein, 2000, p. 74).

Communication Media

Evidence suggests that communication via different media may achieve varying levels of effectiveness depending on the task being undertaken by the team (e.g., Kerr & Murthy, 2004). Face to face and computer mediation

554 • *Theories of Team Cognition*

represent the circumstances routinely faced by teams as they complete their assigned activities and are, therefore, two particular media conditions that have received extensive research attention in the team literature. Whereas face-to-face teams work together in person, computer-mediated teams use computer-supported collaboration tools to interact. Researchers have shown that these media are differentially disposed to passing certain types of content (e.g., Huang, Wei, & Tan, 1999) and prompt specific patterns of communication (e.g., Kerr & Murthy, 2004). To better understand why these differences may exist, we turn to the theories of media richness and social presence.

Media Richness

The seminal work on media richness by Daft and Lengel (1984, 1986) suggests that the capacity to carry interpersonal communication cues varies across media types. Employing media richness theory, Chidambaram and Jones (1993) formulated a continuum anchored by face-to-face interactions at the rich media end and electronic communication at the lean media end based on the types and amount of information carried by different media. Rich media are typified by interactions with multiple channels available for verbal, paraverbal, and nonverbal cues that relay information from a sender, feedback, and socioemotional signals (Daft & Lengel, 1986). In contrast, lean media effectively limit the flow of communication cues due to the restricted number of channels available to transmit information (Daft & Lengel, 1986).

Face-to-face communication, a rich communication medium, has many channels available, such as facial expressions, verbal and nonverbal cues, posture, and eye movements, that inform the speaker and receiver when people meet in person (Tu, 2000). The way communication unfolds may be influenced by the communication behaviors afforded by such a rich medium. Specifically, the interpersonal communication shared in face-to-face interactions may promote a give-and-take attitude from one person toward another. The effect takes the form of turn-taking behaviors during conversations, the withholding of interruptions while others are speaking, and the reciprocation of information exchange or acknowledgement of the speaker's words (Ijsselsteijn, van Baren, & van Lanen, 2003). As such, research has found that teams communicating face to face, rather than through computer mediation, have more cohesive and personal communication (Jonassen & Kwon, 2001).

Alternatively, computer mediation, a lean communication medium, has limited channels of communication (Chidambaram & Jones, 1993). Because the medium is inherently impersonal due to fewer channels, it may better support communication about topics that are task based (e.g., rules, regulations) (Daft & Lengel, 1986). Indeed, research has found that teams using computer-mediated communication, compared with teams using face-to-face interactions, are more task oriented (Jonassen & Kwon, 2001). The communication flow itself, however, may also be impacted by the fewer channels. Because the medium requires more time and effort to send messages because each message has to be input through mechanical means into a computer (Graetz, Boyle, Kimble, Thompson, & Garlock, 1998), team members tend to exchange shorter messages and omit agreement statements, feedback, or acknowledgement that the topic is understood (Boyle, Anderson, & Newlands, 1994). Moreover, the ability to work asynchronously permits team members to share information that is tangential from the last message, adding to the divergence of ideas that can be shared (Murthy & Kerr, 2003).

Social Presence

Social presence refers to the sense people have of others in the interaction (Short, Williams, & Christie, 1976). It is culled by the number of communication channels available to the team members. Face-to-face communication, in particular, provides a fluid medium to foster and build high levels of social presence (Rice, 1984; Sproull & Kiesler, 1991) because people can more easily and quickly communicate nuances of "warmth, personality, sensibility, and sociability" (Alavi, Yoo, & Vogel, 1997, p. 1318). The development of social presence has been shown to support social interactions that build relational links among team members (Warkentin, Sayeed, & Hightower, 1997). These links may help teams in their achievement of different types of tasks. For one, face-to-face team members may better address tasks in which they have to negotiate a solution. Indeed, research has found that verbal and nonverbal feedback during in-person interactions is important for understanding team members and identifying a compromise or consensus as the solution to the problem (Setlock, Fussell, & Neuwirth, 2004). In addition, face-to-face interactions may be crucial in tasks with an executable process. Specifically, team members meeting face to face are better able to sense other team members'

556 • *Theories of Team Cognition*

abilities, actions, and intentions (Andres, 2002). As such, the rich information passed through face-to-face interactions coupled with high social presence among team members may create a cooperative communication environment for achieving task objectives.

When working with only limited channels of communication, such as through computer mediation, social presence may remain at a lower level (e.g., Warkentin & Barenak, 1999). Indeed, research suggests that social presence may be dependent on timely feedback and responses from others, which is less forthcoming in distributed communication (Garramone, Harris, & Anderson, 1986). The low levels of social presence garnered through computer-mediated interactions, however, may also be responsible for uninhibited discussions that support more creative thinking and higher member participation (Wellman et al., 1996). Research suggests that computer mediation facilitates group idea generation (e.g., Wang, Fussell, & Setlock, 2009) because the ability to communicate in parallel by not having to wait for a turn before beginning a response or new information transmission allows the discussion to be more diffuse and grow tangentially (Murthy & Kerr, 2003). Thus, computer-mediated communication has been found to help teams completing tasks that require more concise, parallel conversations in an environment free of social pressure.

In summary, face-to-face communication provides team members with an environment in which to share information across a number of channels. Through such rich exchanges, team members can develop social presence that will facilitate task activities requiring more coordinated activities. Alternatively, computer-mediated communication facilitates more factual communication that may be hindered by strong social presence. These lean exchanges may promote tangential, creative discussions that are not influenced by the personalities in the room. Both media clearly have a role in team functioning. As we have shown, however, the team may be best served by matching the team's activities to the media most appropriate for effectively completing them.

MENTAL MODEL CONTENT

In addition to the ways in which information is exchanged among team members, which we have discussed, the type of task may also influence what information, in terms of content, the members are discussing. Research suggests that shared mental models containing distinct types of content may emerge during collaboration and, as previously mentioned, may be surmised by examining team communication. Cannon-Bowers, Salas, and Converse (1993) designated four mental model types that may be useful to team collaboration: team, team interaction, equipment, and task. Based on this framework, Mathieu et al. (2000) forwarded two broad categories that have been empirically tested. The first category, *teamwork mental models*, includes (a) team models representing knowledge about one's teammates, such as teammates' knowledge, skills, abilities, preferences, and tendencies, and (b) team interaction models that establish how the team will work together in terms of roles, information sources, interaction patterns, interdependencies, and communication channels. The second category, *taskwork mental models*, includes (a) equipment models with knowledge about the equipment and its limitations, operating procedures, and potential failure points, and (b) task models that contain knowledge about the procedures, strategies, constraints, potential alternatives, and probable effects.

These teamwork and taskwork mental models are conceptualized as existing simultaneously (e.g., Marks, Sabella, Burke, & Zaccaro, 2002; Smith-Jentsch, Mathieu, & Kraiger, 2005). Yet distinct types of mental model content may be more relevant to the team's performance of certain types of tasks than others. To identify the various task types that teams may be required to complete, we use McGrath's (1984) circumplex. In his circumplex, McGrath identifies eight types of tasks teams may encounter. Further, he proposes that all team tasks can be captured by four general processes: negotiate, execute, generate, and choose. Thus, we review three studies that have examined teamwork, taskwork, or both types of mental models, and we highlight the potential link between these types of mental models and the tasks being undertaken by the teams in the studies.

Several empirical studies have included teamwork mental models, taskwork mental models, or both. To better understand those studies examining only one type of mental model, we discuss two studies where the team's strategy played a significant role in team performance. On the one hand, Gurtner et al. (2007) found that team interaction mental models (a specific type of teamwork mental models) were positively related to performance when mediated by strategy implementation. For this task, one team member (the commander) could recommend a strategy designed

558 • *Theories of Team Cognition*

to enhance coordination to the two specialists on the team who would then execute the strategy given to them. On the other hand, Edwards et al. (2006) demonstrated that taskwork mental models (i.e., task actions and strategies), assessed in terms of accuracy and similarity, were positively related to performance (i.e., combat success). During training, team members were given four known, effective strategies that would be useful as they completed their missions (Arthur et al., 1995). The team members had to work together to choose the appropriate battle strategies from the given set of strategies. Thus, teams executing a strategy required teamwork mental models, whereas those selecting the strategy were well served by taskwork mental models.

To our knowledge, four studies have included teamwork *and* taskwork mental models as distinct constructs in analyses (Lim & Klein, 2006; Mathieu, Heffner, Goodwin, Cannon-Bowers, & Salas, 2005; Mathieu et al., 2000; Smith-Jentsch et al., 2005). We examine in detail the research conducted by Smith-Jentsch et al. (2005), who conducted a field study examining the mental models shared among air traffic controllers, to demonstrate the relationship between mental model content and the type of task being undertaken. Their teamwork mental model, positional-goal interdependencies, refers to the shared understanding of the interdependencies among the ground, approach, and departure control positions. Their taskwork mental model, cue-strategy associations, captures the perceived probability of success for various strategies that may be used in a given situation. Mental models were assessed in terms of both consistency (i.e., team members possess the same relative priorities across the items assessed) and agreement (i.e., team members possess the same priorities and are, therefore, interchangeable) to performance in terms of efficiency (i.e., flight delays) and effectiveness (i.e., air safety).

Interestingly, no direct relationships between shared mental models and performance were found. Moreover, no interactive effects were found when shared mental model agreement was the construct being investigated. The significant findings of interest in this study suggest that consistency in both teamwork and taskwork mental models is necessary for the team members to effectively function as a team and perform well on their task. Indeed, the highest performing teams had highly consistent teamwork *and* taskwork shared mental models. The worst performing teams reported high consistency across teamwork shared mental models and low consistency across taskwork shared mental models. The authors suggest that teamwork mental models are adequate when the team of air traffic controllers face normal operating conditions. When novel situations arise, however, the controllers must be able to quickly generate alternative strategies and decide a course of action. Under these circumstances, taskwork mental models are the predominant mental models needed to function; teamwork mental models are necessary as well, albeit to a lesser degree.

In summary, teamwork and taskwork mental models are distinct constructs as proposed in the theoretical frameworks proffered by Cannon-Bowers et al. (1993) and Mathieu et al. (2000) and tested in the empirical research undertaken that includes one or both types of shared mental models. The findings from the empirical studies suggest several important points relative to the current research: (1) team's task may be accomplished most effectively when team members have shared mental models about particular aspects of their collective activities; (2) the content of the shared mental models may be dependent on the type of task being carried out; and (3) teams are often asked to undertake multiple types of tasks in their day-to-day operations and, therefore, may require a portfolio of shared mental models that encompass both their teamwork and taskwork.

FACILITATING MENTAL MODEL CONVERGENCE THROUGH COMMUNICATION

In Table 22.1, we expand our understanding of the relationship between mental model convergence and communication by introducing a taxonomy that highlights how various aspects of communication may facilitate effective mental model convergence processes for various types of tasks. We organize our taxonomy using the tasks indentified in McGrath's (1984) circumplex that can be classified around the processes of negotiate, execute, generate, and choose. We use our extant understanding of these task types and processes to ascertain the most effective combination of mental model content, communication flow, and media for each task type.

Our taxonomy does not imply that the identified elements are the only ones necessary. Rather, we suggest that they are the dominant elements that may promote more effective mental model convergence. For instance, Smith-Jentsch et al. (2005) suggest in their study of air traffic controllers

560 • *Theories of Team Cognition*

TABLE 22.1

Taxonomy of Task Type, Mental Model Content, Communication Flow, and Media

Task Type	Mental Model Content	Communication Flow	Media
Negotiate: Cognitive-conflict and mixed-motive tasks	Taskwork	Focused	Face to face
Execute: Contests and performance tasks	Teamwork	Diffused	Face to face
Generate: Planning and creative tasks	Taskwork	Diffused	Computer mediation
Choose: Intellective and decision-making tasks	Taskwork	Diffused and focused	Computer mediation

that taskwork mental models are dominant in cases where novel circumstances must be addressed requiring the controllers to generate options and choose among them, but teamwork mental models also play a role. This example also highlights how teams in the field may be called upon to execute all of the processes included in McGrath's (1984) circumplex at some point during their life cycle. Teams may function more effectively if they intentionally transition among the various content, flow, and media types available as the processes required of them change.

Negotiate

Cognitive-conflict and mixed-motive tasks require the team to negotiate (McGrath, 1984). In cognitive-conflict tasks, team members align in terms of purpose and goals but have disparate cognitive views of a problem that, when resolved, lead to a solution. A common task that often involves cognitive conflict is a jury making a judgment decision. Specifically, the jury members, while sharing the purpose of deciding on a verdict, may have discrepant perspectives regarding the evidence, and therefore, through discussion, they may talk through the differences to arrive at a judgment. Alternatively, when team members' motives do not align, then the task is considered a mixed-motive task (McGrath, 1984). In mixed-motive tasks, merely coming to terms on a mutually agreed upon solution may not be possible; negotiations may require concessions on the part of one or more members. Such tasks are demonstrated, for instance, by top management teams that have to make budget cuts for the next fiscal year. The cognitive dissonance associated with the team members' funding preferences may

Facilitating Effective Mental Model Convergence • 561

require bargaining and negotiation in order to achieve a solution satisfactory to all team members.

Negotiation requires the team to focus their communication on topics that will help them resolve their conflicting cognitive states. Research suggests that resolving conflict and successfully negotiating perspectives may depend on team members' social influences on one another; that is, one party is trying to persuade the other party to share their perspective (Walton & McKersie, 1965). Moreover, the negotiating parties may benefit from multiple channels of communication because they allow the exchange of personal cues such as gazes, nods, and utterances, thereby providing immediate feedback that helps negotiations progress rather than allowing the opportunity for depersonalized or omitted cues that may obstruct negotiations (Andres, 2002). The flow of communication during negotiations must be focused so that the team's perspective hones in on a solution. Through these focused conversations, team members can share task-related information that reduces ambiguity and uncovers areas of compatible perspectives, and more importantly, they can develop a shared sense of understanding regarding the task that facilitates the team's ability to reach an agreement (Thompson, Peterson, & Brodt, 1996). Thus, negotiation processes may be best accomplished via face-to-face, focused exchanges of task-related information.

Execute

McGrath's (1984) circumplex describes a task requiring an execute process as one that involves physical competition aimed at winning or performance against an ultimate goal. In particular, a contest task is one in which the objective is to beat the opponent. Any competitive sports team or military unit physically engaged with their rival is in a contest task. The desired solution is to win the game or battle. A performance task invokes the engaged team to strive to be the best; however, instead of a physical opponent, the performance is measured in comparison to a benchmark or standard of excellence (McGrath, 1984). For example, pit crews execute actions effectively and efficiently to get their racecar back on the track after a pit stop. A crew can compare its time taken to change tires, refuel, and so on, to a benchmark and, therefore, assess its performance. Gurtner et al.'s (2007) aforementioned specialists executing a strategy suggested by their commander provides a second example of a performance task.

562 • *Theories of Team Cognition*

Although understanding the task, including strategies, procedures, constraints, and so on, is necessary, the knowledge held about teamwork, particularly about the way in which the team will interact, may be paramount to successful performance. Stated another way, teams that have shared mental models about teamwork may be able to have implicit coordination (Espinosa et al., 2001) that enables an awareness of what other team members will do at any given moment in time. While the team is engaged in their contest or performance task, communication concerned with teamwork serves to direct actions and facilitates the team's need to adapt to situations in real time. As such, diffuse communication may be most useful because it promotes short exchanges of information that serve as status updates. Indeed, clear, concise communication that draws feedback to ensure shared understanding may build situation awareness and, therefore, be more appropriate to the types of situations where quick adaptation is needed (Salas, Burke, & Samman, 2001). Thus, face-to-face communication about teamwork delivered in a diffuse manner is most appropriate when a team executes a task.

Generate

Planning and creativity tasks require the team to generate outputs (McGrath, 1984). Teams involved in planning tasks cooperatively construct strategies of action for a chosen alternative, such as the air traffic controllers in the study by Smith-Jentsch et al. (2005) who may be required to generate alternative plans of action when novel circumstances arise. Creative tasks require teams to brainstorm alternatives to a given problem (McGrath, 1984). For example, a marketing team that needs a new ad campaign for a soft drink may meet to generate ideas that provide alternatives for the campaign.

Creative tasks involving brainstorming and idea generation have been prominent in the team literature, but research involving planning tasks has been limited. Indeed, McGrath (1984) indicated that few empirical studies of planning tasks had been conducted. To our knowledge, the research specifically examining planning tasks continues to be sparse even after McGrath's call for more research in the mid-1980s. Therefore, we use the research pertaining to brainstorming and idea generation to garner general knowledge from empirical results about teams tasked with generation processes.

Recent research indicates that teams may be more creative than individuals when they collectively generate ideas (e.g., Connolly, Jessup, & Valacich, 1988). One reason for their advantage may be due to their composition. Teams are typically composed of individuals with unique backgrounds. When a set of individuals begins disseminating their unique knowledge and perspectives in a diffuse manner, the conversations become tangential, and the team is able to devise more creative alternatives than any one individual (Kerr & Murthy, 2004). Certain provisions, however, may be necessary to encourage the sharing of ideas on a team (Paulus & Yang, 2000). For instance, evidence suggests that the generation process is more effective when team members are less apprehensive about being evaluated by others; that is, when the social awareness about others is low and the anonymity of participating is high (Connolly et al., 1988). Because the discussion is centered on the task under these circumstances, rather than on developing social presence among teammates, the team members' mental models may be comprised primarily of taskwork content. Therefore, teams assigned work that requires generating plans or creative solutions may function most effectively if their conversations focus on taskwork, are diffuse, and occur via computer mediation where social presence is low and the ability to conduct parsimonious, tangential conversations is high.

Choose

Teams that must execute choose processes are working on intellective or decision-making tasks (McGrath, 1984). Intellective tasks require the team to solve a problem that has a correct answer. The problem may have multiple alternatives that the team must check and eliminate in order to obtain an answer. The answer itself may be determined correct based on fact, proof, or expert consensus. For example, a production team tasked with fulfilling a consumer's order for multiple products may work to allocate resources as needed to meet demand while minimizing production costs. Unless unreasonable requirements are made, a feasible, and possibly optimal, solution exists. Similarly, a decision-making task charges the team with distilling alternatives down to a final solution; however, a correct answer does not necessarily exist, and therefore, the solution is determined via consensus among team members (McGrath, 1984). A human resource team that has to make a hiring decision for the next year provides an example of a decision-making task. Although the team may have many

564 • *Theories of Team Cognition*

potential candidates to consider, the final decision is often made by gaining the consensus of all team members. A second example of a decision-making task can be found in the aforementioned study by Edwards et al. (2006) where the team members had to choose which one of the given battle strategies to implement at different points during their exercise.

For both intellective and decision-making tasks, communication about the different alternatives allows the team to discuss options as they relate to task criteria. That is, in general, the conversation may revolve around sharing taskwork information that may be used to evaluate many alternatives. Focused communication too early in the choosing process may prevent the team from seeing the potential benefits or errors in alternatives by creating groupthink around a selection or strategy (Janis, 1972). Instead, diffuse communication that serves to convey information about all alternatives, even rejected ones, may lead to an appropriate and accurate set of alternatives to consider (Janis, 1972, 1982). After a diffuse discussion of pros and cons associated with the various alternatives under consideration, the team may benefit from shifting to a more focused exchange to garner consensus. With respect to the appropriate media for choose processes, the encouragement of discussions about alternatives may benefit from the same computer-mediated communication that promotes idea generation and creativity, specifically the ability to participate without external pressures of censorship (Henningsen, Henningsen, Eden, & Cruz, 2006). Indeed, evidence suggests that computer-mediated communication results in higher quality outputs compared with face-to-face communication when the task is intellectual (e.g., Schmidt, Montoya-Weiss, & Massey, 2001). Thus, the combination of content, media, and flow that facilitates effective team communication for conducting intellective and decision-making tasks is taskwork mental model content via computer mediation in a diffused manner initially and then transitioning to a more focused manner as the team works toward consensus.

CONCLUSION

In this chapter, we present a taxonomy that relates communicated mental model content and the way in which that content is exchanged among team members to the type of task being undertaken by the team. This research builds on the conceptual work of Kennedy and McComb (2010) that articulates a link between communication and cognition. Specifically, our objective was to highlight how the mental model convergence process can be enhanced through the communication of certain content in a particular manner, depending on the team's task. In doing so, we proposed a taxonomy that synthesizes theoretical and empirical research in this area. Future research is needed, however, to test the taxonomy proffered herein. This research may include: (a) further analysis of the extant shared mental model research examining teamwork and taskwork mental models, such as we did with the research by Edwards et al. (2006), Gurtner et al. (2007), and Smith-Jentsch et al. (2005); (b) designing experiments to specifically test the relationships specified in the taxonomy; and (c) conducting field studies that include a detailed analysis of the task(s) being undertaken by the teams.

Our taxonomy also provides insight for practitioners. Teams may encounter various types of tasks throughout their existence. Therefore, they may need to consider discussing information most relevant to the task at hand and in a manner that will facilitate the most effective exchange of this type of content. Moreover, they may need to change modes of communication at various points throughout their life cycle as the task process requirements change. Such a holistic approach to information exchange has the potential to streamline the mental model convergence process in the short run and enhance team performance in the longer term.

REFERENCES

Alavi, M., Yoo, Y., & Vogel, D. R. (1997). Using information technology to add value to management education. *Academy of Management Journal, 40*, 1310–1333.

Andres, H. P. (2002). A comparison of face-to-face and virtual software development teams. *Team Performance Management, 8*, 39–49.

Arthur, W., Jr., Strong, M. H., Jordan, J. A., Williamson, J. E., Shebilske, W. L., & Regian, J. W. (1995). Visual attention: Individual differences in training and predicting complex task performance. *Acta Psychologica, 88*, 3–23.

Boyle, E., Anderson, A. H., & Newlands, A. (1994). The effects of visibility on dialogue and performance in a cooperative problem-solving task. *Language and Speech, 37*, 1–20.

Cannon-Bowers, J., Salas, E., & Converse, S. (1993). Shared mental models in expert team decision making. In N. Castellan, Jr., (Ed.), *Individual and group decision making* (pp. 221–246). Hillsdale, NJ: Lawrence Erlbaum.

566 • *Theories of Team Cognition*

Carley, K., Diesner, J., Reminga, J., & Tsvetovat, M. (2007). Toward an interoperable dynamic network analysis toolkit. *Decision Support Systems, 43*, 1324–1347.

Chidambaram, L., & Jones, B. (1993). Impact of communication medium and computer support on group perceptions and performance: A comparison of face-to-face and dispersed teams. *MIS Quarterly, December*, 465–491.

Connolly, T., Jessup, L. M., & Valacich, J. S. (1988). Effects of anonymity and evaluative tone on idea generation in computer-mediated groups. *Management Science, 36*, 689–703.

Cooke, N., Gorman, J., & Kiekel, P. (2008). Communication as team-level cognitive processing. In M. Letsky, N. Warner, S. Fiore, & C. A. P. Smith (Eds.), *Macrocognition in teams: Theories and methodologies (Human factors in defence)* (pp. 51–64). Burlington, VT: Ashgate.

Cooke, N., Salas, E., Kiekel, P., & Bell, B. (2004). Advances in measuring team cognition. In E. Salas & S. Fiore (Eds.), *Team cognition: Understanding the factors that drive process and performance* (pp. 83–106). Washington, DC: American Psychological Association.

Daft, R., & Lengel, R. (1984). Information richness: A new approach to managerial behavior and organizational design. In L. L. Cummings & B. M. Staw (Eds.), *Research in organizational behavior* (pp. 191–233). Homewood, IL: JAI Press.

Daft, R., & Lengel, R. (1986). Organizational information requirements, media richness and structural design. *Management Science, 32*, 554–571.

Dennis, A., & Valacich, J. (1999). Rethinking media richness: Towards a theory of media synchronicity. *Proceedings of the 32nd Hawaii International Conference on System Sciences*. IEEE Computer Society.

Edwards, B., Day, E., Arthur, J., & Bell, S. (2006). Relationships among team ability composition, team mental models, and team performance. *Journal of Applied Psychology, 91*, 727–736.

Espinosa, J., Kraut, R., Lerch, J., Slaughter, S., Herbsleb, J., & Mockus, A. (2001). Shared mental models and coordination in large-scale, distributed software development. *22nd International Conference on Information Systems*, 517–518.

Garramone, G. M., Harris, A. C., & Anderson, R. (1986). Uses of political computer bulletin boards. *Journal of Broadcasting and Electronic Media, 30*, 325–339.

Graetz, K., Boyle, E., Kimble, C., Thompson, P., & Garlock, J. (1998). Information sharing in face-to-face, teleconferencing, and electronic chat groups. *Small Group Research, 29*, 714–743.

Gurtner, A., Tschan, F., Semmer, N., & Nägele, C. (2007). Getting groups to develop good strategies: Effects of reflexivity interventions on team process, team performance, and shared mental models. *Organizational Behavior and Human Decision Processes, 102*, 127–142.

Henningsen, D., Henningsen, M., Eden, J., & Cruz, M. (2006). Examining the symptoms of groupthink and retrospective sensemaking. *Small Group Research, 37*, 36–63.

Hinsz, V., Tindale, R., & Vollrath, D. (1997). The emerging conceptualization of groups as information processors. *Psychological Bulletin, 121*, 43–64.

Huang, W., Wei, K., & Tan, B. (1999). Compensating effects of GSS on group performance. *Information and Management, 35*, 195–202.

Ijsselsteijn, W., van Baren, J., & van Lanen, F. (2003). Staying in touch: Social presence and connectedness through synchronous and asynchronous communication media. In J. Jacko & C. Stephanidis (Eds.), *Human-computer interaction: Theory and practice* (Part 2, Vol. 2, pp. 924–929). Mahwah, NJ: Lawrence Erlbaum.

Janis, I. L. (1972). *Victims of groupthink*. Boston, MA: Houghton Mifflin.

Facilitating Effective Mental Model Convergence • 567

Janis, I. L. (1982). *Groupthink* (2nd ed.). Boston, MA: Houghton Mifflin.

Jonassen, D. H., & Kwon, H., II. (2001). Communication patterns in computer mediated versus face-to-face group problem solving. *Educational Technology Research and Development, 49*, 35–51.

Kennedy, D., & McComb, S. (2010). Merging internal and external processes: Examining the mental model convergence process through team communication. *Theoretical Issues in Ergonomic Science, 11*, 339–356.

Kerr, D. S., & Murthy, U. S. (2004). Divergent and convergent idea generation in teams: A comparison of computer-mediated and face-to-face communication. *Group Decision and Negotiation, 13*, 381–399.

Klimoski, R., & Mohammed, S. (1994). Team mental model: Construct or metaphor? *Journal of Management, 20*, 403–437.

Kozlowski, S. W. J., & Klein, K. J. (2000). A multilevel approach to theory and research in organizations. In K. J. Klein & S. W. J. Kozlowski (Eds.), *Multilevel theory, research, and methods in organizations: Foundations, extensions, and new directions* (pp. 3–90). San Francisco, CA: Jossey-Bass.

Kraiger, K., & Wenzel, L. (1997). A framework for understanding and measuring shared mental models of team performance and team effectiveness. In E. Salas, M. Brannick, & C. Prince (Eds.), *Team performance assessment and measurement: Theory, methods, and applications* (pp. 63–84). Hillsdale, NJ: Lawrence Erlbaum.

Lim, B., & Klein, K. (2006). Team mental models and team performance: A field study of the effects of team mental model similarity and accuracy. *Journal of Organizational Behavior, 27*, 403–418.

Marks, M. A., Sabella, M. J., Burke, C. S., & Zaccaro, S. J. (2002). The impact of cross-training on team effectiveness. *Journal of Applied Psychology, 87*, 3–13.

Mathieu, J., Heffner, T., Goodwin, G., Cannon-Bowers, J., & Salas, E. (2005). Scaling the quality of teammates' mental models: Equifinality and normative comparisons. *Journal of Organizational Behavior, 26*, 37–56.

Mathieu, J., Heffner, T., Goodwin, G., Salas, E., & Cannon-Bowers, J. (2000). The influence of shared mental models on team process and performance. *Journal of Applied Psychology, 85*, 273–283.

McComb, S. (2007). Mental model convergence: The shift from being an individual to being a team member. In F. Dansereau & F. J. Yammarino (Eds.), *Multi-level issues in organizations and time* (pp. 95–147). Oxford, UK: Elsevier Science Ltd.

McComb, S. (2008). Shared mental models and their convergence. In M. P. Letsky, N. W. Warner, S. M. Fiore, & C. A. P. Smith (Eds.), *Macrocognition in teams: Theories and methodologies* (pp. 35–50). Aldershot, UK: Ashgate Publishing.

McComb, S., & Vozdolska, R. (2007, March). *Capturing the convergence of multiple mental models and their impact on team performance.* Paper presented at the meeting of the Southwest Academy of Management, San Diego, CA.

McGrath, J. E. (1984). *Groups: Interaction and performance.* Englewood Cliffs, NJ: Prentice-Hall, Inc.

Murthy, U. S., & Kerr, D. S. (2003). Decision making performance of interacting groups: An experimental investigation of the effects of task type and communication mode. *Information and Management, 40*, 351–360.

Newell, A., & Simon, H. (1972). *Human problem solving.* Englewood Cliffs, NJ: Prentice-Hall.

Paulus, P., & Yang, H. (2000). Idea generation in groups: A basis for creativity in organizations. *Organizational Behavior and Human Decision Processes, 82*, 76–87.

568 • *Theories of Team Cognition*

Poole, M. S. (1978). An information-task approach to organizational communication. *Academy of Management Review, 30,* 493–504.

Rice, R. E. (1984). *The new media.* Beverly Hills, CA: Sage Publications.

Rosen, M. A, Fiore, S. M., Salas, E., Letsky, M., & Warner, N. (2008). Tightly coupling cognition: Understanding how communication and awareness drive coordination in teams. *The International C2 Journal, 2,* 1–30.

Salas, E., Burke, S., & Samman, S. (2001). Understanding command and control teams operating in complex environments. *Information, Knowledge, and Systems Management, 2,* 311–323.

Schmidt, J., Montoya-Weiss, M., & Massey, A. (2001). New product development decision-making effectiveness: Comparing individuals, face-to-face teams, and virtual teams. *Decision Sciences, 32,* 1–26.

Schroder, H., Driver, M., & Streufert, S. (1967). *Human information processing.* New York, NY: Holt, Rinehart and Winston, Inc.

Setlock, L. D., Fussell, S. R., & Neuwirth, C. (2004). Taking it out of context: Collaborating within and across cultures via instant messaging. *Proceedings of the 2004 ACM Conference on Computer Supported Cooperative Work* (pp. 604–613). New York, NY: ACM.

Shannon, C., & Weaver, W. (1949). *The mathematical theory of communication.* Champaign, IL: University of Illinois Press.

Short, J. A., Williams, E., & Christie, B. (1976). *The social psychology of telecommunications.* London, UK: John Wiley and Sons, Ltd.

Smith-Jentsch, K. A., Mathieu, J. E., & Kraiger, K. (2005). Investigating linear and interactive effects of shared mental models on safety and efficiency in a field setting. *Journal of Applied Psychology, 90,* 523–535.

Sproull, L., & Kiesler, S. (1991). *Connections: New ways of working in the networked organization.* Cambridge, MA: MIT Press.

Thompson, L., Peterson, E., & Brodt, S. (1996). Team negotiation: An examination of integrative and distributed bargaining. *Journal of Personality and Social Psychology, 70,* 66–78.

Tu, C. (2000). On-line learning migration: From social learning theory to social presence theory in a CMC environment. *Journal of Network and Computer Applications, 23,* 27–37.

VanGundy, A. B. (1988). *Techniques of structured problem solving* (2nd ed.). New York, NY: Van Nostrand Reinhold.

Walton, R. E., & McKersie, R. B. (1965). *A behavioral theory of labor negotiation.* New York, NY: McGraw-Hill.

Wang., H., Fussell, S., & Setlock. L. (2009, April). *Cultural difference and adaptation of communication styles in computer-mediated group brainstorming.* Paper presented at CHI 2009, Boston, MA.

Warkentin, M., & Barenak, P. M. (1999). Training to improve virtual team communication. *Information Systems Journal, 9,* 271–289.

Warkentin, M., Sayeed, L., & Hightower, R. (1997). Virtual teams versus face-to-face teams: An exploratory study of a web-based conference system. *Decision Sciences, 28,* 975–996.

Wellman, B., Salaff, J., Dimitrova, D., Garton, L., Gulia, M., & Haythornthwaite, C. (1996). Computer networks as social networks: Collaborative work, telework, and virtual community. *Annual Review of Sociology, 22,* 213–238.

Section VI

The Road Ahead

23

Commentary on the Coordinates of Coordination and Collaboration[*]

John Elias and Stephen M. Fiore

The contributions comprising this volume address, directly or indirectly, the following basic questions: What makes a team a team, as opposed to just a group? What has to happen for an aggregate of individuals to truly cohere into a team? What are the conditions for this coherence to occur? Various answers to these questions may be posed, as well as various versions of these questions, depending on the particular context, situation, and disciplinary stance. Yet the singular term *team* still appropriately applies in and through these different approaches and contexts, and such apparent consistency of application would seem to indicate a certain consistency of meaning. Several general elements are indeed enumerable, including subordination of members to some common goal, clearly defined roles, and a certain set of prepared and expected actions. But it is the concept of *coordination* that captures many of these characteristics and seems to be at the crux of what we mean by *team*. Furthermore, the concepts of *coordination* and *collaboration*, in their contrast and continuity, serve to mutually illuminate one another, and together provide a means of elaborating and elucidating team process and performance.

In their earlier work, Fiore and Salas (2004) discussed this primacy of coordination in the team cognition literature. They noted that factors such as shared knowledge and member awareness are what lead to a synchronization of teamwork behaviors to enhance coordination. Essentially, team cognition can be conceptualized as the mechanism that "fuses the multiple

---

[*] The views and conclusions contained in this chapter are those of the authors and should not be interpreted as representing the official policies, either expressed or implied, of the Army Research Laboratory, the ONR, the U.S. Government, or the University of Central Florida. The U.S. Government is authorized to reproduce and distribute reprints for Government purposes notwithstanding any copyright notation herein.

572 • Theories of Team Cognition

inputs of a team into its own functional entity" (Fiore & Salas, 2004, p. 237). Metaphorically, they suggested that just as neural firings synchronize to produce conscious experience, cognitive and behavioral components must *bind* to produce coordinated teamwork. Fiore and Salas (2006) went further and argued for a more foundational understanding of *team coordination*, noting that it is sufficiently distinct from other concepts found in the team cognition literature (e.g., "collaboration" or "cooperation"). In particular, collaboration and cooperation simply mean to "work together," but coordination most cogently captures what we mean by effective teamwork. Specifically, the etymological origins of coordination suggest it was derived from three distinct concepts—"arrange," "order," and "together"—thus fitting with how teamwork is conceptualized in the literature. For example, Marks, Mathieu, and Zaccaro (2001) defined team coordination as "orchestrating the sequence and timing of interdependent actions" (p. 363). Following the call by Fiore and Salas (2006) for a deeper understanding of coordination, we elaborate on these ideas to provide more clarity to this foundational issue and demonstrate why coordination is truly at the core of team cognition.

What follows is an attempt to hew to the conceptual character of these terms, in a style akin to the philosophical method of *conceptual analysis*, in which concepts are analyzed, or broken down, into their component parts, in order to gain a more clear and precise sense of their meanings (e.g., Jackson, 1998). Although this approach perhaps smacks of "armchair" philosophizing, it may prove useful for the attainment of conceptual clarity, while also yielding an alternative conceptualization of processes normally described in psychological terms, again in the hope of further delineating and clarifying the concepts themselves. Yet concepts have psychological and behavioral implications, so the separation of the purely conceptual from the psychological will not be absolute but rather interpenetrative and porous. This discussion will then be positioned in relation to the other chapters, thereby adding something of a philosophical dimension to this already interdisciplinary volume.

COORDINATION AND COLLABORATION: CONCEPTUAL CONTINUITIES AND DISCONTINUITIES

The categories of *implicit* and *explicit, unspoken* and *spoken*, or, perhaps more problematically, *unconscious* (or *sub-* or *preconscious*) and *conscious* tend to crop up in attempts to account for the kinds of interactions characterizing fluidly functioning teams (e.g., Entin & Serfaty, 1999; Espinosa, Lerch, & Kraut, 2004). There are obvious reasons for this, ranging from the psychological nature of much of the research in question, to the need to capture processes that indeed seem quite distinct from what may be broadly described as deliberate and deliberative decision making. Yet the potentially vexing question of whether an action or decision occurs *consciously* or *unconsciously* can lead to confusion and distraction. As such, we set aside these psychological or quasi-psychological concerns and hold them constant in order to pursue a more intrinsically conceptual clarification of some of the constructs and processes in question, independently of what may seem to be happening psychologically.

Making sense of concepts *as concepts* is especially revealing with the relation between *coordination* and *collaboration*, which are at once intimately interconnected and yet significantly distinct. Beginning with an etymological investigation into a word's origins and meanings can help cue us to its resonances and relations, and aid in the preliminary clarification of a concept or set of concepts, to get to its core, by getting at its root. Furthermore, we may find multiple meanings running together, informing one another, as though a concept were actually a chord made up of many notes. To start with, then, because the concept of *coordination* is so central to team interactions, submitting it to etymological and conceptual inquiry might yield insight into its centrality.

Consideration of the various strands of meaning of *coordination*, as documented in the *Oxford English Dictionary* (OED, n.d.), reveals emphases on holism, equality of elements, and implications of automaticity and fluidity. According to the OED (n.d.), *coordination*, from *coordinate*, originated in parallel with its opposite, *subordinate*. That they originated together, as an opposition, indicates that the contrast may be key to both their meanings, that each is best understood by the contrasting light of the other. Against *subordinate*, the sense of *coordinate* as meaning "of the same order; equal in rank, degree, or importance (*with*); opposed to *subordinate*" (OED, n.d., italics in original) becomes strikingly clear. Insofar as *coordination* is intimately connected to team cognition, the fact that it entails equality, as opposed to a disparity therein, as in a notion like hierarchy, has implications for our understanding of position and distribution of authority in teams. So, according to the logic of this meaning, although a team may have a leader or authority figure, to

574 • *Theories of Team Cognition*

the extent that a team is coordinated, a quality of equality pervades the interaction.

More generally, though, this connotation is consonant with a common-sense conception of actual teams in action; for, in the process of performing a task, the flow of performance is preferably uninterrupted by explicit, deliberate commands. A quality of harmonious interaction, fluidity, and even automaticity is optimally at work, and any discrepancy in equality might disrupt this sense of fluid harmony, of parts interconnecting together into a coherent, working whole. The work of deliberate goal setting, explicit planning, and the like, although necessary, ought to occur prior, as a precondition, to actual optimal performance. Thus, we can see why expert teams regularly engage in preparatory behaviors (e.g., Fiore, Hoffman, & Salas, 2008; Marks, Mathieu, & Zaccaro, 2001) in service of actual interaction. And, indeed, the very idea of *coordination* implies this preliminary imposition of order, the positioning of elements in relation to each other, in order for the order to then be put to use. That is, coordination must first be coordinated: Orders are made, and order is sufficiently established, as preconditions for coordinated activity. However, once this preparatory phase is complete, and actual activity has begun, deliberate interjection by an authority, especially as perceived as *extrinsic* to the team, might impede performance by interfering with fluidity. We will further elaborate on this point in the following section, with our redescription of what has been called *explicit* versus *implicit* coordination in terms of the contrast and continuity between *collaboration* and *coordination*.

This dynamic is apparent at the individual level as well. Coordinated physical activity, whether athletic or more task oriented, is often and optimally carried out under conditions of minimal conscious consideration. For example, during the back and forth rhythm of a tennis rally or while driving a vehicle, explicit executive control (i.e., top-down authority) is usually unnecessary and, indeed, can be interfering and counterproductive, leading to less than optimal performance (e.g., Wang, Marchant, Morris, & Gibbs, 2004). Rather, a reflexive, immediate responsiveness comes into play, quickly, almost automatically adaptive, unhindered by the comparative slowness of conscious deliberation. So it seems that systems in general, individual and group, in the process of coordinated physical activity, operate according to this principle of holistic fluidity, free from the intervention of an authority unequal or external to the system and not at one with the coordination itself. Although, terms such as *conscious, explicit*, and *executive control* carry potentially confusing or distracting psychological associations, we will attempt in the next section to describe these dynamics conceptually in terms that do not rely on reference to what may or may not be happening psychologically.

This theme or thread of physical activity resonates with the physical imagery of *coordination*, indicating perhaps some metaphorical import to the concept. With regard to team cognition and coordination, we are, after all, referring to a blend of internal mental activity with external social activity, which can be seen, ultimately, as *physical* interactions between people. In addition, the various senses of *coordinate*, permeating through to its purely physical and mathematical meanings too, relate to its use in the human social sphere. For instance, the idea of a *coordinate plane*, the ordering and defining of values "by reference to a fixed system of lines, points, etc;" (OED, n.d.), that is, the unification of some realm of space by the order imposed by a coordinate system, mirrors the unity of team coordination, with members working together on a shared level, occupying an equal plane. Furthermore, the underlying physicality of the concept comes through in the sense of a *coordinate* bond in chemistry, as a shared union of electrons, and in the physiological meaning of *coordination* as "the simultaneous and orderly action of a number of muscles in the production of certain complex movements" (OED, n.d.). Again, the physicalism, the implication of automaticity, and, particularly, the ordering and positioning of parts into a whole echo in the description of *coordinated* social interaction.

In this light, the similarity and contrast between *coordination* and *collaboration* are especially revealing. Both are social, interpersonal processes involving people *working together* in some way. However, whereas *collaboration* implies a more open, independent sort of interaction, in which each individual maintains a significant degree of freedom and autonomy, *coordination* implies a more cohesive, tightly interrelated interaction, in which individuals are inextricably bound into the workings of some (optimally) harmonious whole, with the degrees of freedom limited to the particular parameters of the coordinated activity at hand. Indeed, collaboration connotes those very qualities—autonomy and deliberative freedom—that can be seen as comprising *personhood* or subjectivity. Additionally, the fact that *coordination* meaningfully applies to both *human* and *nonhuman* physical phenomena indicates perhaps the abdication of some degree of personhood, the relinquishment of autonomy, on the part of individuals as

576 • *Theories of Team Cognition*

they enter into coordinated activity, becoming parts of a whole as opposed to independent persons.

Collaboration, then, has a more volitional component, suggesting a willful cooperation among entities. This contrast can be seen by trying to apply the notion of *collaboration* to nonhuman entities, as in, for example, "the collaboration of muscles in complex motion." The readily apparent disjunction indicates its inappropriate application, whereas *coordination* can describe both human and nonhuman, or subject and nonsubject, interaction. This pertinence to both contexts carries the implications of determinism over from the nonhuman to the human, which leads back to the quality of automaticity in coordinated activity and its relationship to authority. "To coordinate" entities, human or not, implies the imposition of order upon them, even if the coordinating comes from inside the group or team itself. For, again, the preconditions for coordination, setting goals, making plans, and other explicit considerations, may be made by either a team leader/participant or the team as a whole, by *collaboration* and consensus. But once coordinated activity actually begins, deliberate consideration, the exercise of explicit executive functioning, is kept optimally to a minimum, with adjustments made as implicitly and rapidly as possible and not by the interjection of an authority. That is, during *coordination*, the locus of explicit authority lies prior to the process itself, as opposed to *collaboration*, which implies the active involvement of autonomous, authoritative decision making in the process itself. But this is not to say that team members, in the flow of coordinated activity, are somehow constricted or *unfree*; rather, within the constraints of the given task, they may *feel* freer and more immediately responsive than when having to consciously think things through. So, from a loosely psychological point of view, one might say that, within coordinated constraints, team members are *free* in the sense of an immediate, almost instinctive responsiveness to a given situation; that is, they are free from the inhibitions of consciousness, in its mode of explicit control. More conceptually, however, the continuum between collaboration and coordination may be broadly described in terms of the consideration of multiple possibilities, and the gradual establishment of a narrowed range of those possibilities, on the collaborative-deliberative end and the carrying out of the activity thereby defined within that constrained range on the coordinative end. Such a process, of course, may be much more complex than this simple linear picture suggests and may involve cyclical, bidirectional interactions between levels of collaborative and coordinative activity.

A concrete example may help ground the relationship between collaboration and coordination. Imagine a band of musicians composing and performing songs. The composition process is collaborative, with band members creating, exchanging, considering, and revising various ideas for songs. That is, they generate and deliberate on multiple possibilities, and insofar as the members are equally involved in the collaborative process, each is free to create and compare alternatives: Indeed, it may be said that the expression and consideration of such alternatives constitute the collaborative process itself. Thus, at the idealized extreme of the collaboration spectrum, we can picture the members as positioned outside the possibilities they propose: As uncommitted deliberative subjects, they are not yet subject to the constraints of some particular possibility or set of possibilities. In this opening state of indefiniteness, where a decision has yet to be determined, the musicians are at their most freely autonomous, with any number of alternative avenues available. Eventually this range of alternatives is narrowed, and they establish determinate parameters for some song or set of songs. At this stage, practicing and performing the composition becomes more properly a matter of coordination. With the ambit of possible options now winnowed down, the degrees of freedom are defined and limited by the established structure of the song, with the parts the members play interdependent in a determinate way.

We can quickly complicate this picture, however. For instance, revisions to the song are likely to occur during the initial practice sessions; thus the coordinated musical activity, as preliminarily established in the collaborative stage, feeds back onto and alters the very conditions that define and bring it about. So something of a blurred boundary between collaboration and coordination is already easily evident, with the relation being not merely linear but cyclical and interactive. In addition, portions of the song may be specifically designated for improvisation, a case where constraints optimally enable a certain degree of freedom; that is, improvisation is made possible, and *meaningful*, by the limitation of possibility imposed by the song. This dynamic is perhaps epitomized by the improvisatory ethos of jazz, where collaborative creation and coordinated performance become inextricably interlinked, with the performance the collaboration, the collaboration the performance. Classical music, by contrast, is generally highly regimented and coordinated, with the authority of the

578 • *Theories of Team Cognition*

conductor leading the orchestra in the performance (Hackman, 2002). We have pursued these musical lines of thought in order to sketch the spectrum between collaboration and coordination and to suggest potential complexities of interaction between constraint and freedom and preparation and performance. In the next section, we will recapitulate and further elaborate this account of collaboration and coordination, proposing it as a conceptual redescription of processes often described in terms of *explicit* and *implicit* coordination.

Reconfiguring Terminology: A Conceptual Redescription

Having conceptualized the continuum between collaboration and coordination in terms of the creation, consideration, and delimitation of possibilities, we will now redescribe the broadly psychological distinctions usually used to characterize these processes. Specifically, the terminology of *explicit* versus *implicit* coordination (e.g., Entin & Serfaty, 1999; Espinosa et al., 2004) may be redescribed, more conceptually and perhaps accurately, in terms of the collaborative deliberation on the eventual details of the coordination versus the actual coordinated activity itself; that is, as the coordination, or *pre*coordination, of coordination. For instance, Espinosa et al. (2004) describe explicit coordination as comprising "task programming" and "communication." The former category can be conceptualized as the collaborative or precoordinative processes of deliberation, consideration, planning, and so on. The latter category may be further analyzed as communication, or *language*, used to collaboratively speculate on or plan for the conditions of coordination, versus speech or language used as action, as part of the process and performance of coordinated activity itself, akin or on par with physical behavior. The former use of communication or language would count as part of *collaboration* (i.e., explicit coordination), whereas the latter would count as part of *coordination* (i.e., implicit coordination). Similarly, the category of *implicit* coordination can be redescribed as the actual coordinated activity itself.

Decision making specifically is also identified with explicit coordination, which further illustrates how we can reconceptualize explicit coordination as collaboration, that is, as deliberation on decisions concerning preparation for or execution of coordinated activity. Espinosa et al. (2004) include "consciously trying to coordinate" (p. 107) as part of the process of explicit coordination, which translates clearly into the collaborative,

Coordinates of Coordination and Collaboration • 579

deliberative process of *pre* or *fore* coordination, the planning and setting of the conditions for coordination proper. And insofar as *administrative coordination* is synonymous with *explicit coordination*, that category too is sensibly describable as the collaboration and deliberation on the preconditions for coordination. However, the question of what *implicit* means exactly is perhaps more problematic. Again, Espinosa et al. (2004) state that implicit coordination comprises "synchronization of member actions based on unspoken assumptions about what others in the group are likely to do" (p. 112), which once more may be redescribed in more purely conceptual terms, without direct reference to the psychological matter of explicit or implicit or spoken or unspoken. *Unspoken*, for instance, may be understood as *established*, as no longer up for debate, discussion, or consideration, and thus, effectively, no longer needing to be *spoken* of. *Synchronization* here can be seen to mean coordination proper and assumptions about what others are likely to do as the conditions under which the possible range of actions has been narrowed, thereby enabling more immediate responsiveness within those constraints (action being facilitated by the limitation of options; e.g., Lynch & Srull, 1982). Yet for truly dynamic coordination, some element of unpredictability, of indeterminacy, must be present as well, a theme to which we return later.

Relatedly, Faraj and Sproull (2000) speak of the importance and benefit to performance of locating expertise *within the team* as opposed to administrative imperatives imposed from without. This finding chimes with our etymological and conceptual analysis of coordination, in that the intrusion of an external authority or force understood as itself not being subject to the same constraints, the same narrowed range of conditions, creates problems with the coordinated system. For the equality inherent in the meaning of coordination, the sense of an equal plane or playing field is obviously disrupted by the entry of an entity not equally subject to the same set of conditions. Thus, conceptual and empirical support converges on the notion that intrinsic, coequal cohesion is more optimally aligned with coordinated performance than explicit administrative or managerial approaches.

Ultimately this discussion leads to the question of where exactly to draw the line between collaboration, the coordination of coordination, and the coordinated activity itself, or as Espinosa et al. (2004) put it, the question of "how explicit and implicit coordination mechanisms complement and interact with each other" (p. 108). The problem may be posed, in our

580 • *Theories of Team Cognition*

terms, as to how the conditions, the enabling constraints, of coordination may to some degree be revised in the process or the extent to which they may be amenable to revision at all. Perhaps the relationship can be seen as one of frameworks within frameworks, as a space within the space of conditions within which further conditions may be considered and created, such as plays planned during timeouts within the framework of the rules of the game of basketball. Additionally, the previously presented scenario of a band composing a song provides an example of the process of coordination, in the form of practicing a composed song, feeding back onto the process of the construction of the structure of the song itself. These considerations tend toward the view that standard input-process-output models of teamwork may be too linearly simplistic or at least not always appropriate, especially for complex and dynamic teams (e.g., Ilgen, Hollenbeck, Johnson, & Jundt, 2005).

To explore the relationship between collaboration and coordination, let us start with the simplest, most determinate manifestation of coordination, what may be called *co-ordered* activity. For instance, individuals may be coordinated insofar as they are each ordered to carry out a particular task or aspect of a task, yet are directed to do so by some initiating imperative or order and operate independently while doing so: Under such conditions, they are perhaps more *co-ordered* than coordinated and coordinating proper. In addition, mechanical tasks, such as an assembly line, can be seen as a *co-ordered* form of coordination, a directly rule-bound and rule-following activity effectively operating by the imperative "Do this!" as opposed to a more dynamic, flexible form of coordination, exemplified by games and perhaps musical performances (at least of certain kinds). Along these lines, coordination has been described as the "effective management of dependencies" (Espinosa et al., 2004, p. 109), as opposed to processes in which elements operate independently. That is, in coordination proper, elements have an effect on one another, varying in mutual dependence, as opposed to operating utterly independently. But with the concept of *management* of dependencies comes the question of who, or what, exactly is doing the managing. Perhaps the activity of coordination itself is in some sense performing this management by managing its own dependencies. Conceived as a multilevel process, the activity of coordination may be contemporaneous with the management or organization of its own dependencies. This view is in contrast to a traditional, nondynamic conception of explicit coordination, which depicts the process as one of task organization, basic scheduling, and the construction of direct orders and objectives that are then implemented and followed through on—that is, a process of preordering and *co-ordering*, rather than coordinated and coordinating. Again for more routine, automated, and *predictable* tasks and subtasks, such a specific, definite, rule-bound ordering of directives may be used; yet even at this seemingly basic level, the question of degree of resolution of rule following and formulation comes into play, problematizing the picture.

Moving from this basic level of co-ordered rigidity to considerations of the continuity between collaboration and coordination, factors proximal and distal to a particular coordination may begin to be explored. Using the terms of Espinosa et al. (2004) as a kind of counterpoint or foil, they include under explicit coordination "complex intellective tasks in which task dependencies are somewhat uncertain" (p. 108). Again, this category may be incorporated into the conception of collaboration detailed here, where *complex intellective tasks* may be understood as broadly involving the creation and consideration of multiple possibilities, and *uncertainty* may be understood as entailing fluid, as yet unset possibilities still under consideration. Espinosa et al. (2004) describe explicit coordination as also comprising "the early stages of a task, when team members are still unfamiliar with the task and with each other" (p. 108). These *early stages* may be seen as collaborative stages involving the creation and consideration of possible conditions for coordination, for some particular coordination to arise. Empirical support for these initial and initiating processes comes from Wholey, Kiesler, and Carley (1995), who found that communication occurs most intensely toward the beginning of the formation of a team, when overarching questions concerning goals and subgoals, the shape of the overall project, the relation of means and ends, and so on, are first formulated. These stages precisely map onto what we describe as the collaboration phases, as the consideration, deliberation, and determination of the conditions under which coordination proper, the actual activity to be coordinated, is to be conducted. Indeed, it was found that the more successful teams tended to taper their communication toward the end, indicating the narrowing down and determination of the conditions for coordination and the eventual entry into these conditions as the process progresses. Again, this comes down to the distinction between collaboration, that is, the deliberation and decision upon conditions for coordination, and the coordinated activity itself. The picture presented then would

582 • *Theories of Team Cognition*

be one of more or less linear progression from one to the other, as in theories of cognition moving from controlled to automatic processing (e.g., Shiffrin & Schneider, 1977), a general model in which, over time, *explicit* mechanisms are substituted by *implicit* ones in the movement from collaboration to coordination, from the creation, consideration, and deliberation of possible conditions for possible coordinations, to the determination and performance of the particular coordinated activity itself. Yet we must concede that, in many cases, something more than a simple linear model is needed, something like a dynamic model of multilevel, bidirectional interaction between these states or stages. These concerns once again bear on the question of the relation between collaboration and coordination (i.e., *explicit* and *implicit* coordination): Is it to be conceived as a simple linear trajectory, moving from collaboration to coordination proper, or as simultaneous interacting levels, or *frames within frames*? To help answer this question, we return to our conception of what constitutes *collaboration*: those processes, or aspects or stages of processes, during which possible conditions for possible coordinations are under question, up for consideration, and thus amenable to alteration and revision. Yet further inflection or refinement is required, as we now come to see that collaboration can occur within some already established coordinative frame and not merely as a prelude to it. The picture might be one of pockets of flexible collaborative activity packaged, so to speak, within fixed frameworks of coordination. In these frames within frames, nested like Russian dolls, space is made for some degree of freedom, some range of individual and collaborative agency, within the constraints of coordination. This notion of *enabling constraints*, a space of possibility at once *constrained* and *enabled by* a certain set of conditions, perhaps helps to account for more dynamic manifestations of coordinated activity. A basketball team not only operates within the rules of the game of basketball, but also within the plays set up by the coach; yet despite, or rather because of, these sets of constraints, the team is able to spontaneously improvise various maneuvers, with members making decisions that appear at one with, that inhere in, the very actions themselves. Obviously this is not a matter of mere rule following in the deterministic sense; rather it is a matter of what might be called *rule use*, in which the rules are being used in the service of creative and collaborative action.

A closer look at this example may illuminate and specify this notion of nested frames. The basketball team cannot ultimately call into question the basic rules of the game of basketball; the rules that fundamentally *constitute* and make up the game are not themselves up for consideration. If the players were to question, reconsider, and reconfigure these rules, they would no longer be playing basketball; they would be creating and playing what amounts to a different game, however similar to basketball it might be. These *constitutive rules* constitute the game (see Searle, 1969) and, by definition, define and frame the game. So insofar as the players want to play the actual game of basketball, they cannot question this constitutive, coordinative frame—the set of rules and conditions that constitutes and coordinates the game space of basketball. Within the overarching coordinative frame of the game, the coach and the players collaborate on different plays, creating and considering various alternatives, by questioning, deliberating, and revising them, and so on. Once a set of patterns and plays is in place, the team enters the game with the intent of implementing these coordinated arrangements. Although unlike the frame of the game itself, the conditions for these coordinations, as frames within the frame of the game, are up for question and consideration and hence amenable to alteration and revision. So if the status of a play changes in the course of the play or if a pattern needs to be altered or thrown out altogether, the team has space to do so, within the constraints of the immediate situation. Although this *space* obviously is not deliberative in the discursive sense, it may be conceived as *collaborative* within a very narrow range of possible actions, with the players rapidly signaling assent or dissent, agreement or disagreement, or preference for one possibility over another by means of *embodied* cues in the flow of the action itself. Thus, these frames within frames, these spaces created by virtue of being coordinated, allow for at least a certain degree of *conditional collaboration*, with the outmost coordinative frame (the rules of the game itself) conditioning and constituting the collaborative activity.

The mathematical sense of *coordinate*, as touched on briefly in our earlier etymological analysis, may help clarify this idea of coordinated space, of spaces of collaboration within coordinated constraints. The Cartesian coordinate plane is a chartable, navigable space precisely because a coordinate frame is in place. The coordinate frame itself is unquestioned and unquestionable, unless the aim is to change the nature of the space itself, for example, by introducing additional axes and dimensions. However, the *functions* plotted on the plane, the equations establishing relations between variables, may be questioned, changed, and manipulated

584 • *Theories of Team Cognition*

according to various purposes. So the plays of the basketball team can be seen as equations plotted onto the coordinate *game space* of basketball, positioning players at particular points and establishing specific relations between them. The *game space* refers literally to the basketball court, a physical space designed in and by the rules of the game, but it also refers to the space of possible actions constrained and enabled by the conditions and rules of the game. It is this *space of possibility* that defines and delineates the range of meaningful action that *makes* actions meaningful by their placement within its coordinates.

The central notion of *team cognition* may be viewed in relation to these considerations. The common underlying view is that of groups as information-processing units where individual-level information processing is used to understand group performance. Team cognition has been conceptualized as comprising interactions and dependencies between intraindividual-level processes and interindividual-level processes (Fiore & Salas, 2004, 2006). As illustrated in this volume, team cognition theories are cast in terms of the component knowledge of team members (i.e., shared knowledge structures). However, they also include the dynamic processes through which teams access and act on stored knowledge (e.g., when sharing information). A foundational construct is that shared mental models underlie expert teams' ability to coordinate their behaviors and anticipate each other's needs while adapting to task demands (e.g., Cannon-Bowers, Salas, & Converse, 1993; Marks, Zaccaro, & Mathieu, 2000; Salas & Fiore, 2004; Smith-Jentsch, Campbell, Milanovich, & Reynolds, 2001). Recent meta-analyses relate distinctions between compositional and compilational conceptualizations of knowledge within teams to process and performance outcomes (DeChurch & Mesmer-Magnus, 2010).

In their discussion of team cognition and coordination processes, Espinosa et al. (2004) define team cognition along the aforementioned lines, noting that it is "knowledge that team members share" (p. 107), that is, knowledge that is already there, to be relied on, as a condition for coordination. But they go further to add a process element to their conceptualization in that they identify *team cognition* as an aspect of what they term *implicit coordination*. In the terms offered here, this may be classified under coordination in its outermost limits. That is, team cognition, as an overarching framework, coordinates and organizes the activity of the team; in this sense, team cognition may be understood as shared knowledge that enables the team to *be on the same page*, to know where members stand in relation to each other within the context of the unfolding activity. Espinosa et al. (2004) also state that "explicit mechanisms both influence and are influenced by the existing level of team cognition" (p. 108), which again speaks to the multilevel, bidirectional interaction of collaborative and coordinative activities, although in this case, the outermost coordinative framework of knowledge must be conceived as provisional to some degree and amenable to question and revision. In this sense, *cognition* generally may be understood in terms of provisional overarching coordinative frames, as the very limits of knowledge, which nevertheless are still subject to addition, adjustment, and revision.

Team cognition also enables and facilitates team *social* cognition. That is, it provides a context for understanding, a set of constraints that endows behavior with meaning and purpose and with directedness and aim, and allows for anticipation precisely by narrowing the range of action. Hence, explanation and expectation, understanding and anticipation, go hand in hand; here a resonance with certain approaches to social cognition, specifically those of an embodied nature, may begin to come into view (e.g., Wilson & Knoblich, 2005). Furthermore, if team cognition is to be distilled or described as some sort of shared knowledge and commonality, then it may be seen as agreement, as constraint, establishing this with this, this as this, and so on. Again, this process may be understood as going all the way down to the normative constraints of language itself. Thus, team cognition may be seen as the commonality that grounds and enables the explanation of the behavior of others, in terms of understanding the overall task (game space or situation space), facilitating expectations (prediction enabled by narrowing of constraints), and the efficient communication of meaning (because of fundamental commonality, but also because of narrowed constraints allowing directedness and determination of action, endowing behavior with narrowly defined meaning and purpose). If the construct of *shared mental models* is incorporated into that of team cognition, then much may be accounted for in terms of the agreement and establishment of a narrowed range of possibilities, a set of enabling constraints.

Summary

So in seeking to delineate and delimit the distinction between collaboration and coordination, we come to see that they are often inextricably

586 • *Theories of Team Cognition*

interwoven and mutually dependent. Although the conceptual distinctions ought to be kept in mind, their relation and interrelation are significant as well. Thus, we find systems of frames within frames, which allow space for collaboration even within the constraints of coordination, in the sense of allowing for at least a certain degree of consideration and reconsideration of conditions and preconditions of coordinations (i.e., some room to collaborate and recalibrate the conditions of coordination). Therefore, our discussion seems to arrive at what might be called *collaborative coordination*, or *coordinated collaboration*. We opened by stating, broadly, that the concept of autonomy is included in, or more proximate to, the concept of collaboration as opposed to coordination. The crucial point, for instance, of subordination of the part to the whole seems to distinguish *coordination* from a concept like *collaboration*. The latter suggests an interaction among autonomous individuals, with a certain degree of independence between them. Indeed, the characteristic of *personhood* seems to inhere much more in the latter than in the former, hence entailing the idea of autonomy. Yet even in the most controlled and coordinated of scenarios, action is never completely and thoroughly deterministic, because when it comes to human agency, there is always an element of indeterminacy, irreducible and ineradicable. That is, our capacity for agency should not be conceived as a simple switch, flipped on or off depending on whether the scenario is collaborative or coordinative. Hence, the need exists to interrelate the concepts of collaboration and coordination, because the element of agency is never entirely removed and conditions and constraints are never totally absent.

The question of conceptual origin and analysis, then, is not a mere academic exercise. At the point of coinage, the original impulse of a word, its reason for being, is especially perceptible, and attending closely to the context and use of words, distinguishing appropriate and inappropriate applications, can refine and clarify concepts and meanings. Conceptual clarity is intrinsic to valid scientific investigation, because our questions come conceptualized and direct us toward the answers that we seek. Furthermore, we hope our contribution in this quasi-philosophical mode of conceptual analysis will contribute to the overall interdisciplinarity of this volume. Thus, in pursuit of clarity and interdisciplinary perspective, we turn now to a discussion of how this conceptualization relates to the theorizing others have offered within this volume.

COORDINATION AND COLLABORATION IN THEORIES OF SHARED COGNITION

Sharpening the Theoretical Clarity

Many of the chapters in this book, in some sense or another, seek to conceptualize and clarify the construct of team cognition. For instance, Kozlowski and Chao (Chapter 2, this volume) present a theoretical conception of the development and application of knowledge in teams. Their characterization of iterative, multilevel processes, in which a later stage of the process feeds back onto an earlier stage that originally brought it about, fits well with our model of collaborative and coordinative stages in dynamic, bidirectional interaction. This multilevel interaction is especially manifest in the relation, and at times tension, between individual and collective processes, which again may be seen in terms of autonomy and the abdication thereof in the movement between collaboration and coordination. Additionally, their emphasis on conceptual clarity speaks not only of a methodological similarity and sympathy with our contribution, but also of the need for such conceptual clarification in the shared cognition field at large. Santos et al. (Chapter 3, this volume) provide a computational model of decision making and comprehension of others' intentions in the high-pressured situation of combat casualty care. Our discussion of the constraints inherent in coordinative processes, the narrowed range of possible actions that define a particular situation, may illuminate the facilitation of rapid decision making under time-pressured conditions.

Mohammed, Tesler, and Hamilton (Chapter 4, this volume) discuss the integral role of time in team cognition and performance. Their exploration, which considers, among other things, the relation between temporality and nonlinear dynamics in team coordinative processes, converges toward the distinction drawn here between collaboration and coordination. As they state: "Indeed, coordination includes a temporal component that is not present in other types of team processes, such as communication and cooperation." This resonates with our characterization of coordination as entailing constraints to a degree that collaborative processes do not. Time here may be understood as a particular kind of *constraint*, a requirement or demand that some particular activity unfold according to definite temporal parameters.

588 • *Theories of Team Cognition*

Poole (Chapter 18, this volume) addresses the meanings of sharing and presents "co-orientation" as a multilevel concept that can be used as a metric for shared cognition, and its variation over time can be used to describe the state of shared cognition in a group at any point in time. This was used to capture the reflexive nature of shared cognition and link it to the formation of a team's collective identity. However, we can also see how co-orientation's reference to different levels of interpersonal perception and the mutual orientation team members have toward an object can help us understand collaboration and coordination. For example, consensus in co-orientation would certainly be foundational to coordination but differentially influence collaboration (e.g., in cases of pluralistic ignorance). Our attempt to address the relations and distinctions between collaboration and coordination, as stages and phases in an extended complex process, and their relation to the overarching construct of team cognition, may aid in this project of conceptual clarification.

Adding to Our Understanding of Process

Others in this volume have focused more on the impact of communication on processes of collaboration and coordination, issues again that we hope our commentary contributes toward. Murase, Resick, Jiménez, Sanz, and DeChurch (Chapter 5, this volume) present a framework connecting leadership functions to the emergence of collective cognition. They differentiate between different forms of leadership as they relate to the facilitation of collective cognition. As we describe in our contribution, the modulation of authority in relation to collaborative and coordinative processes is key to the transition and transformation between them. Again, how authority and leadership relate to both of these processes will determine whether they are facilitated or hindered. Indeed, we might say that an element of equality is necessary for both processes, although in different ways: In pure collaboration, members are equally free, as authorities unto themselves, to contribute to the creative and deliberative process, whereas in pure coordination, members equally abdicate their autonomy and authority upon entry into a defined and determinate activity.

Rentsch and Mot (Chapter 6, this volume) address the development and establishment of similar cognitive configurations when individuals work together. As they point out, such similarity may problematically result in a kind of rigidity, as "similar interpretations may become reified to the extent that people (and groups and organizations) forget that they, themselves, control their similar interpretations and, instead, become controlled by them." Our conception of how collaborative and coordinative processes may feed into and back onto one another may serve to illuminate and clarify this potential problem, by delineating the particular phases in which the conditions for some particular activity are open to question, under deliberation, and when those conditions are deemed established and settled and no longer up for consideration and debate. Ultimately, these phases must be treated as permeable and interpenetrative so as to avoid the inflexibility of unquestioned assumptions. Hinsz and Ladbury (Chapter 10, this volume) consider the sharing of cognitions in team performance. Such shared cognitions, or knowledge, may be understood in terms of the underlying conditions and preconditions necessary for some particular team activity to occur. Because agreement on, and thus knowledge of, these conditions is itself a necessary requirement for entry into the coordinative activity in question, our discussion may help to position shared cognition in terms of the function it serves in the context of coordinative processes; that is, shared cognition functions as a condition for coordination.

Stahl and Rosé (Chapter 21, this volume) consider insights from group cognition in light of computer-supported collaborative learning, with a focus on identifying the conditions under which moments of inspiration are triggered and with the goal of facilitating group innovation and collaborative knowledge creation. Our distinction between collaboration and coordination may aid in determining which stages require which type of technology in facilitating either collaborative or coordinative processes and also whether the communication in question is collaborative or coordinative in nature. Carroll, Borge, Ganoe, and Rosson (Chapter 9, this volume) focus specifically on collaborative processes in complex and creative tasks, particularly those of a unique, one-of-a-kind nature. Again, our discussion of the flexibility and autonomy inherent in *collaboration*, in contrast to *coordination*, may help illuminate the processes involved in creative problem solving. What requires further elaboration are the precise means by which the process of considering possibilities occurs and how possibilities under consideration are eventually narrowed and formed into specific solutions and actions. Ladbury and Hinsz (Chapter 15, this volume) provide an important addition to shared cognition by articulating the role of team member expectations on interaction

590 • *Theories of Team Cognition*

outcomes. In line with our theorizing on coordination processes unfolding dynamically within teamwork, they show how expectations allow teams to coordinate without a need for explicit communication. They add to theorizing on shared cognition by also providing a means of quantification to uncover positive and negative patterns of interaction arising from expectations.

Clarifying Translations of Theory Into Practice

Other contributions attempt to extend theoretical insights into more practical applications. Patterson and Stephens (Chapter 7, this volume) outline five macrocognitive functions: *detecting, sensemaking, planning, deciding, and coordinating*. These unfolding functions clearly parallel our description of the trajectory from collaboration to coordination. The authors proceed to concentrate on the coordinating function specifically, elaborating this phase with theoretical and empirical observations. Our conceptualization of these macrocognitive functions in terms the continuum and interaction between collaboration and coordination may serve as a conceptual supplement and alternative to the theoretical terminology currently prevalent in the shared cognition literature.

Cooke, Gorman, Myers, and Duran (Chapter 8, this volume) point to the central characteristics of interaction and interdependency in differentiating between groups and *teams* proper. In delineating the complex and various manifestations of coordination, we distinguish between so-called *co-ordered* activities and truly *coordinative* activities: The quality of equality and interactivity within a set of shared conditions and constraints can indeed be seen as the key distinguishing factor. Furthermore, the authors differentiate *shared cognition* from *interactive team cognition*, proposing the latter as a more accurate theoretical description of dynamic team activity. Here we can see how our description of coordination as inextricably involving a quality of holism, and hence a certain equality of elements, may relate to this chapter's discussion. Lyons et al. (Chapter 11, this volume) provide an analysis of macrocognition in teams and the ways in which task complexity alter macrocognitive processes. As they describe, macrocognition in teams very much involves a collaborative activity. Its deliberative nature, the planning process, and the creation of knowledge all require a less constrained sphere of operation where member inputs are freely given and taken in service of problem solving. As such, we would expect to see less of a process of coordination as we have conceptualized in this commentary. However, just as task complexity may alter macrocognitive processes such as knowledge building, we similarly suggest that the act of collaboration may also change under the varied conditions they describe.

Espinosa and Clark's (Chapter 12, this volume) characterization of knowledge structured within and across units within a team may similarly benefit from our distinctions. Knowledge of team members, knowledge about a task, and knowledge about how to execute an action will all differentially contribute to coordination and/or have a role in collaboration as we have conceptualized it. Thus, knowledge representations, and the dimensions thereof, could be characterized along the lines of their differing roles in collaboration versus coordination. This, in turn, may suggest alternative or additional means of measuring these varied forms of knowledge or times when they should be measured in the context of a team's work.

Sukthankar, Shumaker, and Lewis (Chapter 13, this volume) describe the rich body of research on cognitive agents and how they do and could act as teammates. In their role of supporting humans, we can see how coordination would come more into the equation in that there is a subordination of responsibility and a limitation of action. However, when conceptualizing agents as teammates, the question becomes the following: What role can they play in collaboration? For example, in the deliberative acts of decision making, planning, and so on, what degree of autonomy will be necessary for agents to freely interact with their human teammates and contribute to the collaborative activity? McNeese and Pfaff (Chapter 14, this volume), in their analysis of shared cognitive approaches, present a comprehensive view of team-related simulations to integrate macrocognitive concepts from various domains. Their review of the Living Laboratory as a research paradigm illustrates the sophisticated ways in which team cognition has been studied. Our conceptual distinctions and interrelations may add to the development of such laboratories by more clearly specifying, for example, how information representation alters collaboration versus coordination or how variations in task complexity change the characteristics of, or trajectory toward, coordination within teams. We hope our conceptual distinctions and interrelations add to the clarification of the practical applications of these varied theoretical concepts.

592 • *Theories of Team Cognition*

Augmenting the Cross-Disciplinarity

Still other chapters take an explicitly and self-reflectively cross-disciplinary approach in addressing the ways in which key constructs are conceptualized. Koschmann, Dunnington, and Kim (Chapter 16, this volume) offer a hybrid approach to studying teams that acknowledges the tradition of psychological research in the field but embraces the academic inheritance of methods from other disciplines. Their discussion of ethnomethodology presents an intriguing way to delve deeper into the core of coordination, helping to uncover degrees of freedom experienced when teams interact freely or within more constrained structural bounds. Furthermore, their description of the choreography of the "tool pass" illustrates nicely our points about the influence of regulation on teamwork and how rules tightly bound the coordinated activity.

Hollingshead, Gupta, Yoon, and Brandon (Chapter 17, this volume) review transactive memory theory, providing a theoretical integration of this important contribution to the shared cognition literature. Our differentiation between collaboration and coordination could be better specified through an articulation of the how transactive memory systems may differentially contribute to collaboration versus coordination. For example, on the one hand, knowledge of expertise distribution may be relied on more explicitly during certain collaboration processes such as planning or decision making. But, on the other hand, in actual execution, reliance on transactive memory fades more to the background, as the essentially automated coordination of teamwork, while still relying upon, may no longer explicitly draw from such a system.

Beck and Keyton (Chapter 19, this volume) use examples from jury conversations to illustrate how macrocognition is communicatively based and can be tracked in team members' message interdependence. Viewing the *message* as the cognitive act provides a methodological lens through which to understand the mutual unfolding of coordination and collaboration. The content of the communications, in general, and their interdependencies, in particular, may illuminate the degree to which we see the more freely interactive form of collaboration or the more regulated aspects of coordination. Musaeus (Chapter 20, this volume) argues that societal institutions validate and shape knowledge, goals, tools, and ideas relevant for high-reliability team problem solving and that these indicators are evident in team checks-and-balances systems. These influenced processes, or cultural tool kits, show how factors outside the team can bound the sphere of interaction and knowledge production within a team. As such, his suggestion that reason derives from institutions and society provides an interesting sociocultural angle to our distinctions between collaboration and coordination.

McComb and Kennedy (Chapter 22, this volume) postulate that the media over which communication is carried out are capable of limiting the amount and flow of information transmission among team members. What is important to understand is how mental model convergence and the process of sharing information occur differently under conditions of coordination versus collaboration. Teams must clearly have some level of convergence to achieve the form of coordination as we have explained it. But does that mean that convergence is a property of only coordination? Is there not convergence, then, during or from collaboration? It seems unlikely for this to be the case, so the question then becomes as follows: What is the degree of convergence necessary for coordination to occur? And, similarly, how does collaboration, in and of itself, lead to, sharpen, or stifle convergence? From these comments, we hope our contribution in the mode of philosophical conceptual analysis will assist in the increasingly interdisciplinary nature of much of what can be included under the rubric of the cognitive sciences.

CONCLUSION

In sum, our goal with this commentary was to add to the contributions comprising this volume. Each contributor addressed, in some way, the basic question of what makes a team a team. In their analyses of aggregations, communication, process, and performance, they illuminated how some form of coherence arises from a team's work. By specifying the processes of subordination of members to some common goal, the contribution of clearly defined roles, and the importance of prepared and expected actions, we articulated how and why coordination occurs and its difference from collaboration. We hope that our more conceptual analysis of the contrast and continuity of *coordination* and *collaboration* helped to shed further light on these theories of team cognition to help us more fully elaborate and elucidate team process and performance.

594 • *Theories of Team Cognition*

ACKNOWLEDGMENTS

The writing of this chapter was partially supported by the Army Research Laboratory and was accomplished under Cooperative Agreement No. W911NF-10-2-0016. We were also supported by the Office of Naval Research (ONR) Collaboration and Knowledge Interoperability Program and ONR Multidisciplinary University Initiative Grant No. N000140610446. We would also like to thank Patricia Bockelman Morrow for editorial assistance.

REFERENCES

Cannon-Bowers, J. A., Salas, E., & Converse, S. A. (1993). Shared mental models in expert team decision-making. In N. J. Castellan, Jr. (Ed.), *Individual and group decision making* (pp. 221–246). Hillsdale, NJ: Lawrence Erlbaum.

DeChurch, L. A., & Mesmer-Magnus, J. R. (2010). The cognitive underpinnings of team effectiveness: A meta-analysis. *Journal of Applied Psychology, 95,* 32–53.

Entin, E. E., & Serfaty, D. (1999). Adaptive team coordination. *Human Factors: The Journal of the Human Factors and Ergonomics Society, 41,* 312–325.

Espinosa, J. A., Lerch, F. J., & Kraut, R. E. (2004). Explicit versus implicit coordination mechanisms and task dependencies: One size does not fit all. In E. Salas & S. M. Fiore (Eds.), *Team cognition: Understanding the factors that drive process and performance* (pp. 106–132). Washington, DC: American Psychological Association.

Faraj, S., & Sproull, L. (2000). Coordinating expertise in software development teams. *Management Science, 46,* 1554–1568.

Fiore, S. M., Hoffman, R. R., & Salas, E. (2008). Learning and performance across disciplines: An epilogue for moving multidisciplinary research towards an interdisciplinary science of expertise. *Military Psychology, 20,* S155–S170.

Fiore, S. M., & Salas, E. (2004). Why we need team cognition. In E. Salas & S. M. Fiore (Eds.), *Team cognition: Understanding the factors that drive process and performance* (pp. 235–248). Washington, DC: American Psychological Association.

Fiore, S. M., & Salas, E. (2006). Team cognition and expert teams: Developing insights from cross-disciplinary analysis of exceptional teams. *International Journal of Sports and Exercise Psychology, 4,* 369–375.

Hackman, J. R. (2002). *Leading teams: Setting the stage for great performances.* Boston, MA: Harvard Business School Press.

Ilgen, D. R., Hollenbeck, J. R., Johnson, M., & Jundt, D. (2005). Teams in organizations: From input-process-output models to IMOI models. *Annual Review of Psychology, 56,* 517–543.

Jackson, F. (1998). *From metaphysics to ethics: A defence of conceptual analysis.* New York, NY: Oxford University Press.

Lynch, J. G., Jr., & Srull, T. K. (1982). Memory and attentional factors in consumer choice: Concepts and research methods. *The Journal of Consumer Research, 9,* 18–37.

Marks, M. A., Mathieu, J. E., & Zaccaro, S. J. (2001). A temporally based framework and taxonomy of team processes. *Academy of Management Review, 26,* 356–376.

Marks, M. A., Zaccaro, S. J., & Mathieu, J. E. (2000). Performance implications of leader briefings and team-interaction training for team adaptation to novel environments. *Journal of Applied Psychology, 85,* 971–986.

Oxford English Dictionary. (n.d.). Oxford English Dictionary Online. Retrieved May 4, 2011, from http://www.oed.com

Salas, E., & Fiore, S. M. (Eds.). (2004). *Team cognition: Understanding the factors that drive process and performance.* Washington, DC: American Psychological Association.

Searle, J. (1969). *Speech acts: An essay in the philosophy of language.* Cambridge, UK: Cambridge University Press.

Shiffrin, R. M., & Schneider, W. (1977). Controlled and automatic human information processing: II. Perceptual learning, automatic attending and a general theory. *Psychological Review, 84*(2), 127–190.

Smith-Jentsch, K. A., Campbell, G. E., Milanovich, D. M., & Reynolds, A. M. (2001). Measuring teamwork mental models to support training needs assessment, development and evaluation: Two empirical studies. *Journal of Organizational Behavior, 22,* 179–194.

Wang, J., Marchant, D., Morris, T., & Gibbs, P. (2004). Self-consciousness and trait anxiety as predictors of choking in sport. *Journal of Science and Medicine in Sport, 7,* 174–185.

Wholey, R., Kiesler, S., & Carley, K. (1995). *Learning teamwork: Emergence of communication and structure in novice software development teams* (working paper). Pittsburgh, PA: Carnegie Mellon University.

Wilson, M., & Knoblich, G. (2005). The case for motor involvement in perceiving conspecifics. *Psychological Bulletin, 131,* 460–473.

24

Some More Reflections on Team Cognition

Olivia C. Riches and Eduardo Salas

There is understandably a great interest in team cognition, and this trend does not appear to be ending any time soon. The science of teams would be incomplete without first considering and understanding team cognition. Appreciating its significance and influence on a variety of domains has resulted in both the expansion and improvement of the field. The field is amassed with literature that is relevant to all disciplines that have a shared interest in team cognition. The difficulty lies in uncovering an effective medium by which these ideas can be shared across disciplinary domains. Experts from a range of disciplines are recognizing the need to merge their array of contributions from their respective fields. This is an important step for team cognition because the disciplines' research questions are beginning to intersect and can work to complement one another. As such, continuing to move forward as individual disciplines would only hinder effective progress in the field.

In 2001, Cannon-Bowers and Salas reflected on the construct of shared cognition and postulated several fundamental questions that needed attention in order to progress the field as a whole. Some of these questions will be discussed further throughout this chapter. Although the field has made notable strides in addressing these questions, the quest for continued clarification and investigation is far from over. Additionally, the increase in the knowledge base of the field of team cognition presents even more questions that require empirical and theoretical efforts. As the field progresses forward, it is in its best interest to acknowledge the need to integrate knowledge of team cognition and unite the myriad of ideas that permeate the field. This volume illustrates that developing a multidisciplinary alliance is a necessary step that is fortunately becoming a reality.

598 • *Theories of Team Cognition*

This volume compiles and organizes a number of perspectives on team cognition from a variety of disciplines. A primary purpose of this work is to disseminate the knowledge that exists yet that remains unshared among experts in the field. As evidenced by the preceding chapters, there continues to be tremendous progress in the team cognition literature. Nevertheless, there is a need to expand the field's current knowledge base and further the cross-disciplinary trend set forth by this volume. The purpose of this chapter is to reflect on the different topics in this volume that are representative of the science of team cognition. First, we extract some themes that have surfaced throughout the book. Our reflections on each of the themes are then presented in the hopes that they will spark further discussion in the field. The themes provide the reader with overarching insights into the directions and progress of team cognition as it stands today. We additionally highlight those areas that are in need of further exploration.

EMERGING THEMES

Team Cognition Cuts Across Disciplines...

Team cognition is a complex construct whose research both advances and informs a variety of domains that have a shared interest in team dynamics. Throughout this volume, many diverse perspectives are presented by authors of numerous disciplines, including cognitive and social sciences, engineering, military science, organizational science, human factors, medicine, and communications. Input from these domains strengthens the position of the field because their contributions offer unique insights that are critical to the efficacy of teams that exist in a variety of settings. For example, the medical field more fully understands how the frequent transfers of information and the constant need to coordinate effectively in medicine influence patient safety (Santos et al., Chapter 3, this volume). Additionally, the field's knowledge regarding the nature of and similarities between team cognition in human teams and agents is now more comprehensive (Sukthankar, Shumaker, & Lewis, Chapter 13, this volume). The array of contributions enhances the field's understanding of team cognition and offers valuable insight into new ways that team processes can be improved.

The purpose of this volume is to provide a medium for research on team cognition to permeate the field. This implicit contribution is perhaps the most essential. Team cognition is a young field, and experts on the subject are uncovering a way for their efforts to be shared and made easily available to other members of the field. Yes, team cognition cuts across disciplines because contributions from one discipline can be just as applicable to another. Unfortunately, the connecting road that allows one discipline to reach another is choppy. In other words, the relationships and connections among the cross-disciplinary ideas that circulate the field are by no means clear-cut. Ironically enough, it can be argued that the shared mental models and transactive memory systems of the field are not fully developed.

Team cognition is a complex and dynamic construct that influences many aspects of a team's combined knowledge, skills, and abilities. As such, continuing to expand into other domains and grow as a field is inevitable and offers the potential for more exciting progress in the field. To do so, a reconciliation of the language used to describe team cognition is sorely needed. The jargon that holds value for each individual discipline is no longer appropriate when dealing with a pervasive topic of this magnitude. Input from a number of domains on the construct of team cognition has led to rich and abundant discussion in this volume; however, a common language is needed to help organize and guide this ever-expanding field. Koschmann, Dunnington, and Kim (Chapter 16, this volume) address this issue of the necessity of a vocabulary that is implemented across disciplines. A more unified language that is decipherable by scholars across disciplines will assist in the development of better conceptualizations of team cognition, while at the same time enhancing collaboration among the domains that comprise the field.

Conceptualization of Team Cognition Remains Fuzzy ...

Cannon-Bowers and Salas (2001) recognized the critical problem that the term team cognition was being used inconsistently. Throughout this volume, it becomes apparent that this problem continues to persist, and its presence is a barrier for effective progress and dissemination of findings in the field. For example, team cognition is just one term used throughout the chapters of this volume. Other terms such as group cognition (Stahl & Rosé, Chapter 21, this volume), interactive team cognition

600 • *Theories of Team Cognition*

(Cooke, Gorman, Myers, & Duran, Chapter 8, this volume), and mental model convergence (McComb & Kennedy, Chapter 22, this volume) are also used. The differences among the various forms of team cognition (e.g., transactive memory systems, shared mental models, macrocognition) are well defined and understood; however, there is a great deal of overlap among different conceptualizations of the overarching construct of team cognition. Before moving onward, as a field, there is a need to improve the collective understanding of team cognition.

Kozlowski and Chao (Chapter 2, this volume) address the lack of conceptual clarity that characterizes the field of team cognition, and they note that the issue of inconsistent conceptualization derives in part from the lack of specificity when operationalizing the construct. They suggest that built into the different conceptualizations of team cognition is the notion that it is understood as both a process and an outcome (Kozlowski & Chao, Chapter 2, this volume). As a process, Cooke et al. (Chapter 8, this volume) define team cognition as the cognitive activities (i.e., planning, decision making, designing, assessing situations, and solving problems) that teams engage in. As an outcome, Beck and Keyton (Chapter 19, this volume) define team cognition as a collective understanding of a concept that stems from the interactions within a group. These are but two presentations of the term, and they serve to illustrate the need to be prudent when clarifying the construct's use and investigation.

When discussing the complicated area of team cognition, scholars should be cognizant of their definitions of the construct. Kozlowski and Chao (Chapter 2, this volume) provide the field with a simple way to solve this dilemma by distinguishing between team learning and team knowledge, suggesting that both are defining components of team cognition; however, learning is the process component of team cognition, whereas knowledge is the outcome component. These guidelines may help to facilitate the discussion of team cognition across and within disciplines. Espinosa and Clark (Chapter 12, this volume) also address difficulties that arise from the different perspectives on team knowledge and argue for the adoption of a multidirectional perspective as a way to elucidate the current understanding of team cognition. Importantly, this perspective acknowledges the influence of sharedness (individual versus shared), domain (taskwork versus teamwork), durability (long lasting versus fleeting), and type (content versus structure). So, although the field is getting better at defining team cognition, some fuzziness remains.

Measuring Team Cognition Is Still a Challenge ...

Although measuring team cognition is still a challenge, progress has been made. Honing the conceptualization of team cognition and implementing it consistently can, of course, provide improvements in how team cognition is assessed, captured, and measured. For example, Kozlowski and Chao (Chapter 2, this volume) discuss complications concerning accurately measuring team cognition because of its complex nature and status as both a process and outcome of team interactions. Rentsch and Mot (Chapter 6, this volume) additionally provide information related to the difficulties that arise when assessing perceptual and structured cognition. They note that both have an entwined influence on team cognition, and this continues to present challenges to research efforts aimed at measuring their combined effects on team inputs, processes, and outcomes (Rentsch & Mot, Chapter 6, this volume).

This volume contributes several methodological advancements that provide valuable insight into how to measure team cognition. For example, Espinosa and Clark (Chapter 12, this volume) suggest a method that accounts for both the content and structure of team knowledge. Using a social network analysis approach, their methodology allows knowledge distributions to be analyzed at levels ranging from individual to team (Espinosa & Clark, Chapter 12, this volume). Kozlowski and Chao (Chapter 2, this volume) also contribute to this discussion by offering some basic guidelines that should be followed when investigating team cognition between or within teams, as well as when using simulations and modeling techniques.

In addition to these authors, a number of other chapters in this volume also suggest that the question posited by Cannon-Bowers and Salas (2001) concerning how shared cognition should be measured has not been ignored. These chapters have correspondingly made the need to continue expanding the field's repertoire of scientifically sound methodologies all the more salient. Measuring team cognition presents complications surrounding the conceptualizations and operationalizations used by researchers. As such, continued and careful consideration of these components should be taken seriously by scholars in the field. More rigorous, robust, reliable, valid, and precise metrics, methodologies, and assessments to capture team cognition are, indeed, the next frontier.

602 • *Theories of Team Cognition*

The Focus on Communication Is a Promising Approach but Is a Big Bucket...

There is no doubt that communication is an inherent process of team cognition. Because communication represents one of the most readily available avenues by which to examine team processes, understanding how it contributes to and describes team cognition is key. Communication is inherent to coordination and interaction within a team, and it serves as a means for the team to regulate its behaviors and activities. The role of communication in a team is that of a conducer of information sharing and knowledge building, and as such, it enhances investigative efforts aimed at exploring cognitive processes (McComb & Kennedy, Chapter 21, this volume).

Several chapters focus on communication and illustrate its status as a promising approach for understanding team cognition. Communication can be used to improve team cognition; for example, Poole (Chapter 18, this volume) explores how feedback and closed-loop communication can enhance co-orientation within a team. Knowing the types of communication that occur in effective teams additionally allows researchers to identify types of communication that are more counterproductive to team effectiveness. Furthermore, communication analysis provides insight into the cognitive processes that teams are engaged in. For example, Stahl and Rosé (Chapter 21, this volume) describe a linguistic-level lens, which is an approach that enables one to analyze the syntax, semantics, and pragmatics of a team's communication in order to gain better insight into the cognitive processes and outcomes that unfold. Beck and Keyton (Chapter 19, this volume) also support the exploitation of communication and describe how message interdependence is evidence that team cognition is present within a team.

As noted, communication is a powerful indicator of team cognition. Over the years, researchers have used it because it is readily capturable in teams via verbal, nonverbal, and electronic forms. The interest in team cognition extends to a number of domains, and this necessitates that the field continue efforts aimed at understanding how communication is manifested in different contexts, how it can be measured and analyzed within these different contexts, and how it can improve team cognition in different contexts. Hollingshead, Gupta, Yoon, and Brandon (Chapter 17, this volume), for instance, found that teams with limited nonverbal cues available to members are hindered because they seek out less task-related information and clarify answers less frequently than members in face-to-face teams. In addition to continuing to explore these questions, another promising avenue for the field to pursue is finding ways to enhance data collection efforts and the quality of data gathered from investigations of team communication. McComb and Kennedy (Chapter 21, this volume) illustrate such improvements with their finding that communication content and processes should be relevant to both the task at hand and the manner of exchange. However, communication indicators are a "big bucket," and methodologies used to digest this bucket must continue to evolve and mature. It seems that what matters is not the frequency of communication, but the pattern that surfaces over time. So, again, a more precise way of diagnosing what the bucket reveals to the field is needed.

Contextual Considerations Continue to Apply ...

There is no doubt that context plays an important role in team cognition. This is evidenced by the abundance of literature that touches on topics surrounding the roles played by a leader, the type of task, and the type of team. Murase, Resick, Jiménez, Sanz, and DeChurch (Chapter 5, this volume) present several propositions around the concept of leadership and team cognition, all of which suggest that leader influences are important contextual considerations for the field. Additionally, different types of team cognition emerge in different environments and teams, thereby making the type of task used in research efforts an important factor to consider. Macrocognition, for example, occurs in environments that are characterized as dynamic and requiring activities such as complex problem solving (McNeese & Pfaff, Chapter 14, this volume). In their discussion of combinations-of-contributions theory, Hinsz and Ladbury (Chapter 10, this volume) further reinforce the importance of context's influence on team cognition by examining the many ways that it determines how relevant team member inputs are to the team's effectiveness.

Exploring contextual variables exposes valuable insights into their impact on team cognition. Moreover, the understanding of context is taken to deeper levels by exploring more specific ways that it can impact team processes. Returning to the topic of leadership, an example of this would be the finding that the particular approach taken by the leader heavily influences team cognition (Murase et al., Chapter 5, this volume).

604 • *Theories of Team Cognition*

Another contextual variable that is receiving more attention within the field is time. Mohammed, Hoult, and Hamilton (Chapter 4, this volume) discuss important applications of team cognition research concerning the concept of time and assert that longitudinal studies may hold valuable insights into the influence of time on team cognition.

In reflecting on such contributions, it is apparent that more exploration is needed. This volume highlights a number of contextual variables that influence team cognition. Examining different relationships that exist between various contexts and how one aspect of a team's context influences another are particular avenues in need of further understanding. McComb and Kennedy (Chapter 22, this volume) illustrate such efforts in their exploration of the interplay between a team's task and communication. Other authors address the need to explore these relationships as well. For example, Hinsz and Ladbury (Chapter 10, this volume) urge the field to become more aware of and flexible toward changes that occur in a team's context and how they are associated with individual members' contributions. Continuing to expand on and deepen the field's knowledge base of contextual considerations will allow for more diverse applications of findings in team cognition. The issues of how, when, and why context matters need more exploration.

Progress Is Exposing Gaps in Current Theory ...

Several significant relationships and moderating factors have been disseminated throughout the pages of this book. Cooke et al. (Chapter 8, this volume) describe how it is the processes of the team, not their knowledge bases, that better predict the team's ability to maintain its skills. Koschmann et al. (Chapter 16, this volume) discuss the nature of individuals' conceptualizations of their social situations and the role of accountability in their social interactions. Murase et al. (Chapter 5, this volume) discuss the nature of emergence and the role it plays in both team mental model and transactive memory research. These are only a few of the valuable insights this volume addresses. In turn, these insights expose copious gaps throughout the team cognition literature that are deserving of the field's attention.

As progress is made in science, new developments subsequently spark even more questions that request the attention of team cognition scholars. Poole (Chapter 18, this volume), for example, addresses the gap that exists in the literature on the impact that a team's identity has on outcomes such as their performance and effectiveness. Similar efforts that recognize and devote attention to such gaps in the literature on team cognition provide direction and guidance to the field. Additionally, attending to such gaps raises awareness about aspects of team cognition that offer new opportunities to apply findings to a variety of teams. For example, uncovering ways that teams can be more proactive in managing and monitoring their own team cognition is an area of the field that is lacking in research, yet deserving of further exploration. Hollingshead et al. (Chapter 17, this volume) discuss the value of research efforts that aim to examine the error-correction process in teams. For instance, how might teams self-correct aspects of their own team cognition (e.g., transactive memory) when they become counterproductive to effective performance?

It is apparent that the field of team cognition is reaching new heights when it comes to uncovering applications of this research. McComb and Kennedy (Chapter 22, this volume), for instance, discuss how the convergence of mental models can be enhanced through the use of a holistic approach to information exchange. Additionally, it is possible for teams to obtain the necessary competencies needed for them to become more aware of their cognition (Carroll, Borge, Ganoe, & Rosson, Chapter 9, this volume). Developments such as these have shed a new light on the field's understanding of team cognition, yet they also open the door to many questions that remain unanswered. Turning attention to such questions has great implications for the field of team cognition. There is more to explore, and this is good news for both science and practice.

CONCLUSION

This chapter has reflected on the work presented in this volume and, in doing so, has identified several themes that have emerged throughout the pages. It is clear that teams matter in organizations and in society at large. This alone strengthens the need to acquire a more comprehensive understanding of both their nature and potential. Because team cognition is understood as both a process and an outcome, its implications are all the more valuable to those sharing an interest in teams. This volume exposes a number of insights that are applicable to teams existing in a variety of

606 • *Theories of Team Cognition*

contexts and domains. Knowledge related to team cognition impacts many different teams in society, whose ability to perform effectively can often result in dire consequences. Many chapters in this volume expose ways for members of the community who have an interest in enhancing team processes and outcomes to go about doing so. As the different disciplines continue to collaborate, the integration of their research efforts becomes a critical consideration for the field of team cognition.

This volume not only serves as a medium for the multitude of disciplines to circulate their findings, but it also illustrates a significant trend that is becoming a reality for team cognition researchers. Efforts that continue to explore themes that surface in the field should maintain the goal of increasing cross-disciplinary collaboration and understanding of team cognition. There is a great deal this field has to offer the literature on team research, and continuing to integrate and combine findings across disciplines is a great way to enable such endeavors. It is the authors' hope that this volume continues to motivate research that enhances the field's understanding of team cognition and the influence it has on team performance.

REFERENCE

Cannon-Bowers, J. A., & Salas, E. (2001). Reflections on shared cognition. *Journal of Organizational Behavior, 22,* 195–202.

Author Index

Adibhatla, V., 361, 362
Aditya, R. N., 127, 131
Adkins, C. L., 122
Ahmed, A., 104
Ahuja, M. K., 291
Ai, H., 519, 543
Alavi, M., 292, 293, 448, 555
Allan, M. B., 448
Alligood, K. T., 191, 203
Allison, L. K., 123
Alterman, R., 197
Altman, I., 248, 387
Alvarez, G., 53
Amazeen, P. G., 193, 195, 196
Ambrose, R., 328
Anand, V., 300, 435, 438
Ancona, D. G., 375
Anderson, A. H., 555
Anderson, C., 391, 396
Anderson, J. R., 22, 40, 44
Anderson, N. H., 250
Anderson, N. R., 146, 147, 149, 155
Anderson, P., 424
Anderson, R., 556
Andres, H. P., 556, 561
Andrews, D., 88, 189
Ang, S., 164
Anspach, R., 506, 510
Argall, B., 323
Argote, L. L., 87, 118, 119, 303, 421, 422,
        428, 429, 431, 435, 438, 448, 449
Arocha, J. F., 498
Arora, S., 519
Arrow, H., 87, 88, 223
Arthur, J., 549
Arthur, M. B., 129
Arthur, W., 97, 123
Arthur Jr., W., 558
Artman, H., 87, 201
Asbury, M. A., 472
Ashe, D. K., 154

Ashleigh, M. J., 432
Atherton, J., 324
Atkin, R. S., 388
Austin, J. R., 121, 123, 149, 428, 431, 434
Avolio, B. J., 130, 131
Azmitia, M., 518

Baer, M., 153
Baguley, T., 99
Bailey, D. E., 245
Bain, P. G., 146, 147, 149
Baker, D. P., 101, 318
Bakhtin, M., 529
Balakrishnan, B., 360, 362
Bales, R. F., 249, 397, 474
Ballard, D. I., 87, 88
Balogun, J., 129
Banerjee, S., 324
Bannon, L. J., 191, 210
Bar, F., 439
Bara, B. G., 474
Barber, D., 326
Bardes, M., 130
Barenak, P. M., 556
Barker, R. G., 346
Barley, S., 295
Barnes, M. J., 319
Baron, R. A., 163, 319
Baron, R. S., 250
Barron, B., 220, 221
Barry, D., 134
Bartel, C. A., 91, 92, 93, 109
Bartlett, C. J., 149
Bass, B. M., 125, 130
Bates, A. L., 164
Bates, D. W., 59
Beal, D. J., 42
Beavin, J. H., 474
Beck, S. J., 471, 472, 482, 491, 520, 592,
        600, 602
Bedny, G., 102

608 • Author Index

Beele, P., 95
Beer, J. S., 391
Beers, M. C., 290
Beersma, B., 149
Begole, J., 235
Bell, B. S., 13, 20, 22, 23, 24, 33, 40, 41, 42, 43, 44, 88, 245, 246, 289, 375, 377, 387, 388, 496, 549
Bell, S. T., 97, 123
Belliveau, M., 435
Benne, K., 474
Benner, P., 507, 509
Bennett, N., 146, 147, 149, 153, 156, 162
Berdahl, J. L., 223
Bereiter, C., 520
Berger, C. R., 477
Berger, P. L., 145
Bergman, J. Z., 391
Bergman, S. M., 391
Berkowitz, M., 518
Bernard, C., 129
Berson, Y., 130
Bhambare, P., 215
Bhasale, A., 53
Bienvenu, M., 195
Bjork, R. A., 218
Black, J., 214
Blandford, A., 107
Bliese, P. D., 147, 262
Bluedorn, A. C., 92, 93, 99
Blumer, H., 473
Bly, S., 294
Bødker, S., 191
Boekaerts, M., 221
Bohmer, R. M., 468
Bolman, L., 102
Bolstad, C. A., 104
Bono, J. E., 130
Borge, M., 8, 209, 219, 220, 222, 223, 225, 226, 234, 589, 605
Botero, I. C., 447, 478
Bougon, M. G., 132
Bourgeois, L. J., 91
Bowers, C. A., 98, 289, 292, 293, 294, 295, 301, 303, 306, 465
Boyer, D. G., 294
Boyle, E., 15, 555
Brachman, R., 329

Bradley, B. H., 130
Brandon, D. P., 12, 303, 307, 416, 421, 422, 429, 432, 434, 435, 436, 439, 592, 602
Brandt, C. J., 119, 121
Brannick, M. T., 364
Bransford, J. D., 348, 349
Braun, C. C., 465
Bray, R. M., 388
Breazeal, C., 324
Brennan, S. E., 215, 539
Brewer, I., 347, 348, 349, 360
Brodbeck, F. C., 255, 257
Brodt, S., 561
Brooks, D., 448
Brown, A. L., 214, 217, 218, 221, 222, 237
Brown, C. E., 355
Brown, J. S., 222, 346, 347, 354, 356, 357
Brown, V. R., 388, 389
Browning, B., 323
Bruner, J., 497, 505, 507
Brunswik, E., 191, 198, 203, 354
Bryant, A., 117
Bunderson, J. S., 41, 43, 464
Bunz, H., 194
Burd, R. S., 508
Burgoon, J. K., 490
Burke, C. S., 6, 13, 100, 117, 123, 133, 134, 147, 271, 346, 447, 465, 557
Burke, J., 326
Burke, L. M., 129
Burke, M. J., 42
Burke, S., 496, 562
Burstein, M., 322
Butler, D. L., 221, 226
Button, G., 408, 409, 410
Byrne, J., 437
Byström, K., 275, 280

Cacciabue, P. C., 272, 405, 474, 501, 512
Çakir, M. P., 520, 527, 528, 538
Caldwell, D. F., 375
Camacho, L. M., 389
Campbell, D. J., 286
Campbell, D. T., 464
Campbell, G. E., 98, 584
Campion, M. A., 41
Campione, J. C., 222, 237

Author Index • 609

Cannon, M. D., 146, 149, 463
Cannon-Bowers, J. A., 3, 87, 96, 97, 98, 99,
    100, 118, 121, 122, 139, 149, 150,
    188, 189, 212, 261, 271, 287, 291,
    293, 294, 328, 378, 379, 405, 416,
    448, 457, 458, 466, 471, 477, 501,
    513, 549, 557, 558, 559, 584, 597,
    599, 601
Carello, C., 198, 199
Carley, K. M., 150, 290, 291, 292, 294, 295,
    306, 429, 549, 581
Carlson, T., 293
Carroll, J. M., 8, 209, 211, 212, 215, 219,
    220, 223, 225, 228, 229, 230, 232,
    233, 234, 236, 589, 605
Carson, J. B., 134
Cazdan, C., 218
Chaffee, S. H., 460
Chakravarthy, B. S., 210
Chalupsky, H., 314, 320, 322
Chao, G. T., 4, 19, 30, 36, 37, 40, 42, 587,
    600, 601
Chatman, J. A., 391
Chatterjee, A., 129
Chaudhuri, S., 519, 543
Chemero, A., 197
Chen, G., 21, 24, 147, 326
Chen, J. Y. C., 319
Chen, L., 320
Cheyne, J. A., 191
Chidambaram, L., 554, 555
Child, J. T., 440
Chin, J., 228
Chiron, B., 448
Choi, J. N., 149
Chomsky, N., 520
Christensen, C., 3
Christian, C. K., 52
Christie, B., 15, 555
Christie, F., 521
Christoffersen, K., 319, 338
Citera, M., 357, 358
Clark, A., 197
Clark, H., 293, 539
Clark, H. H., 212, 215
Clark, M. A., 9, 123, 289, 600, 601
Clark, R. A., 474
Clayton, L. D., 245

Clemson, P., 232
Cloran, C., 522
Code, S., 150, 188
Cohen, P., 314, 315, 317
Cohen, R. R., 42
Cohen, S. G., 245
Coiera, E., 53
Colbert, A. E., 130
Coleman, J. C., 213
Collins, A., 222, 347
Collins, C. J., 153
Collyer, S. C., 188
Colquitt, J. A., 146, 147, 149, 152, 153, 156,
    162, 165
Conant, F. R., 217
Conger, J. A., 126, 133
Connolly, T., 563
Connors, E. S., 347, 357
Contractor, N. S., 441, 442, 443
Converse, S. A., 3, 7, 96, 118, 149, 187, 188,
    261, 293, 338, 378, 417, 501, 557,
    584
Convertino, G., 211, 215, 236
Cook, R. I., 176, 182
Cook, W. L., 381
Cooke, N. J., 7, 8, 13, 97, 98, 187, 188, 189,
    193, 196, 197, 199, 289, 291, 292,
    293, 294, 295, 301, 303, 305, 306,
    328, 379, 416, 417, 496, 501, 507,
    508, 511, 549, 550, 551, 552, 553,
    590, 600, 604
Cooprider, J. G., 289, 293, 294
Cordery, J. L., 448
Corrigan, J., 52
Cosenzo, K. A., 319
Cotton, T. S., 389
Cowen, M., 471
Craig, S., 124
Cramton, C. D., 289, 293
Crandall, J., 324
Cronbach, L. J., 382
Cronin, M. A., 479
Croskerry, P., 51
Crott, H. W., 250
Crowston, K., 176
Cruz, M., 564
Cuevas, H. M., 104, 286
Cui, Y., 519, 543

610 • Author Index

Daft, R., 554, 555
Dalton, A. C., 52
Dalton, G. D., 52
Davenport, T. H., 290
Davis, J. H., 250, 251, 253, 377
Day, D. V., 126, 133, 135
Day, E. A., 97, 123, 549
Dayan, M., 437
DeChurch, L. A., 6, 19, 27, 28, 87, 97, 117, 118, 119, 120, 121, 122, 124, 125, 132, 135, 137, 246, 255, 261, 262, 374, 376, 379, 380, 392, 584, 588, 603
Decker, K., 316
Deckert, J. C., 502
De Dreu, C. K. W., 15, 149
Delia, J. G., 472, 474
Delise, L. A., 6, 151, 164
de Lisi, R., 518
De Long, D. W., 290
Demaree, R. G., 301
Den Hartog, D. N., 125, 131
Dennis, A. R., 257, 553
Dennison, R., 218
DeRue, D. S., 135, 245
DeShon, R. P., 24, 39, 41, 467
Devine, D. J., 42, 118, 245, 247
De Visser, E., 319
Dey, A. K., 235
Di Benedetto, C. A., 437
Dickinson, T. L., 7, 187, 338, 417
Dickson, M. W., 121, 123, 130, 153, 154, 158
Dickson, W. J., 248, 387
Dickstein, E., 509
Diesner, J., 549
Diller, D., 322
Dillon, J. R., 19
Dinh, H. T., 68
Donaldson, M., 52
Donnellon, A., 132
Dorfman, P. W., 164
Doty, D., 135
Dougherty, D. S., 479
Dourish, P., 294
Drabek, T. E., 449
Drake, L. R., 128, 393
Driscoll, P., 505

Driver, M., 551
Driver, R., 219
Duffy, L. T., 150
Duguid, P., 213, 347
Dumville, B. C., 347, 416
Dunbar, K., 510
Dunford, B. B., 245
Dunnington, G., 11, 405, 525, 592, 599
Duran, J., 7, 187, 189, 590, 600
Duranti, A., 530
Dwyer, N., 538
Dyck, C., 153
Dyer, J. L., 145
Dykema-Engblade, A. A., 87

Earley, P. C., 146, 276
Eastridge, B. J., 51
Ebright, P. R., 173, 181
Eden, D., 291
Eden, J., 564
Edmondson, A., 19, 20, 38, 87, 219
Edmondson, A. C., 149, 463
Edmondson, A. E., 468
Edwards, B. D., 97, 98, 123, 549, 558, 564, 565
Egido, C., 249
Ehrhart, M. G., 119, 125
Eiseman, B., 51
Eisenberg, E. M., 479
Eisenhardt, K. M., 375
Eke, A., 196
Elias, J., 15, 271, 571
Ellis, A. L., 251, 377
Ellis, A. P. J., 41, 97, 245, 447
Ellis, L., 327
Elms, H., 134
Endsley, M. R., 102, 103, 104, 105, 106, 107, 108, 109, 229, 235, 249, 294, 347
Engeström, Y., 211, 213, 215
Engle, R. A., 217
Ensley, M. D., 91, 149, 150, 163
Entin, E. E., 502, 573, 578
Erber, R., 428
Erez, A., 134
Ergener, D., 105, 116, 356
Erlen, J. A., 509
Espinosa, J. A., 9, 277, 289, 562, 573, 578, 579, 580, 581, 584, 585, 591, 600, 601
Evans, A. W. III, 319

Author Index • 611

Fan, X., 321, 331, 356, 358, 361
Faraj, S., 289, 291, 292, 294, 300, 303,
 307, 422, 431, 448, 449,
 508, 579
Farooq, U., 211
Faust, K., 290, 296, 308, 443
Federico, T., 99
Feinman, A., 197
Feldman, M. S., 449
Feltovich, P., 411
Ferguson, D., 332
Ferzandi, L., 89, 135, 363
Filkins, J., 90
Fincannon, T., 319
Fine, G. A., 88, 459
Finkelstein, S., 424
Fiore, S. M., 3, 9, 13, 15, 22, 28, 29, 44, 45,
 133, 173, 245, 271, 272, 273, 274,
 275, 283, 286, 347, 405, 416, 475,
 496, 508, 571, 572, 574, 584
Fischer, F., 518
Fischer, U., 13, 496, 502
Fiss, P. C., 122, 125, 129, 137
Fitzpatrick, P. A., 195
Flaherty, S., 51
Flanagin, A. J., 439
Flavell, J. H., 43, 502
Fleishman, E. A., 125, 127, 132, 145
Florey, A. T., 132, 293
Floyd, S. W., 91, 101, 123, 129
Folger, J. P., 468
Ford, D. J., 480
Ford, J. K., 40
Forman, E., 218
Foucault, M., 505, 506, 513
Foushee, H. C., 88
Fox, M., 314
Fraidin, S. N., 427, 428
Franklin, N., 99
Frederiksen, J. R., 214
Freeman, L. C., 37
Freeman, M., 95
Frese, M., 153
Frey, L. R., 472, 491
Fugelsang, J., 510
Fuks, H., 530
Fulk, J., 439, 440, 441, 449
Fussell, S. R., 293, 555, 556

Futrell, D., 123

Gadamer, H.-G., 538
Galanes, G. J., 476
Galantucci, B., 8, 189
Galaskiewicz, J., 443
Gallagher, J. M., 249
Galletta, D. F., 291
Ganoe, C. H., 8, 209, 211, 215, 229, 234,
 589, 605
Garbis, C., 201
Garfinkel, H., 408, 409, 410, 415, 416, 417,
 418, 529, 537
Gargano, G. M., 388
Garlock, J., 15, 555
Garner, J., 438
Garramone, G. M., 556
Garretson, J. A., 129
Gebert, D., 126, 131
Gelfand, M. J., 164
Gentner, D., 261
George, G., 131
Gerras, S. J., 146
Gevers, J. M. P., 89, 91, 92, 93, 94, 95, 96,
 109
Giambatista, R. C., 101
Giampapa, J., 315, 322
Gibberd, R., 53
Gibbs, J., 518
Gibbs, P., 574
Giberson, T. R., 129, 130, 139
Gibson, C. B., 38, 100, 146, 374
Gibson, J. J., 191, 198, 203, 354
Gigone, D., 255
Gil, F., 100, 374
Gilden, D. L., 196
Gillis, L., 422
Gilson, L., 97
Giuliano, T., 422
Glantz, E. J., 360
Gleser, G. C., 382
Glick, W. H., 129, 300, 435
Glisson, C., 149, 154, 155
Golbeck, S. L., 518
Goldberg, D., 332
Gonzalez, C., 104
Gonzalez-Roma, V., 147, 154, 158
Goodrich, M., 324

612 • Author Index

Goodstein, L. P., 354
Goodwin, G. F., 87, 96, 121, 150, 189, 212, 261, 271, 289, 378, 411, 549, 558
Gordon, A., 127
Gorman, J. C., 7, 8, 187, 188, 189, 193, 195, 196, 501, 550, 590, 600
Graesser, C. C., 250
Graetz, K., 15, 555
Grant, L. D., 389
Gratch, J., 320
Gray, B., 132
Green, D., 103
Green, M. L., 52
Greenbaum, R., 130
Greenberg, S., 235
Greeno, J. G., 191, 228
Griffin, M. A., 149, 156, 162
Griffith, T. L., 448
Grojean, M. W., 130
Gronn, P., 126
Grosz, B., 314, 315, 317
Grudin, J., 181
Gruenfeld, D. H., 88, 293
Gu, Y., 323
Gudykunst, W. B., 284
Guise, J. M., 53
Gully, S. M., 38, 42, 118
Guo, Y., 51
Gupta, N., 12, 101, 421, 428, 429, 592, 602
Gurtner, A., 549, 557, 561, 565
Gutwin, C., 235
Guzman, E., 235
Guzzo, R., 245
Gweon, G., 519

Hackman, J. R., 95, 247, 248, 249, 353, 373, 375, 386, 389, 578
Hahn, S., 321
Haken, H., 194
Halfhill, T., 245
Hall, R. J., 98, 164, 289, 293, 294, 380, 391
Halliday, P., 104
Hambrick, D. C., 128, 129
Hamilton, K., 5, 87, 89, 100, 106, 135, 361, 587, 604
Han, Y., 123, 447
Hancock, P. A., 101
Handel, M. J., 294

Hanges, P. J., 6, 19, 119, 121, 145, 153, 164
Hanks, W., 540
Hardin, R., 440
Harding, B., 324
Harkins, S. G., 276, 277, 282, 388
Harris, A. C., 556
Harris, T., 324
Harrison, D. A., 132, 293, 395
Hastie, R., 250, 255
Hauland, G., 106, 107, 108
Haviland, S. E., 212
Healey, P. M., 60
Heath, C., 412
Hedegaard, M., 497, 505
Heffner, T. S., 87, 96, 121, 150, 189, 212, 261, 289, 549, 558
Hegel, G. W. F., 495, 496, 497
Heidegger, M., 537, 540
Heimstra, N. W., 346
Heino, R., 439, 441
Hellar, D. B., 361
Helm, E. E., 98, 189
Helmreich, R. L., 512
Hempel, P. S., 123, 447
Henderson, A., 520
Henningsen, D., 564
Henningsen, M., 564
Henry, K. B., 87
Herbsleb, J. D., 277, 294
Heritage, J., 410
Herman, P., 196
Herndon, B., 435
Herring, S., 530
Hertel, P. T., 422
Hessler, E. E., 196
Hewlin, P. F., 133
Higgins, E. T., 3, 253, 459
Higgs, M., 278
Hightower, R., 555
Hiller, N. J., 126, 129, 133, 134, 135, 137
Hinds, P., 324
Hinsz, V. B., 3, 8, 11, 119, 245, 246, 247, 249, 250, 251, 252, 253, 255, 373, 376, 378, 379, 392, 551, 589, 603, 604
Hinton, G. E., 148
Ho, V. T., 435
Hobby, L., 236
Hoffman, R. R., 175, 354, 574

Author Index • 613

Hoffrage, U., 255, 379
Hofmann, D. H., 146, 149
Hogan, K., 220, 227
Hogan, R., 124
Hogg, M. A., 87
Holcomb, J. B., 51
Holden, J. G., 196
Hollenbeck, J. R., 41, 89, 245, 247, 377, 580
Hollingshead, A. B., 12, 88, 128, 249, 251,
    253, 303, 307, 393, 416, 421, 422,
    427, 428, 429, 432, 433, 434, 435,
    436, 439, 440, 441, 445, 447, 449,
    450, 478, 482, 490, 492, 592,
    602, 605
Hollnagel, E., 175, 272, 405, 474, 501, 512
Horvitz, E., 320, 321, 329
Horwitz, L. I., 52
Hoult, R., 604
House, R. J., 127, 129, 131
Howison, J., 176
Howitt, A. M., 188
Howley, I., 519
Hripcsak, G., 59
Huang, C. C., 121, 447
Huang, M., 447
Huang, W., 554
Huang, X., 121
Hubbell, A. P., 256
Hubert, L., 301, 306
Hudlicka, E., 356
Hulin, C. L., 374
Hullman, G. W., 477
Huot, S. J., 52
Hurwitz, B., 52
Hutchins, E., 3, 183, 191, 201, 202, 203, 353,
    405, 497, 501, 505, 508, 520, 523
Hutchinson, S., 6
Hutchison, S., 145

Iberall, A. S., 193
Ilgen, D. R., 19, 20, 39, 41, 42, 89, 123, 245,
    246, 247, 374, 377, 389, 580
Ilies, R., 127
Imamoglu, S. Z., 437
Ingram, P., 422
Introne, J., 197
Isabella, L. A., 149
Isenhour, P. L., 211

Ishii, H., 235
Iun, J., 121

Jackson, C. L., 146
Jackson, D., 474
Jackson, F., 572
Jackson, P., 435, 438
Jacob, E., 51
Jacobsohn, G. C., 482
Jacobson, E. J., 60
James, L. A., 154
James, L. R., 147, 149, 154, 155, 301, 306
James, N., 104
James, W., 190, 203
Janis, I. L., 138, 394, 564
Jansen, J. J. P., 131
Järvelin, K., 275, 280
Jefferson, G., 411
Jefferson Jr., T., 357, 363
Jenkins, D. P., 51, 102
Jenkins, N. M., 151
Jensen, M., 128
Jentsch, F. G., 13, 315, 319, 496, 508
Jessup, L. M., 563
Jiang, H., 234
Jiménez, M., 117, 588, 603
Jirsa, V. K., 194
Johns, G., 146, 149, 165
Johnson, D. W., 217
Johnson, G., 129
Johnson, J., 315
Johnson, M., 89, 247, 377, 580
Johnson, R. T., 217
Johnson, W. L., 323
Johnson-Laird, P. N., 99, 261
Johnston, J. H., 271
Jonassen, D. H., 554, 555
Jones, B., 554, 555
Jones, R. E. T., 347, 357, 360, 361
Jones, W. M., 102
Jordan, B., 520
Joshi, M., 519, 543
Juarrero, A., 193
Judge, T. A., 127, 130
Jundt, D., 89, 247, 377, 580

Kaiser, M. K., 198
Kaiser, R., 124

614 • Author Index

Kalman, M., 439, 441
Kalra, N., 332
Kameda, T., 3, 253
Kamiya, J., 191, 198, 203
Kanawattanachai, P., 448
Kane, T. D., 126
Kanfer, R., 21, 24
Kang, H. R., 99
Kang, M., 519
Kaplan, D., 214
Karam, E. P., 135
Karoly, P., 21, 44
Kashy, D. A., 381
Katona, L. B., 51
Katz, L., 353
Kearney, E., 126, 131
Keebler, J. R., 319
Keller, J., 435
Kellermanns, F. W., 91, 123
Kelso, J. A. S., 194
Kendall, D. L., 6, 100, 117
Kennedy, D. M., 15, 549, 550, 551, 552,
       565, 593, 600, 602, 603, 604, 605
Kennedy, W. G., 326
Kenny, D. A., 165, 380, 381, 382, 386,
       460, 461
Kerr, D. S., 553, 554, 555, 556, 563
Kerr, N. L., 250, 388
Kerschreiter, R., 255
Keselman, A., 214
Keskin, H., 437
Keyton, J., 13, 471, 472, 475, 480, 491, 520,
       592, 600, 602
Kiekel, P. A., 13, 98, 189, 197, 199, 289, 496,
       549, 550
Kieser, A., 328
Kiesler, S., 327, 432
Kilduff, G. J., 391, 396
Kilduff, M., 37
Kim, K. J., 11, 51
Kim, M., 405, 525, 592, 599
Kimble, C., 15, 355
Kinicki, A., 145
Kiris, E. O., 105
Kirkman, B. L., 146, 149, 156, 162
Kirsh, D., 201
Kivlighan, D. M., 391
Klatzke, S. R., 479

Klein, C., 387
Klein, D. E., 191, 204
Klein, G., 191, 204, 405
Klein, G. A., 173, 174
Klein, G. K., 474
Klein, K. J., 20, 24, 26, 27, 35, 44, 97, 120,
       138, 553, 558
Kleinman, D., 356
Klimoski, R. J., 19, 90, 96, 97, 148, 150,
       259, 289, 290, 293, 294, 295,
       300, 301, 379, 457, 458, 459, 465,
       501, 549
Klobas, J., 435, 438
Knight, D., 91
Knoblich, G., 585
Kobayashi, M., 235
Kobayashi, T., 324
Koch, U., 438
Kocsis, L., 196
Koes, M., 331
Kohn, L., 52
Koopman, P. L., 125, 131
Korolis, A. A., 448
Koschmann, T., 11, 14, 405, 411, 415, 517,
       525, 592, 599, 604
Kovacs, G., 51
Kozak, L. R., 196
Kozlowski, S. W. J., 4, 19, 20, 21, 22, 23, 24,
       25, 26, 27, 29, 30, 33, 35, 38, 39,
       40, 42, 43, 44, 88, 120, 123, 138,
       191, 204, 246, 377, 387, 388, 389,
       467, 553, 587, 600, 601
Krackhardt, D., 290, 306
Kraiger, K., 40, 151, 293, 294, 448, 549, 557
Kramer, M. W., 479
Kraus, S., 314, 315, 317
Krauss, R., 293
Kraut, R. E., 249, 277, 573
Krishnan, R., 119, 428, 431
Kristof-Brown, A. L., 130
Krumholz, H. M., 52
Kuendig, S., 255, 379
Kuenzi, M., 130
Kuhn, D., 214, 221, 226
Kumar, K., 375
Kumar, R., 519, 543, 544
Kurzweil, R., 337
Kwon, H., 554, 555

Ladbury, J. L., 8, 11, 245, 246, 373, 589, 603, 604
Laing, R. D., 460, 463
Landro, L., 52
Langan-Fox, J., 150, 156, 188, 458
Lange, D., 422
Lange, S., 164
Langfield, K., 150
Langfield-Smith, K., 188
Lant, T. K., 133
Larson, J. R., 3
Latané, B., 276, 388
Laughlin, P. R., 250, 251, 252, 253, 377
Lave, J., 347, 354, 497, 501
Lawrence, B. S., 38
LeBaron, C., 411
Lechner, C., 91, 123
Lee, A. R., 460
Leidner, D. E., 292, 293
Lengel, R., 554, 555
Lenox, T., 321
Leonard, H. B., 188
LePine, J. A., 134
Lerch, F. J., 573
Lesk, M. E., 508
Letsky, M. P., 3, 9, 89, 173, 217, 245, 271, 272, 273, 274, 284, 285, 347, 405, 471, 475
Leupp, D. G., 355
Levesque, H., 314, 315, 317, 325
Levesque, L. L., 98, 149, 150, 189, 289, 301, 306
Levine, J. L., 3
Levine, J. M., 253, 375, 405, 422
Lewis, B., 324, 331
Lewis, K., 119, 121, 123, 289, 292, 294, 303, 307, 337, 422, 428, 431, 432, 433, 435, 437, 591, 598
Lewis, M., 10, 313, 320, 321, 323, 324, 325, 329
Lewis, P., 322
Li, D., 51
Liang, D. W., 87, 118, 119, 303, 421, 422, 428, 431, 432
Lim, A., 89
Lim, B., 558
Lim, B. C., 97
Lindell, M. K., 119, 121, 154, 159

Lindoerfer, D., 132
Lingard, L., 53
Littlepage, A. M., 128, 393
Littlepage, G. E., 128, 293, 393
Liu, J., 51
Livingston, E., 410, 418
Looi, C.-K., 538
Lord, R. G., 129, 132
Loring, D., 132
Lovelace, D., 38
Luckmann, T., 145
Luff, P., 412
Luh, P., 356
Lum, H., 9, 271, 275
Luria, G., 119, 122, 130, 146, 147, 149, 153, 154, 159
Lynch, J. G., 579
Lynn, G. S., 437
Lyons, R., 9, 271, 590

Majchrzak, A., 449
Makary, M. A., 53
Malecki, G. S., 188
Mallon, M. W., 196
Mancuso, V., 106
Mandelbrot, B. B., 195
Mandler, J. M., 99
Mann, L., 146, 147
Mannix, E. A., 293
Manterea, S., 54
Manz, C. C., 126, 300, 435
Marchant, D., 574
Marecki, J., 322
Markin, R. D., 391
Marks, M. A., 98, 101, 118, 123, 124, 125, 126, 132, 133, 135, 147, 150, 155, 156, 161, 249, 271, 474, 557, 572, 574, 584
Marrone, J. A., 134
Marsella, S., 314, 320
Marshal, C., 293
Marsic, I., 508
Martin, J. R., 521
Martorana, P., 129
Mason, C. M., 149, 156
Mason, P. A., 128
Massey, A., 564
Masuda, A. D., 126

616 • Author Index

Mathieu, J. E., 24, 87, 96, 97, 98, 99, 101, 118, 121, 122, 123, 126, 132, 150, 151, 161, 164, 189, 212, 249, 261, 271, 289, 294, 295, 301, 306, 378, 474, 549, 557, 558, 559, 572, 574, 584
Mayer, D. M., 119, 125, 130
Mayfield, E., 519
Maynard, M. T., 97
McBeath, M. K., 198
McClelland, J. L., 148
McComb, S. A., 15, 97, 549–550, 551, 552, 565, 593, 600, 602, 603, 604, 605
McCrickard, D. S., 211
McDaniel, R., 508
McDermott, P., 319
McDermott, R., 212
McEntire, D. A., 449
McFadden, R. D., 188
McFarling, F. H., 346
McGrath, J. E., 87, 88, 126, 132, 223, 247, 248, 249, 278, 293, 376, 385, 387, 484, 557, 560, 561, 562, 563
McIntyre, M., 245
McIntyre, R., 51, 465
McKersie, R. B., 561
McLendon, C. L., 42
McLeod, J., 460
McNeese, M. D., 10, 249, 321, 322, 345, 347, 348, 349, 352, 353, 354, 355, 356, 357, 358, 360, 361, 362, 363, 364, 591, 603
McNeil, J. D., 51
Medina, R., 538
Meglino, B. M., 122
Mehan, H., 511
Meisenhelder, H. M., 87
Meister, D., 102
Melner, S. B., 245
Mentis, H. M., 215, 236
Merlo, J. L., 326
Merritt, A. C., 512
Mesmer-Magnus, J. R., 19, 27, 28, 87, 97, 118, 119, 120, 121, 122, 124, 135, 246, 255, 261, 262, 374, 376, 379, 380, 392, 584

Metz, K. E., 219
Michaels, C. F., 198, 199
Michaelsen, L. K., 375
Michinov, E., 448
Miettinen, R., 211
Milanovich, D. M., 98, 584
Miller, C. C., 129
Miller, G., 53
Miller, M., 322
Milliken, F. J., 38, 91, 92, 93, 109
Millward, S. M., 99
Milner, K. R., 24
Mitchelson, J. K., 123
Mohammed, S., 5, 19, 87, 89, 90, 91, 94, 95, 96, 97, 99, 100, 101, 110, 132, 135, 137, 149, 150, 156, 165, 259, 290, 293, 294, 300, 347, 416, 457, 458, 501, 549, 587, 604
Mojzisch, A., 255
Mondada, L., 411
Mone, M. A., 276
Monge, P. R., 439, 440, 441, 442
Montgomery, R., 518
Montgomery, S. P., 51
Montoya-Weiss, M., 564
Moon, H., 36, 40, 42
Moreland, R. L., 87, 118, 119, 303, 375, 421, 422, 428, 431, 432, 433, 435, 437, 438, 449, 450
Morgan, B. B., 465
Morgan, P. L., 104
Morgeson, F. P., 128, 131, 132, 133, 135, 146
Morris, C. G., 247, 248, 353, 373
Morris, N. M., 147, 261
Morris, T., 574
Morrison, E. W., 38
Morse, J. J., 127
Mosakowski, E., 146
Moss, J., 13, 496, 508
Mot, I. R., 6, 145, 157, 164, 588, 601
Moynihan, D. P., 88
Murase, T., 6, 117, 125, 132, 135, 588, 603, 604
Murff, H. J., 59
Murray, R., 130
Murthy, U. S., 553, 554, 555, 556, 563

Author Index • 617

Musaeus, P., 13, 495, 519, 592
Myaskovsky, L., 422, 433, 450
Myers, C., 7, 187, 189, 590, 600

Nadkarni, S., 89, 94, 96
Nagasunder, A., 519
Nägele, C., 549
Nair, R., 314
Nanda, H., 382
Nason, E. R., 38
Naumann, S. E., 146, 147, 149, 153, 156, 162
Nead, J. M., 354
Neale, D. C., 211, 236
Neale, M. A., 293
Negri, A., 58
Nelson, K. M., 289, 293, 294
Nelson-Le Gall, S., 219
Neuwirth, C., 555
Nevo, D., 215, 435, 438
Newell, A., 191, 204, 551
Newlands, A., 555
Newman, D. A., 395
Newman, S. E., 222
Newton, P., 219
Nguyen, H., 57
Nichols, R. G., 466
Nicolis, G., 191, 192, 203
Nielsen, C., 324
Nieva, V. F., 145
Niles-Jolly, K., 119, 125
Nishida, T., 284
Nishii, L. H., 164
Noe, R. A., 146
Nonaka, I., 292
Norman, D. A., 181
Norton, R. W., 468
Nosek, J., 357, 358
Nourbakhsh, I., 331
Nunnally, E., 461
Nutt, P. C., 128

Obieta, J. F., 357
Olivier-Chiron, E., 448
Orasanu, J. M., 3, 13, 496, 502
O'Reilly, C. A., 38, 375
Orr, J., 507
Ososky, S., 319

Ostroff, C., 145
Owens, P., 129

Palazzolo, E. T., 442, 443
Palincsar, A. M., 214, 217, 218, 221, 222
Palincsar, A. S., 217, 219, 226
Palmgreen, P., 468
Pannu, A., 316
Paolucci, M., 315, 322
Parasuraman, R., 319, 324
Park, E., 379
Park, E. S., 255
Parsons, T., 406, 407, 408, 410
Parush, A., 52, 53
Pasmore, W. A., 445
Patel, V. L., 59, 498, 506, 509
Patrick, J., 104
Patterson, E. S., 7, 173, 174, 176, 178, 180, 182, 183, 590
Pattipati, K., 356
Paul, M. C., 147
Paulus, P. B., 388, 389, 563
Payne, S. J., 99, 315
Payne, T., 321
Pearce, C. L., 91, 126, 133, 149, 150, 163
Pearl, J., 55
Pearsall, M. J., 447
Pearson, A. W., 101
Peeters, M. A. G., 93, 94
Peiro, J. M., 147
Pejtersen, A. M., 354
Pellegrino, E. D., 510
Pellid, L. H., 375, 396
Peltokorpi, V., 435, 438
Penrod, S. D., 250
Pentland, B. T., 449
Perusich, K. A., 348, 357
Peterson, E., 561
Peterson, R., 129
Petty, R. E., 276, 277, 282
Pfaff, M. S., 10, 345, 354, 355, 360–361, 363, 364, 365, 591, 603
Philips, J. L., 245, 247
Phillipson, H., 460
Piaget, J., 211, 217
Piccolo, R. F., 127
Pierce, L. G., 6, 100, 117, 396
Pimentel, M., 530

618 • *Author Index*

Pioch, N. J., 57, 58
Pirola-Merlo, A., 146, 147
Pisano, G. P., 468
Plewnia, U., 278
Ploch, J., 278
Ployhart, R. E., 41, 245
Plymale, J., 322
Poole, M. S., 12, 87, 457, 468, 491, 492, 539, 550, 588, 602, 604
Powers, A., 327
Pratt, C. M., 51
Prewett, M. S., 326
Price, R. H., 149
Prichard, J. S., 432
Priem, R. L., 91
Priest, H., 88
Prigogine, I., 191, 192, 203
Prince, C., 101, 318, 364
Pritchard, R., 21
Punamaki, R.-L., 211
Putnam, L. L., 480, 492

Rabinow, P., 506, 513
Radvansky, G. A., 99
Rafferty, L., 102
Rajaratnam, N., 382
Randall, K. R., 6, 117, 123, 125, 133, 139
Rapert, M. I., 129
Rapp, T., 97
Rasmussen, J., 354
Rau, D., 431, 432
Ravlin, E. C., 122
Rawls, A. W., 408, 415, 417, 418
Raymond, P., 428
Reagans, R., 448
Reddington, K., 293
Reichers, A. E., 146
Reick, A., 145
Reid, S., 53
Reimer, A., 392
Reimer, T., 255, 379
Reminga, J., 549
Ren, Y., 429, 435, 437, 438
Render, M. L., 176, 182
Rentsch, J. R., 6, 19, 90, 97, 98, 119, 121, 122, 145, 148, 149, 150, 151, 152, 161, 163, 164, 165, 289, 293, 294, 295, 301, 347, 348, 380, 391, 465, 588, 601

Resick, C. J., 6, 117, 121, 123, 125, 126, 129, 130, 131, 153, 588, 603
Resnick, L. B., 3, 253, 405
Reynolds, A. M., 98, 584
Rice, R. E., 555
Richards, H., 245
Riches, O. C., 16, 597
Rickel, J., 320, 323
Rico, R., 100, 374
Riemersma, J., 467
Ringseis, E., 87, 90, 91, 149, 165
Rittman, A. L., 124
Roberts, L., 321
Robinson, A., 519
Robison, W., 293
Roby, T. B., 353
Roe, R. A., 93
Roethlisberger, F. J., 248, 387
Rogers, T. K. K., 479
Rogers, Y., 202
Rohre, D., 135
Roloff, K. S., 19
Roschelle, J., 539
Rosé, C. P., 14, 54, 517, 519, 521, 543, 589, 599, 602
Rose, D., 521
Rosé, E., 519
Rose, W. D., 54
Rosen, B., 146
Rosen, J., 51
Rosen, M. A., 13, 271, 272, 273, 274, 275, 347, 475, 496
Rosenkopf, L., 128
Rosson, M. B., 8, 209, 211, 215, 228, 230, 232, 233, 235, 236, 589, 605
Roth, E. M., 173
Roth, P. L., 395
Roth, S., 314
Rouse, W. B., 147, 261
Rowe, L. J., 8, 188, 196, 501
Rowley, C., 99
Rubin, R. B., 468
Rubleske, J., 176
Rudnicky, A., 324
Rulke, D. L., 432, 443
Rumelhart, D. E., 147
Runciman, W., 53
Rusch, E., 448

Author Index • 619

Rutte, C. G., 89, 91, 93
Ryan, T., 439

Saavedra, R., 276
Sabella, M. J., 123, 147
Sacks, H., 520, 530
Sadeh-Koniecpol, N., 314
Salas, E., 3, 6, 7, 9, 13, 16, 19, 24, 44, 87, 88,
    96, 97, 100, 101, 102, 103, 104,
    106, 107, 117, 118, 119, 121, 133,
    139, 149, 150, 187, 188, 189, 212,
    249, 261, 271, 272, 274, 275, 286,
    289, 291, 293, 294, 318, 328, 338,
    346, 347, 378, 379, 387, 405, 416,
    417, 447, 448, 457, 458, 465, 466,
    471, 475, 477, 496, 501, 513, 549,
    557, 558, 562, 571, 572, 574, 584,
    597, 599, 601
Saleem, J. J., 173
Salmon, P. M., 101, 102, 103, 109
Saltz, J. L., 119, 125
Salvador, R., 130
Salvaggio, A. N., 121, 130, 153
Samaropoulos, X. F., 52
Samman, S., 562
Sanchez-Manzanares, M., 100, 374
Sanchez Svensson, M., 411, 412, 413
Saner, L. D., 104
Santos, E., 55, 56
Santos Jr., E., 5, 51, 55, 56, 57, 58, 68
Sanz, E., 6, 117, 588, 603
Sarcevic, A., 508
Sarmiento, J., 540
Sarmiento-Klapper, J. W., 541
Sarter, N. B., 103, 104, 107
Sauer, T. D., 191, 203
Sayeed, L., 555
Scerri, P., 315, 321, 322, 324, 329, 331
Schaeken, W., 99
Schatzki, T. R., 501
Schaubroeck, J., 121, 125
Scheff, T., 460, 461
Schegloff, E. A., 416, 528, 530
Schein, E. H., 129, 130
Schelling, T. C., 427
Schermer, T., 250
Schiller, H., 51
Schippers, M. C., 125, 131

Schmidt, A. M., 24
Schmidt, J., 564
Schmidt, R. C., 195
Schneider, B., 118, 119, 121, 122, 125, 130,
    146, 147, 149, 153
Schneider, W., 582
Schoenfeld, A. H., 214, 221, 222, 225
Schooler, J. W., 283
Schraw, G., 218
Schroder, H., 551
Schulte, M., 145, 149, 160
Schultz, M., 290
Schulz-Hardt, S., 255, 257
Schurr, N., 322
Schvaneveldt, R. W., 156
Schwartz, D., 518
Scielzo, S., 286
Scott, J., 290, 296, 301
Scott, M. D., 460
Searle, J. R., 54, 583
Sebanz, N., 8, 189
Seedhouse, P., 418
Seibold, D. R., 476
Semmer, N. K., 549
Senge, P., 405
Serb, D. A., 443
Serfaty, D., 356, 502, 573, 578
Setlock, L. D., 555, 556
Sexton, J. B., 512
Shaffer, C. A., 235
Shaffer, D. M., 198
Shalley, C. E., 276
Shamir, B., 129
Shannon, C., 551
Shapiro, A., 362
Shapiro, D. L., 38
Sharlin, E., 326
Sharrock, W., 408, 409, 410
Shaw, C. D., 191, 203
She, Y., 220, 443
Sheats, P., 474
Sheffey, S., 90
Sheikh, A., 52
Shiffrin, R. M., 582
Shih, S., 51
Shimoda, T., 214
Shimony, S. E., 56
Shmulyian, S., 145

620 • *Author Index*

Shope, S. M., 189, 197
Short, J. A., 15, 555
Shrestha, L. B., 101, 105, 107, 318
Shriver, C. D., 51
Shteynberg, G., 164
Shumaker, R., 10, 313, 591, 598
Shumate, M., 440
Sierhuis, M., 331
Sigman, S. J., 477
Sillars, A. L., 46
Sillinceb, J. A., 54
Simon, H., 551
Simon, R., 54
Sims, D. E., 447, 465
Sims, H. P., 126, 508
Sims, V., 324, 327
Sionti, M., 543
Slaughter, S., 277
Small, E. E., 6, 19, 119, 145, 150, 151, 152, 163, 391
Smith, C. A. P., 173, 245, 271, 348
Smith, C. M., 90
Smith, D. B., 129, 130
Smith, E. M., 38, 39
Smith, F. L., 480
Smith, K., 101
Smith, K. G., 153
Smith-Jentsch, K. A., 97, 98, 151, 160, 271, 274, 315, 448, 557, 558, 559, 562, 565, 584
Smolensky, P., 148
Snyder, D. E., 347, 358
Snyder, W. M., 212
Sofge, D., 337
Sonnentag, S., 153
Soo, C., 448
Sorensen, J. B., 153
Spataro, S. E., 391
Speier, C., 278, 279
Spencer, B., 101
Sproull, L., 289, 291, 292, 294, 300, 303, 307, 422, 431, 555, 579
Squire, P., 324
Srivastava, S., 391
Srull, T. K., 579
Stagle, K. C., 6, 100, 117
Stahl, G., 14, 405, 517, 519, 520, 521, 522, 524, 532, 540, 589, 599, 602

Standifer, R. L., 92, 93, 99
Staniewicz, M. J., 152, 163
Stanton, N. A., 102, 103
Stasser, G., 10, 28, 250, 255, 256, 257, 292, 293, 363, 377, 379
Stein, B. S., 348, 349
Stein, J. H., 447
Steiner, I. D., 28, 248, 376, 388
Stentz, A., 332
Stephens, R. J., 7, 173, 590
Stevens, A. L., 261
Stevens, L. A., 466
Stevens, M. J., 41
Stewart, D. D., 10, 255
Stiegmann, G. V., 51
Stogdill, R. M., 124, 135, 138
Stohl, C., 480, 492
Stone, P., 314
Stout, J. A., 294
Stout, R. J., 97, 293, 328, 379, 416
Straus, S. G., 278
Streufert, S., 551
Stryker, S., 461
Stubbs, K., 324
Stutman, R., 468
Su, C., 443
Subirats, M., 121, 153
Suchman, L. A., 210
Sukthankar, G., 10, 313, 324, 591, 598
Sun, B., 321
Sun, S., 321
Sundstrom, E., 123, 245
Sutcliffe, K. A., 41, 43
Suthers, D. D., 14, 517, 518, 538
Sutton, J. L., 396
Swiecki, C. W., 51
Sycara, K., 320, 321, 322, 316, 320, 323, 325, 314
Sycara, S., 331
Sypher, H. E., 468

Taber, T., 127
Tajfel, H., 36
Takanishi, A., 324
Tambe, M., 314, 315, 317, 318, 321, 322
Tan, B., 554
Tannebaum, S. I., 417
Tastan, B., 324

Author Index • 621

Taveesin, J., 164
Taylor, A. R., 189
Teasley, S. D., 405, 518, 539
Tenne-Gazit, O., 131, 153, 154, 158
Terasaki, A. K., 528
Terrell, I. S., 361
Tesler, R., 5, 87, 587
Tesluk, P. E., 134, 146
Thomas, L. S., 90
Thompson, L., 459, 561
Thompson, P., 15, 555
Thornton, T., 196
Tindale, R. S., 3, 87, 90, 119, 246, 253, 551
Titus, W., 28, 255, 256, 257, 363, 379
Tiwana, A., 448
Tjosvold, D., 124, 447
Tolman, E. C., 354
Tordera, N., 147
Trafton, G., 324
Trafton, J. G., 326, 337
Traum, D., 320, 322, 323
Tremble, T. R., 126
Tsai, W., 37
Tschan, F., 87, 109, 448, 549
Tsvetovat, M., 549
Tu, C., 554
Turvey, M. T., 196
Tushman, M. L., 128
Tziner, A., 291

Valacich, J. S., 553, 563
van Baren, J., 554
Vance, R. J., 126, 133
Van den Bosch, F. A. J., 131
Van den Bosch, K., 467
Vanderstoep, S. W., 132, 293
Van der Vegt, G. R., 464
Van Dyne, L., 276
van Eerde, W., 89, 91, 93
van Ginkel, W. P., 90, 428
VanGundy, A. B., 553
van Knippenberg, D., 90, 125, 131, 428
van Lanen, F., 554
Van Orden, G. C., 196
van Velsen, M., 315
Varcholik, P., 326
Vatrapu, R., 538
Velliquette, A., 129

Veloso, M., 314, 323
Vermeulen, F., 38
Vessey, I., 278
Vinokur, A. D., 149
Vogel, D. R., 555
Volberda, H. W., 131
Vollrath, D. A., 3, 119, 246, 551
Volpe, C. E., 271, 328, 466, 477
Volz, R., 322
Vozdolska, R., 549, 550
Vroom, V. H., 389
Vygotsky, L. S., 191, 211, 218, 497, 522

Wackman, D., 461
Waddock, S. A., 149
Wagner, F. R., 127
Walker, G. H., 102, 103
Wallace, D. M., 246
Waller, M. J., 87, 101
Walter, J., 91, 123
Walton, R. E., 561
Walumbwa, F. O., 121, 125, 131
Wand, Y., 215, 435, 438
Wang, H. C., 519, 543, 556
Wang, J., 324, 332, 574
Wang, Y. C., 519, 543
Warkentin, M., 555, 556
Warner, N. W., 9, 89, 217, 245, 271, 272,
   274, 347, 405, 471, 475
Warner, S. M., 173
Wasko, M., 291
Wasserman, S., 290, 296, 308, 443
Watson, W. E., 375
Watts-Perotti, J., 177, 178
Watzlawick, P., 474
Weaver, W., 551
Webb, N., 217, 219, 226
Weber, T. J., 131
Wee, J. D., 538
Wegner, D. M., 293, 294, 300, 303, 422,
   423, 424, 425, 426, 427, 428, 429,
   430, 434, 435, 444, 445, 446, 447,
   450, 500
Weick, K. E., 6, 117, 137, 504
Weinberger, A., 518
Weingarden, S. M., 126, 129
Weingart, L. R., 38, 249, 373, 377, 479
Weizenbaum, J., 327

622 • Author Index

Weldon, E., 388
Wellens, A. R., 102, 103, 105, 106, 107, 108, 356, 360
Wellens, R., 294, 357
Wellman, B., 556
Wenger, E., 212, 347, 354, 501
Wenzel, L., 293, 294, 549
Wertsch, J. V., 191, 211
West, G. P., 220
West, M. A., 146, 147, 149, 155
Wettergreen, D., 324
Wheelan, S., 87
Whitaker, R., 358
White, B. Y., 147, 214, 218, 221, 222
White, P. R., 521
Whitman, D. S., 126, 129
Whitney, D. J., 42, 118
Wholey, D. R., 98, 149, 189, 289
Wholey, R., 581
Wiechmann, D., 24, 25
Wildman, J. L., 19, 24, 44
Wilkinson, J. T., 56
Williams, E., 15, 555
Williams, K., 38, 276, 388
Williams, K. A., 54
Williams, K. Y., 293, 375
Williamson, M., 316
Wilson, D., 355
Wilson, J. M., 98, 149, 189, 289
Wilson, K. A., 88
Wilson, M., 191, 585
Wilson, R., 53
Winne, P. H., 221, 226
Winner, J. L., 8, 188, 189
Winograd, T., 210
Wittenbaum, G. M., 10, 255, 256, 292, 293, 447, 478, 492
Wittgenstein, L., 523, 524, 537
Wittrock, M., 217
Woehr, D. J., 165, 380, 391
Wolf, G., 301
Wong, B. L. W., 107
Wong, S. S., 435

Wood, R. E., 286
Woods, D. D., 103, 104, 107, 173, 175, 176, 177, 178, 182, 183, 319, 338
Wooldridge, B., 129

Xhafa, F., 528, 538
Xiao, L., 211, 232
Xiao, Y., 13, 448, 449, 496, 508
Xie, J. L., 146, 149, 165
Xin, K. R., 375
Xu, D., 322

Yang, H. D., 99, 563
Yates, J. F., 175
Yen, J., 321, 322, 331
Yoo, Y., 448, 555
Yoon, K., 12, 421, 428, 429, 592, 602
Yorke, J. A., 191, 203
Young, M. F., 348
Yu, F., 51
Yuan, Y. C., 439, 440, 441, 443, 450
Yukl, G., 125, 127
Yun, S., 508, 509

Zaccaro, S. J., 98, 118, 123, 124, 126, 131, 132, 137, 147, 150, 249, 271, 474, 557, 572, 574, 584
Zaff, B. S., 357, 358
Zajac, E. J., 122, 125, 128, 129, 137
Zelno, J. A., 163
Zemel, A., 520, 528, 531
Zeng, D., 316
Zenger, T. R., 38
Zhang, J., 498
Zhang, Y., 87
Zhang, Z., 123, 127, 447
Zhao, Q., 57
Zhou, N., 538
Zohar, D., 119, 122, 130, 131, 146, 147, 149, 153, 154, 155, 158, 159
Zuber, J. A., 250
Zuckerman, C., 256
Zwaan, R. A., 99

Subject Index

A

Accountable, 409
Acquisition, knowledge, 32–33
Actions, 57, 408, 409
Activity awareness, 209–215
  activity theory and, 215
  and collaborative competence,
    relationship between, 216–218
  articulating/guiding development
    of collaboration competence,
    222–228
  developing collaborative
    competence, 219–222
  similarities between macro- and
    metacognition, 218–219
  in collaborative teamwork,
    supporting
  simulating real-world collaboration
    through case-based learning,
    230–233
  toward collaborative activities
    promoting a community of
    practice, 233–235
  and development of macrocognitive
    skills, 219
  as dynamic process, 214
  empirical studies of, 215–216
  exploring relationships between levels
    of, 216
  facets of, 212
  framing, 211
Activity theory, 191
  and activity awareness, 215
  concept of activity from, 211
Adjustable autonomy, 321
Agent communication languages, 319
Agent-only teams, 314
  dealing with dynamic environments,
    316–317
  guaranteeing coordination, 314–316

making agents proactive, 317–319
  team planning, 317
Agent persona, 327–328
Agents' attitude of proactive assistance,
    318
Agents supporting team members, 322
  challenges, individual human, 321
Anti-Air Warfare Team Observation
    Measure (ATOM) model, 315
Applicable principle, 254
Architectural psychology or
    environmental psychology,
    346
Articulating collaborative contributions
    to activity awareness
  activity awareness, 209–215
  empirical studies of activity awareness,
    215–216
  relationship between collaborative
    competence/activity awareness,
    216–218
  articulating/guiding development
    of collaboration competence,
    222–228
  developing collaborative
    competence, 219–222
  similarities between macro- and
    metacognition, 218–219
  supporting activity awareness in
    collaborative teamwork,
    228–230
  simulating real-world collaboration
    through case-based learning,
    230–233
  toward collaborative activities
    promoting community of
    practice, 233–235
Assessing cognitive similarity
  perceptual approach, 152–155
  structured approach, 155–157
Asymmetric sociomatrix, 297

623

624 • *Subject Index*

Awareness, 209–210
Axioms, 57

B

Baseline system, 335
Bayesian knowledge bases, 5, 55–57
  belief revision, 56
  belief updating, 56
  I-nodes and S-nodes, 55
  instantiation, 55
  intent inferencing and, 54
  size of, 67
Behavioral leadership, 125
Beliefs, 57, 146, 260
Betweenness centrality, 37

C

Case study elements, workspace for
  reviewing/debating, 232
Causal reasoning, 58
Centrality, 164
C^3 interactive task for identifying
  emerging situations (CITIES),
  105
  simulation, 360
Classroom BRIDGE, 229, 230, 232
Climate quality, 159
Climate strength, 158
Closed-loop communication, 465
Cognition, 585
Cognition in teams, elaborating, 145–146
  aiming for future, 166
  assessing cognitive similarity
    perceptual approach, 152–155
    structured approach, 155–157
  conceptualizations of similar
    cognitions in study of teams,
    146–148
  developing cognitive similarity
    configurations, 162–163
    cognitive content domains,
      163–164
    forms of cognition, 164–165
    forms of similarity, 165–166
  moving toward cognitive similarity
    configurations, 151–152

operationalizing perceptual and
  structured cognition, 148–150
potential linkages between cognitive
  similarity configurations/team
  variables, 157–162
Cognitive aspects of leadership theories, 124
  approaches to organizational
    leadership, 125–126
  behavioral perspectives, 124–128
  functional leadership theory, 131–133
  shared and distributed leadership,
    133–135
  strategic leadership, 128–130
  transformational leadership theory,
    130–131
Cognitive configuration, 163
Cognitive-conflict tasks, 560
Cognitive consensus, 158
Cognitive content domains, 163–164
Cognitive development, Piagetian theories
  of, 217
Cognitive examples of components, 254
Cognitive fit
  task complexity and, 278
  theory, 278
Cognitive functions, 7
Cognitive psychology and study of teams, 3
Cognitive similarity, 6, 151
  level of, 158
  multiple types of, 6
  types, 152
Cognitive similarity configurations, 163
  developing, 162–163
    cognitive content domains, 163–164
    forms of cognition, 164–165
    forms of similarity, 165–166
  moving toward, 151–152
  and team variables, potential linkages
    between, 157–162
Cognitive systems engineering
  perspective on shared cognition,
  173–175
  assumptions, 174
  case for distributing cognition, 176
  coordination patterns/triggers, 176
    delaying lower priority tasks during
      bottlenecks, 180–181
    emergent workload balancing, 179

Subject Index • 625

escalation of activity, 177–178
increased communication during
nonroutine events, 182–183
proactive investment in coming up
to speed, 178–179
reducing priority of tasks, 181–182
role-based communication,
179–180
macrocognition functions, 174–175
coordinating, 175
deciding, 175
detecting, 174
planning, 174
sensemaking, 174
Cognitivism, 519
Collaboration, 213
in teams, 373
Collaboration competence
articulating and guiding development
of, 222–228
communication, 224–225
critical evaluation, 225
minimizing complexity, 226
planning, 224
productivity, 225
guide, excerpt from, 227
realms contributing to, 224
Collaboration through case-based
learning, simulating real-world,
230–233
Collaborative activities, 223
effective, 223
promoting a community of practice,
toward, 233–235
Collaborative case-based learning, 233
Collaborative competence, 214–215, 221
and activity awareness, relationship
between, 216–218
articulating and guiding
development, 222–228
developing collaborative
competence, 219–222
similarities between macro- and
metacognition, 218–219
developing, 219–222
Collaborative fashion, case studies in, 231
Collaborative learning, "virtual school"
environment for, 228

Collaborative processes, 221, 223–224,
228, 577
effective, 222
instruction, 223
problems associated with, 220
Collaborative Systems Technology
Laboratory, 345
Collaborative teamwork, supporting
activity awareness in,
228–230
simulating real-world collaboration
through case-based learning,
230–233
toward collaborative activities
promoting community of
practice, 233–235
Collective cognition
and leadership, relationships between
types of, 137
promoting, 127
Collective information sampling model,
256
Collective team identification, 464
Combinations, 251, 253, 266
Combinations of contributions, 251–254
aggregation strategies of contributions,
265
combinatorial rule, 265
components/principles of, 253
context, 253
individual contributions, 258
and sharing cognitions in teams,
264–266
social combination approach and, 251
theory, 8, 251, 252, 264
components and principles, 254
implications of, 259
shared mental models,
conceptualizing, 262
Command, Control, and
Communications (C^3), 352
Common ground, 212, 219
Communication, 330–331, 457, 472–474,
551
deconstructed, 552
communication flow, 553
communication media, 553–556
face-to-face, 554

626 • *Subject Index*

facilitating mental model convergence through, 559–560
choose, 563–564
execute, 561–562
generate, 562–563
negotiate, 560–561
message interdependence, 473
network approach, 441–442
group-level variables, 442–443
individual-level variables, 442
during nonroutine events, increased, 182–183
role-based, 179–180
Communities of practice (CoP), 212–213
Compatible situation awareness (SA), 103
Competence, 214
demonstrating, 221
Compilation, 27
Compilational emergence, 120
Complementary knowledge, 285
Complex intellective tasks, 581
Complexity, 275
Complex organizational behaviors, 51–54
case study, 63–66
experimental study, 66–67
action prediction, 74
course of actions in mastectomy, 68
errors in case study, 80–82
evidence for overall inference, 80
experimental results, 69–80
experimental setup, 67–68
general surgeon's competence, validation with inference/influence, 70, 72
inference out of considering experience, 79
inference with patient conditions, 76
inference with patient information combined, 77
inference with status of patient's nipple, 75
most probable potential procedure, 69
size of Bayesian knowledge bases, 67
to validate inference of target variables, 73
validation with patient condition, 70

intent inferencing and Bayesian knowledge bases, 54–58
surgical intent modeling, 59–63
Composition, 26
Compositional emergence, 120
Computer-mediated communication, 15
Computer-supported collaborative learning (CSCL), 14, 517
Computer-supported cooperative work (CSCW), 362
Conceptualizing team knowledge, 27–28
Conflict and controversy, 217
benefits from, 219
Congruent cognitions, 151
Conjunctive aggregation rule, 262
Considering experience, inference out of, 79
Contributions, 251
aggregation strategies of, 266
Convergent expectations, 427
Co-ordered activity, 580
Coordinates of coordination/collaboration, 571–572
coordination and collaboration, 572–578
reconfiguring terminology, 578–585
shared cognition/coordination/collaboration in theories of, 587–588
adding to our understanding of process, 588–590
augmenting cross-disciplinarity, 592–593
clarifying translations of theory into practice, 590–591
Coordinating, 175, 176
Coordination, 537
dynamics, 194
patterns and triggers, 176
delaying lower priority tasks during bottlenecks, 180–181
emergent workload balancing, 179
escalation of activity, 177–178
increased communication during nonroutine events, 182–183
proactive investment in coming up to speed, 178–179

Subject Index • 627

reducing priority of tasks, 181–182
role-based communication,
179–180
theory, 176
Co-orientation, 12, 459, 539, 588
communication and, 461
levels of, 460
team cognition/performance
promoting co-orientation, 465–468
team functioning, 462–463
team identity, identification, and
affect, 463–465
C³ Operator Performance Engineering
(COPE) program, 352
Creative tasks, 562
Cross-disciplinary perspectives on team
cognition, 4–16
Cultural-historical practices, 495
Cultural mosaic, example, 35
Current situation, 210

D

Data, 22
information, and knowledge typology
(DIK-T), 22, 28
Decision making, task complexity and,
278–279
Declarative knowledge, 22
Degree centrality, 37
Developmental processes capture
compilation of knowledge/skills,
40
Diagnostic reasoning, 58
Dichotomized-directed sociogram, 297
Dichotomized-undirected sociogram, 297
Direct perception, 198
ecological psychology, 191
Disjunctive aggregation rule, 262
Distributed cognition, 176, 191, 200–203
approach, 201
Hutchins' theory of, 202
Distributing cognition, case for, 176
Diversity, 278
effects in teams, 375
task complexity and team, 278
on team functioning, impact of
cultural, 396

Domain: taskwork *vs.* teamwork, 293–294
Durability: long lasting *vs.* fleeting, 294
Durable knowledge, 294
Dynamic environments, 316
dealing with, 316–317

E

Ecological psychology, 198
Effective co-orientation, 465
ELIZA, 327
Embodied agent, 313
Embodied cognition, 191
Emergence, 192
"ideal" forms of, 26
knowledge
between team, 34–35
within team, 34
Emergency crisis management, 358
Emergent cognition, 137
and leadership, linking forms of, 136
Emergent collective cognition, leadership
and, 117, 118–119
applied implication, 135–137
cognition, leadership, and
effectiveness, 123–124
cognitive aspects of leadership
theories, 124
behavioral perspectives, 124–128
functional leadership theory,
131–133
shared and distributed leadership,
133–135
strategic leadership, 128–130
transformational leadership theory,
130–131
content of cognition, 122–123
form of cognition, 121–122
nature of emergence, 120
team mental model concept, 120
team transactive memory, 120
Emergent multilevel phenomenon, 24
team compilation as, 40
Emergent workload balancing, 179
Encoding information, 424
Environmental conditions, 194
Episodic task cycles, 39
Escalation of activity, 177–178

628 • *Subject Index*

Ethnomethodology, 410
Execute, 561–562
Expertise, 427
Expert planner, qualities, 218

F

Face-to-face communication, 554
Facilitating effective mental model
convergence, 549–550
communication deconstructed, 552
communication flow, 553
communication media, 553–556
facilitating mental model convergence
through communication,
559–560
choose, 563–564
execute, 561–562
generate, 562–563
negotiate, 560–561
mental model content, 556–559
mental model convergence and
communication, 551–552
Fact space, 22
Focused communication, 553
Foundation for Intelligent Physical Agents
(FIPA), 319
Fractal dynamics, 195–196
Functionalism dynamical/complex
systems, 191
Functional leadership, 125
theory, 131–133

G

Gaining insight into team processes on
cognitive tasks, 373–374
areas of team and small group research
open to investigation using
SRM, 396–397
inferring processes of interacting
teams, 376–381
prediction of team outcomes from
SRM indices, 386–387
quality, 388–389
quantity, 387–388
team sustainability, 389–390
social relations model (SRM), 381–386

SRM applied to shared cognition in
teams, 390–396
team member qualities, 374–376
Garfinkel's critique of Parsonian theory of
action, 406–410
Garfinkel's "empirical theoretic"
approach, 416
Goal content, 43
Goal frames, 43
Goals, 57
Group climate level, 159
Group cognition, 14, 517
in online teams, 517–521
constructing joint problem space,
539–541
event: VMT Spring Fest 2006 team
B, 525–526
forming groups and coconstructing
knowledge artifacts, 541–543
move: showing how to view
problem, 528–529
pair: question/response, 530–531
reference: "it," 533–536
theme: "I have an interesting way to
look at this problem," 527–528
toward enhancing transactive
interactions with automatic
facilitation, 543–544
utterance: question, 531–532
viewing learning and thinking,
536–539
views of learning and thinking,
522–525
postcognitive theory, 519
theory, 520
Group potency, 94

H

Human–agent interaction, 325–331
agent persona, 327–328
communication, 330–331
multimodal interaction, 325–327
mutual adaptation, 329–330
mutual predictability, 329
team knowledge, 328–329
Human–agent intrateam communication,
330

Human–agent teams, using, 322
Human–agent teamwork, 319–320
   models, 10
   primary roles played by agents
      interacting with humans, 320
Human development, 212
   activity theory, 213
Human intent, computational
   representation of, 57
Human–robot teams, 324–325
   teamwork, application of, 331–336
Human teams, agents supporting,
   323–324
Hutchins' theory of distributed cognition,
   202
Hybrid approach to studying teams, 12

I

"Ideal" forms of emergence, 26
Implicit coordination, 584
Individual knowledge, 30, 31
   building, 29
   content pool, 300
Individual metacognitive activities, 222
Individual self-regulation heuristic, 21
Influence of task complexity
   on externalized team knowledge
      processes, 284
   on individual knowledge-building
      processes, 281
   on internalized team knowledge
      processes, 283
   on team problem-solving outcomes, 285
Information, 22
   allocation, 424
   sampling bias, 255
   seeking and use, task complexity and,
      275–276
   sharing in teams, 254–260
   space, 22
I-nodes, 55, 57
   hierarchy of interaction between four
      types of nodes in intent models,
      58
Input-process-outcome (I-P-O) model
   framework, 247, 376, 381
   of team interaction and performance, 247

theory of combinations of
   contributions integrated within,
   252
Intelligent agent, 313
Intelligent Agent Interface (IAI), 333
Intelligent agents as teammates, 313–314
   agent-only teams, 314
      dealing with dynamic
         environments, 316–317
      guaranteeing coordination, 314–316
      making agents proactive, 317–319
      team planning, 317
   human–agent teamwork, 319–320
   research challenges, 320–322
      agents acting as team members, 323
      agents supporting human teams,
         323–324
      agents supporting team members, 322
      application of human–robot
         teamwork, 331–336
      human–agent interaction, 325–331
      human–robot teams, 324–325
Intent, 57
Intent inference, 57–58
   and Bayesian knowledge bases, 54
Intentional states, 54
Intent model, 58
   for surgeon, 60–63
      complexity of procedure, 60
      condition of patient, 60
Interactive team cognition (ITC), 7
   assumptions/theoretical underpinning
      of, 187–190
      preferred unit of analysis for
         studying team cognition,
         200–203
      team cognition as dynamic,
         190–196
      team cognition as tied to context,
         197–200
   influenced by theory of distributed
      cognition, 202
   and team cognition, 8, 189
   theory
      measurement of externalized team-
         level behaviors, 202
      theories/schools of thought
         inspiring, 191

630 • *Subject Index*

Interactive theory of team cognition, 201
Interdependence, recognition, 127
Interlingua, 519
Interpretative cognition, 122, 164

K

Knowledge, 22
 vs. learning, 20
 skills, and abilities (KSA), 41
Knowledge acquisition, 30, 32–33
 and emergence in teams, shaping, 35
  leveraging team member network
   linkages, 35–38
  leveraging team regulation and
   knowledge compilation, 38–44
Knowledge-building processes
 implications for, team, 282
 individual, 281
 implications for, 280–281
Knowledge compilation, 23
 leveraging team regulation and, 38–44
 learning orientation, 42–43
 team cohesion, 42
 team metacognition, 43–44
 teamwork skills, 41
 theoretical foundation, 38–41
Knowledge configuration, 30, 32
Knowledge emergence
 between team, 30, 34–35
 within team, 30, 34
Knowledge formation compiles over
  iterations of regulation process,
  21
Knowledge metrics, 30
Knowledge pool, 30, 31–32
Knowledge Query Manipulation
  Language (KQML), 319
Knowledge representations–assumptions,
  grounding, 28
Knowledge representation typology,
  28–35
 illustration, 30
 individual knowledge, 31
 knowledge acquisition, 32–33
 knowledge emergence (between team),
  34–35
 knowledge emergence (within team), 34

 knowledge pool, 31–32
 knowledge variability, 30, 33–34
Knowledge variability, 30, 33–34

L

Leadership, 6, 117, 124, 135
 behavioral, 125
 and collective cognition, relationships
  between types of, 137
 and emergent cognition, linking forms
  of, 136
 forms of, 125–126
 functional, 125
 linking emergent cognition and forms
  of, 136
 strategic, 125
 transformational, 125
Leadership and emergent collective
  cognition, 117
 applied implication, 135–137
 cognition, leadership, and
  effectiveness, 123–124
 cognitive aspects of leadership
  theories, 124
  behavioral perspectives, 124–128
  functional leadership theory, 131–133
  shared and distributed leadership,
   133–135
  strategic leadership, 128–130
  transformational leadership theory,
   130–131
 emergent collective cognition, 118–119
  content of cognition, 122–123
  form of cognition, 121–122
  nature of emergence, 120
Leadership theories, cognitive aspects of,
  124
 behavioral perspectives, 124–128
 functional leadership theory, 131–133
 shared and distributed leadership,
  133–135
 strategic leadership, 128–130
 transformational leadership theory,
  130–131
Learning
 and development, Vygotskian theory
  of, 218

vs. knowledge, 20
  orientation, 42–43
  as process, 20–21
Leveraging team member network
    linkages, 35–38
Leveraging team regulation and
    knowledge compilation, 38–44
  learning orientation, 42–43
  team cohesion, 42
  team metacognition, 43–44
  teamwork skills, 41
  theoretical foundation, 38–41
Living Laboratory framework, 10, 349
  designs via prototypes, 350
  reconfigurable prototype design and
    technology, 353
Living Laboratory perspective,
    background of
  beginning primitives, 346–347
  Living Laboratory framework, 349–351
  macrocognition, 347–349
Local emergency planning committees
    (LEPC), 159
Longitudinal research
  perceptual team cognition over time, 91
  team SA over time, 103–104
  TMMs over time, 97

M

Macrocognition, 9, 19, 173, 191, 216–217,
    272, 347–349, 474–475
  CSE perspective, 173
  research in Living Laboratory, example
    of current, 364–365
  theories of, 210
Macrocognition, team learning, and team
    knowledge, 19–20
  representing acquisition and
    emergence of individual and
    team knowledge
    foundation and assumptions, 27–28
    knowledge representation typology,
      28–35
  shaping knowledge acquisition and
    emergence in teams, 35
  leveraging team member network
    linkages, 35–38

leveraging team regulation and
    knowledge compilation, 38–44
  theoretical foundation and conceptual
    drivers, 20–27
Macrocognition in teams, 271, 272–273
  framework for, 29
  implications of task complexity for,
    280
    externalized team knowledge,
      283–284
    individual knowledge-building
      processes, 280–281
    internalized team knowledge,
      282–283
    team knowledge-building
      processes, 282
    team problem-solving outcomes,
      284–285
  model for research on, 274
  processes involved in, 273–274
    externalized team knowledge, 274
    individual knowledge building,
      273
    internalized knowledge, 273–274
    team knowledge building, 273
    team problem-solving outcomes,
      274
Macrocognition through
    multimethodological lens,
    looking at, 345
  background of Living Laboratory
    perspective
    beginning primitives, 346–347
    Living Laboratory framework,
      349–351
    macrocognition, 347–349
  contemporary advancement of
    macrocognition and team
    research, 357–363
  example of current macrocognition
    research in Living Laboratory,
    364–365
  historical precedence of teamwork
    research in military operations,
    351–352
  NORAD human factors initiative,
    352–355
  scaled-world simulation, 355–357

632 • *Subject Index*

Macrocognitive processes, 7
  common elements, 7
  complex collaborative environments, 9
  nature of, 217
Macrocognitive regulation, 219
Media, communication, 553–556
  media richness, 554–555
  social presence, 555–556
Medical cognition, 498
Medical error, 52
  communication failure and, 52–53
Member characteristics, 247
Mental models, 147, 160, 260, 263, 549
  accuracy, 161
  content, 556–559
  convergence and communication, 551–552
  convergence process, 551
  similarity, 161
  team, 96–97
    over time, 97–99, 100
    time as part of construct content, 99–100
    time as part of general context, 100–101
Mental model similarity, 155
Message interdependence and team cognition, 471–472
Metacognition, 502
  components, 218
  team, 41, 43–44
Metacognitive activities, individual, 222
Metacommunication, 467
Military hospitals, patient management, 51
MINDS (Multidisciplinary Initiatives in Naturalistic Decision Systems) Group, 345
Moral identity, 498
Motivation, information exchange, 257
Motor coordination, 194
Multidimensional scaling (MDS), 149, 150, 156, 157, 161
Multidimensional sociomatrix, 296
Multilevel modeling, 191
Multimodal interaction, 325–327

Multiple goal, multilevel model of individual and team regulation, 25
Multirobot manipulation task, 331
Mutual adaptation, 329–330
Mutual enhancement model, 256
Mutual knowledge, 293
Mutual predictability, 325, 329

N

NASA's Robonaut, 328
Navy Center for Applied Research in Artificial Intelligence (NCARAI), 326
Negotiation, 561
NeoCITIES, 106, 363
  simulation, 360, 361
Network analysis
  and current approaches to team knowledge representation/ measurement, 305–308
  sociomatrices, 308
  of team knowledge, 300–304
Network configurations, 37
Network density, 37
Network linkages, leveraging team member, 35–38
  team composition and team networks, 35–38
New Trends in Cooperative Activities: System Dynamics in Complex Environments (McNeese, Salas, & Endsley), 347
Noncombat evacuation operation (NEO), 322
NORAD human factors initiative, 352–355
Norm, 408
Normative model of team compilation, 38–39

O

Online awareness, 218
Online group discourse, levels of analysis of, 537
Operating room (OR) environment, 52
  teamwork in, 53
Organizational silence, 38

P

Parsonian theory of action
  elementary unit act, 407
  Garfinkel's critique of, 406–410
  voluntaristic theory of action, 407
Pathfinder, 150, 155, 156, 157
Patterns and triggers, coordination, 176
  delaying lower priority tasks during
    bottlenecks, 180–181
  emergent workload balancing, 179
  escalation of activity, 177–178
  increased communication during
    nonroutine events, 182–183
  proactive investment in coming up to
    speed, 178–179
  reducing priority of tasks, 181–182
  role-based communication, 179–180
Perception–action system, 198
Perceptual cognition approach, 121, 146
  assessing cognitive similarity,
    152–155
  operationalizing, 148–150
    climate research, 149
  vs. structured cognition approach, 148
Perceptual team cognition, 90–91
  over time, 91
  teams over time, 94–95
  time and, 95–96
  time as part of construct content,
    91–94
  time as part of general context, 95
Philosophical Investigations
  (Wittgenstein), 523
Piagetian theories of cognitive
  development, 217
Planning, 127
  effective, 218
Postcognitive theory, group cognition,
  519
Postcognitivism, 519
Postcognitivist theory, 520
Primary operationalization, 149
Primary variance components of social
  relations model, 384
Proactive investment in coming up to
  speed, 178–179
Procedural knowledge, 22

Product and process, workspace that
  integrates support for, 234
Productive agency, 518

Q

Quadratic assignment procedure (QAP)
  correlation, 301, 306, 307

R

Real-world tasks, 22
Researcher bias, 156
Retrieval coordination, 425
RETSINA agent architecture, 315
RoboCup rescue competition, 333
Role-based communication, 179–180
Role clarification, 127

S

Scaled-world simulations, 355–357
  contemporary case of, 359
  at U.S. Air Force Human Engineering
    Division I (1983–2000), 356
Schemas, 147
  structure similarity, 156, 162
Science of teams, 11
Scientific knowledge, 496
Self-regulation, 21
Shared cognition, 3–4, 457–459
  categories, 458
  cognitive task performance in teams, 8
  coordination/collaboration in theories
    of, 587–588
    adding to our understanding of
      process, 588–590
    augmenting cross-disciplinarity,
      592–593
    clarifying translations of theory
      into practice, 590–591
  in hall of mirrors, 459–461
  role of time in, 5
  on time, 91–92
Shared/distributed leadership, 133–135
Shared information processing, 3
Shared knowledge, 293, 306
  and task, 378

634 • *Subject Index*

Shared mental models (SMM), 188, 210, 293
  literature on, 261
  as shared cognition in teams, 260–264
  types, 160
  utility of, 261
Sharedness, 458
  individual *vs.* shared, 292–293
Shared situation awareness (SA), 102
Shared task knowledge, 296, 300, 301
  computation and visual representation of, 302
Shared task representations, 90
Shared team leadership, 126
Shared temporal cognition, 91–94
  antecedents, 93
  components of, 92
  consequences, 94
  teams over time, 94–95
Shared/unshared information, hypothetical distribution of, 258
Sharing, 457
Sharing cognitions, 245
Sharing cognitions in teams,
  combinations of contributions for, 245–246
  combinations of contributions, 251–254
  and sharing cognitions in teams, 264–266
  framework for team functioning, 246–250
  information sharing in teams, 254–260
  shared mental models as shared cognition in teams, 260–264
  social combination approach to teams, 250–251
Short-term knowledge, 496
Similarity, forms of, 165
Simulation-based tasks, 22
Situated cognition/action, 191
Situation awareness (SA), 101–102, 229
  team, 101–103
    over time, 103–104, 106–107
    time as part of content, 104–106
    time as part of general context, 107
Situation awareness global assessment technique (SAGAT), 103, 105

Slaving principle, 194
SOAR-based agent, 323
Social actors, 346
Social capital, 212, 213
Social cognition–based approach for team interaction and task performance, 8
Social combination approach, 250
  to teams, 250–251
Social combinatorial models, 250–251
Social decision scheme (SDS) theory, 377
Social identity theory, 36
Social loafing, 276
Social modes of coconstruction, 518
Social order, 408
Social practice, 501
Social presence, 555
Social relations model/modeling (SRM), 380, 381–386
  applied to shared cognition in teams, 390–396
    I-P-O framework, 391
    team morale/satisfaction, 395
  areas of team and small group research open to investigation using, 396–397
    impact of cultural diversity on team functioning, 396
  indices
    other indices within, 384
    representation of team data and its effects on, 383
  prediction of team outcomes from indices, 386–387
    outcomes, 387
    quality, 388–389
    quantity, 387–388
    team sustainability, 389–390
  primary variance components of, 384
Social settings, 409
Societal knowledge, 497–498, 505–506
Sociocognitive process–oriented roles, 226
Sociocognitive roles, 227–228
Sociocultural theory, 497
Sociograms, 298
  dichotomized-directed, 297
  dichotomized-undirected, 297
  illustration of, 297

Sociomatrices, 297, 298, 299, 301
  illustration of, 297
Software agent, 313
States of co-orientation in group or
  collective, 462
STEAM (Shell for TEAMwork), 315
Strategic cognition/consensus, 123
Strategic consensus, 91
Strategic knowledge, 24
Strategic leadership, 125, 128–130
Structural complexity, 277
Structured cognition approach, 121, 148
  assessing cognitive similarity,
    152–155
  operationalizing, 148–150
  vs. perceptual cognition approach, 148
Structured meaning, 147
The Structure of Social Action (Parsons),
  407
Subgroups, 38
Subordinate, 573
Surgical intent modeling, 59–63
  BKB's capability and elements of
    intent, 59
  example of, 61, 62, 64
  goals of, 63
Surgical workspace, layout, 412
Symmetric sociomatrix, 297
Synchronization, 579
Synergetics, 194

T

Tacit knowledge, 440
Tactical learning, 228
TANDEM target identification control
  and command task, 323
Task characteristics, 248
Task complexity, 271, 275
  and cognitive fit, 278
  and decision making, 278–279
  and information seeking and use,
    275–276
  and task strategies used, 276
  and team diversity, 278
  and team engagement, 276–277
  and team performance, 277
  and technology use, 277–278

Task complexity on macrocognitive team
    processes, influence of, 271–272
  implications of task complexity for
    macrocognition in teams, 280
  implications for externalized team
    knowledge, 283–284
  implications for individual
    knowledge-building processes,
    280–281
  implications for internalized team
    knowledge, 282–283
  implications for team knowledge-
    building processes, 282
  implications for team problem-
    solving outcomes, 284–285
  macrocognition in teams, 272–273
  processes involved in, 273–274
task complexity, 275
  and cognitive fit, 278
  and decision making, 278–279
  and information seeking and use,
    275–276
  and task strategies used, 276
  and team diversity, 278
  and team engagement, 276–277
  and team performance, 277
  and technology use, 277–278
Task content knowledge, 123
Task–expertise–person (TEP) units, 434,
    435
Task priorities, hierarchy, 181
Taskwork, 41
Taskwork mental models, 557
Team and team–customer
    communications, 234
Team characteristics, 247
Team climate, 119
Team cognition, 87, 187, 189, 475–476,
    585, 598
  and accountabilities of tool pass,
    410–415
  Garfinkel's critique of Parsonian
    theory of action, 406–410
  hybrid approach to studying
    teamwork, 415–418
  toward "science of teams," 405–406
  caricatures of perspectives on, 190
  central notion of, 584

636 • *Subject Index*

dynamics and, 192
　complexity, 192–193
　fractal dynamics, 195–196
　synergetics and coordination
　　dynamics, 193–195
　foundation, 476–478
　interactive theory of, 201
　outcome, 482–483
　perspectives on, 190
　process, 478–481
　team as aggregate of cognitive entities,
　　188
　and team performance, 118
　team situation awareness/team
　　performance, 366
　and time, 88
　time and. *See* Time and team cognition
　type of, 13
Team cognition, communication, and
　　message interdependence
　communication, 472–474
　demonstrating three communicative
　　aspects of team cognition,
　　483–487
　　analyzing excerpts in relation to
　　　propositions, 487–490
　macrocognition, 474–475
　message interdependence and team
　　cognition, 471–472
　team cognition, 475–476
　　foundation, 476–478
　　outcome, 482–483
　　process, 478–481
Team cognition, communication, and
　　sharing, 457
　co-orientation, team cognition, and
　　performance
　　promoting co-orientation,
　　　465–468
　　team functioning, 462–463
　　team identity, identification, and
　　　affect, 463–465
　shared cognition, 457–459
　shared cognition in hall of mirrors,
　　459–461
Team cognitive activity, 199
Team cognitive processes, 250
Team compilation model, 39

Team composition, 35–38
　and team networks, 35–38
Team coordination, 199, 572
Team data and its effects on social
　　relations model indices,
　　representation of, 383
Team diversity, task complexity and, 278
Team engagement, task complexity and,
　　276–277
Team–environment systems, 197, 200
Team-focused content, 122
Team functioning, 462–463
　framework for, 246–250
Team initiator, 317–318
Team interaction process, interpersonal
　　expectations approach, 392
Team knowledge, 4–5, 289–291, 325,
　　328–329
　basic underlying dimensions,
　　291–292
　　domain: taskwork *vs.* teamwork,
　　　293–294
　　durability: long lasting *vs.* fleeting,
　　　294
　　sharedness: individual *vs.* shared,
　　　292–293
　　type: content or structure, 295
　building, 284
　　processes, 282, 284
　conceptualizing, 27–28
　constructs and their basic dimensions,
　　296
　emergence, 35
　forms of emergence, 26
　implications for
　　externalized, 283–284
　　internalized, 282–283
　network analysis and current
　　approaches, 305–308
　network analysis of team knowledge,
　　300–304
　preliminary empirical proof of
　　concept, 304–305
　representation, network analytic
　　approach to, 295–300
　representation/measurement, network
　　analysis and current approaches
　　to, 305–308

Subject Index • 637

research, 9
typology to represent, 20
Team learning, 28
and learning as process, 20
orientation, 41, 42–43
and problem solving, 29
and subgroups, formation, 38
Teammate–environment system, 199
Team members
agents acting as, 322, 323
agents supporting, 322
networks and team regulation, 5
Team mental models, 96–97
and knowledge, 97
over time, 97–99
properties, 96
teams over time, 100
time as part of construct content,
99–100
time as part of general context,
100–101
Team metacognition, 41, 43–44
Team networks, 35–38
Team outcomes, factors that influence,
248
Team performance, 365–366
cognitive processes and, 3
and mental models, 262
task complexity and, 277
team cognition/team situation
awareness, conceptual
differences between, 366
Team problem solving, 280
outcomes, implications for, 284–285
Team reason, 497
levels of analysis, 503
at mesolevel, 499
relevance, 499–500
and team cognition, 506–508
Team reason: between team cognition and
societal knowledge, 495–498
illustration of model, 508–511
observing and measuring team
reason, 511–513
organization of argument, 498–499
relevance, 499–500
situating team reason
metacognition, 502

sociocultural tradition and social
practice, 500–501
team macrocognition and practice
turn, 501
theoretical model of team reason, 503
model, 504
societal knowledge, 505–506
team reason and team cognition,
506–508
Teams-as-information-processors
perspective, 249
Team satisfaction/viability, 123
Team situation awareness, 101–103
over time, 103–104
team cognition/team performance,
conceptual differences between,
366
teams over time, 106–107
time as part of content, 104–106
time as part of general context, 107
Team temporal environment, 95, 107
Team transactive memory concept, 119
Teamwork, 3, 11, 346, 471
cohesion, 40, 42
and interdependence, 12
mental models, 557
skills, 40, 41
Technology use, task complexity and,
277–278
Temporal coordination/dynamics, 88, 89
Temporal environment, team mental
model, 100
Temporal perceptions, congruence, 93
Temporal synchronization, 92
Temporal TMMs
teams over time, 100
time as part of construct content,
99–100
Time and team cognition, 87–89
perceptual team cognition, 90–91
over time, 91
teams over time, 94–95
time as part of construct content,
91–94
time as part of general context, 95
team mental models, 96–97
over time, 97–99
teams over time, 100

638 • *Subject Index*

time as part of construct content,
99–100
time as part of general context,
100–101
team situation awareness, 101–103
over time, 103–104
teams over time, 106–107
time as part of content, 104–106
time as part of general context, 107
Time in team research, 88
Time scales of human activity, 191
Tool changes, surgical procedure, 412
Training, 466, 467
Transactive memory, 293, 307
communication-based approaches
and, 444
concept of, 215
content of, 426–428
depiction, 430
development in organizations, 436
effective, 393
extending theory to organizational
settings, 431–439
content of, 434–435
dynamics of, 434–435
emergence and development of,
432–434
misnomer, 429
outcomes of, 428–429
processes of, 423–425
structures of, 425–426
systems theory, 421
Transactive memory theory, 12, 422, 423
communication-based extensions,
439–444
communication network approach,
441–442
depiction of original, 430
original theoretical formulations,
422–423
content of, 426–428

outcomes of, 428–429
processes of, 423–425
structures of, 425–426
as public good, 439–441
as sociotechnical system, 446
and teams, 421–422
theoretical integration, 444–447
Transformational leadership, 125
theory, 130–131

U

Urban search and rescue (USAR), 333
Usability Case Studies (UCS) repository,
230, 232
Usability engineering, 216, 230, 231, 233,
234, 235, 236, 237

V

Validation
with inference of surgeon's
competence, 70
with patient condition, 70
Valued-undirected sociogram, 297
Variability, knowledge, 33–34
Virtual humans, 323
Virtual Math Teams (VMT) Project, 519
"Virtual school" environment for
collaborative learning, 228
Vygotskian theory of learning and
development, 218

W

Warfare, 351
Workspace
integrates support for product and
process, 234
for reviewing and debating case study
elements, 232